THE KAHANS FROM BAKU
A FAMILY SAGA

Cherry Orchard Books

THE KAHANS FROM BAKU

A FAMILY SAGA

VERENA DOHRN

Translated by Uri Themal

BOSTON
2022

Library of Congress Cataloging-in-Publication Data

Names: Dohrn, Verena, author. | Themal, Uri, translator, writer of foreword.
Title: The Kahans from Baku: a family saga / Verena Dohrn; translated by Uri Themal.
Other titles: Kahans aus Baku. English
Description: Boston: Academic Studies Press, 2022. | Series: Cherry Orchard Books | Summary: "The Kahans from Baku is a saga of a Russian Jewish family. Their story also provides an insight into the history of Jews in the Imperial Russian economy, especially in the oil industry. The entrepreneur and family patriarch, Chaim Kahan was a pious and enlightened man and a Zionist. His children followed in his footsteps in business as well as in policy, philanthropy and love of books. The Kahans from Baku takes us through a forced migration history in times of war and revolution and the 20th century's totalitarian regimes telling a story of fortune and misfortune in economy and everyday life of one cohesive family over four generations in Russia, Germany, Denmark and France, ending up in Palestine and the United States of America"-- Provided by publisher.
Identifiers: LCCN 2021041248 (print) | LCCN 2021041249 (ebook) | ISBN 9781644697542 (hardback) | ISBN 9781644697559 (paperback) | ISBN 9781644697566 (adobe pdf) | ISBN 9781644697573 (epub)
Subjects: LCSH: Cohen family. | Kahan, Chaim, 1850-1916. | Jews--Russia (Federation)--History--19th century. | Jews--Russia--History--20th century. | Jewish businesspeople--Russia (Federation)--History--19th century. | Jewish businesspeople--Russia (Federation)--History--20th century. | Jewish businesspeople--Germany--History--19th century. | Jewish business-people--Germany--History--20th century. | Jewish businesspeople--Europe--History--20th century. | Jews--Azerbaijan--Baku. | Zionism--Europe--History--19th century. | Zionism--Europe--History--20th century. | Petroleum industry and trade--History--19th century. | Petroleum industry and trade--History--20 century.
Classification: LCC DS134.92 .D6413 2022 (print) | LCC DS134.92 (ebook) | DDC 947.54/004924--dc23
LC record available at https://lccn.loc.gov/2021041248
LC ebook record available at https://lccn.loc.gov/2021041249

ISBN 9781644697542 (hardback)
ISBN 9781644697559 (paperback)
ISBN 9781644697566 (adobe pdf)
ISBN 9781644697573 (epub)

Book design by PHi Business Solutions
Cover design by Ivan Grave

Published by Cherry Orchard Books, an imprint of Academic Studies Press
1577 Beacon Street Brookline, MA 02446, USA

press@academicstudiespress.com
www.academicstudiespress.com

Dr. Elijahu (Eli) Rosenberg, Strasbourg, 2013

This edition is dedicated to
Dr. Elijahu Rosenberg, z"l, who accompanied my research over the years attentively and promoted it generously and who followed in the footsteps of his great grandfather, Chaim Kahan. Rosenberg was a geologist, a pioneer in oil and gas explorations in Israel. It was he who discovered, in June 1999, Israel's first offshore gas field, *Noa* (as part of the *Tethys field*), the beginning of many gas discoveries in the Mediterranean Sea.

Contents

Acknowledgements

The idea to write about the history of the entrepreneurs and oil wholesalers, the Kahan dynasty, was born in the context of the project "Charlottengrad und Scheunenviertel. East-European Jewish Migrants in Berlin, 1918–1939" at the Free University of Berlin. During a research trip to Israel as part of the project, I was introduced to descendants of the family. They came from Eastern Europe, had lived in Weimar Berlin and therefore fitted into the research field. In the exhibition "Berlin Transit," which our project organized together with the Jewish Museum Berlin, one room was dedicated to the Kahans. During the preparations for the exhibition, I met Jonah Gavrieli and saw the Haimi-Cohen family archive, which he kept. Jonah encouraged me to write about the history of the Kahans. The resulting book was published in German by Wallstein Verlag in Göttingen, but the descendants in Israel and the United States could not read it. Jonah initiated and took over the job to organize the translation project.

The research took me to fourteen countries and to numerous state archives—in Russia, Azerbaijan, Ukraine, Poland, Belarus, Lithuania, Denmark, England, France, Belgium, the Netherlands, Germany, the USA and Israel. Above all, however, my findings are based on the Haimi-Cohen archive. My special thanks therefore go to Jonah Gavrieli.

Jonah and Ittai Gavrieli ceded the Haimi-Cohen archive—partly as a gift, partly on loan—to the Jewish Museum Berlin, which provided me with the source material in digitalized form. Without the generous provision of the archive materials, I would not have been able to write my book. For this I would like to thank Aubrey Pomerance, the archive director of the Jewish Museum Berlin.

Written and oral family stories, numerous interviews and conversations with descendants in Israel and the USA complement the documents. Many have told me impressive and significant stories, shown me photo albums, provided valuable information and made further source texts available to me. In particular I would like to thank Daphna Cohen-Mintz, who introduced me to the Kahan descendants; Efrat Carmon, the historian of the family, who allowed me to share with her recollections of Kahan family saga; Giza Haimi-Cohen, the best storyteller; Dvora Ettinger-Rozenfeld (of blessed memory); Eli Rosenberg (of blessed memory); and Yossi Cohen (of blessed memory)—they gave me the first interviews—as well as Raziel Haimi-Cohen, who passed on many of his mother's stories to me; and Victor Ripp for the collegial dialogues.

I would particularly like to thank Eli Rosenberg for his generosity. For him the project of telling the story of his grandfather's fortune and his family's fate was a matter of the heart. It is for this reason that this book is dedicated to him.

I owe valuable insights to Aner Ater, Hagit Benziman and Anat Tzamir, Amos Cohen, Uli and Miriam Cohen-Mintz, Michal Froom, Naomi Loewenthal, Ylana Miller, Menachem Perl, Paul and Eleanor Ripp, Daniel Ripp, Raphael Romm, Mirriam Rosen and, last but not least, to Noa Rosenberg.

The descendants of Chaim and Malka Kahan supported my research in non-material and material ways. My thanks to the whole family for sponsoring the translation, which made this edition possible.

Furthermore, I would like to thank all my colleagues and contemporary witnesses for their help. First and foremost, I would like to thank Morten F. Larsen and Thomas Glad. I owe them a lot of information about the partnership between Kahans and L. C. Glad & Co. in Copenhagen.

In Azerbaijan I would like to thank Moisei Beker, Parvin Ahanchi, Rudolph Gil and Sabina Hayiev. In Belarus, Yefim Basin, Yevgeny Rozenblat, Olga Sobolevskaya, Alina Dzerevianka and Tatsiana Kasataya. In Bulgaria, Gergana Karadzhova. In Germany, Cornelia Rauh, Cilly Kugelmann, Miriam Goldmann, Leonore Maier, Jakob Stürmann, Hans-Jürgen Ritter, Markus Weber, Ulrich Räcker-Wellnitz, Wiebke Lisner, Teresa Willenborg, Elzbieta Kassner, Benedict Tondera, Elisabeth Piegsa, Gábor Lengyel, Ittai Joseph Tamari, Rachel Heuberger, Maike Strobel, Gisela Erler, Feli Gürsching, Tamara Or, Lutz Häfner, Ravi Kantian, Volkard Bir, Klaus Leising and Stephan Klatt. In Israel, Benjamin Lukin, David DeVries, Michael Beizer, Tamar Eshel, Daniella Wexler and Dorith Carmeli. In Latvia, Nadezhda Pasukhina. In Lithuania, Esfir Bramson (of blessed memory), Aelita Ambrulevičiūtė and Felix Ackermann. In the Netherlands, Erik Schumacher, Ineke and Pim Fenger. In Poland, Ruth Leiserowitz, Stephan Lehnstaedt, Jan Jagielski, Marta Rzepecka and Wojciech Kononczuk. In Russia, Aleksandr Ivanov, Oleg Budnitskii, Natalia L. Kolonitskaia (of blessed memory) and Olga Demidova. In the Ukraine, Yefim Melamed. In the USA, Diana Franzusoff-Peterson, Marion Kane, Gennady Estraikh, Michail Krutikov and Tatyana Chebotarev.

Doron Oberhand and Albina Gamburg helped me greatly in deciphering the Hebrew, Yiddish and Russian correspondence.

The Fritz Thyssen Foundation financed the research project. The German Historical Institute in Warsaw and the Schroubek Fonds in Munich promoted research trips to Poland, Belarus, Lithuania, Russia, Israel, the Netherlands and the United Kingdom. Without the generous support of the Fritz Thyssen Foundation and the interest shown by Wallstein Publishing House, this book could not have been written or published. I am truly grateful to both the Foundation and Publisher.

Many thanks to Uri Themal for his translation, which I was pleased to collaborate with, for the wonderful cooperation.

Last but not least I would like to thank my husband, Henning Dohrn, for his untiring patience as well as for his wise and loving support.

Preface

Jonah Gavrieli

The Book *Die Kahans aus Baku* is an intricate story that goes back to my maternal grandmother, Rachel Haimi-Cohen (Rosa Kahan née Rosenberg). Rachel was a direct descendant of Chaim and Malka Kahan, the founders of the Kahan "tribe," which this book is all about. Since her childhood Rachel was very much involved in the family affairs, and during her entire long life span (1896–1981) she collected and stored every piece of written family material that came her way. The written material was in Russian, German, Yiddish and Hebrew. The accumulated huge bulk of papers was stored without any explanation, description, or classification in a classic nineteenth-century traveling trunk kept in the living room.

My mother inherited the trunk and my father, after his retirement in 1985, tried, without much success, to make sense of the documents.

After the passing away of my mother in 2006, my brother and I inherited the trunk. My brother made it clear that he had no interest in that part of our joint inheritance, which led to me storing the content of the trunk on specially built shelves at my home. My wife, Michal, consistently asked: "What's the purpose of the storage?" and I consistently answered: "One day I will find use for the material …" not knowing what to anticipate.

And then:

The Jewish Museum in Berlin (JMB) decided on a temporary exhibition to portray the Jews from Eastern Europe who had made their way to the West, making Berlin a transit location. The exhibition was to take place in March 2012. In preparation for the exhibition, Ms. Miriam Goldmann, a curator of the JMB, and the historian Prof. Verena Dohrn came to Israel in 2010 looking for relevant artifacts. Prof. Mira Zakai had connected Verena Dohrn through Daphna Cohen-Mintz with Efrat Carmon, and thus contact was established with the descendants of Chaim and Malka Kahan.

Since I am two generations removed from the time the Kahans' descendants who lived in transit in Berlin, I was considered a minor information-source,

thus, only a brief meeting with me in Kiryat Tivon was scheduled. As was anticipated, I was not able to provide historical stories nor meaningful artifacts handed
down from the Berlin days of the family. Just before their departure, I invited
the guests to look into the stored boxes.

And that was the beginning of the book:

Instead of continuing that evening to another information source, Miriam
and Verena spent the evening until late that night and continued into late the
following morning, looking through the content of the boxes.

At this point of time Verena Dohrn decided that the story of building and
maintaining an international oil producing and distributing business by Chaim
Kahan and his wife Malka, and the involvement of their descendants in the
business, was a historic tale worth investigating.

The visit was concluded with thirteen kilograms of cramped papers being
sent to Berlin.

The exhibition took place as scheduled and was very successful. The
museum devoted to the Kahan family a full room in which artifacts and a small
part of the available documents were put on display. After the exhibition the
documents were given/loaned to the Jewish Museum Berlin to be kept for historians and for future generations of the Kahan family.

Verena Dohrn spent years of thorough academic research, learning the
content of thousands of documents and traveling to numerous locations, in
order to put together as a book the story of the "Kahan family from Baku."

The publishing of Verena's book caused great joy and pride within "the
tribe" of the descendants of Chaim and Malka Kahan, but since it was written in
the German language, a language no longer spoken by members of "the tribe,"
very few members could read the story of their family's history. So, in order
to make the family story available here and now and for future generations in
Israel and in North America, an English translation was necessary. I decided to
take the initiative and accepted the challenge of making a translation become
a reality.

For the translation, both a reliable and knowledgeable translator in
German and English language, in Jewish traditions and scripts, as well as
financial means to pay the translator for his work had to be found.

An outstanding translator, who happens to be a very good friend of Michal
and myself, Rabbi Uri Themal, was found. Uri was available and willing to do
the job, and indeed, a very good job he did.

The project was generously financed by various family members
I approached with a request for donations.

Dr. Eli Rosenberg, the only member of the Kahan "tribe" that followed in Chaim Kahan's footsteps as an entrepreneur in the energy field by finding the Israeli offshore gas deposits, was keenly interested in preserving the historical heritage of the Kahans and supported the translation of the book to English at its first steps. Thanks to his daughter Dr. Noa Rosenberg, the publishing of the English translation of the book before you, *The Kahans from Baku,* was made possible. The book is dedicated to the memory of Eli Rosenberg (who passed away in May 2020) in honor of his great contributions.

In conclusion, I wish to thank:

- Verena Dohrn for the great work she did in investigating and putting in writing the story of my family, the Kahan family from Baku.
- Rabbi Uri Themal for a wonderful translation into English of the book written by Verena Dohrn.
- All family members that contributed and made the translation possible.

In Memoriam Elijahu (Eli) Rosenberg

Noa Rosenberg

It is very moving for me to be writing an introduction to a book about the history of my family, beginning with the family's patriarch, my great-great-grandfather, Chaim Kahan, who passed away a century ago, though the memory of his deeds and incredible work still lives on in the minds of his descendants, six generations later. It begins in the late nineteenth century with a small refinery and petroleum trade in a competition with the large company Branobel, the enterprise of the brothers Ludwig and Robert Nobel, in Czarist-ruled Baku, goes on the with the purchase of the Petrol oilfields in Baku in 1912, the establishment of the Nitag oil company in Weimar Berlin by his children and the integration of this company into a European cooperate networks of oil companies with their own fleet of shipping tankers. The history of both the business acumen and the involvement of the Kahan family with the Zionist project is recounted by historian Verena Dohrn in her recently published book, *Die Kahans aus Baku: Eine Familienbiographie*.

I was privileged to be entrusted with writing an introduction to the English translation of this book, a translation that was envisaged and initially financed by my late father, Elijahu Rosenberg, one of Chaim Kahan's great-grandchildren. This will also serve as an apology and homage to my dear, beloved father, whose heart gave out a few months ago at ninety-two years of age, just a few months before the completion of the translation.

Dr. Elijahu Rosenberg reestablished Nitag in Berlin in the early 2000s, after the Kahan family was driven out from the original firm with the rise of the Nazi regime. As a geologist, my father was involved in oil explorations all over the world. His occupation as a geologist was worldwide. The Nitag company he set up in Berlin was intended to extend the scope of his search for oil and gas to Europe. It turns out that geology, deep down in the ground, has no borders—unlike up on Earth's surface.

It is easy to point out quite a few aspects of resemblance between Chaim Kahan ("Grandfather Chaim" to all his descendants) and his great-grandson,

Elijahu Rosenberg. Both of them, being persons of vision and enterprise, were pioneers in the energy market (oil and gas), and in this market they both made their fortunes: Chaim Kahan, a shtetl-born Jew, who in the second half of the nineteenth century already traded with oil from the Azerbaijani capital of Baku, was a pioneer in spreading light to Russia, while his geologist great-grandson was a pioneer of gas exploration and discovery in the Mediterranean. Both were generous people, open-hearted and open-handed, who saw their wealth as an opportunity to give unto others, very often quietly, away from the limelight. Both never forgot their own periods of economic hardships. Both were honest, open and truthful, and their good name preceded them.

Elijahu Rosenberg was born in Berlin and presented his doctoral thesis in geology to the University of Zürich and to the federal technical college ETH Zürich. Decades later, he had heard from the historian Verena Dohrn that she intends to write a book about Chaim Kahan's—and his seven children's— role both in the oil market and in Zionism and Hebrew revival. Although the German was his spoken language, familiar to him, my father offered to help her book translated from German into English—for the benefit of Chaim Kahan's younger descendants, most of whom live in Israel while a few families live in the USA. True to his word, Rosenberg was the first who generously contributed towards the realization of his fondest wish—to commemorate the work of the various Kahan generations and to pass it on to all of Chaim Kahan's descendants, from now on.

It is only right that this book—though he never saw it completed—be dedicated to him.

I vividly recall a conversation with my father, a few years ago, when he stumbled upon two consecutive articles about Chaim Kahan, his great-grandfather, printed in 1917 issues of the Hebrew quarterly *Heavar*. My father was thrilled and seemed to be overflowing with a keen sense of intimacy and perhaps with a sense of the resemblance between the two of them. When I told him that his thrill may be due to his noticing that resemblance and to the realization that this grandparent was the source of his own inspiration, he quickly and humbly rejected this view on the spot.

However, my father explained to me how Grandfather Chaim was "a visionary, who was ahead of his time in realizing the potential of petroleum, following the first oil drillings in America," and told me of his extreme generosity, his frequent donations and his inspired spirit. He quoted from the article on Chaim Kahan: "Many were aided by him, but the relationship between them remained casual and simple, so that it was impossible to tell, who was the benefactor and who the beneficiary" (Meir Aronson, *Heavar* 1 [1917]). My father also said that Chaim Kahan sometimes made donations against his sons' judgement. I smiled. My father then told me a story that used to run in the family, about the occasion when Grandfather acquiesced to a request for a larger donation, just when a huge fire devoured much of his property and fortune. His sons were alarmed when they realized that their father keeps making donations to the needy, despite the fire. Grandfather Chaim's response to his sons was: "True, a lot of money went up in smoke, so you just go ahead and imagine that a little more was burnt." This lesson in family tradition made me realize just how much my father admired his great-grandfather's values and way of life, and how much he made them his own, perhaps even getting a sense of intergenerational epigenetics. Furthermore, his thrill in telling me this made me think of his own generosity, and of the deep, unseen link between him and his great-grandfather. I sensed a subterranean link to a deep, ancient geological layer which tied them both together: my father Elijahu Rosenberg and grandfather Chaim Kahan.

Elijahu was born in 1928 in Berlin to Shulamith (Sulamith née Hurwitz) and Nahum Rosenberg, Chaim Kahan's grandson (on his mother's side). At the age of five, he immigrated to the land of Israel with his beloved family (his parents and his eldest brother, Michael).

Verena Dohrn's book concludes with the observation that of all of Chaim Kahan's descendants, it was his great-grandson, Rosenberg, who carried on his grandfather's work in the field of energy sources, oil and gas. Rosenberg was a geologist, a pioneer in oil and gas explorations in Israel's Exclusive Economic Zone of the Mediterranean Sea. He founded the oil and gas exploration company Avner (the Hebrew acronym of his full Jewish name, Elijahu Son of Nahum Rosenberg). It was he who discovered Israel's first offshore gas field, Noa (the harbinger of further gas finds, as part of the Tethys field). A thrilling climax came on Hanukkah, December 25, 2003, with the beginning of gas production from deep within the Earth, in the middle of the sea. The gas flowed from the offshore platform towards the Israeli shore and to the Ashkelon power plant, and lights went on in Israel's central district. Eli Rosenberg's thorough understanding of the geological and geophysical wonders of gas reservoirs, and his unique interpretation of singular phenomena in the deep-sea electric diagrams, were what provided Israel with gas for electricity. "It was thanks to Eli that Israel came out of darkness and into light," as was said of him in an obituary, upon his death in May 2020.

In conclusion, I would like to add one more trait to the list of resemblances between Chaim Kahan and his great-grandson, Elijahu Rosenberg. As described by Meir Aronson in his account of Chaim Kahan in *Heavar*:

"He was never consumed by the majority, by the crowd, nor did he assimilate into it. Rather, he stood off to one side, apart from the group. He was looking for those single persons, those individuals closest to his heart, with whom he would confer away by the corner, because he was 'solitary' and 'self-possessed,' of deeply-rooted noble spirit, and his soul yearned for 'the solitary.'"

A half-century later, Israel's third president, Zalman Shazar, turned to Eli Rosenberg, who was trying to retire by the corner, inviting him from the crowd to take his place by the president, and said with heartwarming determination: "Even though you are a geologist, do not hide yourself behind the rocks."[1]

BIBLIOGRAPHY

Meir Aronson, "R. Chaim Kahan," *Heavar* [Peterburg] 1 (1917): 33–38.

Efrat Carmon, "Misadut haneft leshchunot Mekor Chaim: Chaim Kahan, po'elo vemishmachto," in *Mekor Chaim. Sipura shel shchuna bedroma shel Yerushalaim*, ed. Yossi Spanier, Eyal Meiron, and Reuven Gafni (Jerusalem: Keren Kayemet Le-Israel, 2015), 105–116.

---

1 A paraphrase of a well-known sentence addressed King Shaul in the Bible: "Do not hide yourself behind the tools."

Translator's Foreword

Uri Themal

My wife, Geraldine, and I first heard about this project from our good friends Michal and Jonah Gavrieli, over a series of Shabbat dinners, when Jonah would entertain us with snippets from his family's history, as they came to light through Verena Dohrn's research. Little did I know how intimately I would become involved in it.

When the book was published in German, Jonah lent it to me to read. I found it fascinating and was delighted when he asked me to do the translation. I considered it an honor and accepted with great pleasure.

The translation itself posed a few challenges. First, there were the names of people and places. The book, by its very nature, contains a large number of those and they needed to be transliterated into an acceptable English spelling. Where the original name was in Cyrillic, I was working from a transliteration into German. With some place names that was easy, for example, *Brest-Litowsk* is already known in English as *Brest-Litovsk*. People's names posed a greater difficulty and we had to agree on a formula for those, especially where it involves the guttural *ch*, as in *Chaim*. Like in this example, the German spelling is usually kept in English texts, but in other cases, *kh* is used, like in *Kharkov*, which is known as such in English.

Secondly, there were the various foreign-language words, idioms, or quotes in Yiddish, Russian, or Hebrew, which were left in their original with a translation in square brackets. In some cases, I needed to see the original text, which added to the excitement of working on this project.

Thirdly, there were the original texts of letters or documents, quoted in the German book. The German translation tried to be true to their original style, including imperfect use of language. Withstanding the temptation to iron those out, I tried to convey the content and style as accurately as possible. So, for example, Chaim Kahan's letters, which are written in his own kind of shorthand, with scant regard for interpunctuation or grammatic accuracy, appear as such in the translation.

However, all these challenges were managed with relative ease through the great collaboration with Verena Dohrn, who had accepted the role as editor of the English translation. Our discussions were always enjoyable as well as enlightening and I am truly grateful to her.

I would also like to thank my wife Geraldine for acting as a subeditor, ensuring that any typing, grammatical and idiomatic errors were eliminated.

Finally, my sincere thanks go to Jonah and the descendants of the Kahan dynasty for entrusting me with the task of making their family history available to the English-language reader.

CHAPTER 1

Jacob Kahan.
Imprisoned. Berlin

September 1914. War had been raging in Europe for a month and a half. It was probably difficult for Jacob to grasp what had happened since then. In June they had gone to the summer resorts. As in previous years, he and his two brothers, their parents, grandparents, aunts, uncles and cousins had come from St. Petersburg, Kharkov, Baku, Yekaterinoslav and Berlin, to spend the summer together, or at least close to each other, as was customary among middle-class Jewish families who were scattered over long distances, even across several national borders. The majority of them had gathered in the Hessian-Franconian-Rhineland triangle. This year the parents took the waters in Wiesbaden, the Rosenbergs in Bad Kissingen, the grandparents in Bad Neuenahr. In Wiesbaden Jacob had learned to cycle shortly before they were leaving due to the outbreak of the war. The past six months had been turbulent and somewhat unreal with the unexpected move of Cousin Rosa from Warsaw to Berlin in late December, the trip to Egypt and Palestine with parents and grandparents in April, the reunion with his brother in Jaffa, the outbreak of war during the summer retreat and now the forced trip to Berlin. He had just successfully completed the second semester in Munich. Now he was stuck in Berlin. The solitary confinement cells in the Berlin-Mitte city jail on Dirksenstrasse were anything but comfortable. Jacob, the student from a well-to-do bourgeois home, had become a prisoner from one day to the next. He had been arrested as an "enemy alien." There was only one person who could have helped him in this situation—his grandfather, but he was far away now, somewhere in the Russian Empire, in St. Petersburg, Kharkov, Saratov, Kislovodsk, or Baku.

Austria-Hungary's declaration of war on Serbia on July 28 had depressed the mood of the Jewish holiday guests in the health resorts. The bad news about the political turmoil had destroyed the idyllic tranquility of the health seekers. News, telegrams and newspapers, which were awaited impatiently by the spa guests, comprising merchants, manufacturers and bankers, arrived only slowly due to the bad postal and rail connections. In the face of the crippling uncertainty, unrest spread at the spring water wells, in the pump halls and reading rooms, at the lunch tables and among the nervously gesticulating groups of people gathering around the meager dispatches. In addition, there was the drop in temperature. Following the hot days, it suddenly started raining and turned cool.

The day after the declaration of war, Rosa complained in her letter from Bad Kissingen to Jacob in Wiesbaden about the bad weather and the frightening political situation: "The war thoroughly spoils everyone's mood and nothing else is heard or talked about." Jacob, equally disgruntled, tried to cheer her up in his letter the next day, encouraging Rosa not to be alarmed and to follow his example. He had been using the time in Wiesbaden to learn to cycle.

When Germany sided with Austria-Hungary, and both declared war on the Russian Empire on August 1, the Kahan and Rosenberg families felt almost excited. While longing for the collapse of the old Tsarist regime, they worried about their economic livelihood, which could be endangered by a European war. At that time, the grandparents were staying in the Villa Daheim guesthouse in Bad Neuenahr in the Rhineland, Jacob with his parents and brothers in the Hotel Ritter, one of the two Jewish "well-managed, ritual hotels" in the old Hessian spa in Wiesbaden, and the Rosenbergs in the Villa Esplanade in the Bavarian Spa in Kissingen. According to memoirs, they "got stuck" in Germany that summer because of the beginning of the war. In order to avoid internment in more uncomfortable places, the grandfather had rented an entire hotel for the family. This was acceptable to the local police. The Kahans and Rosenbergs were stuck in Bad Nauheim.

The sudden outbreak of war caused thousands of Russians to be held back in Germany, Austrians to be expelled from France and Belgium to Germany, and Palestinians to be cut off from their homeland. A few hundred Eastern European Jews, who had spent the summer in German health resorts, were concentrated in Bad Nauheim, recalled Nachum Goldmann, who also bunked there after he had been banished from Frankfurt am Main, as a stateless student and Jew of Eastern European origin, because of insubordination to the state authorities. They were allowed to live in hotels. Since they were mostly wealthy people, they were doing pretty well. Aron Kahan, Jacob's uncle, was already on his way home at the time. The news of the fire at the Kahan refinery in Riga, which he happened to see in a Berlin newspaper, drove him back to the Russian Empire. In his memoirs he wrote about this. Given the many soldiers and nurses, and the presence of the Red Cross at the train station, he realized already then that the situation was more serious than expected: "During our entire trip, military trains came towards us on their way to the border, and in Gatchina soldiers told us that the Germans had just crossed the border into Russia. The world war had started." Most, especially the wealthy Russians, who had been surprised in Germany by the start of the war, were able to travel home over the next few weeks—including the Kahans. Jacob's father Baruch, his brother Nachum and grandfather Chaim returned to the Russian Empire via Sweden and Finland together with relatives from Baku and Yekaterinoslav. But his mother Rosalia and his youngest brother Arusia stayed in Germany with the Rosenbergs and so did Bendet Kahan with his wife and children. These two families had recently moved to Germany and had an easier time coming home. From the summer resort they travelled to Berlin.

As a young man fit for military service and a citizen of the war enemy, Russia, Jacob apparently had the greatest problems. He was not only expelled from the university, but also arrested shortly before the High Holidays. How he got from Wiesbaden to the Berlin-Mitte city jail on Dirksenstrasse remains uncertain. In any case, he was detained there. Postcards, letters and notes from this period are preserved among the family archives. As soon as possible, Jacob contacted his relatives from the prison, and they got in touch with him, conforming to the applicable Prussian regulations: open letters, in the official language, German, and without any critical word about the conditions of his detention.

From one day to the next, Germany shrunk into a single Prussian prison cell for the nineteen-year-old, which he shared with three young Jews from Poland. Many poor Jews from the Russian Empire who saw no way to get home were also held there. In addition, there was the risk of being transferred to the internment camp for civilian prisoners and hostages from the enemy countries in Holzminden, where several thousand people from France and the Russian Empire were held in inhumane conditions during the war years.

The fact that Rosh Hashanah, the New Year, was imminent, exacerbated the predicament for Jacob, who was a traditional and religious Jew. The Jewish community alleviated his needs. Represented by a certain Rabbi Dr. Levy, they cared for the spiritual and physical wellbeing of the prisoners over the festive season. In addition, the rabbi, who lived in Charlottenburg in the immediate vicinity of the Kahans and Rosenbergs, personally sent messages to the families. Jacob also hoped for help from Dr. Ludwig A. Rosenthal, who at that time was highly regarded as an Orthodox rabbi and scholar in Berlin. Rosenthal, from the German-ruled Putzig, Puck in Polish, was born near Danzig. He was a contemporary, coreligionist and fellow traveler of Jacob's grandfather and, in a way, a compatriot of his. Jacob's grandfather, Chaim Kahan, had good connections to the Orthodox community in Germany, which in turn maintained close contacts with the Jews in Eastern Europe. Through his grandfather, Jacob had found accommodation before the war at the Rosenthals in Berlin, 108 Chausseestrasse, and made friends with the family.

> I feel so lonely and abandoned today. I have a great longing for you. When will we see each other again? ... Why didn't you send me anything to eat today? You are supposed to send something every day and a lot. I also need laundry and money. God bless you all, you dear ones! May he send you good luck and save you from such difficult times. Yours, Jacob Kahan

In view of the upcoming High Holidays, Rosh Hashanah and Yom Kippur, when one isolated oneself even more than usual, retreated to services in the synagogue and then to the family, where they prayed and sang together while sharing ritual meals, the pressure on inmate Jacob and his misery in the prison cell was so great that he made a concession to the German authorities and submitted a concrete proposal for his release. He promised to stay in Berlin during the war and not return to either Munich or his parents in Kharkov and suggested that he could rely upon the authority and influence of Rabbi Ludwig A. Rosenthal. However, the family was unable to free Jacob before Rosh Hashanah. Apart from a brief note on the back of a prison form that Jacob received from Uncle Bendet after an unsuccessful attempt to get freed, a card from Cousin Rosa was the first written message from the family. "We are doing everything we can to get you released and hopefully you will be back soon," she wrote. "Your last card broke my heart completely: you are too agitated ... But, Jacob dear, you have to try not to be like that!" Cousins Jacob and Rachel, nicknamed Yasha and Rosa or Roska, were particularly close. Three years earlier, so it is said, when he was sixteen and she was thirteen, they had promised to marry each other, while attending the circumcision ceremony of Cousin Moshe Ettinger in Yekaterinoslav.

After Rosh Hashanah Jacob got in touch again with a long letter from cell number 584 of the city jail: "My dear ones! The holidays are over! We did everything we could to observe them in a dignified manner." He described how fifteen men spent New Year's Day together in one prison cell praying and blowing the shofar under the leadership of a cantor, eating and sleeping. The community had sent not only a cantor, but kosher meat meals on both festival days. According to the letter, Jacob was still angry and hardly more confident about his release, but at the same time he seemed to come to terms with his custody. For the first time, the family found out more about the prison regulations—visits had to be requested from the commandant, visiting times had to be observed—and about the fellow inmates: among them was gentleman with a PhD, who had apparently been stopped in transit and was separated from his suitcase, and there was also someone whose most basic wherewithal was lacking.

With that, the connections on which Jacob and the family had set their hopes became apparent. As Jacob wrote:

> Some rabbis visited us. ... Yesterday Dr. Rabbi Munk was here. He was amazed to see me here because he thought I was already free. He said that Dr. Nathan and Hermann Struck will speak to the commandant for me and that I will be released because my grandfather has donated to the Tachkemoni School, which is under German protection. Is it all true? And when will freedom finally come?

Rabbi Esra Esriel Munk, born in Altona in 1867 and died in Jerusalem in 1940, one of the outstanding fighters for Orthodox Judaism in Germany with influence on the state government and city administration in Berlin, had visited the prisoners. Since 1900 he had served as rabbi and chairman of the rabbinical court of the Orthodox community Adass Yisroel as an expert on Jewish affairs in the Prussian Ministry of Culture and as a leading member of numerous Jewish Orthodox associations. The Kahan and Rosenberg families were closely associated with Adass Yisroel in Berlin and therefore known to Rabbi Munk. Jacob was supposed to have been released due to the intercession by Dr. Paul Nathan and Hermann Struck. Paul Nathan was known as the founder and dedicated director of the Aid Organization of German Jews. From 1900 to 1919, he also represented the Progressive People's Party as a city councilor in Berlin. In those days, at the beginning of the war, he had not only founded the Interdenominational Aid Committee for Jews in the Occupied Eastern Territories, but also a committee to repatriate poor Russian Jews to their homeland. About sixteen thousand people were transported in seventeen special trains. The painter and graphic artist Hermann Struck, best known in Germany for his portraits of eastern European Jews and prisoners of war, belonged to the circle of active religious Zionists in Mizrachi and was associated with the Kahan family throughout his life. A few months before the start of the war, Hermann Struck, Chaim Kahan, Jonas Rosenberg and the librarian Hermann Pick, who was also active in Mizrachi and employed by the Prussian State Library, were sitting together in a Charlottenburg apartment, making plans, and decided to convert the Tachkemoni School into a high school, based on a generous donation from Chaim Kahan amounting to 55,000 gold francs (44,550 gold marks, whereby a gold mark had about five times the purchasing power of one euro today), a handsome sum. The Tachkemoni School in Jaffa had been under the supervision of the western Mizrachi center in Frankfurt am Main for years and was considered a model for the religious-Zionist educational system in Palestine. In gratitude, Struck had portrayed Chaim Kahan in oil—the painting is one of the family's most striking heirlooms—in duplicate, one for the donor without, and one copy for the Tachkemoni School with, a kippah. Shortly thereafter, Jacob traveled to Palestine with his grandparents in a group of Zionist politicians. His grandfather wanted to get an impression of the school.

For Jacob this was the second trip to Palestine. He first got to know the country in the summer of 1911 and met his parents there. Perhaps they had sent him on this trip, shortly after he had cancelled his first stay in Berlin, to learn how to deal with a foreign land and with homesickness. This time, however, Jacob was travelling on an official mission, in a "Zionist Commission," as Kurt Blumenfeld later called it. He was to accompany his grandfather and grandmother. His parents had already travelled ahead. The commission was personally led by Nachum Sokolow, a member of the executive committee of the Zionist Organization. Kurt Blumenfeld, then general secretary of the Zionist Organization, was also part of the tour group. The first stop, as was customary at the time, was Egypt. They looked at the pyramids in Egypt and visited the museum in Cairo before taking the train to Port Said and from there an Austrian Lloyd ship to Jaffa. A photo album from the trip has been preserved, with small, somewhat faded pictures pushed into dark-gray black-rimmed passe-partouts. They give us an idea of how Jacob, while waiting for his release, might have dispelled fear and boredom. The tourist highlights can be seen in these photos—pyramids, camels, a veiled woman, palm groves, the Dead Sea coast in front of desert mountains, the Mediterranean coast in front of Jaffa with fishing boats, the old town, the Temple Mount in Jerusalem, Tel Aviv under construction, Bedouin tents, the railway line from Jaffa to Jerusalem, but also some personal photos—his mother on a camel, grandfather in a horse-drawn carriage, his parents on the balcony of a house, a self-portrait. In addition, formal photos: Grandfather in the middle of the Zionist Commission, visiting the Tachkemoni School among numerous, venerable looking people, mostly men. On one photo, there is Jacob in the back row. Jacob had apparently attended all of his grandfather's important meetings. He wrote to his mother that visiting the Hakham Bashi Chaim Nachum Effendi, chief rabbi of the Ottoman Empire, on his return trip to Constantinople had been particularly exciting. The grandfather was not only a sponsor of the Tachkemoni School, but was also involved in the acquisition of land in Palestine. Jacob had also completed the one-week return trip with only his grandparents, via Port Said, Alexandria, Salonika, Constantinople, Sofia and Vienna. Chaim and Malka Kahan had traveled on from there to Berlin, but he went to Munich, while the parents stayed in Palestine for two more weeks, until the second half of May, when they followed with brother Arusia. In April 1914 Hermann Struck sent Chaim Kahan a postcard with his own etching: "Dear Mr. Kahan, I am very happy to learn from your family here that you have traveled well. Hopefully you are in good health and can tackle our great work there. With best wishes and warm regards, your devoted Hermann Struck." Now, at the beginning of the war, while Jacob was in custody, Struck was a member of the Aid Committee for Jewish Exiles of the Zionist Association for Germany.

Cousin Rosa immediately responded to Jacob's detailed letter with a postcard: "I think you are calmer now and I am very happy about that. There is nothing new with us"—she wrote, once again conjuring up her love for Jacob and invoking the close family relationships and friendships that tied them to Berlin. The ties with brothers and cousins, and with their mutual friends Trude and Rosa, the daughters of Rabbi Rosenthal, represented the good relations of the Kahans and Rosenbergs with the German-Jewish society. For the first time, Rosa's brother Noma also appeared in a short addendum and with a greeting written in Gothic script.

For Jacob, Berlin had previously been primarily associated with the memories of Rosa Rosenthal. During his first stay in the city, she had replaced his mother and cousin, in short, the family, whom he had been missing so painfully. That was almost four years ago, when he was fifteen and his parents had sent him from Kharkov to Berlin so that, like his father formerly in Frankfurt am Main, he could continue his German studies that he had started in Antwerp. In Berlin he was living in the home of Rabbi Rosenthal and prepared for the entrance exam at the Dorotheenstadt High School. He apparently passed the exam, but had barely entered high school when he returned to Kharkov. Unlike in Antwerp, where he had lived with the family, he was alone in Berlin. A photo from 1910, which was probably taken at the Berlin school, shows a slightly disturbed-looking lanky adolescent in a double-breasted jacket. Stand-up collar and tie are tightly bound around his neck.

Jacob remembered Rosa Rosenthal's bright eyes, her kindness and tenderness. Only recently had she expressed her affection for him in a letter, called him "dear brother Jacob" and raved about "big black Yasha with the dreamy black eyes." Rosa was meanwhile married to the merchant Yossel Langer and lived in her own apartment in Schöneberg. Only following her encouragement did Jacob overcome his shyness and confess to her in a carefully crafted return letter, painstakingly composed and written in German, which was probably the reason why it was preserved. His soul was drawn to her, he wrote, like a flower to the sun. Thereupon she had consoled him with a reunion in Palestine, the land of her longing, where she envisaged Yasha as a minister and herself as a visitor. Rosa Rosenthal was obviously Jacob's maternal-erotic love. The bond remained even after he had promised himself to his cousin Rosa Rosenberg.

Finally, his mother got in touch by letter, which she had penned in Berlin Charlottenburg—perhaps quite deliberately—on a bulletin page and under the business letterhead of Max Lew, "General Representative of the Russian-Baltic Mineral Oil Company Inc. (formerly Ch. N. Kahan), St. Petersburg," which revealed Jacob's status as a member of a Russian family of entrepreneurs with proven business contacts in Germany. Max Lew acted as the main agent for the family business in Berlin and was one of the most important players in the business association. His mother wrote: "My dear son! I have read your postcards. It was so unexpected! I'm only too well aware of your innocence. I assure you that your release is expected, and that's why I didn't send you laundry or food." In some parts of the letter, his mother's writing is blurred with tears.

Jacob had sent seven cards and letters from his prison to the family as cries for help, all written in pencil (the ink had run out in the middle of the first card), so that the writing had faded. Mother, cousin and uncle returned just as many postcards, letters and notes to him. The correspondence was kept in two bundles at different locations. What joy when I could put them together. All cards and letters are written in German, in a language foreign to the Kahans, because they were censored by Prussian officials. Jacob's letters not only portray fear and pain, but also report relief in the form of food deliveries and other amenities. "My dear darling mother! I just received your letter and the suitcase with the laundry and food that you sent me. Thank you so much! I was so sad today because I had no news from you. Now I am comforted and patiently await the release that I hope will happen this week. My spirit and that of my cellmates is very high, thanks to the good news."

Jacob was apparently privileged as a prisoner. He made every effort to be a good Jew, an advocate for his fellow prisoners. At the same time, the longing for things familiar in peacetime emanated from his words. His desire to participate in family events, at least from a distance, was made possible, at least symbolically, by the gifts of love that his cousin and mother had enclosed with their letters: another postcard and a letter in a light blue miniature envelope from Rosa, again on Max Lew's stationery, and his mother's lines. As the next High Holiday, Yom Kippur, the Day of Atonement, was approaching, the impatience and unrest about whether and when Jacob would be released grew again. "Dear Jacob! Many greetings and kisses! Sending you food, chess and the laundry you asked for. Enjoy your meal. Bon appetite! Write a few words and send them to me, if possible. Rosa"—"My dear beloved son, Yasha! I'll bring you a bottle of milk and some fruit with butter, including the *tefillin*. How are you with your runny nose? You got a warm jumper. We are very worried about you and all of us hope to hug you on Erev Yom Kippur. Please God! Please return the *machzor* I sent you. That's because you won't need it. I'm waiting for it." Just in case, his mother sent the obligatory festival greetings—*chatima tovah* [may you be inscribed in the book of life], meaning relief from all guilt towards others, and well over the fast.

After graduating from high school in Kharkov as an external student, Jacob returned to Berlin in September 1913 to study there, at about the same time as Uncle Bendet Kahan, who rented a nineteen-room apartment in 36 Schlüterstrasse, in Berlin-Charlottenburg, on behalf of the grandfather. But Jacob preferred to live again with the Rosenthals in Chausseestrasse. When his application for the Friedrich-Wilhelms University was rejected, his father advised him, from the summer resort in Merano, to study in England, France, or Italy, but Jacob decided on Munich. It was not easy for him to deal with the expectations that parents and grandparents had of him as the eldest son and grandson. Added to this was the politically difficult situation and the restrictions on him as a Russian citizen and a Jew.

Nevertheless, Jacob enjoyed the protection and privileges of the family as long as possible. Even in prison, he maintained a bourgeois lifestyle. He took care of his physical, mental and spiritual wellbeing and also looked after his fellow prisoners. From this he drew energy and self-confidence. At the same time, he kept an overview of the situation. He got money from the family to buy food and services for himself and his fellow sufferers. Jacob and another inmate received lunch from a restaurant in the nearby Burgstrasse, an idyllic shopping street on the River Spree in Altberlin, opposite the castle, where the stock exchange and some well-known venues were located, such as the Cassels Hotel, King of Portugal and the Stock Exchange Hotel. Many merchants, agents and stockbrokers lived there, and even more used to come and go. In 1914, the kosher restaurant in the Cassels Hotel & Restaurant, managed by Adass Yisroel and headed by Leopold Pelteson, in which the student Sammy Gronemann and his fellow students from the rabbinical seminar used to dine, had long ceased to exist. The hotel King of Portugal had taken it over. However, the King of Portugal, too, was managed with "strictly ritual cuisine" and an in-house synagogue in accordance with Jewish traditions and regulations under the direction of the wine merchant Richter. There was also the Burg Hotel, at 20 Burgstrasse, owned by S. Lewin. Jacob would get his lunch from one of the two houses.

> 27. IX. 1914. City jail. My dear mother! Although I gave the supervisor my letter from last night half an hour ago, I'm yet writing again because I have thought of something. The vest I asked for should be from the black suit I had made in Kharkov. It is in the big suitcase. I don't need a mirror because there is one in my soap box. Besides that, I want to have a small spirit machine with a small, light cooking pot. In addition, a double spoon for tea. I only drink hot coffee in the morning and I sometimes want to warm up. When I actually get released, these will be of great benefit for my comrades. I also want to have books to read, something serious, Nietzsche or Wedekind's *Spring Awakening*! You have a lot of Russian Universal-Library books. I could give them to my comrades. It might seem strange to you that I supply myself as if I intended to sit here for another month. But who knows? A week ago, my uncle was here to pick me up and wrote that on the next day I'd be free, but I'm still here. If I am not released by Yom Kippur, you must definitely visit me on Tuesday 10–11. You can bring some of the things I asked for tomorrow, the rest then. It would have been good, had you sent me food and fruit. I'm sending warm greetings to everyone and am your Yasha

Apart from the Primus stove with saucepan and tea strainer, chessboard, fresh laundry and warm clothes, Jacob asked that books be sent to prison. He had a special interest in literature. That is why he studied philology. His book requests revealed that he shared the taste of his generation in Germany, but that at the same time classic Russian literature was available to him. Yiddish was his mother tongue, and Hebrew was a must for a Zionist Litvak. Jacob was born in Warsaw, but his family came from the northwestern border region of the Russian Empire, called Kresy in Polish, a place where the St. Petersburg government found it difficult to hold its own. The eventful history of the Russian-Belarusian-Polish-Lithuanian border country testifies to that. There, the national borders were always drawn arbitrarily. They intersect in the Kresy cultural landscapes with ethno-denominational diversity in which the Jewish diaspora was significant and itself diverse for over six hundred years, since the fourteenth century and until its destruction and the murder of the Jews during the Holocaust. The Jews living according to rabbinic tradition in Lithuania were called Litvaks. The Kahans were Litvaks.

The ability to speak multiple languages and live in different cultures was Jacob's asset, worth at least as much as his family's financial wealth. His religious way of life gave him support. But how did he reconcile reading Nietzsche and Wedekind, their revolts, social criticism, individualism and skepticism, with a life according to the Jewish religion and tradition?

> 29. IX. 1914.ערב יום כיפור [Erev Yom Kippur]. My dears! Today I and a few comrades were admitted to the lieutenant, who told us that we were about to be released. He very much regretted that he could not give us the release papers straight away, but promised to do everything, even send telegrams, so that we could be released before dark today. I'm waiting impatiently, but there is still an hour to go till the holiday and the dispatch has not yet arrived. If it comes tonight or tomorrow morning, I will ask permission to stay here for the holiday. Uncle Bendet should wait for me downstairs. I have sent him a note. In any case, I wish you all the best for יום כיפור [Yom Kippur] and חתימה טובה [chatimah tovah] with greetings to you all. Yasha

Jacob even put religious duty above freedom. Already before Rosh Hashanah, when he had the religious duty to take a ritual bath before the High Holidays—his mother had hinted at it in one of her letters—he was unable to fulfil his ritual obligation. Now he was determined to follow his religious duty: should the imminent release take place after dark, after the beginning of Yom Kippur, he would voluntarily remain in prison in order to comply with the requirement to rest on the *yom tov*, the holiday. Nachum Goldmann's memoirs of the interned Russians in Bad Nauheim at the beginning of the war testify to the importance for a Jew to live according to traditional religious regulations. When they were denied ritual baths before the High Holidays in the only accessible *mikveh* in nearby Friedberg, with the argument that there were enough baths in Bad Nauheim, Nachum Goldmann successfully stood up for them with the town major of Frankfurt.

Jacob's correspondence with the family from the city jail on Dirksenstrasse ended in September 1914 with the hurried lines in erratic handwriting scribbled on the eve of the High Holiday, just before the start of Erev Yom Kippur.

CHAPTER 2

Chaim Kahan.
From Orlya to Brest-Litovsk

Chaim Kahn was an unusual person, a rare type. A restless spirit with inexhaustible energy. His head was always full of plans and ideas. He was a talented person with a wild imagination and amazing traits.

—Meir Aronson

Jacob's grandfather Chaim-Moshe ben Nachman, called Chaim Kahan, was the son of Melamed Moshe Nachman Hacohen in *shtetl* Orlya. He was born around 1850, had three older brothers, and grew up as an orphan. The mother died after his birth. It was the time of panic over the arbitrariness of Tsar Nicholas I. As a precaution, the father gave the four sons three different surnames to protect them from military service, which was particularly cruel at the time. He named the two older ones Ahron and Aba Kamenetsky, and the two younger ones, Shaul Falk and Chaim Cohen. The fewer sons registered with the same surname, the more secure they were from being drafted. Early marriage served as a second precaution. Therefore, and because the family was poor, Chaim was married at the age of thirteen, barely having had his Bar Mitzvah.

Although it is said that he came from a family of scholars, and although his grandson Arusia respectfully, and, as was customary, traced the Kahans genealogy back to the seventeenth century, Chaim's father was one of the common people. He was neither a scholar, nor a land or tax leaseholder, an entrepreneur, or a wholesale merchant. He was also not counted among the community's officials or employees, but he was one of the many teachers who taught children under six Torah and prayers and also ran a business on the side, to make ends meet. Among the family legacy there is little evidence of Chaim's childhood.

The place where he grew up was in Grodno Province, near Byelsk, today Polish Orla near Bielsk Podlaski on the border with Belarus. Accordingly, the historical territory of Podlaskie in eastern Poland between the Western Bug and Memel, Łomża and Brest with Bielsk at the center was Chaim Kahan's homeland. Orlya is located on the Orlyanka river.

> The townlet of my birth, Motol, stood—and perhaps still stands—on the banks of a little river in the great marsh area, which occupies much of the province … and adjacent provinces in White Russia; flat, open country, mournful and monotonous but, with its rivers, forests and lakes, quite picturesque. Between the rivers the soil was sandy, covered with pine and furze; closer to the banks the soil was black, the trees were leaf bearing. In the spring and autumn, the area was a sea of mud, in the winter a world of snow and ice; in the summer, it was covered with a haze of dust. All about, in hundreds of towns and villages, Jews lived, as they had lived for many generations, scattered islands in a Gentile ocean.

In the same way that Chaim Weizmann described his birthplace Motol in the Grodno Province, Chaim Kahan also could have described Orlya.

Orlya, or Orla, about an hour's drive south of Białystok, is now a village with two names on its nameplates, one in Latin and one in the Belarusian Cyrillic, like others in the border area. The place has three or four bitumen roads, connected by gravel paths, running through its center. Today, it consists of one-story brown or colorful wooden houses with verandas and benches in front of them, surrounded by vegetable and flower gardens. Has anything survived history so that memories can be pinned to it? There are two Orthodox churches, St. Michael since 1797 and Cyril and Methodius since 1870—and a synagogue that towers over all other buildings like a foreign body.

Although Orlya's Great Synagogue is situated in the middle of the town, it is yet lonely on the edge of a bare lawn, behind a large, empty bitumen area, as if the shabby site had been abandoned, waiting in vain for visitors. The bright Renaissance gable pushes proudly into the sky. The high building is flanked on the right and left by low side buildings. Large arched windows, reaching from the floor of the former gallery to the roof, let the sunlight in. The stone outer walls are plastered, the masonry is exposed here and there, because moisture gnaws at it. The windows of the extensions are boarded up. But the mighty portico stands for durability and grandeur, inviting visitors to enter the building. Chaim has probably passed its threshold regularly.

Unlike Motol, Orlya has a remarkable history that is briefly told on a roadside information board. Its existence has been verified by sources since the beginning of the sixteenth century. In 1500, the Polish king Aleksander Jagiellończyk gave the land to the clerk of the governor of Trakai, Lithuania, so that he could build a city on it. The privilege was confirmed by King Zygmunt the Elder in 1507. This date is considered the year the city was founded. However, one of the actual founding fathers of the city and owner of the Orlya Estate was a Lithuanian treasurer who managed to bring the land under his rule between 1512 and 1522. Nine villages belonged to the Orlya Estate in the middle of the sixteenth century. By marriage, the property went to an aristocratic Polish family from Sluck and probably became part of the Radziwiłł family's assets in 1585.

The golden age in the history of the place began with the reign of Christopher Radziwiłł (1585–1640), who campaigned for this Podlachian property, because Orlya had fertile soil thanks to the Orlyanka and was located in the strategically important border area between Lithuania and Poland. In 1634, under the rule of Janusz Radziwiłł, who was an avowed Calvinist, Orlya received its town charter, a coat of arms and, around this time, also a Calvinist church as well as a synagogue.

The fate of the *shtetl* stood and fell with the Polish-Lithuanian nobles who were landowners, masters of the Belarusian and Ukrainian bonded peasants; for the Jewish residents they were patrons, representatives of state power, employers and customers. The Jewish community played an important role in Orlya. Even after the Cossack Wars of Liberation from the Polish-Lithuanian nobility (1655–1660), which back the development of the city as a whole, it remained a Jewish center, which flourished particularly in the nineteenth century, in the middle of which Chaim Kahan was born. For the year 1765, the community ledgers already listed 1,358 poll taxpayers. In Chaim Kahan's childhood, the Jewish community of Orlya counted more than three times as many, 4,436 souls. At the end of the century, according to the official census, they still made up two-thirds of the total population, but were only half as many as fifty years earlier, 2,310 out of a total of 3,003 inhabitants. The rural exodus had begun.

The Great Synagogue was filled with life for more than three centuries. Shortly before the Second World War, the roof structure burned down. During the war, the Nazis misused the ruins as a camp, but did not destroy them anymore, so that the synagogue could be restored in the 1980s. It has been hosting a small exhibition since 2008. It is both a museum and a memorial, which is managed by the Foundation for the Preservation of the Jewish Heritage in Poland with headquarters in Warsaw. The Renaissance building is the only testimony to the former greatness of the *shtetl*. Surprisingly, the inside displays fragments of colored murals, floral patterns and figurative representations—grapevines climbing up on pillars; fictional birds swinging under the capitals in hanging flower baskets and hoops, while a lively swallow under the roof sails along and screams excitedly; magnificent, almost life-size lions and tigers to the right and left of the Torah shrine; a decorative ribbon at the height of the former gallery with pictures from the Garden of Eden—where deer and rabbits peacefully walk alongside eagles and lions amidst flowers, bushes and trees.

The exhibition on the bare brickwork of the synagogue is dedicated to the prewar period. Photos show the old *shulhoif* [synagogue yard], where several prayer rooms—crouched, dark, one-to-two-story wooden houses—stand close together in front of the magnificent light stone building. Chaim might have gone to *cheder* here once and then attended the *lehrhaus*. Two large photos, stretched on canvas, show the still intact interior of the synagogue, one facing the Torah shrine, the other facing the main entrance. The caption "Phot. Hermann Struck 1916" lays a trail from today's Orlya to Chaim Kahan's hometown. Both photos are by his political companion Hermann Struck. He had been here as a soldier and had captured the interior of the synagogue for posterity. The graphic artist liked to take photos as a template for his drawings, and synagogues in Eastern Europe were among his favorite objects. But on what occasion was he in Orlya and in what capacity? Had Chaim Kahan's stories from *heimatshtetl* aroused his curiosity? Was he there privately, for personal interest, or officially, sent there by the press officer of the Commander-in-Chief East (Orlya was then part of the Upper Eastern Governorate), for which he worked as a censor and translator between March and November 1916, or only later, as a frontline soldier?

The Jewish cemetery in Orlya is now only a meadow on a hill, from which gravestone tips protrude here and there. Only a few can be recognized. Chaim's parents may be buried here together with other ancestors. At least, the meadow is being mowed. The mower takes an afternoon nap under the shade of an elderberry. In the local pub, two farmers drink their midday beer. Tripe soup is being served. The synagogue building, the photos, the cemetery hill, the churches, the tripe soup and memories are probably the only thing left of the old Orlya.

"I am a little bit from Orla," recalls the Polish writer Roman Śliwonik, son of the postmaster of Orlya in the 1930s.

(The original inhabitants there were Jews, Belarusians. It turns out that I too come from Orla.) It happened—and it still happens in me—against the background of the huge setting sun, or maybe in the twilight immediately after the sunset. I was looking from the bridge at dark praying figures beyond the silvery waves of the river. To the left, the huge mill trembled, vibrated, while meadows, white with daisies stretched beyond the bend. Still further, a hill grew out of the meadows with the old cemetery and further still, there was and perhaps still is, the unspeakable. I lived in this town for the first eight years of my life. The original inhabitants were Jews and Belarusians, but also some Polish officials lived here with their families. ... These Belarusians, those big, likeable, mustachioed giants, were stooped, a bit shrill, loud and good to the children. The first illustrations in large folios were shown to me by such a large Belarusian, one of the postmen who worked for my father. He showed them, explained them wisely, with kindness and willingness. Children, little boys, can sense lies. Later they lose that ability and wisdom. Jews, that's my entire childhood, tall, strange, swaying on the riverbank, filling the streets, the shops, my life. Talkative, always wise, honestly feigning indignation. And now I'm supposed to banish all that from my memory, reject it, change it, rework it, just because someone's stupidity is making me angry? At the age of seven, I had more peace in me than now. I watched the Jews who walked from the synagogue to the river, they passed our veranda, and nothing will replace the picture, long black shadows, slowly passing in the sky, where the world's most beautiful sun was setting.

When Roman Śliwonik lived in Orla, or Orlya, Chaim Kahan was long gone. But the place remained the same. Only that instead of the Russian there were now Polish officials.

In May 1864 Chaim was married in Orlya to Malka Basch, the daughter of Eliezer Moshe and Debora Basch from Brest, who was three years his elder. At that time, he was not only younger, but also smaller than his bride and both were almost children. Perhaps the wedding took place in the Great Synagogue. The verse from the psalms on the fresco, *ratz ketzvi*, "running like a deer," could have become Chaim's motto for life. The family says that he was crying when he had to leave home and the *shtetl* to move to his parents-in-law abroad, to Brest. After Białystok in the north, Brest was the next largest city in the south, about eighty kilometers from Orlya. Chaim wrote from Petrograd to Berlin, many years later, apparently hastily, in Russian, with almost no punctuation:

Dear Malke! I doubt that you remember those years when we were board-
ers, as was customary among the Jews in those days, and how we lived?
I can say with some certainty that in any case my life situation was much
worse than my fantasies of my hometown Orlya. I was really happy with
you and my fantasies had completely turned into my wish to make you
happy!

Today the population of Orlya, or Orla, is predominantly of Belarusian and
Ukrainian origin and is Orthodox. A farmer living there told me that people
in Orlya speak their own language, a mixture of Polish, Ukrainian, Belarusian
and Russian. As in many places, the language demarcation does not run
along the state border. Chaim Kahan grew up with that mixture of languages
as his mother tongue. Orlya, the farmer says, had 5,000 inhabitants before
the Holocaust, of whom 3,000 were Jews. Today the population comprises
800 souls. Orlya used to have city rights, today it is a village. There is no work
and people are leaving.

Nowadays, the Polish-Belarusian state border blocks the direct route from
Orlya to Brest; a border crossing is only possible at Brest. Brest-Litovsk, known
as Brisk in Jewish literature, has 330,000 inhabitants and is world-famous for
the peace treaty between Soviet Russia and the Central Powers in March 1918.
It has always been a border town, first between the Grand Duchy of Lithuania
and the Polish Nobles' Commonwealth, and since the third division of Poland,
between Austria and the Grodno Governorate in the northwestern border
region of the Russian Empire, called *Kresy* in Polish. After the collapse of the
empires, it belonged to the First Polish Republic, but after the Second World
War the city again became a border station between the People's Republic of
Poland and the Soviet Union. Today it stands on the border between Poland
and Belarus, the European and the Eurasian Union. Brest is also famous for
its fortress, which Tsar Nicholas I had built after the First Polish Uprising in
1831 where the city stood. Construction began in the late 1830s and continued
into the 1850s. The fortress was still of strategic importance during the Second
World War. Mussolini and Hitler met there. Brest has been a transportation
hub for ages. Here the Western Bug and the Mukhavets flow together and have
formed a waterway from the Dnieper to the Vistula since the completion of the
Dnieper–Bug Canal (1841), which connected Pina and Mukhavets. In 1896,
eleven steamers, several hundred barges and more than fifteen thousand rafts
passed the waterway in Brest. The road from Warsaw to Moscow via Minsk runs
through the city. Most recently, Brest became a railway junction. Trains have

been running between Warsaw and Brest since 1869, and a few years later the Brest–Moscow and Königsberg–Brest–Kiev lines were added. The convenient geographical location of the border crossing, at the confluence of the Bug and the Mukhavets, predestined Brest to be a trading town between Poland and Lithuania, but also beyond, between Russia and Western Europe. Brest was originally one of the largest cities in the Grand Duchy. It was also the center of Lithuanian Jewry from the middle of the fourteenth century until Vilna contested this rank three hundred years later. The daughter of a Jewish entrepreneur, Pauline Wengeroff, née Epstein, describes in her memoirs the life in Brest in the 1830s–40s, the idyll before the fortress was built, the destruction caused by it and the cramped living conditions in the new town, before the "great transition period" 1860s–70s when Chaim Kahan came to Brest:

> This was already the time when the Lilienthal movement had penetrated the broader and deeper population layers. Now you could at least dare to study the "foreign" books; and the young people in Brest made full use of this opportunity. They held meetings in which one read German classics and scientific works, but especially the old Greek literature. Gradually, women were also admitted to these meetings.

Pauline Wengeroff's brother Ephraim Epstein and her brother-in-law Abram Sak, later a well-known banker in St. Petersburg, led the Jewish enlightenment movement in Brest when they were young; this had begun during the 1840s with the mission of the German-Jewish reformer Max Lilienthal, under Tsarist orders. Young Chaim Kahan might have been influenced by them. According to Pauline Wengeroff, her brother-in-law and sister once caused a family scandal when they walked together one Shabbes afternoon on the large Shosseinaya [Chaussée Road, same as the German Chausseestrasse], where most Brest Jews strolled while enjoying the twilight, because men and women had to walk strictly separate from one another. Did Chaim and Malka adhere to the old rules of modesty, or did they stroll together on Shosseinaya?

In Brest, Chaim Kahan lived the first two married years with his parents-in-law *auf kest*, and presumably studied in the *lehrhaus* or the yeshiva like other young men, who were fed on rotation by the congregants. When the first son, Baruch-Tanchum, was born two years later—Chaim was just sixteen—he began to make a living for the family himself. The Kahan family lived in Brest for about three decades since their wedding and until their eldest daughter, Miriam, was married. Nowhere had they been so sedentary as there. The last of the scarce evidence among the family heirlooms of their existence in Brest is Eliezer Moshe Basch's congratulations to his granddaughter Miriam in Warsaw on the birth of her daughter, his great-granddaughter Rosa, in the summer of 1898, under the letterhead of the Brest branch of the Caspian-Black Sea Oil Industry and Trading Company, while Chaim Kahan himself lived already in Kharkov and was working from there.

In the middle of the nineteenth century, the new Brest was built three kilometers east of the fortress, on an area stretching over two suburbs, consisting of one-to-two-story stone houses, with wide, straight streets and elegant shops. Nevertheless, low wooden houses dominated the city. Not all of the streets were paved. The Mukhavets was not only an economical waterway, but also a source of infectious diseases. At least, a large city park made it possible to relax and have fun. The hygienic conditions, like everywhere in the cities and towns at that time, were not good, waste was simply thrown onto the street. A year after Chaim and Malka's marriage, Brest was hit by a cholera epidemic. There were only five wells with suitable water for drinking and two baths, one on the Dolgaya, and the other on Mukhavetskaya Street, both owned by Jews, plus two *mikves*.

When Chaim came to Brest, the Nicolaite fortress was already standing, while a generation had passed since the violent transfer of the city. The fortress covered an area of four square kilometers. The citadel alone, its center, was surrounded by a wall nearly two kilometers long. The fortress was so big that I still hadn't covered the entire area after two hours of walking through it double time. It is the city's destiny. It destroyed the old Brest, its construction drove out and ruined the inhabitants, it brought death, attracted violence and fighters during the war. But in times of peace it provided work, thereby keeping the city alive. Chaim Kahan came in peacetime when Brest prospered again and developed into a transportation hub as well as a center for trade and industry. The Great Synagogue on Millionnaya Street (now Sovetskaya), had just been built.

Brest was the second largest city in the Governorate after Grodno, and the predominantly Jewish population was open to modernization. Brest kept up with the times and in the 1860s had a Litvak-dominated community with a differentiated infrastructure. Even before the Great Synagogue, it owned a hospital larger than the city hospital, a free community school, the Talmud Torah, for five hundred boys. The *maskilim* campaigned for the modernization of education and opened a library. There was a small Jewish state school alongside the traditional *chadarim* and a variety of social and healthcare institutions, especially for widows, the poor, orphans and expectant mothers. In 1889, Brest had two thousand houses and more than forty thousand inhabitants, two-thirds of whom were Jews. With a certain growth, this ratio remained stable over the next decade. Almost all of the artisans in Brest—iron- and tinsmiths, carpenters and wheelwrights, cobblers, butchers, bookbinders, rope makers, tailors, bakers, goldsmiths, hairdressers, watchmakers, fur hat makers, glaziers, soap makers and cutters—were Jews. The military garrison was a major customer for various goods such as uniforms, accessories, building materials, utensils and food. The fortress building prohibited tall factories, but there was industry in Brest that was mainly run by Jews: factories producing turpentine, leather, cloth, soap and food; there were several brick factories, printing plants and steam mills.

That time was a dawn of a new era. Industrialization and railway construction changed the occupations. When serfdom was abolished, the peasants displaced the Jews from the tenant-farmer posts. The railroad made wagoners, innkeepers, smugglers and craftsmen redundant. The accelerated transport of goods and people increased the external competition. Reforms based on the physiocratic concept of productization led to the establishment of agricultural colonies in Brest (1881). Jews began to practice modern agriculture. However, this was only a marginal phenomenon: the restrictions under the May laws of 1882, the ban on land purchase and other restrictions tended to force their urbanization. The majority of the trades in which Jews were employed accounted for forty percent of manufacturing and publishing, closely followed by commerce. Goods such as alcohol, groceries, homewares, farm equipment and tools, building materials, petroleum, wood, paper goods and printed matter were sold in Brest. From the end of the nineteenth century, the city had five libraries and eight printing plants, almost all of them Jewish-owned. Jews introduced book printing in Belarus. At that time there were seven large pharmacies, twenty-three drugstores, several hundred shops on Shosseinaya, many of them owned by Jews, and a shopping arcade on Millionnaya. There were two synagogues and about thirty Jewish prayer houses in Brest.

At that time, Chaim Kahan would have had the opportunity to become a scholar like some of his ancestors. In his day, rabbis were officiating in Brest, whose names were to play a role in the further family history and who were probably his teachers and advisors at the time: Zvi Hersch Ornstein from Galicia (from 1865 to 1874), Moshe Yehoshua Leib Diskin (until 1877) from Łomża, who at the end of his life was a prominent rabbi in Jerusalem, Joseph Dov Ber Soloveitschik (from 1878 to 1892), and his son Chayim Halevi Soloveitschik (from 1892 to 1914). But Chaim Kahan opted for commerce. He began by importing salted herrings, which was not supposed to be missing from any table, in barrels from Holland. Malka resold them in bulk. There is a joke in the family about this: when the herring ran out, Chaim and Malka sold the barrel, bought initially for ten, for fifteen rubles. But the scarcer the goods, the higher the price. When it rose to one hundred rubles per barrel, the barrels were repeatedly sold as lucrative commercial objects, so that the herring stank when it arrived at the consumer and the consumer complained. Chaim Kahan replied, "Why did you open the barrel? It was intended for sale."

Malka still had contacts in Brest and continued to do business there, long after she had moved away, because her sister Riva, married Dubinbaum, lived there with her family and Malka sold soap and soda from Warsaw to friends and relatives in and around Brest. The busy city, with its fast connections to the world, offered Chaim Kahan many trade and craft opportunities to make a living, when he gave up the fish trade after a short time, but instead of dealing in wood or grain, leather, tobacco or fabrics, he decided to do business with a brand new product that was booming in the market—petroleum, light oil. For seven years, since he was eighteen, he had worked as a laborer in various places—in Kiev, Königsberg, Tsaritsyn on the Volga (Stalingrad since 1925, Volgograd since 1961) and other cities until he became a self-employed oil wholesaler in Vilna in 1876/1877. Chaim Kahan was a self-made man from the start, not least because he was flexible and—as he later put it himself—skillfully "combined." Arusia remembered that his grandfather had traveled a lot and later had apartments in many places, besides Brest, in Kharkov, Warsaw, Vilna, Baku, Antwerp and, most recently, in Berlin. He was very often away from home, which frequently brought him in conflict with Malka, who used to be waiting for him at home raising the children. The Kahans often argued about Chaim's business ideas and his rationale for the many places of residence. Nevertheless, he always returned to Brest until the mid-1890s. The family lived there, he had an office there and for all the years until the beginning of the First World War also an oil depot, initially only under his own name and later also under that of the Caspian-Black Sea Oil Industry and Trading Company. His two eldest children, Baruch and Miriam, also got married here in Brest.

Arusia recalled that in Brisk his grandfather owned a large house with an orchard. After the First World War, the house was leased to the Polish police headquarters until Hitler came. Yefim Basin, managing director of the Jewish community and regional historian in Brest, found the property. The Kahan family owned all of the buildings until the outbreak of World War II, while the main building had been leased to the Commandant of the Voivodeship Police in the interwar period. The Voivodeship police was the city's highest civilian police force and was responsible for the entire region. So, it must have been a respectable address. The Kahans owned a spacious, three-quarter-hectare corner property where the Medovaya, the Honey Street, ended in the Shosseinaya. During the interwar period, the Medovaya was called Zygmuntowska in Brześć nad Bugiem, and in the Soviet- and Belarusian-era Brest it became Karla Marksa, while the Shosseinaya—today Praspekt Generala Masherava, was the Jagiellonska Street in the Polish city. It is said that the wars had destroyed Brest almost completely. In fact, there is no old building on the Kahan's former property. In its place stands an eight-story Soviet-style tenement building. However, there still exist numerous prewar buildings, and a picture can be formed by comparing old houses from the Tsarist period in the neighborhood.

Right next door, only separated from Kahan's former property by the Karla Marksa Street, is a magnificent administration building, which today accommodates a tourism agency. Under Russian rule it was the tax authority, in the interwar period the seat of the Voivodeship administration. This is followed by the old post office, today a branch of the Brest Postal Service. On the other side, in immediate proximity, Praspekt Masherava 2, on the corner of Lenina Street, stood the Slavic Hotel, which was converted after the First World War into a Jewish orphanage maintained by the Joint. On Karla Marksa, but also in other side streets, there are still houses from the Tsarist era. They are firmly grounded, broadly stretched, low, with thick walls, decorative bands under the molding, reliefs on the right and left of the windows and entrance portals and balconies with wrought iron railings above them; old, solid town houses in a central location, because the Chausseestrasse started at the fortress and was the thoroughfare from Warsaw to Moscow. The city park was diagonally opposite, and it was maybe a hundred steps to the bank of the Mukhovets. On the other side, also within walking distance, was the train station, and in between, the city center with the Millionnaya where the Great Synagogue once stood, a stately, octagonal, tapered building over two floors for eight hundred visitors. At the beginning of the 1970s it was deformed beyond recognition in a modernistic style, like many synagogues in the former Soviet Union, which function as cinemas in some places. Only in the basement, near the toilets, do massive natural stones testify to the synagogue foundation, which was built from the same indestructible material and in the same solid manner as the fortress, so that the Soviet city government was unable to blow up the building. The Chabad community recently consecrated a Torah scroll in the Belarus cinema and organized a procession through the city, for a moment returning to the building some of its former aura.

The Shosseinaya Street in Brest was probably already paved and also had a sidewalk when Chaim and Malka lived there. At that time, it was already wide, had a median strip with trees, fenced-off areas, perhaps for horses or other pets, and parking spaces for cabs. The street was very busy. One shop was next to the other. Vehicles of all kinds travelled there, even the first cyclists. There were strollers, transients, soldiers from the fortress, craftsmen and traders who were busy in the garrison. People who were going to the administration or the post office were passing by. There was a garden behind the house, because the property was large, so that the children were given fresh air and had space to run, even if they could not go to the city park or the Mukhovets bank. There is another family joke from the Brest period: Chaim Kahan once went for a walk with an acquaintance, an elderly man who occasionally farted. He accompanied every explosive discharge with the exclamation *"Oi, a churben!"* When Chaim looked around, he noticed that a couple was following them. He asked the two since when. They replied, since the *churbe rischn*, the first *churben!* Anyone who laughs here, is at home in Jewish history and knows that *churben* refers to the destruction of the Temple, which was ever since a turning point of history.

According to construction plans, building permits and tax levies, around the turn of the century there were three two-story stone houses, a horse stable and farm building on the property Chaim Kahan inherited from his father-in-law. Which of them they lived in and since when, whether since their marriage or only when Chaim's business became successful, remains uncertain. Perhaps in the stately front building, directly on the main road, with a one-story wing to the rear, in the house in the yard, or the one on the crossroad, the Medovaya. The largest was a semi-detached house, more than thirty meters long, with fourteen windows, except for the main entrance with three doors on each side facing the Shosseinaya. Behind it were the offices or shops. Assuming that the family, three generations, old Basch (his wife was no longer alive), Chaim and Malka, the children, presumably also servants and employees were living in the semi-detached house, they probably lived on the first floor, which was spacious with twelve rooms. Maybe father-in-law Basch also had his own apartment in the wing or in one of the other apartment buildings. There was certainly a lot of life, because of the business and because of the many small children, since Malka Kahan had given birth to eleven in the course of twenty years—first, close together, Baruch, Miriam and Pinchas, then, after a seven-year break, Bendet, Aron, David and Rachel; the names of four are missing, presumably because they died early. Grandfather Basch used to hear the incessant rattling of the spoons with which the children were fed when they were growing up, the family says.

After the Kahans left Brest, they continued to take care of their property in the city, renovated and extended it. Throughout the years, including the difficult times of the First World War, they kept in touch with Brest—with the administrator, Tanchum-Michal Orchow, and the family of Malka's sister Riva. "Again, I'm reminding about brother-in-law Osip Abramovich [Dubinbaum] to pay him 200 marks, to add something for all relatives. Reminding y[ou] about Jakob Orchow he is probably poor help him too," Chaim Kahan wrote on March 3, 1916 from Petrograd to his loved ones in Berlin. According to the address books, there were still some named Basch and Kahan living in Brest in the interwar period, including the dairy owner Szmul Kahan, who worked as an administrator alongside Orchow, and a certain Wichna Kahan, 66 Białystokska Street, where Chaim N. Kahan's successors were officially registered.

What is left of the old Jewish Brest apart from the walls of the Belarus cinema? A memorial to commemorate the 34,000 Jews murdered by the Nazis on the edge of the former Great Ghetto; buildings that no longer display their Jewish history—on Sovetskaya, the former seat of the ORT, the Society for the Promotion of Work among Jews in Russia, the office of the Algemeyner Yidisher Arbeterbund in Lite, Poyln un Rusland, Bund for short, and Beitar, the youth organization of the Revisionist-Zionists; on the bank of the Mukhavets, the Jewish hospital, later the Progress clubhouse; on Masherava, the former orphanage. There is a pile of broken tombstones with Hebrew inscriptions in one corner of the fortress. The Jewish cemetery, opposite the Catholic one on Pushkina Street, was desecrated by the Nazis and destroyed under the Soviet rule. Construction work on the site unearthed broken tombstones, which should be put together and built into a memorial.

CHAPTER 3

Life under War Conditions. Berlin

Fortunately, Jacob Kahan had connections and he used them. The community and self-help organizations had not abandoned the Jewish prisoners in the city prison on Dirksenstrasse in September 1914. Jacob was released after ten days. But the beginning of the war had changed his life.

The Kahans also had an address in Germany, an apartment in Charlottenburg. At that time, Charlottenburg was not yet part of the city of Berlin, but administrated itself and was considered a suburb with a relatively high Jewish population. By the beginning of the war, the Jews had long since spread to the city in western Berlin with the Kurfürstendamm as its central axis, where the Jewish residents were clustered, making up a quarter of the district's population. Even though Jews of all classes lived in Charlottenburg, it was shaped by the Jewish upper middle class. Chaim Kahan had rented the apartment on Schlüterstrasse in the summer of 1913 to get some peace. Berlin was also interesting for him businesswise.

I stopped in Schlüterstrasse and rang the doorbell of the cosmetics school on the first floor of building number 36—to no avail, because it was the weekend. The five-story apartment building looks sedate and, at the same time, captivating, with playful asymmetries on the roof, gables, windows and bays. It is reminiscent of a castle, the round walls of which have been turned into a bourgeois city building. The building, built in 1906 as 32 Schlüterstrasse by the architects Gustav and Hermann Paulsen in the historic style, has retained its character for more than a century.

Even later I was unable to contact the cosmetics school.

Then Chaim Kahan's great-grandson Eli came to Berlin. With him I managed to get into the stairwell and up to the apartment door. But the cleaning lady refused us entry. In the vestibule, leaning against a marble console with a brass grille and mirror attachment, Eli talked of his early childhood in Berlin.

The next time I was passing by, I saw a large construction sign at the building's entrance and found the doors open. So, I went in.

The Kahans had lived on the first floor, on the left. Rubble and stones were swept up in a heap at the entrance. Partitions were torn out, plaster was knocked off the walls, but the stucco on the ceilings of the three representative front rooms—antique miniatures in decorative bands, flower wreaths and spray—were intact, as were the old doors between the rooms, the balcony and the box windows. The chest-high dark wood paneling of the more than forty-five-square-meter *Berliner Zimmer* matched Dvora Ettinger-Rozenfeld's descriptions (Chaim's granddaughter had been living, as a ten-year-old, for a short time at 36 Schlüterstrasse): the walls of the dining room were paneled with walnut at a height of one and a half meters. From the *Berliner Zimmer* I went into the back rooms. With two long wings, the building reaches deep into the courtyard. The apartment used to have ten rooms and a service entrance. But the floorplan in the rear area could only be recognized by torn seams on the ceilings and walls.

The third time I arrived with a group of Chaim's descendants, this time with a proper appointment, guided by a property manager. The apartment building was now completely renovated. Noa Tal recounted for the assembled relatives—the voice of her ninety-eight-year-old mother Dvora by cellphone in her ear—her memories of the apartment: the entrance was magnificent. Wide stairs, covered with a red runner, led upstairs. Only the adults were allowed to use the elevator. The caretaker, Mr. Schwalbe, had his room next to the front door. He paid close attention to who came and went, and provided the police with reports about the residents. Upstairs in the apartment, just behind the front door, facing the courtyard, was the bedsitter, very modern with white lacquered furniture; opposite was the *Biedermeier* room, its furniture decorated with porcelain figures and other knick-knacks the children were not allowed to touch. It also served the women as a prayer room, *esrat nashim*, because religious services were regularly held in the apartment. For this purpose, the adjacent study was converted into a synagogue on Shabbat and religious holidays. Here, mainly Russian migrants prayed with the family. As a rule, a few dozen used to come, but sometimes more than a hundred on festivals. A long corridor led from the dining room to the bedrooms, the kitchen and the maid's room. In the study, there was a mighty bookcase holding the religious and traditional works, an imposing desk and chairs. The furniture was dark wood, awe-inspiring and serious. From here one entered the wood-paneled *Berliner Zimmer*, the dining room, where the *kiddush* took place. On festive occasions, the table would be laid with flowers and fruit. The dishes were made of the finest porcelain, the cutlery of pure silver. The *Berliner Zimmer* was dominated by the bulky buffet cabinet. Persian rugs lay on the parquetry floor and double curtains hung from the windows. What was missing from that bourgeois German salon were paintings with human representations. The entire facility differed only from the usual *Wilhelmine*-apartment interior by its attributes of Jewish observance, with the associated double function as a representative living and ritual space. According to Dvora, the knick-knack figurines had had their noses cut off, in order to adhere to the ban on pictures.

But where did Chaim's and Malka's portraits hang, if not at 36 Schlüterstrasse? Before the beginning of the war, Struck had painted Chaim in oil at his request, perhaps to eternalize the sponsor of the Tachkemoni School for posterity. The entrepreneur is shown larger-than-life, as a sedate gentleman in a black double-breasted suit with velvet lapels. Only the seated posture, the bald head above the gray beard, a tired expression around the eyes and a pince-nez in the right hand softened the impression of status and power. It is highly unlikely that Chaim would have taken the more than one-meter-high picture with him on his rushed return to Russia at the beginning of the war. By contrast, Malka's figure in the armchair appears small and withdrawn, in the painting by an unknown painter from 1917. Calmly, slightly resigned, she looks down at the viewer from beneath her *shaitel* in front of the warm, golden-yellow and Sienna-red background.

This is how the Kahans' apartment, 36 Schlüterstrasse, was described in the 1920s. It didn't look much different, though maybe not quite as splendid, in the early days, before the war and throughout its duration. There was always a lot of activity in the apartment, Roska recalled. At 36 Schlüterstrasse, people not only talked about the Tachkemoni School, but also offered hospitality and donated help. The address developed into a center for Russian Jews in Berlin. The Central Zionist Office, 8 Sächsische Strasse, saw it as a kind of branch, where it sent everyone who needed support. Roska once wrote to Arusia,

> Perhaps you still remember the *ger* [gentleman] who stayed with us for a few days on his way to *Eretz Israel*. He didn't even know the exact address, but asked for the Rosenberg guesthouse and was brought directly there. He also wasn't the only one who visited the guesthouse, or the "food

distribution center." During the difficult years, Mom often got food (in large quantities) "on the sly," which she then distributed to friends and acquaintances (for a fee, of course).

Did Chaim summon his son and son-in-law to the German metropolis, or did they come voluntarily? Be that as it may, Bendet, the middle of the five sons, was the first to move with his family from Antwerp to Schlüterstrasse in Charlottenburg in the early autumn of 1913. A few months later, in December, Jonas Rosenberg followed him from the east, from Warsaw, with his mother-in-law, wife and children. Malka had been living with Miriam, her eldest daughter, who had helped her a lot with the children when they were small and who was particularly close to her. Due to the closed borders between the enemy states, the separation from her husband became permanent. Initially, two families, nine people, plus a cook and maid lived in the Charlottenburg ten-room apartment, so that there was just enough space for everyone. Bendet Kahan was listed in the address register as a tenant in 36 Schlüterstrasse, first floor, since 1915.

Until then, neither Bendet Kahan nor Jonas Rosenberg had proven to be eager employees in the family business. Perhaps for this reason alone they were, at least geographically, separated from the patriarchal business. Maybe that's why they came to Germany.

Jonas was a merchant of the Second Guild, owner of a small chemical factory in Warsaw, but preferred chess, socializing and women over work. Apart from that, he was a pious man, traditionally educated in Talmud and Torah, who led the family services and taught his son and nephews. He came from a prestigious rabbinical dynasty in Łomża and had studied there at the yeshiva. His father, Elias, had already been a merchant. His mother Sarah, née Diskin, a relative of Rabbi Moshe Yehoshua Leib Diskin of Brest, later Łomża and finally Jerusalem, was considered a good businesswoman: When her ledgers, where her many debtors were listed, went up in flames, Sorke, the Rebetzin, as she was called, is said to have recollected their names and sums from memory. Jonas had been married to Miriam since 1894, when he was twenty-four. He was forty-three and in his prime, when the family had moved from Poland to Germany for an indefinite period. His difficult relationship with his father-in-law is reflected in a letter Chaim wrote for Passover in 1916 from Baku:

> Dear Marij and Jonas, don't remember how many Easters we spent with you and do you know Jonas that I on my part outside of business … had a very good relationship with you for a long time and we usually had

nothing against each other at the time did not criticize each other and saw
no moral shortcomings in each other. If material misunderstandings arose
in bad times then even what connected us on holidays became weaker so
be fair and acknowledge that my reservations were only for y[our] own
sake in my opinion you could have been a partner in business matters for
a long time.

The disagreements between Chaim Kahan and Jonas Rosenberg were based
on differences in origin, education, temperament and religious orientations.
There were also conflicts between Bendet and his father. Bendet was the only
son who had defied his father. He had chosen his wife himself and had married in the absence of the family, something his father had reluctantly accepted.
The marriage certificate states that Bendet had married Judith, the daughter of
Mendel and Scheina Lea Bramson, on February 23, 1904, at six o'clock in the
afternoon, in the village of Weissee, Wiżajny in Polish, Sejny District, Suwałki
Province, in the presence of two witnesses from the village, a worker and a master mason. They were married in the Wiżajny synagogue after three notices of
intended marriage within one week. The preliminary contract was concluded
with a notary in Suwałki, while the religious act, without a rabbi, was carried
out by the keeper of the congregation's registers. Both were twenty-six years old
at the time.

Following the 1905 autumn pogroms during the first Russian Revolution,
which Bendet experienced as the branch manager of the family business in
Kursk, he left the Russian Empire with his wife and daughter, never to return.
He wasn't interested in the oil business, which, again, angered his father. Chaim
Kahan summarized his disturbed relationship with Bendet in a letter to Miriam
two days after the attack in Sarajevo. For years he had spoken neither to Bendet
nor of him, and had also quarreled with Malka about him, something which
he now regretted. In deference to his father, Bendet Kahan had been dealing
with diamonds in Antwerp, but without much success. He actually wanted to
publish books. But regardless of the discords, the family business always guaranteed him, too, a living.

Now Bendet and Jonas were living with their families in one apartment.
They knew each other well, because the family held together and Bendet was
particularly connected to his mother and sister following the argument with
his father, but he had little in common with his brother-in-law. In addition, a
new situation had arisen. As soon as they had set up in Berlin-Charlottenburg,
the war began. This brought them closer together, but also caused tensions, not

least as a consequence of the economic uncertainty, because the political situation had foiled Chaim's business plans in Germany.

The relatives in Schlüterstrasse offered Jacob some feeling of home; they gave him shelter. After his release he was there often, but stayed with the Rosenthals. Before the outbreak of the war, he was one of the many students who had moved to Germany because of the *numerus clausus* for Jews at Russian universities. In his case, the family's preference for German education had been an additional factor, but studying was over for Jacob with the outbreak of war.

Three areas of tension created a complicated dynamic within the family in the already politically charged Berlin situation: the difficult relationship between the so differently tempered and oriented brothers-in-law and family heads Bendet Kahan and Jonas Rosenberg, which also affected and influenced their wives Judith and Miriam; the geographic separation between Chaim and Malka, which had existed for two decades due to his mobile business activities, but became irreversible due to the war; and Jacob's endangered situation, which was not made easier by his initially secret love for his cousin Rosa that blossomed during the war in Germany. In Berlin, Malka and Miriam joined by Bendet represented the female line of the Kahans, while the patriarchal one upheld the business in Russia.

After Malka ascertained that most of the mail from Russia did not arrive and that one could only rely on personal messengers, Jacob's mother, Rosa Kahan, informed her husband Baruch in November 1914 that she was in the process of organizing the trip home to Kharkov, because the city commandant of Berlin had granted the Russians, who had been held there since the beginning of the war, leave, and many of her acquaintances were already on their way. Her life under the restrictions as an "enemy alien" in Berlin under war conditions had become hopeless, exhausting and bleak for her. She was longing for her husband. Her youngest, Arusia, was sick and had a weak lung. He had just returned from the warmth of Palestine a few months earlier, and his mother was worried about him. She was in contact with the Foreign Office because she was examining the travel options via Stockholm to Petrograd. Nevertheless, Rosalia and Arusia did not leave Berlin until months later, in May 1915, to return home.

It was different for Jonas and Miriam, Bendet and Judith. They were unsure of what to do. When one couple was toying with the idea of going back to Warsaw, the other did not want to go back to the Russian Empire; neither could they go to Belgium, even if they had wanted to, because Antwerp was besieged by German troops since August 20 and then occupied.

Following Germany's declaration of war on Russia, Russian citizens in the German Empire were categorized as "enemy aliens" and usually interned or deported. Those among them who remained used to be distrusted and watched. Identification and passport systems as well as the policy of "homogenization" under nationalistic pretexts gained in importance. The Kahans and Rosenbergs were initially tolerated in Berlin, but were required to report regularly to the police, initially twice a day, later (since 1916) every two days and towards the end of the war (since 1917) only twice a week. The curfew was also gradually loosened, with its start postponed from year to year; when it came into effect, the hours were changing until it was extended to midnight by the end of the war. In their identity cards, the columns of the date stamps, official tattoos on paper, became clustered. The Frankfurt regulations, which prescribed that "enemy aliens" who had been living in the city for less than ten years would be expelled, were not applied in Berlin. After being deported from Frankfurt, Nachum Goldmann received a residence permit for the German capital from the Foreign Office as a result of some personal references and proof of a job.

In Germany, patriotism and enthusiasm for war had gripped the entire public. The German Jews, too, demonstrated their love for the fatherland and their willingness to participate in the war by reporting for military service, collecting donations and organizing fundraisers, establishing military hospitals and billets in community buildings and former synagogues, forming aid committees and conducting supplication-prayer-services. In this stoked-up atmosphere, Jews from the Russian Empire were in a difficult situation at the beginning of the war. As Russian citizens, they were considered "enemy aliens," but they had no state behind them that could have represented their interests. Various support groups, Jewish and German, international and interdenominational, were formed to aid them.

The situation of Jews from Eastern Europe was more complex than that of many other Russian subjects and therefore more complicated. They were politically and culturally very heterogeneous and could not be easily pigeonholed into the warring parties. In the Russian Empire, they constituted a legally restricted ethno-denominational group, oppressed by the autocratic state. During the war, they lived and fought on both sides of the opposing fronts, more in the East than in the West. The Ashkenazim, the majority of the Jews in the Russian Empire, felt connected to the Jews in Germany, the German language and culture, by language and tradition, as well as the cultural links generated by the Enlightenment and modernity. This was badly resented by the Russian side in the war, and punished with persecution and deportations, which the Germans took full advantage off in those years, by pretending to represent Jewish interests in Eastern Europe. Jews on the Eastern Front were not only used as interpreters and scouts, but also as political mediators. The German Reich aroused the sympathy of Eastern European, German and even American Jews, by the very fact that Tsarist Russia, which denied civil rights to the Jews, was its enemy.

As Russian citizens and "enemy aliens," the Kahans and Rosenbergs in Berlin were now severely restricted in their freedom of movement. They were closely monitored, adhered to the curfew and cut off from relatives in Russia. In addition, Jacob was forbidden to leave Berlin because he was liable for military service, while his relatives were allowed to travel to the resorts for the summer holidays since the second summer of the war. The general secretary of the Aid Association, Dr. Bernhard Kahn, had issued a recommendation for his admission to the Friedrich-Wilhelms University in May 1915, arguing that the family "has always supported the school project of the Aid Association of German Jews, which had the objective of spreading the German language in the Orient," but the recommendation was rejected. Thereupon Jacob gave up his student digs and moved to Schlüterstrasse. While friends of his, like Max Rosenthal or Rosa's husband Yossel Langer, fought as soldiers at the front, Jacob sat idle at home with his uncle and aunt.

Fourteen field postcards from Max Rosenthal to Jacob are preserved in the archival legacy, as well as the pencil drawing of an apparently peaceful moment at the front, dedicated to Rosenthal, dated July 1915, and the portrait photo of a young man in a round black frame, without explanation, which could have depicted Max Rosenthal. The first card dates from January 11, 1915, when he was undergoing basic training at the Camp de Sissonne, Departement Aisne. All are written in pencil. Max Rosenthal was four years older than Jacob. Before the war, he had studied law followed by art history at the University of Berlin and was active in the Free Student Body, the union of liberal students, who did not belong to a student corps. At the end of January he wrote of the wonderful weather, how they had marched to music into the city of Cambrai where they had cigarettes and chocolate for dessert; in March, that they had no sense of Purim in the field; in April, that he celebrated his birthday "with as much fun as possible right in the face of the enemy ... with the help of alcoholic beverages etcetera," sending greetings from the French spring. In May and June, he thanked him several times for sending the *Jüdische Rundschau* newspaper and asked for further deliveries, since he would like to hear the opinions of others, without agreeing with them. In July, he complained that he was receiving the *Rundschau* irregularly and had just spent three days and nights in the horrible ditches near Arras, "lacking all communications, thirsty, thirsty, thirst and dirt with sogginess. Miracle, I'm safe and sound. Back to hell tomorrow night." In August, he wrote that he was having animated discussions about Judaism and Zionism with a fellow soldier, the mathematician Dr. Fränkel.

Max Rosenthal had the risky job of company runner, which meant traveling alone between the front lines and headquarters to deliver orders. He claimed that this position suited him well. The rank was not very important, but put things in perspective, since the promotion of Jews in his current regiment was extremely rare, despite the war. Were he able to speak Russian, like Yasha, he would have had a quiet command by now in the Russian prisoners-of-war camp behind the French lines. The pencil drawing among the field postcards in the archival legacy shows a typical rest break of a frontline soldier: he is warming up by the open fire in a captured, abandoned and ruined house, a bowl of soup, cooked on an open fire, in his lap and his clothes drying over the fire.

From the Third Army Corps, Sixth Infantry Division, Infantry Regiment "General Field Marshal Prince Friedrich Karl of Prussia" no. 64, Fifth Company, Special Formation: Trench; he sent Jacob and the family good wishes for Yom Kippur on September 12, 1915:

> Thanks for the map and the *Jüdische Rundschau*. Our festival services [for Rosh Hashanah] here in Cambrai, in the theater, were strictly conservative, with *krias hatauro, yizkor,* all the *piutim* etc. etc. sermon etc. Dr. Frankel ran everything. Very atmospheric. Lots of participants, many directly from the trenches. Met a lot of old acquaintances. Nice days, completely off duty. Almost all of us stayed together in groups. I don't know yet whether I will come to B. in the last days.

"Max wrote to her [sister Trude] today that he would be going on vacation to Berlin at the end of the month. It will be a joy for the whole family!"—Jacob wrote to Rosa in the summer resort, Bad Harzburg, on September 2, 1915 from Berlin. Max Rosenthal had been promised furlough after the holidays. Instead, his unit was relocated to Serbia to help support the Austro-Hungarian troops in the Balkans. The field postcards to Jacob Kahan are written relatively tersely and calm in tone. Max offered Jacob to read the letters he had written to his parents and siblings, to get a better picture of his situation. Barely four weeks after the holidays, he was dead. He was one of the 12,000 fallen from a total of 85,000 Jewish front-line fighters in the First World War. In the diary kept by Max Rosenthal's sister-in-law Ilma, for and on behalf of her newborn daughter, it is stated that Uncle Max had sent his niece a necklace with a Belgian five-cent coin as a pendant that he had made himself in the trenches on the Aisne, to commemorate the Great War. For this, he received a thank-you poem. About Max's death, it is recorded in the diary that he was shot in the head on October 20.

In the Kahans archival legacy, among the field postcards in the round frame, the head of the unknown young man has no body, as if cut out or retouched, without a neck and shoulders. The artist had signed it with C'OERTEL. Someone, possibly Max himself or Jacob, had photographed the picture hanging on a cord and pinned to a wall with a thumbtack. The eyes look obliquely past the viewer, inwards. Maybe it had its own spot in Jacob's room on Schlüterstrasse.

Jacob Kahan was still a prisoner, only under more comfortable conditions of detention. He kept himself busy and was also studying, as he dutifully wrote his parents, giving friends language and literature lessons, taking the opportunity to study Talmud and Torah with Uncle Jonas and Rabbi Rosenthal, learning Turkish and Arabic elsewhere, but these activities were characterized by a certain listlessness. Jacob wasn't an adventurer, but now and then he played with the thought of returning to Russia—maybe due to pressure by his parents, because he was homesick, possibly to avoid this unsatisfactory and disgraceful wait, or perhaps because the authorities gave him more leeway, providing him with a potential escape route. He also drew up plans for the future and wanted to travel with Rosa to Palestine, the land of his longing. His love for Rosa prevented him from fleeing to Russia. The thought had made Rosa sick. The fear of losing that relationship led her to confess her love for Yasha to her mother.

Despite all the difficulties, the Kahans and Rosenbergs continued to lead a bourgeois lifestyle in Berlin during the war years. They had servants, a cook for the kosher kitchen, a maid and a nanny. Before the war Mali and Selma took care of the household, during the war Lina did the cooking. An acquaintance noted that, wherever they went, the Kahans not only opened an office and rented an apartment, but also hired a cook. "Fräuleins" were looking after the children not only in Baku, Yekaterinoslav and Antwerp, but also in Berlin. By contrast to the cooks, the maids and nannies in Berlin were of German, but non-Jewish origin. Apart from seeking education, one practiced idleness, read newspapers like the *Vossische Zeitung*, the *Berliner Illustrierte Zeitung*, the *Jüdische Rundschau*, as well as the Warsaw *Haynt*, played chess, went for walks, the theater and the cinema, solved crossword puzzles and travelled to the resorts.

Included in the archival legacy are a large number of letters and postcards from Russia, most of them checked by the military censors, to "the loved ones" in Berlin, including an awkwardly worded letter from Chaim, without envelope, from Stockholm, dated July 14, 1915, in *Germyish*, a mixture of German and Yiddish, in Latin script, which is something like a declaration of love for Malka. Chaim was trying in vain to persuade Malka to return to him in Russia. It would have been possible to travel via Sweden or Denmark using the existing connections. Many of his postcards speak of this wish, just as many replies from his children in Berlin dissuade him. No mail from Malka to Chaim has survived. Others describe Chaim's postwar business plans and living together in Kharkov. In their letters from Kharkov, Baruch and Rosa Kahan expressed concern about Jacob's situation and his wellbeing in Berlin. Jacob reassured them.

In August 1915 German troops occupied Warsaw. In Berlin, those who stayed at home (Jacob: "Let's all go there") went to the Marmorhaus Cinema on Kurfürstendamm on August 22 to watch the movie *The Fall of Warsaw*. Jacob refrained from commenting in his letter to Rosa. For the Kahans and Rosenbergs, the surrender of their hometown was a media event arousing ambivalent feelings, which was better not mentioned in wartime Germany's regular mail.

With the occupation of Poland, Belarus, Lithuania and Courland until August 1915, the German Empire gained control over large parts of the Eastern European Jewish diaspora. This power aroused greediness among the new German masters. The German-Jewish community suddenly had more scope and new responsibilities. Various interest groups began to develop design concepts for the Jews in the occupied territories. The Committee for the East, consisting of a broad alliance of assimilated German Jews and moderate Zionists, in which the young Nachum Goldmann was active and about which he might have spoken to the Kahans, assumed that German and Jewish interests were identical. It advocated the establishment of independent states on the former Russian-ruled territory and promised administrative autonomy to the Jews there. "I engaged him [Nachum Goldmann] in a conversation for several hours," wrote Jacob to Rosa, "so that Uncle Jonas even had to wait for me." The committee made a clear distinction between Eastern and Western European Jews, defining the ones nationally, the others ethnically, and linked their attachment to German culture with responsibility towards the Jews in Eastern Europe. In this context, Yiddish was given a new status and was accepted as a language that was closely related to German. Yiddish and Jewish autonomy were supposed to contribute to the Germanization of the East.

On the other hand, leading liberal Jews, businesspeople and philanthropists, took the initiative to form an interdenominational committee, chaired by the Spanish ambassador and led by the Aid Association, to alleviate the need in the occupied Eastern territories. This committee pursued philanthropic goals and provided humanitarian aid during the war, primarily through donations from American Jews. Nevertheless, due to the war and competition with other initiatives, this Aid Committee was politicized. According to its understanding, shaped by the German-Jewish model, education, emancipation and assimilation, rather than nation building, was the solution for the Jews in Eastern Europe. The only question for them was whether the assimilation would be German or Polish, the answer to which was unclear, because it depended on the outcome of the war.

Both committees attracted criticism from the radical Zionists, led by Kurt Blumenfeld, with whom the Kahan and Rosenberg families were politically allied and later also related by marriage. The radical Zionists were the only ones who actually saw the Eastern European Jews as partners and did not functionalize them as objects for political or philanthropic interests. They saw that the war was destroying the world of the largest Jewish diaspora at the time and that a way out had to be found. They also warned against using the Jews as a tool of German power politics at the expense of the Polish-Jewish relationship.

The traditional Jews of the occupied territories in the East were probably influenced politically by Agudas Yisroel, the party of German-Jewish Orthodoxy. According to their program of combining Torah and tradition with modern life, the members of Agudas Yisroel were connected with their Eastern European coreligionists by piety and adherence to the religious commandments. However, they, too, followed the German-Jewish model of regarding Judaism exclusively as a religion and, therefore, had removed all external characteristics from clothing and hair. They wanted the Jews in the occupied territories to live according to the principles of *Torah im derekh eretz*, the old rabbinic motto stating that basic religious and traditional tenets should be combined and taught consistent with worldliness and general knowledge, and to represent German interests. Although they emphasized their attachment to the Eastern Europeans, they were still displaying some arrogance and a sense of mission to "civilize" them. Their primary goal, shared with the Liberals, was to make Jews in Eastern Europe aware of the incompatibility of Judaism with "The Nation." The competing policies of the German-Jewish organizations, for the favor of the Jews in the occupied territories, which had begun with the outbreak of the war, also effected the Jews from Eastern Europe who had remained in Germany and encouraged the Kahans and Rosenbergs to do something for their compatriots.

They started their own social commitment as a family, in parallel to the large aid organizations, campaigning in a big way for Eastern European Jews, prisoners of war, displaced persons and transients in Berlin, as well as for people who lived in the occupied territories. A postcard to Rosa Rosenberg in the archival legacy, delivered by the Austro-Hungarian Red Cross in the spring of 1916, describes the fate of Salo Stock, a prisoner of war in the Habsburg Empire, who was initially jailed in Bohemia as a soldier of the Tsarist army. Salo Stock requested that his parents in Łódź be informed of his transfer to Albania. In her memoirs of Schlüterstrasse, Rosa mentioned the "small company Azbil" (the committee for the procurement of Jewish literature), also called Azbeda, which sent books to Jewish prisoners of war from the Russian Empire, presumably to the camps near Berlin, Döberitz, Rohrbeck and Dyrotz, west of Spandau, or to the vineyard-camp near Zossen, south of Berlin in Fläming. More than half of all prisoners of war came from the Russian Empire, among them many Jews. The board of Azbil included the lawyers Aron Z. Syngalowski and Yuda M. Beham, Zalman Shneour and Bendet Kahan. Syngalowski had ended up in Berlin as a Russian prisoner of war. After the war, he was to become general secretary of the Society for the Promotion of Work among Jews at International Level, the World ORT. The poet Zalman Shneour had studied medicine in Berlin and, like Jacob, had been expelled from the university as an "enemy alien" at the beginning of the war. Yuda M. Beham was the lawyer and a friend of the family from Kharkov. A photo in the archival legacy shows the group: the Board and behind it nine young people: Jacob, Rosa, Noma and unknowns. According to family recollections, Bendet procured prayer books and religious literature for the prisoners. The young people organized the contacts and distributed the books. Even during the war, people looking for help, guests and worshipers were welcome in Schlüterstrasse. The hungry, sick and transients, including prominent rabbis from Poland-Lithuania, were given physical and intellectual sustenance on Schlüterstrasse, sometimes including a night's lodging.

Jonas Rosenberg, by contrast, was responsible for the care of employees, relatives, friends of the family and other needy people in occupied Poland, especially in Warsaw, but also in Zamość, Siedlce, Łódź, Łomża and Aleksandrovo. He regularly sent money to the employees Pisarewicz and Ebin in Warsaw, Friedland in Zamość and to his brother Benyamin Rosenberg in Łódź. Around 100 postcards with petitions and acknowledgments testify to this. Some of those requests, especially for employees or business partners, arrived by mail from his father-in-law in Russia. Again and again, he wrote whether this one or that one had been considered, or whether one amount or another was adequate. Another activity, which also taxed the family's emotions, was writing letters to relatives across the enemy lines, no easy task in view of the war censorship and the interruption of regular mail. Private "mail circles" and "occasions" helped in times of need: courageous travelers who crossed the front lines, soldiers on home leave, helpers from neutral Denmark, Sweden, Norway, or Spain. The families shared the most important things with each other, mostly sparingly: festival greetings, confirmation of mail receipt as a sign of life, information about the whereabouts and wellbeing of relatives relocated from the front to Russia—Elias Rosenberg in Poltava, Menachem Bramson in Tula— and concerning the state of health of all family members in Berlin, Petrograd, Kharkov, Baku, Yekaterinoslav, the financial situation and money transfers.

In the beginning, the days passed without major events or eruptions. When the relatives travelled to their summer resort, Jacob felt the emptiness of the large apartment in Schlüterstrasse, became homesick and was longing for Petrograd and Kharkov. Lessons, visits, walks, most often with Rosa Langer, and correspondence filled the monotonous everyday life of the exile within the narrow limits set by the war regulations. Jacob later told Roska in Bad Neuenahr, in great detail, about his daily routine. Special events were lectures that Jacob attended. He listened to a lecture by Rabbi Yechiel Jacob Weinberg about "The Educational System of the "Eastern Jews," organized by the Association of Jewish Academics, in the Logenhaus—the dignitaries of the Orthodox community were also present, and Jacob made a transcript for Dr. Rosenthal—and Zalman Rubashov in the Herzl Club (co-organizer was the Alliance of Jewish Student Fraternities) on the twelfth anniversary of Theodor Herzl's death on the subject of "Herzl and the Idea of Messianism." He also attended lessons at the Orthodox Rabbinical Seminary. The learned Rabbi Weinberg, as well as the student and prospective Zionist politician Zalman Rubashov, were Litvaks, like the Kahans, and belonged to their circle of family friends. Both were trapped in Berlin as "enemy aliens" because of the war. (Zalman Rubashov changed his name to Zalman Shazar in Israel, where he served as its third president in 1963–1973.)

Jacob regularly gave language and literature lessons to his friend Max Kut, son of the businessman Karl Kut, tobacco products and fur waste, at 8 Jostystrasse, Berlin no. 43. Reading matters were Yehudah Steinberg's *Ba-Yamim Hahem* [In those days], a novel that was to appear in 1920 as *The Soldier of the Tsar* in German, about the fate of a Jewish soldier under Nicholas I, which had regained political topicality due to the war; poems by Chaim Nachman Bialik; the stories and novels by Scholem Aleichem; prose by Yehudah Leib Perez; Mendele Moicher Sforim's *Binyamin Hashlishi* [Benjamin the Third and the Journey to the Promised Land]; translations, too, of Russian novels, popular in Germany at the time, such as Dmitry S. Merezhkovsky's *Julian the Apostate*, part of the cycle *Christ und Antichrist*, and Dostoevsky's *The Idiot*. They would sit down here and there, working not only at home, but also in the Rabbinical

Seminary or whilst travelling on the train. Since Jacob was barred from studying philology, he introduced his Berlin friend to modern Hebrew, Yiddish and classic Russian literature.

The number and names of the visitors at 36 Schlüterstrasse, whom Jacob commented on in his letters, reveal that those who stayed behind were not lonely during those war years; the migrants preferred to stay among themselves, but also had friends and acquaintances in long-established Berliners circles. Once, Yasha wrote to Rosa in *Germyish*, in the middle of a Russian letter: "*Mir seinen alle sehr vertummelt,*" which means something like: "We're all messed up" and then listed the visitors: Rabbi Rosenthal with wife and children; Rabbi Weinberg and legal advisor Beham; apart from Max, a friend from Russia—Abraham Aronson, son of the Kiev Rabbi Shlomo Aronson; young men named Poiluš, Stok, Montano, Mindlich, Eliash, Lifshitz and Lyubman. Other visitors were the Hamburgers, Goldbergs, Mr. Berlin, a relative from Vilna, Frumzhe Hurwitz, a friend of Miriam Rosenberg, and the couple Barkan and Fräulein Basch, probably Malka's relatives. Chaim Kahan's managing director in Germany, Max Lev, was a guest, as was Nachum Goldmann, who was officially employed, at the time, by the Foreign Office as a "lecturer and academic assistant." Jacob and Noma used to make return visits.

The freedom of movement for the Berlin families began to increase from the beginning of 1916. In the summer, the women went to the Bad Neuenahr spa in the Rhineland. Jonas traveled to Poland for the second time. Bendet moved with his family into a holiday home near Berlin. Jacob and Noma Rosenberg also applied for travel permits to go for their summer holidays to Bad Harzburg. The applications were submitted at the Charlottenburg police station and forwarded to the commander's office at the police headquarters. Nachum Goldmann, at the Foreign Office, was asked for help. Nevertheless, the process dragged on. Berlin remained a place of exile for the young men, seventeen and twenty-one years old. They made the best of it. Affluent, sheltered and self-confident, they felt protected, even in the warring Germany, by their grandfather's reputation in the Orthodox community, the Zionist movement and his efforts for the Jewish homeland in Palestine. Despite the official requirements, the daily reports to the police station in the morning and evening and the curfew, they were provided small escapes—trips to the environs of Berlin and a place all to themselves while everyone else was away. With Max, also with others, they cycled to the Grunewald, to rowing regattas on the Wannsee. After a month, their applications were denied, following the medical officer's recommendation, because only those seriously ill were given permission to travel to the spa: Jacob could relax on the Berlin lakes and Noma in the Tiergarten Park, being as "round and stout" as he was. When Max Kut received permission for the trip to Bad Harzburg without any problems, Jacob was offended. Obviously, an "enemy alien" of conscription age attracted special treatment, especially since Nachum Goldmann could not help.

The situation changed two days after the refusal because all relatives, including the cook Lina, were away and the two young men were alone in the ten-room apartment. Jacob's fantasies worked overtime at the unexpected freedom. With exuberance and humor, he described how they managed the housekeeping without giving up the usual conveniences or getting carried away as "bachelors" should. They did not move to Eugenie Kahan's Orient Hotel on the Schiffbauerdamm and also not to acquaintances; neither did they go to the legendary Struck Guesthouse nor to Logenheimer, the branch of a kosher-run Bad Harzburg hotel on Friedrichstrasse, as they had initially contemplated, but lunched instead in the Weinberg restaurant and otherwise got help from Frau Schwalbe, the caretaker's wife, as a maid and *Shabbes goy*. Jacob cooked spinach and Noma baked omelets. They made *smetana* from cream, and nibbles from cucumbers and sardines. In the evening they went out with friends—to the Deutsches Theater, which performed a tragicomic farce; to the movies in the new Unionpalast on Kurfürstendamm; and then next door to the Café Westerland, with Italian opera music. They went to the Volksbühne Theater and sat in the Tauentzien-Palast coffee house until midnight. Berlin, the Entertainment City, offered the young people in their exclusive exile many attractions. But were they able to prepare "a good kosher *Shabbes*"?

The Shabbat seemed like a slapstick film. One mishap followed the next, chaos reigned at home and they made a total mess of the rituals. This culminated in mutual teasing, as to who had caused more nonsense. Jacob blamed Noma for the clogged-up tub drain, the missed bath, the delays and the clutter in the apartment. Noma acted as a moral guardian, revealing that Yasha hadn't written to his parents in Petrograd for a long time, but had instead written interminably long letters to Rosa with stuff Jacob had plagiarized from him. He also denied having had tea with friends on *Shabbes*. Such *goyim* they weren't yet. On that day the traditionally prescribed order became unhinged. The young men were probably inexperienced, because they were in charge for the first time and therefore clumsy, but they might also have been exploring their own latitude in complying with the religious commandments, challenging tradition. Maybe they were also reacting to the political muzzling, so that the rites of passage into adult life ended with a backward flip.

CHAPTER 4

On the Move. Vilna, Warsaw, Kharkov, Saratov ...

Postcard. Opened by the Petrograd War Censorship. Military Censor no. 11. To Mr. Mauritz Tarschis, Stockholm, 35 Götgatan, Sweden, under the letterhead of the Head Office of the Caucasian-Volga Trade-Industry Inc. Petrograd, 6 Stremyannaya Street.

Petrograd, March 4, 1915. My Dear Ones, wanted to share with you that thank God our businesses have been getting better recently thanks to the Nobel shares that have risen. ... This money makes things easier. Chaim.

The Kahans, entrepreneurs and Jews, belonged to the mobile diaspora groups that played a double role in the Russian colonial empire, like the Germans and the Armenians. In the western provinces they belonged to the colonized indigenous population, though not to the mainstream society, but in the areas conquered later, like the Transcaucasian region, they were identified with the colonial rulers, because they had arrived in their wake. The Kahans came from Poland-Lithuania, lived in the Ukraine, most recently also in St. Petersburg (Petrograd in 1914–1924), and, since they traded oil from the new Russian colonies beyond the Caucasus, had a base on the Caspian Sea. In 1917, their operational sphere extended from the Baltic to Baku. However, the end of the empires brought about by the end of the First World War destroyed their life and economy. Chaim Kahan, the entrepreneur, initially experienced the war as an economic success. But simultaneously, it was a personal misfortune, because of the separation from Malka and the torn family.

Chaim went about his business and traveled a lot, mostly by train. When he could afford it, he would have, most probably, taken the fastest trains, travelling first class, in the dark blue wagons with the silk-upholstered seats. The faster the trains, the more expensive the tickets. But the railroad, with its comfortably equipped wagons and elegant train stations epitomizing a new era and a modern civil order in the Russian Empire, was used primarily for military purposes during the war. The trains for civilian passengers ran less frequently, were slower and overcrowded. The journeys now took longer than before. On one such trip from Petrograd to Baku, Chaim Kahan was on the move for ten days. At many of the layovers he stayed in inns. There he would only drink tea because of the dietary kashrut laws, related grandson Arusia. According to one employee's recollections, most business deals were negotiated and concluded in these inns, while consuming copious quantities of tea with sugar. Chaim wrote to his wife and children in Berlin from everywhere. The postcards passed the war censorship and reached their destination via the neutral countries Sweden or Denmark.

> Petrograd, June 27/9, 1915. My Dear Ones! Repeating again. Believing in my responsibility and expressing my opinion in favor of the arrival [of Malka] I will continue to inform you these days going away will be a month outside of Petrograd. Chaim.

Chaim Kahan had started his business in the so-called Pale of Settlement and expanded it into the neighboring Kingdom of Poland to the west, areas where the Jews had been living for centuries. (The Pale of Settlement is usually defined as the area in the western border regions of the Russian Empire in which the Jews were required to live by law.) He had operated from Brest for around three decades, until the mid-1890s, and then gradually opened up new locations, starting with Kharkov in eastern Ukraine. The earliest testimonials in the archival legacy are eight empty envelopes with wax seals—lying there, like ancient hollow pigeons with lean messages, unsealed, but still silent—in a variety of scripts, addressed to a certain Fedor Fedorovich Danilovich, Kharkov, Inspector of the Veterinary Institute on the Bolshaya Nemetskaya Street, in General Mandrykin's residence. One of the wax seals bears the inscription *"Trud i terpenie"* [work and patience]. The letters, which stem from the early years of Chaim Kahan's professional activity, were mailed from St. Petersburg and various small towns—Pereyaslav, Akhtyrka, Kanev, Zaslav, both inside and outside the Pale of Settlement in the provinces of

Kiev, Kharkov and Minsk, which were located along waterways or railway lines. The ongoing contact with the Inspector of the Veterinary Institute is documented by another envelope from 1897. Could Chaim Kahan possibly have worked for him?

> Petrograd, June 1/13, 1915. My Dear Ones! As you can see, I am already here because we are making a merger with Levit to increase the capital of the V. [Volga] society about my return I may go to Copenhagen briefly your Chaim.

Mobility was a basic requirement for a successful entrepreneur in the Russian Empire. This was especially true for the Jews, as they were subject to restrictions of settlement and property, having to comply with strict passport regulations. The state hindered their mobility. Even in the last years of the Tsarist Empire, legislation was largely influenced by snobbery and protectionism. The merchants were the first to be granted the right to stay outside the Pale of Settlement, despite opposition from their Russian competitors. They were assigned to the general professional associations, the Merchant Guilds, of which there were initially three, and after 1863, two. They also enjoyed far greater mobility than other Jewish subjects. According to the decrees of 1804, they were allowed to travel around the empire for the duration of their business needs, accompanied by their wives and children; they were even allowed to travel to the two capitals. The decrees of 1835 refined that privilege, but at the same time narrowed it down: Jews needed permission from the local authorities for business trips to the interior of the empire, lasting a maximum of two months. Only the Jewish merchants of the first two guilds were allowed to travel, twice a year, without special permission: those of the First Guild no longer than six months and those of the Second Guild up to three, which was even reduced to two between 1890 and 1904. They were allowed to travel to the trade fairs in the capitals and port cities—Nizhny Novgorod, Irbit in the Urals, Kharkov, Sumy, to the Korennaya Pustyn monastery near Kursk—and take along up to two Jewish servants. From 1848 the Jewish merchants were allowed to stay in all the cities of the empire. Instead of traveling themselves, they could send an employee. In the capitals and in port cities, they were allowed to sell goods from the Pale of Settlement in bulk, but not foreign ones, which restricted Chaim Kahan, when he was dealing in American oil from Königsberg.

Postcard. Opened by Pyatigorsk War Censorship. To "Messieur" L. C. Glad & Co, Copenhagen, Danie, under the letterhead of the Russian-Baltic Mineral Oil Company, Petrograd.

Kissengen [Petrograd is crossed out], August 11/24, 1915. My dear Malke! For the New Year (*Rosheshono*) I send you best wishes that God has received all your requests and desires your loving Chaim.

Chaim Kahan had business relations with Riga, Reval and St. Petersburg already early on. But in the capitals and port cities, Jews were only allowed to sell their goods wholesale through resident Christian merchants, and imports also wholesale only at trade fairs. Direct sales to consumers or the opening of shops were punished with expulsion and confiscation of the goods, and later with fines. However, it was permitted to have imports cleared at customs by Christian merchants for a commission and also to buy wholesale in the capitals and port cities for sale in the Pale of Settlement. The 1904 trade laws largely abolished the restrictions applicable to Jews during the nineteenth century. However, the ban on sales in shops outside the Pale of Settlement remained in force until the end of the empire. In order to operate successfully, Chaim Kahan had to be familiar with the legal maze, as well as prices, tariffs and complicated tax regulations. And nothing worked without bribery.

Kislovodsk, August 11/24, 19 [15]. Dear Maria Jonas Roske and Nioma! I hope you receive this letter for our New Year, and I wish you that God willing all your wishes and requests will be fulfilled by God in these days you will surely ask for an early reunion with your loved ones. Believe me that with all my heart I'm also longing for you of course in first place for *Mamasha* [mother] then for you your loving Chaim.

Chaim Kahan had grown up in a time of great upheavals and modernization. The Crimean War ended when he was five years old, and the reformer, Alexander II, took over the government. A few years later (1859) the Jewish merchants of the First Guild were given the privilege of living outside the Pale of Settlement. Serfdom was abolished and railway construction began. The first lines connected the capitals, St. Petersburg and Moscow. Subsequent ones were built in the western provinces, the Jewish settlement region, leading to the imperial borders and the Baltic Sea ports so as to connect the capitals with the Western world. Since the suppression of the second Polish uprising (1863), the government had been courting the Jews as loyal subjects in the rebellious northwestern border area. The development of society as a whole had opened up new opportunities for Chaim Kahan and expanded his operational range. He got into the oil business when the sale of petroleum from Pennsylvania in the Russian Empire was booming. Petroleum, used as lighting fuel, was sold, like the herrings, in barrels and transported by rail and on water from the ports to the interior of the empire, bringing light to offices, workshops, factories and apartments. Königsberg was one of the ports for its import, and Chaim Kahan didn't live too far away. The East Prussian Southern Railway reached the border to the Tsarist Empire in 1871. Two years later it was linked with Russia's Southwest Rail, connecting Königsberg with Brest.

> September 6/19, 1915, Petrograd. My Dear Ones! It is very difficult to get anything I assume that if there is no message from you between 2/3 months I will go to Stockholm again although frankly it has become very difficult for me your Ch. Kahan.

The new form of lighting had made it possible to work around the clock. The railroad revolutionized transportation and the telegraph the transmission of messages. The telegraph had been used extensively since the 1870s. A fast message transmission was required for the swift handling of business. From the 1880s, the first manually operated telephone exchanges operated in the capitals, port and trade cities of the Empire, providing St. Petersburg, Moscow, Riga, Odessa, Libau, Reval, Nizhny Novgorod and Baku with the first telephone networks. Chaim Kahan was known for making extensive use of the telegraph and telephone which was, however, not possible across the fronts during the war.

> Petrograd, September 13, [1915.] My dear Malke am very happy about the letter Roske wrote. You can often write with your signature and the like. It is the only thing that I received from you in all that time after my return for my part I often write Chaim.

In the middle of the nineteenth century, the wholesale business and long-distance trade of Jewish merchants was dominated by agricultural products such as grain, sugar, wood and tea. Well-known family names—Efrusi in Odessa, Brodsky in Kiev, Wissotzky in Moscow—testify for this. The well-known saying, "*Chai Vysotskogo, sakhar Brodskogo, Rossiia Trotskogo*" [Tea

belongs to Wissotzky, sugar belongs to Brodsky, Russia belongs to Trotsky]
echoed an antisemitic slogan. Other large merchants ran state-owned enterprises like Pauline Wengeroff's father, earning their money by building forts
and roads or by supplying equipment to the army. The tax farmers, in turn,
were mostly involved in the alcohol business. It wasn't until the 1860s, when
Chaim Kahan's career began, that new lines of business began to emerge for
Jewish merchants—the modern money business in the form of banking and
credit systems, which brought the Barons Günzburg in St. Petersburg prosperity and prestige; the railway construction, in which the Polyakovs invested; and
in addition to the coal, ore and gold production, the oil business. When Chaim
Kahan started in business, the oil industry was in turmoil. Baku had become the
oil metropolis of the Russian Empire in the late 1870s, so that oil from America
was no longer required. While it had been used primarily as a light source until
the 1860s, its use as a strategic raw material for energy generation in modern
technology, industry and warfare was gradually being discovered.

> Petrograd, September 21, [1915]. My Dear Ones! Hurrying to write that I
> have now received Y.[our] good wishes written in an open letter in Russian
> keep up the good work, your loving, Ch. Kagan.

One of Chaim Kahan's greatest skills was his ability to "figure out," as was his
knack to sniff out promising investments and reliable financiers. He initiated
business opportunities, established new contacts, gained partners and employees. In the mid-1870s he set up on his own. For two decades, until the mid-
1890s, he was a partner in the Trading Company Dembo & Kahan in Vilna,
which traded in oil products acquired in Baku, Saratov and other places in the
Russian Empire as well as abroad and sold them within the Pale of Settlement
in Vilna and Brest and beyond, in Warsaw, Riga and St. Petersburg. Since Peter
I, membership in the merchant guilds for wholesalers in the Russian Empire
was the prerequisite for commercial business on a larger scale, regardless of
which ethno-denominational group one belonged to, and, since Alexander I,
three types of companies had provided the traditional legal framework for this:
the "complete company" (polnoe obshchestvo) with at least two equally liable
partners in the same merchant guild, the "good faith company" (tovarishchestvo
polnoe i na vere) with one or several fully liable and silent partners whose liability depended on the size of their contributions and the "share company"
(tovarishchestvo po uchastkam), the forerunner of the incorporated company.
This followed the English model and was introduced under Nicholas I in 1835,

about a decade earlier than in Prussia and France, but took hold slower in the Russian Empire than in its western neighbors. The majority of Russia's medium-sized oil entrepreneurs in Baku emerged from the business community and operated in *obshchestva* and *tovarishchestva*. However, the modern extraction, processing and marketing of the oil wealth required new methods, qualifications and economic forms.

Dembo & Kahan had the legal status of a "good faith company." Chaim Kahan was the silent partner of Abraham Dembo from Kovno, and after that, of his son Osip Abramovich. Like the Kahans, the Dembos were Litvaks, but, unlike them, the Dembos were *maskilim*, modern Jews, while Chaim was considered a nationally conscious and pious Jew. He was the head of the company, according to Meir Bar Ilan in his memoir, "the Jewish gentleman," *idishn gvir*. Already under the Dembo & Kahan label, Chaim competed with the Rothschild and Nobel conglomerates, which led the industry in Baku.

In 1885 there were seventy-nine companies in Baku. Bradstreet's, the New York business-to-business information service, reported about Russian petroleum that Dembo & Kahan were among the top eight in terms of production and trade volume. In 1882 they were the second largest petroleum exporter in Baku with 1,700,000 *puds* after Branobel's with 4,500,000 according to the journal *Export—The Organ of the Central Association for Commercial Geography*. (*Pud* was a Russian quantitative measure for mass.)

Among the Jewish public, the trading house was considered to be worth millions; in fact, they had more sense than money, more entrepreneurship than capital, more willpower than economic clout, according to Bar Ilan. Nevertheless, Dembo & Kahan had to defer to Branobel. In 1886, during the first Baku oil-trade crisis, the latter company went bankrupt. This was reported by Bradstreet's as well as the German *Chemist's Newspaper*. Overproduction, poor transportation, mismanagement, ineffective government policies and excessive draining of capital in view of anticipated rapid earnings across the industry, had led to a price drop that Dembo & Kahan could not cope with. They left behind a debt of four million rubles. The company was bought by Tbilisi merchants. However, it was only in the mid-1890s that the partners finally separated. The family says that although Chaim Kahan refused to invest again in the partnership, he nevertheless granted Dembo a loan at his request. When his children asked why, he replied that the mere fact that Dembo needed him was a sign, which was why he gave it to him. It was less an expression of satisfaction for Chaim Kahan than a manifestation of his generosity.

Petrograd, the 24.9.[1915]. Dear Loved Ones I wrote Y.[ou] that we have received your card with good wishes signed by everyone in a few days I [will travel to Tula and give it] to the Bramson family in Tula will see the respected father of Judis on the way I will often write to you Your Chaim.

Even before he separated from Dembo, Chaim Kahan had "figured out," calculated and expanded his business. The expansion of the company was underpinned, backed by a marriage policy, with the following stages. At the end of 1893 he married off his eldest son Baruch to Rosa Berlin, the niece of Naftali Zevi Yehudah Berlin, known as Hanetziv, head of the Volozhin Yeshiva and Meir Bar Ilan's father, in Vilna, the headquarters of Dembo & Kahan. From 1894, after his daughter Miriam had married the Warsaw merchant Jonas Rosenberg, who, like Rosa Berlin, stemmed from scholarly aristocracy, Chaim Kahan had also maintained an address in the Polish congress capital. After the separation from Dembo, father and son Baruch ran the company from Kharkov and, after the marriage of the second son Pinchas to the merchant-daughter Zina Golodetz in 1900, also from Baku. When the third son, Bendet, married Judith Bramson in February 1904, he already had a branch in Kursk. Five years later (1909) Chaim Kahan opened an additional branch in Yekaterinoslav and had it managed by David Ettinger from Uman, who had married his youngest daughter, Rachel. Two of the weddings were celebrated in Polish-Lithuanian, now Belarusian, railway stations. Bendet and Judith invited their guests for the evening after the unconventional marriage in Weissee, or Wiżajny, to the Porechye station, Pinchas and Zina to that in Baranovichi, because train stations could conveniently be reached by guests from near and far. The splendid, spacious station buildings had elegant ballrooms, which could easily accommodate the wedding party, and were used perhaps also because it was considered chic and modern. The photo of Pinchas and Zina's wedding at the Baranovichi railroad junction is the only surviving family portrait from the period before the war and revolution in the Russian Empire. There are two versions of the invitation to Bendet and Judith's wedding. It was formulated in Hebrew by the bride's father and in German by the bride herself. "Kindly request you attend my marriage to Mr. Benedikt Kahn, on the evening of February 10/23, at the St. Petersburg–Warsaw Porechye train station," Judith wrote, apparently equating "marriage" with the wedding feast.

> Moscow, September 25, 1915. Dear Loved Ones! Received a letter yes-
> terday from Jonas without a date only by good wishes I understood that it
> was written before New Year there is a greeting from Struck, I wrote to you
> that I plan to spend more time here and in Kharkov I would like to open an
> office in Moscow after Saturday I will go to Tula shortly I will be in Poltava
> write from there. Your loving Chaim.

The connections with respected families in Vilna and Warsaw show Chaim's closeness to tradition as well as his to the future-oriented business sense. Vilna, also called the Lithuanian Jerusalem, *Yerushalayim shel Lita*, was the capital of the Litvaks. Vilna and the Polish capital Warsaw were larger cities than Brest and also economically more important. Both can undoubtedly be called the urban centers of the Jewish Pale of Settlement in the northwestern border region. But taking a decisive step in expanding to Kharkov, Saratov, Baku, Yekaterinoslav, areas outside the Pale of Settlement, was risky.

> Petrograd, October 2/15, 1915. Dear Loved Ones! Returned here because
> Pinchos also arrived on Sunday he was in Moscow on Saturday I hurried
> because Rabbi Aronson is here I have not received letters from you Chaim.

Chaim Kahan was officially registered as a merchant in Kharkov from 1869, when the city was connected to the Russian rail network. Kharkov, today the second Ukrainian capital at the confluence of the Kharkov and Lopan rivers, was founded in 1654 as a fortified town on what was then the southern border of the empire. Located at the crossroads of the trade routes from Moscow to Kiev, from St. Petersburg to the Crimea and into the Caucasus, it was not only a garrison town, but, from its inception, also a trading center with its well-known trade fairs, long before the railway was built. Kharkov had a university since 1805, and since 1835 it was the capital of the only Ukrainian province outside the Pale of Settlement, albeit in its immediate vicinity. Since then, Jews have been allowed to do business in Kharkov, and many of them made use of it. Since the end of the 1860s, thanks to Polyakov's investments, Kharkov has also functioned as a railway junction. At the beginning of the reform era, the Jewish population, which now consisted not only of soldiers and merchants, but also artisans, doctors, teachers, lawyers, students and high school students, had grown by leaps and bounds. This motivated the governor, Count Aleksandr K. Sivers, to demand of Tsar Alexander II legal equality for the Jews, something that was revolutionary at the time. From the 1870s, Kharkov had gas lighting, a decade later, sewerage and a horse-drawn tram; it also became a center for science and culture with libraries, museums and numerous educational institutions. The real boom of the city began with the development of iron ore and coal deposits and the emergence of industrial centers in the nearby Donets Basin, where a strong mechanical engineering industry sprang up. At the beginning of the twentieth century, Kharkov had 200,000 inhabitants, more than five percent of whom were Jews. It developed into the Russian city with the second highest Jewish population after St. Petersburg outside the Pale of Settlement. For this reason and because Kharkov was on the way from Brest, Warsaw and St. Petersburg to Baku, it was attractive for Chaim Kahan.

> Kharkov, March 15/28, 1916. Dear Loved Ones! The apartment here is very good, suits us and is very cozy for us together. Now the city of Kharkov is completely Jewish like the Pale of Settlement. I hope I can build-up the business better convert it and Jonas will be busy forever.

The company in Kharkov was called Ch. N. Kahan Manufacture and Sale of Oil Products. Kharkov Branch. Until their escape from Russia, the Kahan family had lived and worked in Kharkov in the historic city center, the hilly neighborhood of Nagorny *rayon*, 21 Pushkinskaya, in a two-story town house, about half the size of the Brest family residence, which has been preserved. Pushkinskaya Street is one of the main streets of Kharkov. Until 1898 it was called Bolshaya Nemetskaya in honor of the German artisan colony initiated by the university founder Karamzin. That's where the aforementioned inspector of the Veterinary Institute was located. At the turn of the century, the Jewish Kharkov had a distinctive infrastructure. Jewish businesspeople held key positions in the financial world. Ninety percent of all First-Guild merchants there were Jews. In Kharkov, the Kahans lived in familiar social settings while living and working conditions were favorable for them in every respect.

Chaim Kahan managed the Saratov refinery from Kharkov, something unthinkable nowadays, in the times of the Russian-Ukrainian conflicts. At that time, however, the cities were neither separated by a state border nor by war, and the rail network was denser in the western border area than anywhere else in the Russian Empire. When the Kahans were traveling by train between Brest, Warsaw, Kharkov and Saratov, they moved largely within Jewish regions, because the Jewish population lived predominantly in this part of the empire. Yiddish was mainly heard in the carriages, on the platforms and in the station halls. The Tsarist prohibition from 1897 for Jews to pray in a public space was evidence of their self-confident appearance. But Saratov on the Volga, located beyond the Ukrainian-Russian border and nowadays more than eight hundred kilometers by road from Kharkov, could be reached in peacetime in the nineteenth and even nowadays, in the twenty-first century, by rail in about twenty-four hours. It is and was a Russian city, belonging to the third category of industrial centers in the empire. Saratov had a reputation for being stubborn because many rebellious subjects lived there—Old Believers, *narodniks* and Social Revolutionaries. The city described itself as the "Capital of the Volga Region" as well as "Athens-on-the-Volga," but dust and dirt was the prevailing impression among visitors.

The center consists of a checkerboard-shaped square of treeless streets, which, here too, has in its midst a Nemetskaya Street [Deutsche Strasse] with elegant shops, cafes and pastry shops. Three gorges, running at right angles to the Volga, flow through the city, which is located on the elevated right bank of the Volga and resembles an amphitheater that opens to the east like onto a stage.

In the late nineteenth and the early twentieth century, Russians made up eighty-five percent of the city's population, and Germans were the largest minority with six percent. There were hardly any Jews living in Saratov. They were not eligible to vote there even if they owned real estate. Jacob Teitel, a contemporary of Chaim Kahan's, and, as he kept saying, the only Jewish judge in the empire, worked there for several years (1904–1912). He recounted that, at that time, there were apparently two educational institutions attracting young Jews from the Pale of Settlement to Saratov—the medical college [*feldsherskaya shkola*] and the technical school [*sredne-tekhnicheskoye uchilishche*]. Apart from that, he considered the pogrom which followed the October manifesto after the 1905 revolution as the only event worth mentioning in the history of the Saratov Jews.

> Baku, April 14/27, 1916. My dear daughter Maria! Received your letter was very happy about it, although you only write about Mama as "satisfactory" when Jonas wrote "comparatively not bad" But what should one do will hope for something better Here t.[hank] God everything is well If I return via Kharkov I will try to go see your father in law and Mr. Mintz. R.[abbi] Akiva [Rabinovich from Poltava] came to me obviously for money. Please write often! Stay healthy and happy with all of yours—your loving you Chaim.

In the early 1870s there were no more than thirty merchants of the First Guild in Saratov. Twenty years later (1895) when Chaim Kahan was one of them, there were three times as many, almost a hundred. Saratov also experienced an economic boom in that period. Since 1871, the city had been connected to the Russian rail network by the Ryazan-Uralsk line, which ran in the direction of the Urals, but only as far as Saratov.

The merchant exchange was opened in 1882. The entrepreneurship was ethnically similar to that of the entire population, among them there were many Russian Old Believers and Germans, steam mill owners, as well as mechanical engineering and cast iron manufacturers, and even a Jewish tobacco producer. Many belonged to Chaim Kahan's generation. Branobel had an office in the Volga city. On the riverbank, in the western suburb of Uleshi, now a small Saratov neighborhood, petroleum, mineral oil and oil residues were pumped from barges, which had arrived from Baku, into huge tanks. Numerous shipping companies were based in Saratov on the bank of the Volga River: alongside the large Kavkaz i Merkury and Samolet, there were also smaller ones, among them Lebed. Lebed, headquartered in Baku, took on freights for shipping to the ports of the Caspian Sea, to all the cities that could be reached via the Volga, Kama and Don rivers, to the port cities of the Sea of Azov and the Black Sea, to all rail connections in Tsaritsyn and to all railway stations of the Zakaspiysk Railroad. The company maintained a passenger line across the Caspian Sea. In addition, it took oil residues and petroleum from Baku to the Volga cities as cargo. The report of the Saratov Stock Exchange Committee for the year 1885 contains a reference that Dembo & Kahan traded a *pud* of kerosene for 0.50 ruble, while Branobel traded it for 0.55 ruble. In the 1890 annual report of the Caspian-Black Sea Oil Industry and Trading Company, the Rothschild group in Baku, Dembo & Kahan are listed as subcontractors of oil tanks in Saratov. So much for the presence of the company there during the 1880s–1890s and their competition with the large conglomerates at that time.

The report of the Exchange Committee for 1900 and 1901 shows a listing for "Kogan, Chaim Naumovich, Jew, Saratov First-Guild Merchant, Member of the Exchange." Chaim Kahan had been on the books as a First-Guild Merchant of Saratov since 1893, although it was only three years later (in November 1896) that he acquired a refinery at the railway junction in Knyazevka, now a district and industrial zone. Three photos in the archival estate testify to this. One of them shows floods on the Volga in front of factories, a group of men in a barge, in the middle Baruch Kahan with a gap between him and the others, the only one with a white hat and holding a cane, with his brother David next to him. The second shows factories in a spacious truck yard, low buildings with crates, sheet metal roofs, tightly built, high smoking chimneys, workers and employees in front of them. On the third, the workforce of more than sixty poses in five rows, in the center the owner Chaim Kahan, flanked on the right and left by his sons Baruch and David and by his son-in-law David Ettinger.

The lease agreement between the Ryazan-Uralsk Railway Administration and the Baku businessman, Lev P. Zilberman, from whom Chaim Kahan took over the factory, gives an overview of the company premises. The refinery, which produced 32.5 tons (2,000 *puds*) of oil a year, had tanks, a pit and halls for the storage of mineral oil and oil residues on the almost one-hectare (2,000-square-*sazhen*) plot at the Knyazevka station; a thirty-cylinder steam engine, a house for the administrator, a branch canal from the nearby Volga with a landing stage, pipes and pumps to transport the oil from the barges to the company premises and the processed oil from the factory into railway wagons. Pipes were also laid underground, with rails running above them. A path connected the factory to the train station. Transportation was based on contracts concluded with the railway administration.

As a result, Chaim Kahan was no longer just a wholesaler but also a medium-sized manufacturer. When he bought the refinery, he followed a trend, like in the 1860s. Saratov on the Volga, a region that had been known for its oil reserves for some time, even if the large-scale yield had not yet been achieved, offered a location advantage from 1871 onwards, when the city was connected to the rail network. Transport by train from there to the capitals and port cities as well as to the industrial areas was much easier, and therefore cheaper than on the weather-dependent waterway of the Volga. Chaim Kahan's economic presence formed the basis for his guild membership in the Volga city. He also had an address in Saratov: First District, Moskovskaya Street, House of Osipov. Since 1896 the company was called Ch. N. Kahan's Knyazevka Factory. Production and Sale of Light and Lubricating Oils, Saratov.

"The property of the Kahan family, which was large, was on a piece of land in the countryside near the factory," recalled a former employee, Ilya Golts. "Most of the year, the Kahans lived in St. Petersburg, but in the summer they came to Knyazevka, their property located on the bluff above the Volga River, from where there was a wonderful view of the vastness of the water and the boundless steppes of the Zavolzhye region." As a young relief accountant, Golts had attended the Sabbath services at the Kahan's house, to which the Jewish employees were invited, comprising almost all of the administrative staff. In Saratov, too, the family lived according to Jewish tradition and maintained an open house. "A general *kiddush* used to be held after the service, during which there was a truly informal atmosphere. There were no landlords there, no employees," according to Golts's recollections. Golts lovingly portrayed Chaim Kahan, describing his relationship with his employees whom he knew by name and whose families he helped. In the years leading up to the October Revolution of 1917, there were no protests, no strikes in the factory, and Chaim Kahan was highly regarded not only in the company, but also in the city of Saratov. He was also so progressive, that he sent one of his engineers—at company expense—to the United States for three years to study the American system of labor organization in the oil processing industry. The engineer not only brought back to the company technical know-how, but also new, effective operating principles and democratic conduct.

> Petrograd, April 29, 1916. Dear Malke! Arrived today I will only stay here for 8/10 days after which I will travel to Saratov. Repeat to reassure you about the material situation, therefore try to placate all our relatives and acquaintances. your Chaim.

It was probably some logistical feat at that time, to manage a refinery near Saratov from Kharkov, when the trains were running relatively rarely and not faster than twenty-five to forty kilometers per hour. Kursk, where Bendet ran the company, was centrally located with its famous trade fair and direct rail connections in three directions, to Kharkov, Kiev and Moscow, and from there to St. Petersburg. The sixth location, Baku, was also more than 2,000 kilometers by rail and several days trip from Kharkov. The seventh, managed by David Ettinger, was the provincial city of Yekaterinoslav (now Dnipro in Ukraine), at the confluence of the Dnieper and Samara rivers; it could be reached from Kharkov relatively quickly, about nine hours by train. Yekaterinoslav, which also had rail connections to the interior of the Empire, south to the Black Sea and west since the beginning of the 1890s, was the second largest city on the edge of the Donetsk Basin after Kharkov to benefit from the accelerated industrialization. Both cities exploded. Unlike Kursk, Yekaterinoslav also had a reputation for being a Jewish city.

> Saratov, May 17/30 [1916.] Dear Jonas! When you see the portrait taken by son-in-law David [Ettinger] in the factory don't envy him as he works in our shop more than we do. Believe me that we hardly differ from him only in terms of you it seems to me that you may have weaned yourself from those non-normalities maybe you can give me moral support which I do not expect from him.

Chaim Kahan's companies expanded in the course of accelerated railway construction and industrialization. He used both the new railways and the reliable waterways. The oil was transported from Baku across the Caspian Sea and on the Volga, on land by rail, at first in barrels, later in tankers, barges and tank-trucks. Dembo & Kahan signed contracts with the Saratov shipping company Lebed to ship oil products in tankers between Astrakhan and Tsaritsyn, but also further north, to Saratov. In Tsaritsyn and in all other Volga ports, Dembo & Kahan set up warehouses and reservoirs jointly with Lebed. From the mid-1890s, Chaim Kahan worked with Mazut, a transport company financed by the Rothschild bank, which was managed by the Pollak brothers from Nizhny Novgorod. During the war he acquired his own fleet of ships. At the large train station in Tsaritsyn, the oil was loaded into tank wagons and transported by rail to the interior of the Empire as well as to the western border region. Two other routes that Chaim Kahan used from Baku were the Transcaucasian Railway to the Georgian Batumi on the Black Sea, which had been operating since 1883 (controlled by Rothschild after 1905 together with Branobel), and the line via Petrovsk, now the Dagestan capital Makhachkala, opened in 1896, to Vladikavkaz, the administrative center of the North Ossetian Terek region in the Caucasus. From Batumi the export went to Western Europe by ship. The domestic market was supplied from Vladikavkaz from where one got directly to Kharkov via Rostov-on-Don. Dembo & Kahan signed contracts with the Russian-Baltic Wagon Factory in Riga for the rental of tank wagons. After the separation from Dembo, Chaim Kahan took over the contracts, expanded them, leased and also bought tank wagons in Riga. The competition with Branobel or perhaps also the consequences of the crop failure and cholera epidemic in the early 1890s forced Dembo & Kahan to dismantle the company. In the following years Chaim Kahan worked alone, but also under other names such as Kaplan & Lev Trading House, Caspian-Black Sea Oil Industry and Trading Company and Tseitlin & Itskovich. In order to remain able to offer goods at a reasonable price, he organized a whole apparatus of agents and commissionaires, especially in the western border district, which linked the Baku oil region with the consumer market.

> Kislovodsk, July 12/25 [1916]. Dear Roske! I am very grateful for your letter that you inform me about the well-being of the grandmother and the mom because I get absolutely nothing from them Let us hope for completely different times that we will all live together staying for about half a month then I will go to Kharkov. Your loving Chaim.

According to the decrees of 1859, also enforced in the Caucasus region since 1860, merchants like Chaim Kahan, who had been admitted to the First Guild after its ratification, had unlimited freedom of establishment, but could not exercise this right before the end of a five-year period. The first cities outside the Pale of Settlement in which Chaim Kahan had officially been granted unlimited access were Kharkov and Saratov. Membership in the First or the Second Merchant Guilds in cities outside the Pale of Settlement gave Jewish merchants the same rights and privileges as Russian ones regarding trade, government contracts, tax farming, the establishment of enterprises and factories, as well as the opening of bank accounts. They were also given the right to purchase real estate in the Empire, provided they had an unblemished record.

The merchants of the First Guild were allowed to take family members, as well as employees and servants, out of the Pale of Settlement, as long as they were registered in their Merchant Certificate. The residence right of the twenty-eight-year-old Baruch Kahan was bound to his father's guild membership when he relocated to Kharkov, as was that of the other sons, Pinchas in Baku and Bendet in Kursk; this applied also to his son-in-law, David Ettinger, in Yekaterinoslav; only Jonas Rosenberg, being a guild member in Warsaw, was able to independently decide on his place of residence. For that matter, the employees Josef Lederman and Leiba A. Lifshitz in Kharkov, Solomon Lvovich Paperno in Saratov and Nechemia Moiseevich Neiman in Baku also remained bound to Chaim Kahan's guild membership. They did, however, have the right to travel freely on behalf of their employer.

Reports mailed by a certain A. Szereszewski (who may have been a relative of the family banker D. M. Szereszowski from Szereszowski Bank in Warsaw) to Baruch Kahan in the spring of 1896 attest to the activity, omnipresence and responsibility of an employee. First, Szereszewski collected bills-of-exchange in Riga, paid bills at the Russian-Baltic Wagon Factory for the rental of tank wagons and informed Baruch about the receipt of forty-eight bills-of-exchange to the value of 65,500 rubles from Baku. A few days later, he reported from Petrovsk about the condition of Kahan's tanks in the Dagestan capital, some of which were filled with their own oil and others with that of the Caspian-Black Sea Oil and Trading Company. He informed Chaim about the Branobel tanks supplied by the Kahans in Petrovsk and Rostov, as well as Branobel's difficulty in delivering oil from Rostov to Kharkov. Furthermore, he was waiting for an instruction as to whether he should go from Petrovsk to Baku in order to brief Chaim or get to Kharkov.

A certain restriction for the Jewish merchants of the First Guild was the legal obligation of employees and servants to be tied to the employer's abode outside the Pale of Settlement. They were only allowed to accompany him once, when they moved out of the Pale of Settlement. After that, they had to remain bound to his place of residence. The longstanding employment of Lederman, Lifshitz, Paperno and Neiman could also be explained by this legal background. In this regard, it was easier for Kahan's employees in the Jewish settlement areas, the branch managers Volf Kamenetsky in Białystok, Gilel E. Turovski in Kiev, Girsh P. Zaidengof in Poltava, Moisei D. Grinberg in Częstochowa, Chackel L. Volovelski in Kalisz, Jakov G. Vainshtein in Sieradz in the Kalisz Province, Simcha Lederman in Rejowiec, Zelman Bash in Chełm, Movsha Shpigel in Zamość, Shmuel Rabinovich in Rovno and Hersh B. Swizer in Brest-Litovsk.

> Kislovodsk, 3/8 [1916]. My Dear Ones! Nothing seems to be holding me here Kharkov is better I telegraphed that I rent an apartment together with an office so that it would be appropriate even for Maria and Jonas and Roske The authorizations for Jonas are almost secured now it depends on y[ou] to come or not to send Chaim
>
> [on the margin in German] sender Kahan.

The merchants of the First Guild acquired their residence permit outside the Pale of Settlement for themselves and their families for ten years. After this period, they received unlimited, permanent residential rights in all cities in accordance with the generally applicable laws and regardless of their guild membership fee. They could also register in other status groups. In 1902 Chaim Kahan moved his guild membership to St. Petersburg. At that time, the household consisted of the three children, Aron, Rachel and David, who were still living with their parents, as well as Baruch, Pinchas and Bendet, who already had their own families; only Miriam did not live there, because she was married to the guild merchant Jonas Rosenberg. After 1900, Chaim Kahan's children were free to choose where to live and work. They lived in different places, but all remained in the father's business, including the youngest sons Aron and David, who were trained in Kharkov. Aron had assisted in Baku since the turn of the century. After Chaim Kahan's death at the end of 1916, he took over his father's position as a merchant of the First Guild of St. Petersburg.

Chaim Kahan was still commuting between the different locations at sixty-five. He sent postcards from anywhere, made appointments, established contacts and arranged transactions that were sometimes more and sometimes less successful. He was interested in business ideas and the wellbeing of family, friends and employees. "Mr. Kahan had his finger on every phase of his business and its personnel" recalled one employee, half of whose family was employed by the Kahans and who would later call himself Martin Kushner.

> Rostov, August 4/17, 1916. My Dear Ones! Not only once did I write to you about relatives and acquaintances that you should increase for them due to the price rises, with us the business t.[hank] G.[od] has changed a lot for the better.

Chaim Kahan used the traditional profile and the privileges as a merchant of the First Guild on the one hand and the innovative field of the oil industry on the other, in order to break out of the old class boundaries and ethno-denominational group restrictions so as to act flexibly and with mobility as a modern entrepreneur by imperial standards. Between 1912 and 1916, two more offices in St. Petersburg and Moscow were added to the aforementioned others. Despite the different profiles, all locations served as distribution points and shipment centers. The boom of the new industry required presence in several locations. The main sales areas were and remained the old Jewish settlement regions of Poland-Lithuania, Belarus and Ukraine in the western border area. In addition to the branches in those cities, Chaim Kahan owned, before the war, fully equipped petroleum and other oil product stores in Łódź, Lublin, Kremenchuk, Grodno and on leased land in Kharkov, Kiev, Brest, Warsaw, Mława (Płock Province) and Czerwony Bor (Łomża Province).

> Postcard. Rossiya—Russia. To Mr. W. Finkelstein, Stockholm, 11 Upsalagatan, Sweden, chez Ion[as].

> [Petrograd] 2/XI [1916]. My dear [Jonas]! Your letter of 7/IX New Style only arrived yesterday and unfortunately you hardly answer the many questions about which we would like to know something with silence you completely ignore the money matters What income does the factory [in Warsaw] have and what income can we expect from Shalom and Volf Kamenetsky [in Białystok] and others [several words were erased] Your Chaim.

The correspondence shows Chaim Kahan's mobility, even after he was already tired of traveling. As Chaim Kahan wrote in a letter to Miriam at the end of June 1914,

> When a certain time has passed, you will feel & know that my living in Warsaw and the branches in other cities, especially Antwerp and Vilna, will have been good for you. Although the situation has improved, thank God, it cannot be felt. But if you look at it a little more broadly from a business perspective, you get a slightly different picture, especially when you consider the number of years with the deficit situation. How did we work … My futile travel and walking around in St. Petersburg. It may also be that my weak heart suffered badly. To be without hope is a special piece of work.

Citizenship and the World of Education—Berlin, Bonn, Frankfurt, Marburg, Antwerp

On January 9, 1931, Bendet Kahan submitted his application for naturalization in Charlottenburg. "I am of the Mosaic Faith," he writes, "and have been a Polish citizen for about 5–6 years; I was forced to accept Polish citizenship because my Russian passport had expired when the war broke out, and since then I have had an identity card that could not be renewed because, in the meantime, Brest-Litovsk had been occupied by Poland." In the application Bendet introduces himself as a publisher and the authorized signatory for Nitag, emphasizing his German education. One reason for the move to Berlin was his intention to give his children a "good German upbringing." The family was proficient in German—both orally and in writing. He had no intention of ever returning to Russia or Poland, especially since he owned real estate and conducted business in Berlin.

His nephews, Jacob and Arusia, had lodged a similar naturalization application in Prussia, Jacob just a few months earlier, on November 18, 1930, Arusia already in autumn 1927. At the time of the respective applications, Bendet was fifty-four years old, Jacob thirty-five and Arusia twenty-eight. Unlike their uncle, the brothers Jacob and Arusia were stateless. Jacob, like Bendet, had submitted his application in Berlin-Charlottenburg, while Arusia had lodged his in Bonn. The forms were not identical, but basically followed the same criteria. They asked for the usual data required to register a person. In addition, they were interested in matters relating to nationality, language skills, military service, schooling, places of residence, membership in associations, social interactions, the applicant's social reputation and their attitude to "Germanness." In particular, they wanted to know, if "despite his previous affiliation with a foreign country, he could be expected to be able to faithfully fulfill his obligations, arising from his newly-naturalized status, towards the Reich, the *Länder* and the municipalities."

Since most of the applicants came from the two multiethnic empires in Eastern Europe, ethnic origin was a criterion for naturalization in Prussia in addition to their previous citizenship. "Is he [the applicant] of foreign origin or German descent? (The descent [nationality] must be specified)," the application form inquired. Bendet and Jacob replied succinctly "Russia"; for Arusia, the appropriate section stated, "presumably Russian," which, in the course of the proceedings, was later changed to "not German." For the Prussian authorities, "Jewish" was not a nationality, but a denomination. All three had not served in the military, neither in Russia nor in Germany. Bendet, like his brothers, was exempted from military service in the Russian Empire as the son of a First-Guild merchant. Jacob declared that he had been too young for conscription in Russia while Arusia was able to provide a certificate of his ineligibility. Regarding the relationship to "Germanness," Bendet, who had spent seven years in Belgium, but had by now been living in Berlin for seventeen years, asserted that he knew different cultures and had "always had a great interest in German culture and science." Jacob used the same arguments. His father Baruch, chairman of the Nitag board, who, like Bendet, had gone to school in Germany, had also given him and his two brothers a German school education. He himself had studied in Germany, where he had been living since 1913. Arusia confirmed these statements in his application. He had been living in Germany from October 1921.

The grandparents, Chaim and Malka, had only attended a *cheder* and were raised, educated and married in the Lithuanian-Rabbinic tradition. Chaim corresponded in Hebrew, Yiddish and Russian. He was a self-made man with international contacts who knew Berlin, London, Paris, Antwerp and Palestine. However, he did not speak a foreign language, even his Russian remained faulty. A family legend has it that when he was planning a trip to Paris at the invitation of the Rothschilds, he was asked how he would manage to communicate there. *Nu*, he answered, he had Malka with him. When asked in astonishment whether Malka spoke French, he replied: "Why should I speak French to Malka, after all, we speak Yiddish to each other."

"Is he [the applicant] and his family proficient in spoken and written German (a written sample might be required)?" the authorities asked in the naturalization applications. Bendet and Jacob answered "yes." "The applicant speaks German and Russian, his everyday language use is German," Arusia stated in his Bonn application. Even though Chaim Kahan himself has only had a traditional upbringing, he obviously recognized early on the enormous worth of a modern German education. Perhaps it dawned on him in Königsberg, which was a magnet for Russians from the nearby border region, a marketing place for merchants, a center of enlightenment for students ever since Kant and his Jewish students had taught there. Maybe Chaim Kahan also knew the value of a German education from Baku, where he had been doing business from the time Bendet was born. At that time, the whole world met in Baku for the oil business. In any case, Chaim Kahan favored the German-Jewish model when it came to the education of his children.

After learning Torah and rituals—the boys also Talmud—and after private lessons in Hebrew and high school subjects, four of his sons, Baruch, Pinchas, Bendet and David, as well as his youngest, Rachel, attended schools in Germany for several years: Baruch and Pinchas in the second half of the 1880s, Bendet in the mid-1890s, David and Rachel around the turn of the century. Only Aron is reputed to have refused and to have returned to Kharkov after a short stay in Germany. "He [the grandfather] sent four of his sons to school in Frankfurt am Main and the two youngest to Marburg," recalled Arusia. The older ones were students of the Philanthropin, while Aron and Bendet, the middle ones, attended the Samson-Raphael-Hirsch school, according to how their children, Aron's son Yossi Cohen and Bendet's daughter Dora Loewenthal remembered it. David, the youngest, was sent by Chaim Kahan to Ze'ev Yavetz's house for classes and then to Marburg. He also sent his daughter Rachel there. The German Reich was considered tolerant towards the Jews from a Russian perspective. So, the children were to acquire a modern education there and learn German, "a language that was recognized among Russian Jewish intellectuals like Yiddish and Russian," according to Rachel's daughter Dvora. "As a boy, my father spent six years in high school in Frankfurt am Main, Germany," added Pinchas's daughter Gita.

There were two well-known Jewish secondary schools with different concepts in the 1890s in Frankfurt-am-Main: the Philanthropin and the Samson-Raphael-Hirsch School. The Philantropin was founded 1804 in the tradition of the Jewish reform schools in Berlin, Breslau, Dessau and Seesen. It was based on the model of two Enlightenment schools: Basedow's Philanthropin in Dessau and the Pestalozzi-Musterschule in Frankfurt. Almost fifty years later, in 1853, a Jewish Neo-Orthodox school was opened by Rabbi Samson Raphael Hirsch, called Realschule der Israelitischen Religionsgesellschaft. At that time, both were secondary Prussian schools limited to six grades. Their goal was to prepare students for the business world. Priority subjects were arithmetic and the foreign languages—French and English. Unlike the Neo-Orthodox secondary school, the Philantropin did not award a high school diploma. Committed to the ideals of enlightenment and humanism, both were open to Jewish and Christian teachers and students. But the schools differed in their understanding of themselves and their religion. The Philantropin educated students to be German citizens of Jewish faith. The Shabbat and festival calendar was adhered to, but, consistent with their humanistic ideals, the Bar Mitzvah was transformed into a Jewish counterpart to the Christian-Protestant Confirmation. The Neo-Orthodox, on the other hand, evaded the denominational dictate while outwardly not touching it as far as state and society were concerned. The Samson-Raphael-Hirsch School was based on the principle of *Torah im derekh eretz*. This affected particularly the Sabbath, dietary laws, worship and gender relations. *Derekh eretz* encompasses the entire social and civic life: being Jewish was not a matter of belonging; it totally governed life on weekdays and festivals, within the family, at work and in public. Therefore, the principle applied: the more the Jews were Jewish, the more universal their views and aspirations; and vice versa: the more humane the culture of the world, the easier it could be reconciled with being Jewish. Samson Raphael Hirsch saw this development accomplished in the humanism and idealism of the German classics. Accordingly, the secular lessons consisted of the Prussian secondary school program. In German classes one read the literature of the Enlightenment and Weimar classics. In history lessons Prussian, German, Greek and Roman history was taught, while geography classes offered homeland instruction about Frankfurt as well as knowledge of the world. On the other hand, the Jewish curriculum of Hebrew, Bible, Talmud and biblical history remained free from reformist liberalization efforts. In addition to the obligatory program, they offered optional Hebrew and Talmud courses.

In the student lists attached to the annual reports of the Samson-Raphael-Hirsch School, names of foreign pupils are noticeable. They come almost entirely from Eastern Europe, often from the Russian Empire. But the Kahans are not among them. For each year, the number of foreign pupils is stated. Usually they amount to no more than a dozen, five percent of two hundred and thirty. The fact that Chaim's sons had attended the Philanthropin and Samson-Raphael-Hirsch School was not submitted as evidence in the naturalization procedures. Since the Second World War, it has not been possible to verify this. The files were almost completely destroyed when the Frankfurt City Archive was demolished in 1944. Even a search for their names in the registry-office files of the Institute for City History is of no avail. In photos of the 1880s–1890s, the teachers and students of the two differently oriented Frankfurt schools look alike. All of them, large and small, pose according to the fashion at the time: they wear dark suits, with watch-chains dangling from the pockets of their vests, white shirts with starched collars and ties. The older students and teachers are clean-shaven or wear neatly trimmed beards. In terms of habits and lifestyle, the Neo-Orthodox Jews had also adapted to the German bourgeois society. A photograph of Baruch as a pupil, presumably together with fellow students and a teacher in a *sukkah*—taken by the Frankfurt photographer "Chr. Lau," preserved among Baruch and Rosa Kahan's Kharkov heirlooms in the National Historical Archive of the Ukraine in Kiev—is the only visual testimony to the Kahan children's immersion in Frankfurt's German-Jewish educational world.

However, one more document from the Frankfurt school days is held by the Cohen-Mintz family archive in Tel Aviv. According to that certificate, Baruch first attended the foreigners' class of the Wöhler School (now the Wöhler-Realgymnasium) in 1884–1886 and then year seven of the associated commercial school. This certificate fits perfectly into the files of Arusia's naturalization procedure kept in the Berlin State Archive. The applicant had submitted it. Thus, a third Frankfurt school gets into the picture. The Wöhler School in Westend, founded in 1870 as a boys' school of the Polytechnic Society, was named after August Wöhler, the president of the Society, founder of the Frankfurt vocational school system.

Since the Middle Ages, Frankfurt has been both a center of traditional Jewish scholarship and lively economic activity. In the second half of the nineteenth century, the percentage of the Jewish population there was higher than in other German cities. The Jewish community was part of the avant-garde and was characterized by diversity. Although the relationship between the Jews of Frankfurt and those from Eastern Europe was not free from prejudice, a distinction was made between the destitute, uneducated and the learned immigrants. The poor constituted the majority and determined the image. But, even after reform and emancipation, it was common practice to employ scholars from Eastern Europe as rabbis. The Neo-Orthodox, who created their first community in Frankfurt, concurred with the traditionalist Eastern Europeans in their practice of religion and lifestyle. The religious Zionist movement in Germany sprang from their midst. Along with the Belarusian Lida, Frankfurt was the second, the western center of the Mizrachi, with whom Chaim Kahan was actively involved.

"Does the applicant belong to any associations, including those that serve German interests to some degree or to such whose members are predominantly foreigners?" Bendet named the Aid Association of German Jews, Jacob, none. Arusia was not asked about an organizational membership. Did they—unlike Chaim—have nothing to do with the Mizrachi? Mizrachi (the acronym of *merkaz ruchani*—meaning "spiritual center"—and also the Hebrew word for "eastern") was an association of Rabbinical and Neo-Orthodox Jews who had joined the Zionist movement without putting at risk the influence of the traditional rules. Theoretically, this is contradictory to traditional Rabbinical Judaism, which condemned the return to Zion before the arrival of the Messiah. But secularization had weakened the religious ban while Jewish Enlightenment justified this development. The emergence of a modern nationalistic idea and movement among the Jews redirected thoughts, emotions and fantasies to a territory, the "land of the patriarchs." In addition, the concrete political and economic hardship motivated the Eastern European Jewish diaspora to become inventive and look for ways out and seek other domiciles.

Thus, the interaction of these three factors led to the emergence of first groups of friends of Chovevei Zion [the lovers of Zion] in the Russian Empire as early as the 1870s. They revived the old idea, repeatedly discussed by Jews and non-Jews alike, of mobilizing Jews from the Diaspora to reclaim their birthright in the land of their Biblical ancestors. It was hailed in the new Hebrew literature that had emerged not in Palestine, but in Eastern Europe, especially in Lithuania. The Zionist idea began to be politicized by the self-defense groups against pogroms, in southern Russia, in the early 1880s. They began to apply it more pragmatically. The Russian Jews in Odessa were the first to organize large-scale emigration to Palestine, called *aliyah*—"going up" (to Zion).

In the course of time, especially after the emergence of political Zionism in Western Europe, the movement became more differentiated. Two distinct factions were formed: the cultural Zionists and the religious ones. The religious Zionists mainly came from Eastern Europe, formed their own respective factions, because traditional lifestyles and ideas had survived longer there than in the West, where the process of modernity promoted the development of a national, rather than a religious, self-image. The representatives of Rabbinical Jews in both Eastern and Central Europe countered the challenges of modernity, which threatened to dissolve the Jewish community in exile, with the idea of Judaism as a national religion that could only be regenerated and saved in the spiritual center of Zion. This idea remained the common denominator of both religious Zionism and Neo-Orthodoxy.

When Chaim Kahan was in his mid-thirties and the father of five children, there were already Chovevei Zion groups in Brest and in the surrounding cities, including those that Chaim did business in: Warsaw, Vilna, Riga, Kharkov, Kiev and St. Petersburg. It is possible that he was already involved, when the Lovers of Zion met for the first conference in 1884 in Katowice, Upper Silesia, now under Polish, but then under Prussian rule; or, maybe three years later (1887) in the Lithuanian spa town of Druskininkai; or in 1889 in Vilna. One year later, they were recognized by the Tsarist government. As a result of the debates about the role of culture at the Fifth Zionist Congress, but above all at the Russian Zionist Conference in Minsk, they founded Mizrachi in Vilna in 1902 in order to strengthen the interests of the religious within the movement. One of the Mizrachi's first major projects was the development of a modern, but tradition-conscious, Hebrew education system in Palestine that began with the founding of the Tachkemoni School in Jaffa, for which Chaim Kahan had given large donations and acquired land in the spring of 1914. Through Mizrachi, he established connections to Germany, to his trading center on the Main. The Tachkemoni School was established and supported from Frankfurt. The fact that Chaim Kahan sent one of his sons, Bendet, to the Neo-Orthodox school was an expression of his commitment to the Mizrachi, his modernity, liberalism and ability to "figure out." However, his choice to send his older sons to the Philantropin and the German Commerce school for their education was rather in keeping with his pragmatism.

"Is the applicant to be considered a desirable addition to the indigenous population? Have facts become known leading to the conclusion that the applicant has completely melted into Germanness?"—asked the Prussian form "Report of Police Station 128 concerning the Attached Application for Naturalization" by Bendet and Jacob Kahan. The answer to the first question was positive, to the second negative. What does "Germanness" mean? Why should applicants in the Weimar Republic have been absorbed into "Germanness" in order to obtain the right to naturalization? According to the Prussian authorities, Jews were excluded from this as long as they considered themselves Jewish. Although they could be German citizens of the Mosaic faith, they could not simply be Germans and Jews.

How might a sixteen-year-old from Brest-Litovsk with 45,000 inhabitants, 30,000 of whom, almost seventy percent, were Jews, have felt about life in the German commercial metropolis, which at that time had more than three times as many inhabitants, where the Jews formed a long-established, respectable, economically active and culturally influential but small diaspora community with seven to eleven percent of the population? The Kahan children did not come as tourists for a few days or weeks, but for years. At that time, they were much further away from their homeland than it may seem today, in an age of fast air connections and information technology. How did pupils from Eastern Europe live in Frankfurt am Main? Where did they stay? Gita says, "My father, Pinchas Kahan, boarded at a rabbi's house." It might possibly have been a rabbi of Eastern European origin.

The Kahan children did not want to stay in Germany and build a career there. They intended to live abroad for a certain period of time, learn German, learn other foreign languages and gain practical knowledge and experience for their future as businessmen. The family hoped that this would provide them with cultural assets. German was lingua franca, the global language. Europe stood for the world. A European education was needed for the global orientation required in the oil business. Chaim Kahan's strategy corresponded to the general trend in Germany. In the course of the nineteenth century it had become increasingly common for sons of businessmen and entrepreneurs to attend secondary school and spend time abroad in order to familiarize themselves with new technologies and modern management, learn the ways of the world and establish business contacts. A Philanthropin graduate recalled that, as students, they had dreamed of their future as businessmen; later on, they really occupied the most important positions from among all foreigners as representatives in all parts of the world or as exporters and stockbrokers on foreign markets.

Chaim Kahan's children had come to Frankfurt and Marburg at different times and were therefore shaped by opposing paradigms. In the 1880s, when Baruch and Pinchas lived and studied in Frankfurt, the Jewish elite there was still oriented predominantly towards liberal society with its press, associations and parties and had even played a decisive role in their founding. The Russian Empire, meanwhile, was hit by the first major waves of pogroms and, following the murder of Alexander II (1881), implemented again a repressive national policy against the Jews. This caused the first Jewish self-defense groups to be formed in response to both.

At the beginning of the 1890s, when Bendet was in Frankfurt, the liberal German-Jewish bourgeoisie found itself in a crisis when faced with increased antisemitism; as a result of widespread fragmentation, its self-confidence changed. Developments in the Russian Empire, especially the expulsion of Jews from Moscow (1891), may have exacerbated this new trend. This turning point was marked in the German Reich by the formation of two interest groups in

Frankfurt: in 1893 the Central Association of German Citizens of the Jewish Faith was founded, and in 1897, the Zionist Federation of Germany, with which the more radical Jewish bourgeois youth was affiliated.

When the two youngest Kahan children, David and Rachel, came to Marburg at the turn of the century, the Zionist movement was already based on a well-organized infrastructure throughout Europe. But why did Chaim Kahan send his two youngest children to Marburg of all places? Compared to Frankfurt, the Jewish community in Marburg was downright provincial. Despite brief fragmentations in the wake of the 1848 revolution, the basically conservative attitude of the Upper-Hessian Jews prevailed and remained dominant. The image of the city was displayed through its university, that of the Jewish community through the commitment of individuals. Both together attracted Jewish students, also from Eastern Europe. Rabbi and politician Isaac Rülf (1831–1902), who later became known for his commitment to the suffering of Russian Jews in Lithuania, came from Hesse and began his career in Marburg, where he founded a Jewish elementary school in the mid-1850s. He became an ally of the Chovevei Zion. More famous than Rülf was the philosopher and neo-Kantian Hermann Cohen (1842–1918), who taught at the University of Marburg for over four decades, from 1873 to 1912. His demonstrative commitment to Germany in the face of the First World War is better remembered than the fact that he was an active member of the Jewish community in Marburg and strongly supported it during his teaching career. He ostentatiously opposed conversion and defended the community, including individual members, possibly even in court, against the antisemitic movement in that region. He promoted education among young Jews and fostered Christian-Jewish dialogue. Hermann Cohen attracted Jewish students to Marburg, including those from Eastern Europe. The most famous of them was Boris Pasternak, who wrote to his parents in May 1912:

> If only this were a city! But it is a medieval fairy tale. Oh, this town! Here one goes to the lectures without wearing a cap. Not because you don't have far to go, but because it's as if you were walking through your own endless garden, which is directly adjacent to your room. You simply walk along the street here—there are no cabs or carriages; the tram only rings to attract passengers, this eternally empty beggar-woman.

When the Kahan siblings were in Marburg ten years earlier, the tram didn't even exist (it was reinstated in the 1950s).

Chaim Kahan's choice of school and location was determined by personal connections. Two such contacts can be identified. One was David's first teacher, the writer, historian and pedagogue Ze'ev Yavetz, who was born in 1847 in Kolno/Augustów District on the Polish-Lithuanian border and died in 1924 in London. Yavetz was a multilingual, much-travelled lateral thinker. He embodied a strange mixture of the romanticism of the Chovevei Zion, Eastern European and Frankfurt Neo-Orthodox Judaism. When Yavetz taught David Kahan in the late 1890s, probably in Vilna, he already had ten years of Palestine experience behind him. It was during this time that he wrote the Mizrachi party program. Yavetz educated David in the spirit of the religious Zionists. He also had good connections to Frankfurt am Main and Berlin.

The second contact was the journalist, politician and philosopher Moshe Glücksohn, whom the Kahans also knew from their Polish-Lithuanian homeland. He was born in 1878 in Golynka, Suwałki County (now Halynka in Belarus) and died in 1939 in Tel Aviv. Like Jonas Rosenberg before him, Glücksohn had studied at the yeshiva in Łomża before moving to the University of Marburg. According to family recollections, David and Rachel Kahan had close relations to Glücksohn, who was a few years older. He was apparently something of a role model and protector for the two teenagers. Glücksohn studied philosophy in Marburg with Hermann Cohen and in Bern with Ludwig Stein. He received his doctorate in Bern in 1907. He is reputed to have headed a Jewish student fraternity, possibly the Zionah, at the neighboring university of Giessen. Zionah was a fraternity that did not respond to any provocation into dueling, because that was considered by them "contrary to Jewish nature." The similarity to Kadimah in Vienna (since 1882) and the Russian-Jewish Scientific Association in Berlin (since 1889) is striking. In all three cases, Jewish students from Eastern Europe created and led cultural-Zionist associations at German-speaking universities that later served as models for German-Jewish student fraternities.

David was not enrolled at the University of Marburg. Maybe he was a guest student or a pupil at a Marburg secondary school. A photo in Dvora's souvenir album, showing him at the side of his sister Rachel, with his older brother Aron and a strange young man behind him, is the only indication that, at one point, all three siblings were in Marburg at the same time. She is wearing a wide-brimmed hat with a voluminous bow, a wide white lace collar over a dark jacket with a matching black skirt; the two young men, also dressed to perfection, are wearing bowler-hats and everything that goes with that: stand-up collars, ties, buttoned waistcoats and suits. What is that silly little purse Aron is holding in front of his chest? Was it his way of poking fun at the photographer for having to pose or was he obeying a fashion trend?

> There are very few straight roads here; there are very few roads at all on the ground here; but this is what you get: you stand still in semi-darkness; old, old houses, piled up and nestled inside each other like pinecones, consisting of levels, as it were: one house ends, and above it begins another; then the fading of lilac wings in the distance, and this same dark pine cone of houses stacked one on top of the other continues, already covering the small old sky. Then, as you find your way around this neat semi-darkness, you notice a crooked, grey little road that runs down from above and flows out in strange, strange bends. There is no remnant of the old Marburg here. I'm studying in the old Marburg. ...

Pasternak's description resembles simultaneously Piranesi's pictures of ruins and Gaudi's architectural visions. The thought of Russian-Jewish students in Marburg, the German historic university town, seems stranger after the turn of the century than what the student Boris Pasternak, perhaps even the Kahan children before him, found exotic. The answer to a haphazardly e-mailed inquiry to a Marburg grammar school, which presents its history on the Internet, provided me with certainty that Rachel Kahan was in Marburg at the same time as Moshe Glücksohn. The schoolgirls' albums of the years 1899–1913 in the archive of the Elisabethschule lists her as the forty-seventh entry for the school year 1902/1903, and the list of pupils shows her as Rachel Kahan, living with a certain Dr. Moses Schlesinger at 8 Wilhelmstrasse.

The Elisabethschule, formerly the High School for Girls, was founded in 1879 as a Prussian educational institution for girls and is now a co-educational grammar school. The thinking of the Wilhelminian period is reflected in the three educational goals of technical expertise, character development and patriotism, which were still applicable when Rachel was a pupil there. What was her attitude towards the required German patriotism? According to Dvora, for her mother Germany was the epitome of liberalism and the rule of law at that time. The Elisabethschule's educational program was shaped by the Prussian reformers, who demanded individual emancipation and at the same time responsibility for the community. It was also influenced by the women's movement, which fought for meaningful graduation certificates and the opening of universities for women, which was only granted in Prussia five years after Rachel had left school (1908). Until then, the High School for Girls was not equal to the Grammar School. The old school building, with its historic Gothic stepped gables, on Universitätsstrasse in the center of old Marburg, no longer exists.

There were two minorities of about the same size at the school during its first four decades: one Catholic, the other Jewish, alongside the predominantly Christian-Protestant pupils. Altogether, one hundred and forty-one Jewish schoolgirls attended the school until the end of the Reich, on average three to four per year, mostly from Marburg and its rural environs. Only four of them came from abroad: one was born in France, another in the USA, two others came from the Russian Empire—Sarah Nagel from Kremenchuk and Rachel Kahan from Brest-Litovsk. In fact, Rachel was the only foreigner in her age group. The Elisabethschule students were also taught by some Jewish teachers. Most of the Jewish women had already left the school before the beginning of the Nazi regime; the last ones had to leave in November 1938. For the sixty-six former students who did not survive the Holocaust, a memorial was erected at the school's main entrance in 1993.

Seventeen-year-old Rachel was immediately admitted to the highest, tenth grade, called Selecta, in preparation for the final examination, where she was taught German, English, French, mathematics and science. She was officially registered at Dr. Schlesinger's, who ran the Israelite Pupils and Apprentices Hostel in Marburg at 15 Schwanallee, located in the center of the school district. The hostel had been opened one year before Rachel arrived. It was established as an initiative of Cohen and the province rabbi (Provinzialrabbiner) to advance Jewish youth from rural Hesse, in order to counter the antisemitic movement. Schlesinger was a graduate of the Berlin Orthodox Rabbinical Seminary. Presumably, Rachel lived with him as a subtenant, like many other foreign students, because girls' high schools with dorms were rare. The nearest ones were in Frankfurt or Kassel.

Would it not have been sufficient to state during the naturalization procedures that the applicants "will faithfully fulfil their obligations to the Reich, the *Länder* and the municipalities"? Did the arguments about the affinity to "Germanness," the understanding of the "German character" in Bendet's, Jacob's and Arusia's applications actually correspond to the applicants' self-image or were they a strategy? The Frankfurt and Marburg experiences had left a profound mark on the Kahan children. For Bendet, the Neo-Orthodox community had exemplified the compatibility of the education and virtue code based on Torah, Talmud and medieval philosophy of religion with post-Christian humanism and German idealism. Neo-Orthodoxy was originally a German phenomenon. In Frankfurt, Bendet had been able to observe the lifestyle of modern Central

European city dwellers, who were able to separate individualism, public and private life, work and family; they cultivated socializing, organized leisure time and brought aesthetics into their lives. He had experienced how gender relations were liberalized whereby women were granted more freedom and rights in the domestic environment. In the Neo-Orthodox circles, he was introduced to new codes. There, the conversation was embellished by allusions to German classical music and quotations from fine literature with traditional Hebrew or Yiddish quotes from Talmud and Torah thrown in. In Frankfurt, Bendet Kahan discovered Neo-Orthodox piety and liberal political understanding, as well as their fragility.

According to Dvora, Bendet was the only pious one from among Chaim's sons. His traditional self-image as a law-abiding Jew was transformed into religious feeling and cultural affiliation under the influence of his schooldays in Frankfurt. His older brother Baruch read Heinrich Heine and Ludwig Börne. David was later connected again with Moshe Glücksohn at the *Haaretz* newspaper. The Tel Aviv daily was financially supported by the Kahans, largely through David's efforts, and Glücksohn was its editor-in-chief from 1922.

Chaim's predilection continued into the next generation. The fact that Baruch and Bendet had sent their children to a German school in Antwerp is cited in their application-forms as an argument for their affinity with the German culture. Dvora recalls that her mother made friends quickly in Marburg, and she herself learned her wonderful German from her, in which she is proficient to this day.

After the turmoil of the first Russian Revolution, part of the family had moved to Antwerp. That city was not only a refuge, but also a business location. At the turn of the century, Antwerp was Belgium's second largest city after Brussels, about the size of Frankfurt am Main, and connected to the world's oceans by the Scheldt. By the end of the eighteenth century, it had been developed into a seaworthy harbor and had since become a first-class international seaport. In Antwerp, the Scheldt is a broad river that already shows some of the spirit of the Atlantic. The city had tamed it with walls, so that the water masses were usefully distributed into numerous harbor basins. Antwerp is one of the largest ports on the eastern Atlantic coast, and since the first pogrom waves in the Russian Empire after 1881, it has also been one of the major centers of the Jewish Orthodox Diaspora, famous for the diamond business from which Antwerp's Jews earn their living. It was they who made Antwerp the world center for diamond production and trade. Bendet Kahan's registration form lists *cliveur de diamant* as his profession.

The business reference point for Chaim Kahan in Antwerp was the Société d'Armement d'Industrie et de Commerce, SAIC for short, the cartel of the two major Baku groups Rothschild and Nobel for the export of lubricating oils to Western Europe, founded in 1900 in the Belgian port city with a share capital of fifteen million French francs. The fact that he had middlemen there and did business with the "syndicate" is evidenced by a postcard from Antwerp, December 1905, sent to him and Jonas Rosenberg in Warsaw, with information on oil prices and planned transactions between Baku, Petersburg, Riga and the port city on the Scheldt.

Throughout 1906, the family arrived from Kursk and Kharkov bit by bit. Bendet and his family stayed a total of seven years, the others only one year. Baruch, Rosa with their three sons, Bendet, Judith with their two daughters, also Rachel, who was still unmarried at the time, were all registered with the police in Antwerp. Chaim and Malka, the Rosenbergs from Warsaw and the Baku Kahans left no traces in the city's Aliens Register.

Antwerp is a well-structured, yet a fractured, multicultural metropolis. In competition for the most striking silhouette, the numerous churches of the Counter-Reformation compete in vain with the Station Cathedral. The Protestant simplicity of many townhouses contrasts with the pompous baroque facades of buildings, signifying status or economic importance. There are Arabic, Indian, Chinese and Eastern European neighborhoods; in the city center there is the Jewish Quarter, architecturally inconspicuous, but clearly recognizable by the appearance of its inhabitants. On Shabbat, the Hasidic Jews in black caftans with magnificent *shtreimels*, dangling *peyos*, women with *shaitels* and hats, many children and prams populate the sidewalks. On weekdays, black-clad Orthodox Jews can be seen buzzing through the streets on their bikes, sometimes with flying coat tails. No more than 15,000 Jews, a little over three percent of a total population of 480,000, live in Antwerp today. Just before the First World War, the number was a little less. So, in terms of numbers, the Jews did not play a major role. Nevertheless, Antwerp was then, and is still today, the largest European center of Orthodox Jewish life in Europe after Paris and London, even though the diamond business has been taken over by the Indians.

In Antwerp, the Kahans did not live in the magnificent district around the Museum of Fine Arts with the main synagogue on Bouwmeesterstraat, not even in the center of the Jewish Quarter, but on its north-eastern edge, in two-to-three-story narrow townhouses. At first, Bendet and Judith lived in Provincestraat (number 77), just behind the zoo where the tram runs. A year later they moved to the quieter Van Diepenbeekstraat (number 7), after that, to the more sophisticated Milisstraat (number 39). Baruch and Rosa, on the other hand, lived for a year on the humble Kleine Hondstraat (number 9), a few steps from Dageraadsplaats. A list kept in the Kiev archive of items they brought with them from Kharkov—linen shirts with broderie and braids, gorget jackets, an Ignatian table cloth, a Karakul pelerine garnished with blue fox, a Karakul hat and muff, a felt hat with an ostrich feather and a net veil, a collar and muff made from marten fur—and things they surrounded themselves with in Antwerp speak of a lifestyle that was already quite elaborate at that time, reflecting their need not only to wear abroad clothes, furs and hats from Russia, but also to equip themselves with linen and silverware to which they were accustomed at home.

Baruch and Rosalia Kahan's sons attended the Allgemeine Deutsche Schule at central Quellinstraat (numbers 31–35), because it had a good reputation, although there was also a German-Jewish school, given the many Jewish children in Antwerp before the First World War. The Allgemeine Deutsche Schule was founded by the German-Dutch Protestant community in the mid-nineteenth century and had a respectable history, representing the German colony led by Rhineland Westphalian merchants and university lecturers, comprising the core of the city's society and business world. The school tolerated religious and cultural differences. On average, half the student body was Protestant, a quarter Catholic and a fifth Jewish. The lessons were bilingual, German and French. Dutch and English were offered as foreign languages. The school was funded by the German government. In 1907, it awarded the *Abitur* (secondary-education qualification) for the first time; also, for the first time at a German school abroad, it was awarded to two girls. It had gained equal status with the schools in the Reich in 1913. Shortly before the beginning of the war, this high school promoted itself with photographic views, boasting thirty classes with eight hundred students and a forty-member teaching staff, half of whom were female. The photos show a stately school building, blended into the streetscape, its bright ballroom with a stage, a gallery, a wide window front, boys training in the gym, girls working in the chemistry lab and a senior classroom with a bust of Goethe. In 1906/1907 Jacob attended year six of the upper secondary school, Nachum and Arusia were in the last preschool grade. The Foreign Office recognised Jacob Kahan's attendance of the German school in Antwerp in his application for naturalization. Bendet's daughters, Dora and Lea, went to a Belgian state school. There, Lea is supposed to have been permitted to write with both her right and left hand, her son Menachem Perl recounted. A draft of a circular letter from their mother Judith to the parents, in French, has been preserved, hinting at her commitment to the school.

Bendet, Jacob and Arusia Kahan presented themselves in their applications as successful entrepreneurs in Germany. They concealed Jacob's imprisonment, his surveillance during the war, Arusia's education in Palestine, Dora's and Lea's schooling at a Belgian state educational institution and Bendet's commuting to Wilno to run the Romm publishing house there. The mobile entrepreneurs had become migrants in a predicament, which is only hinted at in their applications. The Kahans, like millions of others in Europe, had to search for new homes after the collapse of the three multiethnic empires. In view of the enormous refugee streams, the policy of ethnic homogenization was reinforced in the old Western nation states and was adopted by the new Eastern and Central European states. The Jewish minorities were among the main victims of this situation. The League of Nations tried to remedy the situation by establishing the High Commission for Refugees, which implemented an accelerated policy for the protection of minority rights and created the Nansen passport for stateless persons in 1922, but the situation remained precarious. As entrepreneurs, Bendet, Jacob and Arusia Kahan had no chance in the new Bolshevik Russia and had enormous difficulties with the authorities in their new German home. After the founding of the Republic of Poland, migrants who were born or had settled in the now Polish territory were required by the Prussian authorities to acquire Polish citizenship. Thus, Bendet was granted Polish citizenship, while Jacob and Arusia, like their parents and brother, remained stateless Russian migrants with Nansen passports. These were mainly issued at the time to Russian migrants which advantaged them over other refugees. However, the Nansen passports also restricted their freedom of movement because every border crossing required special permits, which was a hindrance for entrepreneurs like the Kahans, operating throughout Europe. Bendet, Jacob and Arusia were the only ones of Chaim Kahan's children and grandchildren to apply for German citizenship. Surprisingly, Bendet and Jacob submitted the application at a time when the weakness of the Weimar Republic in the face of the "Emergency Decrees" was already evident, because by now the Nazis were a serious political force. Did they do so because of the economic hardship of Nitag, which had problems as a result of the world economic crisis?

In their naturalization files, the Kahans were described as "a desirable addition" and their economic situation seemed secure. Their reputation was impeccable. Further information showed them as being conscientious taxpayers and having a clean record. Since Arusia had lived in Germany for less than ten years, he needed a fast-tracked naturalization. Representatives from business, politics and community stood up for him—the mayors of Bonn and Wilhelmshaven, the Bonn customs inspector, even a manager of the competing company Olex. In the spring of 1931, all three proceedings stagnated. The Munich city councilor, who shared responsibility for Jacob's naturalization because of his Bavarian academic year, made it a condition for Jacob's naturalization that his "purely German-blood ancestry be proven beyond any doubt." In April 1931, a memo with almost identical wording was added to the file stating that the applications were to be "resubmitted upon receipt of the new guidelines."

Matters concerning the residence periods for migrants applying for naturalization were generally regulated under the Reich and Nationality Act of 1913 and were the responsibility of the *Länder* until 1935. Binding agreements were first concluded during the Weimar Republic. According to the guidelines of June 1, 1921, "aliens of non-German origin" were to be naturalized after a period of ten years. But Bavaria argued for naturalization after twenty years, which was accepted by the other *Länder* in 1925. Two years later Prussia returned to the ten-year period. This was the time the three Kahans submitted their applications. At the beginning of February 1931, there was again a short-lived agreement on the twenty-year period, in accordance with the Bavarian ideas. But, all provisions aside, applications from Eastern Europeans and Jews were treated particularly restrictively, like in old Kaiser times, especially if they were both. *Ostjude* was the epitome of nationalist xenophobia. Antisemitic tendencies played a role in the naturalization procedures of all the *Länder*. The insistence of the authorities on the residence periods was usually a feigned argument. The regulations served as a welcome political instrument to exclude undesirable groups. Prussia and Baden at least raised objections to a general rejection of the naturalization of Jews, which was the subject of controversy in the Reich Assembly.

Bendet Kahan's application ended with the following file-note: since the applicant is not of German origin, has only been living in Germany for eighteen years and cannot provide evidence of having attended school in Frankfurt am Main, reducing the "regular probationary period" under the Law of February 3, 1931, he is not to be recommended. The application was rejected at the end of April 1932. Jacob's application was to be pursued despite the Munich objection, but he, too, received a negative decision in April 1932. In Arusia's case, the proceedings had been stagnant since the end of 1929. The Prussian Ministry of the Interior had stalled and initiated various new inquiries; the Chamber of Industry and Commerce in Bonn had maligned him by arguing that he was rarely here, was too often abroad and, as an individual, not important for the economy. The rejection arrived only in May 1933, now crudely formulated—"because he is a Jew." Thereupon Arusia withdrew his application. The Kahans did not fit the homogeneity requirements of that national state and certainly not the racist ideology of the Third Reich. German-educated Eastern European Jews were worthless. In Germany, cultural diversity had no value.

CHAPTER 6

To Baku

Unlike his brothers, Aron had gone to school in Germany for a short time only. He was the only one of Chaim's sons to study mainly with private tutors at home. He grew up in Brest and later in Kharkov. As a child Aron is said to have upset grandfather Basch to such a degree that he was slapped by him. Thereupon he ran away from home. They searched for him for a long time and found him only at night. The incident was regarded by the family as an early sign of Aron's pride and stubbornness. At the age of nineteen he was being trained in his father's business. At first he was copying business letters. Later he wrote them himself, explaining to the staff how to make good copies. The correspondence was copied with special ink; the copies were duplicated overnight in metal presses on tissue paper; then the wafer-thin sheets were bundled into booklets:

> The office was headed by our accountant, Mr. Lifschitz, whom I had known since I was a small child and who therefore used to call me by my first name. Slowly, as I began to sign business letters, I noticed that sometimes he didn't call me by my first name, and in the end he would address me only formally. This meant that somehow he already recognized me as his "boss." My first business trip ordered by my father was no more and no less than a trip to Siberia.

Aron showed confidence. He describes emphatically how he rose from copier to scribe and from scribe to the signatory of business correspondence. Did he want to prove to his educated brothers what could be achieved, even without German schooling? His first serious task in the office was to work out the railway tariffs for the calculation of transport costs from Tsaritsyn, Saratov and other Volga ports:

I mastered this "science" within a very short time and was known in the office as a specialist for railway transport tariffs. This is how I made a name for myself, causing my father to want to put me to the test. He asked acquaintances to drink and clink glasses with me at a Purim party and when I was already a little tipsy, they began to test me, asking questions about the tariffs, but I passed with flying colors.

Over time, Aron developed, through practice, a really sensible approach to entrepreneurial business activity. Copying correspondence was not the worst way to get to know the business, and calculating transport costs sharpened his sense for numbers, calculations, transfers, speculating and "figuring out."

He took his first trip to Baku in 1902, tasked with escorting his sister-in-law, Zina, and his newborn nephew home. Zina had given birth in her hometown Shchedrin, Minsk Province, today's Belarusian Shchadryn. A train ride with a baby from Kharkov via Rostov-on-Don and Vladikavkaz to Baku took four days and was an adventurous journey. The twenty-two-year-old Aron enjoyed it. He was glad to see his brother Pinchas again, whom he described as a very kind man; they were very close, although there was a gap of nine years between them. However, he probably also enjoyed the—for those days unusual—long, uninterrupted closeness to Zina, who was his age, charming and spirited. On that occasion, he stayed only briefly. But, merely one year later, he returned to Baku. "I can't remember whether this second journey was initiated by me or whether my brother Pinchas had asked me to come to Baku. The fact is, that this time I didn't come as a guest, but stayed as a resident of the city. There was a place for me in the office on the very first day and my brother accepted me as an equal representative of the company from the outset." Aron enjoyed this position.

Baku. The City of the Winds, a metropolis among the port cities of the Caspian Sea, situated on the flat steppe shore and entrance to the Absheron Peninsula, became legendary for its oil and gas glut. These eruptive mineral resources have been worshipped for two and a half thousand years in the fire cult of Zoroastrianism. This is borne out by travel reports since ancient times. At the turn of the century, even before Aron's arrival, Baku was considered the Pennsylvania of the East. Thanks to the oil industry, it was one of the most highly developed industrial regions, not only in Transcaucasia but in the entire empire, with its economically strong urban population of about one hundred thousand. Aron quickly got used to life in Baku, which was completely different from life in Kharkov. Instead of visiting pubs with friends from student circles, he now met business partners at the stock exchange or in the club. "At the stock exchange, which I visited daily, I was considered a 'young man,' and even at the club the older members looked down their noses at me because of my age." But Aron had grown up. The business took up all of his time and he obviously enjoyed it.

The story of the first Baku oil boom has been viewed from different angles and is still not fully understood. The portrayals of world history from a Western perspective devote to it short chapters with little insight, but a distinctive design. They reproduce the success story of the Nobel brothers and their competition with the Rothschild Bank in Paris. These chapters end with the takeover of the Rothschild companies by Royal Dutch Shell before the First World War and reference to the nationalization of the oil industry by the Bolsheviks in the spring of 1920.

Soviet historiography dealt intensively with the Baku oil boom. It was considered the prototype for the development of capitalism in Russia, indeed, the incarnation of monopolistic capitalism, which had to be destroyed and overcome, as well as the event that triggered the emergence of a modern industrial proletariat. The only one who already then looked at the oil boom pragmatically and critically from the perspective of the Soviet *fin de siècle* was Aleksandr Fursenko. He realized its interdependencies on global competition and its world-historical significance for the economy and politics.

After the collapse of the Soviet Union, there began a competition of interpretations under nationalistic pretexts. The nationalistic elation of being one of the richest gas- and oil-producing countries motivated post-Soviet Russian research to sketch out, for the first time, comprehensive overall representations of the oil economy in the imperially ruled Russia, with the beginnings going back to the burning wells on the Absheron Peninsula in the Caspian Sea already described by Herodotus, although Imperial Russia did not conquer this region of the Persian Empire until the beginning of the nineteenth century.

The young Azerbaijani historiography disputes the Russian appropriation and, atavistically, somehow claims ownership of an oil industry thousands of years old and now prospering anew.

Armenian historiography refutes this, in line with the spirit of the Armenian-Azerbaijani antagonism. It emphasizes the disproportionately large share of Armenian capital in the first Baku oil boom with the aim of asserting restitution claims for the Armenian state. This narrow perspective shrinks the imperial, socialist and nation-state reductionism to a bird's eye view. Attention is focused on the large companies—Nobel, Rothschild, Shell—or the entrepreneurs as the economic carriers of a nation-state.

Dembo & Kahan was one of the medium-sized Jewish companies struggling for independence in the face of legal restrictions and under pressure from large companies. Their room for maneuver was limited. They had less freedom to use aggressive tactics to conquer markets. They could not afford to arbitrarily break contracts, make abrupt U-turns, use the armistice merely to prepare for new battles, declare opponents as allies and once again as adversaries, as was customary in the industry. Chaim Kahan was already drawing oil from Baku in the 1880s, but it was only after the separation from Dembo (1895) that Baku became his business and residence. Pinchas managed the branch and, together with Zina, created a family there. Aron lived and worked with them. He described these years as the happiest time of his life.

The bright light, the soft air, the splendor, the wealth of the Transcaucasian port city is intoxicating. But where is the old in the new Baku? The city is experiencing a second oil boom. Many palaces of the first oil magnates are shining in new splendor. The most bizarre belonged to Musa Naghiyev. The Azeri oil entrepreneur, who started his career as a porter, *hambal*, invested mainly in real estate; he owned more than two hundred properties, making him the largest house and landowner in the city. The Kahans have never owned a palace in Baku. They rented apartments and offices. Today, modern high-rise buildings are being built everywhere in the center—more, faster and higher than in other metropolises. Luxury limousines, powerful off-road vehicles, shop windows of Western designer companies, entrances to posh restaurants—everything is spick and span. Ilham Aliyev's authoritarian state government takes special care of the beauty, order and cleanliness of the city scape; it maintains the wide, kilometer-long waterside promenade with its kiosks, tea rooms, cafés, merry-go-rounds, Ferris wheels, as well as the marble underpasses of the riverside road, the parks and green spaces in the center, all at the expense of the housing estates on the periphery, which are poor and dirty. The oil pumps in the steppes, in Bibiheybət, Suraxanı, Ramana, Balaxanı, Binəqədi frame the city environs marked by misery. However, as reminders of the first oil boom, they symbolize the guarantee of the country's wealth. Today, the rich gas and oil wells lie further to the east, in the sea.

Oil has been found on the Absheron Peninsula since ancient times and was being used as an illuminant commercially since the Middle Ages. Even though the Tsarist state did not initially recognize the benefits of the Baku oil deposits after the conquest of Transcaucasia, and underestimated them for a long time, it secured for itself ownership of the oil-rich country and the production monopoly, for a good fifty years (1821 to 1872). For the first three decades, oil production was state-run, then leased to merchants. But it was not until the introduction of the auction system in 1873 that competition for the most effective methods of extraction and processing emerged, followed by a competitive marketing system. This made the oil industry interesting for private entrepreneurs. But even after the state monopoly was lifted, the government retained control of the oil. It alone had the right to grant concessions and levy taxes. It obtained lucrative revenues from the oil industry through taxation and various other methods of skimming off profits.

Following the end of the Russian-Turkish War (1879), the entire Caucasus region was pacified, so that industry and trade could now flourish without danger. In addition to the shipping route across the Volga and the Caspian Sea, the railway lines Orel–Tsaritsyn (1871), Rostov–Vladikavkaz (1875) and the Transcaucaian line Baku–Batumi (1883) opened up new transport routes both within the empire and abroad. The economic policy of the finance ministers Sergei J. Witte (1893–1903) and Vladimir N. Kokovtsov (1906–1914) also made a decisive contribution to industrialization. Like the governor general of the Caucasus, Prince Grigory S. Golitsyn (1896–1904), they promoted the oil economy in the region and opened the market for foreign capital. This policy, which is still controversial today, led to large investments in the Russian Empire by foreign companies, especially in the oil industry. When Aron's father reestablished himself in Baku, the way was already paved for a large-scale global modern oil industry.

The Khaqani, the ancient Molokanskaya [Molokan, after an Eastern Christian sect] Street parallel to the seashore used to lead to a caravanserai. Passing the Molokansky Garden on the left, I turn into Torgovaya [Commercial] Street, now named after Nizami, that has been converted into an elegant pedestrian zone, and pass the Ali and Nino café, a reminder of the romantic novel by the same name, one of the most beautiful in the world. The neighborhood between the Molokanskaya and Torgovaya Streets was once the Armenian Quarter which becomes more distinctive as one approaches the center. Many Jews also lived there. The main synagogue, today a music theater, which Aron visited almost daily, was located on the corner of Torgovaya and Kaspiiskaya [Caspian] Streets, now Prospekt Rashida Beibutova [Rashid Behbudov Avenue], diagonally opposite the Akhundov National Library, not far from the stock exchange on the corner of Torgovaya Street and the Shestaya Parallelnaya [Sixth Parallel] Street, now named after Magomed Nakhchivani. The Armenian Church, now defunct (adjacent buildings are housing the President's Library), with windows and doors boarded up and locked, was also located on Torgovaya Street in the heart of Baku. The banking and office district stretched from the Molokanskaya Street to the old eastern city wall. The largest, probably most imposing building in its center was the city palace of the richest and most powerful oil magnate— Zeynalabdin Taghiyev. Today it houses the National Museum of History.

The entrepreneurs first had to learn how to deal with the Baku oil, as it reached the surface with eruptive force. At first, there was a lack of means to control the oil gushes. Moreover, it had special properties. Modern production began with the emergence of new oil products when oil was used for innovative purposes and recognized as a strategic raw material. Aron Kahan later wrote an essay in Berlin on the paradigm shift in the oil industry. For centuries, mineral oil had been in demand, primarily as an illuminant, processed into kerosene. For this reason, Baku oil seemed less valuable, because it was heavier than American oil and yielded only forty-percent kerosene instead of eighty-percent. But then a new product appeared—oil residues, called Turkotatarian mazut. Sixty percent of the crude oil extracted in Baku was processed into mazut, compared to only twenty percent of American oil. Mazut is a heavy fuel oil (HFO) of inferior quality that is still produced mainly in Eastern Europe. Heavy fuel oil, used as fuel for large machines, became a sought-after product not only in the coal-poor regions of the Russian Empire, but also in Europe and on the entire world market, primarily because it was needed for the conversion of war fleets from coal to oil—an important factor in the First World War. It is also used for industrial furnaces and heavy diesel engines. Kerosene and mazut remained the main products of the Baku oil industry, followed by lubricating oils, gasoline and other oil products, until the collapse of the Tsarist empire past the turn of the century.

The history of the first Baku oil boom can be divided into three phases and briefly outlined: the long boom after the abolition of the state oil monopoly (1872) until the turn of the century under the protection of Witte's economic policy; a seven-year decline despite the creation of a monopoly due to the economic crisis (1900–1903), the strike movement (1903/1904), the Russian-Japanese War (1904/1905) and the 1905 revolution, which affected Baku's economy until 1907; the gradual recovery until the collapse of the Russian Empire and the subsequent establishment of Bolshevik rule. Between 1895 and 1901, Russian oil production in Baku had overtaken its American competitor Standard Oil, which had been the leader for half a century, with a fifty-three percent share of the world market. By 1914, however, the Russian share was only sixteen percent. Aron had arrived in Baku during the period of decline, experiencing the gradual recovery until the Bolsheviks nationalized the oil industry.

The Kahans lived and worked in the banking and office district of Baku. They were in close proximity to the stock exchange, synagogue, club, business partners and competitors. In the beginning, Chaim Kahan rented an office and apartment on Mariinskaya Street in the Dadashev building, now number 3 on the street named after Rasul Rza, next door to his relative and partner Eliezer Lipman Itskovich. His older brother, Aba Kamenetsky, was related by marriage to Itskovich from Volkovyshki in the Suwałki Province, now Lithuanian Vilkaviškis, and was the first of the three to go to Baku. He worked there in railway construction. His brother and brother-in-law had accepted his invitation. The Rasula Rzy Street begins at the street named after Zərifə Əliyeva, the former Merkuryevskaya, goes along Molokansky Garden and ends at the street named after Mirzagha Aliyev (former Chadrovaya). The Dadashev was one of the first buildings on the right and is still a respectable business location in neo-classical style and good condition.

Ownership and division of labor in the first Baku oil boom were definitely determined by colonial conquest and consequently by the ethno-denominational population component. At the beginning of the nineteenth century, Baku was still a commercial center in an agricultural region. After the conquest, the Tsarist government ceded the land to the local nobility, whereby the Azeri peasants were given a status of dependence similar to that of the Russian serfs. However, in Southern Caucasia, they were freed from serfdom almost a decade later than those in the Russian heartland (1870). Thereafter, in step with the development of the oil boom, began the process of gradually removing peasant land from the possession of the landed gentry. Many a farmer's land, which had been acquired for little money, was unexpectedly rich in oil, and with its discovery the landowners' resistance against the arbitrary privileges of the state grew increasingly stronger. Azeri day laborers and craftsmen, who came from the peasantry, participated in the oil miracle by acquiring land. The strangest, sometimes tragic stories circulated about them: lightning careers, suicides and the difficulty of dealing with the fantastic and immense wealth. Essad Bey described for posterity such fates in his fabulous stories.

No one has presented or described Baku during the oil rush more exotically than Lev A. Nussimbaum, also known as Essad Bey or Kurban Said (1905–1942), who has much in common with the Kahans, with Pinchas and Aron, although they were a generation older, and even more with their children.

He, too, had Jewish parents; his father was also an oil businessman in Baku; and like the Kahan children, being familiar with the German language at an early age, he ended up immigrating to Berlin. At the end of the 1920s he lived in the immediate vicinity of the Kahans in Fasanenstrasse, where he wrote his first work, *Oil and Blood in the Orient*, which captures the first Baku oil boom for eternity. His most beautiful and successful work is the novel *Ali and Nino*. It deals with the love between Ali Shirvanshir, an Azeri Muslim man, and Nino Kipiani, a Georgian Christian woman. Its wit is nourished by the clash of tradition and modernity and the friction of cultures in the Caucasus. No one had written as many books about the region as Lev A. Nussimbaum, giving rise to the suspicion that he was running a writing workshop with destitute migrants working for him there.

The Azerbaijani oil companies were primarily concerned with oil production and less with its processing and marketing. They did not reinvest their wealth in the oil industry, but rather in the regional infrastructure. The richest Azeri oil entrepreneurs, Gadzhi Zeynalabdin Taghiyev and Musa Naghiyev, had buildings, schools and theaters constructed, while leaving the struggle for the world oil market to others. Traditionally, however, Armenian merchants determined the economic life in the region. They were the first oil-well leaseholders and were among the most solvent buyers when the oil fields around Baku were initially auctioned. Many of them adapted their lifestyle and bearing to that of the colonial masters and added Russian endings to their family names. Even after the turn of the century, they were mainly active in the oil industry, ran a third of the oil companies, generated about thirty percent of the oil production and were among the owners of the more valuable real estate in the city, unlike the majority Azeris, who owned the smaller, though largest number of buildings. The most famous Armenian oil industrialists were Aleksandr I. Mantashev, Pavel O. Gukasov and Stepan G. Lianozov. Aron described his socio-cultural distance to the Armenian and Azerbaijani oil entrepreneurs, called Tatar at that time, with the statement: "The Armenians and the Tatars call everybody by their first name."

Baku was located outside the Pale of Settlement. Nevertheless, according to the 1897 census, some three thousand Jews lived in Baku, a unique Azerbaijani mix of backgrounds and traditions, comprising three percent of the city's population. In absolute terms, their number doubled at the turn of the century as a result of the economic boom in the oil industry. Before the First World War, they numbered just under ten thousand, no more than four and a half percent of the urban population, but were disproportionately represented in the middle class and in economic life. Of the lawyers registered in Baku, more than thirty percent were of Jewish origin; of the doctors, more than forty percent; among the merchants of Baku, Jews were in fourth place after Azeris, Armenians and Russians. At least fifteen percent of oil production was generated by Jewish-controlled companies. If Mantashev, Gukasov and Lianozov had the advantage of being part of the regional merchant community in the Caucasus region, Chaim Kahan came to "New Russia" in the wake of the colonial masters. In the Transcaucasian Province on the Caspian Sea, where the antagonism between Muslim Azeris and Christian Armenians was prevalent, the Jews formed a neutralizing element. As foreigners, they were unbiased in the conflict. They also lived and worked there with many other strangers, especially the employees of the large entrepreneurs and foreign investors Nobel and Rothschild. Nevertheless, they were sometimes harassed by the local authorities and also viewed with contempt or hostility by the foreign businessmen. On one occasion (1883), when Dembo & Kahan reported a burglary, the police threatened to expel employees without official residence permits from the city, instead of searching for the thieves. Since then, Itskovich had organized a community fund for bribes among Jewish entrepreneurs. The German industrialist Georg Spies, who had oil fields in Grozny and lived in Baku for several years (1902–1904), regarded the newly arrived Jewish entrepreneurs as an "evil mob," and Ludwig Nobel feared them, together with the Germans and Russians, as competitors, since they—like himself—traded internationally on the stock exchanges and exerted strong influence in the empire's banks. The Jews could not forgive him for his striving for independence, nor for not allowing them to take over all the oil outlets. In a letter to his brother Robert, Alfred Nobel speaks of Jewish greed and intransigence. Nevertheless, Baku offered Jews a relatively large economic scope.

Dembo & Kahan was the first Jewish company in Baku. They opened a refinery and built an oil pipeline between the suburbs of Baku, from Balaxanı to the Qara Şəhər [Black City], which anyone could use for a fee. For several years, from 1883 onwards, their administrator was the sophisticated polyglot chemist and engineer Arkady G. Beilin, who later held a key position in the Baku oil industry. A graduate of the rabbinical seminary in Zhitomir, he had studied at the St. Petersburg Mining Institute and the Charlottenburg Polytechnic, and simultaneously at the Friedrich-Wilhelms University in Berlin. In 1878, he was awarded his doctorate by that university and was granted the title of technical engineer by the Swiss Federal Institute of Technology in Zurich. He returned to Russia and taught at the Mining Institute in St. Petersburg, while at the same time conducting research at the university under the Russian doyen of chemistry, Dmitry I. Mendeleev (1883–1907). Together with Mendeleev, he had gone to Baku after being denied a chair in Petersburg because of his Jewish origins. He accepted the position at Dembo & Kahan because as a Jew he stood no chance in the Baku laboratory for testing oil wells. Dembo & Kahan provided him with professional work, secured his livelihood and gave him a start. Dembo & Kahan was not only a patron for Beilin in Baku. A large number of employees later set out on their own, becoming entrepreneurs or managers in the oil industry, thus contributing to the development of industry on the Absheron Peninsula. Among them were the brothers Vasily and Grigory S. Dembot, who strove for a more nuanced use of oil, and were the first to successfully market mazut from Bibiheybət; until 1887, the black waste was being dumped at sea or flogged off. Instead of the expensive peat, oil residues were now used as heating fuel, first on the steamers of the Volga and the Caspian fleet, then in the locomotives of the Vladikavkaz Railway and the factories of the Volga region, the mills in Samara and Saratov and the sawmills in Tsaritsyn. Following a few years of self-employment, their former employee, David V. Bychovsky, advanced to the position of CEO at Oleum and Shibaev, market leaders among the medium-sized oil companies. His brother Karl V. Bychovsky offered Aron a well-paid position in his refinery, at the end of his apprenticeship. Aron had interpreted this as recognition of his "trading talents," but declined the offer, even though the economic situation of the Kahans was tight due to the oil crisis. Money could not tempt him because he was mainly interested in running his father's business as effectively as possible, which he was clearly successful at.

In the oil industry, Jewish merchants were mainly involved in trade and processing, as the acquisition of land for extraction was denied to them for a long time and remained difficult until the end of the tsar's rule. If Jews or foreigners wanted to acquire land, they needed special permission. It was only after the lifting of the ban on the Caucasus region (1892) that both groups became increasingly involved in Baku's oil production; apart from the two large corporations, numerous Russian and British companies contributed significantly to the first oil boom. Engineers and chemists came mainly from Germany. Siemens & Halske and AEG were the largest German companies in Baku, but smaller ones such as the Hamburg oil companies Stern & Sonneborn or Julius Schindler also established trade relations. In the streets you could hear Russian, Azerbaijani, Armenian, Georgian, Polish, Farsi, Yiddish, Swedish, English, French, German, Greek and many more languages. Essad Bey writes that the multilingual conversations were mixed and muffled by the desert wind and the sand it carried along, and that one had to be an oil entrepreneur to understand the languages of Baku.

Chaim Kahan had come to Baku shortly after the Nobels. Like them he, too, was one of the pioneers of the Russian oil industry. They were his biggest competition. In the second half of the 1870s, the brothers Ludwig and Robert Nobel, machine manufacturers, had been developing a unique, innovative business model from St. Petersburg under the company name Branobel (the acronym of the Russian phrase for "the Nobel brothers"): they had the necessary start-up funds, the technical, scientific and commercial know-how and also developed a sensitivity to social issues. Like Rockefeller, they were less concerned with oil production than with processing, logistics and market control. The core business administration remained close to the government in the capital, St. Petersburg. However, the center of their commercial enterprises was Baku. From there they expanded into other regions of the Empire. Branobel became the largest Russian oil company. The brothers improved oil processing, thus achieving higher product quality. Ludwig Nobel developed the first seaworthy oil tanker in 1878, thus laying the foundation for the company's own Caspian oil trading fleet. He had the first tank wagons put on tracks in 1881 and in the same year built the first paddlewheel-driven tankers for inland waterways, so that the most modern containers were now available for mass transport. In the last few years of its existence, the Branobel company operated with an impressive fixed capital of thirty million rubles. In the end they owned seven oil-processing plants and mechanical factories in the Qara Şəhər, including two chemical ones. They also maintained a workshop for the production and repair of ship engines and other machinery in Baku. They owned seventy-five oil derricks on the Absheron Peninsula, in Bibiheybət and other areas on the Caspian Sea. A diesel engine factory was run under their name in St. Petersburg. They owned a wide network of storage facilities within the empire, initially in the Volga cities. From the beginning of the 1890s, oil from Baku had been the main cargo of the Volga fleet. Routes opened up to other Russian rivers and canal systems via the Volga, as far as the Baltic ports. From the Volga cities Branobel expanded into other parts of the empire. How could Chaim Kahan compete with such a colossus?

A reception: it is a farewell dinner at a conference, hosted by the Azerbaijan State Oil Company SOCAR and the Baku Nobel Fund in the Villa Petrolea between the White (Ağ Şəhər) and the Black City, two decades after the collapse of the Soviet Union. The story of the first oil boom returns to Baku. Men drive up in shiny limousines, greet the guests, open the exquisite buffet and, surrounded by decorative young women, dominate the action within the historic walls. Villa Petrolea was a showpiece, aesthetically, socially and from a business perspective. It was a complex with a palatial building in its center, housing the headquarters of the Baku Branobel companies. It was surrounded by a park, for which the soil was shipped in from afar, from Lenkoran in South Azerbaijan across the sea. It featured flat, one-to-two-story apartment buildings for about one hundred employees, plus non-profit facilities such as a library, theater, canteen, billiard rooms, a telephone and a railway connection to the White City, the historical center of Baku, about eight kilometers away. It was created in the 1880s between the seashore and the mountains to attract Scandinavian specialists, offering them tolerable living and working conditions, given the toxic fumes of the Black City, and designed so that the winds from the sea would drive away the black oil and fire clouds. Today, the villa belongs to the Baku Nobel Fund, accommodating a club and conference center, as well as housing a small museum. This complex is located in the industrial park and is visually separated from it by high wooden fences, making it difficult to reach by public transport. When Aron went to the Villa Petrolea for negotiations with Hjalmar Krusell, one of Branobel's senior executives and Ludwig Nobel's illegitimate son, he would have taken one of the phaetons in front of the Hotel Europa. Branobel were not only the biggest competitors, they also became partners and in a way a role model for the Kahans.

Unlike in the USA and fortunately for Chaim Kahan, the big oil business in the Russian Empire was not in one single hand. Branobel had competitors, the largest being the Parisian bank Rothschild. The Rothschilds had controlled the Caspian-Black Sea Oil Industry and Trading Company since 1883 and the transport company Mazut Inc. since 1898, with a combined share capital of almost twenty million rubles. While Branobel was a company founded by Swedish Protestant-Christian foreigners and run by Scandinavians, the Corporation and Mazut were Franco-Jewish owned companies, but in which Eastern and Central European Jews had a significant influence and for which special conditions applied. Like the Nobels, the Rothschilds also stood in the government's favor. Like them, they found support, albeit to a lesser extent, in the ministries. Throughout their existence, Branobel and the Rothschilds were linked by two interests in the Russian oil business: to challenge Standard Oil on the global market and to defy the revolutionary movement in the Empire. However, the business philosophy of the Jewish banking house, led by Alphonse de Rothschild, was based on a different, yet equally innovative model during the Baku oil boom. Branobel was an industrial concern, while the Rothschilds were a financial institution. The starting point and core business of the Corporation was the lending and consignment business. The company attracted more than one hundred, mainly Jewish oil entrepreneurs—the Dembots, Dembos, Goldlusts, Itskovichs, Tseitlins, Leites, Bychovskys, Pollaks, Kahans and others—and faced Branobel as a kind of block. The Rothschilds' loans were particularly cheap, with an annual interest rate of six percent. The company thus strengthened the financial power of many small and medium-sized local companies, thereby boosting the Baku oil industry. The Nobels initially marketed the oil mainly in the Russian Empire. The Rothschilds, on the other hand, initially aimed to supply the world market with Baku oil and in this way to counter Standard Oil. They organized and maximized exports. In return, they left the domestic market to Branobel until the founding of Mazut.

In the old Jewish Quarter of Baku, between Nizami and Fizuli Streets, near the Old Town, many houses are dilapidated. Desert winds and vehicle exhaust fumes have blackened the brickwork and worn down the wooden balconies. They hang half-broken from the facades. Stars of David in ornamental glass windows, or elaborate decorative bands on the gables, indicate that Jews once lived here. From time to time, the passerby's gaze finds an unscathed villa that has fallen into oblivion in the cluster of decaying houses. At the top of Nizami Street, this section of which was called Gubernskaya [Governorate's] Street in the days of the Tsars, beyond the Ministry of the Interior on the corner of the former Persidskaya [Persian] Street, now named after Murtuza Muxtarov, stands a protruding, light-colored sandstone building in the classicist style. The graceful loggias on the first and second floors, each supported by a column, stretching beyond the corners, are more decorative than practical and attract attention. The long side of the building is covered with mesh at the bottom and hidden behind a wooden framework at the top, so that the high arched windows appear half-blind. The building, constructed in 1888/1889 by K. Skurevich, is being restored. It was the Corporation's headquarters, in form and function similar to the Jewish Town Hall in Prague. The Rothschild offices were once located here, Arkady G. Beilin worked here, and Arnold Feigl, the most respected man in the Baku oil industry, resided here for more than three decades until the October Revolution. The company actually had three directors apart from Feigl. One of them was Alphonse de Rothschild's son-in-law Mavriky Efrusi, also known as Maurice Ephrussi, the representative of the family and a man who hardly ever made an appearance. The actual management was in the hands of Feigl, who also held a considerable number of positions: hereditary freeman and councilor of commerce, chairman of the Congress of Oil Manufacturers, vice-chairman of the Stock Exchange Committee and voting member of the city Duma in Baku. He also sat on the Supervisory Board of the St. Petersburg International Commercial Bank, as well as on the Board of Directors of two factories in Warsaw and an oil industry and trading company in St. Petersburg. Apart from that, as an entrepreneur he owned a small group of active drilling rigs in the Baku region and was a highly qualified specialist; not to be confused with his brother Leopold Feigl, who was an executive member of the company's board of directors. Arnold Feigl came from the Habsburg Empire and was married to the daughter of Heinrich Goldlust, a Baku oil entrepreneur and consul of the Austro-Hungarian Empire. The Goldlust and Feigl families were already in the 1880s active in the oil trade beyond the borders of the Habsburg, Ottoman and Russian Empires and were well connected not only in business but also in family and political terms. The Efrusis in turn, who also owned a bank in Vienna, combined Austrian and French economic interests in the Russian oil business. Chaim Kahan and his sons Pinchas and Aron certainly did not only deal with Beilin but also with Arnold Feigl in their contacts with the Corporation. With the Goldlusts they were in a business relationship.

The Rothschilds had acquired the Batumi Oil Industry and Trading Company (BNITO) from the Russian entrepreneurs Palashkovsky and Bunge, the initiators of the Transcaucasian Railway, financed thousands of tank cars and invested in the newly opened railway from Baku to Batumi. From there, the oil could be shipped more easily to the West than by land and water. The Corporation owned oil storage depots in Baku and Batumi. A few years after its foundation, it opened the first shipping lines for transporting oil to Western Europe and, since the first oil war against Standard Oil (1886), it also supplied the markets of the Middle and Far East in alliance with British oil companies. In 1884 the Corporation had sold 2.4 million *puds* of oil abroad and five years later (1889) it had sold more than tenfold worth thirty million. With the help of the Corporation, the Rothschild Bank controlled and organized the export of Baku oil and, as an exporter, ranked ahead of Nobel (twenty-six to eighteen percent) in 1894.

As a foreign-owned business, the Corporation benefited from an authorization for foreigners to produce oil on their own land. Like Branobel, it acquired extensive areas on the Absheron Peninsula where it bought and founded companies, soon after that law had come into force. In addition, it modernized and expanded BNITO's original plant and built an industrial complex on the outskirts of the White City for the production of petroleum, gasoline, lubricating oils, oil fats as well as waste products such as gasoline, tar and diesel-oil. It also built a gas and electricity works, a seawater desalination plant, repair workshops for the oil production facilities and an oil gallery in Baku, all in collaboration with the great Azeri oil industrialists Taghiyev, Naghiyev and Muxtarov. Arkady Beilin was the technical director of the Corporation since 1885.

Like Itskovich and former employees of Dembo & Kahan, Chaim Kahan took over the management of a BNITO branch in the White City in the mid-1890s, a job Pinchas did, because his father was only irregularly in Baku. He also acted as commission agent and representative of the Corporation for several years, undertaking (1897) to sell to them his petroleum from Baku, which was intended for the Russian market and was transported by water. He agreed not to export his own or otherwise acquired petroleum from Baku on his own authority and to lease his tank wagons to them, with the exception of those in Knyazevka. In return, he was granted the exclusive right to distribute the company's petroleum within the empire, except in Nizhny Novgorod and the two capitals.

The Kahans resided on Mariinskaya until 1911. Then they moved with their office to the Krasilnikov building at 59 Naberezhnaya [Shore Road], in close proximity to the Shestoi Bolshoi Krepostnoi Pereulok [Sixth Bigger Fortress Lane] below the Old Town, just one alley away from the administration of the Baku merchant fleet. At that time the seashore was lined with jetties and the port basin was rugged. All major shipping companies had their locations and offices there, including Mazut. The transport company was managed by the Nizhny-Novgorod steamship owners Pollak, acquaintances of the Kahans, with whom they remained connected even after the escape from Russia, and brothers-in-law of Arkady Beilin, who was also engaged in oil distribution since he got married to Grigory A. Pollak's daughter. Here too, this kinship underpinned and expanded business interests. Like the Nobels, Pollak and Beilin demonstrated a special talent for effectively combining commercial experience with modern science, technology and logistics. Beilin persuaded Pollak to shift the business he, like Dembo & Kahan, had been running since the late 1870s entirely to oil transport. At the beginning of the 1890s, Pollak opened an office in Baku and took over oil transports by sea to Astrakhan and from there, over the Volga water system, into the interior of the empire. When the mazut started, he leased Persian sailing ships especially for this transport.

Beilin, in turn, organized a syndicate of Baku manufacturers for the export of Russian petroleum to compete on the world market with Standard Oil. Anticipating the economic situation on the domestic market, he persuaded the Rothschild Bank to join the creation of a divergent oil distribution and storage system within the Russian Empire as well as product diversification: the production of petrol and other derivatives. In 1897/1898, the bank acquired a majority stake in the Trading House G. A. Pollak & Sons and renamed it Mazut. From then on, Beilin managed the company. The Pollaks retained control, with a twenty-five percent shareholding. Mazut increased the Corporation's share capital. The increasing diversification of the crude oil production increased the yield, so that sometimes the Rothschilds even exceeded the production of the Nobels in Baku. Thanks to the energetic leadership of Poliak and Beilin, Mazut covered the Russian Empire with depots as far as Finland; two hundred and fifty of them before the war. Many Jewish oil entrepreneurs worked with them. Chaim Kahan and a relative, Isidor Berlin, also became agents, one in Kharkov and Yekaterinoslav, the other in Vilna. Since the founding of Mazut, Rothschild had also competed with Branobel on the Russian market. The company now had its own offices in the Volga cities, the Baltic States and Belarus, and had tanks in the Polish capital. A dozen tankers sailed for Mazut on the Caspian Sea and even more on the Volga. By the end of the century, the Rothschild and Branobel companies together controlled seventy percent of Russia's oil trade. A few years later, the crisis of 1903 motivated them to form a cartel thereby creating a monopoly in the industry within the empire. Thus, Nobmazut was born.

According to Aron, it was a mistake that Chaim Kahan rejected Branobel's 1880s offer to divide the markets among themselves. He should have established himself in areas "without a Jewish base" east of the Volga. Consequently, after the establishment of the Nobmazut cartel, agreements with Branobel only occurred from time to time. Chaim Kahan purchased from Branobel a certain percentage of the petroleum he needed for distribution and undertook transports of their petroleum from Baku. In return, the company let Chaim Kahan sell his own and purchased petroleum to numerous Polish cities. Thus, David and Goliath became partners. According to family legends, Chaim Kahan was lucky that Branobel, too, made mistakes.

Dembo, Kahan and the other Jewish oil industrialists were merely small planets circling around the big companies, says historian Moisei (Mikhail) Bekker in Baku. The Kahans did not even always operate under their own name, changed their partnerships and worked in Baku under Kaplan & Lev or Tseitlin & Itskovich until they entered into a partnership with Eliezer Lipman Itskovich in 1903. But the image of the small planet does not do justice to Chaim Kahan. His was only one of the many medium-sized companies among the almost two hundred oil industrialists in Baku. The letterhead was more modest than that of Kharkov or Brest; dazzling advertising was not Chaim Kahan's cup of tea anyway. But in the wild cosmos of Baku's oil industry, where the war for the black gold was fought by all available means, understatement and clever negotiations contributed to success. Chaim Kahan was a pioneer and patron in Baku. He also operated on an imperial scale as an innovative entrepreneur. Already as a commissioned agent of the Rothschilds he was self-employed and head of the company Ch. N. Kahan, Production and Sale of Oil Products, ran the refinery in Knyazevka with his son Baruch, integrated his sons-in-law Jonas Rosenberg in Warsaw and, from 1909, also David Ettinger in Yekaterinoslav into his business and maintained an office and refinery, run by Pinchas and Aron, in Baku. From the early 1890s, he traded his own and foreign oil in bulk, which he had transported in tank wagons of the Russian-Baltic Wagon Factory, following the example of Nobel. In addition, he also owned the oil tanks at various railway stations. His business advantage over the large foreign investors in the oil business was that he combined modern economic and technical know-how acquired through mobility and experience; he also possessed socio-cultural assets and language skills as well as local knowledge and insight into human nature.

Making deals with the Rothschilds and the Nobels, as well as his Jewish, Russian and Armenian partners in Baku was most successful for Chaim Kahan, but his business activities did not remain limited to that region. They materialized elsewhere, especially in the northwest frontier region, later also abroad, and there were also other deals he made. In order to survive, medium-sized companies were forced to adapt, negotiate interests, find and exploit niches and learn from the big corporations. Chaim Kahan adopted their marketing strategies and transport methods. He organized partnerships, syndicates and distribution networks, within his own ethno-denominational group, as was customary at the time; equipped himself with tank wagons, tankers, jerrycans at the ports of Riga, Odessa and Batumi, which were strategically well situated in terms of marketing strategies and renounced market shares. Chaim was content with those markets the large corporations left him and with the freedom that resulted from competition. Competitors became business partners with whom deals could be made.

Aron arrived just when the economic crisis began. Nobmazut began to monopolize the Russian oil trading market so that even the medium-sized companies had to reposition themselves. He learned from his father to run the business under difficult conditions and to develop strategies to free himself from dependence on the overpowering monopoly.

CHAPTER 7

Zina and the Oilfields. Baku

The Old Town on the hill above the waterfront, dominated by the Maiden Tower, is the landmark of Baku. Its mosques and bathhouses, the shops of the carpet traders, the ruins of the Shirwan Shah Palace on the hilltop are protected by a high wall of sandstone from the Absheron Peninsula. From here Baku may have evolved as early as the seventh century, but no later than the twelfth century.

The Azeri name for the Old Town is İçəri Şəhər, Inner City, in contrast to the Outer City, Bayır Şəhər, which only grew rapidly under Russian rule. For the young storyteller Ali Khan Shirwanshir in Kurban Said's *Ali and Nino*, they were as different from each other as a nut from its shell. The Outer City on the other side of the wall, with wide streets, high buildings and noisy people chasing after money, was the shell. It was built on desert oil, had theaters, schools, hospitals and libraries. There were policemen and beautiful women with bare shoulders. According to Ali, if there was a shooting, it was always over money. Europe began in the Outer City. Nino lived in the Outer City. But inside the Old Town, streets and houses were narrow and crooked like Persian dagger blades. Minarets pierced the milky moon, markedly different from the oil-well derricks of the surroundings. The Maiden Tower stood and still stands adjacent to the eastern wall. Legend has it that Mehmed Yussuf Khan, Lord of Baku, had it built for his daughter, whom he desired to marry. The daughter avoided this by throwing herself from the tower. But enough of the legend and let's leave Kurban Said's Ali. When Pinchas, Zina, Aron and the children lived in Baku, the Old Town was the Azeri Quarter. But they lived and worked, like Nino, in the Outer City.

Nino was the daughter of a Georgian prince, while Zina Kahan, nee Golodetz and nicknamed Zlata—"the golden," after her grandmother—came from a dynasty of Hasidic wood wholesalers, who worked and lived in Shchedrin as if to the manor born. Hasidism is usually associated with piety, and not with economy and prosperity. But the Renewal Movement also attracted wholesale merchants. The Golodetz family made their fortune by selling timber from Belarusian and Ukrainian forests and having it shipped on the Dnieper to the south of the Empire. Ali would have called Zina a forest-person, like Nino. The estate was part of an agricultural colony founded in 1830 by Jewish craftsmen in the name of the Lubavitcher Rebbe Mendel Schneerson. If pious thoughts come to a businessman's mind, cause him to study a little, pray, do good, they were sent to him by a *tzaddik*, taught Abraham Joshua Heschel, the Apter Rebbe. Zina's great-grandfather had removed the former manor house from the communal property thirty-five years later and had resided in it ever since. He had a synagogue built next door and ran his household on a grand scale. Gradually, homes were built nearby for his children and his children's children. Thus, half a kilometer from the *shtetl*, a few hundred people lived together on just three streets, in the manor house and sixteen large wooden houses. They were concentrated, like only a few Jewish families in the Russian Empire were, with the sexes strictly separated in public. Shortly before Zina's birth, her grandfather had also acquired Lyalichi, a castle with estates near Surazh in the Chernigov Province, originally a gift from Catherine the Great to one of her servants. The patrician lifestyle in rural seclusion, in the midst of a large family, had shaped Zina just as much as undisputed conduct according to Hasidic tradition, piety and schooling, because only Jews, followers of Chabad lived in Shchedrin. The Golodetzs demonstrated social responsibility for the community, provided a good infrastructure, hired a doctor, midwife, special governesses and tutors for their children, who introduced them to modern knowledge and even heretical ideas. Thus, Zina had learned Russian at the age of nine, but got to know electric light only after her marriage at twenty. Zina and Pinchas were not like Nino and Ali, in love with each other and not worlds apart, although they had grown up in different milieus. When she was presented to him for the first time in Bobruisk, she seemed too young to him—the age difference was ten years—but the marriage still went ahead. Zina remained the only one from a Hasidic milieu in the anti-Hasidic Kahan family. Zina lived with Pinchas in Baku from the turn of the century. Two years after their marriage, her first child, their son Leon, Leonid, called Lolia, was born in her parents' house in Shchedrin.

The difficulties of the first Baku oil boom were caused as much by the colonialist-autocratic regulations, the impassability of the empire, the backwardness of Russian industry, the peculiarity of the oil deposits and their composition, as by the explosiveness of the ethno-sectarian constellations and the resulting social conflicts. Ethno-sectarian affiliation, as manifested in the censuses, was in the Russian Empire—as in all colonial systems—not only a subtle criterion for socio-cultural demarcation, but an administrative category. It regulated social status. The highest criterion for the hierarchization of subjects was the distinction between "true believers" and "heretics," the latter subjected to another ranking order. At the bottom of the hierarchy were the Jews as "Christ murderers," followed by the Muslims, who, as former subjects of the hostile Persians and Ottomans on the southern border of the Empire were to be acculturated as potential sympathizers. Catholics were equated with the Polish nemesis, while Protestants, following the example of the Baltic Germans, were regarded as civilized, qualified, loyal, cooperative and therefore useful and harmless. In traditional Russian society, the subjects moved within the boundaries of ethno-denominational groups, unless one was forced out or privileged to cross them for the sake of earning a living. Ethnicity and denomination were closely related to territorial concentration, social status and also to certain professions and economic sectors.

The oil metropolis of Baku was an oasis in the agricultural hinterland, an industrial city in the corporative state, in which the old barriers were eroded but had not disappeared; instead, they were given new attributes, becoming emotionally and socio-politically charged. Traditionally, mainly Azeri smallholders and Armenian merchants lived in the city. In an effort to Christianize Transcaucasia, the St. Petersburg government presented its conquest as the liberation of the Georgians and Armenians from Persian Muslim foreign rule. As long as the Armenians did not strive for national autonomy, they took on a supportive function. Therefore, many Armenians from the Ottoman and Persian Empires flocked to Transcaucasia in the hope of gaining more freedom and recognition here. For the Azeris, however, the Tsarist government constituted a foreign regime, and the discrepancy in these interpretative patterns created the basic Azeri-Armenian conflict that has dominated Baku's fortunes ever since.

Due to the oil boom, there was a gold-rush atmosphere in Baku, which attracted job seekers of different origins from all over the empire, neighboring countries and the world. Native and Persian Azeris, Persians, Russians, Armenians, Lesgines, Kazan Tatars, Georgians and a few Jews formed the workforce. A large number of them, especially those from Persia, were legal and illegal migrant workers, who came and went with the change of seasons and work opportunities. The Baku of the first oil boom disintegrated not only into an inner-and-outer, but also into a White and a Black City. The workers lived—unlike Pinchas, Zina and Aron—on the northern edge of Baku or in the oil fields, in the part of the city blackened from the emissions of the factories.

Zina Golodetz was not a Caucasian beauty with fair skin, large sparkling eyes and narrow waist like Nino Kipiani; she was a strong woman of proud demeanor, with long dark brown hair that was thick until old age, stately breasts, charm and temperament. She posed for a Baku photographer in an elegant dark, long and narrow-cut high-necked dress with a flowing train and fur-trimmed cuffs, her hair held together by a wide pearl-embroidered crown-like ribbon. She appeared very European and impressive in her feminine appearance. Zina had not come to Baku for the oil, but for marriage. Little is known about her relationship to the city. "For strangers, our city is only hot, dusty and oil-soaked," Ali told Nino, but the years in the Transcaucasian port metropolis were for Zina among the best of her life. "Business was always very speculative, like the stock market," she said in old age. "If there was a *fontan* [gusher of oil], prices went down, or they went up. In Baku, there were constantly *fontans*. And as a result, the trifles of life did not play such a big role. So, you live a little longer."

In Zina's memories the oil workers feature as well. She believed that the workers in Baku earned more than anywhere else in the Russian Empire. She probably had Armenians, Russians, or Jews in mind, who were usually skilled workers and employees. Muslims were usually given the simple, heavy, badly paid work. Zina remembered the small horse-drawn carriages, *brichkas*, "very good carriages," which belonged to employees and brought them to work, because they did not live near the factories, but in the White City. The air at the refineries was bad, it smelled of gas. However, the Kahans' contact with the working class was kept to a minimum. Aron related that he used to be driven, to inspect the factory in the Black City, every Sunday by an Azeri, whose phaeton was waiting for him in front of the Hotel Europa on Malygina (now Gadzhi Z. Taghiyeva) Street, where the Russian Lukoil now resides in a massive new building. Zina, however, probably stayed away from the refinery and oil fields, as befits the wives of entrepreneurs.

To the "oil-baptized" entrepreneur's son Lev Nussimbaum, who took the pen name Essad Bey, the oil fields around Baku appeared to be the most beautiful industrial area in the world, a fantastic fairy-tale forest in which thousands of slender, narrow, dark wooden derricks, standing close together, towered into the sky; where air and earth, soaked in oil, even had a healing effect on the people. Ali compared it to an evil dark forest where machines tortured the earth and interfered with the eternal forms of the landscape. The Menshevik Eva Broido, however, experienced it as hell in the revolutionary year of 1905, just as the traveling reporter Maxim Gorky had done a decade earlier. Dense, black, caustic clouds of oil dust rose up from countless dark drilling rigs and chimneys, soiling skin and clothing. In between, stood low huts with wire mesh instead of glass panes in the window cavities; at the boreholes and oil pits moved figures of dark, greasy, shiny Persians in long skirts, with high lambskin caps; others with naked upper bodies blackened by the oil were bracing themselves against the elements and equipment under the scorching desert sun: devilish images of boiling pitch pots above the never-ending purgatory. The soot in the stuffy heat made breathing difficult. The oily sandy ground offered no support for one's steps. The fire-breathing earth, the flammable sea became a source of wealth in the industrial age, when the oil rigs and refineries surpassed Ateshgah, the temple of Zoroaster, but they also created social flashpoints. The devastating living and working conditions in the oil fields ignited a firestorm in the Black City, like the oil gushers and the strong desert winds.

Initially, the young Kahan family lived in the old Armenian Quarter, on Mariinskaya in the Dadashev building, and Zina easily got used to the big new city life. "With *Dedushka* [Grandfather], sometimes he had money, sometimes not, though the last years were very profitable. Materially, we lived well, though not luxuriously." They were not attached to Hasidic traditions, but the family ran a kosher house and celebrated the Sabbath and festivals. Zina, Pinchas and Aron only visited the synagogue on the High Holidays, although Dembo & Kahan had, at one point, played a decisive role in the development of a large, lively synagogue community from the small prayer-room congregation of Nicolaitan soldiers, thanks to the arrival of relatives and staff in the early 1880s in Baku. Russian was spoken within the family, but Yiddish was also spoken among the adults. They moved in Russian-Jewish circles of friends and acquaintances.

While the bourgeois upper class in the White City around the Old Town Hill represented their interests in the Association of Oil Industrialists and ruled the economic metropolis by mutual agreement with the authorities, the workers radicalized themselves and came into contact with the revolutionary movement, which had organized itself at the beginning of the new century in parallel with the concentration of the corporations. The gulf between the rich and the poor deepened in Baku. In addition to class and property lines, it also ran along ethno-sectarian boundaries and differences, so that these intermingled with and aggravated the social conflicts, even if alliances between workers of different origins were temporarily formed during strikes and demonstrations. In February 1905, Aron and Pinchas witnessed one of the first massacres of the

Armenians perpertrated by the Azeris in Baku. From their balcony on Mariinskaya, they saw people being shot in the street and police officers standing by, watching. Everyone knew that the government had tolerated the pogrom, if not provoked it itself. Whether Zina stood with the men at that time remains uncertain. She later described herself as "pretty democratic," because, unlike her cousin, she had friends among the simple *shtetl* inhabitants in Shchedrin. But she was not interested in politics like her older sister-in-law Rosalia and was never a revolutionary like Eva Broido, who was the same age and also from Lithuania. Eva came from a poor family, had a job and a political mission; she lived undercover and spread revolutionary propaganda among the oil workers in Baku. Neither was Zina like her younger sister-in-law, Rachel Kahan, who at that time was enthusiastic about the revolutionary movement in Warsaw, for which she was even briefly imprisoned.

The composition of the oil workers was not mentioned by Aron in his memoirs. Essad Bey, however, differentiated between the Russian skilled workers, who had difficulties living abroad, felt downgraded and formed a restless, rebellious potential, and the unskilled Muslim workers, who were used to the climate and felt socially privileged through employment in industry compared to their fellow countrymen. Many Muslim workers could neither read nor write and therefore did not make any demands. In any case, the migrant workers regarded themselves only as fleeting guests who came to earn money and return to their families as soon as possible. Nevertheless, many of them brought revolutionary ideas home from Baku. As a Menshevik, Eva Broido paid particular attention to the social and mental differences between the local and the migrant workers in the oil fields within the undercurrents between the workers' movement, government policy and business interests. For both factions of the Russian social democrats, the Bolsheviks and the Mensheviks, a critical stocktake of the workforce was a prerequisite for successful revolutonary agitation in view of the concentrated, well-organized mass of industrial workers in Baku's oil industry. The companies would have preferred to hire the local Azeris, often small owners of houses and land, using their local patriotism and sense of ownership, to provide private security on the oil fields, rather than the mostly indifferent migrant workers from Persia and Dagestan. These "private Muslim security forces" supported the Cossack police. It was only when the massacres and revolutionary uprisings began that they unexpectedly turned against the guardians of public order.

In her early childhood, Zina had always spent the holidays with her parents in the Russian-Baltic province. In July 1905, Zina and Pinchas and their son Lolia enjoyed a German summer resort. Aron had remained alone in Baku. When the pogrom began and the first shots were fired, he took a packet of cigarettes, wrapped it in a handkerchief, something he had never done before, and went to the parents of his friend Yossi Lev, so as not to be left alone. There they played cards for almost two days and nights without a break while being kept informed by telephone about the pogroms as well as the workers' rebellion in the oil fields and in the Black City. One employee narrowly escaped execution on the street because he succeeded in convincing Azeris that he was not Armenian but Jewish. In the months that followed, yields declined. In October, after the publication of the manifesto on legal reforms in the Tsarist empire, unrests broke out again. This time they were intermingled with anti-Jewish pogroms, which at that time spread like wildfire throughout the empire. Zina, Pinchas and Aron decided to take refuge on deck of one of the tankers of the transport company Mazut in the port of Baku. They told little Lolia that he had to keep quiet so as not to upset the ship's captain. They stayed only one night, because peace returned quickly. After that, there were more frequent robberies and blackmail attempts, also in the Kahans' offices. Chaim Kahan had always cared for his employees in a paternalistic way, in line with the Jewish practice of *tzedakah*. The story goes that when the factory in Knyazevka burned down at one point, and the workers there lost everything, he sent them money, although he was not obliged to do so, arguing that adding a little bit more to his losses wouldn't make much difference. But how much he himself cared for or paid attention to his oil workers in Baku, or whether he left that to his local sons, is unknown. Aron was not particularly interested in the work processes in the oil fields and in the factories, or in the situation of the workers. That was what the administrators were there for. He did not see the unrest of 1905 as a reaction to social problems, but as ethnic conflicts that were cleverly exploited by the government. Aron Kahan was a passionate businessman, not only as an observer of events, but also when he himself was affected by them.

The factory site of Itskovich & Kahan in the Black City occupied three lots, numbers 512, 516 and 517, located between the Devyataya and Desyataya Zavodskaya [Ninth and Tenth Factory] Streets and the Vtoraya and Tretya Chernogorodskaya [Second and Third Black City] Streets, far away from the sea. A railway feeder led from there to the main tracks, to the freight station on Aktsiznaya [Tax] Road. The factory was located conveniently for shipment on tank wagons. Itskovich & Kahan oil fields and refineries were located in Balaxanı. A large part of the workforce lived on the oilfields, close to the factories. The unskilled workers, in particular, did not indicate their place of residence in the personnel lists. The migrant workers lived in damp, dark, dirty barracks, where they slept crammed together on wooden plank beds. Otherwise there was no furniture, hardly any room for aisles; there was only water for drinking. Never had Gorky seen so much dirt around human dwellings, so much broken glass in the windows, or bitter poverty in the rooms that resembled caves. Not a flower in sight, nothing green. The better-off workers lived near the refineries in the Black City, in low houses with courtyards, with communal seats under canopies, toilets and water-pumps in the middle. Each apartment had a door and window to the courtyard with two small rooms behind them—a kitchen with a clay floor and a bedroom. The apartments, about fifty of them in each courtyard, were all alike. Only for the local workers did the staff registers include addresses in the White City.

Aron fondly remembered the Baku years, his happiest time, as he wrote, because of the business successes and the warm relationship with his brother Pinchas and his family, especially the children, who were still small at that time. Zina is hardly mentioned in his memoirs. When Aron would come from the barber, little Lolia was always allowed to smell the aftershave on his arm. When his sister Gita, seven years his junior, was able to walk and talk, their uncle invented the morning ritual of mourning his hair loss together with her, something he never forgot until old age. Gita grew up on Nikolayevskaya, one of the most representative streets of Baku, which surrounds the old town in the north. The family lived on Nikolayevskaya, today Istiglaliyyat [Independence] Street, until September 1920, when they left Baku. That's where Musa Naghiyev's Ismailiyya Palace stands, nowadays the seat of the Academy of Sciences, a showpiece of Venetian Gothic in the middle of Baku, designed by a Polish master builder. Naghiyev, the oil baron, humanist and Bahai devotee, had bequeathed it to the Islamic Benevolent Society in memory of his only son Ismail, who died young. The magnificent town hall is close by. Then comes the City Park, where the French governess would take little Gitushka for a walk, perhaps also where the private tutor would have dismissed her brother, Lolia, from his lessons. On the corner of Niyazi, the former Sadovaya [Park] Street, directly opposite the Kahans' residence, the oil industrialists used to meet in the Summer Club, one of the most magnificent architectural structures of Baku with its domed hall and amphitheater. Pinchas and Aron regularly went there to play whist. The club was the ideal business exchange. Before the Summer Club was built, they had belonged to the English Club in the Gurdov house somewhere in the Bayıl District, between the Torgovaya Street and the Naberezhnaya.

Today, the Baku high society meets for musical events in the Philharmonic Hall (2 Istiglaliyyat Street) in the Mikhailovsky Park. Surrounded by fountains, the Philharmonic Hall is bright and light thanks to its flat construction and generous window areas. For this park, too, the earth had been brought from far away, from Persia, with great effort. Ali saw only sparse, sad trees, asphalt covered paths, three flamingos under dusty palm trees, a big round basin without water or swans, staring eternally empty to the sky. In the City Park where he had been waiting for Nino, he saw the futile attempt at transplanting a European park into the desert. Today, tall trees with sprawling canopies provide shade in the Park. Lovers sit on benches around the cool fountain in the round basin. Parallel to those parklands, on the Niyazi Street, which runs from the Istiglaliyyat Street down to the sea, stands the former Rothschild Palace, now the National Art Museum, where the Parisian bankers used to reside when they visited Baku.

As long as she could remember, Gita lived with her parents and uncle at 1 Nikolayevskaya, where her grandfather had rented the apartment; he used to come to visit sometimes. The house was new then, like the Summer Club and the Ismailiyya Palace. It belonged to the Sadıqov brothers, oil industrialists, and, like all the buildings where the Kahans lived in Baku, it was constructed in the historic, oriental Baku style, with loggias and balconies, four stories high. It was magnificently restored a few years ago. Gita later remembered well the large apartment, the building with the elevator on the elegant street, opposite the club and the City Park. The Kahans' furniture was certainly not covered with red silk like in the Kipiani salon, but there may have been palm trees and flowerpots in the corners. The walls were certainly not roughcast or covered with carpets, but rather wallpapered. The family drank their tea, similar to the Kipianis, but unlike the Shirvanshirs, from large Russian tea glasses or painted porcelain cups. Nevertheless, the Baku taste and lifestyle had left its mark on the Kahans. The story goes that Chaim lived modestly, had no interest in money or splendid buildings, never gave Malka furs or jewels either, because she deserved better— what that was he never did say—but he had a weakness for carpets from Isfahan or Kashan, only that in his case they covered the floor instead of the walls. Chaim trampled the carpets underfoot, as Ali would have said. "The only thing he needed were rugs, because he liked to walk in the house in comfort," his children remembered. Barely recognizable are the carpets' ornamental pictures of gardens and lakes, forests and rivers, hunting scenes and knights' games, with verses woven into the edge of the carpet in elaborate writing, the colors having been extracted according to ancient recipes from herbs collected by women in the thorny undergrowth of the desert. The weavers spent years working on such a work of art.

Zina employed two domestic servants and was active in charitable organizations. Her daughters remembered that she had power and talked a lot. All three, Zina, Pinchas and Aron, loved to dress elegantly, to live well. Tailors and seamstresses came to their house. They loved to travel first class and stayed in the best hotels. Pinchas may have brought this preference with him from Frankfurt, Aron may have imitated his brother, Zina may have inherited it from her grandfather Leib, who, as she said, was an aesthete, always paying attention and dedicating time to the furnishing of his house at Shchedrin as well as to the choice of his clothes and his appearance. He owned a large number of precious *streimels*, had a servant, a horse and liked to ride out in the company of his nephews. But perhaps they simply cultivated Baku glamour and style.

It was only a stone's throw from Nikolaevskaya to the Rothschild offices, along the Persidskaya Street, which bears today the name of Murtuza Muxtarov, past the fairytale Gothic villa of the Azeri oil baron of the same name. The offices on the Naberezhnaya and on the Staropolitseiskaya [Old Police] Street were also within walking distance. Since the Kahans had acquired Petrol and lived on Nikolayevskaya, they had their main office at 24 Staropolitseiskaya Street. Despite its dark past in Tsarist Russia, this street, which is now named after Yusif Məmmədəliyev, is one of the most beautiful old streets in the banking and office district of Baku, with cobblestones, trees and wooden balconies on the buildings, where vines creep around the windows.

The beginning of the First World War disrupted many in their summer resorts—Ali and Nino in Susha, Nagorno-Karabakh, Zina, Pinchas and Aron in German spas. The French governess had left the family. The police searched the apartments for Austrians and Germans. But the Kahans—like the Shirvanshirs and the Kipianis—resumed their daily life. Baku was far from the war fronts, and business was even better than before. In the summer of 1915, Zina gave birth to Chaim Kahan's fourteenth grandchild, Lia, called Lili, in the Caucasus spa town of Kislovodsk. Nine months later Sasha Sokolova came to the house as *nyanya*, the nanny.

It was a heavy blow to the family when the patriarch Chaim Kahan, who had spent two war summers with them in Kislovodsk instead of Kissingen, died of a heart attack in Petrograd in November 1916.

It was not until the revolutionary year of 1917 that riots began again in Baku. In those autumn days, when the Bolsheviks took power in Petrograd, Pinchas unexpectedly fell ill with meningitis, succumbed to the disease and followed his father. Aron describes the shock in his memoirs. For him it was the first encounter with death. He did not move from the side of his brother's sickbed, having been particularly close to him, helping him and watching over him until the very end, probably himself suffering his first retinal infarction in the presence of the dying man. Aron was thirty-seven, Pinchas forty-seven and Zina thirty-six. But how did Zina react? There is no record of her reaction. Nobody seems to have dealt with that. Even how fifteen-year-old Lolia coped with his father's death remains unknown. For the eight-year-old Gita, it was more painful than any other experience after that. Lili had never met Pinchas. From then on, Aron took over the role of father.

In 1915, 46,347 people were employed in the Baku oil industry, more than thirteen thousand of whom came from Persia. Ten thousand were Russians, almost nine thousand Armenians, five thousand Lesgines, almost two thousand Kazan Tatars, five hundred Jews and four hundred Georgians. More than half of them (29,030) were laborers, thirty-six percent were skilled and twenty-five percent unskilled, the rest were craftsmen and administrative staff. The Azeris from Northern Persia, the Persians, the Lesgines from Dagestan and the autochthonous Azeris made up the majority of the unskilled workers in the oil fields. The Russians, Armenians and Georgians were mostly artisans or skilled laborers who worked mainly in the factories. The majority of the Jews belonged to the white-collar workers. About half of the workers in total were Muslims. The workforces of Petrol in Balaxanı and of Itskovich & Kahan in the Black City corresponded to the general composition, even if the Kahans did not employ ten thousand like the Branobel and also not predominantly Russians, but altogether only "a few hundred" (Aron) predominantly Muslim workers. In 1918, there were one hundred and sixty men employed by Itskovich & Kahan and one hundred and four men by Petrol. As a result of the war, the revolution and the frequent regime changes in the hard fought-over city, the numbers fell in the following years. In the beginning of 1920, there were ninety workers and employees, and at the end of the year, only seventy-five. In 1918, Petrol's workforce in the oil fields and in the factory in Balaxanı consisted of seventy-one Muslims (Persians, Azeris, Tatars and Lesgines), twenty Russians, twelve Jews and one Armenian. Of the two inspectors and six administrators, all but one, who was probably of Armenian origin, bore Jewish names. Their names were Sheingait, Slutskin, Levin, Kiterman, Lifshits, Neiman, Melnikov and Shneider. Locksmiths, fitters, machinists, laboratory assistants and stove fitters were mainly Russian, while those doing the rough work, such as distillers, stokers, lubricators, cleaners and security personnel, were almost exclusively Muslims.

An exception were the Zaks, Jewish by name, one of whom was a guard, and *arobshchiki*, drivers of two-wheeled high-axle carts, pulled by donkeys or oxen. During the last two troubled years, before the start of Soviet rule in Baku in the spring of 1920, the guards of the Petrol company comprised up to eleven people, Azeris, Persians and two Jews.

Later, Aron as well as Gita remembered Passover 1918, when the Bolsheviks fought over Baku and the Armenians took advantage of the situation to take revenge for the 1905 massacre and, supported by the Bolsheviks, murdered thousands of Azeris. In the streets people were shooting with pistols, rifles and cannons. The Nikolayevskaya Street was located in the immediate vicinity of the Azeri Quarter in the Old Town, the center of the pogrom. Windows burst under the hail of bullets. Fortunately, nobody from the family was injured. During a ceasefire, Aron, Zina and the children set out to seek shelter in the Petrol office in the Armenian Quarter. Aron went ahead with Lili in his arms and a bucket of eggs in his right hand. Zina, Sasha and Gita followed, each carrying something in their hands—matzah, salmon and other food. The way from the Nikolayevskaya Street along the old city wall to the Staropolitseiskaya Street, on foot no more than a quarter of an hour, was life-threatening in this situation and may have seemed to them longer than ever before. Lolia had fortunately already taken refuge with friends in the Armenian Quarter. The revenge of the Azeris in September of the same year, when the Ottoman army conquered Baku, was not experienced locally by Zina, Aron and the children. Like Ali and Nino, who had escaped across the sea to Persia, they fled shortly after Passover from the interim rule of the Bolsheviks via Astrakhan, Saratov and Moscow to the Ukrainian city of Kharkov. When Azerbaijan came under British rule after the collapse of the Ottoman Empire, Zina and the children, like Ali and Nino, returned to Baku, while Aron was on the move across the war fronts in search of a safe haven for family and business, only temporarily staying with them.

After Pinchas's death, Aron took over the management of the business and the leadership of the family in Baku. He had no obligation to undertake a levirate marriage, but was responsible for his brother's widow and the children who had become fatherless. However, there was more at stake. The story goes that Aron desired Zina. It is uncertain from when or how she reacted to it. Zina gave people the feeling of understanding them, of being there for them, as her granddaughters express it. Coming from the Hasidic tradition, could she have obtained sanctity from a physical relationship? She impressed men easily, but remained obstinate. Aron had to persuade her at length to flee from Baku. Nino fled to his native Georgia, but Ali could neither go to Persia, his father's homeland, nor to Europe, which he hated, but which, coming from Baku, was part of him. He stayed. Zina ultimately gave in, came to Berlin and became dependent on Aron.

Aron recalled that during his last brief stay in Baku, from November 1919 to the end of January 1920, he recognized the precarious situation, whereby the oil workers constituted a danger to the entrepreneurs. They received starvation wages in the face of galloping inflation and rising food prices. The Russian workers threatened to strike if the oil deliveries to Russia were not approved. Aron reacted to this by appeasing the workers with cheap bread baked on the company premises. His recommendation to the Association of Oil Industrialists to do the same went unheeded. Maybe that was why the Russian workers defected to the Bolsheviks, he assumed.

Ali is, supposedly, buried in the courtyard of the mosque in Ganja. He died, somewhere behind the Armenian houses, to the sounds of the Budenny March, defending in vain the young Republic of Azerbaijan at the bridge that connected the Azeri and Armenian Quarters in Ganja. I walked across the Jewish cemetery of Baku. But like Victor Ripp, the only one of the Kahan family who came back to the oil metropolis in search of traces and wrote about it, I could not find Pinchas's grave.

CHAPTER 8

Aron and the
Black Gold. Baku

During the days of the great upheavals in Russia, on October 1, 1917, barely a year after his father's death and a month before Pinchas succumbed to fatal meningitis, Aron wrote a ten-page letter to his eldest brother Baruch. It was a business letter, but full of reproaches and demands. Aron was thirty-six at the time, and Baruch fifty-one. After their father Chaim Kahan died, Baruch took over the management of the company, running the businesses in Kharkov and Petrograd, assisted by David. Pinchas and Aron ran the company in Baku. Now Baruch was attacked by Aron.

Aron liked to play cards in the summer club of the oil industrialists on the edge of the City Park. "He loved gambling and many times went to the most famous casino in Monte Carlo," Gita recalled. "He was dreaming of one day having 1,200,000 pounds sterling—he needed 200,000 to spend and 1,000,000 for security." Aron probably saw the casinos of Monte Carlo only later when he would be going there from Berlin or Paris, but his talent, his passion for winning in the oil business as well as in gambling, evolved in Baku.

The cards were dealt. The game was on. What role Pinchas played in it fell into oblivion, as he died too soon and left little behind. Until his death, the brothers worked together in Baku, with the older one shouldering more responsibility, and the younger one most likely doing more work. Aron did not have an exceptionally good hand, but it wasn't the worst either. Above all, like his father, he had unbridled energy, a sharp mind, courage, brilliant ideas and ambitious plans. According to his cousin, the publisher Abram Saulovich Kagan, he was a brilliant businessman, while his nephew Moshe Ater (Ettinger), business editor of *Haaretz*, described him in his obituary as "the most talented of Chaim

Kahan's many sons." A bony, tall figure who clearly expressed his iron will and firm character, dry, reserved, mocking, unmarried, a man for whom feelings did not exist, but whose eyes shone when it came to money; this is how Shalom Asch described the naphtha wholesaler from Baku in his trilogy *Before the Flood*, in which he condensed the Kahan brothers into the fictional character of Boris Chaimovitch Goldstein, who bears Baruch's name and David's love of Palestine, but above all Aron's traits.

However, the initial idea of expanding his father's oil business to Siberia proved to be a flop. It was the one thing that enabled the barely twenty-year-old to make an extended, but ultimately boring and fruitless trip to Tomsk and Irkutsk. I read in Aron's memoirs that the economic situation in the company remained very tense, for a long time, after the revolutionary year of 1905. But the biggest problem was the formation of cartels by the large corporations. They held all the trump cards. After the turn of the century, Branobel as producer and Rothschild as distributor had founded the Société d'Armement d'Industrie et de Commerce (SAIC) in Antwerp, a syndicate for the export of lubricating oils to Europe with a share capital of fifteen million French francs. By joining forces, this paved and secured the export route from Baku to the West for both of them. Three years later they opened the Nobmazut transport company, thereby strengthening their position on the domestic market. Here they controlled more than half of the petroleum trade, over forty percent of the sale of oil residues and two-thirds of the lubricating oil business. In the following years, from 1904 to 1907, the two Baku companies gave in to a concerted anti-American action by the German Emperor with the consent of the Russian government. They merged with the Deutsche Bank, Bleichröder Bank and Deutsche Disconto Gesellschaft into the European Petroleum Union for the purpose of trading on the West European market. Oil from Baku, Romania and Galicia was meant to make Europe independent from the American market, from Standard Oil. The European Petroleum Union was the first European cartel for the sale of petroleum. The main shareholders were Deutsche Bank (fifty percent), Rothschild (twenty-four percent), and Branobel (twenty percent). It was officially only a petroleum and diesel distribution company. Trade in other oil products was free. But in fact, the European Petroleum Union functioned as a European oil corporation. In view of the growing demand, where there was petroleum, other products were available. In 1907, the alliance of Branobel and Rothschild was joined by the merger of Russian and English companies. Thus, the Mantashev Group and Shiboleum were created, which relinquished the Russian market in favor of Nobmazut. After that, the Baku oil business was played with a stacked deck by the major European corporations in collaboration with banks and governments.

In the letter of October 1, 1917, Aron complained about the inexplicable silence of his older brother, about incomprehensible letters and decisions that had not been agreed upon, which led to misunderstandings. It was not the right time for new business deals. The chaos, which followed the military attempt to overthrow the Provisional Government a few weeks earlier, caused correspondence to be erratic. The instability of the political situation following the failed coup, named Kornilov Coup after its leader, confronted the entrepreneurs with new risks and imponderables. Aron found it disconcerting how Baruch reacted sorely to every inaccuracy, while simultaneously arrogantly ignoring their demands from Baku, even with regard to important matters, and reminded him of the quote from the Sermon on the Mount about the mote in his brother's eye, while ignoring the beam in his own eye. He accused his brother of the arbitrary, nonsensical sale of shares that were stable, and wanted to know why Baruch had not sold others, less profitable ones instead and why he had not informed Aron of the exact proceeds from the sale.

As a medium-sized company, owned by a legally restricted Jewish subject, the Kahans had to play their low cards skillfully in order to be in the right position when an opportunity opened up in the game. Chaim Kahan had joined the concerted actions of the corporations to conquer the Western European markets as a small partner, as best he could, hoping that something would fall away from the big business for him. This was not the least of his reasons for taking up residence in Antwerp (1906) and later in Berlin (1913) and employing agents in both places. At the same time, he had always resisted being bullied by the corporations wherever possible. In Baku Itskovich & Kahan were actively involved when, in 1906, entrepreneurs were fighting against Branobel's control of the sulphuric acid trade. Sulphuric acid, obtained from crude oil and necessary for its further processing, was produced in several Baku factories and was sold to various companies, with prices, timing and volume of deliveries controlled by Branobel. Without sulphuric acid, the refineries were at a standstill. The Kahans were contractually obligated to purchase the sulphuric acid they needed from Branobel. Pinchas and Aron rebelled, in the name of their father of course, and gathered other entrepreneurs behind them. They wanted to form a syndicate of sulphuric acid manufacturers. From Branobel's point of view, that broke the rules. The company punished Itskovich & Kahan with higher prices and a halt to deliveries. The political unrest and strikes, which had paralyzed production and distribution, helped to destroy the old order, but not to build a new one. There were attempts of this kind in Baku until 1919. But the Kahans remained dependent on Branobel's sulphuric acid supplies. About this episode, Aron didn't say a word in his memoirs.

Aron had his first chance to show what he was capable of in 1908/1909 when he learned that the Indirect Taxation Department in the Ministry of Finance had run into difficulties due to a deferral of payments. It had granted a large loan to the company Vacanto for a mortgage on a Volga ship, which it was unable to repay. Aron went to St. Petersburg, bought the ship for the amount of the loan and also obtained a deferral of the oil tax. Shortly afterwards he sold the ship to Michael Pollak, the managing director of Mazut. This brought Kahans a loss of 30,000 rubles, but the whole operation brought a net profit between 300,000 and 400,000, because the best card was the tax deferral.

That same year, Aron, again on behalf of his father, courted disparate players, large and small companies, promising successful partnerships in various directions. According to his own statements, he planned to establish a syndicate of the five Baku refineries that produced lubricating oil—Itskovich & Kahan, Rylsky & Shifrin, Goldlust, Leites and Vartepetov. In the Soviet collection of documents on Baku's oil economy there is a letter, signed by Chaim Kahan, owner of a petroleum and oil refinery in Baku, to the Mazut Department of Branobel's Baku office, dated December 16, 1908; possibly Aron's first memorandum of the many he wrote in his life. It provides information about trade relations, size, yields and prices of the refineries. It proposes to merge their lubricating oil sales and not to tolerate any further companies in this field. He presented the Itskovich & Kahan company as the largest supplier of lubricating oil, with a yield of 1.2 million *puds* per year, selling half of it on the Russian market—Itskovich 400,000 and Kahan 200,000 *puds*. This time Aron first secured the necessary approval from Branobel. The negotiations with the individual manufacturers, in which Aron presented himself as an independent buyer, were conducted discreetly. Two years later, the first lube-oil-syndicate was formed in Baku. In this way, the smaller companies were able to confront Branobel in a united manner, which also saved the group from negotiations and provided security. The Kahans took on a spokesperson and mediator role in this game. "The success of my plan brought us great profits and helped us to establish our corporate fund," Aron recalled.

In his letter of October 1, 1917, Aron asked his older brother for precise information on business transactions. What he found quite incomprehensible, even outrageous, was a contract that Baruch had signed with the most powerful of the Armenian oil magnates, Leon Mantashev, for the sale of shares in the

French Bank, a batch worth approximately one and a half million rubles with a deferment period of a whole year. Aron demanded explanations. Baruch had undoubtedly received large sums of money. Since the brothers were supposed to work together, Pinchas and Aron had a stake in "this little deal"; therefore, all of them should, firstly, know all the conditions and, secondly, receive their share. He asked his brother to keep him up to date.

Aron did not only aspire to greater heights, he also wanted to spread his wings. But did he really have an overview of the game, did he really anticipate the consequences? "One clear day in 1909, the post office brought us a letter from Copenhagen in which L. C. Glad & Co, a company we didn't know at all, approached us. They asked us for an estimate for 3,000 buckets of mazut made from crude oil in Balaxanı." All the refineries in Baku had received such a letter, but, accustomed to selling the products locally, none of the owners had ever thought of exporting on their own, so they did not reply. "My brother also raised his hand to throw Mr. Glad's letter into the bin. But I stopped him by saying that it would be worthwhile to start something direct with foreign countries. 'Who knows,' I said, 'maybe this is a way for us to find a window into Europe.' In time, though not until a decade later, it turned out that my mouth had spoken a prophecy."

L. C. Glad & Co, founded in 1880 by Lars Christian Glad, was the oldest oil company in Denmark. It processed and distributed oil that it obtained from the Russian Empire. Pinchas and Aron wanted to discuss the matter with Glad personally in Copenhagen. Their common language was German. The following summer they combined their holidays with a business trip to the Danish capital. The event was etched in Aron's memory. For their initial disappointment that no one was meeting them on the platform, because of a wrong arrival time as it turned out later, they were compensated by Glad's hospitality. The gentlemen dropped their work and dedicated the whole day to them. They took them to the club, where they were served caviar on ice, as befitted Russian guests. Back in Baku, the brothers did their utmost to get the required mazut to Glad from Batumi, which proved to be difficult. The mazut, suitable for further processing in the Danish refinery, was obtained from a particular type of crude oil produced in Balaxanı and Ramana, stored separately and shipped by rail via the Caucasus to Batumi, where it was awaiting transport on the tanker *Harry Wadsworth* from Copenhagen, which arrived in Baku six months later, together with the return visit of the Glads. The Glads, in turn, combined their business with a trip to the Caucasus. Pinchas and Aron returned the favor of the Danish oil company by showing them Branobel's and all the other refineries in the

Black City. In the end they parted as friends. The first deal was to be the last of its kind, but it was the beginning of a far-reaching, even life-saving partnership.

Pinchas and Aron now began to look for higher stakes and bigger profits. Their first deal of this kind was the attempt to acquire the Armenian oil industry and trading company Aramazd. Aramazd was founded in 1901 and named after the god of creation in the Armenian mythology influenced by Zoroastrianism. It was one of the many medium-sized companies with drilling rigs in the Baku region and an extensive pipeline network on the Absheron Peninsula in Balaxanı and Ramana. Therefore, it was attractive for Pinchas and Aron. They needed four million rubles for the business, which they did not have. In secret negotiations—Aron did not show his cards—they reached an agreement with the main shareholders, accepted the demanded price under the condition that they would be given an option of three months to buy Aramazd shares worth 75,000 rubles. If the option remained unused, the invested money would go to Aramazd.

The deal achieved the desired effect: it attracted attention on the Baku stock exchange and increased the value of the Kahan companies. Aron's hope of finding investors on the European stock exchanges was not unfounded. Stepan Lianozov did the same for the establishment of the Russian General Oil Corporation (RGOC), only on a slightly larger scale. The RGOC, founded in London in 1912, registered as an English company in order to mobilize financial resources on the European stock market, was an alliance of Russian, mainly Armenian entrepreneurs with English investors against the large corporations in Baku. Aron travelled to Berlin and London, but without success. The deal did not go through. Later, he blamed this on political factors, such as the outbreak of the Balkan war. In his memoirs, he described his efforts to at least save the down payment on the option, possibly even making a slight profit, as a lesson and an adventure: how the general manager of the Siberian Trade Bank hurt his pride when he tried to squeeze the price of the Aramazd shares, how the Private Trade Bank in St. Petersburg finally approved the bid and how one of Aramazd's main shareholders made it clear to him that he would have received his money back in any case, when the Nordic Bank in Baku handed over the shares. This incident apparently left a bad impression about the Kahans' business practices in Baku business circles.

Following the botched game with the Aramazd shares, Pinchas and Aron were criticized by their father for acting on their own authority. "Last night, I had a fight with Aron Meir I was annoyed that Pinchas sold Mantashev shares without asking me," he wrote from St. Petersburg to his wife in Warsaw on

May 21, 1912. Aron, whom he called Aron Meir, or Meir for short, had also sold other Caucasus shares without his consent and to his annoyance; when questioned by his father, he defiantly replied that he could deduct those from their holdings in Baku. Pinchas and Aron held special positions in the company. They were sitting at the source of the oil, in the seething, hotly contested center of the oil industry, which entailed a high degree of responsibility. It meant quick money, but also a great deal of risk, and required immediate and decisive action, far from their father's decision-making power and yet bound by it. The incident with Aramazd cost Chaim Kahan money and also harmed his health. It prompted him to divide his assets.

By then, he had been struggling for some time with signs of exhaustion and depression. Chaim was in his early sixties at the time and his fourth decade in business. He was tired of traveling, increasingly less able to cope with the pressure of making fast and momentous decisions, but could not get rid of his restlessness. That's why he had fled from his business seat several times, to Pinchas in Baku or to Miriam in Warsaw or abroad to German spas. A good partner and friend, Ilya Pines, an employee of the Russian oil export company Viktor I. Ragozin & Co. in Moscow, was worried about him: he saw Chaim Kahan as a very special person with an exceptionally lively spirit, great kindness and an unusually sensitive soul. Perhaps this was the tragedy of Chaim's life, Ilya said: it existed within Chaim and was now unfolding at a cruel speed which could not escape anyone familiar with him. Chaim's friend, Rabbi Aronson from Kiev, whom he had asked for advice, could not help him either. To calm down, Chaim considered to engage a teacher, to study Torah, or to travel with Malka again, provided she did not try to patronize him.

For two years, Chaim Kahan had been trying to establish a new company for processing oil and wood to trade the products at home and abroad. In this way, he wanted to merge the trading house and refineries, while expanding his business activities. However, the name, form and function of the company were the subject of long negotiations. At first, Chaim envisioned the rather modest format of an incorporated company with partners and registered shares. The desire to invest in the traditional timber industry alongside the innovative oil business points to a plan based on security, perhaps even sentiment. The company was to be called Ch. N. Kahan & Sons. Its share capital was to amount to one million rubles, divided into 10,000 shares of 100 rubles each, and, apart from the existing refineries in Knyazevka and Baku, it was to acquire, build, lease and open offices only where Jews and foreigners were allowed to do so. The headquarters were to be in Kharkov, Chaim's main residence. But then,

someone, we don't know who, brought into play a new name, a more sophisticated profile: the Caucasus-Volga Industry & Trading Company. Chaim
retreated from the idea of running a wood industry, at the same time insisting
on strong management. The dispute between Chaim and his Baku sons over
the Aramazd affair had erupted during these negotiations. In the summer of
1912, the family was summoned to St. Petersburg, where a contract for the division of property was drawn up in the presence of the adviser Meir Yakovlevich
Aronson, a brother of the Kiev rabbi: half was given to the children, but the
management remained with Chaim Kahan. Aronson was also charged with
finding a wife for Aron Meir, now thirty-four years old, to bring the hothead to
his senses and curb his recklessness.

However, Aron did not get married yet at that time. Pinchas and he got
a new trump card. They acquired for the family Petrol Inc., a company rich
in tradition that produced, processed and sold oil. Petrol, founded in 1898,
had been in existence for fourteen years, owned oil fields on the Absheron
Peninsula in Balaxanı and elsewhere, all of which belonged to Princess Anna
Pavlovna Gagarina, wife of the Governor General of the Georgian city of
Kutaisi; they were part of the oil-rich land that Alexander II had excluded from
auctions and granted in 1879 to nobles he favored, like Gagarina. "I was active
in the matter, but the initiative came solely from my father," Aron recalled. The
purchase probably came about thanks to the longstanding relationship with
the entrepreneurial Dembo family. The brothers Isaak and Vulf Dembo were
among the previous owners and board members of Petrol. At the beginning,
fifty percent of the shares were in private hands. The Kahans invested 15,000
rubles for the option to acquire twenty percent of the shares at their nominal
value within six months. The company's share capital and total value amounted
to almost two million rubles, although ninety-five percent of that amount was
spent on unsuccessful drilling operations. Petrol's yield in Balaxanı amounted
to a maximum of 50,000 *puds* per month, which was barely enough to cover
the expenses. The company had no debts, but also hardly any disposable funds,
about 50,000 rubles according to Aron's recollections. As far as numbers were
concerned, his memory was still working well, even in old age.

The unprofitability was noticeable, he wrote. They were warned that it was
a bad business; better to forego the already invested 15,000 rubles and not to
spend even more. As Aron recalled,

> I remember sitting in a hotel in Berlin, reading a letter from my brother in
> Baku, telling me that Vladimir Galperin (his best friend) had visited him

and warned him not to buy Petrol shares. Vladimir Galperin was a very talented engineer and was only involved in drilling for large oil companies, so his claims could be considered as reliable. I replied to my brother in response to this letter that even though Vladimir Galperin was a great expert and the Petrol company itself seemed to be dubious about the chances of greater returns, I was convinced that the purchase of the Petrol shares would bring us millions.

The Kahans paid for the shares within the agreed time and acquired the remaining half from the State Bank, so that by the fall of 1912 they owned the company outright. On October 12, 1912, Chaim Kahan wrote to his wife in Warsaw that Pinchas would not leave him alone because of Petrol. Before the purchase was completed, he was to come to Baku. But he considered the journey difficult, and the business was becoming a nuisance to him; he wanted to travel abroad as soon as possible.

According to Aron, the acquisition of the unprofitable Petrol proved to be a trump card for two reasons. The articles of association did not contain the usual restrictions for Jews—the non-admission to management and the prohibition to acquire oil fields without special permission. A Jewish lawyer, Yakov Tobias, had already been among the founders, and, during the last two years before the Kahans' acquisition, three of the five board members were Jews, Yakov Tobias and the brothers Isaac and Vulf Dembo. The participation of a Jewish entrepreneur at Petrol was practically an established tradition. In addition, the company was able to account for the roughly two million rubles spent on drilling not as a loss, but as an equity, debit and tax-free investment acquisition. The purchase of Petrol brought the Kahans large profits and a leading position among the medium-sized oil companies. As a result, they gained a certain notoriety and also attracted the attention of the Yiddish writer Shalom Asch. He called his protagonist Boris Chaimovich Goldstein, based on Kahan, "Russia's Oil," crowning him the naphtha king, picking up and expanding on the infamous triad "tea belongs to Wissotzky, sugar belongs to Brodsky, Russia belongs to Trotsky."

Baron Alexander G. Günzburg, son of the St. Petersburg banker and sponsor Horace Günzburg, took over the chairmanship of the board of directors; he figured as a trustee without being a major shareholder, since his name was well known, had prestige, provided security and guaranteed a good reputation. Only once, in an emergency situation, did he invest generously in the company. Aron was appointed managing director alongside his father and two directors who had been kept on. The bookkeeping remained in reliable hands. The head office was located in the office block at 6 Stremyannaya in St. Petersburg.

Petrol's purchase and conceptional design was the responsibility of Pinchas and Aron in Baku. Chaim was more concerned with the oil and timber company in which he wanted to merge his assets. The change of name from Ch. N. Kahan & Sons to Caucasus-Volga Industrial & Trading Company did not suit him. He wanted to undo it. Throughout his life, he had managed under his own name, with the help of his sons. This was known to all banks, business partners and competitors. The name Ch. N. Kahan & Sons was trustworthy. A few weeks later he returned to his desire and his plan to get into the timber business. Neither of these were granted to him because the founding of the company was postponed by the takeover of Petrol. In December 1912, the Kahans joined forces. Petrol took over Chaim's company shares, the refineries near Saratov and in Baku, precisely half of the Knyazevka factory for the production and sale of kerosene, lighting and lubricating oils and a third of Itskovich & Kahan, which affected Chaim's plans to found the Caucasus-Volga Industrial & Trading Company or, if he had insisted on the name, Ch. N. Kahan & Sons. The refineries were excluded from this, which may have been economically advantageous for both, but may have hurt Chaim's pride.

Caucasus-Volga Industrial & Trading Company's inaugural meeting finally took place on September 12, 1913. Chaim transferred to it eleven warehouses for petroleum and other oil products on his own land comprising equipment, buildings, tanks and moveable property, as well as twelve warehouses, including all accessories, on leased land in Congress Poland and the Western Borderland, plus one hundred and forty tank wagons. At that time, Chaim estimated his total assets to be worth 950,000 rubles. On average, the company consisted of eleven or twelve shareholders. Chaim Kahan with his children Baruch, Aron, David, Pinchas and Rachel were major shareholders, with Baruch owning by far the most shares. Chaim and his four sons served as directors. Prospective directors were his son-in-law Jonas Rosenberg in Warsaw and son Bendet in Berlin. The company operated as a family business which was not listed on the stock exchange. Chaim Kahan's wish to consolidate the assets he had amassed in a family business run under his name, as the crowning glory of his success, was only partially fulfilled. Shortly before the end of his career, Petrol had put Caucasus-Volga Industrial & Trading Company in its place and overtaken it. Although Aron was one of the major shareholders and directors of Caucasus-Volga Industrial & Trading Company, neither it, nor the Russian-Baltic Mineral Oil Company in Riga, also founded by his father in September

1913, were worth mentioning in his memoirs. Aron wrote only about his own merits. He demanded new business methods; he was striving for higher realms.

In his letter to Baruch of October 1, 1917, Aron zeroed in on the management of the refinery at Saratov. Because of the distances and traffic conditions, it was not easy to decide who exactly was responsible for it—Baruch and David in Kharkov or Pinchas and Aron in Baku. Aron got this problem off his back, by insinuating that Baruch had failed to go there and look after things himself, but was rather relying on the employee Solomon L. Paperno, whom Aron actually distrusted. To replace Paperno, Aron had suggested his own people: the engineer Nechemia M. Neiman, his commissioned agent in the Petrol's oil fields, who was well versed in technical matters, and Caucasus-Volga Industry & Trading Company's branch manager Yakov G. Vainshtein, who was supposed to make himself useful in Knyazevka for one and a half to two months. Aron had let his ticket via Rostov expire, stopping-over instead in Saratov to inspect the refinery in Knyazevka. But why should he have spent his one-day stay there, as Baruch had asked him in retrospect, to keep order there? Aron did not understand Baruch's relationship to the Saratov refinery. He feared that father and son Paperno would use the power of attorney for their own interests, which was not be tolerated under any circumstances, and by criminally neglecting their obligations, would lead to the ruin and destruction of the plant. Therefore, the quarrel had to be put to an end; a reorganization of the refinery had to be undertaken. Aron had at first suspected that Baruch was postponing the question of evacuating the administration to the city of Saratov and Moscow due to the political unrest, but there was no sign of that. Aron now urged the fastest possible evacuation. Waiting until the zeppelins flew over the city would not be a good idea. Therefore, he went himself in search of a suitable twelve-room apartment in Saratov. Even if they had to sublet it, it wouldn't be a great loss for them.

With the announcement of the increase in ownership, Petrol had applied to the Ministry of Commerce and Industry for a capital increase—the doubling of the share capital from two million rubles to four million rubles—on the basis that the two refineries contributed to the corporation. The files show the long procedure: a shareholders' meeting, examination by the Ministry and approval by the Governing Senate. The capital increase was granted to Petrol one year after the takeover and half-a-year after the application, in the summer of 1913. Petrol and Itskovich & Kahan ranked seventh in the Baku oil industry in terms of processing and transport, but headed the list of twenty-one processing companies in the production of high-quality products, lubricants and solar oil. Among the forty-eight transport companies, they ranked seventh, eighth, or ninth, depending on the product. They delivered by rail on the Transcaucasian line to the Black Sea port of Batumi; on the Baku–Petrovsk route, to Russia and the Caucasus; by ship, to Astrakhan and to places in the Baku region; across the Caspian Sea, to Persia and to other neighboring countries, as well as to Petrovsk, today's Makhachkala. In the Congress of Oil Industrialists, they had a combined vote of five out of a total of three hundred and sixty-seven, while Branobel had eighteen. The company now had a share capital of four million rubles in the form of 40,000 shares of 100 rubles each. The advantage of the Petrol shares proved to be that they were listed on the St. Petersburg Stock Exchange. For years no one had made use of this right, Aron recalled, because business had been bad and no interested parties could be found. The Kahans went public. "I was given access to the stock exchange through a deal with two gentlemen, where they were now offering the Petrol shares. As the son of a First-Guild merchant, I was allowed to visit the exchange, and I was present when our shares were first listed there. Within a short time, forty percent of the total was sold at the standard price."

Officially, Pinchas headed Petrol's Baku branch; Aron was on the board of directors. In 1913, Baruch took over a vacant directorship. Thus, in the second year after the acquisition, three of the directors belonged to the family: Chaim, Aron and Baruch. Baruch remained in this position until the end, thus ensuring the continuity of management. Aron was replaced by Pinchas in 1916 and now took over the management of the Baku branch. Was he too rebellious for his father or was he withdrawn to be available for other tasks?

After the reprimand for the uncoordinated sale of shares and the neglect of supervisory duties in Saratov, Aron informed Baruch on October 1, 1917 of unauthorized transactions:

> We are conducting negotiations concerning two major companies—the lease of the Rylsky plant and the purchase of the Guliev oil pipeline.— Pin[cha]s will be writing more about this in detail.—We seem to have to close these two deals without waiting for your answer, because the deal with Guliev could slip through our fingers and as for Rylsky, one has to cater to his whims. Although it is possible that by the time you receive this letter, the contracts will already have been signed, we would still ask you to let us know your opinion about it immediately by telegram via Moscow.— If you do not approve of our position, you cannot stop us, but if you agree, we want to know as soon as possible.

Up to three dozen shareholders were involved in Petrol. Before the war began, Kahans held the majority stock, 15,511 of 23,351 shares, Chaim 6,726, David 3,526, and Aron 2,964. Major shareholders included a certain Mark I. Lifshits (3,375), who also held shares in the other two Kahan companies, and Vulf Dembo (2,640), who had been a director of the company before the takeover, a merchant of the First Guild living in St. Petersburg since 1914.

In those years, the Baku oil entrepreneurs obtained government permission to acquire shares in other companies. The share trading, which now began to flourish, was a game with new rules for the brothers. After ten years of apprenticeship, Aron, as managing director and major shareholder of Petrol, was holding a good hand and had developed strategies that enabled him to anticipate the flow of the game and apply a combination of tactical moves. In addition, his father had passed the zenith of his entrepreneurial career, enabling him to take the management out of his hands more easily than when his older brothers were at their best. Was Aron already the main family strategist when the Kahans, like Asch's Goldstein, took part in the 1913/1914 "New Russia" project at the RGOC, surpassing Branobel, even forcing the market leader to start operating on credit, and in the rush of success and in concerted action with the Russian-Asian Bank, the largest in the Empire, twice attempting to take over the company? Be that as it may, the Kahans, with the help of a third Dembo brother, Boris Dembo, worked closely together in a covert action and on the stock exchanges in St. Petersburg, Berlin and London, speculating with the Nobel shares. Both attempts failed. However, as a letter shows, Chaim blamed for the resulting losses not his sons, but rather the circumstances. There is nothing in Aron's memoirs about the attempted creeping takeover and nothing about the fact that the family had lost the majority as Petrol share-holders in the meantime.

When the Kahans took over the corporation, it was, as already mentioned, in a desolate state. Estimating the land value of the plants and oil fields in Balaxanı, it had no debts, but was unprofitable and badly managed. The machines were outdated and consumed too much heating oil. In addition, there were new boreholes that had not yet yielded a profit and old ones that had not been maintained. Pinchas and Aron developed plans, raised money and invested. They bought five Lietzenmayer machines with four-stroke engines, built in Sormovo near Nizhny Novgorod, whose fuel consumption was much lower than that of steam engines. This enabled them to drill wells and increase the yield from the production. Thanks to the two refineries, Petrol was able to process both foreign and its own crude oil in house, selling its products directly to Russia and abroad instead of having to sell them cheaply to exporters. In addition, there were the tank wagons owned and leased by Chaim Kahan, as well as trade contracts for petroleum and oil sales on the domestic market. In the oil business, consolidation drove up prices, especially for petroleum, gasoline, lubricating and cylinder oil. Only processing companies could operate profitably.

Initially, Chaim Kahan had been Petrol's only creditor. The loans were repaid with stock from further share issues as a result of capital increase. In early 1913, the ministry had approved a new issue of additional shares for the corporation: 10,000 for the sum of one million rubles, at 100 rubles per share, and in September of the same year the new issue of additional shares, a second series of the same amount and at the same price. In the early summer of 1914, new private investors were attracted: the Finnish businessman Richard G. Menzbir, who thus became a member of the board of directors and also had a stake in the Russian-Baltic Mineral Oil Company, and a certain S. Yu. Muchnik, both owners of the St. Petersburg-Tver Oil Industry Company, with a contribution of 180,000 rubles. I wonder if Aron had instigated this.

In addition to a certain D. G. Pernik, who was also a shareholder of Caucasus-Volga Industrial & Trading Company, two Petrograd banks were major shareholders in the summer of the second war year: the United and the Private Trade Bank. Chaim owned barely more than each of them, only 2,713 shares, Aron about half that many. Petrol had maintained business relations with the Azov-Don Trade Bank at least since 1909, and with the Private Trade Bank since 1911. Petrol also received loans from the Siberian Commercial Bank—twice between June 1915 and April 1916, in the total amount of 950,000 rubles—in the form of tax receipts to pay the excise duty on petroleum to the Moscow Government Treasury. By January 1916, Petrol was not yet back under the control of the Kahan family. The group around Chaim (4,075) with Baruch, Pinchas, Aron and Rachel, who together owned just six hundred and fifty shares, was only the second largest shareholder in the corporation after Vulf Dembo (5,100). But already at the time of the following shareholders' meeting, in June 1916, Chaim (4,505) and his four sons (2,000), while not owning the absolute majority, had regained the relative majority of the Petrol shares, followed by the Petrograd branch of the United Bank (2,565).

At that time Aron only held one hundred Petrol shares, which was irritating. What tactics was he applying, or had he lost a game? At the same time, he left the company's board of directors, but remained in the Baku branch management. Was he slowed down, reprimanded by his father and brothers? In a letter to David in Petrograd on June 27, 1916, Aron cryptically hinted at various activities—he wanted to do some more work in the pay of the "French Oil Company" (presumably the Caspian-Black Sea Oil Industry and Trading Company), had himself put up for "election to the council" and hoped that this would please the chief representative, his father. "Think of me as an experienced and well-educated oilman (*neftyanik*)." Aron was now heavily involved socially, and was therefore terribly busy, Rosalia Kahan reported to Berlin; she was probably not thinking of his proven activities in a St. Petersburg housing association, but rather of his presence in the oil lobby. Whether Aron succeeded in being elected to the council of one of the last congresses of the Baku oil industrialists, remains unclear. At the end of his letter to David, he mentioned "the most important thing": the flipflopping performance of the Petrol shares. The brothers in Petrograd were to sell as many as possible, 1,500 to 2,000, provided that the price had risen, so that the course of more than 100 rubles per security could be maintained by buybacks. In this way they would achieve security in the event of a new stock issue.

Barely three months later, in September 1916, the Kahans succeeded in bringing Petrol back under their control. They had the absolute majority of shares, Chaim owning 13,185, Aron 3,174 and his siblings holding the remaining numerically significant, but much smaller share packages. The circumstances were apparently back to normal. Business was now going so well that in January 1917, immediately before the February Revolution, Petrol was authorized to increase its capital again, doubling its stock from four to eight million. However, it took four months to implement, so that it was not done until after the fall of the autocracy, in April 1917. The political upheaval did not seem to affect the economic developments, at least not in the essential wartime industries. Nonetheless, events in the petroleum industry intensified to a similar extent as in politics. In June 1917, the corporation applied for a further capital increase, the third doubling of the share capital from eight to sixteen million. It was granted two months later, in August 1917, which, in retrospect, seems audacious if not futile.

At the end of his letter of October 1, 1917 to Baruch, Aron mentioned the new issue of Petrol stock in the course of the last capital increase, the details of which had eluded them in the political chaos. He was concerned about the subscription, publication. and distribution of the shares:

In general, I wanted to know more about this distribution. Did you determine that voluntarily? What were you guided by in this instance and why did you not ask us? Or is it possible that there is some new rule for this consideration? However, aren't you nevertheless obligated to inform us immediately after the first publication about the distribution and not, following the Nobels' principle, leave it for clarification by a bunch of dregs?

Aron suggested complaining to the bank that they had been unable to subscribe in view of the disrupted postal connections, and demand their money back, including interest. The management could then set a new deadline for the delayed shareholders. It was also necessary to ascertain whether the banks had not subscribed the shares on their own account. "We know full well that there have been such cases. We would also like to know exactly how many Petrol shares we currently own, and whether the last issue is guaranteed, and at what cost." Shortly before the Bolsheviks overthrew the Provisional Government, Aron showed clear ambitions to take over the management of the Kahan operations.

Photo 1: The Kahans travelling in Palestine and Egypt, 1914.
Jüdisches Museum Berlin, Archiv Haimi-Cohen

Photo 2: Malka Kahan. Portrait by H. Dietrich. Berlin, 1917.
Giza Haimi-Cohen, Tel Aviv

Photo 3: Chaim Kahan. Portrait by Hermann Struck. Berlin, 1914.
Giza Haimi-Cohen, Tel Aviv

Photo 4: Chaim and Malka's golden wedding anniversary portrait in an ornamental frame. Jerusalem (Bezalel), 1914. Ittai Gavrieli, Mevaseret Zion

Photo 5: Yasha Kahan. Berlin, 1910. Jüdisches Museum Berlin, Archiv Haimi-Cohen

Photo 6: Roska Rosenberg. Berlin, 1914. Jüdisches Museum Berlin, Archiv Haimi-Cohen

Photo 7: Yasha Kahan. Charlottenburg, 1916. On the back there is a dedication to Roska Rosenberg: "To my darling girl on our anniversary". Jüdisches Museum Berlin, Archiv Haimi-Cohen

Photo 8: Baruch Kahan (back row center) and classmates in the *sukkah*. Frankfurt am Main, between 1884 and 1886. Tsentralny Derzhavny Istorichny Arkhiv Ukrainy, Kyiv

Photo 9: Miriam and Jonas Rosenberg. Warsaw, c. 1894. Jüdisches Museum Berlin, Archiv Haimi-Cohen

Photo 10: Pinchas Kahan marries Zina Golodetz (back row center). Baranovichi, 1900. Efrat Carmon, Jerusalem

Photo 11: Cousins, from left to right: Noma Rosenberg, Yasha Kahan, Roska Rosenberg, and Nachum and Arusia Kahan. In the Russian Empire, c. 1905. Jüdisches Museum Berlin, Archiv Haimi-Cohen

Photo 12: Miriam and Jonas Rosenberg with their children Roska and Noma. Antwerp, c. 1907. Jüdisches Museum Berlin, Archiv Haimi-Cohen

Photo 13: David Kahan with nephews; from left to right: Arusia, Nachum, and Yasha Kahan. Kharkov, 1911. Jüdisches Museum Berlin, Archiv Haimi-Cohen

Photo 14: Refinery in Knyazevka near Saratov, 1909. Jüdisches Museum
Berlin, Archiv Haimi-Cohen

Photo 15: Staff of the refinery in Knyazevka near Saratov, 1909.
Efrat Carmon, Jerusalem

Photo 16: Baruch and David Kahan with others on the Volga. In the background the refinery in Knyazevka near Saratov, no date. Jüdisches Museum Berlin, Archiv Haimi-Cohen

Photo 17: Zina Kahan. Baku, no date. Jüdisches Museum Berlin, Archiv Haimi-Cohen

Photo 18: Baruch Kahan as Circassian warrior. Baku, 1896. Jüdisches Museum Berlin, Archiv Haimi-Cohen

Photo 19: Rachel Kahan as Circassian warrior. Baku, 1909. Ettinger-Rozenfeld family, Ramat Gan

Photo 20: Pinchas and Zina Kahan with their son Lolia, 1907.
Daniel Ripp, New York

CHAPTER 9

Summer Resorts during the War: Bad Harzburg, Bad Neuenahr, Bad Polzin

"Polzin 15. 8. 17. My beloved ones," Rosa wrote to Berlin, "it is more than strange that I have never written to you from here before. Because I have enough time and an even greater urge. But I simply didn't get around to it because we wanted to get better acquainted with this strange backwater. So, now I want to write to you in detail."

E ven during the war, the Rosenbergs used to go to the summer resorts from Berlin, but mostly to less well-known and expensive places. As in previous years, the ladies took the waters in Bad Neuenahr, but none of them would travel anymore to Bad Kissingen, Wiesbaden, Bad Reichenhall, Franzensbad, St. Moritz, Merano, or Menton; instead, they went to Bad Harzburg, Polzin, or Bad Salzbrunn. Presumably, the family was aware of the lists of antisemitic resorts published by the Central Association's weekly journal, but they were not deterred. After all, there were also spas that traditionally catered for Jewish visitors, who preferred to stay there as part of their regular guests.

As of 1915, the Rosenbergs obtained travel and residence permits for summer resorts. After the beginning of the war, it was almost impossible to undertake harmless journeys to the spas in the German Reich as patriotism demanded anything but summer retreats at a spa. Tourism had decreased. The Germans, but above all the wealthy foreign guests, stayed away. The towns became desolate; hotels were transformed into military hospitals. But the Rosenbergs, whom Yasha Kahan had joined, had stayed in the country and were now outsiders in the double sense of simultaneously being "Eastern Jews" and "enemy aliens." For them, the summer resort had become increasingly more significant. It was a retreat where the appearance of normality, continuity, peace in times of war could be maintained to a certain extent. Their legal adviser and friend, Dr. Yuda M. Beham from Kharkov, who had been living in Berlin-Charlottenburg since 1916, expressed understanding for the fact that Yasha enjoyed the Bad Harzburg summer retreat: the poetry of the Harz Mountains was particularly important and helpful in times of war and revolution.

Rosa continued,

> Mom and I were very happy about yesterday's phone call. Maybe you felt the same, and so now you know more or less how we are set up here. I'm not sure what there is to tell you about Polzin. Do you know what is paradox? To travel to Polzin first class. Because I think that when we, *im yirzeh hashem* [God willing], will go home, the Polzin ticket clerk will certainly not know what first class actually means. Polzin is a kind of big village nestled among the hills. The good Lord has accidentally blessed it with good peat so that sanatoriums could be built. There is a municipal sanatorium and there are also private sanatoriums that have in-house baths. (There is no public bath house.) The people who come here enjoy full board and take the waters in the same building. Apart from the sanatorium where they live, they have absolutely nothing here. There is a nice park, but most of the time you sit in the guest house, which, fortunately, is in the park.

Połczyn-Zdrój, the former Bad Polzin, is a small town in Poland, in the Pomeranian Switzerland, with less than ten thousand inhabitants (before the First World War it was half as many), which bore the title "Bad" officially since 1926. It is situated among hills, forests and lakes in a lowland area, which is divided by two small rivers. Since the middle of the nineteenth century, Polzin has been a recognized mud-bath resort with precious mineral springs. Having been linked to the railway network in 1897, it increasingly attracted spa guests until the war began. "Rooms like you, dear daddy, fantasize about in your imagination, remain a fantasy here, too," wrote Rosa. "Of course, we wanted to take the most beautiful rooms of the g[uest house], but there are none. They are all the most primitive rooms you can imagine and there is no choice. The sanatorium is full of military personnel, just like all houses, which are full of soldiers. At the Finkelsteins, too, there are many soldiers billeted. The only slightly nicer sanatorium is the Luisenbad, but it's out of town, making it impossible for us to stay there."

Like educational journeys, the summer retreat, copied from the aristocratic ideal of idleness, was part and parcel of the bourgeois lifestyle. It was, however, adapted to the work ethic of the middle class, where idleness was confined by time and space. The European summer, being the most joyful season, a symbol of vitality, provided the appropriate time frame. For the busy urban middle class, summer recreation served primarily as a respite from work. Nature was cultivated for this purpose, and in the course of the nineteenth century special premises were created in the form of spas, where new businesses, gastronomic, medical and technical facilities were developed. The spas presented themselves as paradisical fountains of youth and at the same time formed social spaces for the self-promotion of the bourgeoisie. People wanted to see and be seen; they discussed politics; they negotiated business and personal matters in a protected bubble away from everyday life. Well-known spa resorts such as the Bohemian baths, Baden-Baden, or Cabourg, provided material for works of art. Marienbad became the epitome of the Jewish spa.

Just as the German middle-class had copied the aristocracy, so the Jewish bourgeoisie imitated the German middle-class in terms of the summer retreats, the educational ideals and the entire lifestyle. Like the trip to the Promised Land, the summer retreat was a journey to a different world, a better one. Even in the German Reich, resort life was very popular with Jewish entrepreneurs, writers and the well-educated. Hotel and guest house advertisements, travel reports in the press called *Badebriefe* [spa letters] and memoirs bear this out, just as much as the negative resort antisemitism, a phenomenon that already existed before the turn of the century. The wealthy East European guests presented a spectrum of the entire Jewish society at the time: Orthodox and liberal Jews; Zionists and assimilated German, Polish and Russian Jews; Jews with more traditional lifestyles, giving rise to the now famous antisemitic clichés.

In the third summer of the war, the dramatic year of the Russian Revolution, from mid-August to mid-September 1917, the Rosenbergs, and with them Jacob Kahan, enjoyed four weeks of summer retreat. Father Jonas and Grandmother Malka had stayed at home, Rosa with her mother, Miriam, enjoyed the mud baths in the Pomeranian Polzin, Yasha and Noma were in Bad Harzburg. The summer retreat offered them a place to relax in a kind of sheltered sanctuary—beyond the war front, far away from revolutionary Russia and from the starving big city. Rosa had spent every summer of the war with her mother and grandmother in resorts—1915 in Harzburg and 1916 in Neuenahr. The young men were allowed to leave Berlin, for the first time since the beginning of the war, a few days after the women in 1917. Yasha's first letter from Bad Harzburg to Rosa in Polzin reflects the enthusiasm about being able to finally move more freely after three years. He experienced the departure in a turbulent frenzy. The police permit had only been granted at the last moment, directly before the planned departure, so that they had to leave hastily. There was a dispute with Uncle Jonas and Noma, who both urged a speedy departure, while Yasha wanted first to celebrate the receipt of the permit and the farewell with friends, which he actually succeeded in doing. He described for Rosa the last hours before the journey via Magdeburg to the Harz Mountains in all details. He liked Bad Harzburg, unlike Noma, who was disappointed by the place and the weather and wanted to return to Berlin immediately. The town and its surroundings reminded Yasha of Bad Reichenhall, where he had relaxed with his parents in the summer of 1909. The guest house was good and relatively inexpensive, the food was the best in the whole of Bad Harzburg, the room was spacious and had a balcony. They paid only seventeen marks per day per person for full board. The ladies paid even five marks less. All of Polzin could probably be bought for a few thousand marks, Rosa wrote.

The Harz mountain range was a popular recreation region at that time and Bad Harzburg, situated on its northern slope, was a first-class spa, the most elegant summer resort there, even if it could not compete with the southern German and Bohemian spas. In 1907 it had about 17,000 spa guests (in Polzin there were between two and three thousand at the same time), mostly North Germans, but also Dutch, British and Russian tourists, plus 21,000 day trippers. While the Jews were a noticeable group among the spa guests, they were only a minority of less than a thousand. Bad Harzburg offered comfortable accommodation and ozone-rich air. The center of spa life was the *Kurhaus*, which could accommodate eight hundred guests. It featured tasteful reading and games rooms, as well as music halls staging regular concerts and dance events on weekends. The municipal baths, called Juliushall, was a monumental building, one hundred meters long. There, salt water, pine needle, malt, steam, hot air, light, hydroelectric and carbon dioxide baths were administered in seventy cells. In addition, there were also inhalation facilities. The large foyer opposite offered a drinking cure. In the middle of the hall was a saltwater drinking fountain, named after the Saxon Germanic god Krodo, which was supposed to have a laxative effect, cure catarrhs of the throat, stomach and intestines and be good against hemorrhoids, indurations, obesity, fatty heart and gout. The surrounding area with parks and gardens, the castle on the hill, the deep valley of the Radau and miles of promenades to the theater, horse racetrack and tennis courts, provided open invitations for walks and picnics in the woods. Rosa knew Bad Harzburg and could make the comparison; she was therefore shocked by the state of the Pomeranian town, which she called a village and considered an insult to the guests. When they arrived, they found all the rooms occupied by soldiers, because the spa town was accommodating a military hospital with more than a thousand beds.

> Apart from the mud baths, Polzin has nothing. No reading room, no light, no concert—*keyn leyb un keyn leben* [as dull as ditchwater]. It's not to be taken seriously at all. A band comes once in three weeks. "When it has time and can get away," they say here. But there's a substitute concert— cows in the morning and chickens in the afternoon. All the people here are complaining about boredom, but since almost everyone is famished, they are happy to be fed. It's possible to eat one's fill, although it's nothing to crow about. There are no surprises here for us, but for others who are already used to worse, it's very good.

After a few days of temporary accommodation, Rosa and her mother got a room at the *Kurhaus* Finkelstein. The "1st class hotel, *kosher*, all baths inside the house, central heating, WINTER TREATMENT!—Four-cell baths, electric massage, galvanization, faradization etc., sunlamp, electric radiation (under medical supervision), modern furnishings" was only built a few years before the war. It was a stately three-story building with balconies, loggias and verandas, the only one situated directly in the spa park. It was one of the three Jewish-run houses that shaped the townscape. At that time Polzin had a small Jewish community, over a hundred years old, with a cemetery, synagogue, twenty to thirty households and one to two hundred members, comprising about two percent of the town population. The *Kurhaus* was probably run by the family of J. W. Finkelstein, who was the community's teacher, cantor and butcher. Polzin was said to be a popular destination for Jewish spa guests from Poznan.

In Bad Harzburg, the health resort continued to operate despite the war. Yasha and Noma reported daily to the police; a curfew was imposed from 9 p.m., but one could talk to the city council and be exempted from the regulations. Everybody did so. The city council was "relaxed," as was the Harzburg police, Yasha wrote to Rosa. The reporting was reduced to twice a week, and the curfew was not in effect until 11 p.m., which was completely sufficient for them, because at that time the streetlights were already out anyway, and the town was steeped in darkness. Rosa did not say a word in her letters about police checks in Polzin. Miriam Rosenberg had duly deregistered in Charlottenburg and registered at the health resort, as she had done for every summer retreat during the war. But not so Rosa. Was she only considered an underage travelling companion?

Yasha and Noma were staying in the Parkhaus, since 1894 a hotel for Jewish guests. It was initially run by Max Hecht, then by M. Fifar, had a kosher kitchen, a wooden synagogue in the garden, central heating and electric light. Sammy Gronemann had once celebrated his engagement there. In the *Jüdische Rundschau* as well as in the *Israelite*, the Zionist and Orthodox press, it was advertised, even during the war, as a highly recommended hotel in one of the most popular summer resorts. In 1917 it had 200 beds. Only few Jews lived in Bad Harzburg, which had no established Jewish community. But since 1899 kosher slaughtering was allowed there, thereby fulfilling a requirement for offering hospitality to Jewish guests. Unlike Braunlage, Herzberg, Zellerfeld and Hahnenklee, which had been attracting attention for their antisemitic advertising since the turn of the century, Bad Harzburg was considered the health resort in the Harz Mountains where Jewish paying guests were welcome; consequently, it was known as a "Jew Bath" in the jargon of antisemitic propaganda. This was possibly one of the reasons that motivated extreme right-wing nationalistic groupings to convene a meeting with the Nazi leadership there, for the purpose of creating a political force to topple the government. This became known as the "Harzburg Front," formed at this convention on October 11, 1931; it made the town much more famous than the fact that it was a popular holiday resort for the Jewish bourgeoisie.

From the summer retreat in August 1917, at the same time that General Kornilov was preparing to overthrow the Provisional Government in Russia, Rosa Rosenberg in Polzin and Yasha Kahan in Bad Harzburg entered into an intensive correspondence. Letter-writing was part of the daily routine throughout the years, even during the holiday season. They wrote to those who stayed at home and received reports from them. Letters from Yasha's parents and other relatives in Russia were forwarded to them in the holiday resorts via Copenhagen or Stockholm. Rosa and Yasha exchanged those with each other, without asking for them to be returned. They sent congratulatory letters to relatives and acquaintances on birthdays, name days and religious holidays; because it was the custom; because they were worried about family and friends, torn apart by war; to keep the circles together. Probably also because in the precarious situation of a police-controlled resort, shared joys and sorrows, even second- or third-hand, made life easier. And because sometimes, especially when it rained, the summer retreat was boring. They wrote letters to each other in Russian and postcards in German; to her father, Rosa would write letters in German, or— like her mother—in Hebrew and Yiddish. In the first summer of the war they had conducted their correspondence only in German, in the second, they had gradually switched to Russian. From year to year, the fear of censorship seemed to diminish.

Rosa and Yasha wrote to each other because they were in love. Since they had been separated, they exchanged letters summer after summer, as often as they could. They even phoned each other, despite bad connections. In the beginning, these were secret letters sent via the post office box of their mutual friend, Trude Rosenthal. They read particularly sensitive when Rosa wrote, in the woods, with a pencil to her "black boy," like the one from Bad Harzburg to Berlin in the summer of 1915: "… all of a sudden, I wanted to see you, dear, so much that I certainly wouldn't mind flying to you in an airship." Her mother could sense the feelings of her seventeen-year-old daughter since that summer, when they had stayed with their grandmother, probably to save money, in the Albrecht Haus at 6 Dommesstrasse, with only six rooms, ten beds and no kosher kitchen. Despite the separation from Yasha and the simple accommodation, Rosa had enjoyed her first summer break after the beginning of the war. "I sit on the veranda and write," she said. "The weather is beautiful. Clear skies, sunshine and an enchantingly light and pleasant wind. A big chestnut tree protrudes with its branches all the way up to my table and it's so wonderful to write!" That summer, they had decided that Rosa from Bad Harzburg and Yasha from Berlin would send a photo to their relatives in Russia as a discreet indication of their relationship. By the following year, when Rosa, her mother and grandmother were taking the waters in Bad Neuenahr in the Rhineland, the relationship had intensified. She had already been bored then, as she was now in Polzin. She had longed for Yasha, even more than the year before, almost getting sick with desire. The daily telephone calls, the clandestine correspondence under her mother's nose or the open letters in view of the censorship, were an almost unbearable substitute. At that time, Rosa and Yasha had exchanged postcards on the subject of "spring awakening" and "first love," which depicted silhouettes of antique sculptures, veiled nudes and nymphs; his were hidden in an envelope, hers were open, because she knew that Yasha and Noma were alone in Schlüterstrasse. At that time Rosa had invented the most diverse, sometimes untranslatable nicknames for Yasha, her tomcat, her black, golden boy—Kisik, Kisya, Kota, Yashulya, Yashulenka, Chernenky, *malchik moi zolotoi*. And yet, she wrote to Yasha, she understood that a Russian prisoner of war who had left his loved one behind at home and had gone fighting in the field, not even receiving news from his relatives, was a thousand times worse off than she was. She had realized that it was selfish of her to cry over her being separated from Yasha for four weeks. Yet she did not stop crying on the first day.

Rosa's letter from August 15, 1917 continues:

> So, as you can see, Polzin is not an ideal place to stay, especially because it has not been developed as a spa. If Mommy doesn't need to take the waters here, we'll find somewhere more interesting to relax. But I certainly hope that, with God's help, Mom will recover well here, because the mud is highly praised. Mama has already taken the second bath today, yesterday a spruce needle bath, and today a mud bath. The doctor says Mom doesn't have to stay here for more than 4 weeks, because the baths are taken with great frequency.

Miriam Rosenberg had come to Polzin because of a foot problem. During previous retreats, she had primarily taken care of her mother, who suffered from diabetes. For years, Malka Kahan had therefore travelled to Bad Neuenahr in diverse company. That resort specialized in the treatment of diabetes.

"Carlsbad on the Rhine," Bad Neuenahr, also used its mineral and medicinal springs for spa treatments since the middle of the nineteenth century. Their Apollinaris Fountain and alkaline thermal baths were advertised as "acid-quenching, liquefying, mildly loosening and strengthening the organism." Like Polzin and Bad Harzburg, it had experienced its heyday before the war, registering at that time about as many guests from the European aristocratic elite and the German and Russian upper middle classes, among them many Jews. Neither village nor town, Bad Neuenahr had everything that Jewish guests needed in a resort: in addition to the sanatorium, bathhouse, theater, orchestra, casino and spa gardens, it also had restaurants with kosher cuisine, a *shochet* and a synagogue. In addition to a scant *minyan* of local Jews, it was home to several thousand Jewish and two dozen non-Jewish spa guests, a Jewish doctor, four doctors of Jewish origin, twenty-one more, according to a *Badebrief*. Diabetes, which Bad Neuenahr promised to cure, was then considered a "Jewish disease." Medical debates were conducted with distinctly ethnic overtones for over half a century. Research attributed the disease, especially among the Jewish bourgeoisie, to multiple factors, but above all to economic prosperity, everyday life in the big city, the tradition of consanguineous marriage and extreme nervousness.

From a Zionist perspective, diabetes was a consequence of the oppression of the Jews in the Diaspora, in the dingy and suffocating ghetto.

Bad Neuenahr was booming at the time when the Kahan's companies began to prosper. At the beginning of the century it experienced a gold-rush atmosphere similar to Baku. Fortune hunters and Rhineland cliques with contacts to the imperial family were among the investors. Huge spa facilities rose up from the meadows along the river Ahr. Hotels, raised quickly, showed off their proud facades and sumptuous interior decorations. By 1907, some of the Kahans, coming from Antwerp as well as from Baku, had already met in Bad Neuenahr, staying at the Villa Hedwig. Likewise, in 1911, when they had travelled from Antwerp and Kharkov, they had taken lodgings in Bonn's Kronenhotel and in the Villa Regina. Since then, they came almost every year. In 1912, they registered one after the other in the Grandhotel Flora and in the Bade- und Kurhotel. That summer Malka had been taking the waters together with Chaim, while Miriam stayed with Jonas in St. Moritz, until Chaim fled to Baden-Baden to escape the regulations and Malka's endless ramblings about illnesses. The Rosenbergs had then driven on from St. Moritz to Bad Kissingen. In the summer of 1913, before Chaim travelled to Vienna for the Eleventh Zionist Congress, he was a guest, with Malka, at the Villa Sanssouci. A group photo, presumably with arriving spa guests, shows Chaim Kahan in the first row, with proudly and worldly worn bowler hat, watch chain across his chest and cane in his hand. Before the beginning of the war, after their return from Palestine, in the summer of 1914, the two of them stayed, for the last time together, in the Villa Daheim; in 1916 Malka lodged without her husband, but with her daughter and granddaughter, in the Villa Rembrandt. Both houses were situated, like the Villa Hedwig, on the banks of the Ahr with a view of the spa gardens, park and casino. The war had begun in the immediate vicinity with the invasion of Belgium and had devastating consequences for both the Rhineland and Pomeranian spas. Workers left Neuenahr and joined the army. Parts of the Kurhotel and numerous guest houses were converted into military hospitals. The Apollinaris Fountain had been closed since the beginning of the war. Though the spa operation had not been stopped, it was severely restricted. The wealthy guests stayed away; instead, wounded soldiers were arriving, like in Polzin. From year to year there was less food, unlike in the "Pomeranian Switzerland."

Now and then, Rosa did take a bath in Polzin, but probably only because she was bored. Taking the waters was not close to her heart; she merely accompanied her mother, as was customary and appropriate for a Jewish daughter from a "good family." From Bad Harzburg, Yasha and Noma said nothing about treatments. The young people were not interested in the therapies, but rather wanted to have fun, to socialize, to seek tenderness—a central topic of their correspondence. Yasha met fellow members of the Association of Jewish Academics, but they left shortly after his arrival. He and Noma enjoyed the company of Max Lew and his wife for a few days before these returned to Berlin. During mealtimes, they talked to Mr. Cohen, a member of Bet Va'ad, the association for the revival and cultivation of the Hebrew language in Berlin, in which Rosa and Yasha were members. When he welcomed the first Sabbath in Bad Harzburg in the circle of *frumer daitscher* [pious German] Jews who, instead of waiting for darkness, had begun to pray while the sun was still high in the sky, Yasha became melancholy. They ditched, as soon as they could, their compatriot, who had already been living in exile in Germany for ten years and assimilated to such a degree that the cousins nicknamed him "gutta-percha" after the rubbery substance. Yasha was glad when he made the acquaintance of Herr Fuchs from Leipzig. "A Russian Jew—that's something else entirely," he wrote to Rosa. Herr Fuchs lived in the same hotel, was a Zionist and received all kinds of Jewish and Yiddish newspapers. He perked up when Zalman Shneour arrived, the globetrotter, Hebrew and Yiddish publicist and writer from the dynasty of the Lubavitcher Rebbe. Although already thirty, eight years older than Yasha, Zalman Shneour had also been interned during the war as an "enemy alien" of conscription age and belonged to the circle of family friends. Yasha characterized him as a difficult but flexible person with whom they could do something like going on excursions. In none of his letters to Rosa is there any mention of the Harzburgers and their reactions to the foreign guests during the war; nothing like Thea Sternheim's diary descriptions that describe how people would abuse her, on her way to the dairy, by yelling "*Russ, Russ*," while leaving her very fair companion unmolested.

Yasha and Rosa were excluded from the patriotically buoyed-up German public. They kept to themselves, in Jewish, preferably Eastern European Jewish circles. There are no Polziners in Rosa's letters either. Her mother, she wrote, enjoyed the village life; she was used to it and had often been to smaller towns. She refers to the spa public as "so-so." She stopped being bored when acquaintances from Berlin arrived or when she met young people from Königsberg, but above all when she made the acquaintance of Walther Freund, dentist in the military hospital. During the first summer of the war in Bad Harzburg, Max Kut, Yasha's friend from Berlin, had entertained her, showing her the Harz Mountains; during the second, in Bad Neuenahr, she would often be out and about with Mina Levstein from Łódź, alone or in company with their mothers, who were friends. Twenty-four-year-old Mina was recommended to Rosa's mother that summer by Grandfather Chaim, on the advice of aunt Rosalia, as a good match for Aron, and the marriage, which actually came about after the war, was perhaps initiated at that time in Bad Neuenahr. Match-making was a tradition in the spas. But the planned meeting of the two marriage candidates in Kislovodsk did not take place because of the war. The Caucasus spa had also changed to its detriment since the autumn of 1914. It was flooded with impoverished ladies, hard-up artists and young men from Moscow and St. Petersburg, who loved to ride through the streets on hired horses, wildly gesticulating, as Gaito Gazdanov relates in *An Evening with Claire*. Instead of Apollinaris, people in Kislovodsk drank Narzan and came to cure heart disease instead of diabetes, which is why Chaim Kahan sought help there in his last summers. During those years, the Baku Kahans regularly thought treatment in the Caucasian Kissingen. In the summer of 1917, they wanted to stay until after the New Year holiday, wrote Pinchas to his loved ones in Berlin and notified them of the arrival of a parcel.

Meals were eaten together. Yasha and Noma had their meals in the Parkhaus, Rosa and her mother Miriam at Finkelstein's. In the afternoons, the young men enjoyed visiting the Café Peters in Bad Harzburg, where they had the most delicious apple pies. Together with friends and acquaintances they strolled in the pumphouses, walked along promenades, under pergolas, through the small towns, spa parks and environs. Everywhere, there was opportunity for conversations of all kinds, about which the letters remain silent, however. Rosa briefly told Yasha of a long conversation about matters of the heart with her new friend, Fräulein Reiss, during a walk around Polzin. In Polzin, there was no reading hall, like in Harzburg or Neuenahr, where newspapers and magazines with rebus and crossword puzzles were displayed. Yasha would go to the Kurhaus in the evening to study the *Berliner Tageblatt* and the *Berliner Zeitung*. But the press that interested him most, the *Jüdische Rundschau* and the *Yeschurun*, he received by mail; it was also on display at Fifar's or in Mr. Fuchs's room. Once or twice in the evening the cousins went to the cinema, diagonally opposite the Parkhaus, which featured, to Yasha's delight, the brand-new film comedy *The Queen's Love Letter* with Henny Porten; it inspired him to imagine his marriage to Rosa as a sequence of spats and making-up, like in the movie. Other times they spent the evenings reading, writing, or playing cards and dice with Shneour in the hotel. Rosa did not write much about her evenings in Polzin. In Yasha's letters one can read that she often could not be reached by telephone. In Bad Neuenahr the Rosenberg ladies were spending the evenings in the Kurhaus with the Levsteins or, occasionally, also with one of the doctors, Dr. Albert Goldberg, and his wife. They had once been invited to an Erev Shabbat at the Goldbergs'. The concerts in the Kurhaus had not interested Rosa—she did not like spa music—and the military concerts in the park had even disturbed her letter-writing. She had gone to the Kurtheater once. They performed the operetta *A Waltz Dream*, which, like *The Queen's Love Letters*, was light entertainment about the compatibility of etiquette and emotions in an idyllic aristocratic world. On another occasion, she went with Mina to the spa's Great Entertainment Hall to watch the shadow theater *Living Silhouettes*, an event of the Bad Neuenahr Red Cross Foundation and Patriotic Women's' Association, where wounded soldiers presented the war in the last act.

The crowd that liked to meet in Polzin's only café in the evenings also included the dentist, Walther Freund, who, as Rosa reported, was wonderful at entertaining them. He had hundreds of "party pieces" ready and wrote many of them down for her. He called her Sonya because that was his favorite of all the Russian names. Together with seven letters she kept the poem "Love. Love is the greatest deity, it's the most beautiful religion …," which he had dedicated to her. At the end of the third week she wrote to Yasha that this summer retreat was one of the most beautiful. No other place had pleased her so much. The reason for this was the dentist whom she had already mentioned. Independently of each other, the two obviously enjoyed themselves in their summer resorts. While Rosa was beguiled by Walther Freund in Polzin, Yasha developed tender erotic fantasies in Bad Harzburg. In the family archives, two draft letters are preserved, to a certain Regina Petruschka in Leipzig, whose address he found carved into the balcony railing: "It was a pleasure for me to imagine that, a year ago, a young lady lived in the same room and had the same wonderful view from her balcony." The second letter was to a young lady whose name and address were written on a bench on the path to the chalet. Leaves one wondering if luring pen pals was common in the summer idyll in those days. Gaito Gazdanov's narrator remembered Kislovodsk as an "air temple" on the mountain, whose white walls were littered with sentimental inscriptions.

Rosa and Yasha would go on excursions from Polzin and Bad Harzburg respectively, to explore, in company, the surroundings, sending each other the usual postcards from well-known lookouts as souvenirs, waving to each other from idyllic distances. Most of them came from the Harz Mountains—from the Dairy, the Waterfall, the Harzburg ruins and the Bismarck monument on castle hill; the Rabenklippe, Eckertal and Brocken; the town halls in Wernigerode and Goslar and the Hotel Silberborn. Yasha was out and about more often than

Rosa, roaming with Shneour and Noma. The ladies had once hiked from Bad Neuenahr to Walporzheim and the Bunte Kuh, a rock in the vineyards above the Ahr valley. From Polzin, Rosa took a boat trip to Fünfsee. Ten, maybe twelve people participated. Walther Freund was also on board. Rosa sent Yasha a postcard from there, with greetings and signatures from all the day-trippers.

Political news trickled into the letters from the wartime summer resorts like isolated fragments of an inexorable reality, at first only in hints such as: "It's really bad when you think about it a bit. But you're a Jew, and you mustn't lose hope."

In the summer of 1917 Yasha learned from Trude Rosenthal that her brother Arthur was still stationed at the Küstrin garrison. An empty envelope, addressed to Jacob Kahan, Bad Harzburg, sent by a certain Field Auxiliary Doctor Aron, Münster, from Charlottenburg, indicates that Yasha also received news of the war from other sources. In his letters to Rosa he was now able to take a more concrete stand. He expressed his joy at the loss of territory by the Ottomans; quoted State Secretary Richard von Kühlmann's hopeful words that after careful consideration he could say that they were entering the final year of the World War; was delighted that Reich Chancellor Georg Michaelis spoke of the internationalization of Palestine. This mattered to them (with three exclamation marks). He took heart from the reaction by the two newcomers in the Reich government to the Pope's appeal for peace, before the main committee of the Reichstag; it promised a turnaround. He was glad that Rosa was interested in politics.

Both were active in the Zionist and Hebrew movements and belonged, like their grandfather, to the Russian religious faction. Yasha's "social" activity, as Rosa called it, found its first public expression during those weeks in a comprehensive publication on "the National Demands of the Jewish People in Russia and its Political Parties," which were serialized over two editions of the Orthodox *Yeshurun*, following a lecture Yasha had given in the Association of Jewish Academics. This publication, Yasha's joy, Rosa's pride and the object of Rubashov's praise, provides comprehensive information about the political structures of Eastern European Jews and is a surprisingly light and easy read even for today's reader. It was the subject of some of Rosa's letters. A year earlier, the idea of returning to Russia had been a disturbing fantasy for Rosa. The big political events of the summer of 1917 obviously gave hope to her and Yasha. Germany's territorial gains in Poland, Lithuania and the Ukraine made it possible to resume connections with Eastern Europe from Berlin. The fall of the autocracy opened up new life and economic prospects for Russia. The losses of the Ottoman Empire were a step towards the realization of the establishment of a Jewish home in Palestine. On September 2, Rosa congratulated Yasha— the best Zionist she knew—on the opening of the American Jewish Congress, which she wanted to celebrate as a "national day." Both hoped that the Congress would bring "much good," which for them probably meant peace initiatives and the strengthening of Jews as a nation in the family of nations. But the Congress was postponed, something Yasha was aware of; it did not take place until after the end of the war.

In Polzin, Rosa dreamt of Palestine. She was considering taking a four- to-six-week course in Berlin about "flower arranging," to become an "arts- and craftswoman." She was glad that Yasha liked the idea. They had the same taste after all. So, for the sake of Palestine, she said, it was nice to know something about it. For the time being she was content to strengthen the feeling of togeth- erness and anticipation by eagerly reading the *Jüdische Rundschau*, where the news on the last pages under the headings "Emergency Action for Palestine," "Golden Book," or "Herzl Forest" had a similar function to the social net- works of today. For example, on these pages, Yasha expressed his thanks with a donation for the recovered pince-nez that he had lost during a trip to the Torfhaus, which he made in the luggage rack on the roof of the bus, because there was no free space inside. Congatulations were also published there. From the "Emergency" section Rosa learned that Rubashov's then-protégé, Gerhard (Gershom) Scholem, had been exempted (from military service in Allenstein) and was back in Berlin, thank God.

The correspondence with Yasha's parents beyond the Russian front arrived as contraband via Stockholm or Copenhagen, causing Yasha and Rosa to dis- cuss censorship. Rosalia Kahan had complained bitterly about Yasha's bland letters. She had not seen her son for two years. Yasha apologized, explaining that the mail was censored so heavily during the war, going through so many hands, that he was not able to write about intimate thoughts under these cir- cumstances. He envied his mother who was able to do this. But Rosa countered that he shouldn't care about the censorship. Nobody could know who was read- ing the letters. His mother's tightly written eight-page-long letter touched and affected him. He wrote to Rosa that it was nice to finally receive such letters, despite the criticism.

Rosalia Kahan had spent that summer with her family in Tsarskoe Selo, the former seat of the tsars near Petrograd. "We live in a luxurious dacha," she wrote, "how nice it would be if you, Yashunya, were with me too; how good it would be to sit and chat together in the pretty little garden." Arusia, her youngest, was with her, studying with a tutor to make the grade, as was her nephew from Baku, the fifteen-year-old Lolia. Rosalia was afraid that Yasha would become alienated from her; she was worried about him. "You definitely need versatile interests, serious occupations and company; life has something for everyone. I often doubt whether you have all that. The years go by. The best, the strongest, the brightest." Rosa understood Yasha's mother. He should finally write to her about their love, which was no longer a childhood friendship, but had taken on concrete forms in the last two years, if for no other reason, than to obtain her consent.

Contrary to Yasha's mother, Rosa's mom was in the know. So Yasha was all the more surprised that Aunt Marie, as Miriam was called at that time, had suggested in Polzin that Rosa should join Yasha and Noma in Bad Harzburg for two weeks, since the mountains had always done her good. She had always been against it, and now she was for it? But Rosa, as much as she would have liked to be with Yasha, did not want to leave her mother alone and stayed in Polzin, which she increasingly liked, thanks to Walther Freund's stimulating company. He had obviously fallen in love with Rosa and she had given him hope. The exchange of letters after her departure, which lasted for months, encouraged him to think about a reunion, making the connection. Shortly after the peace treaty of Brest-Litovsk, in April 1918, a letter from her, after a long pause, had stirred his soul into turmoil. Once again he tried to conquer her. Neither a convinced Zionist nor a pious Jew, he hoped that he was her only "friend of the heart" in contrast to her companions who were "friends of the spirit." She would know what he felt for her. When he read in the newspaper about prisoner exchanges, Bolshevik atrocities and pogroms, he was worried about Rosa, he said, and assumed that she was no longer in Germany. He would be happy if she came back to Polzin. All military hospitals have been reequipped, Finkelstein's as well.

The magnificent multi-story Parkhaus in Bad Harzburg with its ornate wooden Art Nouveau style frontage on Herzog-Wilhelmstrasse, now a pedestrian mall, has been thoroughly restored, and now only the façade remains. The Labor Exchange has rented the mezzanine floor, while the rest of the building has been divided into condominiums. A memorial plaque on the street commemorates the kosher-run house. The wooden synagogue in the garden no longer exists, but the Café Peters does. The Villa Daheim at 8–10 Lindenstrasse, Bad Neuenahr, became the Lilac Residence retirement home. The Villa Rembrandt at 8–9 Georg-Kreuzbergstrasse is still a guest house today. The restaurant Kowalski on Poststrasse, where the ladies used to have lunch and made their telephone calls to Berlin, has been replaced by a supermarket. During the second half of the twenties, the Kurhaus Finkelstein in Polzin had been bought by the Polzin doctor, Dr. Neuberg, and renamed Parkkurhaus. After 1933 it became property of the Council and served, for a long time, as town and spa administration. Now, it is the Parkkurhaus again. The spas have lost their charm, their aura was destroyed by the wars. Today, thermal and water treatments are only marginal aspects of the wellness program.

In the last summer of the war, Rosa and her mother actually went to Polzin again, but Yasha and Noma did not go to the Harz Mountains; they went instead to Bad Salzbrunn. However, no report from Yasha, about the Silesian summer retreat, has survived, while Rosa's letters from the Polzin summer of 1918 open a new chapter. She announced her engagement to Yasha. After the war, Walther Freund settled in Polzin as a dentist. In his last letter to Rosa in May 1919 he congratulated her on her marriage.

CHAPTER 10

Economic Management in Times of War and Revolution. Petrograd

What did Jacob Kahan live on in Berlin or in the summer resorts? How did Jonas Rosenberg and Bendet Kahan finance the livelihood of their families during the war? Although they had founded an investment company in 1915, nothing is known about its activities. Companies owned by "enemy aliens" were threatened with expropriation, which explicitly affected Russian citizens from autumn 1917 onwards. The Kahans and Rosenbergs were cut off, not only from relatives, but also from businesses and accounts in Petrograd, Kharkov and Baku. The war front ran between Russia and Germany. The border was impassable for civilians and closed for money, merchandise and mail traffic.

On February 17, 1917, immediately before the great unrest in Petrograd, the strike at the Putilov factory, the food riots and the overthrow of the autocracy initiated by the workers' demonstrations, Rosalia Kahan wrote a letter to Jonas and Miriam, Bendet and Judith and to her beloved Yashenka (by which route it arrived in Berlin is not revealed): "What an abyss of time and events lies between us, my dear ones, since that day when I sent you my last letter. I have pondered so much and lived through such a lot, which I cannot convey in one letter. Now you have already understood my silence. ... How hard even silence is in such bitter times." In addition to war and general unrest came personal suffering: the separation from her oldest son and from relatives; the death of her father-in-law. In her letter, Rosalia described the last months of his life. Already in January 1916, Chaim Kahan had suffered a severe heart attack, was bedridden for three weeks and recovered only gradually. Nevertheless, he had gone to Baku for Passover, then to Kislovodsk and from there back to Petrograd. Two weeks before Rosh Hashanah, he had had another severe heart attack and despite all his efforts he had not managed to regain his strength. He felt weak and barely got up. From time to time he went out for a drive, but finally he did not go out into the street at all, receiving only a few visitors at his bedside. On the holidays, a *minyan* was called for him into the house. Mentally he remained present until the end, but emotionally he was unstable, mostly depressed. On his last day, November 28, he was better than during the preceding days. He felt good, went for a walk, ate and drank. He could sleep again, which was already rare. On that day, his doctors examined him and found his condition satisfactory. They recommended a change of scenery, a trip to Baku. Rosalia and Baruch had already begun planning the trip. "In the evening, there were guests for tea, who left at half past eleven," wrote Rosalia. "Suddenly he wasn't feeling well. We called the doctors, but by a quarter to two in the morning he was no more, our unforgettable father, our pride and joy."

Chaim Kahan spent his last days at 23 Troitskaya, today Rubinshteina, Street, which is located in the historic business district of St. Petersburg. Chaim had rented an apartment for the family there after the acquisition of Petrol in 1912. Before that, he used to stay in the Hotel Severnaya on Nevsky Prospekt, just around the corner, when he was in the capital. 23 Troitskaya Street was at that time a brand-new Art Nouveau residential complex with a forecourt and six floors, which belonged to the St. Petersburg Merchants' Association. It was renovated a few years earlier and is as magnificent today as it was then. The apartments at 23 Troitskaya Street were spacious, four to seven rooms, with a parlor, maids' chambers and two toilets. Like in the apartment of the famous lawyer in Asch's *Petersburg*, the Kahans gathered around a table that took up almost the entire length of the parlor-like dining room, with dignitaries, relatives, friends and acquaintances: the St. Petersburg Rabbi Moshe Eisenstadt; Rabbi Shlomo Aronson from Kiev, who had coorganized the Beilis trial, and his brother, the businessman Meir Aronson; the lawyer Oskar Gruzenberg perhaps, who became famous for his defense in that Kiev trial; Michael Pollak of the transport company Mazut, who had an office in the capital; and Shalom Asch. Asch was in St. Petersburg in 1912 and met Pollak there, who donated a lot of money to a publishing project, invited Asch on a trip to Palestine and promised to introduce him to Rothschild. It is possible that Asch was introduced by Pollak to the Kahans and the world of the Baku oil industrialists.

It was not easy to recover after that blow, Rosalia wrote. "God sent us sorrow and gave us strength to bear it. We found it difficult to keep calm, despite the consolation by our friends who did not leave us alone. We struggled for a long time, not being able to find our way back to reality; but the circumstances of life are stronger than we are. Slowly we resumed work and it was as if life was getting back on track." In the office, work had been piling up, which the administrators began to tackle listlessly, working in harmony with the employees. Meanwhile, business was flourishing. "Baruch went to Pinchas to familiarize himself with the new shareholder business. I accompanied him," said Rosalia.

Chaim Kahan's death was the end of an era. The patriarch had left the family when the oil economy was booming, his companies were expanding and the old order was collapsing. "There was general jubilation, especially in the big cities, when the tsarist regime was deposed, and I myself witnessed in Baku, how strangers were hugging and kissing with joy in the streets," Aron remembered. Rosalia and Baruch experienced this at the center of power, in Petrograd, but in both the open and closed letters to Berlin, they hardly said a word about the tumultuous political events—the general strike, the demonstrations against the bread shortage, the mutiny by the war-weary soldiers, the escalation of the protest to revolutionary upheaval, the abdication, later the arrest of the tsar—the first signs of the disintegration of the empire. They also did not mention the power struggle between the Duma and the workers-and-soldiers councils, the formation of the Provisional Government and its first measures: the lifting of ethnic, sectarian and permanent restrictions, the declaration of civil rights and freedoms and the promise of a constitution. As of March 22, 1917, Jews were legally equal under the Russian civic administration. A positive omen for the Kahans. Nevertheless, the businessmen in Shalom Asch's Petrograd and Moscow were worried, wavering between hope and fear. The times were deceptive. Nothing was certain, everything seemed open. The political parties and social interest groups were locking horns, but none was able to take power to end the provisional state of affairs. The war had developed a dynamic of its own, and the transitional government proved too weak to counter this, to successfully conduct peace negotiations. In this mind-boggling situation, time seemed to be condensing, in contrast to the German summer holidays during the war. The Kahans in Petrograd had to reorientate themselves after Chaim's death and make decisions. In general, the government's demand to the oil industry continued to apply: "Increase production! Send more crude oil! Bring as much as possible to Petrograd! Make yourselves independent of English coal! Avoid the railways! Navigate the waterways." As entrepreneurs in the industries vital to the war effort, the Kahans, like Asch's naphtha king Goldstein, used their opportunities as best they could and for as long as they could. They showed themselves to be patriots, but they also didn't put all their eggs in one basket. They made use of their new rights and freedoms, politically too. They participated actively in the organization of the first officially authorized Zionist Congress from May 24 to June 6 in the Great Hall of the Petrograd Conservatorium with more than one hundred thousand participants. "And that without Poland and Lithuania," as Yasha wrote in the *Yeshurun*. The *Jüdische Rundschau* gave it detailed coverage, which enabled the Berlin relatives to follow the proceedings. There was no talk of leaving Russia, although after the brutal treatment of the Jews at the hands of the tsarist army in the war-front region, instigating expulsions and pogroms, many Jews in Petrograd adopted Germanophilia over patriotism. Politically, their status remained uncertain. The loyalty of the Jews had been a public issue since the beginning of the war. The connection to relatives on the other side of the war front could have been interpreted as treason, and they were running the risk of being defamed as "enemy aliens."

After the death of his father, Baruch took over the management of the company according to patriarchal tradition and had his younger brother instruct him in the "new shareholder business." On May 24, 1917, he reported from Tsarskoe Selo via Glad & Co in Copenhagen to Berlin:

> My dear ones! We have relocated here to the dacha and are very happy. May it please God that we receive frequent messages from you. At the moment, the subscription for the issue of another four million Petrol shares is in progress. Because of the general mood, we thought the public would not accept them, but that did not happen at all. The public has subscribed to some of the shares and we have taken the rest.

Barely four weeks later, one day after the start of the Kerensky offensive, by which the Provisional Government broke the promise to negotiate peace, the Petrol's corporation semi-annual shareholders' meeting took place in Petrograd, at 6 Stremyannaya, on June 19 at 11 a.m. Present were the Chairman of the Board, Baron Alexander von Günzburg, Director Baruch Kahan, his deputy and brother David, his sister Rachel Ettinger and three other shareholders— the employee and engineer E. V. Yegorov, a certain I. S. Günzburg and the lawyer Berngard L. Trachtenberg. Mark I. Lifshits took the minutes.

Stremyannaya is a side street parallel to Nevsky Prospekt, between Fontanka and the Moscow train station, a few minutes' walk from Troitskaya, also in the historic business district of St. Petersburg. At that time, it belonged to the First Section of the Moscow District. It has always been the seat of Petrol. 6

Stremyannaya is still an office building. Before the war, several corporations had their offices in this sprawling four-story edifice with its five impressive entrance gates and austere facade, built in 1870 by August I. Lange in the classicist style. The best known was the Russian Transport and Insurance Company Inc. The Kahans used the Petrol office as their headquarters. What satisfaction, what a feeling of elation it must have been for Chaim Kahan to move into rooms in the dignified office district of the capital, where he had often knocked on doors, petitioned, or negotiated in vain. Thanks to his success on the periphery of the Empire, via the detour to the port city of Baku on the Caspian Sea on the other side of the Caucasus, he had created a position for himself as a Jewish merchant of the First Guild, in the center, in St. Petersburg. Although the Kahan's oil companies were among the outsiders in the industry, even during the war, they were able to hold their own successfully.

Three and a half years earlier, in this office, Chaim Kahan had founded Russian-Baltic Mineral Oil Company about the same time as the Caucasus-Volga Industry & Trading Company. Since then, it too had been managed at 6 Stremyannaya, while the plants were located in Riga, which is why this corporation bore a German name, Russisch-Baltische Mineralölwerke, until the beginning of the war. Chaim had paved the way between Baku and Riga since the early 1890s, when he rented and purchased tank cars from the Russian-Baltic Wagon Factory there. With the refinery in Riga, 30 Kronenstrasse, on a one-hectare plot of land, which he had leased at first from Richard Menzbir, then bought, for 172,000 rubles, in the summer of 1914, he had created a third location for oil processing in the north of the empire, alongside Baku in the south and Knyazevka on the middle Volga.

On January 28, 1914, an account for the Russian-Baltic Mineral Oil Company was opened in the State Bank with half of the share capital of 375,000 rubles. On the same day, the shareholders, Chaim Kahan and those invited by him to participate, owners of the 7,500 shares with the right to 750 votes, had met in the afternoon, between 2 and 5 p.m., at 6 Stremyannaya. David chaired the meeting; Chaim welcomed the shareholders, summarized the history of the company's foundation and presented the official authorization of the Ministry. Richard Menzbir and Aron and David Kahan were elected as directors, and Baruch Kahan and Chaim's son-in-law David Ettinger as their representatives. Mark I. Lifshits took the minutes on that occasion, too. Menzbir resigned after the purchase of the refinery. Baron Günzburg took over the chairmanship of the board as he had done with Petrol, while Baruch got promoted to the position of third director. The corporation was a relatively small family business, the existence of which had to be certified upon request by the Ministry, in case of doubt. The Kahans controlled it without having an absolute majority of the shares. The company did not make too much profit, but was going to come in useful. Before the war, it was represented in Berlin by Max Lew. A few days after the outbreak of war, the refinery was in flames; the fire and the danger of German occupation caused the share capital to be halved. Fortunately for the owners, the factory had been evacuated to Russia with their own funds, helped by Petrol and the Vacuum Oil Company in the autumn of 1915. Because of the war with Germany it was renamed—like the Russian capital—and now bore a Russian name, Obshchestvo Russko-Baltiiskikh neftepromyshlennykh i torgovykh zavodov, or Rubanito for short. Yasha, the Rosenbergs, Bendet and Judith Kahan had witnessed the founding of the company in the last year of peace, but not what happened to Rubanito during the war and the revolution. In October 1916, Baruch had let his brother and brother-in-law in Berlin know that he would send them two powers of attorney from Rubanito through Gerson Oppenheim, an employee of the Danish company L. C. Glad & Co.

From the summer of 1916, 6 Stremyannaya was also the office of the Binəqədi Oil Industry and Trading Company, Kahan's fourth corporation. The successor to the Pétroles de Binagadi (Bakou) Société Anonyme, founded in Brussels in 1899 with Belgian capital, had existed since 1908. Aron speaks in his memoirs of "Totalité shares of Binagadinskoye." In 1914, its share capital was one million rubles. It owned oil fields with industrial facilities on its own land in Binəqədi, which were among the oldest and most profitable on the Absheron peninsula. For this purpose, the corporation had its own sixteen-kilometer pipeline from Binəqədi to the refineries in the Black City. The Kahans acquired the majority of the Binəqədi Oil Industry and Trading Company shares in the middle of the war, half a year before Chaim died. "The purchase was my father's initiative," Aron recalled. But, according to the company's articles of incorporation, "Russian subjects of the Jewish denomination" were not allowed to hold executive positions. They were not allowed to be elected to the shareholders' meeting or the board of directors or the management, nor were they allowed to manage or administer the corporation's real estate. So how did the Kahans manage to get on the board of the company, nevertheless?

Already during the second year of the war (1915), the Ural-Caucasus Inc. and the Trading House Stuken & Co. had been the main shareholders of the Binəqədi Oil Industry and Trading Company. The Ural-Caucasus, established in 1912 in St. Petersburg (with a share capital of four million rubles) bought and sold iron, pipes and machinery; it built oil production and other technical plants. Stuken & Co. in Moscow, with a branch in Baku, traded in optical equipment under the management of Charles E. Stuken, merchant of the First Guild and hereditary honorary citizen. The chairman of Binəqədi Oil Industry and Trading Company in 1915 was the aristocratic technician Yury M. Tishchenko, partner and senior manager of P. O. Gukasov & Co, a company owned by Armenian Baku oil magnates, the brothers Pavel, Avram and Arkasha Gukasov (Gukasyan), which traded in iron and cement. The Binəqədi Oil Industry and Trading Company's board of directors also included the cement manufacturer Aleksandr D. Zeifert, the administrator of Gukasov & Co. Tigran A. Khandamirov and Gustav L. Nobel, a son of Ludwig Nobel, who had been in charge of Branobel in Baku since the summer. Most of them were working in the Baku industry and all of them claimed to be Christian-Russian subjects, some of them of Armenian origin, except for Nobel, who was a Swedish citizen. But even then, Jewish shareholders were already involved, without appearing by name in the official papers: the Baku industrialists, Heinrich Goldlust and Rudolf Lammaraner had held leading positions at Binəqədi Oil Industry and Trading Company until the beginning of the war; one as a member of the board, the other as the director. Lammaraner and Goldlust's son Emil, like his father honorary consul of the Habsburg Empire in Transcaucasia and partner of the trading house Goldlust & Sons in Baku, as well as a certain Mayer-Galler from Germany, owned shares in the Ural-Caucasus. Although being of Jewish origin, they were considered foreigners and were thus exempt from the restrictions imposed on Jews in the Russian Empire. However, after the outbreak of the war, in the summer of 1915, a Jew with Russian citizenship had joined the game as the major shareholder of Binəqədi Oil Industry and Trading Company, the third largest after the Ural-Caucasus and Stuken & Co. This was Savely L. Shifrin, the owner of the chemical factory for the production of sulphuric acid and mastic asphalt in Baku, which had a department for oil processing. He was to be included in the board of directors. The company had already applied for the admission of Jews to the executive committee before the war began.

Since the beginning of the war, the attention of state supervision had shifted. Despite the public discussion about the loyalty of the Jews in Russia, it was not them but the "enemy aliens" in the economy that were the problem now. Appropriate restrictive clauses, prescribed by the Council of Ministers, were inserted in the company statutes. At first, the "unwelcome" securities belonging to the "enemy aliens," Goldlust, Lammaraner and Mayer-Galler, could still hide behind the company shares of Ural-Caucasus. But it was only after the situation was revealed and the Ural-Caucasus had withdrawn from the corporation, in the summer of 1917, that Binəqədi Oil Industry and Trading Company received permission for a second capital increase of four million rubles.

Rudolf Lammaraner, who was three years younger than Baruch, had worked for Goldlust & Sons since the age of twenty (1885) as an accountant, correspondent and finally as an authorized signatory and had represented Honorary Consul Emil Goldlust in his absence. He was arrested in Baku in 1916 and interned as an "enemy alien" in Tsivilsk, Kazan Province. He died of pneumonia in the local hospital on March 5, 1917. Emil Goldlust had been out of the country when the war began and had not returned to Baku. After 1918, he lived in Vienna.

The Kahans bought the "unwelcome" securities and acquired the controlling stake of Binəqədi Oil Industry and Trading Company in that precarious situation. Chaim Kahan had maintained business contacts with the Goldlust and Shifrin companies from the 1890s. Like his own, they were among the smaller Jewish oil companies in Baku. All three were connected by their work for Rothschilds' Caspian-Black Sea Oil Industry and Trading Company and their competition against Branobel. Since the summer of 1916, Pinchas Kahan and Vulf Dembo had been on the board of directors not only of Petrol, but also of Binəqədi Oil Industry and Trading Company. The chairman was Gustav L. Nobel. Of the old board members, Khandamirov and Zeifert were still on the board. They were joined by Nikita A. Melikov, son of the Armenian oil entrepreneur Andrei S. Melikov. David Kahan was a candidate. The audit committee consisted of two Jewish and three Russian shareholders. The managing director in Baku was Genrikh L. Gertsberg. The main shareholder of Binəqədi Oil Industry and Trading Company was now *Petrol Inc.*

Unlike the three companies the Kahans had already controlled before the war, which I identified by means of letterheads in the archives, I found Binəqədi Oil Industry and Trading Company only mentioned in a few letters and diary passages as a family property. On October 12, 1917, Yasha wrote to his parents that he had recently received a greeting from them by finding the balance sheets of three of their companies printed in the newspaper: Petrol, Binəqədi Oil Industry and Trading Company and Caucasus-Volga Industry & Trading Company. "It was a pleasant surprise for all of us, especially the good result." On October 21, Jonas Rosenberg followed up by saying that he had read in the newspaper about the dividend payments of their companies and would be extremely grateful to his brothers-in-law if they deigned to inform him about the business. Presumably, Yasha and his uncle had read this information, which had appeared in the difficult to obtain *Petrograd Stock Exchange News*, in the Trade Agreement Association's journal *Der Deutsch-Russische Wirtschaftskrieg*, to which Yasha had cryptically referred to in his letter as TAAJ. The Trade Agreement Association was founded in 1900 by Georg von Siemens to promote German exports and an economic policy supporting them. It provided its one hundred and sixty members—chambers of commerce, trade associations and industrial associations—with information about the financial market and industrial production beyond the front lines during the German-Russian economic war. Two of the Kahan's corporations, *Petrol* and Binəqədi Oil Industry and Trading Company, had oil fields, were companies with tradition and were listed on the Petrograd Stock Exchange as owner-managed companies. Except for the Russian-Baltic Mineral Oil Company, they had expanded and increased their share capital during the war, thus keeping pace with the inflation rate.

The war brought to light the weaknesses of the Russian economy: the excess of state control and foreign debt. Before the war, the state had steered the economy by a lending policy, not least due to the dual function of the state bank as a trading bank and an underwriter; during the war it did so by placing orders with industry. Both strategies were largely financed by government bonds in Great Britain and France. The declaration of war had come at a moment of deep depression of the Russian financial market. The stock exchange was closed, and it was forbidden to sell stock. But from mid-1915 the situation was reversed. During 1916, a war economy had emerged: a hunger for goods, price hikes and inflation. Most of the industry worked for high prices on the basis of government orders. The profits of the companies rose steeply.

Petrol's shareholders meeting in June 1917 opened with a management report of its activities. The company was in the black, had votes in the Congress of Baku's Oil Entrepreneurs and also had an office in Moscow. In 1916 it had made a surplus of 1.3 million rubles. The selling price of crude oil had risen by a few kopecks during that period. The production costs, however, had almost doubled, labor and materials had become more expensive. By February 1917 the price of goods had risen fourfold, and the purchasing power of the ruble had fallen dramatically. The ruble had only a quarter of its prewar purchasing power.

The price increases for oil products were caused by the growing demand for mazut from companies that were essential for the war effort. Petroleum was also in greater demand among the population, which in some places had increased by refugees from the frontline area, as lighting material and, due to the high price of firewood, also as heating fuel for stoves and ovens. Prices were even driven up further by the withholding of goods.

More corporations than ever before developed lively activities with enormous capital input, reviving the stock market. The reasons for this were manifold. With the beginning of the war, the ruble had collapsed. War-related government orders drove up industrial production. Because of the abundance of free capital, interest rates fell and stock prices rose. The demand for shares to be invested in the revalued monetary capital also increased. New, fast-changing alliances between banks and financial capital groups were forged. Companies that had been dependent on foreign corporations before the war and had now accumulated free capital merged and acquired share control packages of other companies. After the "enemy aliens" among the shareholders had been driven out of the Russian financial market, their Russian favorites, like Binəqədi Oil Industry and Trading Company, took over the ownership and management of the orphaned companies, by taking advantage of the vacuum.

Petrol's management reported to the shareholders' meeting in June 1917 that, due to the war, less oil was being transported by rail and the industry's needs could therefore not be met—with the result that production had to be restricted. The Baku and Knyazevka plants operated with interruptions. In the past six months, the corporation had exported a good six million *puds* of petroleum and oil residues from Baku to Astrakhan by water, but was only able to ship three-quarters of them further because of the chaos in the Volga traffic. The rest was sold in Astrakhan.

There was a substantial lack of war-essential materials such as oil and steel on the market. "Oil hunger" became the buzzword. While the demand for war materials grew, production decreased, as technical standards could not be maintained due to obsolete machinery and lack of skilled maintenance workers. Many engineers, stigmatized as "enemy aliens," had left the country. In addition, there was a lack of income from oil exports, especially to the countries of the Central Powers, from which technology used to be bought previously in return. Because of inflation, there was a shortage of iron and steel as raw materials. The production of quality oils declined, but the supply of inferior oil, mazut, increased.

In the summer of 1917, Petrol wanted to further increase its own fleet on the Volga and Caspian Sea in an effort to expand the company, while at the same time, strengthening its influence over other companies. However, the available funds were not sufficient for this purpose, so another capital increase was requested. According to the minutes of the shareholders' meeting, this did not have to be done immediately, but since the process of planning and implementation was taking time, the company wanted to apply for a new share issue, of eight million rubles, as soon as possible. In view of the "extraordinary circumstances" and the desired investments, the company asked the Ministry to be allowed to bypass the usual cost estimates. It also planned to acquire buildings in Baku, Astrakhan and Saratov. In return, it requested permission to take out a mortgage of up to four million rubles.

The speculative bubble, which was driven up by the hunger for goods, further increased the accumulation of money by companies. On the one hand, the free market was restricted by government orders, which weakened the corporations, and on the other hand, the increased economic power led to the formation of new companies, including in the oil industry. The accumulation of enormous monetary capital, resulting from inflation, had found no investment possibilities in industry; as a result, it went into the money market and expanded it enormously. For the first time in Russia, an independent market of speculative securities emerged on the basis of the war-inflationary economy without the intervention of the banks. This gave rise to a new type of dividend holder: instead of pensioner, there appeared the industrialist and the powerful trader, who had accumulated large amounts of monetary capital, invested in shares and did not depend on bank loans.

In view of the generally precarious economic situation and the phenomenon of "oil hunger" the Russian government, in particular, attempted in various ways to influence the oil industry, which was financially strong and important during the war. In the spring of 1915, it developed a project for state oil production on the Absheron Peninsula, but this was thwarted by the merger of oil companies and joint production in new oil fields. In the summer of the same year, as a concerted action with banks and corporations, she initiated the establishment of four different commissions to regulate the most important areas of the national economy: industry, transport, heating materials and food supply. Nevertheless, the biggest problem, the high price of oil, remained unsolved. By the end of 1915, the government had countered this with fixed prices, but only a few months later, in March 1916, the oil industry forced another price increase. As a result, the oil tax was extended, and from then on it was levied on processing, oil products and crude oil. Sales and distribution were to be organized by the state, but was not implemented. Attempts to regulate the transport from the oil fields, the Volga depots and the distribution of petroleum, mazut and other oil products to consumers by means of licensing procedures were also made in vain. The plan to make state purchases of Romanian oil failed as well. In short, in the oil industry, no cooperation between government and industry was achieved, neither state monopoly nor imposed management was enforced.

The corporations operated largely uncontrolled, sometimes under devastating production conditions.

Encouraged by political events, the Petrol board of directors requested in June 1917 that discriminatory provisions from the Tsarist era, restricting economic freedom for Jews, be removed from the company's statutes. The board was particularly concerned about the provision that land for oil production outside the Caucasus region, could only be acquired with the special permission of the responsible ministries. The minutes list all the relevant authorities by name: the Ministry of Land and State Property, the Ministry of Finance, the Ministry of the Interior and the Provincial Administration of the Caucasus, as well as the Ministry of War with regard to the Districts of Ter and Kuban. Petrol demanded the lifting of the ban on acquiring real estate outside the port cities and certain urban settlements, outside the towns and *shtetls* of the Pale of Settlement. The publications of the joint-stock company were to appear only in the *Trade and Industry Journal* and no longer in the various government gazettes. The deadlines for invitations to shareholders' meetings were to be shortened. At general shareholders' meetings, the presence of shareholders with papers worth one-fifth of the share capital was to be sufficient. The passage stating that the managing director could not be Jewish should be deleted. The company no longer wanted to have to operate "with the permission of the Ministry of Land Management and State Property." Instead, the approval by the Ministry of Trade and Industry should be sufficient. In short, they wanted to operate more freely.

As far as the commitment of Petrol to its workers was concerned, it had clearly increased over the years and had become clearer. While the corporation had spent no more than a few hundred rubles on "medicines and treatment for employees and workers" in 1914, more than five thousand rubles were invested in a relief fund during the following year. By January 1917 the corporation had already budgeted twice that amount for a Savings, Credit and General Relief Fund. Now the Relief Fund was to be converted into a cultural and educational fund, endowed with 50,000 rubles, in memory of the recently deceased director and main shareholder, Chaim Kahan.

Despite depreciation due to fire damage, a regular occurrence in the oil industry and distribution difficulties caused by the war, Petrol's business was good during the war and the revolutionary year, as evidenced by the balance sheets of 1916 and 1917 and the renewed capital increases at the beginning and in the middle of 1917. The ownership of factories, conveyor equipment, loading stations, administrative buildings including furnishings, tank wagons, freighters and barges increased steadily. The 1914 balance sheets still showed a capital of four and a half million rubles, which had increased to around five million in 1915 and to almost six million in 1916.

The Kahans initially experienced the adaptation to the Russian war economy as a development opportunity. An early advantage resulted from the convergence of a war economy with favorable employment opportunities. At Petrol, Jews were admitted as main shareholders and directors. This gave the oil wholesalers access to production. In addition, Petrol was exempt from paying taxes for several years due to the investments it had made. For the first time, it was possible to combine extraction, processing and distribution and to operate comprehensively. As a result of inflation, the hunger for goods and transport bottlenecks, it was now feasible to achieve a certain independence from large corporations and public transport. The Caucasus-Volga Industrial & Trading Company sold part of its tank wagons. Petrol bought ships, making itself more independent of the railways, which, because they were primarily used for war purposes, were only available to a limited extent for the private sector.

The overall revival of the economy, due to government contracts, had a particularly beneficial effect on the oil industry, which was vital to the war effort. The Kahans' companies, too, supplied the war industry. The military proved to be a generous customer. A letter, signed by Baruch Kahan and dated November 8, 1916 from Petrol to the Special Executive Committee for Governmental Supervision of Commercial and Industrial Enterprises, states: "the Corporation supplies heating fuel to the Izhorsk factory of the Maritime Office to the Petrograd Public Administration and various other factories working for state defense." In the Russian Empire, fleet building was carried out mainly in state-owned enterprises. The Izhorsk factory near Petrograd was one of the two oldest and largest state factories for the production of armored warships in Russia.

The extension of locations from Riga to Baku, from the Baltic Sea to the Caspian Sea, had advantages and disadvantages. From the 1870s, Kahans' companies had expanded from the Pale of Settlement in the north-western border region to the Volga, to Transcaucasia, to the edge of the prosperous industrial region of the Donets Basin in eastern Ukraine and to the Baltic region. At the beginning of the war they maintained offices in Petrograd, Warsaw, Brest, Kharkov, Baku, Yekaterinoslav and Riga. A disadvantage was that some of the company's locations were in the war zone and could no longer be managed due to the loss of Russian territory. The advantage was that the factories, depots and offices could continue to operate at the remaining sites in Petrograd, Baku, Kharkov and Yekaterinoslav despite the restrictions of the economic landscape.

The exclusion of "enemy aliens" from the economy reduced the competition, especially in the oil industry where foreign capital was concentrated, causing business takeovers. Already at the beginning of the war, under the banner of official patriotism, a powerful regrouping of Russian oil companies in the RGOC had occurred, including an attempt to take over the Nobel concern, in which the Kahans were actively involved. When the Habsburg and German oil industrialists were driven out of Baku during the war, the Kahans had acquired Binəqədi Oil Industry and Trading Company.

Jacob, the Rosenbergs, Bendet and Judith Kahan had only vague ideas about all this. They had to make do with brief news about business developments in the Russian Empire, which became even rarer when there were no postcards from Chaim after his death. Often they consisted of only one sentence: "Thank God our business is doing very well." The question was, in what way, to what extent did the Kahans and Rosenbergs in Berlin share in that prosperity, given the closed borders.

Seven postcards and one letter arrived from Baruch during the revolutionary year. Until the summer he wrote monthly and after that again in October. On June 5, 1917, he had asked Jonas Rosenberg, via W. Finkelstein in Stockholm, to collect dividends with the help of Glad & Co. in Copenhagen; on July 5, he complained about Jonas's silence and briefly reported on the July Bolshevik uprising and the state of emergency in Petrograd. On October 17 he wrote an eight-page letter to his brother-in-law in Berlin, which was long by his standards. Aron recalled that on that day, in St. Petersburg, the National Assembly was to be opened, whose members belonged mainly to the left-wing parties, which pursued similar goals to those of the Bolsheviks, only without bloodshed. However, the so-called Red Guard, led by Lenin and Trotsky and their comrades, had torn the assembly apart. A Military Revolutionary Committee had been formed in Petrograd a few days earlier following the threat to the city from German troops. The overthrow of the fragile interim government by the Bolsheviks was imminent. Baruch had apparently received a letter from Jonas and was furious:

> After almost a year and a half of silence, you justify that silence and promise to write in future. This is how you end the letter and that's it. Couldn't you have said more? I believe you absolutely, I am fully aware that life for you is very uninteresting, but the facts alone should make it possible to fill five pages. How are you doing with all this, in particular, how does our good mother feel? How are Mary, Bendet, Judith, your children and Bendet's children and, last but not least, my firstborn?

Baruch reported that, with the help of their broker, an acquaintance had purchased 200 Petrol shares for the unit price of 145 rubles, that Petrol had experienced major fires in Baku, Saratov and Astrakhan, that they had suffered an enormous loss despite the compensation from the insurance company, but that, thank God, this was hardly noticeable in view of the successful business. "Why don't you report anything about the state of your material situation, about how production is doing? Is production at a standstill? What about the money? Can't you work in the depots?" He inquired about the employees and businesses in areas occupied by the Germans: whether the Berlin families are benefitting from Abraham Ledermann in Riga and whether they worked with Volf Kamenetsky in Białystok. Baruch was seriously concerned about a dispute between Bendet and Jonas over money. "I don't even want to know what so much is needed for, but if Bendet is against the expenditure and won't sign, it means it's not necessary." Apparently, Jonas Rosenberg and Bendet Kahan had access to money transfers from Russia, but they were only paid out against signatures from both, which is what they were arguing about. This made Baruch angry and worried, not only because of the money. Nevertheless, he asked Jonas why he needed such a large sum of money. Then, he changed the subject to business, briefly announcing that he had acquired two-thirds of the capital stock of the Widow and Brothers Romm printing house in Vilna, together with the Petrograd banker Noy (Noe) Abramovich Gordon. Romm was the largest and most respected publisher in the Jewish world at the time. "I am trying to send you a power of attorney for the management of the publishing house and a request for a report from the people in charge there," he promised and provided information regarding the management, budget, wages and book prices. The sale was to be carried out under Jonas's and Bendet's leadership, through the mediation of Mr. M. Barlas and publisher Levin-Epstein, both in Warsaw. They were not to sell too cheaply, to justify the wages. In Russia, Jewish books cost ten to twenty times more than before the war and newspapers were five times more expensive. Often they were not available at all. Finally, Baruch asked to keep him informed about the administrator. Shortly before the Bolsheviks had come to power, nationalizing the industry, defaming and persecuting the business class as *burzhuis*, bourgeoisie in the Marxist jargon, the Kahans acquired another company, this time—to the surprise of the Kahans and Rosenbergs in Berlin—not an oil company on Russian territory, but a publishing house with a printing plant on the other side of the war front. At that time the management of the companies was still in the hands of Baruch.

CHAPTER 11

Across the Front Line—Berlin, Warsaw, Baku, Moscow, Vilna, Kharkov, Kiev

"My dear ones! We received the letter from dear Rose, in which she reproaches me most severely for not writing, and Baruch complains in his telegram that [he] has not received a letter from me for almost a year. I am infinitely sorry that I have such bad luck with my letters, be[cause] in fact, [I] have written several times in the past few months. It seems that, unfortunately, all my letters must have been lost," Jonas Rosenberg replied to his brother-in-law and sister-in-law on October 21, 1917, in the letter in which he also expressed his interest in the dividend payments of the Kahan companies.

When asked why he did not inquire about the business, he replied that he did not know how and what to ask for. It would be much easier for the relatives in Russia. They would always have something interesting to say and yet they don't do it.

> Recently, I have received a trivial postcard from d[ear] Baruch [after] many months, from David we haven't even seen a sign of life for three years, I know too well that they have a colossal amount of work to do there, while I'm not doing anything and just trying to kill time, but a short letter once in 4/5 mon[ths] would be enough to keep me from slipping away completely. It's sad enough when you have to spend three years without any use [either] to yourself or to others, but what can you do, you have to hope [times] will change.

Jonas Rosenberg complained bitterly about his situation. The merchant of the Second Guild, owner of a small chemical factory in Warsaw where lubricating oil and other products had been produced before the war and which belonged to the fifth category of the trade tax code (6,000 to 20,000 rubles profit per year), was now trying under the most difficult circumstances to keep the family business alive by being dependent on payments from relatives in Russia. He thanked Rosalia and Baruch for arranging a due payment for him and reassured them that they should not be angry about his Bendet incident, since the matter was not new, and they knew him well enough. They should also not worry about possible speculations. There was no reason for it. The expenses for the household are enormous at the moment, plus salaries for employees like Swiżer and Kamenetsky in addition to their many donations.

In January 1916, Jonas Rosenberg and Bendet Kahan had travelled for the first time to the former Russian territory, the German-occupied Warsaw Province, perhaps with special permission, under the protection of the Neo-Orthodox Mission, legitimized and commissioned by the German civil administration. Jonas had stayed at the Hotel Krakowski, 7 Bielańska, in Warsaw. Bendet had travelled on to Białystok, where cousin Volf Kamenetsky managed the Kahan depot. In August of the same year, Jonas had been in Poland again, in Łódź, perhaps in Warsaw. He had crossed the border in Skalmierzyce. What Jonas and Bendet experienced and did in Poland can be seen indirectly from entries in the passports and more than a hundred postcards addressed to Jonas and Miriam Rosenberg, Malka, or Bendet Kahan at 36 Schlüterstrasse, Charlottenburg, which had been duly checked by the war censorship. The postcards came from Warsaw, Zamość, Siedlce, Łódź, Łomża, Aleksandrovo, were written in *Germyish* from forty-five different addresses. A few dozen letters and cards, which alternated back and forth between the relatives across the front line, provide further information. However, the letters fail to describe the content of parcels sent to the west by Pinchas from Baku, Rachel from Yekaterinoslav and Rosalia from Petrograd or Kharkov.

WARSAW

Chaim Kahan had had an office in Warsaw since 1894 and Jonas was managing the production there with changing partners, more or less successfully. Relatives, acquaintances and employees lived there. Most of the obituaries and eulogies for Chaim Kahan were published in Warsaw—in Yiddish and Hebrew in *Moment*, *Hatsfira* and *Haynt*, signed by Yehudah Schulmeister, the brothers

Michael and S. Stock, Moshe Pisarewitz, M. Barlas, Chaim and Zvi (Hersch) Swizer; in German in the short-lived Neo-Orthodox *Warsaw Journal*. There had been business connections to Stock's Steam Laundry and Crystal & Soda factories for years. Barlas was to participate in the distribution of books from the Vilna publishing house Widow and Brothers Romm, which the Kahans had acquired together with a St. Petersburg banker after Chaim's death. The employees Moshe Pisarewitz and Yehuda Schulmeister in Warsaw and Hersch Swiżer in Siedlce were receiving monthly subsidies between 50 and 300 marks from Jonas in 1917; likewise, a certain H. Friedland in Zamość and Benyamin Rosenberg in Łódź, a brother of Jonas, who was managing the Kahan cotton processing plant and perhaps their tank depot as well. Jonas Rosenberg had been in regular contact with all of them since the beginning of 1916. He was having the receipt and distribution of the funds confirmed and was learning about their daily hardships, the inflation, the diseases that had been spreading as a result of the misery, the restrictions and the almost insurmountable difficulties in doing business.

Chaim Kahan's connection with Warsaw is authenticated by his business dealings with the Caspian-Black Sea Oil Industry and Trading Company from the mid-1890s and later with Branobel. The oil market in Congress Poland was his first trading region. When Miriam and Jonas got married in Warsaw in 1894, his business was in a state of upheaval. The partnership with Dembo was dissolved, while he was about to gain a foothold in Baku. Two years after his daughter's marriage, Chaim acquired the refinery near Saratov. Since then, things were on the upswing again. At this time Jonas's father, Elias Rosenberg, was also registered as an entrepreneur in Warsaw. Initially, Baruch and Rosalia had represented the trading house Kahan in Warsaw, living at 19 Nowolipki. In 1895 Yasha was born there. Shortly afterwards, the family moved to Kharkov and Chaim followed them. Malka stayed with Miriam, supporting her daughter as she had once helped her. In 1898, Roska was born, followed by Noma a year later. Jonas took over the management in Warsaw. The trade directory of 1909/1910 listed the following under "*Oleje mineralne i smary*" [Mineral Oils and Lubricants]: Rosenberg, 4 Jonas Skórzana Street. In the trade section of the *Adresy Warszawy* of that same year under "*Nafta*" and "*Naftowe produkty*": "Kahan Ch., owner Jonas Rosenberg, wholesale," 3 Ogrodowa Street.

During the war, under German occupation, the Polish capital was grey, sick and hungry; it was hardly recognizable. In November 1916, the part of Poland that had been under Russian rule until the expulsion of the Tsarist troops, with Warsaw as its capital, was declared the Kingdom of Poland by the

German and Habsburg emperors. Since then, the Polish elites were trying to wrest governmental authority from the occupying forces. The economy got off to a slow start. The export of oils and fats was only possible with the permission of the War Raw Materials Agency. The German administration kept watch over the petroleum monopoly. In Warsaw the textile industry worked after a fashion, the leather factories stood still, knitwear was exported to Germany, partly by coercion. The stock exchange was officially closed, but in its lobby there was speculation, and nowhere in Europe was the ruble traded as highly as in Warsaw, because the triple currency of the German mark, Polish mark and ruble confused people, who held back the tried and tested Russian money because of the uncertain outcome of the war. The new Polish currency was to be imposed in the spring of 1917. In Germany, the import and export of rubles was prohibited, except for rubles from the occupied territories and the import of gold rubles, which Jonas and Bendet might have found interesting with regard to currency exchange in Warsaw and money transfer from Russia via Poland to Germany.

Many Jews had fled to Warsaw during the war, others had left the city in a hurry because hunger and typhus were rampant and there was a danger of being drafted for forced labor. Jonas's father had ended up in Poltava; he was either deported by the Tsarist army or got there in the wake of the Russian withdrawal. In 1916, there was not much left of the Warsaw where Miriam and Jonas had spent their best years and which had been Roska and Noma's childhood home.

The dynamic metropolis had left its mark on the Rosenberg family. At the end of the nineteenth century, it modernized at a rapid pace, like many European cities, developing into a city of almost a million inhabitants by the beginning of the war; 337,000 of the population, more than a third, were Jews. At that time Warsaw was the third largest city in the Russian Empire, with the largest Jewish community in Europe. The Jews were attracted by the distinctiveness of Warsaw's ethnic and religious mix and its central position between East and West. Warsaw was now located in the border area of the Russian Empire, a region that had been densely populated by Jews for centuries. All this had led to the creation of a diverse, pulsating Jewish diaspora center northwest of the royal old town in the slipstream of ongoing tensions between imperial foreign rule and national resistance. There in particular, Warsaw was densely populated, four times more densely than St. Petersburg. There the *shtetl* competed with the big city. Rural and urban Jews, poor and rich, lived and worked closely together in rapidly rising four- and five-story apartment buildings with an average of 116 inhabitants per complex, compared to St. Petersburg where that number was 32. They were separated by busy courtyards, noisy streets and market stalls. The most powerful group in terms of numbers were the Polish *Hasidim*, but the Lithuanian *Misnagedim* also attracted attention as political players who provoked in various directions. The *maskilim*, like the entire middle class, adapted the bourgeois lifestyle in a Polish, Russian and German way, without touching the ethnic and religious boundaries, which were also strictly drawn in terms of space. Before the First World War, one third of the total population of the city, more than ninety percent of the Jewish population, had lived on one fifth of the area the ghetto was built in during the Second World War. After the uprisings in the spring of 1943 the entire area was completely destroyed. What remains are photographs, memoirs, stories by Shalom Asch and the siblings Esther, Israel, Joshua and Isaac Bashevis Singer as well as Yiddish novels.

My apartment was located on the southern edge of the former ghetto, in Bagno Street, a few steps from Grzybowski Square. Whenever I would leave the house in Bagno Street walking across Grzybowski Square, I would find myself facing the high facade of an empty multi-story building, which is a memorial now. The erstwhile inhabitants would be looking at me from the raw brick wall; oversized photos on huge canvases. I would go to the Mirów Halls to buy vegetables. Raspberries, blueberries, cherries and strawberries were offered directly in the streets. I would go jogging in the Saski [Saxon] Park.

The Rosenbergs had lived and worked in this area. At first they lived at 3 Ogrodowa, from 1912 at 8 Karmelicka, and as time went by they moved to the center, to Marszałkowska, the main shopping street. During the last years, the Kahans' office bore the address 43 Królewska, the same as the Caspian-Black Sea Oil Industry and Trading Company, opposite the magnificent guild-house. The factory addresses were 12 Graniczna [Boundary] Road and 4 Skórzana [Leather] Road.

Graniczna connected Grzybowski Square with Żelaznej Bramy Square, the Square of the Iron Gates. In the middle of the nineteenth century, the largest trading place in the city was established there, and around it formed the first compact Jewish settlement. When Jonas and Miriam settled in Warsaw, Graniczna became a Jewish street. The houses there were up to six stories high. On the ground floors there were warehouses and shops. The streets and plazas were crowded. The first modern market hall, a round building with arcades made of cast iron columns, was built on Żelaznej Bramy Square. One of the streets leading to the square is Skórzana. In one of the courtyards between Graniczna and Skórzana was Jonas Rosenberg's factory. Not far from there, when the

Rosenbergs were newly married, Warsaw's largest market halls were built, the Mirów Halls, where Miriam and the cook might have done their shopping. At the same time, the Nożyk Synagogue on Graniczna was constructed, the only synagogue in Warsaw to survive the Holocaust. During Jonas's and Miriam's lifetime, there were more than seven hundred synagogues and prayer houses in Warsaw, but also rebellious young people who were demonstrating on Grzybowski Square, during the revolutionary year of 1905, against autocratic foreign rule as well as traditional Jewish life. Twenty-year-old Rachel Kahan was possibly among the demonstrators. Family tradition has it that after she had returned from Marburg, she was enthusiastic about the revolutionary movement. Whether she belonged to the left-wing Zionists or was in the *Bund*, is not known. She had been arrested by the Tsarist police and spent several months in prison. Father Chaim is said to have bought her freedom and supported her fellow Jewish prisoners while he was at it.

It is almost impossible today to imagine the life of the Rosenbergs before the First World War in Warsaw. The buildings were razed to the ground by the Germans. After the Second World War, new prefabricated high-rise apartment blocks were built in Wola, Mirów, Muranow and Nowolipki Districts, which cover the area of the ghetto over several square kilometers. Roads had been moved. In my search for prewar photographs, I initially found ghetto pictures, taken by Nazi photographers or German soldiers, out of curiosity, for documentation, as a trophy of oppression, or a memento of victory. In these pictures, the streets are full of people rushing by. People and buildings appear gloomy and poor. I tried to look through the misery and found later other testimonials, such as postcards from peace times, pictures of the family, studio and pageant photos, as they were fashionable at that time everywhere in bourgeois Europe. Miriam and Jonas in front of a painted backdrop of an idyllic, natural park with trees, with a pond and a flower field; these were probably taken before the turn of the century, a few years after their marriage. Miriam stands slightly to the side, behind Jonas, perhaps to conceal the fact that she was taller than him, while he is sitting on a decaying little wall, adapted to the backdrop. She is no longer wearing a *shaitel*, unlike her mother, showing straight blond hair. His cropped hair is dark and frizzy. Wrapped in a dark silk dress reaching down to the ground, with long, wide sleeves, the buttons tightly fastened up to the chin, she appears stately and looks serious. The slightly lowered corners of her mouth reinforce that impression. By contrast, Jonas is a daintily built, elegantly dressed man with a well-groomed short beard, wearing a bow tie instead of a tie. His eyes smile mischievously. Later photographs show that the right corner of Miriam's mouth had dropped further over time. She had put on weight. Big wagon-wheel hats, lushly decorated with feathers, adorned her plump stature. Jonas now seemed somewhat lost at her side. His hair had turned grey, which made his eyes look even darker.

Rosa and Noma are dressed to the nines in all the photos, to such a degree that their faces pale against the outfits. The earliest picture was taken in 1902. They are both in thick winter coats, his with fur collar, hers with pelerine. The small four-year-old girl wears a high bonnet, tied under her chin with a large ribbon and holds a muff; the three-year-old Noma wears a fur cap. Both wear felt boots. He leads a muzzled toy dachshund on a leash. A photograph showing her standing with her father on either side of her enthroned mother, was taken around 1907 in Antwerp, the family's place of refuge during the first Russian Revolution. The Rosenbergs must have been in Antwerp without having their own address and without registering with the authorities, maybe only for a visit. In 1909, they posed again in a Warsaw studio, in front of an idyllic landscape— Rosa in a large plaid dress, Noma in a sailor's suit—with Aunt Rachel, who was sixteen years younger than her sister Miriam. This time, Aunt Rachel wears a wagon wheel on her head, which appears huge by comparison to the children's straw hats. Perhaps it was a farewell photo. Rachel got married that year and left Warsaw to move to Yekaterinoslav with David Ettinger. In 1910 Miriam and Jonas sent a photo of themselves with greetings from Bad Kissingen to their children, who had spent the summer together with Uncle Pinchas and Aunt Zina from Baku in Cranz by the sea in East Prussia. Rosa kept a photo of the whole family in front of snow-covered mountains from the 1912 summer retreat in St. Moritz, which the Rosenbergs sent as a picture postcard to friends in the Russian-Polish Międzyrzec, today Ukrainian Mezhirichi; one can only wonder how it got back?

Rosa and Noma grew up differently from Isaac Bashevis Singer and his siblings on Krochmalna, and certainly did not live in a two-room apartment. They didn't attend any *cheder* or school; they received private lessons, even though Noma was later photographed in a school uniform, with a satchel. Their parents, themselves traditionally educated, gave them a modern, secular education. They had a governess, Mademoiselle Chlenov from Nowozybkov, nicknamed Smoczek, which means "little dragon" and also "Smoocher." They learned French and Hebrew and received piano lessons. The Rosenbergs belonged to the Lithuanian-*Misnagedim* families in Warsaw, who lived according to the laws of the Torah, but in moderately modern and enlightened ways. They spoke Russian and Polish in addition to Yiddish and Hebrew. Parents and children maintained close written contact with relatives in St. Petersburg, Kharkov, Yekaterinoslav and Antwerp, also with friends in Warsaw when they went to the health spas in summer. Rosa corresponded particularly often with Jacob and with Aunt Rachel, after whom she was named. Once, when Cousin Nachum was ill and probably bored, he sent her from St. Petersburg a doll's bedroom cut out of paper and glued together, comprising a bedside table, washstand, tiny pillows and blankets; it was a gift she kept for the rest of her life. The children grew up well, not least thanks to their social status and their grandfather's financial support, though he would have preferred for his grandchildren to receive a formal education. But Jonas Rosenberg had his own ideas, maintaining a certain independence from his father-in-law, being a guild merchant in his own right.

BERLIN

In May 1916, a certain S. Ebin from Warsaw complained that the power of attorney sent by Jonas Rosenberg was insufficient and requested that Mr. Kahan provide him with a notarized plenipotential authority. In Berlin, Jonas and Bendet had received a power of attorney from Baruch in Petrograd, via L. C. Glad & Co in Copenhagen, to access the family capital. However, that was effective only if the instructions were signed by both of them. Apparently, this had caused strife. Bendet refused to sign for months on end, claiming that Jonas was using the money not only for the household, but also for dubious business. On the first anniversary of Chaim's death, in late November 1917, the brothers-in-law made up. But of what use was the power of attorney to Jonas Rosenberg and Bendet Kahan as "enemy aliens" in Germany or in occupied Poland in 1916/1917?

Like Jacob, they received regular financial support from relatives on the other side of the front line via the Royal Spanish Embassy in Berlin. Neutral Spain was a protective power for the Russian Empire during the First World War, primarily for the Russian prisoners of war in Germany. According to entries in the passports, Jonas Rosenberg and Bendet and Jacob Kahan had received major payments from Russia via the Spanish Embassy in the first winter of the war, from January 1916 until October 1917; from then on, they got 400 marks each month, which was hardly enough to cover their living expenses.

Financial help also came directly from L. C. Glad & Co. "Your relatives have learned from another source that you are in financial trouble, even in debt," wrote Glad's employee Gerson Oppenheim to Bendet Kahan in Berlin on November 23, 1916. Should that be the case, he asked them to write to the company, which would send them a certain amount. According to Aron's memoirs, he had transferred that year 300,000 Danish kroner from Baku to Glad for his mother, brother and sister, since he knew that they had no income. One year later, on October 19, 1917, Mr. Oppenheim reported that there were only 48,000 Danish kroner left from the money Aron had deposited with Glad for the family. If those sums are right, Bendet and Jonas had spent a considerable sum in Berlin within a short time. Oppenheim said that the money had been transferred from Russia to Copenhagen with great difficulty and no more would be forthcoming. The Berliners should only use it for household expenses, and if that is not possible, then only for normal business. He also warned against stock exchange transactions.

BAKU

After the Bolshevik Revolution of 1917, the entrepreneurs Kahan also got into financial difficulties in Russia. The quest to save lives and capital had begun. Immediately after the Bolsheviks seized power, Aron brought a large sum of money to safety, a coup he proudly described in his memoirs: he shipped petroleum in canisters from Baku to Enzeli, today's Bandar Anzali, the largest Iranian trading city on the Caspian Sea; he acquired additional money orders from Persian merchants in Baku, drove with them to Enzeli, sold the petroleum, cashed the money orders, acquired Persian tumens, which weighed heavily, loaded them into a car with the help of porters and transported them to Russia; there he opened an account at the Imperial Bank of Persia, where he deposited the money. Since then, the Kahans tried to adapt their business to the new circumstances, evading the Bolsheviks whenever and wherever possible, and circled the wagons.

The collapse of the Russian Empire was a gradual, discontinuous, convoluted process involving heterogeneous movements and events, comprising warfare, revolution, power usurpation and anarchy; there were struggles between monarchist, bourgeois and socialist pretenders for state leadership, as well as secessions with the intervention of both the Allies and the Central Powers against the Bolsheviks. In war circumstances, political and market-economic conditions differed from region to region. This gave the Kahans some room to maneuver for a certain period of time, until the expansion and consolidation of Soviet power, despite the fragmentation of the economy and the associated restrictions and risks. They were risking their lives by making use of that situation. It proved to be an advantage that their companies were spread over a wide area. While the main office was located in the center of the Bolshevik Revolution in Petrograd, the oil fields, refineries, warehouse and branches were located far away, most of them on disputed land, on the fringes of the former empire, with more or less free markets.

One of the first measures taken by the Bolsheviks was the expropriation of industry. The oil industry in Baku was of particular interest and value because of its profits, monopolistic structure and strategic importance. However, the Bolsheviks' dominion emanated from the capitals and was initially limited to the central Russian territory. On December 1, 1917, Baruch and all his relatives got in touch from Baku. The family had left Petrograd, abandoned their office on Stremyannaya and the elegant apartment around the corner at 23 Troitskaya. Baruch, David and Rosalia had fled with Arusia to their relatives on the Caspian Sea, where it was still quiet. There they wanted to stay for the next three months, until Pesach. Only David went back to Petrograd a few times to see how things were going. Baruch wrote that even in the politically threatening situation, business was excellent.

In Baku Arusia had taken his school leaving examinations externally and was congratulated by Yasha. But by Easter 1918 the coup had already reached the port city on the Caspian Sea. The Armenian massacre of the Azeris, provoked by the Bolsheviks, ended with the proclamation of the Baku Commune. Baruch, David, Rosalia and Arusia probably left the city before Pesach. Anyway, Aron did not mention them in his memoirs of those dramatic days. Shortly afterwards, Zina fled with the three children and the nanny, *Nyanya* Sasha, via Astrakhan and Saratov to David in Moscow, the new capital. They wanted to obtain papers for departure from Soviet Russia, to register as Ukrainians. Aron had planned the escape, but remained until the Bolsheviks proclaimed the nationalization of the oil industry on May 1. Then he followed the others.

MOSCOW

In Moscow, where Petrol had an office and the Kahans had an apartment, the fugitives from Petrograd and Baku were reunited. They stayed there for a few weeks and, according to Aron, had their employee, Mr. Farber, supply them with fresh *challes* and other food from Saratov, since supplies in Moscow were scarce. They were planning to move to the independent Ukraine, to Kharkov, where Chaim Kahan had opened his first office and had had his first residence with Baruch and Rosalia. Ukraine in those days had become a source of hope for all those who were disillusioned with Russia, because it was governed democratically and granted economic freedom as well as minority rights. The naphtha king Goldstein in Asch's novel also set off for Ukraine. An employee was entrusted with the task of finding an apartment for Zina and the children in Kharkov, and to reserve a hotel room for Aron. "The residents are in a pitiful state," observed a traveler in Moscow during those weeks. In front of the German consulate, people stood in dense rows, with petitions and requests for passports and for support. The legation received visits from anxious aristocrats, previous millionaires and former civil servants, honest people and provocateurs. People were pining away with fear of the next day. The same probably happened in front of the Ukrainian consulate. For the time being, the Soviet government did not prevent anyone from applying for a passport of the now foreign Ukraine. That summer, however, Baruch and Rosalia had to do without the planned six-week summer retreat in the Caucasian spa Yessentuki.

Following the Brest-Litovsk peace treaty between the Bolsheviks and the Central Powers, on June 11, 1918, Baruch wrote from Moscow, since incredibly, postal traffic with Germany was getting back to normal. From Kharkov, a rapprochement with companies in the West looked promising. He reported about money transfers from Kharkov and Kiev and planned to send an employee from Moscow to Romm in Vilna. Everything was still in flux, and the borders were not carefully guarded, so it was easy to get passes there. But only nine days later, on June 20, 1918, the situation changed. The Bolsheviks expropriated the oil industry. The refinery in Saratov was not affected by this at first, because it was located on land controlled by the Whites. But, probably, the Kahans did not manage to get to Saratov as they had planned and as the Berliners had assumed before the Bolsheviks seized the region. So the refinery was lost. The uprising of the left-wing Social Revolutionaries in Moscow, less than three weeks later, on July 6–7, in the course of which the German ambassador Graf von Mirbach was assassinated, changed the situation once again. Aron was visiting one of Moscow's best tailors to try on a new suit when a bomb exploded nearby. Stations were closed, the Kahans were stuck in Moscow, unable to start their journey to Kharkov as planned. Supplies were cut off. In most districts of Moscow, the daily ration of an eighth of a pound of bread was not distributed, neither were the groats, which had been promised as a substitute. One pound of bad brown bread now cost twelve rubles, sugar cost twenty-eight, sausage, between eighteen and twenty-eight. Potatoes replaced bread.

KHARKOV

Only a few days after the assassination, all the Kahans succeeded in leaving Moscow and escaping to Kharkov, where the family from Baku settled down near Baruch and Rosalia. Zina's eldest, Lolia, went back to school and graduated from high school in Kharkov. But peace in the Ukraine under the government of Hetman Skoropadsky was only guaranteed at that time with the support of the German army. The entrepreneurial family resorted to any security that was available, preparing for new activities. Women and children went to the summer resort as always, this time they made do with Slavyansk, where Rachel and David Ettinger owned a *dacha*. In view of the close relations between Germany and the Ukraine, there were hopes for an early family reunion. The men drew up business plans.

BERLIN

On July 5, Bendet wrote a letter from Berlin to Baruch in Kharkov with suggestions on what to do with the branches in the German-occupied territories, the refineries in Riga and Warsaw and the oil depots in various places. Production was not possible there during the war, as no deliveries of goods were permitted: "no German, Galician, or Romanian naphtha products will be released." As soon as Poland would become an independent state, he would get provisions from Galicia and Romania commissioning old, tried and tested companies to do so; there would be no room for new companies there, certainly not Jewish ones. He called to mind the antisemitism fomented by the National Democrats in prewar Warsaw. There will be a boycott against Jewish businesses, as there was then. He advocated the sale of the branches to Deutsche Erdöl AG, with whom Max Lew was already involved in negotiations. He himself was planning a trip to Vilna and Riga, which would only be possible with special permission. He did not write what should become of the textile factory in Łódź.

VILNA

While the Kahan's Riga-based enterprise, the Russian-Baltic Mineral Oil Company, had been evacuated to Russia in time before the German occupation in the autumn of 1917, the family owned an active business, the publishing house Romm, in Vilna, which had been part of the Upper East administrative region since November 1915. Gerson Oppenheim wrote from Copenhagen that the acquisition had been Chaim Kahan's wish. Baruch had given the Berlin branch of the family instructions for the management of the publishing house, and Bendet had accepted responsibility for it. He had probably travelled to Vilna in the summer of 1918 for the first time since the war began.

Vilna, known as *Yerushalayim shel Lita*, had been an important point of reference for the family for many years. Chaim had set up his own business there, cofounded the trading company Dembo & Kahan and joined the Berlin family through his son's marriage. Twenty years later, at the end of 1913, he had toyed with the idea of making Vilna once again the center of his business, because things were going badly in Warsaw due to the antisemitism of the Polish National Democrats, which was poisoning the social climate; their hate was directed against all foreign immigrants, in particular Lithuanians who had assimilated to Russian culture and were politically active. After the elections of the Fourth Duma in the autumn of 1912, the populist incitement to hatred against Jews had intensified and their participation in city councils had been restricted. The National Democrats had called for a boycott of Jewish businesses, and the Liberals distanced themselves from their former Jewish allies. This was the reason why Chaim Kahan had recalled Jonas Rosenberg from Warsaw, abandoning the branch. On December 1, 1913, he wrote to Malka and his sons that he had had no intention of returning to Warsaw from Antwerp anyway, saying that he had bowed to the wishes of others in the family, by which he could only mean Jonas, Miriam and Malka.

The nostalgic rather than coolly calculated idea of settling once more in Vilna was born when Chaim founded the Caucasus-Volga Industrial & Trading Company, calling it Chaim Kahan & Sons, because he also wanted to trade in wood. Although the multiethnic city was the center of the Litvaks, it was, in economic terms, an enclave, far away from the stock exchanges and the big land or sea routes for the oil trade. In addition to 36 Schlüterstrasse in Charlottenburg, Chaim Kahan rented an apartment at 10 Zhandarmsky Pereulok [Lane], today Jogailos Street, in Vilna. He had actually been registered at this address in the address register under the name Caucasus-Volga Inc. for a year before the war began. At that time, Chaim still assumed that St. Petersburg would remain his main business base. In the triangle of St. Petersburg, Vilna and Berlin, he wanted to do business in "European style" together with Jonas and have *hana'ah* [pleasure] in it. Arusia, born in 1899 in Vilna, had certainly spent a lot of time with relatives there during his childhood. Later he wrote that his grandfather had rented a spacious apartment in Vilna, where Persian carpets were displayed—gifts from his uncles in Baku—but which was otherwise empty.

The Zhandarmsky Pereulok connected Georgievsky Prospekt [George Avenue], today Gedimino Prospektas [Gediminas Avenue], with Zavalnaya [Wall] Street, linking the new and the old city. In today's Vilna, it is a busy thoroughfare to the Gediminas Avenue, the central road of the bourgeois new town since the middle of the nineteenth century. At the turn of the century, wealthy merchants and entrepreneurs had stately four-to-five-story mansions built there in various historicist styles. Right on the corner of Zhandarmsky Pereulok and Georgievsky Prospekt stood the magnificent George and Bristol Hotels.

The trading house Dembo & Kahan had had its offices on Wall Street, in the immediate vicinity of the old town, near the market hall, but close to the railway station, with excellent transport connections. At that time, it epitomized the economically emerging middle class within the estate-based society. All the petroleum traders, the large multiregional companies, Branobel, Ter Akopov, Shibayev, Mazut, as well as the smaller, local ones, were at that time spread over the area between the old town, the market and the railway station. 43 Zavalnaya (today 49 Pylimo) Street is a massive, broad, two-story-high classicist building from the first half of the nineteenth century, striking because of its two mighty columns, to the right and left of the entrance gate in its center. During the Dembo & Kahan period, it was a commercial building with shops, workshops and offices; after the turn of the century, it housed a grammar school and was restored in the 1960s. Today poor people live there in cramped apartments. The building is decaying. Arusia's maternal grandfather, the merchant and small businessman Chaim Yakov Berlin, had storage rooms for herrings and salt just across the street. His workshop for the production of brushes, the Vilna Mechanical Scraping Factory, was located further away, on the Novogorodskaya arterial road in Asinovsky's house. Chaim Berlin and his wife left Vilna to die and be buried in Palestine, as was customary among the pious, when Arusia was young, recounted his niece Efrat Carmon. But Chaim's son, Rosalia's brother, Isidor Berlin, remained in Vilna. He was also active in the oil wholesale trade, and before the war was a representative of the transport company Mazut at 10 Shopenovskaya [Chopin] Street, near the railway station. Over the years, the Kahans also maintained close business contacts with him and his family.

In autumn 1913 Chaim Kahan had given the Rosenbergs the choice of moving from Warsaw to Vilna or Berlin. They chose the German metropolis. Perhaps because Jonas Rosenberg, who was considered a Litvak in Warsaw, felt that he was a Polish Jew in Vilna and did not feel at home there. Perhaps also because Jonas and Miriam, who were used to the good life in the big city, preferred the West, if only for the summer retreats. In the summer of 1918, the only member of the family to return to Vilna, was the disobedient Bendet, who was not interested in the oil business. At the time, Vilna was the capital of Lithuania under German occupation and was renamed Vilnius when Bendet took over the management of the Romm publishing house.

KHARKOV AND KIEV

In the period between the Bolshevik Revolution and the establishment of Soviet power, the Kahans' scope for economic activity was increasingly restricted. During the struggles for territorial domination, the Russian cities were highly insecure locations faced with violence and anarchy. After Petrograd, Saratov and Baku were taken by the Bolsheviks, the family withdrew to the Ukraine; Kharkov became its hub. The Ettingers remained in Yekaterinoslav. Aron and David decided to build another business base in the new capital of the independent Ukraine, Kiev, where they already had warehouses and an office at 139 Bolshaya Vasilkovskaya, in the industrial area on the main road to the south. They moved into an apartment in the upper town, at 6 Nikolayevskaya, today Arkhitektora Horodetskogo, a side street off Khreshchatik, popularly known as "the Paris of Kiev," because there were beautiful buildings—architectural works of art. The magnificent apartment building number 6 was flanked on one side by the Hyppo Palace, the horse circus and on the other by the Hotel Continental. Yeliseev's delicatessen shop was located at the beginning of the street when viewed from the center. At 6 Nikolaevskaya, Aron and David met Ornstein, a young officer of the Austro-Hungarian Empire, and field rabbi Dr. David A. Winter. Like Khreshchatik, the street was largely destroyed during the Second World War. But building number 6 stands today in new splendor.

That was the time when Aron began to deal with socio-economic problems. He drafted a reform project that has since disappeared, in which he warned against the devaluation of the *karbovanets*, the new Ukrainian currency, and the influence of the Russian ruble on the Ukrainian market. Instead, he recommended the introduction of a new currency linked to the German gold mark. He asked Mikhail I. Tugan-Baranovsky, Minister of Finance of the First Ukrainian Central Rada, later professor at the Kiev University, to review the proposal from an academic point of view and had it printed and sent to the Ukrainian government.

On August 12, 1918, Moshe Pisarewitz reported to Jonas Rosenberg in Berlin from Warsaw that Ebin was back and had brought "great capital" with him. Ebin had obviously been a trustworthy business partner throughout the war years. In early September, Bendet and Jonas travelled to the Ukraine via Warsaw. For the first time since the beginning of the war, the brothers and brothers-in-law met at Baruch's in Kharkov and at Aron's and David's in Kiev. They stayed for two months until the end of October and discussed the new situation; they were considering the import and export business of oil products from Baku, Galicia and Romania via Kiev to Germany. Obviously, they also talked about the sale of the branches in the German-occupied Polish territories.

On November 5 Baruch wrote from Kharkov that they were anticipating the deals planned by Aron and David in Kiev. A few days later the German Reich collapsed. The withdrawal of German troops from the Ukraine had begun, on which Rosalia commented in a letter of December 17 from Kharkov, written to Jacob in Russian, but quoting in German *"Wir haben gemacht die Rechnung ohne den Wirth,"* which means "we had counted our chickens before they were hatched." On December 26 David Kahan wrote from Kiev that they had learned from Kharkov that Jonas had bought fifty Nobel shares in Berlin at a price of about 2,500 marks per share, complaining that he had not bought more at this favorable price. They had received 100,000 rubles from Ebin, a profit which was to be shared between Ebin and them. The mark was worth about the same as the ruble in Kiev at that time. So, David asked if the relatives in Germany could help realize the yield. He mentioned, by the way, trade transactions with the Don region, where the Whites still ruled, foreshadowed Ornstein's arrival and reported about a meeting with the Ukrainian Minister of Trade and Industry concerning the sale of "two million oil products," which could probably not be achieved at the moment in this difficult situation. In a few days, Aron and David were planning to leave for Kharkov and continue from there in all likelihood to Baku, where they intended to settle. Since the destruction of the Commune in Baku at the end of July 1918, it had become once again an accessible and sought-after place for entrepreneurs. The relatives were supposed to recommend locations with good connections to Berlin and tell whether the routes from Germany to the Black Sea ports or to Copenhagen were passable. If so, they would travel via Berlin. They received news from Baku relatively regularly. Everything was in order there. David's letter was delivered by a personal messenger to 36 Schlüterstrasse in Charlottenburg, utilizing an "occasion" with the assistance of Mr. Ebin.

The borders between the warring nations were more permeable than is generally assumed. Just like Jonas and Bendet, others, relatives, friends and acquaintances, moved with special travel permits from Berlin to the German-occupied territories of the former Russian Empire, meeting family members and confidantes beyond the front lines. Mrs. Puschtinsky was there, according to one letter; according to another one, Mr. Levstein had brought several thousand rubles and Beham would be stopping by. In 1918 Rosa mentioned in one of her letters from the summer retreat in Polzin to Yasha in Salzbrunn that her father had "taken a large, very large sum of money with him from Poland, transferred a large capital abroad." Conversely, friendly soldiers such as Ornstein from the armies of the Central Powers provided courier services. The occupied territories served as sluices for the Kahans and their helpers.

On January 8, 1919, Baruch reported that the connections from Kharkov to Yekaterinoslav and Baku had been disrupted because of the fighting between the Whites and the Reds; the business Mr. Ornstein had been talking about would probably not materialize now. The new political situation, the occupation of Kharkov and its environs by the Bolsheviks, had changed everything. In this situation David tried to get from Kiev directly to Baku, while Aron, worried about Zina and the children, was trying to get to Kharkov. When Aron arrived there, the Bolsheviks were already ruling the city. Ten days later, on January 18, Rosalia informed Yasha indirectly that after losing the refinery in Saratov, their depot and office in Kharkov had also been taken from them. What remained was the property in Baku: "a good source for us all." But Aron advised them to leave Kharkov for Berlin.

Photo 21: Roska and Noma Rosenberg. Warsaw, 1902. Jüdisches Museum Berlin, Archiv Haimi-Cohen

Photo 22: Noma Rosenberg with satchel. Warsaw, c. 1906. Jüdisches Museum Berlin, Archiv Haimi-Cohen

Photo 23: Silver Viennese centerpiece with elephant on wheels from the Ettinger home in Uman. Ettinger-Rozenfeld family, Ramat Gan

Photo 24: Rachel Kahan with niece Roska and nephew Noma Rosenberg. Warsaw, 1909. Jüdisches Museum Berlin, Archiv Haimi-Cohen

Photos 25 and 26: Picture postcard, front and back. Miriam and Jonas Rosenberg. Bad Kissingen, 1910. Jüdisches Museum Berlin, Archiv Haimi-Cohen

Photo 27: Miriam and Jonas Rosenberg with their children Roska and Noma. St. Moritz, 1912. Jüdisches Museum Berlin, Archiv Haimi-Cohen

Photo 28: Picture postcard. Arrival of the guests. The gentleman with bowler (center front) could be Chaim Kahan. Bad Neuenahr, summer 1913. Photo: Hans Barten. Courtesy of Heinz Schönewald, Bad Neuenahr

Photo 29: Roska and Yasha Kahan on their honeymoon. Memel, 1919. Jüdisches Museum Berlin, Archiv Haimi-Cohen

Photo 30: The Azbil team, from left to right, sitting: Aron Z. Syngalowski, Yuda M. Beham, Bendet Kahan, Zalman Shneour; standing: Yasha, Roska, Noma, and unknown persons. Berlin, 1922. Jüdisches Museum Berlin, Archiv Haimi-Cohen

Photo 31: The brothers Nachum and Arusia Kahan with friends. Kharkov, 1921. Efrat Carmon, Jerusalem

Photo 32: Women, children, and nannies of the Kahan family at a summer resort. Probably Ahlbeck, 1923. Jüdisches Museum Berlin, Archiv Haimi-Cohen

Photo 33: Mina Kahan and son Joseph with Lotte Kleinert. Berlin, c. 1925. Michal Froom, Ma'agan Michael

Photo 34: Baruch and Rosalia with sons, daughter-in-law, and grandchildren. Berlin, 37 Schlüterstrasse, 1927. Jüdisches Museum Berlin, Archiv Haimi-Cohen

Photos 35: Statuettes of Bendet Kahan and Jonas and Miriam Rosenberg. Berlin, 1924. Naomi Loewenthal, Ramat HaSharon. Jüdisches Museum Berlin, Archiv Haimi-Cohen

Photo 36: Noma (Nachum) Kahan in front of the map of Eretz Israel. Berlin, 1926. Efrat Carmon, Jerusalem

Photo 37: Aron Kahan. Berlin, no date. Jüdisches Museum Berlin, Archiv Haimi-Cohen

Photo 38: The Kahan family. Birkenwerder near Berlin, 1926.
Jüdisches Museum Berlin, Archiv Haimi-Cohen

Photo 39: Noma Kahan and Lolia Kahan with brides at Alkazar, Reeperbahn.
Hamburg, 1927. Jüdisches Museum Berlin, Archiv Haimi-Cohen

Photo 40: Chaim Avinoam. Berlin, no date.
Jüdisches Museum Berlin, Archiv Haimi-Cohen

Photo 41: Lily Kahan and Chaim Avinoam Kahan, with a teddy bear,
on a balcony of one of the attic apartments. Berlin, 1925.
Jüdisches Museum Berlin, Archiv Haimi-Cohen

Photo 42: Eli Rosenberg (in the middle) with his brother Michael and cousin Malka and an unknown boy. Berlin, 1931. Noa Rosenberg, Tel Aviv

Photo 43: Eli Rosenberg with his brother Michael and cousins Malka and Chaim Avinoam Kahan on the balcony in 32 Wielandstrasse. Berlin, 1932. Jüdisches Museum Berlin, Archiv Haimi-Cohen

Photo 44: Group photo of the Nitag staff. Berlin, 1927.
Jüdisches Museum Berlin, Archiv Haimi-Cohen

Photo 45: Trademark of the company Chaim Kahan's Successors.
Israel, 1925–1930. Efrat Carmon, Jerusalem

CHAPTER 12

Expulsion from Russia. Baku, Kharkov, Yekaterinoslav, Moscow

The expulsions started immediately after the Bolshevik Revolution in the territory of the former Tsarist empire. The families fled from place to place to escape from the Bolsheviks—from Petrograd to Baku, from there via Moscow to Kharkov in the Ukraine and back to Baku. Only the Ettingers, Rachel, David and the four small children stayed in Yekaterinoslav as long as possible until they had to flee head over heels to Kharkov in the summer of 1919. By then, Moshe was eight years old, Shalom seven, Dvora five and Chaim two.

The escape in the spring of 1918, when the Bolsheviks first seized power in Baku, is etched in Gita Kahan's memory for life. She was nine at the time. Their luggage almost got lost on the way. There were no regular train connections. They had to change trains at some place and were not allowed to take their luggage. *Nyanya* Sasha rescued them—the Russian woman talked to the people and found a farmer who helped her by hiding them and their luggage in his rack wagon, under the straw. Aron managed to escape on one of the company's tankers thanks to the good will and loyalty of the crew, who could have mutinied against the *burzhui* boss. When he left Moscow for the Ukraine in the summer of 1918 together with Zina, *Nyanya* Sasha and the children, he fell ill on the way. They interrupted the journey and stayed with friends. Ready to travel again, they continued in a cattle car loaded with people. For hours Aron and the three-year-old Lily stood in the crowd, one leg on the ground, the other on a suitcase. Being on the road at that time was not only exhausting, but also life-threatening. There was chaos and violence on the streets. Right from the start the steppe was sometimes "Red" and sometimes "White," the railway line was interrupted while marauding soldiers and gangs made the area unsafe. Travelers did not know which papers to show, whether they should identify themselves as Bolsheviks travelling on official business or by their own names. On one occasion, when trains were not running, Aron was on his way by horse-drawn carriage from Kharkov to Slavyansk, to Zina and her relatives in the summer resort, when two men approached him in the open field, ordering him with drawn pistols to undress. Fortunately, a wagon that appeared on the horizon put the bandits to flight. They robbed Aron of his cash, shoes and the new Moscow suit, but he escaped unharmed. When the Red Army captured the Ukraine city by city in early 1919, Aron was on his way by train from Kiev to Kharkov; the journey took three days instead of the usual ten hours. Exhausted, he fell asleep after his arrival. When he woke up sixteen hours later, the Bolsheviks had caught up with him—Kharkov was already in their grip. "Our Aaron came here a week ago, and has now got his route to Baku interrupted, which we are very sorry for," Baruch wrote to Berlin from Kharkov on January 8, 1919. Continuing his journey to Baku had become unthinkable for Aron.

Since fleeing Baku in April 1918, the family corresponded about Zina and the children leaving Soviet Russia. David wrote from Moscow to Berlin, asking his relatives to obtain an entry permit. This threw the family into turmoil. Yasha spoke of "incalculable consequences" because, after Zina's arrival, "the misfortune can no longer be concealed." Jonas warned of the stresses and strains of such a journey, although he would be happy to be able to hug "our d[ear] Zina here." Bendet, too, advised that if her or the children's state of health did not make it absolutely necessary, it would not be advisable to come. The reason for the turmoil, caused by the news of Zina's travel plans, was the double taboo on Schlüterstrasse of talking about the deaths in the family on the other side of the war front. The fact that Chaim had died was being concealed from Malka, and Pinchas's death was kept secret from Miriam. With Zina's arrival without her husband, the secret would be revealed. It was necessary to lay the groundwork for the women. Were they afraid of taking responsibility for the widow? David and Aron had suggested an escape route via Libau, the Latvian Liepāja, but the Berlin relatives advised against it. There were no safe transport facilities. After that, for a long time, from July 1918, there had been no more talk of Zina leaving the country.

In the autumn of 1918 Baruch and Rosalia planned to travel to Berlin to celebrate Yasha and Rosa's wedding in December, the day of their silver wedding anniversary. Nachum and Arusia wanted to come along. The attempt to obtain passports for them delayed the trip and ultimately failed, as the two were liable to military service. One war ended, another began. When Kharkov fell to the Bolsheviks at the beginning of 1919, the way to Baku was blocked. Aron advised Baruch and Rosalia, once again, not to move to Baku, despite all the difficulties. But what was to happen to Nachum and Arusia, who were now denied permission to leave the country more than ever? Aron, together with his young employee, Mr. Farber from Saratov, set off for the West to organize an escape for Zina and the children, as he wrote later. Another reason was his concern about the future of the companies in Baku and that he was threatened as a committed industrialist and political advisor, as Zina remembered. For *burzhuis*, things had become increasingly risky under the Bolsheviks, and his proposal to reform the Ukrainian fiscal policy put Aron in particular danger. A stamp with the inscription "Workers' Soviet of the Caucasus-Volga Inc." provided them with the necessary permit; Farber had put it on the company's application for permission to travel on business to branches in Vilna, Kovno and Grodno, which in reality did not exist, allegedly to buy oil for the city.

Aron described the adventurous escape in his memoirs. Having apparently learned from the previous summer's holdup, he was dressed as a Russian farmer, in a *tulup*, a sheepskin coat and earflap cap. Accompanied by Farber, he arrived by train from Kharkov in Vilna, which was also occupied by the Bolsheviks at the time. Train journeys were harrowing, with interruptions between stations, or in crowded stations where wagons were shunted, uncoupled and connected again. The Russian railways travelled at a leisurely, infinitely gently swaying speed; with sleeping soldiers, peasants and market women seated on wide, worn wooden benches, with raw mattresses, dirt on the floor, broken windows and luggage boards without brackets—traces of war and revolution, which despised people and things. Aron may have encountered some of that along the way. In addition there was the fear of inspections and robberies.

In Vilna, Aron paid a visit to the business acquired by the family, the Romm printing works, which continued to operate despite the new rule, not without immediately assisting with a guarantee of 100,000 rubles, which he was to cover a few months later, in autumn 1919, from Copenhagen, when Romm Inc. was founded. With a local *balegole*, a Jewish carter, the two men reached Poreche without incident, where Bendet and Judith had once celebrated their wedding, but where now the war front ran right up to the German border. In order to continue their journey to Berlin, they needed new papers. Aron asked around and learned by chance that Field Rabbi Winter, whom he had met in Kiev, was stationed in Grodno. So he sent Farber to Winter on the Tenth Army base in

Grodno, and within a day he got them German visas so that they could travel on to Berlin unhindered. There Aron stayed until Yasha's and Rosa's wedding, which took place without the groom's parents on March 14. Then he travelled on to Copenhagen, where he and Carl Frederik Glad founded a new corporation within a few weeks, the COC—Caucasian Oil Company; he had also begun planning Zina's escape from Soviet Russia.

Already during the war, the L. C. Glad & Co. had helped the Kahans and many other Russian families to cross the borders between the enemy countries via neutral Denmark without danger—in person, with news, or consignments of goods. Three hundred people are mentioned in the company's corporate history. A thank-you note on parchment, kept by the entrepreneur Thomas Glad in a large brown leather folder from his grandfather, was signed by thirty people, including five Kahans: Chaim, Rosalia, Baruch, Aron and David; Zina had signed with her maiden name Golodetz; other signatories were friends and business partners—Rabbi Aronson; I., S. and V[ulf] Dembo; the Mazut representatives M[ikhail] and O. Poliak [Pollak]; N., M. and S. Friedland; and W. Finkelstein. Special thanks in form of a poem and the gift of a Caucasian sword came from the Danish vice-consul Heinrich Warnecke in Batumi, who was a German from Bremen and whom the Glads had met on their trip to the Caucasus in 1910. At the beginning of their trade relations with the Kahans before the war, Warnecke had ensured smooth communications, customs clearance and shipping. The Glads rescued the German officer from Russian captivity in Vyatka and helped him return to his workplace in Batumi. Aron recalls that there was a folder in Glad's office with all the responses to the inquiries from these "special customers." In the middle of the war, in 1916, Aron and Pinchas had gone to Copenhagen with the expressions of gratitude and gifts—a silver tea service that included a samovar with a rhymed thank-you engraved in Danish. On that occasion, Aron had given a golden cigarette case to the junior boss Carl Frederik Glad.

In mid-May 1919, when then the formation of the COC was official, Aron, in Copenhagen, turned his attention back to the family. L. C. Glad & Co. had applied for an entry permit for Zina and the children from the Danish Ministry of Justice, but the Ministry rejected the request. Aron now provided the Glads with arguments to persist with the request. He refuted the reasons for the refusal—food shortages, the fear of Bolshevik propaganda in the country—arguing that a woman with three children posed no danger to either of these. He appealed once again forcefully to humaneness and cited his partnership with Glad as a bond with the country and its people in order to obtain permission for the entry of his sister-in-law and her children, whose guardian he was after his brother's death. As reasons for his flight from Ukraine to "Europe," as he wrote, he listed the atrocities committed by the pogrom movement against Jews there, citing facts and figures: four thousand victims in Proskurov alone, three hundred of them children of a Jewish school.

The pogroms in Ukraine, perpetrated after the collapse of the Empire by the various parties—Ukrainians, Poles, Russians, Whites, Reds, Nationalists, Communists, Anarchists—in the struggle for supremacy, posed a real threat to the Kahans in Kharkov and Yekaterinoslav. They were ostracized as *burzhuis* and as Jews. The pogrom in Proskurov on February 15, 1919 had been particularly cruel. A brigade of Ataman Petlyura had attacked the Jews there. The soldiers had robbed them, plundered their homes, raped their women and murdered them. Brutalized by the war, freed from obedience to autocratic rule and inflamed by the lust for power of self-appointed potentates, they used the old antagonistic image of the Christ murderer that appeared in the revolutionary hype as a capitalist, and in their enemy's propaganda, as a revolutionary. It was a pretext used by all sides for attacking the Jews. In the pogroms, up to two hundred thousand people were injured and at least sixty thousand were killed. After the murders of the Armenians in the Ottoman Empire at the beginning of the war, the pogroms in Ukraine prepared the ground for the next genocide, as it were. At that time, dedicated Jewish contemporary witnesses desperately tried to draw the attention of the European public to the breach with civilized norms, which might have been the reason for the fact that the Ukraine did not belong to Europe on Aron's mental world map.

Assuming that Yasha would be more interested in the fate of his relatives than the other members of his family in Berlin—after all, this was also about his parents and brothers—Aron appealed to his nephew to play a more active role in their rescue from the Ukraine, which he himself was working feverishly on. Aron was staying at Aagaard's Seaside Guesthouse in the coastal town of Skodsborg, twenty kilometers north of Copenhagen, writing on the letterhead of the capital's most noble hotel, the D'Angleterre. His considerations revolved around three helpers, who were to make their way to his relatives by various routes—via the Scandinavian countries and Poland to Kharkov and Yekaterinoslav: Farber, a certain Buch and a Dane whose name he did not mention. The plan was to bring them to Germany via Lithuania. Aron, in a tone of sharp criticism and insulting allegations, accused the Kahans and Rosenbergs in Berlin of indifference, suppression of the problem and apathy towards the fate of their own in Sovdepia, as Soviet Russia was scornfully called by emigrants.

He alleged that Rosa's interest in this matter would have amounted to only fifty percent, while she would have been worrying more about her home furnishings, and her concern for all the other problems would have amounted to only twenty-five percent. During his visit, he had learned more than enough about the Charlottenburg psychology. That's why they would misunderstand him and weren't able to cope with Farber's offers of help. It wouldn't be enough to ask the Zionist office for a letter to the Danish Red Cross. Yasha would have to take the initiative himself in word and deed; he would need to be courageous and take care immediately of documentation, helpers, routes and stopovers for the escape; he would need to proceed in a variety of ways, to be flexible and thoroughly think everything through. Experience would be less important than seizing a good opportunity.

Already in Kharkov, Aron had the idea of seeking help from the Red Cross in Copenhagen. The connection was to be made by an oil industrialist, Ernst Michaelsen, the director of Vacuum Oil for Scandinavia and Russia, whom he knew from Baku. In Copenhagen, Carl Frederik Glad, Michaelsen and the Copenhagen rabbi Professor David Simonsen introduced him to Einar Sørenson, who had proved himself as a human trafficker from Soviet Russia. The Dane, a man of Aron's age who had lived, worked and gained experience in Russia for almost a decade before the war and who had helped prisoners of war in Russia during the war as a representative of the Danish Red Cross, undertook spectacular expeditions to Russian revolution and war zones during those years. He had taken part in the White Army's march on Moscow, smuggled weapons to south-east Russia and Siberia for the self-defense of Danish envoys against the Bolsheviks and advised the Azerbaijani government on questions of agricultural reorganization until his escape from Soviet rule in 1920.

In the disputed border area, the rulers changed often and quickly in those years, like scenes from a drama. Immediately after the establishment of the Transcaucasian Republic, consisting of Georgia, Armenia and Azerbaijan, the Bolsheviks had seized power in Baku, which they held for three months, until the region was reconquered by the British army and its naval forces for the opponents of Soviet rule. Since the end of July 1918, Baku had been the capital of the Democratic Republic of Azerbaijan under British rule, except for a three-month interruption in the autumn of that year, when the Turks, with the help of the Azeris who had taken revenge on the Armenians for the April massacre, asserted their claims to Baku and Transcaucasia until the collapse of the Ottoman Empire in November. After that, Britain and France took control of the borderland between the former Empires, Europe and Asia, Baku and the Black Sea ports, and divided the territory among themselves.

David had managed to escape from the Bolsheviks in Kiev directly to Baku and had been in the oil metropolis for three and a half months, since the end of February 1919. He was concerned about the wellbeing of his Ukrainian relatives. On June 11 he inquired after their welfare and advised them to come to Baku. There it was quiet in every respect. He promised to send in a few days to Rostov the entry document that Zina needed. Beyond that, by way of involving his relatives in his activities, he asked about business deals and informed them about oil exports that had gone to Constantinople via Batumi. In the meantime, since Aron was no longer there, David had taken over the management in Baku and at the same time, like his brother Aron, was concerned with bringing the family to safety and reorienting the trade.

Just over a month later, on July 16, Baruch wrote from Yekaterinodar, now Krasnodar, to his relatives in Berlin, from whom he had heard nothing for eight or nine months. He had known since May of Aron's arrival in Germany through an acquaintance, Dr. Eisenstadt. He inquired after their health, especially that of his mother, son and daughter-in-law. All of them, Rosalia, Nachum and Arusia, but also Rachel and the children were, thank God, healthy. Two weeks earlier, in early July, Zina, *Nyanya* Sasha and the three children had managed to leave Kharkov, the Bolshevik domain, and escape southwards into the territory controlled by the White Army. "I was helped when I was getting out. I gave a bottle of cognac to one [of the] Cherkes. So he gave me permission to leave. It was not that hard. We left on a freight car, and the road was pretty bad," Zina remembered. Except for Arusia and Nachum, who were stranded in Kharkov, all of them, Baruch and Rosalia, Zina and her entourage, had temporarily found refuge in Kislovodsk, which harbored wealthy opponents of the revolution. Zina wanted to leave for Baku as soon as possible. Baruch was travelling on business in southern Russia from the Caucasus resort in Grozny, to Yekaterinodar and Rostov, the provisional capitals of the White Military Dictatorship. At that time, Southern Russia was the main scene of the warlike conflicts for the succession of the empire between the Reds and the Whites; participants were the Cossacks in Don, Kuban and Terek; the small Caucasian mountain peoples, the Transcaucasian nations, but also Great Britain and France, each according to their interests. From Kislovodsk, Baruch worked with David in Baku as best he could. Business as usual, even during the expulsion. "What we went through in Kharkov and in general cannot be written, we will discuss it orally, God willing, at the appropriate time." Then he got down to business. He said that, in these times, there is a great capacity to seize and use opportunities. He advised Jacob to learn to seize them firmly. He then said that he learned of Rachel and David Ettinger's escape from Yekaterinoslav en route to Rostov. They had come to Kharkov on July 7 as refugees without any belongings. There had been a pogrom in Yekaterinoslav, for the second time that year. In May, soldiers of the Ataman Grigoryev had raged there. At the beginning of July, Cossack units of General Shkuro were fighting on the side of the Whites. Locals had taken part in robbing the Jewish population, putting the fear of God into them. There had been casualties. The conditions in Yekaterinoslav had become unbearable, but they already regretted having fled so suddenly; they were already thinking of returning, Baruch wrote. He was glad that Rosalia was better off in Kislovodsk. "The lifestyle in Kharkov is very difficult now; we have not had electric light for months. Bread is much cheaper now, and yet it costs 12/13 rubles, the pound of meat 20/25." He gave the letter, with the concluding sentence "we hope for better times, and may God help us depart soonest, which would be the greatest happiness for us all," to a businessman who took it to Constantinople and sent it by post to Berlin.

At the end of July, Rachel wrote a long letter from Kharkov to Zina, who had meanwhile returned to Baku. It was the answer to a letter that Rachel had been very happy about. She did not often receive mail from her sister-in-law. There are very few written documents from Zina in the family archives. The letter to Rachel is not among them. Rachel described to Zina the difficult situation as a refugee in the house of her oldest brother in Kharkov, without means or prospects. They did not want to stay with Rosalia in Kharkov, but they did not want to return to Yekaterinoslav under any circumstances. The Bolsheviks there were particularly good at mocking the *burzhuis*, she wrote. And then there was the cold. Last winter they were freezing because there was no firewood. This year would be no different in the current situation. It was unbearable there with the little ones. She and David had aged from worry and misery. At first, they were hoping to stay in rest homes where the cost of living was lower, but then they planned to move to Baku for the winter. However, things had turned out differently. It was now too late for rest homes, and there were no apartments to be had in Baku, not even for a lot of money. An acquaintance who had just come from there said so. Rachel was desperately seeking a way out and a refuge. For her, the only options were areas dominated by the Whites—the Caucasus or the Crimea. She only thought of escape, which she called "exit," and in her mind played through all the possibilities. But worse than anything else for her was the to-ing and fro-ing. "Yesterday I decided categorically that we'll go to

Crimea and I am now quite relieved. … We're going to Sevastopol and will look for some rooms for the winter and from there to Balaklava for 1 ½ months." She wanted to wait only for eight to ten days for the things from their Yekaterinoslav apartment to be delivered. In the meantime, the children were able to recover from the flu, which had weakened them all, but especially Shalom, who was also suffering from an inflamed middle ear. At the seaside, in the sun, on the beach of Balaklava they would get well. But Rachel found it difficult not to go to Baku to see Zina and her relatives. "What can we do? Now our lives are determined by the circumstances; we can't create them according to our wishes. I can't imagine that we'll see each other again soon, probably not before spring; that's terrible for me. You are partly to blame for that, my dear. Had you written and informed me that you were leaving, everything would have been different." Finally, Rachel asked if what an acquaintance told her was true: she heard that Zina's apartment had been requisitioned, that some of the furniture had been transferred to the office where David was now living, and that Baruch and Rosalia intended to leave for Baku as soon as Nachum had recovered.

A second detailed letter from Rachel to Zina followed only a few days later. She wrote that the situation had suddenly changed. A Dane had arrived with letters, news and completely new plans. This referred to Einar Sørensen, who had apparently reached Kharkov before continuing to Baku via Kislovodsk. The Ettingers no longer doubted that Zina would leave for Constantinople in the very near future. In view of the new situation, Rachel and David Ettinger now changed their own plans. "In principle, and before Aron decides anything else, it is clear that we are leaving Russia. Our destination is Palestine, of course. With small children who are brought up in the national spirit and are to grow up as free citizens, anything else is out of the question," Rachel wrote. "Clearly, the question is how we are going to set ourselves up materially in Palestine, but we think that given the resources we have, now is the time to get something going in Palestine as well. There is no argument about that. The second question, whether we will acclimatize there, can only be answered by trying, and we have decided to take the risk."

She assumed that Sørensen would also help them to leave the country and explained her ideas. Since entering Palestine without connections was more difficult than ever, they wanted to go to Constantinople first. In the time it would take Sørensen to obtain the necessary papers, they would wait in Sevastopol, preparing to leave the country. Zina was to inform Aron, discuss the plan with him, look for an apartment for all of them after their arrival in Constantinople and make a list of what was worth taking with them. She asked to give Aron her letter; she would not write to him separately. He should inquire about entry possibilities for Palestine and about the connections between Constantinople and Berlin. She wanted to see her mother again before leaving for Palestine. At the same time, her husband David Ettinger wrote to his brother-in-law David, Rachel's brother in Baku, lamenting his suffering and explaining the escape plan once more. He had left behind warehouses and orders in Yekaterinoslav and could not return there, because the roads were unsafe and travelling with the children was dangerous, but also because he was unable to go back to where the Bolsheviks were in charge while the *burzhuis'* hands were tied. They now wanted to go to Crimea, from where they would go somewhere to relax for a few weeks; they were only waiting for the necessary documents. Rachel and David probably gave their letters to Sørensen.

Rosalia also used the Danish helper as an "occasion," entrusting him with a letter of congratulations for Yasha and Roska on their wedding. She wrote that Mr. Sørensen had come to take her to Europe on behalf of Aron. But that wasn't what she had in mind. While she would like to visit Yasha and Roska in Berlin, if it weren't so difficult, living in Europe from one day to the next was something neither she nor her sons wanted. At the end of August Arusia got in touch from Kharkov and informed his father in God-knows-where—Kislovodsk, Rostov, Baku (the envelope and address have not been preserved)—about unfinished business and incoming claims; he asked him and Uncle Aron to send letters, for example in matters of COC, no longer to the office, but to his mother's private address. The company had not yet been inspected, but they did not want to attract attention or arouse suspicion.

It took quite a long time until Aron in Copenhagen received the first news from Baku. "I was following every morning the movements of the Bolshevik troops and Denikin's armies in the Danish newspapers, recording them on a map that was hanging over my bed, until I finally got the reassuring news that Zina and the children had managed to get back to Baku," he writes in his memoirs. With more occasions in mid-September, the letters from Baku to Berlin became more frequent. David, as well as Baruch and Rosalia, now in the only safe place left for them, were writing. Einar Sørensen had arrived, bringing with him the lawyer Hans Frederik Ulrichsen, who had been an employee of the Danish Embassy in Constantinople during the war and was an expert on the region under the difficult conditions. The first rescue operation organized by Aron was for Zina, the three children, Baruch and Rosalia. But, apparently, they could not yet decide to leave the country. Zina only sent away her eldest, Lolia, who, according to family legend, would have preferred to volunteer for the White Army—but *Nyanya* Sasha had fortunately been able to pull him out of the line of applicants in the recruitment office in time. However, Zina herself and her daughters stayed with Baruch, Rosalia and David in Baku. David announced Lolia's arrival to the family in Berlin, asked them to care for Zina's son, and commended his education to them offering some suggestions. From Copenhagen, Abraham Ledermann, Aron's first coworker at COC, announced Lolia's imminent arrival in Berlin and that for the time being there would be no family reunion. Indeed, in early autumn 1919, Sørensen and Ulrichsen, as diplomatic couriers from the Danish Foreign Office, managed to get the eighteen-year-old Lolia Kahan, who was fit for military service, from Baku via Constantinople to Berlin for the price of 10,000 crowns.

Shortly thereafter, in October, Aron himself set off once again to Baku to sell caustic soda, which was needed for oil processing, on the assumption that it was in short supply there. He was not able to send anyone. Perhaps he wanted to persuade Zina to flee, to bring her and the two girls to the West. Already in June he had announced his arrival by telegram from Copenhagen to Yekaterinodar. The journey was long and difficult: by ship from Copenhagen to London, where he received a visa for Azerbaijan, from there to France, in order to secure a loan for the purchase of a tanker in Paris, and on to Rome and Taranto, where he boarded a Lloyd Triestino steamer to Constantinople and Batumi. He arrived there on November 12. Two days later he was in Baku and spent two and a half months there. In his memoirs, Baku, where he found the family safe and sound, was once again associated with a joyful time for him, perhaps the happiest period of his life. The work in the two offices of Petrol and Binəqədi Oil Industry and Trading Company was apparently without any problems. Four authorized signatories did their job. In his memoirs of those months, Aron did not mention any of his brothers. It is possible that the jealousy scene between David and him had occurred in the competition for Zina's affection back in Baku. After all, David and Zina had been living at close quarters without him, she in the old apartment, he in the office. Aron had even pointed a pistol at David, the family says. Aron left again at the end of January 1920—without Zina and the girls. At least he managed to secure contact between Copenhagen and Baku through an officer of Lloyd Triestino and the COC office in Batumi.

It was a shock to the family when news came in early May 1920 that the Bolsheviks had taken Baku. Apart from Crimea, there was now no place of retreat for *burzhuis* in the former Tsardom. The entrepreneurs feared for life and limb while their remaining property was threatened. That was when David, and probably Baruch and Rosalia as well, began their flight from Azerbaijan.

When exactly and how they managed to leave Baku in order to get to Berlin is not documented in the family archives. The only thing certain is that David was already in Constantinople on June 12, while the COC sent requests for help to the Danish and German immigration authorities on July 23 and 26 to save Zina and her daughters from the Soviet Russia. Twice people with diplomatic passports came to get them out, Gita remembered, but her mother did not want to leave. Finally, a Soviet Russian officer, who was billeted with Zina, helped her get the necessary exit papers. "I went with Sasha, Lily and Gita to Batum. We had to wait for a boat to Italy. We lived in a *dacha*. We spent Rosh Hashanah in Rome," Zina remembered in old age. "I got to Germany because Farber was a big *makher*. I got a Georgian passport."

Zina, Sasha and the children fled from Baku, first to Georgian territory. The British Army had withdrawn from Batumi and environs on July 7, 1920, leaving it to the Georgians. The Georgian army had successfully defended the territory against the Bolsheviks until February 1921. Aron immediately arranged Danish residence permits for the refugees. This was necessary because it was uncertain whether they would receive documents for Germany. At the same time he contacted Zina through the Danish branch manager of the COC in Batumi and the officer at Lloyd Triestino via Batumi. He informed her about his actions and asked her to persuade Sasha to come with him to Berlin, which worked. Shortly afterwards he received the news that Zina and the children had already crossed the border together with Sasha and were now in Batumi. On August 11 he received a telegram with the urgent request to send visas for Zina, the children and Sasha, otherwise they would not be able to leave Batumi. It took him some time, but with the help of Rabbi Simonsen, he managed to obtain an unlimited residence permit for Zina, Sasha and the children in Denmark, except for Copenhagen. In the meantime, he applied through COC and the Danish Ministry of Foreign Affairs to the Italian Embassy in Paris for a visa for a business trip to Batumi via Paris, Rome and Constantinople. This, too, was an obstacle course. The Italian consul in Paris initially refused him the visa to continue his journey. He only received it with a certificate from the COC, which identified him as a director of the company, attesting to the necessity of the business trip. In Rome, with the help of his old friend Boris Dembo, who had gone there, he obtained a letter of recommendation from the Minister of Foreign Affairs, Carlo Sforza, to the Italian Allied High Commissioner Eugenio Camillo Garroni, one of the four representatives of the governing allied powers in Constantinople, following the collapse of the Ottoman Empire. The letter to the High Commissioner and the permission to enter Copenhagen helped Zina, Sasha, Gita and Lily to leave Batumi. Aron met them in Constantinople in September 1920, from where they were all able to travel by ship to Taranto, from there to Rome and from Rome by train to Berlin.

Now it was a matter of rescuing Arusia and Nachum Kahan from the Bolshevik-controlled territory. Nachum's daughter Efrat remembered that the two of them had considered that time in Kharkov as an adventure of which they later told stories. The young men had been living alone, for a year and a half, from the summer of 1919 until the spring of 1921, in their parents' apartment at 21 Pushkinskaya, in a mansion on one of the city's boulevards. Arusia was—according to the certificate—exempted from military service since May 6, 1919 and Nachum might not have received the desired document at all or just shortly before leaving the country. The time in Kharkov was a tough experience for them. They defended the large apartment against the threat of confiscation and against the mob. They took people from their circle of acquaintances as subtenants trying to protect their property—furniture, books, clothes, silver—from being looted. In winter it was so cold in the rooms that the water in a carafe on the table would freeze overnight, breaking the glass. Since firewood was not available, they burned the furniture. With the help of a dentist friend of theirs, they disguised the entrance hall as a dental clinic in order to prevent billeting. They were starving, so they traded silver and furs on the market for food. In order not to be persecuted as a capitalist, Nachum obtained a job at the Office of Statistics and a certificate of employment providing him with the right to exist in Sovdepia; he indicated his new status on the name plate of the apartment door. In this way he was able to cope with life in the Russian environment under extreme conditions. Perhaps it paid off that he attended a Tsarist grammar school, because, unlike his brothers and cousins, he had been considered difficult to bring up. The brothers had a division of labor: Nachum had the certificate of employment, Arusia procured the food. At the market he offered *galoshkes* for eggs. A photo, perhaps as a farewell to friends, shows the two of them in a small group of young people in front of bare trees. It may have been taken in a Kharkov park at the beginning of spring 1921. Some people are wearing their winter coats already open, others are getting along without them. The men are dressed, politically correct, with their peaked caps. Arusia, the only one standing—the others are sitting on the edge of a fountain—is wearing commissar boots. Nachum and Arusia are conspicuous in their stiff shirt collars and ties under their coats. Everyone looks into the camera. Nachum looks leaner than Arusia, who is the only one laughing.

The two wanted to get to their parents in Berlin as soon as possible. But they could not leave Kharkov. Maybe they felt the total attachment to their place of residence in *Sovdepia* at that time as enslavement, strangling them? The more Soviet power became consolidated, the more difficult it became to escape. About two million people left their homes in those years in groups, families, or alone, although under Tsarist rule they had been antagonists—monarchists, democrats, or left-wing revolutionaries. They went on odysseys, fled on foot, in horse-drawn carriages, by train, or by ship in all directions. Nachum and Arusia lost contact with parents and relatives in Berlin and Baku. Letters from Aunt Rachel, who had not fled to Crimea or Baku, but had returned to Yekaterino-slav, arrived only irregularly, sometimes not at all. "Occasions" were risky, often unreliable. The post office was no longer functioning. When correspondence was back to normal, it was censored by the *Cheka*. At that time, a letter within Soviet Russia was usually on its way for a month. At first, for half a year, the two of them, like Rachel, were hoping for the arrival of a *malach ha'osher*, an angel of good fortune and a savior, like Sørensen, but that did not happen.

From February 1920 they had been relying on Yuda M. Beham, a young lawyer from Kharkov who was active in Zionist and revolutionary student groups for which he was arrested and deported. Beham was a friend of the Kahans, advising and helping them since the outbreak of the war. He travelled frequently between Berlin, Petrograd, Moscow and Kharkov, as long as that was possible. His wife worried about him and sometimes inquired after his welfare in letters that alternated between the Kahans across the front line. Beham was apparently with his family in Kharkov when the Bolsheviks took over the rule of the city and country; he had been supporting the two young men since their parents had left. He accepted a post at the People's Commissariat for Foreign Trade to open up escape opportunities, perhaps to reach the West on a business trip, be it via Romania or Georgia. But the plan failed. The family that was sup-posed to flee with him, in which he included Nachum and Arusia, was too large to leave the country unnoticed.

The summer months passed, and nothing happened; disappointment began to set in. Shortly before Rosh Hashanah, at the beginning of October 1920, the idea of a departure for Palestine, a return to the homeland, arose. Beham put together a group. Liaison officers from the Jewish Committee for the Assistance of War Victims obtained documents and established contacts with the Lithuanian Embassy, which was to enable the departure. The Ambas-sador at that time was the poet Jurgis K. Baltrušaitis. Under his leadership, the embassy helped many, including the historian Simon Dubnow, to escape.

Friends, relatives and Jewish politicians in Lithuania contributed to this. Their uncle in Vilna, Isidor Berlin, also lobbied the embassy for Nachum and Arusia, perhaps prompted by Aron and Yasha in Berlin. They were registered out of turn. The *Cheka* checked particularly thoroughly Lithuanians from the Ukraine who wanted to leave the Soviet region, because Lithuania at that time still recognized the independent Ukraine. Thanks to a go-between, they managed to pass through all official channels without any problems. The group was to depart shortly after the High Holidays, on October 20, when the Polish military took the Lithuanian capital Vilna, allegedly to protect the Polish minority there. The new political situation changed everything. Departures to Lithuania were stopped, Arusia wrote in a sixteen-page letter to Uncle Aron. At that time, only those who could prove a place of birth in Lithuania received an entry permit, as Efrat had later heard from Uncle Arusia and her father. But both of them were born in Vilna (Vilnius), which was now occupied by Polish troops and was called Wilno. Her uncle then studied the geography of Lithuania in the library in order to find a suitable place of birth.

Some more weeks went by. Then came the winter, the cold, so that travelling was out of the question. During the winter the two young men received some important letters from abroad. One came from Uncle Aron with a recommendation that turned out to be a flop. The second letter, according to Arusia's report, came on *a sheinen pesach morgen* [on a lovely Passover morning] from Farber with documents for them and for Aunt Rachel with her family, which they forwarded to Yekaterinoslav by "occasion." Further letters from Farber followed with the information that he had sent them money and organized help for them. But no one came, and they did not think at the time that their relatives in Berlin could still help to save them. Until the last moment, however, they believed in the possibility of a "business trip" to Batumi or to Moscow, authorized by the People's Commissariat for Foreign Trade, from where group trips were being organized. Beham was involved in this. Again, the Lithuanian Embassy came into play. The plan was to join a group of Jewish dignitaries and intellectuals who were to leave out of turn. In those days, in late March 1921, a letter arrived from Yasha in Berlin, informing them that Farber had spoken with Baltrušaitis and an embassy employee, Dr. G., in Moscow on their behalf. A little later they received a letter from Dr. G. with the request to come to Moscow. He had documents ready for them.

Confusion was caused by further letters and contradictory information from go-betweens. It remained unclear whether group trips to Lithuania were planned only from Moscow or also from Kharkov. It was unclear where the money, which the relatives had sent to the Lithuanian Embassy via Farber, went. Dr. G. allegedly knew nothing about it and made dubious offers, proposing to lend them 500,000 rubles. They were only to come along, and *alles werd rekht zain* [everything will be OK]. They would even be allowed to leave without a group. Nachum and Arusia became suspicious, but decided after all to leave Kharkov and go to Moscow. In the capital it would be easier to get a visa. However, one had to get there first. They needed exit documents and train tickets for a train that was actually going. By chance, Nachum met a former schoolmate on the street who was Jewish like him, but had become a Bolshevik, and he got them the necessary exit documents, said Efrat.

A few days before their departure, Nachum and Arusia received a letter from Farber, which had been on the road for four months, since the end of December, informing them that Dr. G.'s go-between had received one million rubles for the organization of their journey from Kharkov to Moscow. What had happened to it, they did not know. No one had contacted them. On April 25, 1921, Nachum and Arusia left Kharkov for Moscow like new *sovburs*, the Soviet *burzhuis* on business trips, in a first-class carriage provided to Beham by the People's Commissariat for Foreign Trade. A few days later, right on Russian Orthodox Easter, they arrived in Moscow. Arusia's report and his later stories are silent about where they stayed, whether in the former Petrol office or elsewhere, and how they coped with everyday life in the foreign metropolis. Although there were drop-in centers for migrants, things became tight for them when immigration to Moscow was halted at the beginning of June due to overcrowding in the city, and the shelters were gradually closed. They wandered around, got information from acquaintances or from more or less dubious contacts, but first and foremost from Dr. G., about *makhers*, traffickers and about the conditions for leaving the country. They found it laughable that this man wanted to give them unlimited credit, with forty-percent interest, to finance their further escape. It had cost a lot of money, time and health to get to Moscow, Arusia wrote in his report to Uncle Aron which he drafted on July 20, 1921, in Kaunas, the new Lithuanian capital. Nobody knows exactly how, when and with whose help they finally crossed the border and how they actually got there. It is certain that the Lithuanian Embassy in Moscow had helped them. From the applications for a Nansen passport later in Berlin, it is clear that they entered Germany as Azerbaijani citizens. From Kaunas they first moved to a *dacha* in the countryside to recover from their tribulations. Uncle David and, a little later, brother Yasha arrived from Berlin to welcome them. Although sums were known, the cost of the escape for Nachum and Arusia cannot be quantified precisely, in view of the different and rapidly fluctuating exchange rates of the currencies in Berlin, Warsaw and Moscow and the inflation in Russia as well as in Germany at the time. However, Uncle David told Efrat later that it had cost a lot of money to rescue the two boys from being stuck in Russia.

Arusia's letter was a report to account for the expenses of the escape, but also to provide information about the Ettingers, who were now the last of Chaim Kahan's descendants to remain in Soviet Russia. At the end he summarized his thoughts about ways to help Rachel and David. The two young men had thought a lot about them, had also kept in contact with them through "occasions," had passed on documents, information and tips, but had not seen their relatives again. When Nachum and Arusia left Soviet Russia, the Ettingers were still in Yekaterinoslav. The two warned that time was running out; soon it would be over with what they called *sidrat haplitim*, the organized rescue; it was essential to provide their uncle and aunt with money and persuade them to leave the city as soon as possible; they had enough documents. Dr. G., who only wanted to fleece them, had already collected 75,000 marks from the Kahans.

Escaping via Constantinople to Palestine remained a dream for Rachel, which was shattered by the long, cold winter in Yekaterinoslav. In the spring of 1921, at the end of April, they might have received Arusia's request to contact the Lithuanian Embassy in Moscow to help them get away. But the Ettingers hesitated to go down this road at the time. Her father did not want to leave, Dvora recounted, relying on the recollections of her oldest brother Moshe. David Ettinger considered the Bolsheviks to be a temporary phenomenon, and also had no hope of obtaining a Lithuanian visa, as he was from the Ukraine. Rachel dreaded the journey with her four small children. The Ettingers lived in Yekaterinoslav in a beautiful big house with an orchard. Next door was the girls' grammar school. In peacetime they had played croquet in the yard. Then came the war with the German occupation. Since the Bolshevik Revolution, Yekaterinoslav was changing hands quickly, and pogroms broke out there like everywhere else in the Ukraine. The Ettingers had prepared themselves for this. They entrenched themselves on the upper floor, packed their valuables in suitcases and hid them in an invisible compartment under the stairs. They left the defense of the ground floor to the maid Nastya, who betrayed them, however, so that the suitcases were stolen. David Ettinger grieved over the loss and Rachel consoled him. At the market, where she struggled to buy some food, stolen goods from her house were offered for sale, which she, fearing for her life, overlooked. At that time she had fallen pregnant and gave birth to her fifth child. But they suffered from food shortage. The child died. Hard times were about to begin for Rachel. She took care of the household and children by herself. The daily food consisted of kohlrabi and *psheno*, millet porridge. Dvora recounted that her mother had brought home a sack of flour once and baked bread, but forbade them to show themselves with it at the window to avoid arousing envy. They were also not allowed to play outside. In winter it was so cold that Moshe had frostbite on his feet. Boots were sewn for him from a rug. His father wanted to send Moshe to the market, but he was afraid to go out into the street because he was being beaten up by boys. Arusia wrote that Rachel had asked them to come to Yekaterinoslav, but this was impossible. Nachum and Arusia could not help their aunt; they tried to persuade her to go to Moscow where they wanted to rent her a *dacha* for accommodation. In May, Rachel asked her nephews in Moscow to prepare a place for her to stay, as she could not travel with her "baggage" on a whim. But this did not materialize all the time they were in Moscow because of the bad connections and the ban on residence permits.

It was not until the end of 1921 that David Ettinger set out on the dangerous journey to the capital to prepare their escape. In Moscow he fell ill with typhus. Rachel went to him and nursed him back to health. At the beginning of February 1922, both returned to Yekaterinoslav and took the children to Moscow. There the family was living from then on in a two-and-a-half-room apartment in the basement. The four children shared two beds. This went on for two long years. The chief rabbi and David's sister Bella, who had also fled to Moscow with her family, supported them. But despite all the hardships, Moshe also remembered some wonderful experiences: a visit to the Tretyakov Gallery and the performance of Maurice Maeterlinck's play *Blue Bird* in the MKhAT, the Moscow Art Theater. His father did not want to give up hope of being able to stay and work in Soviet Russia. Like in Yekaterinoslav, he tried to do business on the black market, which had received a brief boost under the conditions of economic liberalization during the NEP, the New Economic Policy. In the end, Rachel prevailed and the Ettingers were given the opportunity to escape, again through the Lithuanian Embassy, organized and financed by Aron with the help of a Danish diplomat.

Dvora kept the documents—the travel regulations and her father's passport with the emblem "Proletarians of all Countries, Unite"! David Ettinger was forty-nine years old at the time, the boys twelve and eleven. The passport photos reflect misery, presenting emaciated, haggard and frightened faces. The Soviet regulations concerning items that could be exported were strict and detailed. The last remaining valuables such as a silver centerpiece, made in Vienna in the 1860s, from David Ettinger's parents' house in Uman—an elephant on wheels, carrying four jars of pepper, salt, vinegar and oil on its back, guarded by a Chinese man with an umbrella—was dismantled therefore, and carefully hidden; jewelry was worked into suitcase locks; securities were placed between pages of books. Their preparation for departure had taken three months. On November 21, 1923, they crossed the border and reached Berlin without changing trains, on a visa from the Lithuanian Embassy, according to Dvora. Not much was said during the trip as they were afraid of causing a stir.

Fresh Start in the West. Caucasian Oil Company. Copenhagen, Berlin, London, Hamburg, Wilhelmshaven

In his description of the economic new beginning in the West, Aron sets the tone. David has only a weak voice, and others have little or no say. Aron's memoires claim to be the true account, the master narrative of this event. In it, the author has the role of the key witness for his own merits, his own success. And indeed, Aron had shown foresight in the face of the acute danger that the Bolshevik rule meant for the *burzhuis*, and thus for the Kahans. Over a period of four years, from 1919 to 1923, he successfully operated, organized and financed the risky, protracted and expensive rescue operations of his relatives. He gave himself similar credit for the restart of the family business. Even during the rescue operations, he participated in the establishment of companies in the West.

Aron recounted in his memoirs that immediately after his arrival in Copenhagen he learned that the money he had deposited with L. C. Glad & Co. had been spent. He quickly became aware of the family's hopeless financial situation resulting from their emigration and energetically set about finding new sources of income, all the more so as he felt obligated to provide for the family, especially his mother. Although he had professional experience in the Russian oil industry and knew about refineries, tank wagons, tankers on the Caspian Sea and tankers and barges on the Volga, business in Western Europe was *terra incognita* for him. He wanted to get back into the oil business, anything else was out of the question for him. As a first step, he ventured into trading with the newly founded Baltic republics in the former Russian border area, where his father had been working from the beginning, where they knew their way around and had their networks. Aron knew that Latvia and Estonia needed oil. The political break with Soviet Russia had cut traditional economic relations and opened up a new perspective, a niche for trade from West to East. But shortly after the war and the revolution there were no regular connections between Western Europe and the Baltic states, neither by mail or telegraph, nor by ship. At some point, Aron learned about a cable link between Copenhagen and the Latvian Liepāja, the former Libau. He remembered an address of acquaintances there, 14 Mariinskaya Street, where the mother and brother of his friend Fanny Rabinovitch were living. By cable he asked Julius (Yulchik) Rabinovitch, if he wanted to deal with the sale of petroleum, which would be sent to him in barrels. The answer came back the same day: Yulchik didn't have a clue about such things, but his brother-in-law Zirinsky, also in Liepāja, was willing to enter into the business. Thus the first connection was established. Now it was necessary to procure means of transport. Aron contacted schooner owners in Copenhagen, found some who were willing to take on board petroleum in barrels, transport them to Liepāja and other Baltic ports and get the goods paid for in foreign currency and silver rubles after unloading. He was back in business. Aron initiated and Glad financed Det Danske Petroleum Inc., which supplied mineral oil, gasoline, and petroleum. Det Danske Petroleum Inc., since 1952 Dansk Esso A/S, was one of the major Danish petroleum sales companies controlled by the Standard Oil Co. of New Jersey (Exxon). Initially the goods were exported to Liepāja in batches of five hundred and later one thousand barrels. The captains were honest Danes, Aron tells us, who punctually brought home the foreign currency from each voyage, as well as sacks of silver rubles, which were traded under the code name "ashes" and sold to the merchant bank Samuel Montagu & Co. in London.

"I founded the Caucasian Oil Company early on," he says in his memoires. According to its articles of association, the COC's objective was to become involved in the production and trade of the oil industry, engage with relevant companies and deal with products of such companies at home and abroad. Inspired by its acronym, its emblem—a rooster—might have been designed by Margrethe Glad, the artistically gifted wife of the Danish entrepreneur. The COC started with a share capital of one million kroner and had its headquarters in Copenhagen. Aron Kahan received an office on the premises of L. C. Glad & Co. on Gothersgade. Gothersgade starts in the center, not far from the Hotel

D'Angleterre, passes the Botanical Gardens and leads to the old New Town of Copenhagen beyond the northern city gate. The four-to-five-story apartment and commercial buildings there have a European metropolitan flair. Building number 175 is located at the end of Gothersgade, and is part of a prestigious ensemble that recreates Parisian streetscapes. In mid-May 1919 the shares were subscribed, the capital paid up, the company registered. The business-man Aron Kahan, Baku, currently Copenhagen, the wholesalers Carl Frederik Glad, 175 Gothersgade, Copenhagen, and Johannes Erik Glad, Charlottenlund, acted as founders of the company and also formed the board of directors. Carl Frederik Glad was the managing director. The director alone or two board members were authorized to sign, and in the event of the sale or divestment of real estate, the entire board was authorized to sign. Therefore COC was not, in fact, founded and run by Aron alone, but by him and the entrepreneurs Glad, who in case of doubt had the majority against him.

The COC was initially a pipe dream, nothing more than a promising idea, which had originated from Aron, no doubt. He said that, initially, the share cap-ital was provided almost entirely on the basis of goodwill, based on a letter he had sent to the company. In it, he had referred to the Kahan's four corporations in the former Russian Empire, Petrol, Caucasus-Volga Industrial & Trading Company, Russian-Baltic Mineral Oil Company and Binəqədi Oil Industry and Trading Company, although, in the spring of 1919, they only operated and controlled the Baku oil fields and the refinery in the Black City, despite sales difficulties and increased risk. But why should the "dead souls," as Essad Bey called the Russian stocks in exile, have been less sought after in Copen-hagen than in Paris, New York, London, or Berlin? The COC also benefited from Aron's experience, his business acumen and knowledge of commodities, his connections in the oil industry as well as the German banks. But didn't the company benefit from as much goodwill due to the reputation of L. C. Glad & Co. in Denmark? Had Carl Frederik Glad helped Aron Kahan to obtain a loan? Glad never financed the COC, writes Morten F. Larsen, the biographer of the Danish enterprise. The first million kroner of share capital was fully paid up in May 1919. In order to put his merits in perspective and emphasize his role as a risk-taking and far-sighted entrepreneur, Aron introduced opponents, scep-tics and pessimists to this story: Johannes Erik Glad, the senior member of the board of directors, had only reluctantly participated in this project. On the day the company was founded, Aron by chance ran into Glad in the stairwell on his way to the office. Glad had wickedly joked that Aron better hurry quickly upstairs, because a million shares were waiting for him there. Aron replied optimistically that in a year's time Mr. Glad would no longer be able to buy COC shares at their nominal value.

L. C. Glad, the company, was founded in 1870 by Lars Christian Glad as a chemical factory. It initially produced butter yellow and rennet and later processed oil. It had maintained trade relations with Baku since the beginning of the century. "12 June L. C. Glad anno 1901. København—Baku" is written on the Danish merchant's plaque: the edge is decorated with flowers and two Romanesque window arches providing a view of drilling rigs, a factory and sandy oil fields under a blue sky. It is possible that the company was involved with the Copenhagen agency of the traditional and internationally known Moscow Company for Mineral Oils Ragozin & Co., which produced machine and other quality oils. It was famous for its *oleonapht*, which it distributed throughout Europe. They had laboratories in Moscow, Paris and London and Chaim Kahan, too, had connections to them. Doing business with the Kahans ushered in a new phase at L. C. Glad & Co. From then on, they were importing oil independently from the Russian Empire. This turning point is recorded in the company's history by a telegram in German, from St. Petersburg, dated September 27, 1910, documenting the Kahans' first business deal with Glad for the delivery of 180,000 *puds* of naphtha residue, although they found the price offer too low. When Aron came to Copenhagen nine years later, probably for the third time, Carl Frederik Glad was already on the company's board and obviously had confidence in the Baku merchant. The two businessmen apparently understood each other. They belonged to the same generation, were sons of company founders and represented maverick companies in the oil industry, competing with the three big companies, Standard Oil, Royal Dutch Shell and Anglo Persian Oil, the Big Sisters. Both obviously loved the game and the risk. But Carl Frederik Glad was not only a partner who trusted his Baku colleague, generating goodwill for him; he was also Aron's mentor and teacher. Aron says that working with Carl Frederik Glad became for him a school of the oil business in the West, at first concentrating on Scandinavia, England and Germany, then expanding to the whole European trade and later also looking at production in Romania and America.

Aron's memoirs convey the impression that the management of the COC was in his hands alone while Glad had only shown some interest. He recounts that work at the Copenhagen office increased rapidly. That's why, shortly after the company was founded, he decided to hire an employee—Abraham Ledermann from Riga, the son of a veteran employee in whom he had confidence. His father, Noech Ledermann, had managed Chaim Kahan's warehouse in

Vinnytsia, Galicia, while Abraham Noechovich had already represented the Russian-Baltic companies in Riga. But it was not easy to bring the young man to Copenhagen, as the Latvian authorities did not allow military personnel to leave the country. For this feat Aron engaged Hans Frederik Ulrichsen— apparently for the first time—as a courier. The Danish diplomat, who officially requested Ledermann for the COC, achieved the desired effect in Riga and obtained an exit visa for him. Immediately after his arrival in Copenhagen, the Russian Jewish employee began to learn Danish and was able to communicate well after only a few months. In addition, there was another, Elias Feldmann, who came from Łódź, allegedly from the Kahan's circle of employees, just like Ledermann. He had come to Copenhagen in 1914 as a student. Ledermann was given power of attorney and became head of the office, while Feldmann became an authorized agent. Aron continues: Ledermann was able to run the company in his absence under the supervision of Carl Frederik Glad, who "was also interested in the business." In fact, the COC's correspondence handed down is signed by Aron or Abraham Ledermann. But officially Glad was the managing director. The COC bought all the oil products that came from the USA and also from Russia, chartered the tankers and made all the important decisions in this regard, while the sales were mostly arranged by the Kahans in Berlin, according to L. C. Glad & Co's history. Is it conceivable that Carl Frederik Glad took a back seat when contracts were finalized while Aron was running the COC, even long after he had gone to Berlin, leaving the Danish partner on the spot to merely provide the necessary backing?

The launch of a second company in Copenhagen was certainly Aron's doing alone. Five months after the opening of the COC, in mid-October 1919, he made good on a promise and founded the Publishing and Printing House ROM with a share capital of 10,000 kroner, the amount he had promised its senior manager, Shraga Feigensohn, earlier that year for the rehabilitation of the publishing house in Vilna. Compared to the COC, ROM was a minor project for Aron, which he only pushed ahead with out of respect for his father. But here too, Glad's support was of benefit to him. Apart from Aron, the founder of the company was Gerson Oppenheim, an authorized signatory at L. C. Glad & Co., the Kahan's contact person in the company since the beginning of the war, and Jacob Eskjeld Salomon, a Copenhagen civil servant and Aron's contemporary, whom he may also have met through Glad or through the Jewish community. The board of directors was composed of Oppenheim, Salomon and a certain Yudel (Julius) Goldberg, who is introduced as an author and also acted as managing director.

Aron's dream at the time was probably to combine the new business in the West with the old one in the East. The Baku companies produced and processed oil in the Transcaucasian Republic of Azerbaijan under British sovereignty in a more or less free market and sold their products to the region, to the areas controlled by the Whites, across the Caspian Sea and beyond Caucasus Minor to the West, as well as the Georgian Black Sea port of Batumi, occupied by the British. When the war ended, they had access to the world's oceans again.

One day, an old acquaintance from Russia, Karl Emil Quarnström, arrived from Stockholm in Copenhagen with an idea for Aron. The Swede had learned the oil business at Branobel, after which he ran his own refinery in Baku, but had moved back home in 1918 because of the upheaval caused by the revolution. His suggestion now was to use the Kahan's office in Baku to determine the demand for goods in the Transcaucasian oil metropolis. He provided two million Swedish krona for the purchase of trade goods and a ship for their transport there; it was to carry oil products to Scandinavia on the way back from Baku. He wanted the COC to share the profit without risk. The Baku oil industry was functioning; what was missing were the postal and telegraphic communications necessary for business transactions. With the help of the manager, Michelson, Aron successfully telegraphed David in Baku, via Vacuum Oil's office in Tehran, forwarding Quarnström's proposal to him. David immediately replied that Aron should come to Baku and that a decision would be made there. "This was a real blow for me," Aron said. He did not speculate about David's reaction, which had botched the deal for him. This was embarrassing vis-a-vis the Swedish businessman and annoying for him, because he had expected a lot from that deal without risk or investment. He turned down the offer, adapted the idea and undertook this venture on his own. He borrowed 40,000 kroner from Glad and bought one hundred tons of caustic soda from a Marseille company, on the assumption that the Baku businesses were cut off from the product they needed to refine the oil. The Marseille company also took care of the transport to Baku. He described his journey from Copenhagen via London, Paris, Rome, Taranto, Constantinople and Batumi to Baku as an adventurous business trip. In London he got to know the tanker market; in the emigrant circle of Russian brokers and bankers in Paris he found a financier for the purchase of a Norwegian tanker, but when he went to Constantinople to withdraw the deposit for the ship from the Banca di Roma, he learned that the money was not there, the promise had been a sham. But the deal with the caustic soda, which was doubtful until its arrival at its destination, apparently became a success. According to Aron, he sold the goods in Baku at three times the purchase price.

This daring transaction with personal commitment probably remained the only such import deal into the Transcaucasian oil metropolis.

David does not feature well as a businessman in Aron's narrative, and there is no mention of Baruch. They themselves have left no accounts, only raw material in letters and family legends provide a few fragments. Baruch and David Kahan, the oldest and the youngest of Chaim's sons, attempted in 1919 to carry on business from the Caucasus and from Baku under dangerous conditions and open up trade routes in various directions. Baruch wrote in July in one of his letters to Berlin that they were hoping for a recovery of the oil prices and to buy goods, but for the time being they were still far from their goal. In November/December, he had already sent ten to twelve wagons of various naphtha products via Batumi to Poti, to be shipped on to Crimea, including Odessa. However, due to the political situation, the wagons were stuck in Poti. They were facing colossal damage because high taxes and levies were now being imposed in Baku. When imports to Russia by water and rail, from the Caspian and Black Seas ports, to Petrovsk, Poti and Odessa, were blocked because of the fighting, they had goods shipped to Constantinople by a confidant, the son of the Baku oil entrepreneur Shifrin. It looked as if the business was going well, Baruch wrote. But David described the difficulties in investing the proceeds of the oil products sold in Constantinople in return transports that would promise a profit. The value of the pound sterling was falling. Shortly after Rosh Hashanah, on September 17, 1919, two days after Sørensen had left with Lolia for Batumi, David wrote a long business letter to relatives in Berlin, which he gave to Ulrichsen. Evidently, he wanted to send oil products to the West that autumn, perhaps for the first time after the war and revolution. He asked for information about the market in Germany. As far as he knew, the prices for their products in Europe were very low, and in view of the high cost price and taxes, it was hardly worth exporting there. According to information from Aron, the prices in Denmark were somewhat better. Nevertheless, they found Denmark and Germany interesting for export, because they urgently needed foreign currency for their expenses in Baku and Berlin. He agreed with Aron. Despite the difficulty in obtaining freight wagons from the railways for the transport from Baku to Batumi, he promised to send five wagons with machine oil and three with mastic asphalt, perhaps also with cylinder oil, in a few days. In twelve to fourteen days the goods would be in Batumi and from there they would be transported to Germany either directly or via Denmark. At that time there was no direct line from Batumi to Hamburg or Copenhagen. Therefore, his relatives were supposed to find a shipping company to move the shipment on, preferably to the port of a neutral country, such as Rotterdam. For the return transport they were to buy electrical equipment from the proceeds of the oil products in Germany, including laboratory equipment and a few dozen hydrometers for the Baku company. As additional cargo, David wanted Russian books printed in Germany. There was a lack of them in Baku, and they were cheap in Berlin. If Berlitz produced in Germany, his relatives should send along textbooks for English and French and, if possible, a typesetting machine with Cyrillic and Hebrew letters. David was obviously as interested in books as he was in oil, and at the time, in the fall of 1919, he was far from thinking about giving up the company and fleeing Baku.

Batumi, the Georgian border town and port, belonged for a long time to the Ottoman Empire, then to the Russian Empire since the Berlin Congress of 1878, and again to the Ottoman Empire since the peace treaty of Brest-Litovsk. When that collapsed and British troops, including the Royal Navy, occupied the region, it became the gateway to the Western world for people and goods, especially for the Baku oil. At the end of 1919, the COC opened a branch in Batumi, which was managed by a certain Wilhelm Stehr. In their letters to Berlin, the Baku Kahans had been using Stehr as a contact address since August: 23 Sadovaya [Garden] Street. The branch office had the task of forwarding oil products from Baku to the importing countries. Stehr had the power of attorney for all the COC business and property in Batumi and environs covering all of Georgia. The COC was now equipped to export oil from Baku via Batumi to Copenhagen and Berlin. The Kahans continued their prewar business, which put Aron in a position of having something to offer Carl Frederik Glad— business connections to Baku. Glad benefitted from this. But without David, who was holding the fort in Baku, Aron, in Copenhagen, would not have been able to do business with Caucasian oil.

In mid-January 1920, when Aron just happened to be in Baku, L. C. Glad & Co. bought a load of Russian machine oil, the Kahans' specialty, which was to be transported westwards in barrels via Batumi. Was this the cargo that David had sent on its way in Baku at the end of September, or was it already another? The first shipment for Glad arrived in Copenhagen in June, and the next one went to large companies in Sweden, Axel Christiernsson and Wahlen & Bloch, which was the start of business dealings there for the Danish oil entrepreneur. A few months later, in early April 1920, Glad purchased five thousand tons of Balaxanı mazut for the enormous sum of almost 200,000 Danish kroner, which was still stored in Baku tanks when, two weeks later, the Bolsheviks brought the city under their rule.

Now Batumi was beginning to get dangerous for the Allies as well. On May 23, Stehr, like all the representatives of the oil industry, was given an ultimatum by the British Control Authority to export all oil products from the city by the end of June, otherwise there was a threat of confiscation. Thereupon, the COC agent in Batumi pulled out all stops to secure the Danish company's property. He asked the head office in Copenhagen to protest against this course of action. At 175 Gothersgade, Abraham Ledermann took up the case. He sought the support of the Danish Foreign Ministry in applying to the Foreign Office in London for travel documents for David Kahan in Constantinople, who wanted to get to Batumi, to dissolve the COC depots and transport the goods on company ships, as the letter states. The Danish foreign ministry only intervened after the embassy in London confirmed on June 17 that Batumi was still occupied by British troops, promising the COC support. Unfortunately, the COC branch did not provide any information in its letters about the company's own ships, nor about the inventory. According to the letters, it was possible to export the stored products by the deadline. But the five thousand tons of mazut that had already been paid for did not reach L. C. Glad & Co. from what was by now Soviet Baku.

On July 7, 1920, the British Army withdrew from Batumi, leaving the town to the Georgian Army, which defended the territory for another seven months before it was conquered by the Bolsheviks in February 1921 and incorporated into the Soviet Republic of Georgia. To what extent David and Baruch used their time in Baku to transfer movable property, oil products and tankers to the West remains uncertain. It is also uncertain whether Aron was able to contribute to the COC in Batumi from Constantinople in the summer of 1920, when he had travelled there to meet Zina and her daughters, or how long the branch continued to exist. Court records from Copenhagen show that Stehr unlawfully disposed of COC funds in early 1921, during the unregulated period of transition. The article in the March 1921 edition of the Oil Paint and Drug Reporters, stating that the COC was operating in Grozny, was probably based on outdated information in those times of upheaval. The Kahans did indeed have oil fields in Grozny and David and Baruch were still operating their property there during the last year under White rule. But by March 1921, the Caucasus city was already under Bolshevik control, and the Kahans had left Baku and Batumi. It remains doubtful whether they already suspected then that their possessions there were lost once and for all.

The work in Copenhagen increased steadily and with it the prospect of success, Aron recounts. He admitted for the first time, that circumstances were playing into his hands. It was a happy coincidence, that he had chosen neutral Denmark as the starting point for his business activities in the West and not the defeated and internationally discredited Germany; that the bad image of the German companies, which before the war were among the most active in the oil industry, but now had difficulties getting back into business, was to his advantage. The Danish COC used its locational advantage, filled gaps in the European market that had been torn by the war and supplied Scandinavia and the new republics in the East as well as the defeated Germany with oil.

After Abraham Ledermann's arrival in the summer of 1919, the COC began exporting to Riga, according to Aron. It activated the Kahan's old offices and the refinery in the Latvian capital, according to Glad's company history. The Russian-Baltic Mineral Oil Company, also called Russian Baltic Mineral Oil Rectification Works, which had its administration in 1922 at 7 Arsenāla iela and advertised in *Latvia's Address Book for Trade, Industry and Commerce*, was the successor to Rubanito and accommodated the COC office. Aron again cites a skeptic in his self-promoting narrative: "when we sent the first cargo to Riga, I went to the port with three employees, including Mr. Goldberg ... to watch the ships leave. It was excellent spring weather, the sun was shining, and it was windless. Going back, I remarked what nice weather we were having. Then Mr. Goldberg, a persistent pessimist, looked around and said, 'Yes, yes, it's fine for now.'"

The COC also used the Kahans' traditional connections to the Estonian capital and began deliveries to Tallinn. The largest quantity of petroleum imported into Estonia in the second half of 1920 came from a Danish company. This was undoubtedly the COC, because Det Danske Petroleum had no contacts with Estonia at that time, Shell was busy building a distribution network in Denmark, and the Danish subsidiary of the Anglo-Iranian Oil Company, formerly Anglo-Persian Oil, had not been established yet. This may also explain why the COC rented oil tanks in Tallinn at the beginning of the twenties. The Caucasian Oil Co., 17, 3, Wene tänav was listed in the *First Reval Trade Directory* (Tallinn, 1921), under the headings "Gasoline," "Oils and Fats," and "Petroleum" as one of the major oil suppliers. Even though Estonia was a small country, the COC's exports to Tallinn would have generated good income. As early as the beginning of September 1919, the company increased its share capital by one million kroner, of which only 600 were paid in cash and the remaining 999,400 kroner in the form of Caucasus-Volga Industrial & Trading Company shares in Petrograd at a nominal value of 526,000 rubles. At the end of May 1920, one year after its foundation, the COC increased its share capital for the second time by the same amount to now three million kroner, which were registered as "fully paid up." This, again, raises the question: where did the capital come from?

Only a few weeks before the second capital increase, Aron Kahan had learned of the Bolsheviks' capture of Baku when his brother David had fled the city and abandoned their business there. It was precisely in those days that the former Russian oil magnates successfully sold their securities to their Western competitors in Paris. The trade with the "dead souls" reached its boiling point between spring and summer 1920. The cafés of the French metropolis, where White Russians sat together, were bubbling with rumors from their homeland at that time. They resembled brokerage offices in which securities from the aftermarket, icons, works of art, jewels and other treasures were changing hands, like in the Baku bazaar. In literature, this illustrious trade is described in a malicious way. At that time, the Nobels succeeded in the spectacular sale of a large part of their shares worth 11.5 million dollars at a price of no less than 9 million to Standard Oil, New Jersey. Following the Nobels, other Russian oil entrepreneurs, Mantashev, Lianozov and Gukasov, sold their shares to Dutch Royal Shell. Did these big deals in Paris provide the COC backing with lenders in Copenhagen? It was not until the financial and economic conferences of Genoa and The Hague and the incidental Treaty of Rapallo, two years later in spring/summer 1922, with which two outlawed states, the Weimar Republic and Soviet Russia, sought to rehabilitate themselves internationally, that Russian oil shares were finally devalued, disillusioning the Big Sisters as well as the emigrants. They sanctioned the expropriations by the Bolsheviks on the territory of the former Russian Empire. But apart from fanciful values, the Kahan shares—those of Caucasus-Volga Industrial & Trading Company and Russian-Baltic Mineral Oil Company—were partially covered by real assets such as warehouses, installations and employees in cities now belonging to the republics of Poland and Latvia.

Although the political situation in Germany had calmed down, inflation and reparations demands by the Allies caused economic turbulence. Mineral oil products were in short supply. International demand increased. The share prices for oil on the world's stock exchanges rose accordingly. In 1920, the Allies lifted the blockade, and the compulsory petroleum production controls were loosened. The Big Sisters, which had fended off the introduction of a state oil monopoly, tried to regain prewar quotas. The German-American Petroleum Inc. controlled by Standard Oil, the German Mineral Oil Inc. and the German Petroleum Trading Company, the former representative of the

European Petroleum Union, whose main shareholder was Deutsche Bank, shared the market. It was in this situation that the Caucasische Handelsgesellschaft mbH, a subsidiary of the COC, began operations as an outsider in the industry, with a share capital of 100,000 marks in late autumn 1920, at 36 Schlüterstrasse in Charlottenburg. Its declared aim was to import naphtha and naphtha products from the Caucasus countries into Germany and to distribute them. Although this was not feasible under the political circumstances at the time, it was an expression of the hope that the Soviet rule would soon pass like a nightmare. The merchants Max Lew and Jonas Rosenberg were named as shareholders and managing directors. "Representation is by each managing director acting alone" according to the commercial register, but according to Aron's memoirs, he and his office were initially located at 36 Schlüterstrasse in Berlin, where he had entrusted a certain Michael Herzberg and Max Lew with the business. Not a word about his brothers Baruch, David and Bendet, or his brother-in-law Jonas, all of whom were also now in Berlin. However, in the commercial register there is no reference to him as founder, board member, or manager. Sometime between the fall of 1920, when he came to Berlin with Zina and the children, and the spring of 1921, when the compulsory petroleum production was completely abolished and he married Mina Levstein, Aron gave up commuting between Copenhagen and Berlin. Since then he was living and working in the family circle in Berlin. The fact that he initiated the Caucasische Handelsgesellschaft becomes obvious when one remembers that the company was a subsidiary of the COC, which is also not mentioned in the German commercial register. The initiator apparently left the management to his confidants—brothers, brother-in-law, employees—and kept himself in the background.

Max Lew had already managed the business in Germany for Chaim Kahan before the war, representing the Russian-Baltic Mineral Oil Company (Rubanito) in Berlin. During the war he and his family belonged to the close circle of friends of the Kahans and Rosenbergs. Born in Volkovysk, Grodno Province, in the Russian Empire, the son of a timber merchant, Lew was just under a generation younger than Chaim Kahan. Like Chaim Kahan, Lew was a Litvak by birth, but had grown up in Switzerland. He had attended high school in Germany and completed an apprenticeship in Frankfurt am Main. It is possible that he was related to the oil entrepreneur Lev in Baku, who was one of Kahan's acquaintances and business partners, and thus connected with the family. Max Lew had English, French and Russian language skills and had gained experience on extensive travels in Europe and Central Asia—Turkestan and

China—according to his obituary in the *German Business Guide*. Aron called him a living encyclopedia.

Three quarters of a year after its foundation, the Caucasische Handelsgesellschaft quadrupled its share capital to 400,000 marks. Baruch and David Kahan joined as new managing directors. One month later, at the end of November 1921, the company opened a branch office in Hamburg, on the third floor of 7 Ditmar-Koelstrasse. The management was taken over by Jacob Kahan and Berl Rosenberg, a nephew of Jonas and son of Benyamin Rosenberg, who represented the Kahan's factory and warehouse in Łódź.

According to Aron's description of the beginning of the business in Hamburg, they were searching for a tank facility in the Hamburg oil port, when Max Lew put them in touch with Dr. Ernst Lehner, who knew Aron from Baku. Lehner had given them permission to use a facility, tanks belonging to the German Petroleum Trading Company (GPTC), the distribution center of the European Petroleum Union, in the Hamburg oil port for their exports. This provided the wholesale company with a footing. Having connections in the diaspora obviously paid off for the revolution-refugees and entrepreneurs in exile just as much as Baku's cosmopolitanism had done for them during the first oil boom. The Kahans found trustworthy employees in the West and received start-up assistance here and there from oil industrialists they knew from pre-war Baku. Ernst Lehner, a doctor of chemistry from the Habsburg Empire, who was ten years older than Aron, had headed the electricity company Elektrosila, which belonged to AEG, in Baku since 1900 until the beginning of the war, where he got to know Russian life and Russian literature. During the war Lehner had worked as an oil expert for German Petroleum Inc. in the management of the Romanian concern Steaua Română. After the end of the war he had a Berlin address and was apparently with the GPTC. From 1926 he was a member of the board of OLEX, the German subsidiary of the Anglo-Iranian Oil Company, until he was dismissed in 1937 because of his Jewish origins and had to leave Germany.

Aron recounts that, due to his inexperience at the time, he didn't even know that oil prices could easily be obtained from the London weekly *Oil News*. So he asked Herzberg to write to his acquaintances in London to ascertain the prices of petroleum and gasoline. David, cited here by Aron as the third opponent and pessimist, initially objected to this, arguing that one could not bother people with such stupid questions. It turned out that London promised high selling prices, and that it was worth exporting there in barrels, especially if the turnover of the goods took place in Germany, where prices were low due to inflation. The answer to the "stupid question" led Aron to appoint the brother-in-law of Herzberg's acquaintance from Baku, David Filitz, and his company Filitz & Bahaturianz to represent him in England. Filitz & Bahaturianz at that time ran the London office of the emigrant magazine *The New Russia*, which was published by the Russian Liberation Committee. Business in England had started.

The transport to England was to take place in wooden barrels, Aron recalled. David and he had thirty coopers brought to Hamburg from Königsberg, who made barrels in piecework. These were filled with petroleum and sent to London, Glasgow and other English ports on the orders of the Filitz & Bahaturianz company. Each barrel of petroleum sold in England brought the amazing profit of one pound sterling. "At Manchester the Caucasian Oil Co. Ltd., received 330,400 gallons of kerosene in bulk from Hamburg," the *National Petroleum News* reported in the last quarter of 1922. At the same time, business was developing for the sale of gasoline in Stockholm and Copenhagen, Aron said. Thanks to continuing and increasing inflation, it became possible to buy gasoline in iron barrels from Rhenania, which belonged to Royal Dutch Shell, for payment in marks. When resold to Sweden and Denmark they made the fantastic profit of eight to ten öre per kilogram.

There is a letter, in the family archives, from Jacob Kahan to Berl Rosenberg, who had initially shared a rented room with him in Hamburg. The letter reads like a handover from Jacob, who had gone back to Berlin, to Berl bringing him up to date. The two of them were responsible for the storage and handling of the goods in the oil harbor, which was supervised by a port inspector, a cooper. The letter states that they used new and used barrels supplied by the Flick company; they also employed quartermasters—warehouse keepers who rented premises in the port, but also worked for importers on behalf of others—from the Arbeitsnachweis, the Hamburg employment agency. The Kahans apparently used the local infrastructure of the port city right from the start under postwar conditions.

"The more the business developed, the more we felt the need to have our own tank facility," Aron recalls. The "living encyclopedia" Max Lew claimed that they could purchase the government-owned tanks that had served war purposes and were not used any longer. Aron asked Lew to scout around. So Lew took to the road and found out that there was a large tank facility for submarines in Wilhelmshaven. It is not possible to say who had tipped Max Lew off, whether it was Ernst Lehner or Hans Ornstein, who was meanwhile working at OLEX in Berlin. Perhaps he was attracted by the advertising campaigns of the

Jade City, which was urgently looking for an industrial use of the former naval port. It is possible that the just published brochure by the Rüstringen Municipal Industrial Office, *The Oil Container Facilities in Rüstringen-Wilhelmshaven*, had fallen into his hands. This was followed by months of on-the-spot investigations, negotiations with the Reich Treasurer, the State Finance Office of Unterweser, Bremen, and the Reich Property Office in Wilhelmshaven. Could the Kahans, these entrepreneurs whose career had begun in the Transcaucasian Baku, end up with the Copenhagen COC subsidiary, the Caucasische Handelsgesellschaft, in the northwest German port city?

The City on Command is the title of Jens Graul's dissertation, which deals with the first transformation of the Reich Naval Base into an industrial port. Even the founding of the city in 1869 had a purely military purpose, and is thus unique in Germany. Consequently, Wilhelmshaven experienced the political changes in German history with particular severity. After the World War, the naval shipyard and garrison were drastically reduced. The industrial core consisted of the state-owned naval shipyard and the privately run Rüstringen Plant of the German Works, where warships were being converted for civilian shipping and new ships built by a total of 10,000 employees in the former submarine and torpedo port. Household goods and even furniture were also being produced there. Industrial offices were created especially for this purpose: in 1919 in Rüstringen, in 1920 in Wilhelmshaven and a Joint Industry and Trade Office of the Jade Cities in 1922; they campaigned for the conversion of the remaining area to be independent of the naval shipyard. They proposed that the freight hub, with its central location on the main waterways and its power supply still operated by the Navy, would maintain a deep shipping channel. The industrial port was to be leased primarily to companies that were handling or importing bulk goods transported by tramp shipping in large ships and possibly upgraded by manufacturing. The city must constantly reinvent itself, says regional historian Ursula Aljets. That's how it was back then, after the end of the First World War, and that's how it is still today.

Wilhelmshaven is again on hold. The city seems sleepy, the old port facilities are tidy and empty, the new ones are located far from the center. They are waiting for customers. I asked Jens Graul, the author of *The City on Command*, about the Kahans and the Caucasische Handelsgesellschaft. He couldn't come up with anything. However, the city archives provided research assistance. Wilhelmshaven consists of two parts: the administratively planned Prussian port facilities and the historically grown Oldenburg Rüstringen, where the Reich shipyard workers lived, who took part in the uprisings that had led to the fall of the monarchy in November 1918. This resulted in political differences which are still effective today. The story goes that Wilhelmshaven was built like a ship from east to west, with the Kaiser-Villa on Birkenweg as the command bridge, the city tenements for the officers in the middle, followed by the barracks for the crews and the shipyard workers' housing estates in Rüstringen to the west. The road led across the Kaiser-Wilhelm-Bridge, past the Arsenal Harbor into the villa district surrounding Birkenweg, where the rather inconspicuous Kaiser-Villa, which the Emperor never inhabited, still stands today (number 4), and back through the Kurpark to the city center.

Wilhelmshaven port facilities with warships, oil freighters, barracks, shipyards, oil tanks, pumping stations and an airport were truly imperial and imposing, but only as someone's brainchild, designed on the drawing board. They seem downright crazy and out of place on the flat land and the green, damp meadows far away from the big cities on the East Frisian Marshes on the banks of the Jade Bight. The land connection is still poor. By the time Max Lew, followed by David Kahan, presumably arrived in Wilhelmshaven, the Kaiser had fallen, the war was lost, and the naval port had become redundant. But nothing was destroyed, like later in the Second World War. All buildings and equipment were still in place, awaiting new use. How must the Jewish entrepreneurs from the Russian Empire have felt, not having been in Germany for long, who knew the oil ports in the Volga cities, in Baku, St. Petersburg, Riga, and also in Copenhagen, seeing these facilities in Wilhelmshaven now, bursting with military equipment that had been directed against their countries of origin until recently?

In 1920, the Admiralty and the Reich Property Administration agreed to open the port area west of the Kaiser Wilhelm Bridge for commercial and industrial development. An eastward extension toward the torpedo wharf and the sluicegate was envisaged. The seven-kilometer-long area comprised one thousand hectares of land and two hundred hectares of water, making it larger than the Duisburg-Ruhrort ports at the time, the second largest port after Hamburg. It was also in good condition, as it had only been completed ten years earlier. In addition, there was a rail connection to the Sande freight station, as well as numerous hangars, workshops, storage areas, oil tanks of various sizes and refueling facilities, so that goods could be handled between ship and rail without any problems.

The disadvantage was that the cargo flow had to work in reverse. In the naval port, the ships had been filled with oil from tanks, the tanks from railway wagons. In the industrial port, the oil was to be discharged into tanks from ships and from there into wagons. Problems were also caused by the low capacity of the Ems-Jade Canal as a connection to the hinterland, which was also economically weak and not accessible to traffic. The branch canal to the Weser-Ems Canal was not even planned at that time. The contract conditions also had disadvantages for the entrepreneurs, who were denied hereditary land transfer or building rights; only leasing was possible. If necessary, the navy could demand the land back. For the first four years after the war, the salvage business dominated. At that time Wilhelmshaven was considered the "largest scrap yard in Europe." Even the Rüstringen Plant only lasted until the end of 1924, and plans to convert Wilhelmshaven into a fishing port failed due to the already established competition.

The Kahans began to deal with the tender by the Reich Treasurer in Berlin for ownership of the former naval dockyard at the beginning of December 1921. This emanates from a separate account in the files of the Federal Archives in Berlin-Lichterfelde. They were one of five applicants. In an eleven-page letter, signed by David Kahan and Max Lew, they outlined their project. They presented themselves as the distribution agency of the Copenhagen COC, controlling four Russian corporations—Petrol, Binəqədi Oil Industry and Trading Company, Caucasus-Volga Industry & Trading Company and Russian-Baltic Mineral Oil Company—which was only nominally correct at the time. They further claimed that the COC would also become the central distributor of the American Sinclair Corporation in Europe, with both being managed at the top by the Union Petroleum Company in Philadelphia. The Sinclair Corporation, founded by the oil maverick Harry F. Sinclair in Kansas, had only existed for four years at the time, was also a newcomer in the industry and was expanding. The COC had previously conducted its business in Germany via Hamburg, where it was leasing tank space from GPTC. Up to now, the business had consisted of transferring American naphtha products to the Scandinavian countries and the countries bordering the Baltic Sea. They claimed that in 1921, they had handled around 20,000 tons of petroleum and other naphtha products for the European traffic on sea barges, tank wagons and above all in wooden and iron barrels. The tank facilities rented in Hamburg would be too small. The COC wanted to expand and do trade in Mediterranean and Oriental countries. Hence the interest in Wilhelmshaven. There they were planning, first, to import naphtha products of all kinds from the USA on a large scale to Germany and abroad, and secondly, to finally implement an old prewar plan—the production of Russian naphtha products, especially quality oils, for distillation and refining. By retaining quality labor, premium oil products were to be produced from the raw material. Despite the unresolved political situation in southern Russia, the COC had already purchased large quantities of Russian naphtha products and continues to do so. The Russian raw material would be supplemented by American raw material. Since the company primarily would want to trade with foreign countries, it needs a lot of storage space for packaging materials—wooden barrels, iron drums and zinc bidons. They would also need repair workshops. Local businesses were to help set up a cask producing and packaging industry. Their annual requirement would amount to 100,000 wooden barrels and 10,000 iron drums as packaging material.

The Kahans were referring to a preliminary agreement with the Reich Treasurer for the lease of three tanks on the south bank of the West Harbor, initially for seven months (December 1, 1921 to July 1, 1922), and the torpedo warehouse at Gazelle Bridge for six months (January 1 to July 1, 1922), with the prospect of providing the COC with additional storage and manufacturing space nearby. They expressed their interest in renting the tank facility in Sande for the duration of the 1920s, as stipulated by the Ministry, on condition that both lessor and lessee would have the right to terminate the lease in the tenth year. Under certain circumstances, they would also lease separately the three tanks and associated machinery in the West Harbor, but not the other six. They promised to start operations as soon as possible, but pointed out the short-term nature of the tender and asked for a postponement, as they would first have to reach an agreement with their American partners. They also expressed the wish that they be granted the option of expanding the company premises or of keeping the properties leased under the preliminary contract. This was to comprise the site at the three tanks in the West Harbor, the former torpedo storage hall, the former drill hall next door, the storage yard opposite, workshop buildings, woodsheds and the ship's stoking station with the associated open spaces and the bridges on the canal bank just a few steps away. Another lease option was for additional oil tanks: number 4–10 on the south quay of the Great Port and number 1–2 at the first port entrance before the lock. All these details had been discussed in the Reich Treasury by a small working party, in the presence of Privy Councillor Dr. Weissmüller as spokesman for the owner, Lord Mayor Nollner and Senator Leiske as representatives of the City of Wilhelmshaven-Rüstringen, and Max Lew and David Kahan as representatives of the COC at the beginning of December.

Negotiations for the lease of the facilities in Wilhelmshaven dragged on for well over three months until an agreement was reached. The Kahans were awarded the contract. Three of the other four applicants—Hugo Stinnes Inc.

for Shipping and Overseas Ports in Hamburg and Deutsche Erdöl AG (DEA) and the engineer Immo Glenck in Berlin—were out of the game. Stinnes had failed to develop a conclusive concept, DEA had withdrawn, and the engineer had not been given a good reference by the Berlin Chamber of Commerce. The fourth applicant, Deutsche Petroleum-Block GmbH, which dealt in Romanian oil, was given leases for tanks in another part of the former naval port, the Great Harbor. The founders of the COC, Aron Kahan, Carl Frederik and Johannes Erik Glad, were assessed by the Reichsbank as "respectable and well regarded." The company, which had branches in Libau, Riga and several other cities, was trading in oil, petroleum and other products, and had also done good and profitable business in the Baltic states that year. Accordingly, the Caucasische Handelsgesellschaft company also benefited from the goodwill that L. C. Glad & Co. contributed.

There was resistance within the local authorities against the leasing of the port facilities to the Caucasische Handelsgesellschaft. The State Finance Office in Bremen, as well as the Reich Property Office II in Wilhelmshaven, referred to a large number of existing leases on the land in question—mostly to small businesses and allotment gardeners—and expressed reservations about the fact that "the Caucasians" would be leasing almost the entire shore of the West Harbor, so that no other industries could set up there. If leases were to be given to foreigners, then at least commensurate prices should be charged. Nevertheless, the contract was signed. The Kahans were creative entrepreneurs who were looking for a new start in the West and needed to secure a livelihood for their family. In this crisis, the entrepreneurs and the city found each other. That was the only reason why the Baku merchants were awarded the contract.

Aron recalls that the price charged for the lease of the Wilhelmshaven facilities was ridiculously low according to his standards, which were not based on the German mark but on the value of gold. The whole tank plant with a total capacity of seventy thousand tons, located at Sande, was to cost about eight to nine thousand kroner a year in rent. "When Mr. Lew asked me by telephone how much of the 70,000 tons of tanker space we should take, I replied: 'All of it.' And so we built *our own* fuel depot in Wilhelmshaven [emphasis in the original text]." That's exactly what his son Yossi had been told. This account became famous traditional family lore. It is supported by archival materials, but Aron does not appear there. It ends with a contract in which he is not mentioned by name. He remained in the background.

The Caucasische Handelsgesellschaft leased six oil tank facilities in the large port of Rüstringen with a capacity of fifty thousand tons as well as tank facilities in the western port at the Sander Tidelands, today a local recreation area. It opened an office at 14 Elisabethstrasse, the former drill hall, named Jahn-Halle after the father of gymnastics in the 1930s, today the Coast Museum on Neckarstrasse, in the immediate vicinity of the Ems-Jade-Canal, at Bontekai. The company also leased the former torpedo storage hall right next to the museum, which was used for various purposes after the Second World War and has now been reconstructed into a theater, a café and apartments. On the corner of Parkstrasse and Marktstrasse there is a memorial to the synagogue, which was destroyed in November 1938, and to the deportation of the Jews of Wilhelmshaven. But this did not happen until the next war. The line of sight extends from one stately statue to the next, flanked by ponderous administrative buildings in classicist style, while the path leads through the magnificent Adalbertstrasse, past the Neckarstrasse and into the Weserstrasse with its uniform urban development parallel to the old trading port. I walked once again along Bontekai, where three oil tanks stood, and to the Fliegerdeich along Jadeallee, over the dyke bridge and the Grodendamm, which has separated the former Westhafen, now Banter See, from the Grosser Hafen since the end of the Second World War.

The negotiating parties began to create the conditions for the commissioning of the western port, clarified the fire protection regulations, the terms for the supply of electricity and water in the port area, agreed on the contractual requirement that the COC should establish an "operating company" in Wilhelmshaven. One of the two managing directors should be a German, preferably from the local merchant community. The representative of the Caucasische Handelsgesellschaft for the following four years was the merchant Paul Niehuss (1883–1955), who owned shops for household appliances in Gökerstrasse and Marktstrasse and who at that time was committed to the industrialization of Wilhelmshaven. The contract was concluded on April 1, 1922. Just four weeks later, on April 28, the first oil tanker, the freighter *Lucellum*, built in 1913 in Liverpool, entered the industrial port with six or eight thousand tons of naphtha cargo from the USA. The ship sailed under the English flag and had spent twenty-eight days sailing from the Gulf of Mexico to Newport, Rhode Island, and from there across the Atlantic, through the English Channel, to the mouth of the Jade. When it arrived, it was greeted by the head of the Wilhelmshaven Department of Trade and Industry, the directors of the Caucasische Handelsgesellschaft, Niehuss with another councillor, representatives of the press and numerous onlookers. The newspaper reported on the following day that a bridge had been built between the New World and Wilhelmshaven with the arrival of the *Lucellum* for the Caucasische Handelsgesellschaft. Efrat Carmon said she had heard in the family that in honor of this event, the city issued a special emergency money note for one hundred marks, which a member of the city archives actually found. It shows the picture of a tanker, framed by a dynamic blue, black and white wave-and-star ornamentation with stylized sea and sky motifs. The company was obviously a beacon of hope for the city, now that the oil entrepreneurs Kahan had arrived in Germany.

CHAPTER 14

Family in Exile. Berlin

Four months after the proclamation of the Republic, on March 14, 1919, Roska and Yasha got married in Berlin. The event was celebrated in the Lodge House and a few days later was reported in the *Jüdische Rundschau*, the central organ of the Zionist Organization, which was preferred reading for migrants from Eastern Europe, including in the homes of the Kahans and Rosenbergs. The wedding was celebrated in the meeting place of the B'nai Brit lodge, a favorite meeting place for the Jewish upper crust, where all kinds of events used to take place, often organized by and for migrants; it also used to be rented out for family celebrations. Roska had probably been dreaming of this day for months, thinking about it and planning it, ever since she had been told on the phone by Mrs. Kustow, during her last days in Bad Polzin, that Yasha's parents had agreed to their marriage. Who was this lady whom Roska had named so formally in her letter to Yasha, sent from Polzin to Salzbrunn, and who was entrusted to pass on such intimate information that not even her mother was supposed to be aware of? In the Berlin address register I found the entry "Kustow, Anna, née Levstein, widow, Charlottenburg, Sybelstr. 45."

Rosalia and Baruch Kahan had given their consent to the union of their son and their niece only after some hesitation and long negotiations, conducted by the lawyer Yuda Beham across the war front, traveling back and forth between the Russian Empire and Germany. They would have preferred for Yasha to have studied abroad and seen the world before marriage. But he had made it clear to them that as long as there was war between Russia and Germany, he was not allowed to leave Berlin. When the end of the war became imminent, he immediately applied for a place at the Friedrich-Wilhelms University, which indicates that he did not want to leave Berlin and Roska, even under such new circumstances. In the spring of 1919, one month after his marriage, he resumed his studies of philology, which had been interrupted by the war. After one semester he transferred to the law faculty.

In June, when the end of the war was officially announced in Paris, the newlyweds went on their honeymoon to Memel in the Baltic States. The only photo of the young couple from those days in the family archives was taken, as noted on the back, when they visited friends: Roska and Yasha in a circle of four women in long dresses, which were out of fashion at that time, and a little girl with a ribbon in her hair, in a rural setting, in front of a monument with its inscription covered by their bodies. They look serious. Both are wearing dark clothes; Yasha is perfectly dressed in a jacket, buttoned waistcoat, tie and a stiff shirt collar. The striking difference in size between the small, somewhat chubby Roska—also called "tiny Rosa" to distinguish her from her mother-in-law and aunt—and the tall Yasha is not noticeable in the picture.

Roska and Yasha's wedding took place without the groom's parents and relatives who were stuck in Kharkov, Ekaterinoslav and Baku, because of the political situation, although they had been hoping otherwise.

The fall of the monarchy in Germany in November 1918 had shifted the fronts, changed the balance of power in Russia, brought the Bolsheviks to power and sparked a new war on the territory of the former Tsarist Empire, rendering the borders impassable. Of the relatives from the East, only Aron, a student of the "Charlottenburg psychology," took part in the festivities after he had managed to escape from the Bolsheviks in Kharkov at the beginning of the year. However, he did not stay, but continued his journey to Copenhagen.

The next family member to arrive in Berlin as a refugee was Lolia, Zina's son, in the autumn of 1919. A winter and a spring passed before David, Baruch and Rosalia arrived in Berlin from Baku in the summer of 1920, and a few months later, in the fall, Zina arrived with her daughters and nanny under Aron's protection. Nachum and Arusia joined them only a whole year later, in early August 1921. The arrival of the relatives from Russia dragged on for years; it was a long process. Although there was no war, no revolution anymore, the family was living in a provisional state, in an environment that was suffering from the consequences of the lost war and could not find peace. German society was mentally insecure and, in its reality, still very much involved with the past—its government blocked, driven by the reparation demands of its former enemies, inflation, price hikes and overpopulation in the cities as a result of returning soldiers, as well as the arrival of migrants from Eastern Europe. More numerous than the Russian revolution refugees were the ethnic Germans and those expelled from the border regions. There were also students and Polish itinerant workers, not forgetting the prisoners of war who were still in the country. The young republic was confronted with a migration wave, surpassing anything that had ever been seen before.

Berlin has long been an important transit station due to its favorable geographic location. More than two and a half million Jews had left Eastern Europe for the West since the 1880s because they were oppressed and persecuted, poor and thirsting for education, but Berlin had rarely been their destination. Even Chaim Kahan had only used it as a base until the beginning of the World War. When the great migration wave reached Germany after the war and the USA had almost closed its borders to immigrants, the situation changed. For many refugees from war, pogroms and revolution, Berlin not only remained their first stop in the West, but became a place of residence for a longer period of time. This was also true for the Kahans and Rosenbergs. Weimar Berlin developed into a Jewish emigration center, one of the largest in Europe. Out of over half a million migrants registered in the Republic, a small group, some tens of thousands were of Jewish origin, of whom more than half had been living in Berlin between the wars, for ten years and more. The migrants made the city into a metropolis. They were also an indicator of how much foreignness the Germans could tolerate and were an impetus to the economy and culture of the republic, which continues to have an effect till today.

Unlike most oil industrialists from Baku, the Kahans did not go to Paris, but to Berlin. Unlike most of those fleeing revolution, they had local knowledge and language skills, financial means and, from the beginning, an address in the German metropolis. Not in the poor Scheunenviertel, but in the bourgeois Charlottenburg, in the west of the city. 36 Schlüterstrasse was not a place to go to, a temporary asylum, an emergency accommodation, a boarding house or rooms for subletting, but a luxurious rented apartment that offered them a home. "It was a kind of *Talpiot* for us, a safe haven," Arusia recalled later. The neighborhood of *Talpiot*, where Eliezer Ben Yehuda and Shai Agnon, the founding fathers of intellectual Israel once used to live, is considered a fine location in Jerusalem.

The Rosenbergs welcomed them all. All stranded relatives found shelter one after the other in the spacious ten-room apartment that Chaim Kahan had rented for himself and his family before the war. From September 1920, more people than ever before had lived there. In addition, one of the rooms in the back served as an office for the Caucasische Handelsgesellschaft. Baruch, Rosalia and David, Aron, Zina, Sasha and the three children, nine in all, joined the six Kahans, Rosenbergs and the staff, consisting of the cook Bliuma and the maid Lina, just at the time when Roska gave birth to her first child, Chaim Avinoam. Only Bendet Kahan lived separately with his family, Judith and the three daughters, from the summer of 1917, but in the immediate vicinity of 36 Schlüterstrasse—first at 67 Niebuhrstrasse and since 1921 at no, 10. Yasha had been posted to Hamburg in the summer of 1921 to set up a branch of the Caucasische Handelsgesellschaft there, which brought some relief. He interrupted his studies for this purpose, and since then—to Roska's chagrin—had rarely been at home.

As for Zina, Aron recalled that a furnished apartment was rented for her, the children and Sasha, at 25/26 Württembergische Strasse in the spring of 1921, but without the approval of the Housing Department. As in many other German cities, the rental apartments in postwar Berlin were regulated due to lack of space, instability of the currency, devaluation of the property, or poverty of the tenants. Access to existing housing was begrudged among the migrants, especially to the so-called "Eastern Jews." For years there were debates in the Reichstag about this and the need to introduce special laws for foreigners, because they allegedly were taking away the housing space of the Germans. The landlady had to spend several days with them time and again so that her neighbors would not report her for illegally renting to foreigners. Consequently, they were living in constant fear. Many migrants reported problems with the Berlin housing shortage. Anecdotes of usurious rents and nasty landladies, often widows of officers who were financially forced to rent out rooms, became legendary.

At the beginning of the twenties, Russian emigration to Berlin reached its peak, and the housing issue now occupied the Kahans as well; it became too cramped for them at 36 Schlüterstrasse. Although the joy over the reunion and the cohesion was great, it was above all the women who insisted on running their own households. Roska reported the situation to Yasha in Hamburg. From July 1921 to July 1922, sixty-seven letters written in Russian have been preserved in the family archives, in each of which she reported some family news. There was always talk of quarrels between Rosalia and Baruch over the housing shortage or of her own unhappiness for not having a quiet corner of her own. Every three minutes uncle David was knocking on her door. Father-in-law Baruch made it clear to her that she was not the first one for whom an apartment was being sought. Sometime in the spring of 1921, the opportunity arose to buy the neighboring building, number 37, from the owner of 36 Schlüterstrasse, building contractor Paulsen. Inflation and rent control had probably forced him to sell. The family acquired it under the legal structure of Schlüterstrasse 37 Real Estate Ltd., successor to the investment company founded in

1915, which had a share capital of 300,000 Reichsmark and was owned jointly by Jonas Rosenberg and Bendet Kahan. Did the two of them primarily have in mind to invest their assets in Germany in the form of real estate, which was advisable and also customary at the time? Or did they want to settle down like others fleeing the revolution, who bought buildings in Berlin, such as the garage and workshop owner Nikolai Paramonov, the photographer Roman Vishniac and the merchant Feivel Grüngard? Probably, the purchase of the building was simply an attempt to provide living space for the family. In her reports to Yasha, Roska repeatedly discussed the question: is the apartment she was looking for a temporary or permanent home, a *makom keva*? But the purchase of the building did not entitle her to claim an apartment at 37 Schlüterstrasse for her own use. Her search for a place to live in Berlin lead to conflict with tenants, lengthy negotiations with the authorities and court proceedings.

The summer resorts provided relief, but when Arusia and Nachum arrived at the beginning of August, the problem became worse. The family doctor, Dr. Rosenthal, recommended a four-to-six-week trip, anywhere, for the two of them to recover from the strains of the last two years. Their parents sent them to Badenweiler. They, themselves, rented a *dacha* in Babelsberg, where they spent the summer, where Roska also went with little Chaim Avinoam after returning from a vacation with Zina and family in Bad Harzburg. But the two young men were back in Berlin sooner than planned. The housing problem was compounded by another—the clarification of their residency right. Apparently, the police did not allow them to undertake extended vacation trips and they were denied a stay in the spa town of Bad Harzburg. There was no immigration law in Prussia, but according to the regulations in force, anyone who could prove an address and useful employment was tolerated. With Azerbaijani passports, documents from a state which no longer existed, and having arrived from Lithuania, they were seeking recognition as Lithuanian citizens on the grounds that they were born in Vilna.

Legitimacy has been an age-old problem for Jews in the diaspora, which was exacerbated in times of persecution. At that time, all family members had an unresolved legal status. Lolia, too, had travelled to Berlin on Azerbaijani documents; his mother Zina, on Georgian; David, and probably Baruch and Rosalia, on provisional British passports; all others arrived with passports from the Tsarist empire. Georgia, like Azerbaijan, was occupied by the Bolsheviks, who had declared all these passports invalid. A decree by the highest legislative body of the Russian Socialist Federal Soviet Republic (RSFSR) of December 15, 1921 stated that all citizens who had been abroad for more than five years would lose their citizenship unless they applied for new passports at the diplomatic missions of Soviet Russia. Those who did not opt for the RSFSR became stateless. General international law denied them any diplomatic, labor, or private legal protection. They had no political or civil rights and no guarantee of their human rights. This meant that a guarantee of residence permits and freedom of movement no longer applied. None of the family opted for Soviet Russia, all became stateless. Even Yasha, who had lived in Germany for many years, since 1912, was to face problems with his residency permit in the spring of 1922, when the Weimar Republic recognized Soviet Russia in the Treaty of Rapallo. Arusia and Nachum had received passports at the beginning of October 1921, but for some reason these were not in order. At the end of the month the brothers registered in Berlin, but their legal status remained unclear. The Kahans' helpers, such as Farber from Saratov, took care of the tiresome administrative formalities concerning their residency and domicile. Some Berlin residents, who had competence and influence, also supported them in all official matters. The Kahans were advised by Judicial Councilor Ignatz Holz, who lived around the corner on Fasanenstrasse and was involved in the community; Dr. Alfred Cassierer, with his office on Kurfürstendamm, and Dr. Bruno Goldberg, lawyer at the District Court on Wilhelmstrasse, undertook their legal representation; the engineer Bruno Uhl on Leibnizstrasse supervised their construction work; the land surveyor and estate agent Eugen Funcke negotiated on their behalf with the Housing Department, where one day he actually received a sympathetic hearing from a senior official who, like Funcke's father-in-law, had served with the hussars. Apart from this rather bizarre coincidence, it turns out that the family was already well-connected in Berlin at the time, but this was only of limited help to them in their situation.

At the end of October, Rosalia and Baruch finally managed to rent two furnished rooms in the same building as Zina on a floor above hers for a few months, with the prospect of adding a third room after a few weeks and then having the whole apartment to themselves. Arusia and Nachum wanted to rent their own rooms, but stayed with their parents to start with. Thus, 36 Schlüterstrasse became emptier, but remained a family center, where people dropped in daily, warmed themselves up when it was too cold and uncomfortable in the rented rooms, where the Sabbath and the holidays were spent together, where family meetings were held, where the office and the telephone were located.

In November 1921, Schlüterstrasse 37 Real Estate Ltd. acquired, in a foreclosure auction, a second tenement building in the block of 32 Wielandstrasse and 36 Schüterstrasse, which were back to back across a courtyard thereby forming a passageway. The building was not as stately as 36 Schlüterstrasse, but also had five floors, was middle-class and had two spacious six-room apartments on each floor. With the purchase of the two tenements, the Kahans and Rosenbergs had joined the circle of Berlin real estate and landowners. This was a step towards integration into German society. But even in 32 Wielandstrasse, there were initially no apartments available for them.

Roska suffered from the separation from Yasha, from not having a normal family life. The trips to Hamburg were also uncomfortable for her at first, because she had to ask Uncle David and—through Zina—Uncle Aron for permission to possibly travel with them and because she had to leave the little one behind. Yasha was busy and often seemed absent on weekends. She found his rented rooms there uncomfortable. The uncles talked about moving Yasha and Roska permanently to Hamburg. Roska was dreading it. When the contracts with Wilhelmshaven were signed, there was talk of moving to the Jade City, which she categorically ruled out. In the meantime, Arusia was obtaining for his big brother, time and again, the semester registration stamps at the Friedrich-Wilhelms University. For the time being, Yasha apparently was not considering dropping out of his studies. His brothers, on the other hand, were having difficulty making their home in the German metropolis.

The Russian emigrants were swarming like flies around the Gedächtniskirche, it says in Viktor Shklovsky's *Zoo or Letters not about Love*; they were living in droves among the Germans like a lake between its banks. With the arrival of the revolution refugees from Soviet Russia, new conflicts arose at the among members of the Kahan and Rosenberg families, overlapping the old dispute between Bendet and Jonas, drawing fine cracks into the protective shell of the family unit. Nachum and Arusia, who had experienced hunger, cold, violence and fear of death in the last two years, apparently shared Uncle Aron's feelings about the "Charlottenburg psychology," which they found difficult to cope with. Roska recounts that accompanied by Arusia's mother, she had gone with him to the concert ball of the Association of Russian Jews in the Marble Hall in the Zoo District. The Association had been a short-lived entity of the Russian Berlin in the early twenties. For Arusia it was the first ball in his life. Roska described his strong reaction to the Association, which she called "bourgeois"—the ladies with frilly hairstyles, lavish jewelry and deep necklines. He was upset. He had believed that such things only existed in pictures, found it vulgar and repulsive and could not calm down for a long time. The Yiddish poet and migrant Moische Kulbak described such a ball in Berlin as the writing on the wall—"and gentlemen in tails lead silken ladies to the dance floor ..."

Roska spent a lot of time with Arusia, who was twenty-two, a year younger than her and who resembled his big brother, her husband, to such a degree that one can hardly tell the two apart on photos from back then. Together they dispelled the boredom that Roska felt without Yasha, and Arusia, without occupation. They played with little Chaim Avinoam and went to concerts and the theater together. She wrote to Yasha candidly, apologetically, that sometimes she would kiss Arusia out of joy, as a substitute for him. Shortly before, Yasha himself had given her an example of his own frankness and promiscuity, which caused problems, also for Roska. Sulamith Hurwitz had been in Hamburg during Yom Kippur, the first in seven years that Roska and Yasha were apart, and she stayed overnight with him, thus arousing the landlady's ire. Sulamith was the daughter of a childhood friend of Roska's mother's and was seventeen at the time. Following this incident, Yasha had asked Roska to write the landlady a letter, explaining who the young girl was, and that she herself saw nothing objectionable there. However, Roska criticized Yasha for his recklessness. Not everyone was as progressive as the two of them, and certainly not German landladies; "progressive," *fortgeschritten*, was written in German in the Russian letter. Even people of their ilk could have said that Yasha's and Sulamith's behavior had been shocking. A friend later gossiped that Sulamith was driving the boys crazy. The discussions about free love and the emancipation of women in Soviet Russia as in postwar Berlin were also held among the Zionist youth, even if— like Roska—they had been brought up strictly according to tradition.

In this complicated situation Arusia fell in love with his cousin and sister-in-law. Three days after the concert ball, he couldn't stand it any longer, took the night train alone and travelled from Berlin to Wiesbaden, where the family had spent several summers before the war in the ritually run Ritter's Hotel Pension at 45 Taunusstrasse. He was pleased that even the old owner, the unattractive Theodor Baum, was still there. During the next two days he wrote from there three letters to his mother, brother and Roska, two of which have been preserved. "My dear "friend,'" he wrote to Roska, "who has always accompanied me, you are with me even now! I am sitting in a café, people talking around me and yes, I'm talking to you, my one and only." She herself would know that she's the only one for him now, she having even joked about it the day before. For his only "sister-in-law," using the German word in Cyrillic, his wild and spoiled little one, he found many passionate words. But first he described for her his journey, which had begun adventurously, as a clandestine escape, but then was easier to complete than he had imagined. During the train journey, his glasses were broken, so that he could hardly find his way around. He had felt helpless

like a wet chicken, but an optician in Wiesbaden had fixed his glasses the very
day he arrived. How good it was that he could talk to Roska without arguing.
At the end his caresses and jokes came thick and fast. In doing so, he mocked
Roska's conventional morality, which was acquired in the educational bourgeois theater, and, in contrast, put forward Marxist and mathematically based
triangular theories. The mothers at 36 Schlüterstrasse were not unaware of the
arrival of the letter, which was something like a declaration of love. Rosalia was
anyway waiting restlessly there that day for a message from her son. Mother
Miriam tried to take the letter out of Roska's hand, but she wouldn't have it,
as she wrote to Yasha, reassuring him that Arusia would come to his senses
again—become *vernünftig*, in German—and that everything would be all right.
The letter caused a small scandal in the Kahan and Rosenberg household. What
had Arusia written to his mother, one wonders?

One day later, Yasha, in Hamburg, received a letter from his brother, written
in Ritter's Hotel, Wiesbaden, on November 26, 1921, in which Arusia also dealt
with some fundamentals: "Dear Yasha! It so happened that I decided to come
here. But this journey was not at all terrible. I left on Thursday night (24. XI.)
and will probably return this evening. I just had to deal with one little thing
here. It seems I've already done it." What that meant, he didn't write. Actually,
Nachum and Arusia had planned to go to Wiesbaden together in order to be
on equal footing with all the refugees on their return, whatever that might have
meant, but this is what they had told Roska on the phone. Since Nachum Kahan
and Nachum Rosenberg had the same first name, both were called Noma, and
the family distinguished between them by calling Noma Kahan *kharkovsky* [the
one from Kharkov] or by referring to them as "big" and "little" Noma. The big
Noma was probably privy to Arusia's plan, because he invited Roska to a concert that very evening, of all nights, when Arusia returned to the place where
they, brothers and cousins, used to spend happy times as children; where they
had arranged get-togethers and *shloifn baizam* [sleepovers], where the family
council met. In his letter to Yasha, Arusia invoked the memory of that bond in
order to forge a new one. Terrible years had passed since then. The World War
had torn apart not only the bonds that connected humanity, but also family ties.
He knew that even before the war, not everything had gone smoothly. But the
rifts between the family members had become deeper. The death of their grandfather, this great man, their focal point, had started the decline. The crisis that
the family was experiencing was inevitable, though it was taking too long. There
will probably be even more serious quarrels, simply because they had increased
in number. But he could never accept that the five of them—he, Yasha, Roska

and the big and the little Noma—would be torn apart. He had now been in Germany for almost four months, but had not yet been able to talk to Yasha. They were now further estranged from each other than before, during the years of separation. The only one he felt close to was Roska, although he didn't want to write about that, but rather about the fact that he wished to be in one place with Yasha, not only physically, but also mentally and intellectually. So that "the Five," the handful, would not become an empty name, but a symbol of unity.

With Arusia, the third generation was making itself heard. His criticism was explicit. He made massive reproaches to his brother, shaking his self-confidence and calling on him to take part in a revolt against their fathers and uncles: in the seven years of separation they had grown up, everyone had changed and developed different attitudes to life. He spoke in a Russian-Hebrew-Yiddish language mix of *shmaterovschchina*, "forced baptism," in order to tear apart the "Charlottenburg psychology." The family was living in a metropolis. Life was broiling, societies were being transformed by revolutions, millions of people were being killed. But all this was passing the Berlin family by, wasn't effecting them one iota. Yasha as well as their cousins and friends were sleeping their lives away without noticing it. Roska and Nomek, little Noma, had no formal education. Should Nomek fail, that's the reason why. That would be a pity for him because he was talented. It was also a pity for Roska because she had brains, but those were so childish, wild, dark and only came into their own in the family. People were asking a lot of Yasha, they had high expectations of him. But he was behaving like a big child. All three of them were behaving like children who did not want to understand what it meant when thirty people were dependent on two! If the two were to fall out, things would be looking bad for all of them. All in all, they were wasting their lives. They, like many others their age, should have been shaping the future, fulfilling their obligations to themselves and to others. May Yasha forgive him this letter.

Arusia had taken stock. He was proud of the big family. But he did not like the dependence on Uncle Aron and Uncle David, who had taken over the leadership. He wanted the five of them, the young generation, to formulate demands and to go their own ways. How did Yasha react to this letter? Hardly anything of his correspondence from the Hamburg period has survived; the few things that have are barely legible, written in pencil, or have faded away. One learns about him only indirectly. What did his recalcitrant little brother expect him to do? At that time, Yasha was trying to accept responsibility as a family man, to meet the expectations of his uncles and to prove himself a good businessman, although he was not trained for this and it did not correspond to his inclinations. This is probably why he delayed the suspension of his studies and did not pursue the possibility of working for Uncle Bendet in his publishing house. Roska appreciated Yasha's even-tempered character, but encouraged him with Hillel's famous Talmudic dictum *im ein ani li mi li*—if I don't take care of myself, then who does? She encouraged him to be more courageous and self-confident, but also chided him for rejecting the offer to take over the management of the Berlin office of the Caucasische Handelsgesellschaft when the employee Michael Herzberg resigned.

In addition to the housing and residence problem, there was the problem of vocational training for young migrants. Roska herself had been brought up as a good daughter in the Polish-Jewish tradition, had mastered Hebrew, Yiddish, Polish, Russian and German and had learned French. She demonstrated common sense, character and assertiveness. However, she was in fact financially dependent on Yasha and the decisions of her uncles, due to her lack of formal education and a profession. The housemaid Lina relieved her of the burden of being a mother so that she had time for herself. She did not pursue the training as a florist that she had dreamed of. Instead, she helped an acquaintance to open a candy store and then enrolled in a course at a tailoring school. In order to educate herself, to be edified, to be informed, to have a say; in order to forget the daily turmoil, she would read, go to the theater, concerts and the cinema. Berlin was already enjoying itself at the beginning of the Golden Twenties, the years of uncertainty, and had a wide range of cultural and entertainment activities to offer, even extreme ones, like cabarets, nightclubs, gay bars and drug and sex joints. However, that wasn't Roska's Berlin. She was taken with Chekhov's *Three Sisters*, which she saw in a guest performance of the Moscow Art Theater in early December 1921 on a stage on Königgrätzer Strasse. Enthusiastically she told Yasha about the performances of three artists who were popular at that time. She saw the Viennese Fritzi Massary as Princess Olala in the Berlin theater. Massary, who was able to do everything, did everything, and with what ease, presented a delightful parody of all operetta dances in the world, said Peter Panter, known as Kurt Tucholsky, in the theater magazine *Weltbühne*. Massary, Roska wrote, also fascinated Arusia and Nachum. In the Komödienhaus she experienced Maria Orska in the boulevard play *The Merry-Go-Round*, a *ménage-à-trois*, to which she was particularly receptive at the time. Orska unfolded her most brilliant gifts, kissed, loved, frolicked and lied; she showed herself in fabulous outfits, all with culture and grace and, not least, with good acting, Carl von Ossietzky wrote in the *Berliner Volkszeitung*. Roska's friends, Jettchen and Mademoiselle Kleppfisch, referred to the resemblance between Orska and

Roska and encouraged her to make herself look like the actress from southern Russia in order to enchant Yasha. At the beginning of May 1922 Isa Kremer performed in the concert hall of the Academy of Music, and Roska went there. Born in Bessarabia and raised in Odessa, the singer was one of the first to perform Jewish folklore publicly in Yiddish. With Jettchen, Roska attended a ball in the Palais de Danse in Behrensstrasse, a plush noble dance hall. Of her readings, she mentioned Georg Hermann's *Die Nacht des Dr. Herzfeld*, the story of someone despairing of his existence, which was read in Zionist circles at the time as an analysis of diaspora existence. Apart from that, she was moving in the microcosm of the family, which at that time was still busy with its reorganization in exile in Berlin. She talks about regular visits to relatives—to Mina, and to her Aunts Judith, Zina and Rosalia, but rarely about invitations to friends and acquaintances from among the migrants. Only her two best friends she was going out with apparently came from the German-Jewish community.

What else did Roska notice about Berlin that year? Events that affected the fate of the young republic were hardly a topic in her letters to Yasha; neither the assassination of the center-politician Mathias Erzberger in August 1921, nor the subsequent declaration of a state of emergency, or the recognition of Soviet Russia in April 1922. But she did mention the inflation in the fall of 1921 and the railway strike in February 1922, events that directly affected the family. Now they had to stand in line in the department stores like others, even though inflation had a positive financial impact on the family business, since it had its headquarters in Copenhagen. The strike prevented business trips. She saw Yasha even less often. Uncle Aron spontaneously rented a car and drove to Cologne in order to take the train to Paris from there.

For Roska, flirting with Arusia was a welcome distraction, but became unpleasant when the "triangular story," the "*dreieckige Geschichte*," as she wrote in German, came to light, and he withdrew heart-stricken when she played it down. Her mother stood by him, calling her angrily a *sindenwicht* [wicked wretch]. Roska fought for her dignity, but she did not complain about a lack of education. No one, except Arusia, demanded more from her. Her brother Nomek, on the other hand, who was the same age as Arusia and looked like his mother, was a worry to his parents and sister. His father wanted him to occupy himself with something, be it even with languages. Roska tried to get him a traineeship in various Berlin businesses, but Nomek tried to cop out as long as possible. He had never attended school either, but was multilingual like his sister. Under pressure from his parents, his sister and probably also his uncle, he sat examinations for the external *Abitur*, but failed. He agreed to attend commercial school, but, encouraged by Pilwitscher Raw, a friend of his father's, he flirted with the idea of taking the *Abitur* at the private Neo-Orthodox Carlebach School in Leipzig. But when he learned that the school was not recognized by the state, he rejected this plan. Next came the idea, also inspired by the Pilwitscher Raw, of doing a doctorate in Giessen without the *Abitur* and examinations.

Unlike Roska and Nomek, Arusia and his brother Nachum had a formal education. Both were enrolled at the Handelshochschule, the commercial college, a few weeks after their arrival in Berlin. Arusia enrolled in November, although he had hesitated due to his lack of language skills; he was just altogether disoriented. When he enrolled, he was looking like a bridegroom in his black suit, Roska said. She hoped that his soon-to-be graduation would also lead him to the *chuppe*, the wedding canopy. His Baku high school diploma was apparently recognized in Berlin, but not that of his brother, who had already studied medicine in the Russian city of Perm. Nachum had to take an entrance examination at the commercial college, which he passed in November 1921, but did not take advantage of it. In the summer semester of 1922 he enrolled at the engineering school in Zwickau together with his cousin Lolia Kahan. Their Uncles David and Aron, having the economic interests of the family in mind, probably meddled in their nephews' education plans. Arusia grumbled, Lolia tried to escape the pressure, Nachum remained inaccessible and awkward, which Roska sometimes complained about. She was all the more astonished when she met him at Sulamith Hurwitz's and learned that the two regularly attended concerts together. She was happy when Nachum once came to 36 Schlüterstrasse and talked to her for an extended length of time. There are only a few letters from him preserved in the family archives. Nachum looked different from his brothers, was smaller and leaner than them, had a long, narrow nose and showed a slightly ironic smile on photos from those years. He liked to speak in quotations and insinuations that Roska did not always understand. For example, to his letter from Zwickau dated April 28, 1921, Nachum added the lines "... the king once sent a southern city dweller to us in exile ..." from Pushkin's poem *Gypsies* as a kind of motto. "There it is, my dear Yasha, the sad chorus in my song. This is how it sounds in my head all the time—the sense of being driven away. Suddenly in 24 hours it accumulated and didn't stop and neither did 'The angry God is punishing me for the crime.' In essence, the crime is nothing more than that at the age of 24–25, I still don't know what I want."

From the end of the nineteenth century, mechanical engineering, electrical engineering and related subjects were taught at the engineering school in Zwickau, Saxony. The coal industry needed skilled workers. In the first few days Nachum was apparently moping in Zwickau. To give his loneliness and melancholy weight, form, an escape and support, he borrowed, in a letter to his brother, voices from Russian literature in which he seemed to feel at home. He saw himself as the outcast from the *Gypsies*, like Pushkin himself, as an exile; with the poet Krylov, he promised to do things differently from that fabled picky bride who was duped because she couldn't make up her mind, by trying to fall in love with his studies, even if the conditions were not ideal; he felt abandoned—"the taste on the tongue, fleeting and stale"—like the poet Sasha Chorny in the Ligurian seaside resort of Santa Margherita in 1910. He had noticed that the engineering school was not a so-called "higher" schooling institution; that he was sitting in the middle of a less intelligent German audience calculating $a^3 + a^4 = a^7$ or $a^0 = 0$; that he had to listen to algebra, geometry, trigonometry, analytical geometry and differential calculus—all well-known subjects. With Chekhov, he asked himself: why? Why spend six years studying unpleasant things when you don't know what to do it for? Unfortunately, he could not enter at the level of the fourth or fifth semester, as Yasha had suggested, but had to start all over again. His internships at Petrol in Saratov existed only on paper and all purely technical subjects were completely foreign to him.

But the next day, when the sun was shining, his tone had changed; he had rented two good rooms that day: a bedroom and a study, and the landlord assured him that he would provide him with full board. He had already spent two days in "lectures," or rather, in classes, from six to half past twelve and from two to four (only twice a week in the afternoon). At ten he went to sleep. He noticed, at a glance, *a aitsisher kuk*, that about fifty Russian Jews lived in Zwickau, technologists and skilled workers. He had enrolled in the mechanical engineering department, but was thinking of switching to industrial engineering. He had been persuaded to enter the second semester straight away, but that would mean a lot of work; the second semester would be the hardest and he would have to catch up from the first. He did not yet know whether he wanted to take on such an adventure. As for Lolia, he had not yet found a room, but he was happy so far, and Zwickau was good for him.

About Uncle Aron, Roska sent snippets of gossip to Hamburg, *dvarim shel mah bechach*, as Yasha apparently liked to hear them. Aron, who was forty-one years old, had got engaged on New Year's Eve 1920, in a Hotel de la Poste, probably in some resort. Not to his sister-in-law Zina, who had been close to him for a long time, but to Mina, ten years younger, daughter of the businessman Joseph Levstein from Łódź and his wife Etta, a friend of Miriam Rosenberg and the sister of Anna Kustow, the lady who was the first to announce Roska's happiness in Polzin. The marriage of Aron and Mina had been initiated by Chaim Kahan during his last stay in the Caucasus spa Kislovodsk in the summer of 1916. The son who had resisted marriage for so long was fulfilling the wish of his late father. He married Mina some months later, on April 17, 1921, at the registry office in Wilmersdorf. The local historian Yefim Basin found the document in the archive of Brest-Litovsk. Aron had sent it to his hometown in the mid-twenties together with the application for Polish citizenship. Siblings of the bridal couple, Baruch Kahan and Anna Kustow, were witnesses at the wedding. On February 16, 1922, Mina gave birth to a son, named Joseph after her father, who later became Yossi. Unlike Yasha and Roska, Aron and Mina did not announce the marriage or the birth of the son in the *Jüdische Rundschau*. At first they lived at 4 Darmstädter Strasse on the other side of Kurfürstendamm near Olivaer Platz, a few minutes walk from Schlüterstrasse. When Joseph was born, Lina was assigned there as a nanny. Chaim Avinoam, who was just under one and a half years old and whom she also looked after, moved with her; since then, Roska was commuting between two apartments, about which she complained bitterly to Sasha: her little family was living in three places now. The peak of the provisional arrangement was reached when she had to cede her cot in Darmstädter Strasse to Lolia, who had fallen out with his mother, Zina, and had moved in with Aron and Mina.

Uncle Aron's son was still very small, but already there is a story to tell about him, Roska wrote to Yasha in Hamburg on March 21, 1922. She had seen a pram standing in Joseph's room today: Mina had asked Aron for a dark-blue Brennabor pram, but Aron didn't agree. Mina insisted. So Zina intervened and convinced Aron to buy the pram because otherwise Mina's brother would do it. When the pram was delivered, there was already a dark blue pram of the desired fine brand there. Madame Kustow had bought it in her brother's name. So Zina's fears had come true sooner than expected. This pram was then quickly sent back.

A week later, Roska told Yasha about an argument with Uncle Aron, whom she rarely saw because he was travelling a lot, to Hamburg, Wilhelmshaven, Paris, Copenhagen, and who—unlike Uncle David—hardly ever spoke to her. Aron had noticed that Roska never ate at their place on Darmstädter Strasse, so he questioned her about that, asked for the reason and insisted that she stay for dinner. But Roska refused, arguing in German about moral constraints, *Gewissenszwang*. Mina did not keep a kosher kitchen. Even Lina had noticed that. So Aron went out and bought new dishes. But for Roska, as long as Mina didn't change her behavior, things wouldn't get any better. She kept refusing. She felt sorry for Mina, whom she liked after all. But, then, Aron put her even more under pressure. If only she had her own place, Roska complained. Two days later she stayed for lunch with Aron and Mina. Her uncle had impressed her. He was truly a remarkable person, he was attentive to all sorts of things, there was enough time for everything. That day he put the new dishes on the table, stayed with Mina in the kitchen for some time himself and probably showed her how to keep the kitchen kosher. But Roska didn't like her role as the moral guardian, which she understood in her own way: she was no lover of revolutions, and she certainly didn't want to lead one.

More than any other relatives, the Rosenbergs believed in tradition. Roska vividly described to Yasha how they had prepared for Passover at 36 Schlüter-strasse in April 1922. The apartment was thoroughly cleaned of all leaven, and even the furniture was rearranged to create additional sleeping places for the family members from outside. Uncle Bendet had already brought his sleep-wear over. The whole family, including Berl Rosenberg, was invited to the Seder night. Roska also invited her two friends, Jettchen and Mademoiselle Kleppfisch, to experience a real Passover.

The relationship with the servants had always been kind and humane. A postcard from Lina to Yasha in the summer resort is preserved. Lina's health, her fat feet, were a topic of Arusia's as well as Roska's correspondence. Roska discussed with Yasha, in detail, the question of how they would be able to take part in the wedding of Dodo, the cook Bliuma's daughter; she decided that they should not go, so as not to embarrass Bliuma and Dodo; she visited the bride on another day instead, which apparently was not something Dodo had taken for granted.

The provisional arrangement and the fight with the Housing Department for a *makom keva*, a permanent home, had accompanied the family for some time. In early March 1922, Aron rented a second, furnished, seven-room apart-ment for a few months at 36 Württembergische Strasse. In mid-May, Mina and Aron were to vacate the apartment in Darmstädter Strasse. Aron intervened unsuccessfully with the Rent Regulation Office, and the case went to court. Whether he achieved anything, and they continued to live there for some time, or whether they rented a furnished apartment elsewhere on Württembergische Strasse, remains unclear. Tenants leave no traces in the address registers. Baruch and Rosalia were also moving several times from place to place. Roska's letters mentioned apartments on Wilhelmstrasse in Halensee, on Ansbacher Strasse near Olivaer Platz and in Passauer Strasse. In December 1921 they escaped to

Wiesbaden for a few days, staying this time in the Hessischer Hof at 11 Kranzplatz, a house for people with sophisticated tastes. Roska was talking about the expansion of two apartments, probably in the newly acquired buildings on 32 Wielandstrasse and 37 Schlüterstrasse. In the summer of 1923, Baruch stated 32 Wielandstrasse as his address. As for Zina, Aron found a way out. According to his memoirs, he went to London, met with Zina's relative, the wholesaler Michael Golodetz, and arranged to fit out an apartment for her at his own expense, which was to be rent-free for six years. For about one thousand dollars, a six-room apartment—free of official restrictions—was then added to the top floor of the building at 47 Kurfürstendamm. At that time, thousands of such apartments were created in Berlin under an expedited procedure. The Kahans also had the attics at 32 Wielandstrasse and 37 Schlüterstrasse refurbished. "Several months passed before Zina and the children moved into the apartment, where they lived quietly for 6–7 years, in the immediate vicinity of Schlüter 36, undisturbed and without fear of the Housing Department," Roska continues. Arusia probably didn't get his own address for a long time, but from the spring of 1922 he had been living with his parents at 17 Passauer Strasse, in the middle of the Russian Berlin. "They had moved to Passauer Strasse, on the corner of Wittenbergplatz, opposite the famous KaDeWe ...," says Andrei Bely. There, the Russian emigrants had opened a delicatessen, a bar, a club, a St. Petersburg fashion house, a boarding house and a lending library. Arusia forbade Roska to visit 17 Passauerstrasse, and there is no record of how he experienced Berlin after he had withdrawn from her. But, like his brother Nachum, he was certainly drawn more than his other relatives to the Russian emigrants who used to congregate in cafés and would find themselves thinking of Russia as the most beautiful country in the world, though it had abandoned them, and of the Russian revolution, which had determined their fate, as the greatest of all times, and for which, according to their experience, nothing seemed impossible. For Roska and Yasha, too, no solution to the housing question was in sight. For the time being, they were staying with their parents at 36 Schlüterstrasse, but after the contract with Wilhelmshaven, there was no longer any question of moving to Hamburg. The City of Jade no longer seemed "ominous" to Roska, after her father-in-law Baruch had checked it out together with Aron, David and Yasha at the beginning of May 1922 and, completely satisfied with the successful conclusion of the contract, had commented positively: it was perhaps not exactly beautiful, but still likable.

From the relatives in Soviet Russia, Rachel and David Ettinger, the family received signs of life now and then—a telegram, a letter by "occasion" or a postcard: November 1921—they were sitting on packed suitcases, waiting for the next group of emigrants to be assembled; early February 1922—David Ettinger was released from hospital and they were now returning from Moscow to Yekaterinoslav. The Berliners reacted immediately and telegraphed: the Ettingers were not to leave Moscow without talking to Prof. Coolidge, and take the children there. The pioneer of Russian studies in America, Archibald Cary Coolidge, was in Moscow at the time to buy books for the Harvard University Library. At the same time his first student, Frank Golder, was working for the American Relief Administration in Russia. The Kahans were probably hoping for help from Coolidge. Apparently, they had a diplomatic connection to Golder or to him. At the end of April a postcard from Rachel arrived with the news that they were hoping to leave the country soon. But they did not arrive in Berlin until a year and a half later, the last of the family to get there. Rachel did not live to see her mother. Malka died on January 15, 1922 and is buried in the Adass Yisroel cemetery in Berlin-Weissensee.

The Ettingers arrived at a turning point when hyperinflation and unrest in Germany had just been halted by the introduction of the new monetary unit, the Rentenmark. Similar to Uncle Aron and cousins Nachum and Arusia, the Ettinger children were alienated by the "Charlottenburg psychology." As soon as they had stepped off the train onto the platform, they laughed at the gentlemen in top hats who looked like they were going to a funeral, until their relatives indignantly enlightened them about Berlin fashion. The Ettingers had themselves registered as "Palestine Immigrants" by the Austrian consul general. They, too, were accommodated first at 36 Schlüterstrasse and later next door, in number 37. Now Chaim and Malka's children were all gathered in Charlottenburg. The reunion of the whole family was symptomatic of Jewish emigration and a sign of its irreversibility. Although the Kahans, Rosenbergs and Ettingers had always kept in close contact with each other in the vast Russian Empire, they now found themselves in a new situation that brought conflicts, but also gave them security in the adverse climate.

CHAPTER 15

Nitag. Berlin

"Dear Uncle Aron, after my conversation with you today ... I would like to express my views on various issues recorded in your memoirs and recurring in conversations. I ask you to consider my statements objectively, since, as I also pointed out at the family meeting, the 1932 'period' is only of theoretical interest to me." With these words, Nomek Rosenberg began a letter to Aron, which was over four pages long, typewritten in single-spaced German and dated March 7, 1961. By then, Nomek was already over sixty, lived in Tel Aviv, had two adult sons and grandchildren. He owned his own small company in Israel, Penguin, which produced carbon paper, but was not doing well. The letter to Aron was about the end of the family business centered around Nitag.

Let's go back to Nitag and its beginnings. It was founded in Berlin on July 7, 1922, three months after the conclusion of the lease agreement between the Caucasische Handelsgesellschaft, the Reich Treasury and the City of Wilhelmshaven. This was done in the wake of the Genoa Conference and the Treaty of Rapallo, perhaps in response to their repercussions—the international recognition of the state-owned Soviet oil industry, thereby legitimizing the expropriation by the Bolsheviks. This was the Kahans' final farewell to their Russian companies. The new company owed its name, Naphta-Industrie und Tankanlagen AG (Nitag) to the facilities in the Jade City. Its purpose was the storage, trade and dispatch of crude oil and other mineral oils; transactions of all kinds which appeared to be useful for achieving the company's objectives, such as the acquisition and sale of land; partnership in other companies; the acquisition, manufacture and utilization of tank facilities, particularly in Wilhelmshaven; entering into community interest agreements; the establishment of branches at home and abroad. It never implemented its original objectives of extracting, processing and utilizing crude oil and other mineral resources.

Nomek wrote the letter to Aron a few months after his uncle had distributed copies of his memoirs to the family on his eightieth birthday. He distinguished between two aspects to make his point—Aron's merits with regard to the business and the material claims he derived therefrom. His uncle was blending the two. Nomek had no doubt that Aron had to be credited with the lion's share of initiative, commercial vision and entrepreneurial energy. Without him, the business would probably not have been established. But it bothered him that his uncle derived financial claims from it. "If I may be permitted to slip into the psychological realm" he wrote, "I cannot shake off the impression that, for you too, the financial side of things is not as important as you make out, but that you regard the reality of your financially stronger position as recognition of your exceptional business skills. ... It particularly disturbs me that you want to cash in on your intellectual qualities." The family's paradigm had been based on *shutfut* [collaboration], following the ideals and values their grandparents had lived by. The liquidation of the family business in 1932, he alleged, had been unlawful. Nomek had never accepted it, not even after nearly thirty years. He had lost property due to the company's arbitrary liquidation—buildings in Poland and assets in Israel. With this letter he was apparently calling his uncle to account.

Nitag's initial capital had amounted to 1,045,000 Reichsmark. Where did the Kahans get that money? In the family archives I found a handwritten interim receipt dated June 11, 1923, which states that Messrs. Bendet and Baruch Kahan, as well as Jonas Rosenberg, had jointly acquired preferential Nitag shares to the value of five million marks; at that time, in the year of hyperinflation, the capital was already seventy-five times higher than the initial sum: seventy-five million Reichsmark. The personal contribution by Nomek's father, as well as his Uncles Baruch and Bendet was relatively small. On the back of a handwritten drafted *drashah*, a sermon, presumably by Jonas Rosenberg about the four sons in the Passover *Hagadah*, I found the printed communication of June 11, 1923 from Nitag to the shareholders of the Caucasische Handelsgesellschaft, saying that it had taken over the shares of the company and would continue to conduct its business in the usual manner. It invited everyone to participate.

According to Nomek, the establishment of a corporation requires five essential things: equity investment, expertise, risk distribution among the partners, competitiveness and goodwill. According to these criteria, he analyzed the situation in which the family business had started up in Berlin in the early twenties. At that time, no one believed in a permanent rule of the Bolsheviks, with the Caucasus not yet under their control. Therefore, everything that had been in Russia had belonged to the family business. This included the depots in Poland and the Baltic States. The goodwill had already been created by their grandfather, especially through his position in the bulk oil trade. Aron had maintained old business connections with the petroleum sales to Latvia and the partnership with Carl Frederik Glad. In addition, there was Max Lew's expertise; he had represented the Russian-Baltic Mineral Oil Company for his grandfather in Berlin before the war and had had his office at 36 Schlüterstrasse. The starting capital, too, had come from the family. It included the shabby remainder of the Danish kroner that had been deposited with Glad during the war and the sale of Caucasus-Volga Industrial & Trading Company shares. There was also the profit from the *Salahadji* cargo—*Salahadji* was the name of a Dutch tanker which had brought a load of oil products from Baku to Constantinople for the COC in 1921. Then, there were the proceeds of mazut sales to Glad and Julius Schindler from depots in the Caucasus.

Julius Schindler was an entrepreneur from Hamburg who had started out as the representative for the whole of Europe at Oelwerke Stern-Sonneborn AG (Ossag), one of the first lubricating oil factories in Germany. In 1908 he founded the Handelsfirma Julius Schindler and made a name for himself with the worldwide exclusive sales from one of the most important mineral oil refineries in Russia. The Kahans probably already knew Schindler from Baku. They had already done business with him in Germany before Nitag was founded. According to Aron's memoirs, one of their first profitable business relationships was when Schindler sold the German National Railway large quantities of cheap Mexican fuel oil, which he had stored at the Caucasische Handelsgesellschaft's depot in Wilhelmshaven after the miners' strike had forced the Railway to switch to other energy sources in May 1922. Caucasus-Volga Industrial & Trading Company's shares were still invested in the Copenhagen COC in the spring of 1920, when Baku had already been captured by the Bolsheviks and the oil industry was expropriated. One wonders, who would have bought them, who had assessed their value like other "dead souls"?

The Reorganization of the German Petroleum Trade after the War is the title of a thirty-three-page German-language manuscript in the family archives, dated "Berlin 1924." In it, Aron carried out an industry and market analysis, based on the latest specialist literature, which was probably groundbreaking for Nitag. Based on data, he began by describing the structural changes in the energy industry from kerosene and coal through heating oil to diesel and gasoline. It may seem paradoxical today, but at the time, compared to coal, this meant ecological as well as economic progress—it was easier to use, was better for the boilers, produced less smoke, had a higher energy value, was simpler to transport, required less storage space and left no slag behind. Technological advance—the replacement of the steam engine by the combustion engine, the conversion of trains and ships to oil based fuel, the introduction of motor vehicles and airplanes—had been accelerated by the war, which needed to make its destruction and murder machines more effective.

Although Aron was the creator of Nitag, he had left its management to David and his associate, Max Lew, until the latter's death in late 1929. Together with Baruch, they had jointly signed a letter from the board of Nitag to the shareholders of the Caucasische Handelsgesellschaft, dated June 11, 1923. Baruch, as the eldest of the brothers, had been chairing the board of directors for a long time. Aron was his representative. Other family board members were Nomek's father and initially also sister-in-law Zina. "My original intention was to set aside a certain portion of the profits for my mother and also for the other members of the family for their livelihood. In the business itself, I thought to include only David and Zina—Zina because I was planning to take care of her and her family anyway, and David because I was still counting on his cooperation at that time," is how Aron justified himself. However, Zina had not accepted this honor, causing him to involve the whole family.

Nitag's letter to the shareholders of the Caucasische Handelsgesellschaft was also signed by Dr. Jakob Rabinowitsch and Jacob Kahan as authorized signatories. Rabinowitsch was a lawyer, a relative of Zina's, a revolution refugee like the Kahans, who had already been employed in the oil industry in Baku. Yasha had had a job in Berlin from January 1923, was promoted and held a responsible position at Nitag. The reference the company issued him upon his mandatory dismissal in October 1933 states that he had been active in both their German and international operations: he had been responsible for the supply of the inland depots and had set up and supervised several subsidiaries and branches. As a sales correspondent, he had also handled larger foreign business transactions overseas and in south-eastern Europe. He was a skillful negotiator, and the successes in the domestic German trade were partly attributable to him. Yasha had become a leading manager.

Aron had been on the Nitag board for a long time. In his memoirs he presented himself as the founder of the company:

> The years 1921–1923 were years of feverish activity for me. Spurred on
> by the enormous inflation, which in addition to its harmful effect on the
> economic situation of a large part of the population of Germany was at the

same time a favorable basis for the processing of foreign trade thanks to the reduction in administrative expenses, I made Nitag in Berlin the center of an extensive international oil trade.

About his brother David, who had only come to Berlin more than a year after the founding of the COC, Aron states that in the early days David had been more interested in Yalkut, Bendet's publishing house, than in the oil business.

Nitag founded a branch and subsidiaries. It acquired the majority of shares in other companies and tried its hand at other industries. Already in this early phase, at the beginning of 1924, during the currency reform, it took over Vollbrot, a bread recycling company in Berlin, which was also managed by Max Lew and David Kahan. However, Vollbrot remained irrelevant to the development of the oil trading company. Immediately after its foundation, Nitag opened a branch in Hamburg, which was entered in the commercial register as a corporation with a share capital of seven million Reichsmark in the year of hyperinflation. Five years later (1927) it expanded its tank facilities in the Hamburg petroleum port. Nitag advertised in the trade directory of the Hanseatic city as an importer of petroleum, gasoline, gasoil and lubricating oils with its own tank wagon fleet, headquartered in the old town, at 8/10 Speersort, postal address 19/21 Mönckebergstrasse, in the Hulbe arts and crafts building. This was an impressive building in the style of the Dutch Renaissance—with its stepped gable, an eyecatcher among the office buildings. The manager was Dr. Berl Rosenberg, a relative of the Kahans, who had previously represented the family interests of the Caucasische Handelsgesellschaft in Hamburg. Berl Rosenberg, born and raised in Vitebsk, had studied medicine in Königsberg and Berlin after graduating from high school in 1912. In 1921 he graduated with a degree and a doctorate, after which he reoriented his career. He was a migrant and a self-made man in the oil business. For thirteen years he managed Nitag's business in Hamburg, the most important branch office, including the leased mega plant in the petroleum port. He managed the entire shipping department, took care of extensive foreign business, transporting consignments not only on his own tankers, but also on chartered ones and schooners. When he had to be summarily dismissed in 1934, Nitag credited him with being a highly intelligent and prudent employee. A few days after Hitler became Reich Chancellor, Berl Rosenberg held a wedding in Hamburg with all the trimmings—flowers, champagne and relatives. Wedding photos from the archives show a petite man. Despite his tailcoat, top hat and large, strong glasses, his resemblance to his uncle, Jonas Rosenberg, is unmistakable. His son, a professor at the Technion in Haifa, told me that his father had never spoken about his time in Hamburg.

Nitag's competitive advantage did not only consist of tax and customs concessions, the "reduction of administrative expenses," as Aron called it, but also resulted from the possession of foreign currency, which the Kahans had at their disposal thanks to COC in Copenhagen and the United Caucasian Oil Company Ltd. in London. Aron wrote that the business in London, which was expanding rapidly, was particularly demanding. The United was founded in London at the beginning of 1924, just at the point in time when the German currency was being reformed and the Reichsbank in Berlin was temporarily blocking economic loans. The United was based in the business center of London—in the Museum Station Building at 133 High Holborn, in central London and was represented by Filitz & Bahaturianz, with whom the family had been in business for several years. In addition to David, Filitz and a certain Mr. H. K. Newcombe from Britain, the Danish partner Carl Frederik Glad and Aron and David Kahan served as directors. Like Nitag, the United was financed by COC shares. It developed a lucrative business activity, which, as Aron noted in his memoirs, placed a heavy burden on him. Neither he nor his brother spoke English. On July 25, 1925, the *Petroleum Times* reported on the oil industry in Barrow, a port town in northwest England: "... a new company has commenced operations at Barrow, namely, the United Caucasian Oil Company." The United, a major oil importer, had only appeared in Barrow in April of that year. It had a storage capacity of 3,000 tons of oil, had taken over five of the large tanks owned by Shell-Mex and had just opened new offices in the town. The business was reported to be stable and had good prospects. Shell-Mex was the marketing arm of the Big Sisters in Great Britain. In 1926, the United changed its name to United Oil Importers, Ltd. In early 1927, it had a share capital of 150,000 pounds sterling and several tank facilities along the British coasts. "... during the past few weeks several cargoes have arrived for its requirements, principally from Romania. During 1926 it dealt with over 92,000 tons of petroleum, making profits of nearly £18,000," reported the *Petroleum Times* in January 1927.

Nitag reinvested the profits resulting from its competitive advantage and strengthened its position with parent and sister companies, which were referred to as affiliates in the trade magazine *Petroleum*. Caucasische Handelsgesellschaft and Schlüterstrasse 37 Grundstücks GmbH, also known as Kahan Vermögensverwaltung in Berlin, continued to be included among those affiliates.

With regard to the demand for fuel in the German postwar economy, Aron wrote in his paper about the structural change in the oil trade that urbanization reduced petroleum consumption, but increased gasoline and diesel consumption for trucks even more than for automobiles. The development of air traffic was progressing, albeit more slowly than in other countries, as aircraft construction was only unblocked in May 1921 and was still restricted. Ships were gradually switching to fuel oil, while the war fleet was still fueled by tar, a coal derivative. Industry machinery required more and more diesel and lubricating oils. In order to cover the demand, fuel would have to be imported, as the production of crude oil in Germany was low. After the loss of the production area in Alsace, from which forty-five percent of the oil consumption had been covered before the war, only one remained in the Lüneburger Heide, where mainly lubricating oils were produced. During the war, when the German entrepreneurs were cut off from the oil-exporting countries, they had resorted to coal derivatives from their own production—tar, benzene, solar oil and lubricating oils. Despite the general replacement of coal derivatives by mineral oil, the coal oil industry was able to survive regionally, especially in Germany. The oils extracted from lignite were the main products, those from hard coal were by-products.

Aron understood the global situation of the oil business. The San Remo Conferences in the spring of 1920 had enabled the victorious powers, England and France, to divvy up the market in the Middle East among themselves; the Genoa and The Hague Conferences as well as the Treaty of Rapallo had brought a new competitor onto the world market—the Soviet Union. Aron was now mainly interested in the economic structure of the petroleum industry in Germany, which had been recovering slowly since the end of the war. He apparently wanted to identify Nitag's competitors on the domestic market, and introduced in his paper the three leading companies at the time: the Deutsch-Amerikanische Petroleum AG, controlled by Standard Oil, which had to give up parts of its fleet to France in the course of reparations, but was given preferential treatment by the Reich government and received support from its parent company; Deutsche Petroleum AG, which, together with Deutsche Petroleum Verkaufsgesellschaft, had represented the oil interests of the Deutsche Bank from 1922 and the old European Petroleum Union; Deutsche Erdöl AG, which had saved part of its assets by moving them during the war to Switzerland, had gained strength in 1921 by merging with Swiss, French, Czechoslovak and Polish partners in the International Petroleum Union. In 1921 the three had agreed on the following quotas: Deutsch-Amerikanische Petroleum AG, seventy-three percent, Deutsche Erdöl AG and Deutsche Petroleum AG together with Deutsche Petroleum Verkaufsgesellschaft, thirteen and a half percent each. Aron stated that the latter two companies had changed fundamentally as a result of the war: having been forced, more or less, to sell off foreign ownership, they changed over to oil substitutes made from coal. In addition, another company, Hugo Stinnes, aroused his interest: the similarities in their orientation concerning the oil business with Nitag were obvious. Like Nitag, Stinnes, a coal entrepreneur and benzene producer before the war, was leasing, *inter alia*, tank facilities of the same size from the former Reich Navy, not in Wilhelmshaven, but at a location at least as strategically convenient—in Brunsbüttel-Ostermoor on the Kiel Canal, not far from the mouth of the Elbe. Stinnes imported petroleum products, had drilling done in Argentina and developed a lively bunker business, the trade in fuel oil for ship diesel engines.

In the last part of the paper Aron talked about trade, the sector of the industry in which Nitag was active, and he stated that in Germany it was now less about petroleum than about oil products of various kinds and more about logistics and distribution. Both import and sales were concentrated and centrally organized while consumers were receiving their goods directly from the wholesaler. He described the distribution arrangements in detail. Similar to the old petroleum trade, gasoline for motor vehicles was sold directly to private customers, by sales agencies affiliated with production companies at outlets, for which fitters' workshops, bicycle stores, garages and motels were particularly suitable. The quantity of gasoline sold at those outlets was fluctuating according to seasonal vagaries and the days of the week; unlike petroleum, it sold better in summer than in winter, on public holidays than on weekdays, in the cities and their environs than in the countryside; it was doing particularly well in the Berlin region. Public and industrial transport customers would buy diesel and gasoline directly from the wholesaler. Heating and fuel oil were being transported in tank wagons directly to the factories from the tank facilities located in the seaports. Small companies were receiving them by the barrel from the national tank facilities. Fuel for ships was being stored near the coast in so-called bunker depots and delivered from there. In the last part, Aron's paper reads like a handout to Nitag's management in its early days.

In his memoirs he did not delve any further into the situation of the German oil market. He only described briefly and succinctly how the hyperinflation was defeated by the currency reform at the end of 1923, as a government measure that was based on an apparently effective fiction, commonly called a "miracle"—the coupling of the transitional currency, the Rentenmark, to land as a cover and substitute for the gold standard that had been in force until the beginning of the war. However, he had his own ideas about the reform of monetary transactions in Germany which he spelled out in an essay published in Berlin in 1923. Based on his perspective as a major, internationally active entrepreneur, he recommended the immediate and direct transition to gold currency. Based on his own experience and in his own interest, he reckoned that during the years of paper money hyperinflation in the country, many billions in gold and foreign currency had accumulated in safes and foreign banks, which, for their egocentric reasons would flow towards the public good when the restrictions on foreign currency trade would be lifted. He had many objections to and practical suggestions for economic policy concerns regarding the unresolved restitution issue, the deficit in the state budget and the predictable inflation as a result of the reform, which could lead to unemployment, a reduction in competitiveness and industrial standstill: the conversion to the Goldmark would improve Germany's international standing. With sensible tax legislation and provided that there was general austerity, the budget was not a bad one in comparison to the prewar budget, he wrote, because it did not have to bear the enormous expenses for the army and navy. Unemployment was an unavoidable transitional phenomenon, but could be alleviated by grants, which Aron called "restoring people's savings." The Reichsbank was to be relieved of the obligation to finance the state budget. The Reichsbank and State Bank were to be separated, and the shortage of money in the Reichsbank was to be compensated for by the inflow of the retained foreign currency. This would enlarge its ability to control the money supply and increase the amount of money in circulation. As a first measure, he recommended selling Reichsbank shares to help the treasury help itself and, possibly, using the psychological effect of privatization, also selling them abroad, or issuing "government bonds." Capital that was productively employed in industry and business should be given preferential treatment during the devaluation of paper money and speculators should be compelled to issue gold bonds. The explanations of the reform proposal were followed by a nine-paragraph draft law concerning the regulation of monetary transactions. The only locatable copy of the document is in the library of the Prussian Cultural Heritage Archives in Berlin-Dahlem. Did Aron Kahan send it to the authorities for careful reading and had a ministry official taken an interest in it? The fate of that essay can no longer be determined.

According to the Company Registry file, the Nitag's share capital amounted to 125 million Reichsmark in July 1923 as a result of the galloping inflation. After the currency reform, the conversion of the company was accompanied by a moderation of the share capital to the initial sum of 1,045,000 mark, which was again called Reichsmark at the end of August 1924. At the same time, the company was expanding. During the hyperinflation and currency reform, Aron had written two further essays on current economic and financial policies, this time on the question of restitution, one of which remained a German manuscript, the second, entitled *New Scheme for Settlement of Reparations Problem*, was published in English in London in 1923. The emigrant and oil businessman thus demonstrated social responsibility and political commitment, as he had done in Ukraine several years earlier, but this was not listened to in either Germany or England. Aron's proposal to solve the reparations problem was based on an original idea. He realized that it could only be dealt with intercontinentally, since European creditors were themselves debtors of the USA. All European states, including those that had been neutral during the war, plus Canada and the USA, were to establish a kind of reinsurance to guarantee Germany's reparations payments, because a peaceful solution to the problem was in the economic interest of all nations. He assumed that the nations, acting as an insurance community, could exert particularly strong pressure on Germany to meet its obligations. Moreover, in the event of non-payment, it would be easier for the individual nations to jointly compensate for the missing amounts. Such a construction would also be acceptable to the USA. According to his recollection, a leading employee of the Midland Bank Group in London reacted to this after all, writing to him that the idea of mutual insurance was ingenious. Unfortunately, there was a lack of suitable diplomacy to implement such a plan.

"You told me that the decision to liquidate was taken by the whole family," Nomek wrote to Aron in 1961. "This assertion stands in stark contrast to what was said that evening [in 1932] by Uncle Baruch in the presence of Uncle Bendet and Aunt Judith; Aunt Rochele was not present at the time, while Uncle David used to speak to me until 1939 in a manner which excluded any doubt that he did not share your point of view." Nomek felt, that a *decision* to wind up was not a winding-up *order*. Aron should have been aware that Nomek would lose his job if the business were liquidated. He had been employed by Nitag since January 1923, first for one year as a volunteer in Wilhelmshaven, then a second year in Hamburg. From there he moved to the headquarters in Berlin, where he headed the sales department for the city and region of Berlin until his mandatory dismissal in June 1933. In addition, following an affidavit by his cousin Yasha, he acted as an authorized representative in the compensation proceedings for two subsidiaries, Anhaltinische Kraftstoff GmbH in Dessau, and from July 1932 also for Niedersächsische Betriebsstoff GmbH in Hanover. After graduating from the Engineering Academy in Oldenburg in 1924, cousin Lolia worked for the United in London, then for various subsidiaries and branches and from April 1932 to March 1933 as managing director of Mitteldeutsche Kraftstoff GmbH in Halle an der Saale.

Parallel to the expansion of the tank facilities in the two German North Sea ports, Nitag also extended its inland distribution system to Hanover in the west, Halle and Dessau in the southwest, Bonn and Cologne in the south and Dresden and Königsberg in the east. It also built up a network of gas stations in the vicinity of tank facilities in the regions of Oldenburg, Hanover and Berlin, as well as in the *Länder* of Saxony and East Prussia, which in the mid-thirties consisted of six hundred and fifty stations. Nomek was responsible for the gas stations in the Berlin region. In April 1925, when the currency in England was converted to the gold standard and prices there rose, which also affected the United, the Kahans founded the Rheinische Naphta Industrie AG and in the same year the Niedersächsische Betriebsstoff-Gesellschaft. In 1928 they acquired the Deutsche Betriebsstoff-AG (Debag) in Dresden, an import and distribution company for fuels of all kinds, in order to show a presence on the Saxon market, and the Berliner Bau und Handelsgesellschaft für den Nahen Osten, which they renamed Orient Mineralölwerke GmbH, with the ambitious goal of building refineries in the Middle East beyond the oil trade. At the same time, they expanded their branch in Wilhelmshaven, which was managed by Wulf (Vulf) Dembo. At the beginning of 1931, the Mitteldeutsche Kraftstoff GmbH was added. It was impossible to determine, when the Anhaltinische was established in Dessau, from when on it was controlled by Nitag, whether Erdöl-*Handel G.m.b.H. Königsberg* and the corporation for mineral oil products, Milag, in Berlin had already belonged to Nitag before 1933.

Until spring 1934, the Niedersächsische Betriebsstoff had its office in the center of Hanover, just behind the railway station. The tanks and depots were located in the industrial estate, probably on the National Railways site in Hanover-Leinhausen. During the last year and a half of the Weimar Republic, the management was in the hands of Max Lew's son René. He had started at Nitag in Wilhelmshaven and had worked for the company in Cologne before moving to Hanover. The Rheinische, based in Bonn and since the summer of 1927 in Cologne, was the largest subsidiary with a share capital of 150,000 Reichsmark. It owned tank facilities at the Rhine Port and had an office in Cologne, in the Gereonshaus, one of the most magnificent office buildings in the old town. The founders were Aron Kahan, the Nitag authorized signatory Jakob Rabinowitsch and three other residents of Berlin—an engineer and two merchants, two of them with East European Jewish names: Benjamin Halpern and Ilya Ginsburg. The board consisted of the Nitag employees Max Lew and Israel Estrin. Like

Filitz in London and Berl Rosenberg in Hamburg, Estrin was a migrant from the Russian Empire and was three years older than Yasha. He came from Bobruisk in the Minsk Province and had been living in Germany from the spring of 1914 and in Berlin from 1917 to the end of 1937. He was working as an accountant for Nitag. The Rheinische operated a large tank facility, as well as a wholesale and retail business. During the first two years the company was still experiencing some difficulties. Even though the share capital of 37,500 Reichsmark was merely a downpayment, the business was nevertheless expanded.

The fact that Arusia had successfully completed his studies in the spring of 1925 may also have contributed to the foundation of the Rheinische. He was the first of the third generation to obtain a university degree in Germany, which was useful for the family business. Now he was available as a junior manager. He had been registered as living in Bonn from early May 1925. He was representing the Rheinische locally. "David's and Aron's efforts enabled us to build a large factory in Europe," he recalled. "Aron was the driving force. Most of the money from Russia was gone. So Grandma sold her jewelry. Additionally, their old business friend in Copenhagen and Baron Günzburg's family bank in Amsterdam helped them as well. Our business was doing very well." It seems that Arusia had come to terms after all with Uncle Aron's leadership of the family and the business, contrary to what he had demanded of himself and his brothers, Chaim's grandchildren, some years earlier. After Max Lew's retirement in October 1929, he had joined the board of directors. At that time, he was the first of the family to apply for German citizenship in order to be able to travel freely and operate across borders as a German businessman, for which he received the support of key local politicians. The Mayor of Wilhelmshaven certified that Nitag's activities had contributed significantly to the promotion of business life in Wilhelmshaven. The Land-President in Cologne confirmed that the city of Bonn was generating considerable income from the business operations of the Rheinische at the Rheinwerft shipyard and that Arusia Kahan was known to the city administration of Bonn as an efficient, reliable and conscientious businessman. Besides Arusia, Yasha, Lolia, Nomek, Berl Rosenberg and other relatives were also earning their living as employees in the family business. Dora, Bendet's eldest daughter, was employed there in the same year as Arusia. "From 1925 until my emigration, at the end of 1932, I worked as an executive secretary at Nitag. ... The position in the million-dollar company Nitag was very pleasant and I had promotion prospects," she stated in her restitution application.

By the end of 1926, Nitag had increased its capital by one million to 2,050,000 Reichsmark. New shares were issued: 960,000 Reichsmark for ordinary shares, 45,000 for preferred stock. Of these, the COC in Copenhagen took over ordinary shares to the value of 100,000 Reichsmark, but the Banking House Hardy & Co. in Berlin acquired the bulk of the equity at 860,000 Reichsmark for ordinary shares and 45,000 preferred stock. The Banking House Hardy & Co. at 36 Markgrafenstrasse, founded in 1881 by the brothers James and Ludwig Hardy with Fritz Andreae as managing director and partner, was the largest private bank in Berlin at the time. The larger private banks, which financed industry and trade and issued national and international government bonds, made an enormous contribution to the modernization of Germany as a business hub. After the war, their main activities revolved around the provision of venture capital and funds for international trade, thereby being able to establish themselves successfully in innovative, high-risk market niches. In view of the acute shortage of domestic capital, traditionally good international contacts enabled them to play a central role in arranging urgently needed foreign loans for German largescale industry. Banks and bankers were inseparably linked to each other both internally and externally by personal management and regional ties. Half of all private banks in Germany at that time were owned by Jewish bankers. From 1926, Hardy & Co. was Nitag's largest creditor and commercial bank, being represented on the board by banker Charly Hartung. Carl Frederik Glad represented the COC there and the businessman Vulf Dembo, now also in Berlin, represented the continuity of old business connections originating in the Russian Empire. In May 1927, David Kahan joined the board. To replace him, the management was taken over by the Kiev engineer Dr. Boris Schirman, eleven years older than David, who was well-known in Berlin migrant circles for his commitment as a judge in the Permanent Russian Arbitration Court and as a member of the Association of Russian Jews. In the summer of 1927, Nitag went public.

As of that year, Nitag had three tankers with a total capacity of about 10,000 gross register tons. To finance and manage the tankers, it founded the Limicana Schiffs-Gesellschaft GmbH in July 1927, whose management was taken over by Max Lew and Dr. Hermann Leising. Leising, a Catholic, born in Westphalia, was an oil industry expert in the banking sector, an employee of Hardy & Co. and the Kahan's contact person there. He also took on a management position in one of their companies. He was probably the only leading employee in Kahan's company who was not Jewish and not a migrant. Until 1927, Nitag had operated with chartered ships, for example with the Swedish 7,000-ton *Oljaren*. It acquired its first own tanker, a converted Italian warship, in 1926 and named it *Grete Glad* in honor of Glad's wife Margrethe, an indication of Aron and

David Kahan's attachment to their Danish partner. Two more ships followed in the following year, in 1927, a German schooner converted into a motorboat and an English transport steamer of the Shell group. One was named after their mother, M/T *Malkah*, the other after their father, Ch. N. Kahan, which had by far the largest capacity with almost 6,000 gross register tons. There are photos of these two tankers, the stately *Ch. N. Kahan* and the smaller *Malkah*. A pretty colorful model of the *Grete Glad* is now under glass in the boardroom of L. C. Glad & Co. in Copenhagen. Particularly their own tankers provided valuable capital. In addition, there was a fairly significant investment in tank wagons. Thus, Nitag had its own transport capabilities at a time when the established German traders had to charter ships until the end of the twenties, having had to sell their freighters as part of the reparations framework.

Nitag, like the Kahans' previous companies in the Russian Empire, was one of the outsiders, dependent on building up a personal network. It had to act as inconspicuously, quickly and efficiently as possible in order to survive against the dominating corporations. It bought its goods at low prices wherever they could be acquired, sold cheaply and distributed easily. It collaborated with its parent and sister companies, the COC and the United, bought from outsiders such as the American Sinclair Group and even from its competitors, the big corporations at home and abroad, in London, Hamburg, the Gulf of Mexico, California and Romania. The oil imported into Germany was transported via Wilhelmshaven by the German National Railways to Hungary, Czechoslovakia and Austria, and by tankers from Wilhelmshaven and Hamburg to the Baltic states, Scandinavia and Palestine. The company's own and chartered tankers sailed between America and Europe while the smaller ones headed for the coasts of Northern Europe and the Mediterranean. Despite the fierce price war on the German market, Nitag was able to make good profits until 1930. In 1928 it increased its share capital again by 500,000 to 2,550,000 Reichsmark. The six-percent dividend were not paid out in cash, but were issued to shareholders in the form of bonus shares by the Banking House Hardy & Co. At the peak of its development, in 1930, before the world economic crisis was also felt in the oil industry, Nitag was processing thirty-five oil tankers with a total cargo capacity of 118,000 gross register tons in Wilhelmshaven and Hamburg.

Nitag offered family members, acquaintances and migrants a place of work. "At the beginning of 1925 I took up my last position in Germany, at 'Nitag,' Naphta-Industrie u. Tankanlagen Aktiengesellschaft …," explained Gita Rosenzweig from Kalarash, Bessarabia, today Călărași, Moldavia, during her restitution proceedings. She had worked as a shorthand typist at the headquarters in Berlin. Her family had left the Russian Empire after the Kishinev pogroms of 1905, and Gita graduated from high school in Königsberg in 1914. After that, the Rosenzweigs moved to Berlin, where Gita had graduated from commercial college. Similarly, Sara Gerszgorn, née Rubinov, from Białystok, who, before coming to Berlin and graduating from commercial college, had studied mathematics in Kharkov for a year, worked as a commercial clerk at Nitag in Berlin from 1928 to June 1933. For a short time, for one year (1928/1929), Vera Alexander, born Muravchik, from Borisov, Minsk Province, in the Russian Empire, was also employed as an accountant at Nitag in Berlin. She had gained her high school diploma in Riga and had studied at the Psychoneurological Institute in St. Petersburg from 1914 until the October Revolution. The three women vouched for each other during the restitution proceedings. "The businesses that had sprung up during the Schlüterstrasse period," Arusia recalled, "not only fed us for 15 years, but also provided work for about 100 Russian refugees." In the late twenties, the management declared double the number of employees, which means that half of them were migrants. The personnel policy of hiring primarily employees from their own community, which was shaped by religion, tradition, origin and fate, was in line with the ethical and political attitude of the entrepreneurial family.

The apartment at 36 Schlüterstrasse had soon become too small for business activities. Nitag rented office space in Schöneberg, at 31 Kleiststrasse, directly opposite the Lodge Building. In late summer 1927, it moved a few streets further, to 11 Keithstrasse between Tauentzien and Kurfürstenstrasse. Both buildings no longer exist. "Our main office in Berlin had 30 rooms," Arusia remembered. A photo of the inauguration of the new rooms on September 13 has been preserved. The photographer captured a group of about sixty festively dressed people, women and men, among whom most of the family and management members are well positioned, and therefore easily recognizable. Seated in the middle of the first row is the chairman of the board and eldest of the brothers, Baruch Kahan, and probably Max Lew at his side. Aron Kahan and Jonas and Miriam Rosenberg join on the left, while to his right are Rosalia, Zina Kahan and, next to her, cousin Daria Moiseevna Golodetz. Sitting on the floor in front of them, framed by lush, picturesquely arranged chrysanthemums, are three young ladies—Bendet's daughters Dora and Lea and their cousin, Zina's eldest, Gita Kahan. Uncle David looks out from behind brother Aron and brother-in-law Jonas. Nomek, Salomon Ripp, Gita's future husband, and Sulamith Hurwitz flank the group with Yasha and Roska standing clearly visibly in the back row. Which of the women is Gita Rosenzweig, I could not find out and lack the names of the other faces. The Nitag family radiates pride and self-confidence. Nine days after the inauguration, on a Thursday afternoon, the company hosted in the new office an auction of fifty Rheinische shares at 1,000 Reichsmark each, together with dividend coupons, "highest bid on instant payment." That was the first year the subsidiary was in the black.

To be a successful entrepreneur in the Weimar Republic, in the face of political instability and even more so as a migrant, required vision, agility, networking skills and a special degree of expertise—qualities Aron had already demonstrated in Baku and Copenhagen. However, as an internationally operating entrepreneur who owned foreign currency, he also enjoyed certain advantages over German entrepreneurs. He had followed with interest how much hope the German fuel industry, which was poor in crude oil, had pinned on the production of coal derivatives, while he, guided by the international economic development, stuck to mineral oil. By 1924, the oil industry had again changed considerably internationally, but above all in Germany, from the time Aron had written about its structural change. From the mid-1920s onwards the competition in the petroleum industry was shifting, as the Big Sisters—Standard Oil, Royal Dutch Shell and Anglo-Persian Oil—entered into new partnerships with the German groups specializing in derivatives, thus strengthening their influence on the German market. Nitag's biggest competitors in Germany were now called Rhenania Ossag, Deutsch Amerikanische Petroleum AG and Olex. Ossag had been taken over by Shell; Deutsche Petroleum AG, Deutsche Erdöl AG and Olex by Anglo-Persian Oil. The two petroleum unions, the European and the International, had failed. Deutsche Bank withdrew from the oil industry. The Hugo Stinnes group disintegrated after his death and became part of Deutsche Gasolin.

The global economic crisis changed the situation again. Too much oil was being produced in the USA—the main importer at the time—which did not affect production, but it did affect trade. This led to a fierce price war in the oil industry among the Big Sisters and thus to a general drop in prices, particularly affecting the German import business, which had been suffering from a lack of foreign currency since the introduction of foreign exchange controls. The general crisis impacted primarily the transatlantic oil trade, but also affected German producers of derivatives, whose modus operandi was often outdated. The state was reacting to pressure from German fuel producers with protective tariff policies, countered in turn by the Big Sisters with fuel price accords. As early as 1928, they had agreed on a price cartel, making trading conditions more difficult for outsiders like Nitag. In the spring of 1931 they concluded a quota convention for Germany with the participation of the twenty-one most important producers and importers, which was renewed in August 1932. At that time, Arusia was Nitag's expert on fuel cartel issues, conducting the negotiations for the company. He was given an excellent testimonial about this when he had to be summarily dismissed: "We are losing in him a diligent and energetic employee who has rendered outstanding services to the development of the company and, more recently, especially to its representation in convention matters," it states. Arusia had been a prudent and energetic employee with quick perception and good manners. He was well liked by his colleagues. He himself recalled the time with a certain pride: "In Germany we were the biggest among the smallest. We held 3% of the syndicate." According to records in Anglo-Persian Oil, Deutsch Amerikanische Petroleum AG and Rhenania-Ossag, that is, Standard Oil and Shell, each held 21% of the fuel cartel, the Benzolverband, 16%, Olex, that is, Anglo-Persian Oil, 10.6%, Deutsche Gasolin, almost 7% and Nitag, just under 3%. The Kahans had already held the largest position among the smallest companies in Baku. They kept holding on to this status in the West as well. The tank facilities in Wilhelmshaven, which were among the first of their kind in Germany after the First World War, played a decisive role in making the company and its founders known among Europe's petroleum importers. Hans Ornstein, an old acquaintance and now an employee of the competition, acknowledged in the late 1920s that the Nitag Corporation was an important fuel and oil import and distribution organization and that it was undoubtedly of considerable importance to the German economy in this sector. At that time, Ornstein was a member of the board of directors of Olex, a company belonging to the Anglo-Persian Oil.

In his letter to Aron, Nomek did not mention the company by name. He only spoke of the family business, which was allegedly liquidated in 1932. Did he have in mind Nitag, the beating heart of the family business where he himself had been working, or the COC in Copenhagen, which was the only company he mentioned by name in the letter with a dig at his uncle? Aron was supposed to have "sided with the Caucasian's creditors in Copenhagen." Did he understand the relationship between the COC and Nitag, the intertwining within the company? In his memoirs, Aron did not establish a direct connection between Nitag's debt and the COC. "NITAG, to which we owe mainly our well-known reputation as perfect petroleum experts," he explained, "has expanded into a large business that was the envy of many, but of which no one could have guessed that it was actually a loss-making business." Apart from the German retail business and the tanker plant in Wilhelmshaven, the three tankers regularly made large profits, but despite this, large losses had to be hidden every year by increasing the share capital. In July 1931 Nitag had increased its share capital by another million to 3,550,000 Reichsmark. "Our large personal financial liability to NITAG was gradually covered by us issuing shares, so that the entire responsibility for NITAG was ultimately transferred to the Banking House Hardy." In December 1931 Aron and David left the board of directors and moved to the board of management. Banker Theodor de Günzburg, Amsterdam, son of Chaim's partner Alexander G. Günzburg, replaced the Kahan brothers on the board of directors.

Was this change a sign that the Kahan brothers had already lost control of Nitag or was it a sign that they wanted to maneuver the company out of the crisis by themselves? How can the Kahans' "large personal debt" to Nitag be explained? Didn't the major economic and political factors, the global economic crisis and the rise of the National Socialists in Germany, play a role in Nitag's decline, though on Aron and David's watch? What was the position of the Danish company in the winding-up process that Nomek did not want to recognize as liquidation? "Even if you were convinced that one could simply retain assets for debt, without accounting, without setting a deadline—don't you think you had the moral obligation to inform me about my material situation? The only explanation I can give for this omission is that no liquidation was intended. ... I now claim that no liquidation took place in 1932," Nomek put to his uncle. Did he argue like that because he thought the Kahans' companies in the West were a family business, although they had long been part of a transnational group of companies that had developed their own dynamics? Only in view of the global economic situation, political events and the fact that Nitag and the COC together formed the center of a ramified network of companies can the misunderstanding about the "1932 period" be explained and the end of the Kahans' control over Nitag be understood.

CHAPTER 16

Devotion to Books. Petrograd, Vilna, Berlin

"What do oil and books have in common? They both bring light to the world." For generations this anecdote was told in the family. It is attributed to Bendet, but perhaps stems already from his father or his brothers Baruch and David. Chaim Kahan was considered a traditionally learned and modern-minded man, who was a shrewd thinker and a dreamer until his old age. Except for Aron, all the men in the Kahan family of the second generation, including Chaim's sons-in-law, were interested in books and were engaged to varying degrees in publishing houses. After Chaim's death in November 1916, in the middle of the war, the children gave the tithes of their assets to a good cause, at his request, as has been the tradition among Jews since biblical times. They donated the considerable sum of 800,000 rubles to publish writings, traditional canonical texts on the one hand, and modern contemporary topics from a Jewish perspective on the other.

Chaim's children took part in the publication of the *Togblat*, a Zionist newspaper in the Yiddish language, initially called the *Petrograd Togblat* and published from 1915 to 1918. David Kahan was one of the three editors. In the period between the February Revolution and the Bolsheviks' coup d'état the Kahans established the *Chaim Publishing House* in Petrograd in their father's honor with the magazine *Heavar* [The Past] under the editorship of the journalist and historian Shaul Ginsburg, which attempted to continue recording the history of the Jews and Judaism in Eastern Europe under the new political conditions in Hebrew. In *Heavar*, the first and, for many years, the last generation of Russian Jewish historians, self-made men of science, such as Simon Dubnow, Israel Zinberg and Ilya Cherikover, published in Hebrew; most of them also published in Russian or Yiddish. The journal was launched with two eulogies about the family founder by the Petrograd chief rabbi Dr. Moshe Eisenstadt and Chaim's friend merchant Meir Aronson. Rabbi Eisenstadt praised Chaim Kahan's extraordinary generosity and willingness to donate while Aronson traced his life's path, describing the human being within the businessman with all his sensitivities and ambiguities. By the end of the war, two issues had been published. The journal was later continued by the Hebrew University in Jerusalem.

The most significant acquisition in that historic year was the publishing and printing house Widow and Brothers Romm in Vilna, which was facing bankruptcy. This might have been arranged by Rabbi Eisenstadt. The Kahans shared the purchase with Noe (Noah) Gordon, then director of the Russian-Asian Bank in Petrograd, both becoming joint managers. Arusia recalled that they wanted to save the most valuable possession of the publishing house: old manuscripts. "The substance of these proceedings is the restitution claim for damages against the German Reich for the seizure and transfer of books, printed matter, master plates, printed material, manuscripts and other assets which belonged to the 'Rom' publishing house in Vilna," states a letter from the lawyers, lodging claims with the Restitution Office in Germany on behalf of the Kahan and Gordon families, forty-four years later, on June 17, 1961. "The confiscation took place in the years 1941/42 and the transfer took place at an unknown time. Details are stated below."

The Widow and Brothers Romm was considered one of the largest and oldest publishers in the Jewish Diaspora. Its beginnings go back to 1789, the year of the French Revolution. By the time it was acquired by the Kahans and Gordons, it had already existed one hundred and thirty-eight years. In the 1870s and 1880s it had become world famous for its Talmud, Mishna and Midrash editions. Romm also published classics of modern Hebrew and Yiddish literature, as well as Hebrew translations of world literature. The scholar Shmuel Shraga Feigensohn was the director of the publishing house from 1867 and introduced the relief printing plate, the stereotype, to Romm. From printed pages that had been set with movable letters, stencils were made and, by casting them in a metal alloy, complete printing plates were produced. These were archived so that the books could be reprinted quickly if necessary, which was as innovative then as digital letterpress printing is today. Feigensohn instigated the publication of the Babylonian and Jerusalem Talmud and introduced new forms of editing for this purpose, by having manuscripts, incunabula, first editions and first prints searched for in the archives of the Vatican, private collections and the British Library, comparing and copying the various versions of texts. More than one hundred printers and fourteen editors were involved in the project. When the last volume of the Vilna Talmud was published by Romm in 1886, the edition had 13,000 subscribers. Two years later, Feigensohn pulled out and the decline set in. After the death of the widow, Deborah Romm, in 1903, he returned to the publishing house once again, found a sponsor in Baron David Günzburg from St. Petersburg and paid off the debts, but when the baron died a few years later (1910) there was still a lack of capital. The war intensified the crisis.

Following the peace treaty of Brest-Litovsk in the spring of 1918, the Kahans in Berlin, Petrograd and Kharkov contacted their new company in Vilna, which, as Roska had written to Yasha from the Polish Summer Resort, merely possessed a "philanthropic character," probably implying that it would not be generating any profits. In the summer of 1918 Bendet travelled from Berlin to Romm in Vilna for the first time. In September, a certain Mr. S. Ittigin wrote to him that he had been employed for the last three years at the Caucasus-Volga Industrial & Trading Company in Petrograd, but now, due to the conditions there, mainly because of the food price spikes and after consultation with Bendet's brothers, he had gone with his family to Vilna, where he intended to work at the Romm company for the time being. "We are impatiently awaiting the arrival of one of you. There are questions that only the business owners are able to solve," he wrote. He had made a similar request to David, who was traveling back and forth between Petrograd and Kharkov at the time. At the beginning of December 1918, Abraham Ledermann, who had headed the Russian-Baltic Mineral Oil Company before the war and was later to take over the management of the COC in Copenhagen, came from Riga to Romm in Vilna, where he, too, was awaiting directives from the Kahans, who had meanwhile fled from the Bolshevik-occupied Petrograd to Kharkov. A few weeks later, in January 1919, when Kharkov, too, had been conquered by the Bolsheviks, Aron, fleeing westward, stopped in Vilna and sat down with Feigensohn, who by now was over eighty and had been employed at Romm for over half a century. Aron helped the publishing house with a guarantee of 100,000 rubles, which he was to cover a few months later, in the autumn of the same year, when Rom Inc. was founded in Copenhagen.

"The publishing house 'Rom' was formed as a corporation under Polish law and had its headquarters in Vilna until the company was destroyed by the German occupation authorities. The fate of the company is no longer known," stated the letter from the lawyers during restitution proceedings. The founding of Romm Inc. in Warsaw in October 1923 came about when there was no doubt that Vilna—now officially Wilno—would remain part of the Second Polish Republic. It was listed in the official gazette *Monitor Polski* at the beginning of January 1924 and its charter was published there. The brothers Rafał and Michał Szereszowski, owners of the Kahans' merchant bank in Warsaw, and a certain graduate engineer Dr. Gustav Birsztein, a close friend of Jonas Rosenberg, were listed at the bottom of the charter as founders. The share capital of five hundred million Polish marks, which after the currency reform four months later was converted into 100,000 złoty, was divided into 10,000 shares of 10 złoty each, half of which belonged to the Kahans and half to the Gordons. As evidence of this, the lawyers cited on April 6, 1956 the list of the corporation's shares, belonging to the Kahans, in the amount of 46,500 złoty kept by Banking House Hardy & Co. in Frankfurt am Main, bundled in a wrapper. The Gordon shares had been lost in the war. Even after the corporation had been opened in Warsaw, the company of the same name, founded by Aron in Copenhagen in 1919, continued to exist. It ceased its activities in April 1922 and was to be liquidated, but the decision was withdrawn in September 1927, the articles of association were amended in January 1933, and only in 1955 was its entry deleted from the Danish Commercial Register. The family archives include a letter from Birsztein to Jonas Rosenberg, some shares and dividend coupons. They confirm the articles of association and the information provided by the lawyers.

Baruch's brother-in-law, Rosalia's brother Isidor Berlin, who had already been associated with the Kahans in the oil business before the war, supervised the company on site until 1935, probably until the end of his life. From 1920 to 1941, until he was abducted and murdered by the Nazis, Mattityahu Rapoport, allegedly one of Noe Gordon's cousins, was the managing director. According to the sworn testimony by his daughter Emilia Bloch during the restitution proceedings, the company comprised four buildings in the old town: a printing plant, storerooms, an office building, as well as a library and archive building secured against burglary and fire. In addition to books, this building was housing the master plates, incunabula and all manuscripts, except for the most valuable ones, which were kept in a safe in the director's office: Hebrew first prints from Mantua and Upsala; correspondence with authors; autographs by Chaim N. Bialik, Achad Haam and Sholem Aleichem; the first editions of the publishing house since 1789. The Soviet Russian occupying forces had not touched all these things in 1940, leaving her father to continue working undisturbed until the Nazis arrived.

In the restitution file, Bendet Kahan is named as the first director of the publishing house, which is confirmed by the family records. But how present was he in Vilna? How often did he travel back and forth between Berlin and *Yerushalayim shel Lita*? His brother-in-law Jonas Rosenberg was also involved. Six letters to him fom Mattityahu Rapoport are preserved, which informed him in detail about the business operations and share prices in 1929/1930. But Jonas Rosenberg was not particularly interested in business matters. Since Bendet had cofounded the Azbil company, distributing books to Jewish prisoners of war from the Russian Empire in the camps around Berlin, he had been a bibliophile. In 1920, he founded his own publishing house in Berlin, Yalkut [Satchel], which published about fifty titles within ten years. He was also a member of the Soncino Society, which had been cultivating the traditions of Jewish book art since 1924.

The three trunks of the cabbalistic tree of life, like palm trees, between water and starry sky in Yalkut's signet symbolize Bendet's publishing ideas. Only a few documents and pictures of him have survived: the applications for citizenship and restitution in the public archives, some letters, photographs and personal papers in the family archives. In a letter of August 1925 from Carlsbad, on the finest embossed blue paper to his daughter Dora, he asks for newspapers, if not the *Tageblatt* and the *Illustrierte*, then at least *Haaretz* and *Haolam*. The photographs in these heirlooms depict him as a middle-aged man with a moustache and bald head in a grey suit with a waistcoat, his tie tied tightly under his shirt collar, and reveal that he was a smoker. In the illustrations for Arusia's memoirs in the *Heavar*, he is the only one of the siblings with a pipe in his mouth. On one of the small photo statuettes, which were made in Berlin of Chaim's children, he casually holds a cigarette in his left hand.

The Romm publishing house distinguished itself above all by its editions of rabbinic literature. Their Babylonian Talmud consists of twenty-three volumes and the Jerusalem Talmud, of eight; the halakhic codex *Shulchan Arukh* [Laid Table], which regulates the everyday life of pious Jews, and which usually would not be absent from any religious Jewish home, appeared in seven volumes, all in lavish folio format. The Vilna Talmud, as the Romm editions were called, was known all over the world and became the model for later publications. "From 1920–1941, other publishers also tried to compete with them but not in the works mentioned above," Chimen Abramsky testified during the restitution process; he was the bibliographer and managing director of the Shapiro, Valentine & Co. publishing house in London and appeared as an expert on Jewish books in these proceedings. He estimated that between 1803 and

1941, more than one thousand titles had been published, many of them in several editions; that in 1928, they had in stock more than four hundred volumes; 15,000 print sheets, equal to 240,000 printed pages; printing plates and characters of 12,000 print sheets, equal to 192,000 pages; fifteen printing presses for fast printing, two large electric and two medium-sized printing presses. At the end of the 1920s, Romm employed more than 300 people after its old status had been restored and the company's rights in the Jewish publishing world once again secured. In the thirties the Romm publications were selling as well in the diaspora as before. Under the Kahans' management, Romm did not change its profile or expand its program, but it is thanks to them that the books found their way back to their customers. Compared to Romm, Yalkut was a small, short-lived publishing house, but fulfilled an important mission. "The publishing house Yalkut was less concerned with the publication of books than with the distribution of publications by the publishing house Romm," recalled Rubin Mass, whom Bendet Kahan had hired in the early 1920s. "We received the editions of *Mishna, Midrashim, Chumashim* and their commentaries, by the trainload, all without bindings. We had the books bound in one of the big binderies in Berlin." Even today, one can find the great *Mishna* editions in eighteen volumes with black linen covers and leather spines, in libraries and in many private homes all over the world. The Romm editions with the Berlin binding are universally known and loved.

"As a consequence of the war there was a lack of religious literature in Germany, which was exacerbated by the mass immigration of Eastern European Jews," Arusia recalled. Inspired by the acquisition of Romm, Bendet founded Yalkut with the intention of establishing a center for the distribution of *sifrei kodesh* [holy books] in Germany. His aim was to spread Jewish knowledge, especially prayer books. At that time, people were queuing up to buy a prayer book. Yalkut published literature in Hebrew, Yiddish and German. It ran the bookstore by the same name at 46 Kantstrasse in Berlin-Charlottenburg. David joined Bendet as the second shareholder of the publishing house immediately after his arrival in Berlin in the early summer of 1920. Bendet was running the business. As a distribution center for the Romm publications, Yalkut held large stocks of books, mostly on credit. It was the general agency not only for Romm, but also for two other publishers: Boris Kletzkin in Vilna and Abraham Stybel in Warsaw, until the latter moved to Berlin in 1922. In 1927 Bendet sold the bookshop to Rubin Mass, the employee, but kept the publishing house. "From the advertisements in the Berlin Yiddish press, one gets the impression that the Yalkut bookstore in Charlottenburg wanted to address a Berlin audience in addition to the export business it operated," wrote librarian Maria Kühn-Ludewig about the Yiddish publishers in Berlin between the wars.

One of the most unusual titles published by Yalkut was the *Directory for the Jewish Book Trade*. Three hundred and sixty-five bookshops in Europe, the USA, Palestine, South America and Africa were listed there. Most of them were in Poland and Germany, followed by the USA and Palestine. Many countries, such as Italy, Bulgaria, Soviet Russia, Estonia, Yugoslavia, Libya, Tunisia and Brazil, had only one or two addresses listed. The directory could have been taken from Romm's distribution list. However, it reflected the global Diaspora of the Ashkenazim at that time. Yalkut's most beautiful edition is, without a doubt, the *Haggadah shel Pesach*, the book with the story and the instructions for Passover, which is read on the eve of the festival, commemorating the liberation of the Jews from Egyptian bondage. The Yalkut edition is illustrated with the striking pictures of the Art Nouveau graphic artist Otto Geismar. I saw it in Naomi Loewenthal's home in Ramat Aviv. Naomi looks after the legacy of Dora Kahan, her mother-in-law, Bendet's eldest daughter.

Yalkut opened with the *Kitzur Hatalmud*, compiled by Chaim Tchernowitz (Rav Za'ir), a rabbi and liberal-minded Jewish scholar of Bendet's age from Vitebsk, who had founded a modern yeshiva in Odessa in 1905, the year of the first Russian Revolution, where secular knowledge was taught alongside the Talmud. Like Bendet, he had left Russia because of political difficulties; he was awarded his doctorate from the University of Würzburg in 1914. Shortly after the publication of the *Kitzur Hatalmud* by Yalkut, he went to New York and taught at the Hebrew Union College. Yalkut also published the songbooks by Abraham Zvi Idelsohn, born in the Russian-dominated Latvia in 1882, one of the early experts on Jewish music. Idelsohn, who had arrived from Kurland and, like Tchernowitz, had studied in Germany, recalled how he had met Bendet Kahan at the Twelfth Zionist Congress in Karlovy Vary in 1921. Bendet had bought the copy rights to the first volume of *Sefer Hashirim*, his songbook, and the second edition of *Shire Tfillot*, the sung prayers. The songbook included the first-time publication of *Hava Nagila* [Let Us Rejoice], a Hasidic melody from Ottoman Palestine, which later became the most popular folk song both in Israel and the Diaspora. Yalkut also published religious literature in Hebrew: song and prayer books, as well as Torah and Talmud volumes. Only one work was published in German—*The Festive Prayers of the Israelites* in four volumes, reviewed, translated, explained and edited by Michael Sachs, *maskil* and rabbi in Prague and Berlin. His poetic translation of the *Machzor*, the festival prayer book, was so popular that it appeared in many editions which can still be found on the antiquarian market today.

Yalkut also published a completely different kind of non-fiction, written by a woman, Feiga Shargorodskaya—a system of Yiddish shorthand. The book might have strayed there due to Bendet and Judith Kahan's commitment to ORT. The Society for the Promotion of Work among the Jews, which had been expelled from Russia after the October Revolution and had reestablished itself as a global organization in Berlin in 1921, may have provided the space where publisher and author met. ORT had a social-democratic orientation. Educational work and the emancipation of women were part of its core program. Bendet was connected to ORT through his collaboration with Aron Syngalowski in Azbil. Apparently, he was one of the participants in the founding conference of World ORT in Berlin in August 1921, when Syngalowski was elected its Secretary General. The list of participants registered a person named B. Kahan, a delegate from Vilna. Already in the Vilna Address Register of 1914 a certain Bentsel Chaimovich Kagan was listed. Could Bendet possibly have had a residence in *Yerushalayim shel Lita,* like his father, before moving to Berlin? Since the end of the war he had been associated with that city due to his management of Romm, but apparently he no longer owned an apartment there.

Like Bendet Kahan, Chaim Tchernowitz and Abraham Z. Idelson, Feiga Shargorodskaya had moved, from Uman in the Russian Empire, to the West, when she was young. She had studied philosophy and education in Zurich, Paris, Berlin and Vienna, and was awarded her doctorate in 1914 in Zurich, before returning to revolutionary Russia. After an unsuccessful attempt to contribute to the development of a Soviet pedagogy, she left the country in 1924 and went to Berlin, where she made a living as a teacher and journalist. There she possibly became involved with ORT, as she had been in St. Petersburg, and met Judith and Bendet Kahan. Judith was a born Bramson and probably a distant relative of ORT's founder, Leo Bramson. Both stem from the Suwałki Province in the northwestern borderland of the Russian Empire. Judith Kahan was working for ORT in Berlin, as can be seen from a letter written by Bendet to his daughter, Dora.

Bendet, who had attended the Neo-Orthodox school in Frankfurt, got to know the compatibility of piety and a modern way of life. He had internalized the maxim of *Torah im derekh eretz,* had entered into a love marriage, had separated himself spatially from the family and had a wife who was the only family member of her generation to work. He found his fulfillment in the publishing business. With his books full of Jewish knowledge, wisdom and tradition, he established a way of Jewish life in the desert of the Diaspora for himself and his coreligionists. Remarkable are the reprints of the classical writings and medieval Jewish religious philosophy in the publishing program, which formed a basic introduction to the edification of the *maskilim* in Eastern Europe rather than for those in the West. In Moorish-ruled Andalusia, but also in Christian Spain before the Inquisition, Jewish scholars had made the first attempts to provide secular knowledge—history, language, literature, culture—and to adapt religion to the changing, modernizing world, to find common denominators between Jewish and Christian doctrines. Bendet published Yehuda Halevi's *The Kusari*, an epic about the king of the Khazars, whose empire had stretched between the Black Sea and the Caspian Sea around 800 AD and who had declared Judaism the state religion; he reprinted Joseph Albo's *Ha'ikarim*, a programmatic work on the compatibility of Jewish monotheism with the Trinity of God in Christianity, as well as Bachya Ibn Pakuda's *Chovot Halevavot* [The Duties of the Heart], which understood religion as emotion and piety. He published the main philosophical work of Maimonides (Rambam), the *Moreh Nevuchim* [Guide to the Perplexed], an engagement with Aristotle, in two volumes, as well as two additional programmatic writings of the scholar from Cordoba: *Shemona Perakim* [Eight Chapters] in which the Rambam drafted an extension on the *Pirkei Avot* [Ethics of the Fathers], and the *Biur Milot Hahigayon* [Logica], with a commentary by Moses Mendelssohn. Modern Jews found these titles old-fashioned, though they were still part of the curriculum at the Orthodox rabbinical seminary. However, in the concept of the Zionist movement they took on a new meaning, forming part of the national canon that first took shape in Berlin, not in Tel Aviv. Bendet Kahan was actively involved in this. The formation of the modern Jewish nation, comparable to other nations, was not necessarily conceived of as the State of Israel at that time in Berlin, but was primarily understood as a global political organization and cultural process. It is fitting that Yalkut published, in two volumes, *Toldot am Israel vesifruto*, the latest research on the history of the Jewish people and its literature from the beginnings to the completion of the Talmud, by Meir Bałaban, who had started his career as a teacher at the Tachkemoni School of Mizrachi in Warsaw. At the same time, Bałaban published the first works on the Polish history of the Jews—in Yiddish in Vilna and Polish in Warsaw. Bendet's idea about publishing was to produce inexpensive pocket-sized editions affordable to everyone, according to his niece Dvora Ettinger-Rozenfeld. I saw a whole series of these handy, rather unimpressive volumes, in Naomi Loewenthal's bookcase.

The national canon also included fiction, but Bendet published only a few works of fine literature in Hebrew, Yiddish and German, mostly reprints, almost exclusively by authors from his circle of acquaintances, like the biblical and Talmudic stories entitled *Bamidbar* [In The Desert] by the classic author of modern Hebrew literature, David Frischmann, who had died shortly before in Berlin. These were popular and were often reprinted. Yalkut also published wistful migrant prose and poetry, for example, two works by the family friend, Zalman Shneour, the Yiddish translation of the novel *Ahin: Shriftn fun a selbstmerder* [A Death: Notes of a Suicide] and the German translation of the *Vilna Poem* with lithographs by Hermann Struck. Both works were originally published in Hebrew in Vilna. Arusia remembered that his father loved Shneour's poems. Salomon Aminyu Z. Rosenblum, a cousin of Zalman Rubashov, who was a frequent visitor at 36 Schlüterstrasse and later became a well-known physicist at the Marie Curie Institute in Paris and a friend of Albert Einstein, had his early work published in German by Yalkut. It was the only volume of poetry he wrote in his life called *In der Fremde* [In Foreign Lands], which dealt with the painful yet liberating existence as a migrant. Apart from the *Register of the Jewish Booktrade*, Yalkut published two catalogues that expressed Bendet's love of books and the presence of Jewish media in contemporary Europe—Josef Lin's *The Hebrew Press*, the Jewish Exhibition publications at the Pressa Faire in Cologne in 1928 and Sigfried Bernfeld's *Methodical Catalogue of Modern Hebrew Literature*—the former title in German, the latter in Hebrew.

In November 1922 the publisher Abram Kagan arrived in Germany from Petrograd on the second of the so-called "Philosopher Ships." More than two hundred well-known politicians, scientists and writers, persecuted, imprisoned and labelled as enemies by the Bolsheviks, had been expatriated from Soviet Russia in quick succession. David Kahan had welcomed the publisher, who was his cousin, in Stettin, now Polish Szczecin, and took him to Berlin, together with the Russian literary historian Nestor Kotlyarevsky, who had shared a cell with Abram Kagan in a Petrograd prison. Abram was thirty-three at the time, seven years younger than David. In an interview by the historian Marc Raeff, a few years before his death, he spoke of this family relationship. His father was Chaim Kahan's brother Shaul, like Chaim, a *neftyanik*, involved in the oil industry. Initially he had managed the depots of the Armenian entrepreneur Mantashev in the northwestern border region, acquiring them later for the family business Petrol in St. Petersburg where he worked. According to archive files on the Caucasus-Volga Industrial & Trading Company, Shaul Natanovich Kagan had been in charge of the depots in Vitebsk. Abram had spent his childhood in Vitebsk.

One photo shows him as a young man, in half-profile, self-confident with an alert, firm look, his right hand on his heart under the jacket lapel. His face, expression and posture, that of a Kahan, greatly resemble Aron. Abram, unlike his cousins, had been a student and graduate of the Law Faculty of the University of St. Petersburg. In Berlin he was "Professor Abraham S. Kagan." Being denied an academic career as a Jew in Russia and, like Bendet and David, a lover of books, he founded the publishing house Nauka i shkola [Science and School] in Petrograd in the year of the revolution and opened Petropolis a little later, in early 1918, together with the siblings Raissa and Yakov Bloch.

The Kahans had rented rooms for him, his wife and children in a boarding house in Rankestrasse, while accommodating Kotlyarevsky at 36 Schlüterstrasse. His relatives were proud to be able to accommodate this renowned literary historian and held a reception for him at which the whole family was present, as Abram Kagan told Marc Raeff in the biographical interview. He said that after arriving in Berlin, he wanted to get Petropolis going again, but he needed new capital. He had discussed the situation with his relatives who, as oil industrialists, already had lucrative connections to Europe before the war and the revolution, and who then reestablished themselves as owners of Nitag in Berlin. Of the four Kahan brothers, however, only two were active as entrepreneurs—Aron, whom he called an "exceptionally brilliant businessman," and David. Aron had used the opportunity inflation was offering, leasing tank facilities in Hamburg for Nitag and acquiring large cargo ships with passenger compartments. Some details became blurred in Abram Kagan's recollections. He referred to his cousins as uncles, probably because of the noticeable age difference, and confused Hamburg with Wilhelmshaven. Nevertheless, his recollections complete the mosaic of history. Abram Kagan was hoping for active support in the publishing business. David had shown interest, he continued, pointing out David's commitment to the *Togblat* in Petrograd and to Romm in Vilna, and also mentioned Yalkut, as well as a Jewish newspaper in Kaunas, with which the Kahans were connected, though he failed to mention Bendet, who, like him, loved books. David had founded the publishing house Obelisk together with his cousin and had taken a share in Petropolis. While initially renting rooms from Nitag, the official address for both Russian publishing houses was 37 Schlüterstrasse, in the building that belonged to the Kahans. Abram, in turn, had helped David to obtain illustrations and photos for the Kaunas newspaper from the *Berliner Tageblatt*, with which he was connected. The Kahans had supported him with a very large loan. According to the commercial registers, David Kahan was one of the partners in Obelisk until 1934 and, together with his brother Baruch, in Petropolis.

In the early twenties, Berlin was a veritable publishing hub. Anyone who had foreign currency during the inflation years could produce large quantities of high-quality books there. Migrants from the Russian Empire created a publishing landscape in the German metropolis that was second to none. The slavicist Gottfried Kratz identified 275 printing firms and publishing houses for the entire interwar period, which had published seven thousand titles in 1923 alone. There were some fifty publishers that specialized in Yiddish literature and a few in Hebrew. They were producing for the Russian migrant communities in the Baltic states, Poland, Czechoslovakia, Yugoslavia, China (Harbin and Shanghai), but also for readers in Soviet Russia, Berlin and other German cities. "It's hard to believe that, at the time, more Russian than German books were published in Germany," Abram Kagan recalled. "I didn't believe it either, until I was convinced by the statistics of the German Publishers & Booksellers Association."

Petropolis and Obelisk were able to compete with other renowned publishers such as Ladyshnikov, Grzhebin, Slovo, Skify and Grani. How great the Kahan brothers' interest in the two Russian exile publishers in Berlin, run by their cousin, actually was, and whether they actively supported Abram, is anyone's guess. David and Baruch, unlike brother Aron and Cousin Abram, left no memoirs. Bendet had turned his back on Russia at an early age and had renounced everything Russian and, according to his niece Dvora Ettinger-Rozenfeld, had paid Russia no heed. He was the only one of the siblings to apply for German citizenship, and is supposed to have been the only really pious Jew in the family.

Obelisk published mainly Christian philosophy of religion by authors that Abram Kagan had already published in the Petrograd Nauka i shkola, including Kotlyarevsky's memoirs, in which Berlin and the Kahans do not feature. Petropolis published Russian literature, both classical and contemporary modern fiction, as well as memoirs and non-fiction in which Soviet Russia, as a theme, was dominant. Unlike Bendet, Abram Kagan cultivated his love of Russian literature beyond the Bolsheviks' coup d'état. He did not shy away from contact with the new Russia that had cast him out. What made Petropolis special was that it published both Soviet and exiled Russian authors, including many who were or were to become famous, such as Ivan Bunin, Vladimir Nabokov, Ilya Ehrenburg, Boris Pilnyak, or Yury Tynyanov. The publisher recalled that the connections to Soviet Russia had not been severed, and that authors who had arrived in transit or had emigrated were constantly offering manuscripts. It had been convenient for them, he said, because that was how they could secure their copyrights under the Berne Convention, especially the right to translation into other languages, which the Soviet government, if it printed them at all, had denied them. The Berne Convention of 1887 for the Protection of Literary and Artistic Works had established the intergovernmental recognition of copyright, which Russia did not accept either before or after 1917. Abram Kagan travelled to Poland, the Baltic countries and Czechoslovakia, visiting Russian exile bookstores, antique booksellers and libraries in search of books and manuscripts in order to gain customers, authors and sponsors. The trade with antique books became his second mainstay. It is possible that he handled it via Russkaya kniga [Russian Book Inc.], which existed from 1922 to 1928 and in which he also had a share. As he was keen to publish anti-Soviet migrant literature as well, but without falling out with the Bolsheviks, he founded further publishing houses—Parabola and Granit—in the early 1930s. Granit published a number of Leon Trotsky's works in the Russian original—his autobiography *My Life* and the *History of the Russian Revolution* in two volumes each, the *Stalinist School of Forgery* and the programmatic work *Permanent Revolution*.

Bendet was similarly passionately committed, but represented a completely different concept. He supported Hebrew and Yiddish publishing houses when they got into financial difficulties as a result of the currency reform and, later, the economic crisis. David, however, helped both sides, brother and cousin. Bendet acquired the remaining stock of Shveln, planned the participation in a new Hebrew publishing house and rescued Stybel. In 1928 he revived the publishing house Chaim. The small publishing house with the Yiddish name *Shveln* [Thresholds] in Berlin-Charlottenburg published large-format artistically designed books, including picture books for children, in the Yiddish language. Its signet, designed by Isser Ber Rybak, a stylized spiral staircase leading upwards, as well as titles with prints by El Lissitzky and Rybak, indicate avant-garde ambitions. The program was designed by refugees from the Ukraine. When David Ettinger arrived in Berlin at the end of 1923 and saw the flourishing migrant publishing scene, he got involved with Shveln, perhaps because memories of the pogroms and experiences of violent antisemitism in the Ukraine caused him to bond with the publishers and authors, or perhaps also because he was interested in books, just like his brother-in-law David, but wanted to go his own way. In the summer of 1924 Shveln changed its name to Rubicon, but no longer published books. Yalkut took over the remainder of the books. Yalkut was also named in the *Directory for the Jewish Book Trade* as the distributer for the publishing house Ayanot [Springs], which was founded in 1922 by Simon Rawidowicz, a student of philosophy and one of the spokesmen of the Hebrew movement in Berlin. According to the *Directory*, businessman David Kahan was a shareholder of Ayanot. The Kahans had been closely associated with the Hebrew Movement since the war. Roska and Yasha were active in the association Bet Am Ivri [House of the Hebrew People], which was initially called Bet Va'ad Ivri [House of the Hebrew Synod], which offered language instruction, literature and culture. In the beginning the family had provided the apartment at 36 Schlüterstrasse as a meeting place. Lea Kahan, Bendet's second daughter, served as secretary of the Ladies' Committee at Bet Am Ivri in 1931; she was twenty-four at the time. When Ayanot fell into crisis, Rawidowicz, who had by that time received a PhD, and who was well acquainted with the Kahans, gained Bendet's support for a new publishing house—Hotzaot Sefarim Meuchadot [United Publishing House], which the two founded in 1925 during a visit to Palestine on the occasion of the opening of the Hebrew University in Jerusalem. The publishing house planned to publish books on science, art and literature in Hebrew and other languages. In addition to Bendet, his eldest daughter Dora and Rawidowicz, who registered Berlin addresses, a publisher from Haifa and three members of the Kahan family living in Palestine were also involved. In letters to his future wife Esther Klee, Rawidowicz described Bendet, who was then about forty-six years old, as an enthusiastic, but also difficult person, who was sometimes very happy about the founding of the United and who expected a lot from it, who could sometimes be very hard and yet very optimistic, who was full of ideas, but then again very quiet and suspicious. In September 1925 Rabbi Professor David Simonsen wrote to Rawidowicz in Copenhagen about the new publishing house as a fait accompli, but it was probably only a nice idea.

Bendet had more success with the Stybel publishing house. The largest Hebrew publishing house since the new Hebrew literature came into existence had gone through a severe crisis, according to the *Jüdische Rundschau*. With Bendet's financial involvement, it was revived and reorganized as a limited company at the beginning of September 1927 in Berlin. Stybel was now publishing in Berlin and Tel Aviv. Managing directors were Abraham Josef Stybel, Bendet Kahan, the journalist Benzion Katz and Rawidowicz. The share capital was 20,000 Reichsmark. Stybel had been founded ten years earlier, in the revolutionary year 1917, in Moscow by the leather wholesaler Abraham Josef Stybel, who had made his fortune as the main supplier of boots for the Tsarist Army. The Soviet government had confiscated the publishing house. Stybel relocated to Copenhagen and moved the company to New York, Tel Aviv, Warsaw and Berlin. However, by the mid-1920s it was already in the red. Various problems were cited as reasons for this: mismanagement, high book prices in Europe, an economic crisis in Palestine and the declining demand for Hebrew books in the Diaspora. The publishing house was 75,000 dollars in debt and needed an investment of at least 10,000, wrote the *Jüdische Rundschau* before the take-over by the Kahans. Shortly before, Abraham Josef Stybel had repositioned himself as a wholesaler in Berlin and, together with a Munich businessman, had founded Redelta Leder-Im-und-Export GMBH, also with a share capital of 20,000 Reichsmark. From the very beginning Stybel's aim was to publish and distribute classical and modern world literature in Hebrew translations— Anacreon, Homer, Sophocles, Shakespeare, Wilde, Byron, Emerson, Flaubert, Maupassant, Goethe, Schnitzler, Pushkin, Dostoevsky, Tolstoy, Sienkiewicz, Mickiewicz and so forth. Stybel wanted to expand the education of native speakers without foreign language skills and inspire new Hebrew literature. In addition, the publishing house published modern Hebrew literature and, with interruptions until 1950, the magazine *Hatekufa* [the Era], which attracted writers by paying good fees. Its signet, a plant in a flowerpot, appeared modest by comparison with that of Petropolis' jumping horseman, a reminiscence of the Iron Horseman, the symbol and statue of Tsar Peter the Great in St. Petersburg, which found its way into the signets of several publishers in exile. Contemporaries described Abraham Josef Stybel as one of the most important representatives of the Hebrew movement, which fought for a modern, cosmopolitan Jewish culture in Hebrew on the basis of a humanistic aesthetic. Bendet worked with Stybel for two and a half years. In 1930 he sold the publishing house to Nachum Tversky in Tel Aviv.

In the family archives I found only a few meager Stybel documents from the time after the sale—a bill of exchange for fifty Palestinian pounds, issued in Tel Aviv, dated May 1930, payable in October of the same year, signed by Jonas Rosenberg; another bill for 1,000 Reichsmark dated September 1930; "Order of the Dresdner Bank in Danzig Banking House D. M. Szereszowski," also signed by Jonas, payable in February 1931 in Berlin, 5 Dahlmannstrasse, by Bendet Kahan; an overdue notice of the same period from Stybel, Tel Aviv–Berlin; and a complaint addressed to Jonas about the unpaid bill of exchange.

In 1928 Bendet and David revived Chaim Publishing in Berlin and published *Talmud Vechokhmat Harefuah*, a book on the medical wisdom of the Talmud by Yehuda Leib Benjamin Kazenelson, called Buki Ben-Yogli. In doing so, they let the readers know on the back cover of the title page that they were fulfilling a promise made to their father, who had read the manuscript shortly before his death and requested its publication. The author Kazenelson, a *maskil*, a graduate of the rabbinical seminary in Zhitomir, a doctor and a scholar, one of the editors of the thirteen-volume Russian *Jewish Encyclopedia* and cofounder of the Courses of Oriental Studies and Jewish Studies in Petrograd, had not lived to see it. He had died already a year before Chaim Kahan. His son, Baruch Kazenelson, added there that the book had been ready for printing at the end of 1916 and advertised in January 1917, but could no longer be published in Russia due to war and revolution. The Berlin edition of this rare and precious work remained for years the only one.

With Yalkut, Chaim Publishing, Romm and Stybel, Bendet was controlling for a short time in Berlin, Vilna and Tel Aviv, large parts of the traditional and modern Hebrew publishing activities at the end of the 1920s. From his portfolio, which also included titles by Shveln and Ayanot, he distributed old Jewish writings as well as the treasures of world literature that Stybel had brought into the Hebrew-language world. At the same time, but over a longer period, Cousin Abram distributed the wealth of Russian literature from Berlin. "One publisher after another began to fall into my hands. The most important acquisition was the publishing house Slovo, which belonged to the renowned company Ullstein," he proudly recalled. In 1932, Petropolis surreptitiously acquired the Ullstein majority of shares in Logos Inc., the sole supplier of Slovo Ltd., which, like the publishing house and bookshop Slovo, had already been dissolved five years earlier (1927). This way, Kagan secured an import route to Soviet Russia. With his competitors, the Mosse Group, which published the daily *Berliner Tageblatt*, he opened up business channels in the opposite direction. Mosse, like Ullstein, ran an Esperanto and a Russian department, which was headed by the former St. Petersburg lawyer, Dr. Samuel Shklyaver. Mosse published address books and travel literature, but above all a series of popular statistical information works for which there was demand in the Soviet Union—*Ves mir v tsifrakh* [The World in Numbers] by Vladimir S. Voitinsky. It was first published in 1925, in Russian, by the Znanie publishing house founded by Shklyaver, which Mosse owned, and then from 1925 to 1929 in German in seven volumes as *Die Welt in Zahlen* [The World in Numbers]. Lastly, Mosse published *Ten Years New Germany: A Complete Overview in Numbers* by the economist and revolution refugee from Russia, Voitinsky, who was to head the statistical department of the General German Trade Union Federation from 1929 to 1933. The *Berliner Tageblatt* also sold well to the Soviet Union. When Shklyaver complained to him that the proceeds of the Mosse publishing house sale could not be transferred by monetary means and were gradually becoming worthless, it was his idea to buy publications, including antique ones, in the Soviet Union and export them by way of compensation, recalled Abram Kagan. In the contract he subsequently concluded with Shkyaver, he undertook to purchase literature from the Soviet Union exclusively through Mosse, who in turn promised to accept such orders only from him. He resold the books to migrants in Prague and Paris as well as to libraries in Florence and New York. It seems that Abram took the publishing business even more seriously than his cousin Bendet, who was twelve years older. Unlike his cousin, he was dependent on his companies making a profit, because he did not have a profitable industrial enterprise in the background and always had to look for financially strong partners.

The National Socialists' seizure of power increasingly restricted the Jewish publishing houses. Although Yalkut existed on paper until early 1936, Bendet Kahan apparently stopped publishing books in Berlin after 1931, while Abram Kagan was active as a publisher there until 1938. Petropolis existed until 1938, Obelisk was not extinguished until 1940, and on the day when Petropolis celebrated its tenth anniversary in Grunewald, the Reichstag in Berlin burned down. With the onset of Nazi rule, all so-called "non-Aryan" publishing houses in Germany had to be registered. But Abram Kagan recalled how he had ignored this by merely changing his strategy. Petropolis began to transfer books and money abroad, to Paris. This was helped by a Russian bookshop, Dom knigi [The House of the Book], and a Russian literary magazine, *Sovremennye zapiski* [Contemporary Notes], both in Paris, as well as the Parabola publishing house, which apparently had an offshoot in the French metropolis. Between 1933 and 1936, Petropolis published ten of the twelve volumes of the Ivan Bunin Complete Edition and two novels by Vladimir Nabokov: *Kamera obskura*, which provides the prototype for Lolita and was later published in German under the title *Gelächter im Dunkel* [Laughter in the Dark], and *Otchayaniye* [Despair]. Nevertheless, the publishing activity gradually came to a standstill. His partners Raissa and Yakov Bloch left Germany and found refuge in Paris. Through friends, the Kagans received Belgian visas in March 1938. The plan to continue his publishing activities in France did not work out. Abram Kagan immediately contacted his authors again in Brussels, found a Russian printing house, a company that was importing Soviet books, published books under the Petropolis label and procured contacts. But shortly afterwards, in early 1940, the family had to move on.

Romm continued to print and publish under Soviet rule until summer 1941, when the Wehrmacht occupied Vilna and in their wake the

Einsatzgruppen began to rob and murder. Under Soviet occupation the printing and publishing house had survived, but was forced to print propaganda.
In the restitution proceedings "Kahan vs The German Reich," witnesses testified under oath to the looting of Romm, about which there is much less known
than about the book theft in the Strashun Library and in the Institute for Jewish
Research in Vilna, known under the acronym YIVO, where the looted property from Vilna was concentrated. The taskforce of Reichsleiter Rosenberg
plundered and confiscated books and sent the loot to the Institute for Study
of the Jewish Question in Frankfurt am Main. The taskforce was led locally by
experts—the librarian Dr. Herbert Gotthard and the Jewish studies scholar,
Dr. Johannes Pohl, who had studied at the Hebrew University in Jerusalem. In
one of the first major portrayals of the Vilna Ghetto, Pohl is reported to have
released the Talmud master plates from the Romm printing works for street
sale. Jewish work brigades sorted and transported the looted material, rescuing
some of it at the risk of their lives into the ghetto, where some of it survived the
Holocaust. But the odyssey of the books continued. Many survived another
forty-five years—the Soviet era—in the basement of the Lithuanian National
Book Cabinet, until they were brought back to the light of day after the fall of
the Berlin Wall, expertly and lovingly catalogued by the librarian Esfir Bramson
and her colleagues.

Anna Rapoport, the widow of the former managing director, said that
she had been taken back twice from the ghetto to the publishing house for
interrogation. She had been asked about precious manuscripts and customer
addresses in the USA. She had seen a number of boxes in the courtyard in
which manuscripts, books and master plates were packed. The way they were
packed showed that they were intended for a long journey. She cited two other
witnesses, a Polish acquaintance and a former maid who had visited her in the
ghetto and taken her in after the war. The Polish acquaintance had observed
that the safe in the manager's office on the ground floor of the building had been
broken into and its contents carefully packed in crates, while the maid saw that
a large number of crates had been taken from the publishing house and loaded
onto wagons for shipment to Germany.

The witness Eliyahu Schlossberg, a former employee of Romm Inc.,
asserted that the Soviets had not touched Romm. Akiba Gerschater, who had
been a bank official in Vilna before the war, confirmed these reports. He had
sorted Hebrew books in the YIVO during the German occupation as a Jewish
slave laborer under Gotthard and Pohl. Many thousands of volumes of the
Romm publishing house had passed through his hands. Others from the ghetto,

who were used as porters, testified that for months they had loaded zinc plates and matrices into waiting railway wagons destined for transport to Germany. After the war, the head of the Department for Jewish Cultural Heritage in the Diaspora at the Jewish National and University Library in Jerusalem had sifted through books from Vilna in Wiesbaden and Offenbach, and the Netherlands Reich Institute for War Documentation had given a detailed account of the raid by the Rosenberg staff. The former Yalkut employee Rubin Mass and the bibliographer Chimen Abramsky had testified about the profile and significance of the publishing house. Abramsky quoted the *Standard Jewish Encyclopedia*, edited by Cecil Roth and published in London in 1966, stating that the Romm editions had been sold by the Germans for dollars during World War II, because the Nazis needed foreign currency. In the restitution proceedings, the damage suffered by the Kahans and Gordons was estimated at 700,000 marks, without taking into account real estate, autographs, manuscripts, stencils, printing plates, copyrights, or securities, but only counting the value of the books that had gone missing. Years earlier, in the 1950s, the Kahans had appealed to various official institutions for compensation for the Romm shares to the value of 46,500 złoty; the securities, which by then had only a nominal value, were actually recovered from the Banking House Hardy & Co. in Frankfurt am Main. At the end of the restitution proceedings, in the summer of 1967, the Romm printing and publishing house and everything connected with it had melted down to the paltry settlement sum of 60,000 marks.

Photo 46: Picture postcard. Tanker *Ch. N. Kahan*. Courtesy of
Morten F. Larsen, Copenhagen

Photo 47: Picture postcard. Tanker *Grete Glad*. Courtesy of
Morten F. Larsen, Copenhagen

Photo 48: Picture postcard. Tanker *Malkah*. Courtesy of
Noa Rosenberg, Tel Aviv

Photo 49: From left, sitting: Ida and Simon Dubnow, Jonas Rosenberg;
standing behind them: Anna Kazhdan and others. Berlin, 1932.
Jüdisches Museum Berlin, Archiv Haimi-Cohen

Photo 50: Jonas Rosenberg, Yasha, and Roska Kahan with their children Chaim Avinoam and Malka. Versailles, spring 1934.
Jüdisches Museum Berlin, Archiv Haimi-Cohen

Photo 51: Arusia Kahan with the Nisse family. Riga, December 1937.
Marion Kane, Toronto

Photo 52: Aron and Zina Kahan, Gita and Monia Ripp with their sons Paul and Victor, and Sasha Sokolova. Mont-Dore, summer 1939. Paul Ripp, New York

Photo 53: Sasha Sokolova with Paul and Victor Ripp. Les Sables d'Olonne, July 1939. Victor Ripp, Princeton

אבן כספּ(?) ברוך נ... לבל "חולם" (?) ...
גבּאים(?) ...

Photo 54: Arusia Kahan as chief financial officer of *Haaretz*. Tel Aviv, 1935.
Efrat Carmon, Jerusalem

Photo 55: Aron and Zina Kahan with Zina's children and grandchildren.
New York, 1950. Jüdisches Museum Berlin, Archiv Haimi-Cohen

Photo 56: Zina Kahan and David Kahan. Israel, 1956. Daniel Ripp, New York

Photo 57: The Kahan family and their descendants. Petah Tikva, June 1959. Raziel Haimi-Cohen, Springfield/NJ

CHAPTER 17

36 Schlüterstrasse. Expulsion from Paradise. Berlin

Berlin, 19. 09. 1933, [28.] Elul 5693. Third expanded and improved edition. Dear guests! First of all I would like to thank you very much for coming to my celebration. Under other circumstances, this celebration would have been a happy family event, because I, the first great-grandson of R. Chaim Kahan of blessed memory, am celebrating my Bar Mitzvah. But fate, as well as the political events of recent months, have unfortunately determined that only a much smaller part of our large family could participate at this venue. So, it is all the more appreciated that at least you, my good friends have remained at all.

On September 19, his thirteenth birthday, Chaim Avinoam, or Chaim for short, celebrated his Bar Mitzvah in Berlin-Charlottenburg at 32 Wielandstrasse. Some items, kept by Giza Haimi-Cohen, Chaim's widow, remind us of that celebration—the gift from Grandfather Baruch: six thick volumes of the Babylonian Talmud, bound in black linen, published by Romm in Vilna in 1931; handwritten manuscripts of his *drashah*, a two-page address in German; in Hebrew, thoughts on that day and his words of welcome. It was a memorable, sad day in September 1933, not just a farewell to childhood.

A lot had happened in the past thirteen years. There were the to-and-fro between Hamburg and Berlin, Darmstädter Strasse and Schlüterstrasse; the housing shortage his mother had complained about in letters to his father; the question of his father's and his uncle's education and career choices; the risks of the economic new start in the West. He had not consciously experienced all these adversities and uncertainties that the family was repeatedly confronted with in the first postwar years in Berlin. He did not even get to meet his great-grandmother Malka, who had died of diabetes when he was sixteen months old. He probably had no memory of the scandal when Uncle Aron left Mina and Joseph, shortly after he and they had been the first of the family to move into their own apartment building at 32 Wielandstrasse—sixth floor on the left, where the attic had been converted into apartments. The family was outraged and had tried in vain to prevent it at the time. Joseph, who was later known as Yossi, told his daughter Michal that his father had merely married to produce an offspring. Incidentally, what remained completely unknown to Yossi and his children, was that in November 1922, when Joseph was ten months old, an apartment building had been purchased in the name of his mother, Mina Kahan, at 2 Gutzkowstrasse, Berlin-Schöneberg. It was five stories high, twelve windows wide with stucco work on the facade and has survived war and renovations. According to the purchase contract, Aron was the procurator and Lolia the administrator. As a wife, Mina was denied the right to dispose of her own property. But why, of all people, was Lolia, Zina's son, appointed as the administrator? Because Aron had left Mina to return to Zina. Was the house Mina's dowry or was it meant to be a settlement for her? Aron did not divorce his wife, but continued to provide for her and his son. On Shabbat and the festivals, he would appear with Joseph at 36 Schlüterstrasse. Every Sunday he took him and Chaim to Zina's home, Chaim's widow Giza would recount. The family mattered more than everything so that the broken marriage and differences of opinion were of secondary importance.

For a long time, 36 Schlüterstrasse, the home of the Rosenberg's grandparents, was Chaim's home, with his relatives in the immediate vicinity and neighborhood. His parents were still living there. His Grandparents Kahan had been living since 1925 in the tenement building next door, at 37 Schlüterstrasse, which the Kahans had also owned since 1922. Grandfather Baruch's siblings were living nearby, too. Aunt Rachel with her family had been living at 37 Schlüterstrasse, even if only for a short time. Uncle David was living at 43 Schlüterstrasse, while Uncle Aron was living with Aunt Zina in the attic apartment at 47 Kurfürstendamm, which had been especially fitted out for them after his separation from Mina. Two years later the two of them moved to 32 Bleibtreustrasse nearby, into a seven-room apartment. Chaim didn't have far to go to Uncle Bendet, Aunt Judith and his cousins, at first in Niebuhrstrasse, later in Dahlmannstrasse. He had grown up in the family circle, enjoying a sheltered childhood in a generously run open house.

The extended family had been living close together from the mid-twenties, for the most part in their own property. The apartments at 36 Schlüterstrasse and 32 Wielandstrasse were connected to each other by a passage across the backyard. Two of the buildings in which relatives were living, 32 Wielandstrasse and 37 Schlüterstrasse, belonged to the Kahans. There they also managed their assets and maintained offices of their real estate company, which was renamed Kahan Vermögensverwaltung in June 1927. A handwritten copy of the amended articles of association, drafted probably by Jonas Rosenberg, is preserved in the archives. It states that the purpose of the limited liability company was the administration and utilization of their own property and the remaining assets of Chaim Kahan's descendants. The share capital had been doubled from 300,000 to 600,000 Reichsmark. The sale of shares would henceforth require the consent of at least a two-thirds majority of the partners. Baruch, Aron and David had joined the existing managing directors, Jonas and Bendet. Of the new capital stock, Baruch contributed the lion's share, 143,000 Reichsmark, Zina, 106,000, and Rachel Ettinger, 51,000. The amendment was announced in the *Berliner Börsenzeitung*. This guaranteed the coherent compliance with the inheritance law and secured the material basis for the maintenance of their high standard of living.

"The apartments were furnished for eternity," said Dvora, "Aunt Miriam had furnished 36 Schlüterstrasse well, with furniture and accessories, crockery, table and bed linen. She liked to go shopping. The story became legendary in the family, how she purchased in passing, presumably from Wertheim, several Rosenthal sets for her own and her siblings' households—'the entire display.'" Parts of the crockery are still displayed today in the cupboards of her descendants in Israel and America. By comparison, the furnishings of the other family apartments in Berlin look dignified in photos, but still plain. A Bezalel carpet, representing Zionist arts and crafts, with a floral Art Nouveau ornament depicting the panorama of the holy city of Jerusalem, was the only wall decoration in Baruch and Rosalia's Biedermeier living room. Yasha and Roska, who had furnished their last Berlin apartment in the same style, decorated their walls with a few framed photographs, depicting religious and family motifs. One wonders who might have come up with the idea of having the small photo statuettes of all seven second-generation Kahan siblings made? On the back it says: "Imitation prohibited." Were they standing together in one of the front rooms at 36 Schlüterstrasse or were they distributed among the siblings, each one receiving a statuette of themselves? The miniatures seem to have been more than a decorative gimmick—they might have been talismans for strengthening, even invoking cohesion.

In her memoirs, Roska described life at 36 Schlüterstrasse in detail. From the time Chaim Kahan rented it in 1913, the ten-room apartment had been a residential property, a house of prayer and study, a manager's office, a meeting place and a literary salon. "Our home was a meeting place for rabbis who came to Berlin," she wrote and listed: Rabbi Shlomo Aronson from Kiev, who was a close friend, Rabbi Chaim Grodzenski and Rabbi Isaak Rubinstein from Vilna, Rabbi Abraham Dow Shapiro from Kovno and Rabbi Chaim Joshua Kasovsky from Jerusalem. They would often come to Berlin to receive medical treatment. The story of the rabbis who were sleeping on tables at night, because there were not enough beds available, also became legendary in the family. Rabbi Yechiel Weinberg was a frequent guest. He was a former rabbi in Pilwiszki in Poland, in the Suwałki province, and had been living in Berlin since the war. The same goes for Zalman Shneour. Every evening, throughout an entire winter, the poet used to be looking for fellow card players. No sooner had he stood in the doorway than everyone knew that he wanted to play "twenty-one." He was also a gifted actor and often performed pantomimes.

In Roska's memoirs, 36 Schlüterstrasse became the epitome of a communal paradise in a carefree, satisfying era. The mere enumeration of names of prominent politicians, artists and writers, to whom the house was open, proves the point. According to tradition, Zalman Rubashov (Shazar), later President of Israel, was among the visitors; as were the publishers and editors of the *Encyclopedia Judaica*, Jakob Klatzkin and Nachum Goldmann; Kurt Blumenfeld, President of the Zionist Association of Germany; the sculptor Henryk Glitsenstein; the Sephardic singer Bracha Zefira; actors of the Hebrew theater Habimah; as well as the duo Spiwakowsky with the brothers Jacob (piano) and Tossy (violin), who had played at Roska's wedding. "Incidentally, even strangers used to celebrate their weddings in our home," she remembered. A highlight was the marriage of two Habimah actors.

36 Schlüterstrasse used to attract many other guests, Russian but also well-known, liberal German Jews, especially on the holidays, over one hundred, during the services organized by her father Jonas. As Roska recalled, "Papa's glorious *daven* [leading the service] soon became known throughout the town." There they got an impression of an East-European Jewish home. It can't be excluded that Gershom Scholem was a guest there, too, before he left for Palestine. Roska remembered how the painter Budko was explaining the Seder ritual to his lady friend on Passover Eve. Once Isaak Steinberg, a former commissioner of justice under Lenin, also prayed with them. On Shabbat and festivals, many guests—Roska calls them "congregation"—used to dine

with them at the large table in the dining room, then sang Jewish songs in an excellent mood, and at the end of Yom Kippur, for example, a beautiful melody of *Hamavdil*, taught to them by Abraham Herzfeld, who had arrived with Rubashov. Roska apparently played a central role at 36 Schlüterstrasse, accepting responsibility and hostess duties. "She had impeccable taste, and used to set the table for the *kiddush*," Dvora remembered. "When one came into the dining room after prayer and saw this solemnly laid table, it was an image that cannot be forgotten. The culture of the home revolved around the traditional life at the table."

The open house at 36 Schlüterstrasse was a well-known address in East European Jewish Berlin. It conducted fellowship in the semi-public sphere. Several other houses and pubic spaces played a similar role. Dubnow's home, for example, became a pilgrimage site for its followers at every residence of the historian in Berlin, comparable to Tolstoy's Yasnaya Polyana. Or David and Helene Koigen's Philosophy of Religion Study Group, also in Charlottenburg, 3 Mommsenstrasse, right next door. In Schöneberg, the merchant Feivel and his wife Bracha Grüngard, both active in the Hebrew movement and Zionist circles, ran a salon; the one run in Dahlem by the psychoanalyst Max Eitingon, was called by Anna Freud "Hotel Eitingon" in a letter to her father. Mark and Eva Broido's apartment in Grunewald became the center of the Menshevik colony, while the editorial office of the Jewish Telegraphic Agency, run by Michael Wurmbrand in his apartment in Wilmersdorf, became a meeting place for migrants who were earning their living as journalists. This list could be continued. Every publishing house, editorial office of a newspaper or magazine, every café in the metropolis could fulfil this function. Prager Diele, Romanisches Café, Café des Westens were popular venues and became a mythological part of the Russian Berlin. Every home had its unique convention. For the Kahans it was based on the communal meal around the traditional table. In their case, traditional and modern Jewish community life created a symbiotic relationship: the traditionally religious community, committed to *tzedakah*, welfare, care, and charity, could be enriched with new, national-political content thanks to the *klal Israel* idea that all of Israel belong together. Both were overlaid and aesthetically refined by the bourgeois sociability of the salon culture, excellently led by educated Jewish women, well known in Berlin from the beginning of the nineteenth century. Thanks to their economic prosperity, the family had the necessary space within their private home. As an open house, the Kahans did not integrate themselves socially into the Weimar Republic, as opposed to their integration into the economy with Nitag.

Weimar Berlin offered young people, including young immigrants, many opportunities for diversion and orientation. The impulses for economic, political and cultural renewal emanating from the young capital and metropolis might have unnerved and provoked the migrant family with its strong ties to tradition under the fragile conditions of the foreign, the transitory space. The modern metropolitan society made it possible to free oneself from family ties and the migrant milieu, which could have easily led to loneliness. But it also opened up new community structures in the form of the social movements that revolutionized the relationship between the sexes and generations. Chaim and Malka's children were hardly touched by this. Gathered together in Berlin, they were already in the middle of their lives or even beyond. All of them, even Jonas and Bendet, who had been living in Berlin for some time, were moving with their portable habitat, in family, migrant, religiously orthodox and Zionist circles. Jonas connected the family with the rabbinical world in Berlin, Eastern Europe and Palestine. Bendet opened up the world of Jewish Bibliophilia for them. With her work for ORT, Judith maintained the connection to Diaspora social politics, which had its beginning in the Tsarist empire. Rosalia, whose uncle was a famous Lithuanian scholar, cultivated the *yichus*, the family's spiritual nobility. Baruch enjoyed his retirement, allegedly preferring to read Heine, Börne and the Hebrew cultural magazine *Hatsfira*. Miriam kept up the domestic traditions. Aron concentrated on business. David kept the communication between the siblings, the generations, the different interests going, and was more involved in the Zionist movement than his older siblings. But how did the youth, the third generation, behave? They probably tasted, some more, some less, the lure of the big city. Lolia, in particular, is known to have been able to enjoy himself. A photo shows him and cousin Noma, both with their fiancées, at the Alkazar on Hamburg's Reeperbahn. Apart from that, Chaim and Malka's grandchildren took part in activities offered by the Jewish youth movement and the Zionist organization, but within the framework set by their parents, uncles and aunts.

The Jewish holidays and the summer retreats continued to govern the annual calendar. One went, in different constellations, to Merano, Monte Carlo, Venice, Salzburg, Prague and to the Bohemian and Baltic seaside resorts, the Slovakian High Tatras, Bad Aussee in Styria, but also continued to go to Bad Harzburg, Kissingen and Wiesbaden. "My dearest! I greet you all very warmly and wish you a good *Shabbes* [the last word in Hebrew letters]! We are well, except that we are longing for your letters like heavenly manna. Please write often! All the best! Your Rosa"—thus begins a family letter from August 1923 to those at home in Berlin. "Dear Mama and Papa ... How are you? I'm fine in Swinemünde, but the only bad thing is, that you are not here," it continues in Russian. "Here we go to the beach, but we haven't bathed yet. I am already red from the sun, Fima too. Thank God everyone is healthy here, Lily, Sasha and Fima are all tanned, and Auntie has also got a tan. Mama, please tell Dudi that I forgot what he told me to tell Aunt Zina. Regards to everyone else! Lots of kisses, your Dora." Dora used the German word for "beach" but wrote it in Cyrillic script. The letter ends with regards for her uncle and aunt from Lily. That summer Roska, Zina and Sasha were apparently travelling with a whole group of children, not only their own, but also with Rachel Ettinger's youngest, Chaim, nicknamed Fima, as well as Bendet's and Judith's daughters. Dudi was David Kahan's nickname.

In Berlin the family expanded. At the end of 1924 Nomek married Sulamith Hurwitz, the youngest daughter of the merchant Michael Hurwitz from Minsk and his wife Fruma, a friend of Miriam Rosenberg's. Sulamith had grown up in Königsberg and had lived in Berlin since the war. When Nomek asked for her hand in marriage, she was studying piano at the conservatory and lived with her sister Jenny, who was married to Kurt Blumenfeld. Nomek's parents had reservations at first, but Rabbi Aronson had mediated, recounted Giza, Chaim's widow. Two Nomas courted Sulamith, called Shula, according to the family—Noma Kahan and Noma Rosenberg. Luckily, she chose Noma Rosenberg, or else they would both not have been born, joked their children Eli Rosenberg and Efrat Carmon.

Chaim was four at the time. Did he remember the wedding? It was celebrated, like that of his parents, in the Logenhaus. Dvora, who was a few years older—she was eleven at the time—remembered the bridal couple's carriage ride from Schlüterstrasse along the Kurfürstendamm via Wittenbergplatz into Kleiststrasse. For her the wedding was like a fairy tale. *Drai Kepelech* [Three Heads] is the title of a Yiddish occasional poem by Zalman Shneour about the Hurwitz sisters—Jenny, Esther and Shula in the literary salon at 36 Schlüterstrasse:

Three heads of women combed and crimped
In the evening light—golden and matt:
One head like silver, the second like bronze,
The third—like black agate.
Like chrysanthemums on human necks,
In vases of silken dress,

The black one looks childlike, the bronze one coquettish,
The white one is serious with stress.
Three ages, three colors, three moods—
A coincidence, harmonious and neat.
But the red one is missing, and the blonde one is missing,
So the bouquet could not be complete …
The unsaid, even deeper and sweeter
Stimulates the taste by what's absent;
Art stands alone in the shadows
Observing, enjoying the scene they present.

Three amusing photos of Chaim are from that year: on one of the many KaDeWe Berlin passport photos in the heirlooms, you can see a little boy in a buttoned dark shirt, with a blossom-white collar and a pocket handkerchief in his breast pocket. His big brown eyes, slightly irritated, are looking rather inwards than into the camera; they look out from under a towering brown curly head of hair, in a finely cut, pointed face, framed by large ears. Next to it are photographs of Purim in the Berlin Zionist Association: Chaim in costume, sometimes as Mordechai from the Book of Esther, sometimes as a Hasid with side locks and caftan bent over a Talmud folio. Among the heirlooms are also some of his witticisms from when he was five, which his parents had printed as a fanfold, according to year and month: "Do motorcycles have spinning parts?—What is spinning? Well, the gramophone is spinning, the radio is not." Or, in Aunt Zina's toilet: "I'd rather do it at home. Would be a pity to do it here. It's too clean here."

The young Rosenbergs first moved to Hamburg, where Nomek worked for Nitag. After their first son Michael was born on March 25, 1926 / 10 Nissan 5686, Nomek was offered a position at the headquarters. Nomek and Shula returned to Berlin. The family also moved to 32 Wielandstrasse, to the attic apartment, sixth floor on the right, across the landing from Mina and Joseph. In the same year, on November 28, 1926 / 22 Kislev 5687, Chaim's sister was born and was named Malka in honor and memory of her great-grandmother. Now there was again a couple named Chaim and Malka, this time as siblings. Thus, three little children, two Kahans and one Rosenberg, were living at 32 Wielandstrasse when Nomek and Shula had their second son, Elijahu, called Eli, two years later, on May 6, 1928 / 16 Iyar 5688. The children obviously liked to live close together, something Yossi and Eli enjoyed remembering in old age. Now there were five small children in the family. However, the generations were shifting. Chaim was two years older than his uncle Joseph, while Michael, Eli

and Malka were only a little younger than him. All five of them followed chron-
ologically the last Ettinger son, also called Chaim, who was born in 1917 and
still belonged to Joseph's generation. Bendet's and Zina's daughters, then young
adolescent girls, insisted on participating in the upbringing of their cousins,
nephews and nieces. In a photograph taken on one of the attic-apartment balconies in the summer of 1925, ten-year-old Lily is cuddling five-year-old Chaim
Avinoam who is clutching his teddy bear in his arms.

Unlike Lily, to whom the Russian *nyanya* Sasha Sokolova remained faithful all the way into exile, all the little Kahans and Rosenbergs were brought up
by German Christian nannies in Berlin—Chaim by Fräulein Krause, Joseph by
Lotte Kleinert, Michael and Eli by Fräulein Anna, called Aja. Lotte Kleinert
came from Bischofswerder, part of Liebenwalde in the Oberhavel District of
Brandenburg. Yossi said that he used to spend a lot of time with the Kleinerts
in the Havelland region and learned to ride a bicycle in Bischofswerder. He
showed me photos, the portrait of a young woman with bright laughing eyes
and an open gaze. Another photo depicts the three of them, Joseph with Mina
and Fräulein Lotte, as if they were both his mothers. Even at an advanced age he
remembered going to the cinema with Fräulein Lotte at Savignyplatz, where a
silent film, a nature documentary about elephants was being screened. Eli said
that Aja had wanted to leave Germany with them in 1933. His request to take
her along had presented his parents with a conundrum. As he learned later,
Aja's brother was a Nazi. Lotte Kleinert's father was also a member of the party,
according to Yossi. The Fräuleins became part of precious childhood memories
for Chaim and Malka, Yossi, Michael and Eli. They never forgot them, their
names and the stories associated with them. "Thank you for all the beautiful
letters, my beloved grandfather and grandmother," wrote Chaim clumsily with
a pencil in Hebrew to Baruch and Rosalia, who were probably traveling. "Malka
and I are well. I love my sister Malka very much. She is still very small. Joseph
is also well. He's my best friend now. I'm already learning *Vayetze*. I am writing
a short story about my book every day, except on Saturday and Sunday. On the
days when it's not raining, I go for a walk with my teacher. Shalom and happy
Passover to you from Chaim Avinoam. Shalom also from Fräulein Krause."

The Hebrew *Vayetze* is the first word of the seventh weekly Torah portion in the annual cycle of weekly Torah readings, comprising Genesis chapter
28, verse 10 to chapter 32, verse 3, dealing with Jacob's flight to Haran, his life
with Laban and his return from there. There, little Chaim Avinoam would have
read about Jacob, to whom a ladder, reaching to heaven, appeared in a dream,
who met Rachel at a well, worked for Laban, lived with Leah and Rachel, who

bore him children, and about Jacob leaving Laban, with his wives and his children. One wonders what the stories he wrote about them looked like? Chaim Avinoam and Malka, Joseph, Michael and Eli were introduced to the basic Jewish teachings and traditions at an early age. This was in keeping with Eastern European Jewish custom and the family's commitment to religious Zionism as well as to the Hebrew movement, which had started in Weimar Berlin. One Shabbat, Yasha wanted to play "rocking horse" with his little daughter Malka, as Roska had noted in a booklet with Malka's funny sayings. Malka replied: "Today is Shabbat, we are not allowed to play 'rocking horse' today." When they would have guests and the table was set, she would ask "Is it Shabbat today?"

At 36 Schlüterstrasse, the cook Bluma Altbaum worked in the kitchen. The maid Lina took care of the housekeeping. Every Sunday the seamstress, Frau Feldmann, came to the house. The caretaker couple Schwalbe guarded the entrances. Although the Kahans lived in the bourgeois west of Berlin, they kept in touch with the Scheunenviertel neighborhood around Grenadierstrasse, where the destitute migrants as well as their traditional compatriots and co-religionists were living. There were many prayer rooms in that area, as well as the large synagogue in Oranienburger Strasse and other Jewish institutions such as the Orthodox Rabbinical Seminary and the Hochschule für die Wissenschaft des Judentums in Artillerie-, today Tucholsky-Strasse. Once a week, a Polish Jewish woman, Mrs. Pusztinsky, and her son would buy groceries for all the Kahans, Rosenbergs and Ettingers in the Scheunenviertel. Only those coming from there were considered kosher. The fact that Mr. Pusztinsky was a tall boy who had a speech impediment due to a hole in his throat had made a deep impression on Yossi. Later, in Israel, he met him again. Dvora still remembered the huge quantities of food that the Pusztinskys would regularly fetch for the large family and then store in the kitchen and pantry at 36 Schlüterstrasse. A greeting card for the New Year, inscribed in Hebrew and German, unlike the other business and greeting cards in the archives, with a colorful picture in the upper left-hand corner, a wreath of pink roses, with a purple and white floral arrangement, is a further indication of the faithful service that the Pusztinskys used to render the family.

Already during the war, Roska and Yasha had participated in the founding of Bet Va'ad Ivri, the association for the dissemination of modern Hebrew language and culture, where the teachers were young people, children of the first Jewish settlers in Palestine, who had come to Berlin to study. One of them, Zilla Feinberg, who was studying horticulture and agriculture and worked in the Botanical Garden in Dahlem, belonged to their circle of friends. In the beginning, the Rosenbergs had provided the association with rooms for meetings at 36 Schlüterstrasse. Another initiative was the opening of a kindergarten in their apartment. "We started with 8 children," Roska remembered, "and because the space at home was too small, we only added a few children. But it was really the elite that participated. ... The *gan* [kindergarten] was well known in Zionist circles." For example, they took in Noemi, Jenny and Kurt Blumenfeld's daughter. The kindergarten at 36 Schlüterstrasse, referred to by Roska in shortened Hebrew as *gan*, was not the first of its kind in Berlin. However, according to the family, it was one of many in the movement's educational system that were guided by the idea of a modern, worldwide spiritual Zion, in which the State of Israel would form one of its centers. "*Zeh tinok yehudi* [This is a Jewish baby]," Chaim Avinoam responded to his kindergarten teacher, Lea Krupnik, when she showed him the *yud*, the smallest of all Hebrew letters, Roska recalled.

After kindergarten, the little ones attended the Jewish community school in the nearby Fasanenstrasse. The older ones went to the grammar schools in the area—Bendet's daughters Dora, Lea and Röschen with Zina's youngest, Lily, to the Fürstin Bismarck School, today Sophie-Charlotte Oberschule in Sybelstrasse; Chaim Avinoam and Joseph went to the classical Bismarck-Gymnasium in Pfalzburger Strasse, where Hebrew was taught (today the high school campus of the Nelson Mandela comprehensive school); Moshe and Shalom Ettinger studied at the Russian Grammar School in Wilmersdorf. Gita said that immediately after her arrival from Baku—she was eleven at the time—she was put into a German school without any knowledge of German, which was hard for her. In addition, as an "Eastern Jew," she did not feel accepted by her fellow students. Her only friend, who came from Danzig, was not allowed to visit her at home because the grandmother, with whom the friend was living, disapproved of the relationship. Gita left the grammar school before her final examination. Her younger sister Lily did not like to remember her school days in Berlin. On the gable of the Fürstin Bismarck School in Sybelstrasse there were two inscriptions, a fellow student recalled: Kant's "Two things fill the mind ...: the starry sky above me and the moral law within me" and—in Greek—"I was born to join in love, not hate—that is my nature" from *Antigone* by Sophocles. But this philosophy was in sharp contrast to what had happened there since 1933.

Lily liked to think back to the Shabbat evenings and Festivals at 36 Schlüterstrasse in the family circle. Uncle Aron had loved her like a daughter, and Cousin Röschen, almost the same age, had become her best friend. Gita's wish to attend evening school was rejected by her mother, who argued that this was not appropriate for a Jewish girl. Gita attended a school of interior design for a year. Afterwards she went to Paris to study Bauhaus arts and architecture.

Dvora was eleven when her parents decided to go to *Eretz Israel*. She had been happy to escape the control of the family, nannies, the dress code and conventions. In Haifa, she said, things were much more relaxed.

The family continued to grow when more of Chaim and Malka's grandchildren got married—Noma Kahan in Berlin in November 1927, two years after completing his studies at the Engineering Academy in Oldenburg, which he had begun in Zwickau. He married Rita Kahn from Memel, with whom Roska had become friends in a summer resort. Because the authorities did not allow the stateless Noma, who had only been living in Prussia for six years and who had come from Azerbaijan, to marry locally, the civil wedding ceremony took place in the Free Hanseatic City of Hamburg, and the Jewish one in Berlin, his daughter Efrat recounted. Rita had relatives in Hamburg. Noma and Rita announced their marriage in the *Jüdische Rundschau*.

I could not find an advertisement for Lolia's wedding there. That same year he married Eugenia Pines, possibly a granddaughter of Chaim Kahan's business friend Ilya Pines, an employee of the Moscow oil export company Ragozin & Co. whose family had fled to Riga after the Bolsheviks came to power. Eugenia, called Genia, was also employed by Nitag. All the Kahans and Rosenbergs of the third generation, who got married during the Berlin period, entered into love marriages. Nevertheless, origin and convention remained important. In all cases they married Jewish East European women from their circle of acquaintances.

The family's bond with *Eretz Israel* was traditionally strong. For this reason, but probably also in order to distance themselves from the Kahan brothers and the "Charlottenburg psychology," the Ettingers drew the obvious conclusion from their love for Zion and moved on to Palestine in the spring of 1925, when the Hebrew University was opened in Jerusalem. Noma and Rita followed them shortly after their marriage. Efrat recounted that after the experience of hunger, deprivation and violence in Russia, her father had not been able to come to terms with the sated Berlin lifestyle, where a common pastime was solving crossword puzzles. She showed me two photos of him from that time: on one of them he is holding the *Berliner Illustrierte Zeitung* towards the photographer with an amused smile, flanked by two elegant young women nestling against him. On the other, with crossed arms and a self-confident look into the distance, he is enthroned in front of a map of *Eretz Israel*.

In August 1931, much too early, at sixty-one, nine and a half years after her mother, Miriam Rosenberg died of cancer. She died when the economic crisis of the Kahan companies had reached its peak and found her final resting place next to Malka at the Adass Yisroel cemetery in Berlin-Weissensee. The death of Miriam, then called Marie, meant the end of the family center at 36 Schlüterstrasse. The ten-room apartment was abandoned. Roska and Yasha moved with Chaim Avinoam and Malka to 32 Wielandstrasse, where all five Kahan and Rosenberg children now lived together. After the death of his wife, Jonas Rosenberg was more in Riga than in Berlin.

"Wiesbaden, Hotel Restaurant *Kronprinz*, 3 March 1932. Dear Daddy! How are you? I am fine. The day before yesterday, we were in Mainz. It was very nice there. In the old town there are such narrow alleys that a tall man can touch both sides with outstretched arms. There is a whole district of such alleys there," wrote Chaim Avinoam from the summer retreat to Berlin, describing the old town of Mainz with its cathedral, fair, the old and the new synagogues. "It was a huge shindig. We drew lots and of course we didn't win anything. I couldn't get away. Then the tram pulled away from right under our noses." At the end he told about his visit to friends in Mainz, whose nanny didn't believe that he could speak German, because he talked Hebrew with the son of the house. In Berlin the language habits of the polyglot family were changing. Hebrew was still cultivated, Yiddish was also spoken. Chaim Avinoam had attended the Hebrew kindergarten and had later received private Hebrew lessons. It was similar with the other Kahan-Rosenberg-Ettinger children. But gradually the Russian language was replaced by German. The children were hearing it from their Fräuleins, at school and sometimes from their mothers. Two of the women who married into the Kahan and Rosenberg families, Sulamith Hurwitz and Rita Kahn, had grown up with German, one in Königsberg, the other in Memel. Mina Levstein from Łódż spoke German with her son. German was also the colloquial language in Bendet's family. "I only know myself as being Russian," said Dvora in old age. Eli, on the other hand, describes himself as a Yekke, as the immigrants from Germany were called in Israel.

The last two marriages were celebrated by Kahans and Rosenbergs in Germany a few months before Adolf Hitler's appointment as Reich Chancellor and shortly afterwards—in October 1932 in Berlin and in February 1933 in Hamburg. Gita married Salomon Ripp from Grodno, whom she had met in Paris, and Berl Rosenberg married Bina Warschawski. Now only two men in the family, David and Arusia, were still single. Naomi Loewenthal brought to one of our meetings hectographed sheets in A4 format, which turned out to be the wedding booklet for "Gita KAHAN and Monia [Salomon] RYPP," with verses, speeches and jokes in German. It is said that the Kahans had cast a spell over all those who had married into the family, which proves their power of integration—a view that was passed on in the family. "Monia, what's your name?"—"Ettinger"—"Why aren't you called Kahan?" was, according to Roska's notes, one of the dialogues between her little daughter Malka and Moshe Ettinger, who was also called Monia by the family.

According to the wedding booklet, Moshe, Rachel's eldest, twenty-two, active in the Zionist Blue and White Youth and Hiking Federation, gave a speech. He and his brother returned a few years after the family had moved to Palestine, Moshe to study economics at the Friedrich-Wilhelms University and Shalom to the agricultural college in Berlin. In his speech Moshe compared the family history with the history of a people divided into antiquity, the Middle Ages and modern times, structuring it into a Russian, a German and an international period. In October 1932, the international period had already begun for him. The wedding was marking the transition. He referred to the Kahans as "Nohaks," not "Nitags," after Nohaka (Algemeen Noord-Hollandsch Handel-skontoor), the company Aron had just acquired in Amsterdam. He described them as principled and conservative, tradition being literally their imprimatur. "Educated in the principles of the natural bourgeois order and imbued with an awareness of the advantages of private property, they were unable to join the dreary egalitarianism of the communists," which is why they had moved abroad. Moshe described Berlin as the place where most of their medieval period had taken place, and where the family was reunited in response to the earlier scattering. In the pointed, caricaturing form of parody, he summed up the lifestyle and self-image of the family in Berlin: the "Nohaks" preferred to live here in one and the same street, so that the furthest corners of their pale of settlement were no more than a quarter of an hour's walk apart. He was alluding to the Berlin postwar regulations that were intended to remedy the lack of housing. A powerful urge had even forced the Kahans to live on top of each other, crammed into low, uncomfortable attics. For him, this was an indication that their spiritual needs were stronger than their physical ones. In contrast to the attic apartments, Moshe described 36 Schlüterstrasse as the seat of the Spiritual Head and paradise.

In his speech he also addressed the internal organization of the "Nohaks," which had developed in the Berlin Middle Ages. As all nations emerged from the patriarchy, they had "modified" themselves in Western Europe—not with a written constitution, but by forming a people's assembly according to the federal principle, which decided important questions by an equal number of votes for each tribe, regardless of its size. The tribes were to be represented by their elders. As in other modern nations, there were diverse authorities. Without naming their officials, he alluded to Jonas's role as spiritual leader, Aron's as head of government, David's as head of personnel, Roska's as judge and head of protocol. Roska was also nicknamed the "cooking spoon" in the family because she was said to be meddle in everything. Yasha is portrayed in the wedding booklet not as a manager, but as a philologist and Schiller fan, and Bendet as someone who is out to make money from books. Zina has *chokhme*, wit and wisdom, because you can always get advice from her. Baruch is responsible for housing matters. In Berlin, the "Nohaks" had maintained cohesion and unity. Dvora later put it more clearly: "Aron was a very strong character who led the whole family. The entire family life developed in Schlüterstrasse and the kitty was shared. … There was obedience in the family. What Aron Kahan says gets done and that's how it ought to be."

According to the wedding booklet, the children, Chaim Avinoam, Joseph, Malka, Michael and Eli had put on a show. The five recited verses, written by the two older ones, and presented gifts to the bridal couple: Joseph, gasoline from Africa, Chaim Avinoam, newspapers, Michael, a cake, Malka, flowers, Eli, the youngest one, dressed as a Bedouin, oranges. Less than a year after Gita and Monia's wedding, a few months after the advent of the Nazi Regime, Chaim Avinoam was preparing for his Bar Mitzvah. In Hebrew he recorded thoughts on the subject:

> I will read the *Haftarah* and perhaps write a *drashah*. I will certainly not give a speech. I can't speak in public. I don't know who, which and how many people will come. Uncles, aunts, rabbis, relatives and probably five or six children. The rabbi will say that I come from a righteous, respectable and good Jewish house, but he says that about everyone. I will receive many books, but no bicycle. That's bad because I want a bicycle and no books.

When the time came, he welcomed his guests in Hebrew and apologized in advance that some might not like his speech. Then he got to the heart of the matter: this year he would grow up. The Torah made him an adult just as it made Israel a nation. Two things had to be added to nation-building—language and land—the Holy Language because it was the language of the People and the only characteristic of Judaism during the Nation's exile, and the Land, where his ancestors had been living, and where he wanted to live with his family. He was hoping to see all the guests again soon in *Eretz Israel* and to become a loyal son of his nation and country. One wonders, who had helped him in the formulation of these sentences?

David and Rachel Ettinger, Noma and Rita Kahan had emigrated. All the other Kahans, Rosenbergs and Moshe and Shalom Ettinger were leaving Germany in a hurry, even though they had the opportunity to pack some particularly valuable and familiar belongings into one or two *lifts*—containers in today's language. A few weeks after Hitler's "seizure of power," Mina Kahan was the first to decide on leaving with Joseph, who had just turned eleven. Within the family, they were in the most difficult situation, but were probably the easiest to extricate from the unit. Mina and Joseph, as well as Bendet and Judith with Lea and Röschen left Berlin after the April boycott. Both families travelled first to Poland, because they had Polish passports and wanted to say goodbye to the relatives there—Mina to her siblings in Łódź and Judith to her parents in Losewicze near Suwałki. A few weeks later they left Warsaw for Palestine. Bendet wrote in his CV for the restitution proceedings that, as a publisher of Hebrew literature, he had been particularly exposed to persecution. The harassment had already begun a year earlier. In April 1932 his application for German citizenship had been rejected as was Yasha's. Arusia withdrew his application in May 1933. Nomek and Shula Rosenberg, together with their sons Michael and Eli, had already left Berlin before Passover and before the April boycott, on March 28, 1933. They had gone directly to Palestine via Italy. "This happened," said Eli, who was barely five at the time, "shortly after Michael's birthday." His brother had turned seven.

No one in the family held a German passport. Most of them—Mina and Joseph, Bendet and family, all the Rosenbergs—had Polish documents, including David and Zina, who had entered Germany, with the children, as Georgians. Like Aron, they had obtained Polish citizenship upon application in the mid-twenties. Only Baruch's family was stateless, proving their identity with Nansen passports. Shortly before Gita's wedding, in September 1932, Zina had been deprived of her Polish citizenship. The Berlin police had thereupon declared her and her children stateless. Their passports were only valid until the summer of 1933. The threats by the Nazi Regime, their uncertain legal status, the boycott of Jewish shops on April 1 and an assault on Lolia, who was beaten up by an SA man on Kurfürstendamm because he had not taken off his hat to him—all this was the impetus for the Kahans and Rosenbergs to leave. Germany was no longer their domicile. In early May, Zina left Berlin in a hurry for Paris.

"Berlin, 11 June 1933. Dear Daddy! I really feel very guilty because I have not written to you in detail for such a long time. But it has not been possible for me. Soon after our arrival at home I already had a lot of work and so I didn't get around to writing you a letter," Roska wrote to her father, Jonas, in Riga. They had returned rested and sunburnt from a family trip to Hamburg and Travemünde. The short trip had been a nice change from everyday life in Berlin, which was now dominated by the departures, she reported. In the meantime, Lolia and Genia had left for Lisbon. In mid-June Aron followed Zina to Paris. David and Arusia fled to Palestine. "I myself was director of Nitag-Inc. together with my brother David Kahan," Aron wrote in his application for restitution. "In 1933, I was forced to give up my life's work and leave Germany due to Nazi persecution." Nitag Deutsche Treibstoffe AG Hamburg certified that he had been a board member of the company until early April 1933. No reasons for his resignation were given.

From June 1933, the only members of the Kahan and Rosenberg families to remain in Berlin were Chaim Avinoam and his sister with their parents and the Grandparents Kahan. Baruch and Rosalia had also intended to leave Germany for Palestine, but were probably in no hurry. They had planned a summer retreat in Marienbad with a follow-up in Druskininkai, the oldest and most popular spa resort in Lithuania, where Rosalia's siblings from Vilna also wanted to go, and then a longer trip to Paris. "As for us, our employees must report to the Labor Office this week. So, I suppose that by the end of the month it will become clearer how things will pan out at the office. I'd like us to go to Karlovy Vary in July, if we can," Roska continued as they were in need of a holiday. She didn't write anything about her own departure plan from Germany. In the end she gave her father Zina's address in Paris: 20 Mac Mahon.

During the spring of 1933, the Charlottenburg Paradise was disbanded—after ten years of being together, the family was once again driven away and dispersed. In his Bar Mitzvah speech, Chaim Avinoam came to the conclusion that, in their fateful year of 1933, the "Jewish question" could not be solved by assimilation and fine speeches. Like many German Jews and some of his relatives, he soon set off on a journey to a new, foreign exile, but always with Palestine in mind, where most of his relatives had moved to, and he was hoping to go there in the foreseeable future.

Eleven days after Chaim Avinoam's Bar Mitzvah, on September 30, 1933, at the end of Yom Kippur, his grandfather, the sixty-six-year-old Baruch Kahan, was arrested. A neighbor had denounced him as an enemy of the people. "My father was still in his tuxedo from the synagogue services and had just eaten something after the heavy day of fasting," Yasha explained during the restitution proceedings. "It was 1–2 days before he intended to emigrate; his *lifts* were already in front of the building." Baruch Kahan was detained for one month in the city jail on Dirksenstrasse in Berlin-Mitte, the same prison where Yasha had been imprisoned during Rosh Hashanah at the beginning of the war, nineteen years earlier. Yasha and the other Jewish Nitag employees were dismissed in October 1933. Only Berl Rosenberg in Hamburg remained on duty for the time being. Nitag's testimonial states that "regrettably" Yasha had decided to leave. On October 31, when Baruch was released, Yasha and Roska, too, fled to Paris with their children and parents.

CHAPTER 18

The Mavericks between the Wars—European Corporate Networks: Berlin, Hamburg, Copenhagen, London, Riga, Paris, Amsterdam

At the end of 1931, Aron and David had left Nitag's board of directors. They remained members of the executive for a while, but soon left the management completely, David at the end of 1932 and Aron a few months later, in April 1933. The Kahans were no longer Nitag's main shareholders. The shares now belonged to the Banking House Hardy & Co. Aron later explained in his memoirs that the withdrawal was caused by the bankruptcy of the company, but gave neither political nor economic reasons for the decline. Perhaps he assumed that these reason were known to the family. Perhaps he also wished to keep his cards close to his chest, even in retrospect, to make him the only one capable of keeping track of the company's management.

Included among the heirlooms is a Hebrew-Russian-German picture story on fifteen sheets entitled *The Ahron-Scroll. Subjects worthy of Aivazovsky's Brushes* and labelled "Purim, Cologne, 1928." These must appear like hieroglyphs to all who are not familiar with the three languages and cultures—the Purim story in the scroll of Esther, the Carnival in Cologne and the light-and-water paintings of the Russian-Armenian painter Ivan K. Aivazovsky from Feodosia in Crimea. The title is framed by a painted scroll, similar to those read in the form of the *Megilat Esther*, at Purim, the Jewish carnival. It is the festival when Jews recall the persecution of their people under the rule of the Persian King Ahasuerus by the courtier Haman and their rescue by the Jewish woman Esther, who had become the king's favorite wife. "Text and music by me, Arusia," is written on the last page, "Technical execution: Ing. S. Kamenka."

The picture story begins with a joke, which is manifested on the second sheet as "gallows humor" and annotated in Yiddish "*tatte* [daddy], you'll laugh." This is followed by a cascade of allusions. "*Mipnei ma* [why] …" is the ritual question on the third sheet, sung, in major and minor, as a song from the drama *The Dybbuk* about unhappy love and the transmigration of souls in the *shtetl*, which was popular in the Jewish world at the time. Why does God punish the pious, the *hasidim*? While they were still dancing in 1927, they were sitting around the table in 1928, resigned, gesticulating and pulling their hair. "My Purim" is the title of that picture. It is followed by "My Carnival," with all the trimmings—"Wine, Woman and Song …," from the *Book of Songs* by Heinrich Heine. In the face of a "bankruptcy book," the Rhenish cheerfulness disappears, together with the music, and gives way to the "*Via mea dolorosa*," the image of a man who, quoting from the Russian play *Woe from Wit*, notes: "… on Saturday I'm going to Schmidt's for a 'cup of tea'; he's not bankrupt, but I reckon. …" The company sign of the Rheinische Nitag, Bonn, is underlined with a music score—the opening line of the Russian ballad "I don't know why and for what this needs be. …" The chansonnier Alexander Vertinsky used to sing this against war and revolution. Vertinsky left Russia and went around the world with his songs, consoling the migrants.

On sheet eight, the narrator gets down to business—competition in the Fuel Convention which is depicted as a hand-to-hand battle between the corporations in the form of canisters and pipes with human limbs—the Benzene Association harassing the *Big* Sisters and bringing Nitag to its knees. With a quota of sixteen percent in the Convention, the Benzene Association, which became known as Aral, was the largest fuel distribution organization in Germany without foreign participation. It had introduced a new product, benzene, a derivative-mineral oil mixture, and advertised that it was selling German fuel, which was only half-true. In July 1928, the Association signed a contract with the Soviet Foreign Trade Organization to buy 485,000 tons of oil at extremely low prices. The members of the Fuel Convention tolerated the agreement, but the strengthening of the Benzene Association had a devastating effect on Nitag, which primarily imported American oil to supply its network of filling stations and had a quota of no more than just under three percent of the cartel.

The subsequent sheets tell, in pictures, the story of the Kahans' corporate network in the twenties: one chart shows the roller coaster development of the "freight-listings on the tanker market," in ups and downs, which goes up from 1925 to 1927 and then falls steeply. Under the label "Modern Capitalism or Much Ado about Nothing," on sheet ten, a hand holds a tangle of twenty-seven circles, which look like balloons on a string. The three largest in the middle are called COC, NITAG and the United, and are connected to each other. But the hand only holds the COC balloon directly on the string, while NITAG and the United are hanging on to the COC, with all the others hanging on the three big balloons and only a few also on small ones. The names refer to companies in which the Kahans had an interest or with which they were connected in 1928, businesses in eleven countries and on three continents—Germany, Denmark, Great Britain, France, Poland, Lithuania, Latvia, Estonia, Palestine and, allegedly, even India and Australia. The impressive network of companies is presented jokingly in the picture story as an expression of modern capitalism and as fragile. It threatens to dissolve into nothing if the hand lets go of the string. At the time, Arusia was an expert on the Fuel Convention issues at Nitag and had an insight into its business affairs. He made it clear that Nitag with its subsidiaries in Germany and the Kahan Vermögensverwaltung, including the publishing houses, had been dependent on the COC. So, here he was hinting that while the collapse of the company network had begun with the COC, Nitag's bankruptcy was part of a larger picture.

Contrary to how Nomek Rosenberg had described it retrospectively in his 1961 letter to Aron, Nitag was not the central family business in the interwar period. The focus of their activities was the COC, the parent company, which had subsidiaries and branches in almost all European countries. It included Nitag with its tank facilities in Wilhelmshaven and the United Oil Company in London. The company history of L. C. Glad & Co. from 1930 states that the COC was a worldwide company selling gasoline and had a petroleum business of international repute with its headquarters in Copenhagen. Carl Frederik Glad organized the purchases and chartered the tankers from Copenhagen. The Kahan brothers in Berlin were responsible for the sales. The COC was importing mainly American oil, but also Russian oil even before the agreements on oil exports had been reached between the Soviet Union and Western countries. In the summer of 1920, one year after its foundation, a few months after the Bolsheviks had taken Baku, the Danish company ran a bold advertising campaign about its locations in "Baku, Batum, Białystok, Constantinople, Libau, Memel, Petrograd, Reval, Riga and Saratov."

In the first years after the war, impressive business was achieved in the Baltic countries and for customers in Germany, England and France, according to the company's history. In the mid-twenties, the COC's sphere of activity extended as far as the Middle East and Egypt. At peak periods, twelve of the company's tankers were simultaneously sailing the seas with cargoes worth more than ten million Danish kroner. The situation had consolidated in the second half of the twenties. The COC's main markets, with its own import facilities and numerous filling stations, remained Germany and Great Britain. The company operated a considerable freight business, chartering tankers for its own and other companies' cargoes on a temporary basis, which required good knowledge, experience and tact. In addition, the company owned four ships of its own, besides the three Nitag tankers, the "Oljaren," which had initially run charters for it. So far the Danish company history.

In his memoirs, Aron set different priorities. For him, the COC was his creation, which Carl Frederik Glad had contributed to. The first subsidiary was the Russian-Baltic Mineral Oil Company, Rubanito for short, in Riga and Libau, the only one of the Kahans' companies to survive both the First World War and the Russian Revolution. With the help of the COC, Aron had founded the Union Caucasienne des Naphtes in Paris in 1921, Nitag in Berlin in 1922 and one year later, in 1923, the United Oil Company in London—all as subsidiaries of the Copenhagen company. In the Paris Union, with a share capital of 200,000 francs, Marguerite Rouvier, M. D. Dembo and M. S. Bruni sat on the board. Marguerite Rouvier was the widow of the former finance and prime minister Maurice Rouvier, a renowned patron of the arts. Aron and David Kahan, as well as a Mr. Trachtenberg, were the directors. Companies named Dembo and Trachtenberg had already been partners of the Kahans in Baku. In Paris, Abram Schirman, the brother of the Nitag employee Boris Schirman, represented the Union. Aron wrote in his memoirs that he had hired Abram Schirman, who was looking for work at the time, for the Parisian business. It was also at that time that the public tank facility CIM, Compagnie Industrielle Maritime Stockage et Services Pétroliers, in Le Havre was completed. "I was the *first* in France who rented tank space from CIM," Aron claimed. "The Union Caucasienne des Naphtes held a special meeting last week for increasing capital from 200,000 francs to 1,000,000 francs," the *Petroleum Times* reported on April 2, 1927, and on October 8 of the same year—that the company had changed its name to Union Generale des Naphtes and made a net profit of 36,274 francs in 1926/1927. In June 1928 it had increased its share capital a second time, now to five million francs.

In 1928, its director Aron Kahan, sitting in Berlin, developed a master plan for the Union in Paris, in view of the new constellations on the global market that threatened the Kahans' companies. The Big Sisters were facing new competition on the European market from Soviet imports and derivative products. They protected themselves against this by forming cartels and buying derivative patents. France, as a country without its own oil reserves, countered the Big Sisters' dictates that year with economic policy measures. France had been importing cheap oil from the Soviet Union from 1924. In 1928, the French government passed a law about national stock reserves for times of crisis and war, requiring the retention of a three-month supply calculated on the basis of sales in the previous year—an easy matter for larger companies, but a burden for smaller ones, of which there were many in France. According to Aron, the Union, which was one of the larger companies—like the Kahans' companies earlier in Baku—aimed at buying the products of the small companies through third parties, thus increasing their sales quotas, and required reserve stocks, thereby squeezing them into a financial corner and then offering to sell them the stocks and the right to import. Under Aron's direction, the stock reserve became an instrument for holding his own in a cut-throat competition, a means of cleaning up the market and strengthening his own business. The mavericks in the Kahan oil business were apparently defying the Big Sisters in the European markets.

"In the twenties, the Kahan family set up a company in Western Europe to market oil," wrote Arusia. "Its center was Berlin. The head of the concern, Aron Kahan, suggested bringing oil through the Bay of Haifa to Eretz Israel. The running of the enterprise was put in the hands of David Ettinger." Although this came about in 1925, it was not easy to implement Aron's idea, he said, because Shell was effectively monopolizing oil imports into Palestine, and the British Mandate government did not want a Jewish competitor. However, the Kahans were granted a license. In September 1925, the Official Gazette of the Government of Palestine reported the founding of the United of London with David Ettinger as its local representative. Thus, the subsidiary, Yorshei Chaim Cohen [Chaim Kahan's Successors], was registered in Haifa. Arusia said that, when the company's first deliveries of gasoline arrived in Eretz Israel via Egypt, Shell had reacted by lowering the prices. Under David Ettinger's direction, a few months after the company was founded, a more than 300-metre-long pipeline with a diameter of three and a half inches (just under nine centimeters) was laid on the seabed of Haifa Bay parallel to the road from Haifa to Acre. The *Circulaire Mensuelle* of the Ottoman Bank in Istanbul and the Jewish Telegraphic

Agency reported that the United owned three tanks, each with a capacity of 500 tons, for storing gasoline, kerosene and lubricating oils, with connections to a pipeline so that the oil could be pumped directly from the ships into the tanks. The pipeline made unloading and shipping easier and more profitable. The first delivery by this route was made in 1927 from Constanza in Romania, Arusia wrote, and Shell, once again, drastically reduced its prices to undercut the new competition.

The drawings on sheet eleven in Arusia's picture story are divided into two columns and three rows, six fields in total. The pictures in the left-hand column project optimism, those in the right-hand column, depression. In the first field, one hand holds a sack of money, bulging with 500,000 Reichsmarks and next to it, the *Handelsblatt* of February 1927 reporting from London that the shares of the United were in great demand, "fourteen times oversubscribed." In the second field, labeled "1928," there is a yawning void with nothing to be seen. Beneath it, in the third field, is a drawing of match-stick pyramids, steeply set up and delicately linked, which collapse like a house of cards in the fourth. In the third and last line, an Armenian joke serves as a caption under the two fields: "how different the view from the desert to the pyramid … / than from the pyramid to the desert. …" On the next page, page twelve, the tanker *Grete Glad*, which was still sailing on the calm Baltic Sea at the beginning of 1927, got into stormy waters. The commentary: "… and luck was so close. …"

When the competition with the Big Sisters intensified on the European market in 1928, the United ran into financial difficulties. It could not maintain its prices because of the fierce price war in England. As a result of oversupply on the market and dumping prices for the Soviet oil, the profit margin was too small. For the first time, the company was in the red. In 1929 things seemed to be on the upswing, but already during the following year it became clear that bankruptcy was inevitable. The COC was primarily affected, but other companies linked to it and to the United were affected, too.

The Kahans then sold the Paris Union to the French Petrofina for 350,000 dollars, to pay off the debts of the United and the COC, according to Aron. Next they lost Chaim Kahan Successors in Haifa. On April 12, 1930, the COC sold its subsidiary in Palestine to the Egyptian branch of the Anglo-Persian Oil for 22,500 pounds sterling. The purchase agreement stipulates that the Kahans were obligated to cease all activity in the Palestinian oil business for the next fifty years. However, the sale of the Haifa-based company could not avert the bankruptcy of the parent company. The COC became insolvent, which also affected L. C. Glad & Co. The Glad family had to sell their villa in Hellerup, a suburb of Copenhagen, and their summer house on the north coast of the island of Zealand. The company had to be restructured.

On sheet thirteen, Arusia's picture story shows a rooster, the trademark of the COC, stretched out exhausted on an armchair, a burning cigarette in its beak; in front of it a flaming spirit stove, accompanied by the sentence: "they have earned from spirit," which can also be understood in the sense of "they have earned to be burned by spirit." In the fall of 1931, the United and the COC filed for liquidation simultaneously, but before this could actually be finalized, a group of Norwegian shipowners, creditors of the COC, demanded that it declare bankruptcy instead of being liquidated. The company agreed to this and filed for bankruptcy in early March 1932, but did not accept the amount of nine million Danish kroner in claims for unfulfilled freight contracts. There was a trial at the Danish Maritime and Commercial Court in Copenhagen, from which the COC emerged with a settlement due to lack of clear evidence regarding the amount of the damages.

In the course of the collapse of the COC and its subsidiaries, *Nitag* in Berlin became insolvent, too. The COC's shares collapsed, adding to the distress caused by the strengthening of the Benzene Association. In December 1931, Aron tried to arrange Nitag's sale. The American company Standard Oil Company of Indiana, Stanolind for short, intended to acquire a 4.5 million Reichsmark stake in Nitag through its subsidiary Pan American Petroleum and Transport Co. The *Frankfurter Zeitung* reported, quoting experts, that in view of the threat of a petroleum duty on imports into the United States, Stanolind wanted to expand its market for oil products from Venezuela to Europe. In response to the global economic crisis, the American government, under President Hoover, began to regulate economic activities in the USA, for the first time since 1931. It was controlling production volumes in the oil industry in order to stop overproduction and falling prices. In particular, the states with large oil reserves in the southwest of the USA imposed import duties on foreign oil imports. American companies that produced in the Gulf of Mexico switched to the European market in the face of these price increases. In this situation, Aron and David moved from the Board of Management to the executive. In their time of need, they took the helm themselves. The Banking House Hardy & Co. and the Kahan family worked closely together; the shares of the German minority owners were to be "pooled." In order to accommodate Stanolind, the bank—instead of the owners and without referring to the Kahans by name— asked the Prussian Ministry of Trade and Commerce to waive the capital tax that was levied when a corporation changed owners and names. The Ministry was prepared to reduce the tax by half. But then Stanolind withdrew and the investment failed, perhaps because it did not want to compete with its sister, the Standard Oil Company of New Jersey, which had a strong presence on the European market. In any case, after the withdrawal of Stanolind, the Nitag shares remained with the credit provider, the Banking House Hardy & Co.

After Nitag's bankruptcy, David and Aron Kahan no longer had the opportunity to rebuild the company in Berlin unlike Carl Frederik Glad in Copenhagen. They had lost the first generation of their companies to Soviet Russia. In Germany, they were strangers, Jewish refugees from Eastern Europe, who encountered hostility whether they were entrepreneurs or paupers. The resentment grew into violent antisemitism towards Jews at the end of the Weimar Republic, when the Nazis gained more and more influence on society, politics and the economy. The migrants were in the crosshairs even earlier and more intensely than the German Jews, even though as foreigners they were initially better protected legally. Antisemitic prejudices were fixated on them, and they were branded the quintessential foreigner.

Asked during the restitution proceedings, in January 1955, why he had already left his post as director of Nitag at the end of 1932, David Kahan had his lawyer state that he had resigned from the board of management because he feared that the growing strength of the Nazis would soon make it impossible to obtain public contracts if he remained in this position as a Jew. These fears had been intensified by the pressure major banks inflicted at the time, threatening to stop credits for the pre-financing of extensive gasoline and oil imports under these conditions. "Nitag could only exist in close cooperation with the authorities, because it was dependent to a large extent on import permits. Even the sale of the products and the utilization of the tank facilities could only be successful in friendly cooperation with the authorities. A silent boycott of Jewish companies and the relevant Jewish managers of such companies had begun long before Hitler came to power." In contrast to David, Aron remained director of Nitag until March 1933. Did the brothers judge the situation differently, or did David only find a pretext for his relatively early departure from Nitag?

Plans to increase the state control of the oil industry were publicly debated, under the Brüning government, from the beginning of 1930, just as before the First World War. The battle over petrol prices had unleashed an increasingly nationalistic debate, which motivated members of the Reichstag to call for the introduction of a trading monopoly for fuels. The Reich government pursued a decidedly protectionist course towards foreign interests. It introduced the mineral oil tax and increased import duties. Influential government agencies, like the Reichspost and the Reichskraftsprit [Reich Fuel] appeared on the scene as governmental trading agencies in the oil industry. A new player in state oil production was added in the form of Preußische Bergwerks-und Hütten-AG, Preussag for short. The government was gradually taking a firmer grip on the private energy industry. At the same time, the fuel convention system was being undermined. In May 1932, its members tolerated an inflated valuation of the Benzene Association, which became the German market leader overnight with a quota of twenty-seven percent. At the same time, an oil conference of the German Geological Society in Hanover turned out to be a nationalistic advertising campaign for a self-sufficient Germany in terms of energy. Experts spread the word that the country was rich in oil deposits and that one only had to find ways and means to exploit them. One of the participants at that conference was Dr. Karl Leising, a brother of Hermann Leising, who was a Kahan confidant, employed by Preussag and—unlike the latter—had a National Socialist orientation. Thus, Aron and David Kahan might have quickly learned about the results of the conference from internal sources.

In that year the governments changed three times. Under Reich Chancellor von Papen between June and December, the self-sufficiency debate heated up. During the election campaign for the Reichstag elections at the end of July, conditions on the streets resembled civil war. A few months later, in September 1932, the economic conference of the NSDAP took up the subject of oil and passed a resolution about the expansion of so-called "domestic" crude oil production. These tendencies must have had a disturbing effect on Jewish entrepreneurs, whose creeping displacement from the German economy had already begun anyway. Polish Jews or stateless persons, employing workers from the same cultural group, had a particularly difficult time under these circumstances. When their security and room for maneuver as economic citizens and as human beings was dwindling in the spring of 1933, the Kahans fled westward once again, but tried to continue to operate in Nazi Germany as long as possible, by means of confidants.

In October 1936, Hermann Göring became Minister of The Economy. He enforced the banishment of Jews from the German economy. The Kahans' commercial bank, Hardy & Co., which had become dependent on the Dresdener Bank after the world economic and banking crisis and was gradually "aryanized" by the Nazi fiscal policy, was to be ninety-percent owned by the Dresdener Bank by 1936. In the previous year, 1935, it had sold Nitag to Wintershall AG. Wintershall, originally a drilling company for the production of potash salt, today Germany's largest producer of crude oil and natural gas, had only been involved in oil production for a few years. "Through the acquisition of Nitag, Wintershall AG has secured for itself an extensive tap mechanism for the sale of its gasoline production," reported the magazine *Öl und Kohle* in its "Corporate News" column. In 1936, Nitag, which now belonged to Wintershall, also incorporated the Rheinische Naphta Industrie AG, and in 1938 the company was renamed Nitag Deutsche Treibstoffe AG. It owned 1,660 gas stations that year, far more than double the number in 1935.

As oil entrepreneurs and migrants, the Kahans operated in the global market. While they were forced by political conditions to become mobile again after 1933, they continued to maintain the unity of business and family life under patriarchal leadership, hiring mainly, like before, coreligionists and compatriots as employees. In this way, they fitted into the pattern of traditional ethno-denominational family and business structures, which had been so typical until the end of the nineteenth century and important for the emergence of transnational trade. The Kahans had agents at all business locations. They would either activate existing contacts, or send employees. Everywhere, they would contact banks, open accounts and present their business concepts to financial institutions for the purpose of borrowing; they would obtain legal advice about corporate practices, the market and prices, from among Jewish migrants if possible; they would win supporters with influence and sponsors with capital from within the local population. While David always put the brakes on, Aron kept the capital flowing. The enormous expansion of the family business between 1919 and 1928, in barely ten years, had been his work. If a company was doing well, he would borrow from it, invest the capital, thereby obtaining a new business, and hire employees.

Little can be learned from the archives about what happened to the family businesses after the collapse of the COC network. Aron hardly ever said a word about it in his memoirs. He mentioned Rapide, a French company that was already depicted in Arusia's 1928 graphic as a subsidiary of the Union, as well as Nohaka in Amsterdam and subsidiaries in Latvia and Lithuania, which had provided them with the most income until the beginning of the Second World War. This is probably why Moshe Ettinger had called the family "Nohaks" in his wedding speech in the fall of 1932. What has been preserved are copies of some letters from the spring of 1939, when it was already foreseeable that Germany would involve the world in a huge war. According to these, Aron was making plans and David was reporting business transactions.

In mid-February 1939, Aron presented a proposal to a certain Mr. A. Aufhäuser in New York, on four closely typed pages, to jointly build and operate a network of gas stations and auto repair shops, first on Long Island and then in the New York region. He wanted to invest in the USA, thus creating a refuge for himself, and also provide jobs for his nephew and other Jewish refugees from Europe. "Alfred Aufhaeuser ... started the petroleum wax business, which is now owned by me. He did own several service stations for a short while in the 1940s," his nephew, the New York entrepreneur Keith Aufhauser, wrote to me. His grandfather, Professor David Aufhäuser, had been a well-known chemist in Hamburg, where he ran a laboratory making quality measurements for oils. The Kahans had probably already known David Aufhäuser and his son Alfred from there. After 1933, Alfred, who was twenty-nine years old at the time and belonged to the generation of Aron's nephews, had fled like Aron and Zina to Paris and from there to the USA in 1939. Perhaps they had been in contact with each other during their Parisian exile.

One month later, in mid-March 1939, Aron wrote to his relative and former Nitag employee Jakob Rabinowitsch, who was now in London, and told him that his attempt to export to distant countries was well under way. Nohaka had succeeded in selling two hundred barrels of gasoline to England, where the buyer had already opened a letter of credit, that is, concluded an agency agreement with a bank; the trade was thus legally and financially secured. A company from the Gold Coast (today's Ghana), with administration in Liverpool, had ordered fifty canisters of gasoline and petroleum on approval. He was also going to have lubricating oils added. Through the Liverpool company, he had already obtained information about the use of oil products and prices in West Africa, including freight on passenger liners. The shipping company Elder Dempster & Company in Liverpool had already made him a favorable offer. He was asking Rabinowitsch in London to conduct further research, to inquire about additional freight and return loads. He himself had already corresponded with companies in Madagascar regarding this question. Aron envisaged a trade with the British colonies, the territories of present-day countries Sierra Leone, Nigeria, Gambia and Ghana. The freighters would pass by there anyway, if they were avoiding the Suez Canal, he wrote. From Liverpool, overseas trade would be conducted in the same economic and currency area, making things easier. In his opinion, cement or asphalt were possible as additional export goods, whilst corn or exotic hardwoods could feature as return freight. He already had initial information, but was asking Rabinowitsch to obtain more from the representatives of the colonies in England, enquire about the ports, prices and businesses through the Bank of British West Africa, with which Nohaka had business relations. Aron concluded: "all these plans, the chartering of the ships, outbound freights and return loads may, of course, seem quite fantastic. But that does not mean that they should not continue to be pursued with full vigor."

It remains uncertain what became of the project with Alfred Aufhäuser in New York. The plan to enter into trade relations with West Africa could probably not be implemented before the beginning of the Second World War. But what happened before that? How did the Kahans earn their living in the meantime, from 1930 to 1939? What is the explanation for the almost ten-year information gap in the archives about the family's activities? The Danish historian Morten F. Larsen found out that the COC had a successor in whose activities the Kahans were also involved. In late 1930, even before the COC's network of companies collapsed, Danish wholesalers, owners of the trading company H. C. Gildsig's Eftf. who owned filling stations in Copenhagen and environs, founded the A/S Gica AG with a share capital of 60,000 kroner. They wanted to build a network of filling stations in Denmark, together with a businessman by the name of Behr Katz, also known as Bernhardt Cohn, and Elias Feldmann, until then an employee of the COC and a trusted representative of the Kahans. The Gildsig filling stations collaborated with a purchasing company, which had turned on the Big Sisters cartel and was being supplied by the COC. The name A/S Gica is also linked to the COC. It is an abbreviation of **Gi**lsig and **Ca**ucasian. Gica took over a large tank depot from the COC and, following the COC's bankruptcy, established its headquarters in the COC's former office in Gothersgade. From early 1932 Gica had an exclusive contract for gasoline deliveries with Nitag, which was to run until 1937. Gica functioned as the successor to the COC without assuming its central role as the parent company in the corporate network. Carl Frederik Glad had already been identified by the competition in July 1932 as the manager who was pulling the strings in the background. In mid-1935, when the company fell into a crisis and Elias Feldmann left his post, Glad officially took over the management. Was Gica Aron Kahan's idea and was he responsible for Gica's exclusive contract with Nitag?

Various other sources make clear that when the COC bankruptcy became predictable, the Kahans reinvested in six countries—Latvia, Lithuania, the Netherlands, France, Germany and Palestine. The companies that emerged from these investments formed the basis for a new network of companies that the family controlled from Paris in the 1930s. In Latvia, where Rubanito had been working steadily since the early 1920s, the Kahans gained a creative collaborator, Aron Nisse, with whom they founded a second company in Riga—Latruss. The companies operated according to a division of labor. In 1937, the *Der Osteuropa-Markt*, the organ of the Economic Institute for Russia and the Eastern States in Königsberg, reported about the two companies that jointly held the import monopoly for Soviet oils. They were backed by Nohaka in Amsterdam and an oil company in Paris, both financed by the Kahan brothers. Aron and David, although revolution refugees, apparently did not shy away from doing business with the Bolsheviks and, like the Benzene Association and other buyers, benefited from Soviet dumping prices. Rubanito processed the oils in its own refinery. Latruss sold them in its Latvian network of gas stations.

Nisse, a farmer's son from Jēkabpils, southeast of Riga, about ten years younger than Aron and David, was an enterprising self-made man. During the First World War he used to train Tsarist military armored car drivers in Petrograd, such as the futuristic poet Vladimir Mayakovsky, according to his daughters' recollection. After the war, he earned his money on the black market by converting military vehicles for civilian traffic, for which he served a jail term. Afterwards, he went to Latvia, which had become independent, where he imported and processed coffee together with his brother-in-law, the engineer Fritz Berner, until they both joined the Kahans in the oil business. At the end of the 1920s, they were so successful that they took a stake in their Riga businesses and became the majority shareholder with sixty percent of the shares, recounted Nisse's youngest daughter, the American philosopher Judith Shklar, in an interview with the historian Judith Walzer about her life story in 1981. She spoke of the Kahans as decadent financiers, who from a distance, in Paris, had not paid much attention to their business in Riga. The Nisses were so wealthy in the early 1930s that the family moved into a large posh apartment on the elegant Elisabeth Street, Ruth, the older sister, who was seven or eight years old at the time, told her daughter Marion Kane, who posted her mother's memoirs on her website. Family photos on the website prove that the Kahans and Nisses also knew each other personally.

"They both enjoyed making money, but not its accumulation," Judith Shklar described the business philosophy of her father and uncle. "So they decided to buy a whole lot of things, and their principle was simple—since it had worked for them before—you buy a controlling minority share and set up the business." This was in line with Aron's and David's approach. While still in Berlin, they developed a plan, together with Nisse, to invest capital in a chocolate factory in Palestine, where the Kahans were now denied the oil business. Thus, in October 1933, Elite was founded in Ramat Gan, near Tel Aviv, under the leadership of the confectioner Eliyahu Fromchenko, who had founded Laimas in Riga. Both brands are still known beyond the borders of Latvia and Israel. The Kahans now appointed David Ettinger as their representative and senior employee at Elite. The company expanded in the thirties. At the beginning of 1941, Elite acquired the majority of shares in Priman, a company producing canned vegetables. The Kahans were shareholders until the 1970s.

In April 1931, shortly after the COC's bankruptcy, the Kahans acquired the majority of shares in Nohaka in Amsterdam. The business with the Netherlands had developed gradually during the 1920s, as Aron later explained this purchase. With Nohaka, the family made itself independent of German lenders. According to Moshe Ettinger, Nohaka was the family's beacon of hope in the fall of 1932. At that time, the idea was to send him to the company in Amsterdam. From May 1931, the engineer Benno Hanemann had been running the business in the Netherlands and was joined by his brother Moses, also called Moritz or Mau in 1937. The Hanemanns came from a Jewish family of wood wholesalers in Memel. The First World War had prevented Moses from graduating from high school. From the early twenties, he was living in Berlin, studying and working in a bank. It was there that Aron and David might have met him.

Nohaka had been founded in October 1930 by the Dutchman Johannes H. Gaukstert, a banker, associate of the Banking House Patijn, van Notten & Co, who took over the financing of the company. It was located in the banking and business district of Amsterdam, on the Heerengracht and Koningsplein between the Heeren and Singelgracht, and from December 1930 at 14 Koningsplein. The building no longer stands. The Koningsplein is a bustling plaza with heavy traffic. The streetcar runs there, and the flower market is right next door. The building Nohaka moved into in August 1939, 487 Heerengracht, looks more magnificent, more powerful than the building on the Koningsplein. Nowadays it is surrounded by banks and well-known organizations, such as the Handelsbank and VW Finance. Nohaka's board consisted initially of Gaukstert and Lolia Kahan. At the end of 1932, Baron Theodore de Günzburg, who lived in Amsterdam after fleeing Russia, joined them, followed in 1939 by Aron Kahan. When Benno Hanemann emigrated to the United States in the spring of 1940, his Brother Moses took over the leadership and Gaukstert became his deputy. Until the invasion of the German Wehrmacht in May 1940, Nohaka was importing mainly gasoline and petroleum from the USA. Before the war, Standard Oil and Shell accounted for ninety percent of the gasoline imports to the Netherlands, followed by Nohaka with no more than one percent, and only half a percent of the petroleum imports. But the company wrote positive balance sheets. Nohaka's turnover at that time amounted to well over one million Dutch guilders.

The files about the expropriation by the German occupying power in the Amsterdam Institute for Holocaust Research state that Nohaka's share capital during the war was 500,000 guilders, one fifth of which had been fully paid up. More than ninety percent of the shares were in Lisbon and Palestine at the time. Therefore, the Dutch Corporation for the Liquidation of Enterprises had no access to them, which did not prevent it from handing over the business to a trustee. The trustee, a Dutch Nazi, had forwarded the names of the owners to the Corporation for Expropriation in The Hague, to which the company was assigned: accordingly, Zina Kahan owned almost half of the shares, and her son Lolia, almost a quarter. Aron's and David's shares amounted to a few thousand and were negligible. The remainder, also just under a quarter, belonged to the family in Palestine. Aron apparently wanted to provide primarily for Zina and her children in this way, but also for the rest of the family. According to Moses Hanemann's statement in 1964 to a New York lawyer, Nohaka originally belonged to Aron Kahan, Zina Kahan, "and perhaps the deceased brother of Aron Kahan—David Kahan in Tel Aviv"; how many shares they each held was unknown to him.

Smaller company foundations were added to the larger ones. "Nohaka owned 90% of the shares of a company called Litpetrol, domiciled in Klaipėda (Memel), Lithuania, with a capital of Lit[as] 100,000 = $10,000, and furthermore owner of 90% of the shares of Litoil, domiciled at Kaunas, Lithuania, with a capital of Lit[as] 50,000 = $5,000," Moses Hanemann remembered after the war. "The shares of these two companies were not in hands of N.V. Nohaka, but they were under trust with the manager of these companies. The intrinsic value of the two companies was a multiple of the nominal capital."

The building in which Litpetrol had its headquarters in Memel at 20 Marktstrasse [Market Street], is a four-story-high cube, built in oriental style of light stone; it still rises majestically above all the other buildings on the Turgaus gatvė. After fleeing from Berlin in early summer 1933, Aron founded a network of gas stations in Paris, where the Kahans had controlled the oil importer Rapide since 1926. The network was modelled on the Nitag in Germany, Gica in Denmark, Latruss in Latvia—the Cie des Carburants du Centre, or CCC for short, with headquarters at 17 Rue de la Bienfaissance and a branch in Orleans, which was headed by a young migrant from Moscow, Emmanuel Racine.

Even before the COC's declaration of bankruptcy and before Aron and David had withdrawn from the board of Nitag and taken over its management in early February 1931, a new oil import company, Europäische Tanklager- und Transport AG, also known as Eurotank, appeared on the German market. It was founded in Berlin. Its share capital was initially 2.4 million Reichsmark. The Kahans left only a few traces of their involvement, but Baruch Kahan was on the board until spring 1933, more than two years later. In 1934, Israel Estrin appeared on the scene as a shareholder, according to the Commercial Register. Estrin had already been working as an accountant at Nitag for eleven years, when David and Aron took out a life insurance policy for him in April 1932, and a few months later, at the end of October 1932, gave him power of attorney. After the Kahans' flight from Germany until his own dismissal in 1936 and flight to South America in 1937, he had acted as their proxy, according to an assertion by the Deutsche Nitag during the restitution proceedings the Kahan Vermögensverwaltung claimed against the company. Estrin held a quarter of a million Reichsmarks worth of shares in Eurotank. Where did the money come from? The authorized signatory himself had hardly any assets when he left Germany. During the restitution proceedings, he merely claimed back the fifty percent "transfer tax" on the settlement of 12,500 Reichsmarks that he had received as severance pay upon his dismissal in 1936. It cannot be ruled out that he had operated with the Kahans' capital, financed from the mortgages of the two buildings at 37 Schlüterstrasse and 32 Wielandstrasse from Hardy & Co. The mortgage was 260,000 Reichsmark, the share control package 250,000. Did the Kahans want to save their lives' work in Germany with Eurotank? The 1935 audit report by German Trust spoke of Eurotank deals to put Nitag back on its feet.

When the Banking House Hardy & Co. became the property of the Dresdener Bank, which had sold Nitag to Wintershall, Estrin had left, and other Jewish employees had been ousted from the company and the bank, Eurotank listed the share control package anonymously as bank property. It is striking that not only was Hardy & Co. the commercial bank of both companies, Nitag and Eurotank, but that their boards were almost identical in composition of their non-Jewish members. Thus, Hermann Leising, a leading employee of the bank, was also a leading employee of the Kahans and had held, temporarily, positions of responsibility in all three companies; Aron and David remained in contact with him throughout the war.

The Kahans' contact person at the Banking House Hardy & Co, and also director of their shipping company Limicana, Dr. Hermann Leising, managed

Nitag in 1934/1935 and Eurotank for ten years, from 1931 to 1941. His son Klaus, born in 1927, whom I visited in his hometown in Lower Saxony, told me that he had once accompanied his father on a flight from Berlin to Hamburg, a sensation for the ten-year-old that he never forgot; his father had shown him around the refinery. Both wartime antagonists interrogated Hermann Leising, during the war about his activities after 1933—first the Nazis and then the US authorities, for "doing business with the enemy." In 1941 he was summarily dismissed and sentenced to six months in prison; later his assets were confiscated in the USA. Hermann Leising testified as a witness on behalf of leading Nitag employees from the Kahan family during the restitution proceedings. After the war, he met with Aron in Paris. Did Leising possibly transfer assets to the USA not only for himself, but also for the Kahans?

It had been assumed within the Kahan family that Wintershall was Nitag's sole successor. In reality, Wintershall had taken over only seventy-five percent of the filling station network from Nitag, while Eurotank got the remaining twenty-five percent. The former Nitag filling stations were responsible for selling Eurotank products on the German market. Eurotank acquired the Nitag subsidiaries Debag and Caucasische Handelsgesellschaft and the three tankers *Ch. N. Kahan*, *Malkah* and *Grete Glad*. In the thirties, they operated from the tank facilities in Wilhelmshaven and had a branch in Hamburg and trade relations with Scandinavia as well as the USA. From spring 1933, an American, William Rhodes Davis, was the owner of Eurotank. Like the Kahans and Glad, Davis was one of the outsiders in the oil business, and was a rising star. At the end of 1932, supported by the First National Bank of Boston, now Bank of Boston, he founded the Foreign Oil Company, Foil for short, to develop trade with Latin America and Europe. Davis financed Eurotank with loans from the Boston Bank. He developed Eurotank into an integrated oil company with a refinery, a condition of his purchase of the company, which he implemented in the 1930s. But this could only happen with the support of the highest Nazi authorities. Davis proved to be not only an unscrupulous businessman, but also an antisemite and a Nazi supporter.

From 1933, Eurotank was expanding its capacities. By the end of 1934 the refinery was already located in the New Oil Harbor on the left bank of the Elbe. In 1935 it doubled its original share capital, which now amounted to five million Reichsmark. The plant became one of the most modern in the Third Reich, supplying the German Luftwaffe and war fleet, being a compliant instrument of the military machinery until the USA entered the war. Davis negotiated exclusive oil supply contracts for Nazi Germany with the Mexican government.

He took advantage of the Nazis' protectionist financial policies, which controlled the foreign exchange trade making it difficult for foreign companies to transfer their profits from Germany. With loans from the Bank of Boston, Eurotank purchased crude oil in America and Mexico, imported it, processed it in Hamburg and sold the products in Germany and on the free markets of Scandinavia. With the proceeds from the German market it bought technical equipment, which it sold on the global market, receiving foreign currency that was convertible into dollars to pay back the loans in Boston. Key employees were the twin brothers Carl and Werner von Clemm, who stemmed from Austrian nobility, had relatives in the Nazi elite and, like Leising, were both representatives of the Banking House Hardy & Co.—Carl in Berlin and Werner in New York, where he had been living since the early 1920s and was married to an American banker's daughter. Carl was a member of the board of Eurotank and head of the subsidiary Eurohandel, which brought foreign currency to the Third Reich by exporting diamonds, semi-precious stones and costume jewelry to the USA, from which the Reich also profited. Foreign currencies were under strict economic control. Even the National Socialists had a need for freely convertible currencies, so that the German control authorities overlooked currency offences. The 1941 audit report by German Trust expressly ignored Eurotank's foreign exchange violations, arguing that the wider global political situation made investigations abroad very difficult. Werner von Clemm also worked closely with his brother in this business and, after having previously been employed by Davis, he founded and managed Eurohandel's partner in New York, the Pioneer Import Corporation. In addition, Eurotank benefited from compulsory sales of Jewish companies. Like Leising, who also worked for Eurohandel, Carl von Clemm was accused by the Nazi authorities two years after the beginning of the war, as a member of the board of directors and shareholder of Eurotank, of obscure transactions with enemy foreign countries. He was accused of improper personal enrichment and dismissed in 1941. His brother was prosecuted in New York after the war.

At the end of 1935, there was a trial before the court of arbitration in Berlin, the headquarters of Eurotank, between the American entrepreneur Davis and the Kahans' Danish partner Carl Frederik Glad, concerning the companies Foil and Gica. Eurotank was in crisis at the time, and Davis, in search of the causes, had discovered the preferential treatment of Gica through the exclusive contract with *Nitag*. Glad won. At the same time, Davis, who had gotten into a crisis with Foil, began to establish a new base in Europe, first founding a company in London, Crusader Petroleum Industries with Carl von Clemm at the helm, and a few months later, in April 1936, creating a second company, Parent Petroleum Interests. He acquired new capital and, together with its partner, the Thames Haven Company, built up an oil empire based on Parent, in competition with the Joint British Marketing Shell-Mex, which included twenty-one networked companies in the USA, Mexico, Denmark, Germany, Norway and Sweden. These included the Eurotank refinery, a service station network in Germany, port facilities in Malmö, Sweden, and tank depots in Finland, which supplied the three Baltic states. When Davis resold his Parent shares under pressure from his British partners in June 1938, he received, in return, Parent's property in Germany and Scandinavia. In the fall of 1938, Davis, now represented by Crusader in London, appealed against Glad and Gica before the Court of King's Bench, a civil court. At the same time, the Kahan brothers, together with Jakob Rabinowitsch, who had moved from Nitag to Eurotank in Hamburg and who had been an employee of Davis from 1933 to 1938, negotiated the purchase of a small factory in Denmark, the H. C. Frost Factory in the small town of Strib near Fredericia on Funen, which was heavily in debt. Glad was to take over the management while Rabinowitsch was to be employed by him. The negotiations dragged on until early 1939, but failed because of the lack of approval by the main shareholder. The plant was sold to the Danish Esso, that is, the Standard Oil. Rabinowitsch emigrated to London instead of Denmark. Glad lost the case in the appeal proceedings. Gica went bankrupt. This marked the end of the long-standing cooperation between Carl Frederik Glad and Aron Kahan, the Danish and the Jewish businessman. What happened between them since the collapse of the COC remains unclear.

The thin bundle of letters from the spring of 1939 in the family archives provides little information about the risky, grueling activities of the Kahan brothers in Paris, shortly before the Nazi Germany carried out its last great aggressive blow before the war, annexing further parts of Bohemia and Moravia as well as the Memelland after the occupation of the Sudetenland in the spring of 1938. These are copies of business letters that David and Aron had sent without mentioning company names to Alfred Aufhäuser in New York, Jakob Rabinowitsch in London, Moritz Hanemann in Amsterdam, and to others, unknown persons—Ch. Karl Kondor in Antwerp, A. Milman in Bucharest and Helge Lühr in Malmö. At least one trace leads once again to Davis and his empire. Helge Lühr (or Lyhr), whom the Kahans were supplying with oil at the time, was a Norwegian who was employed by Foil. He managed the tank depot Skanditank in Malmö, which was the Scandinavian distributor for Eurotank's oil products in Hamburg. I first learned about Aron's function at Eurotank from postwar documents.

Aron's memoirs vouch for the fact that in May 1939, the Kahans sold Rapide to the French company Desmarais Frères for $100,000. The family was able to live on the proceeds for several years. The Kahans' last major financial transaction in Europe before their third expulsion, was probably the acquisition of Nohaka shares in February 1940. These were invested in the Rapide company, thereby paying Rapide's debts to Nohaka.

CHAPTER 19

The Third Expulsion. Paris, Lisbon

In May 1933, Zina fled to Paris to live with her daughter Gita. Aron followed her a few weeks later. Paris, city of cities was a migration center like Berlin. At the beginning of the twenties it had been a marketplace for trading Baku oil industry shares, as well as art and other treasures. There, too, all sorts of Russian revolution refugees had gathered, opening cafés and stores, founding publishing houses, associations and magazines and creating a refuge, like in Berlin. After the currency reform, many had moved on to Paris, because Berlin had become too expensive. By the beginning of the 1930s, most of them had run out of money, even in France, so that they were forced to earn their living as unskilled laborers. After the end of the Weimar Republic, new refugees from Germany had joined them—those persecuted because of their origin or for political reasons. The Russian refugees had Nansen or Polish passports, while the German ones had forged documents at best. "The Russians have established themselves better than we have," says a character in Remarque's novel *The Night in Lisbon*. "But they were fifteen years ahead of us in emigration. And fifteen years of misfortune are a long time and provide a lot of experience." The exiles were part of the Parisian population, but, like in Berlin, they remained unsettled, in limbo, in the shadows, a community within itself; they would sit on the park benches in the Jardin du Luxembourg, frequent the large cafés on the Boulevard du Montparnasse or the small ones in the Quartier Latin and Montmartre; they were living in seclusion, in furnished rented rooms and apartments.

Following the humiliations and ordeals of the second expulsion, Zina arrived in Paris together with Sasha and Lily, probably upset and exhausted. In her restitution application, the family doctor, Dr. Leon Dinkin, who, like her, had fled from Berlin to Paris, testified that in June 1933 Zina was suffering from "massive heart problems." Zina was fifty-two at the time. He also testified that Aron's shock about his displacement had caused him visual disturbances associated with high blood pressure. The only thing Aron mentioned in his memoirs about the Parisian exile was his eye disease. For years he had firmly believed that, when he witnessed the departing of his brother Pinchas's soul in November 1917, he saw a small human-like figure flying out of him. Only twenty years later did he realize what had caused that phenomenon: it was probably the first bruise in his eye caused by the shock. In 1938/1939, there was another hemorrhage, which developed into a disease that ultimately became the greatest misfortune of his life because of the outrageous negligence of a professor who had been particularly highly recommended to him.

After his arrival in Paris, Aron began to build on old relationships and open new businesses as an "oilman of European stature," as he called himself, with Nohaka in Amsterdam and the two Baltic companies behind him. As founder of the Cie des Carburants du Centre (CCC) and Rapide, the international entrepreneur, unlike most migrants, did not need a work permit. The investments legitimized his stay.

Zina arrived with two lifts. Most of her furniture was left in Berlin. As during her first escape, she had a place to go to. Gita and Monia were living at the time at 19 Boulevard de la Somme in the Seventeenth *arrondissement* and they took her in. Monia Ripp came from Grodno and had come to Paris in 1925 with a diploma from the Handelshochschule Berlin. First he had lived with his brother Aronchik in a small appartment on Montmartre and then at 14 Rue Jacob. Later his sister Sula had joined them. Rue Jacob runs through the artists', writers' and university quarter of Saint-Germain des-Prés, along the Seine, in the oldest part of Paris, the Sixth *arrondissement*. Gita was reunited with the three siblings there. Immediately after their arrival in June 1933, Aron and Zina rented an apartment at 20 Avenue Mac Mahon, a few blocks from the Boulevard de la Somme towards the center, in the same *arrondissement*. Gita and Monia gave up their apartment and moved in with Aron and Zina. In his application for restitution from 1933, Monia listed 20 Avenue Mac Mahon as their address. The family lived under this arrangement for the next few years—not in the Fourteenth or the Fifteenth *arrondissement* south of the center, where the Russian migrants were concentrated, but rather in upper middle-class neighborhoods, always centrally, changing apartments several times. In 1933, they moved from Mac Mahon to the vicinity of the Eifel Tower, 6 Rue Jean Carriès in the Seventh *arrondissement*. This way, Aron provided them with a prestigious address in the heart of elegant Paris, in the immediate vicinity of the Faubourg Saint-Germain, where the aristocracy, the financial elite and the assimilated Jewish upper middle class resided, whose salons and soirées Marcel Proust described as "Sodom and Gomorrah." Faubourg Saint-Germain was the epitome of perverted assimilation for Hannah Arendt, who had drawn inspiration from Proust's material for her book on totalitarianism and antisemitism. This had robbed the Jews of all natural political instincts and led to modern social antisemitism taking on "sadistic forms" in the salons of Faubourg-Saint-Germain, beginning at the time of the Dreyfus Affair. Hannah Arendt was a close friend of Kurt Blumenfeld and had gone to school with Rita, Noma's wife, in Königsberg. Like the Kahans and Ripps, she was in Paris as one of the persecuted.

In early November 1933, Chaim Avinoam also reached the French metropolis with his grandparents, parents and sister. His parents stayed, while for the Grandparents Kahan Paris was only a stopover on their way to Palestine. It is being said that Aron wanted it that way. He needed Yasha's work capacity. Yasha was the only nephew who apparently allowed himself to be swayed by Aron at that time. Chaim Avinoam lived with his parents and sister in the Sixteenth *arrondissement*, at 1 Villa George Sand, in an elegant tenement building, constructed in the Haussmann style at the turn of the century. He and his father Yasha described the situation in terms of both compulsion and dependence. "I was completely uprooted there and without sufficient knowledge of the language I could not gain a foothold in the milieu that was completely foreign to me," Yasha explained during the restitution proceedings.

> 18 September 1934. Paris Hell. Department: Letters (dedicated to the Palestinian relatives).

> "Mornin." This is how Lucifer, the Devil in Chief, greeted the head of the Letters Department of a newly opened branch of Hell. "How are you?"

> "Makes me wanna puke, ..." replied the head of department.

With these words begins a scene that fourteen-year-old Chaim Avinoam typed on a typewriter with a German keyboard, a copy of which has been preserved. It provides an insight into his Parisian typing workshop and sheds light on his view of things. The setting is hell. The protagonists are Lucifer, the head of department and some scribes, that is, sinners, who, controlled by Lucifer, answer letters piling up next to them in stacks, but do not know what to write and are therefore sweating blood. But Lucifer remains implacable and rebukes them. The letters are family correspondences. One of the writers, a fat, bald man, in life the general manager of a giant corporation—"500% dividend, best relations"—is wondering what his pious paternal great-grandmother would have said had she known that her great-grandson was burning in hell. Lucifer refers him to the biblical verse that his great-grandmother could have quoted at him: "In the sweat of thy brow shalt thou eat bread." At the end, the scene changes and we see the uncles and aunts, who enjoy a blessed posthumous existence in paradise, drinking nectar and calmly reading the abundant mail that keeps arriving. They are not required to answer.

A few days later, Chaim Avinoam wrote a letter to his Grandparents Kahan in Tel Aviv about his writing workshop, divided into paragraphs, which distinguished between easy and difficult, letters written out of politeness and reports to relatives, which he also categorized into easy and difficult letters, giving them names and enumerating them. He pointed out that for report letters one needed material, but he wasn't a gangster to whom something new happened every day. He had to gather the material, which was time-consuming.

In Chaim Avinoam's fantasy, his own and his father's situation were mixed into a horror vision. In the adolescent's Parisian writings, the fate of the family mutated into a compulsive relationship that threatened to come apart. At the same time, in the fall of 1934, the proceedings for the foreclosure auction of the buildings at 32 Wielandstrasse and 37 Schlüterstrasse had begun in Berlin.

In late 1934, the disagreements among the Parisian Kahans had escalated into open conflict. In a letter, Jonas Rosenberg accused Aron of insulting him in the presence of Roska and Yasha, his daughter and son-in-law, and worse, of refusing him funds from the family treasury and of blocking his access to the family fortune. Jonas Rosenberg had repeatedly asked Aron for money for business and livelihood in Riga to which Aron responded with silence. Jonas accused Aron of cruelty and heartlessness, hatred and boundless anger and was even moved to say that this "affected him psychologically." But then he changed his tone, asked Aron for forgiveness, showed remorse for his sins, especially against his deceased wife Marie—"*Irren ist menschlich* [to err is human]," he quotes in German in the Russian letter. He invoked their bond through Chaim N. Kahan of blessed memory—Aron's father and his own father-in-law, promised to leave Riga, go to Palestine and open a guest house or sanatorium there. Since they obviously could not solve the conflict alone, he called for a rabbinical arbitration court.

A bundle of Hebrew and Russian letters written by Aron Kahan in Paris, Jonas Rosenberg in Paris and Riga, Baruch Kahan in Tel Aviv, and letters from arbitrators, also in Russian, from 1934/1935 document the conflict. Aron and also David, who supported his brother, accepted the proposal, probably in order not to lose their good name in the Jewish world. According to the Jewish tradition, three arbitrators were appointed, at least two of whom were prominent figures in the Russian Paris. The former tobacco entrepreneur from Rostov-on-Don and White Guard politician Abram S. Alperin served as the leading referee. Aron's lawyer was the politician Israel Yefroykin from Kovno, who was advocating Jewish nation-building in the diaspora. A certain Rabbi D. Burshteyn stood up for Jonas. On March 18, 1935, they proposed a settlement: Jonas was to leave the family business and receive compensation. But Jonas refused because the compensation offered seemed too small to him. He turned again to the arbitration court and to his brother-in-law David. His advocate, Rabbi Burshteyn, now made the conflict public, which was certainly damaging to the reputation of Aron and David. In addition, Jonas involved Rabbi Moshe Eisenstadt, a longtime friend and advisor to the family, who was now the head of the Russian migrant community in Paris. Incidentally, Gita and Monia had met at his house. The rabbi was acquainted with Monia's father; both had originated from the Litvak *shtetl* Nesvizh, which today belongs to Belarus. The dispute dragged on for more than a year, until early 1936, when Baruch mediated from Tel Aviv. As Aron's oldest brother and Jonas's co-father—they were connected by the marriage of their children and had grandchildren—he was close to the Kahan and Rosenberg families. His mediation probably brought about an agreement. In March 1935, at the height of the quarrel, after a sixteen-month stay, Yasha and Roska left unloved Paris with their two children. They moved to relatives in Tel Aviv, as Chaim Avinoam had wished. Yasha enjoyed his father's proximity for just over a year. On April 9, 1936, Baruch died at the age of sixty-eight. After Pinchas and Miriam, Baruch was the eldest and the third of the Kahan brothers and sisters to leave this world.

What had turned Aron against Jonas was not only his lax handling of money, but also a personal conflict. As Jonas had already indicated in his letter to Aron, it was about wounds they had inflicted on each other years ago and that now opened up again. Aron accused Jonas of having cheated on his wife Miriam, Aron's sister, for years. Jonas, in turn, had not been able to forgive Aron for leaving Mina, because the marriage had been arranged by the Rosenbergs, according to Raziel Haimi-Cohen, Jonas's grandson. Moreover, Jonas's lover, the widow Anna Kustow, was Mina's sister. Now, after

Miriam's death, Jonas began to distance himself from the family through his liaison with a certain Anna Kazhdan in Riga. Jonas had probably already met the Latvian doctor in the twenties in her sanatorium during a summer retreat in Bilderlingshof on Riga Beach. There is a photograph in the family archives—a print of which is in the YIVO in New York—showing a group of Russian-Jewish migrants gathered around a coffee table, including Anna Kazhdan, Jonas Rosenberg and the couple Simon and Ida Dubnow. The acquaintance with the historian had begun in Berlin and lasted until the late 1930s, when Dubnow lived in Riga while the Kahans resided in Tel Aviv and Paris. The photo was taken before 1933 in Berlin, where Anna Kazhdan had been visiting several times. Standing diagonally behind Jonas, who presides at the table next to Dubnow, she is only dimly recognizable in the photo as a rather small middle-aged lady with a rounded face. Also preserved are more than a hundred letters from Jonas to Anna Kazhdan from 1932, as well as numerous other missives and documents of this affair, which had aroused Aron's displeasure.

From 1935 and until their escape in 1940, Aron and Zina lived with their family in the noble Sixteenth *arrondissement*, not far from the Bois de Bologne, in a quiet side street at 3 Rue Marbeau, where the consular section of the German Embassy is located today, but for most of the time and during the last year they were living at 19 Boulevard Delessert. Surely, they would have only moved again out of necessity. For a few years, the French metropolis offered Zina a domicile where at least her small family was gathered around her. During that time, the family grew larger as Zina became a grandmother. In January 1935 Gita gave birth to a son, Arié Paul. Lily, who had been torn out of her Berlin secondary school in year nine, had gained her university entrance qualification and was studying at the École libre des Sciences Politiques. In November of the same year she married Alfred Feiler, her friend from the Jewish Revisionist Zionist youth group Beitar in Berlin. The two young people were renting their own apartment. Paul's brother, Victor Vitali, was born in June 1938. Paul and Victor spent the first years of their childhood in Paris. Paul had little memory of it. He was five, and Victor two, when the family left the city. Paul finds it difficult to distinguish between his own memories and what he heard or saw in photographs. When I met him in Manhattan, Upper West Side, overlooking the Hudson River, he told me that they had recently flown back to Paris and walked through the city, to the house where he was born, and also to the last address before the escape. With his mother, he said, he had already gone on a search for the places of his childhood in Paris. "I have a connection to Europe," he said, "a strong European connection. But from childhood I have always identified as an American." Victor's attitude to Europe is shaped by his mother's attitude, who did not only refuse to visit Germany after the war, but also declined to buy any German products. Cousin Alexandre, who was about his age, as well as other relatives in Paris and in Grodno got murdered during the Holocaust. He has recorded the events in a book entitled *Hell's Traces*, thereby saving Alexandre from oblivion. Victor showed me an album with photos that had survived turbulent times. The pictures show two little boys, in a baby carriage, in a cart, in a playground, with their parents in the forest, with *Nyanya* Sasha at the seaside—non-specific situations. Sasha was by now looking after the next generation, as she became Paul's and Victor's nanny. Victor did not show me a picture of Alexandre.

At the Nazi Party Rally in Nuremberg in September 1935, the laws for the so-called "Maintenance of the Purity of the Arian Race" were proclaimed, while the Kahans' companies were being liquidated in Berlin: in December 1935 the Vermögensverwaltung, in February 1936, the publishing house Yalkut, and gradually the connections with Germany were cut off. The family was now commuting between Paris, Haifa and Tel Aviv. Even after the emigration of the one or expulsion of the other, the Kahans, Rosenbergs and Ettingers remained closely linked across national borders and the Mediterranean. Joseph visited his father Aron during the summer vacations. From distant memory, his impressions of the French metropolis shrank to a few flashes of light. His father had had little time for him, had been a stranger to him. Joseph was fourteen when Aron wanted to send him to college in England. He refused. For days he walked the streets of Paris alone and without understanding French. He was impressed by the Place de l'Etoile, the Star Square, today Place Charles de Gaulle, the largest square in Paris, where many wide streets converge, with the Arc de Triomphe in the middle. Avenue Mac Mahon, where Aron and Zina initially lived, is one of them. The way from Rue Marbeau to the center also led through the Place de l'Etoile. A highlight for Joseph was the small World Fair, Exposition Internationale des Arts et Techniques dans la Vie Moderne, which took place in Paris in 1937. He had particularly liked the German pavilions. After Dora, Bendet's eldest, had accommodated her parents to Palestine, she also went to Paris for several years, of which she later revealed little. At that time she was married to Izchak Gurvics from Latvia. Did she also work for the family business in France? Cute little hats, opera glasses, a fan made of mother-of-pearl and white ostrich feathers, kept by her daughter-in-law, suggest that she was having fun at that time.

As long as the borders were permeable, family members who were in business, especially the independent bachelors David and Arusia, commuted back and forth between Palestine and Paris. Arusia probably felt more at home in Tel Aviv, where he had gone to school for a year before the First World War. David remained torn between Zina, Aron, the family business and Zion. "Between 1933 and 1935 I met him [David Kahan] in Paris," reported the journalist Gershon (Hermann) Swet, recalling invitations to the Kahans on Shabbat evenings or at their office in the Rue de la Bienfaisance, Eighth *arrondissement*, where the CCC was based at number 17, next to the office of the Anglo-Iranian Oil Company. On Shabbat evenings, he got to know the customs and traditions of the house and met the circle of friends and acquaintances. Many Jewish migrants went in and out of the Kahan home, and the Shabbat nights seemed to him like an *aliyah*, an ascent to Berdichev or Jewish Warsaw, as if they were not in Paris at all. Since 1933 the city was full of exiles. Among the friends at the Kahan home were also intellectuals from Germany, wrote Swet. Could Hannah Arendt or Walter Benjamin have been among the guests as well? Certainly Dr. Dinkin from Berlin, and Rabbi Eisenstadt from Petrograd. Swet mentioned by name the lawyer and writer Sammy Gronemann and the journalist Georg Bernhard. Gronemann was organizing in Paris the refugee aid for Jewish migrants from Nazi Germany who wanted to go on to Palestine, as well as the Keren Hayesod fundraising committee and the French branch of the World Organization of Zionist Women, WIZO. After his flight from Germany, the former editor-in-chief of the *Vossische Zeitung* and Reichstag member, Bernhard had founded together with friends the *Pariser Tageblatt* and took over the editorial management. The paper was gaining a reputation as a platform for refugees and a newspaper in exile. Did David Kahan possibly participate in the newspaper? Gershon Swet, who had worked for the Jewish Telegraphic Agency and other press organs in Weimar Berlin, became one of their most important Palestine correspondents. The creation of the Palestine Section of the *Pariser Tageblatt* might have been decided in the Kahan home, as was Swet's employment by *Haaretz* in Tel Aviv in 1935. For a while, the *Pariser Tageblatt*, a newspaper that was critical of Nazi Germany and on the outside, was filling a niche in the market in Palestine, providing the Yekkes with information about world politics as well as about domestic events. Swet was connected to David Kahan, because he was a lifelong supporter of the Hebrew press and the Zionist movement. In the Kahan home, Bernhard had met with the *Haaretz* editors. The great political events were discussed there, Swet wrote in his obituary of David Kahan.

In their second exile, too, the Kahans were apparently running an open house and there was continuity despite their expulsion. They were meeting friends and acquaintances in Paris. Like in Berlin, Dr. Dinkin remained their family doctor and Rabbi Eisenstadt, whom Chaim Kahan had met in 1912 in St. Petersburg, their trusted advisor. One wonders if the furnishings of the apartment reminded them of Berlin? "There, clustered around, was the large, old-fashioned, uncomfortable, too ostentatious furniture," says Lion Feucht-wanger in his novel *Exile* about the evening parties at the home of editor-in-chief Heilbrun, the character based on Georg Bernhard. "Visiting for the first time, Anna had already noticed that they were placed in the same arrangement as in Berlin. She had also noticed immediately that people were eating from the same, far too opulent dinner set, as they had done in Berlin. And today, as always, the same people were there like in Berlin and were talking about the same things." In any case, at the Kahan homes in the Rue Jean Carriès and the Rue Marbeau, people were served with Rosenthal bowls, cups and plates. Victor wrote about the apartment: "the apartment had a maid's room and another for the live-in seamstress and the two in the attic that the family still wasn't sure what to do with. The apartment was big. ..." "We were living in the best area of Paris, had a car, several permanent servants, and our expenses were not less than 20,000 Fr. per month," Gita stated during the restitution proceedings. But the Kahans, unlike the Jews in the Faubourg Saint-Germain, were immune to assimilation, in France like before in Russia and Germany. "I do know that the family never felt embraced by the French. After all their years living in Paris, Gita said she had never been invited to a French person's home. However, she never mentioned any overt anti-Semitism towards her before the war," Eleanor Ripp, Paul's wife, wrote to me.

Following Yasha's departure, Aron was the only businessman in the family who had remained permanently in Paris. Zina's sons-in-law Monia and Alfred, called Ali, earned their living in other ways. Ali stated in his application for restitution that after the forced discontinuation of his medical studies and the escape from Berlin, he had worked in various professions. According to Monia's own statement, he was the manager of a fur trading company until his marriage. "But ultimately Monia was drawn into the Kahan sphere," Victor wrote. "He could not resist my granduncle Aron's offer." Aron financed a new business, a self-service restaurant on Boulevard Haussmann called Kwik, a novelty ahead of its time. However, it was not successful. "Monia threw himself into the job, substituting energy for knowledge," Victor described his father in this situation. Kwik went bankrupt, though sometime after that, Monia and his brother opened a stencil manufacturing company which was reasonably successful until the war. In the application for restitution, Monia did not write a word about Kwik, but instead that he and his brother had invested in the stencil firm in 1937.

Aron's eye condition worsened. Consultations with renowned specialists in Paris and Zurich led to lengthy, serious and expensive treatments. He was injected with hormones and other substances to save his eyesight, which did not help and led to consequential damage, so that he had to undergo surgery. It is likely that in this situation he received help from his brother David and nephew Arusia. In the last two years before the war, 1938/1939, the two were probably living more or less permanently in Paris. Aron was dependent on their support.

But first Arusia got married in Riga. He wrote to his brothers- and sisters-in-law in Tel Aviv on November 12, 1937, in German, so that all four could understand:

> Am I happy, very happy? "Happy" is such a dangerous word. I only know I am in a frenzy. I also know that Edith is edging deeper and deeper into my heart and my life every day. I feel that she will soon be indispensable to me. I am as intimate with her as if I had known her for years, and yet it is only five days since we spoke and exchanged the word "yes" between us. *Mi milel le-Avraham henika banim Sarah* [Who would have told Avraham that Sarah would still be nursing children! (Gen. 21:7)]. Who would have believed that a twenty-four-year-old girl, in her youthful fire, would give herself to a thirty-four-year-old?

Edith was the daughter of the lawyer and politician Paul Mintz in Riga, who had played a leading role in the drafting of Latvia's constitution. She was a successful sportswoman, a promising Latvian tennis star. The marriage had come about through Aron Nisse's matchmaking. He was the manager of Rubanito and Latruss, the Riga-based family business, explained their son, Uli Cohen-Mintz, in Tel Aviv. Arusia had met Edith and her family only in November 1937. Until their wedding, Arusia had been living at the Nisses' on Elisabeth Street in Riga. This is when the photos were taken that Aron Nisse's granddaughter, Marion, published on her website. They show Arusia in the middle of their family. The wedding took place in Riga on December 19, 1937. Of the Kahans, only his mother, Rosalia, was present. Afterwards, Arusia took his young wife via Danzig and Berlin to France, accompanied by his mother. The young couple went on their honeymoon to Nice. Rosalia visited Aron and Zina in Paris before returning to Tel Aviv. After their honeymoon in the south of France, Arusia and Edith arrived in Paris. Edith was not well received by Zina in Paris, Giza told me. She came from another world, a world that was also foreign to Arusia: "and how do I get into this milieu," he wrote, "an *osobnyak* [villa] (a là Grunewald) in which the family life of one of the formerly richest families in the city within the last forty or fifty years took place. A milieu where hundreds of people marched by with congratulations while the word *mazel tov* was never even uttered once? Father-in-law—a professor and former minister in the first Latvian cabinet." The Mintz family was part of the establishment in Latvia, secular and German-acculturated. Arusia wrote a total of four letters about the events in Riga to his brothers- and sisters-in-law in Tel Aviv, thereby sharing with them his exhilaration and enabling them to participate in the festivities.

By contrast, everyday life in Paris was sobering, becoming ever more unpleasant in the face of Nazi Germany's increasingly aggressive policies after the so-called *Anschluss* of Austria in March and the capture of the Sudetenland in September 1938. With the Munich Agreement, Great Britain and France had accepted the annexation, creating for some the illusion of the continuation of peace. A series of business letters in the archives, written by David and Arusia in the course of 1939 shows their effort to keep the business going in this politically explosive situation. David continued to look after his parents' house in Brest-Litovsk, which was rented to the Polish province police and managed by the trusted Eiasz Sliozberg. Apart from selling oil and coordinating the company's activities in Amsterdam, London, Riga and Paris, purchases in Romania and sales in Scandinavia, they apparently organized the trade in pomelos from Palestine—probably fruit from Noma Kahan's plantation—with England, Belgium and the Netherlands. They started selling the fruit after Roska and Yasha had told them that Noma, despite hard work, could not yet live on its revenue. One of his addressees and middlemen was the Berlin acquaintance and former Nitag employee René Lew in Antwerp. Along the way, they sent Nomek and Yasha, who had set up their own business in Tel Aviv, money for investments, checked accounts, collected information for both of them through established networks and established contacts. David blatantly expressed his displeasure about his nephews, who reported inadequately, did not cooperate with him as expected and even compared them to saboteurs and traitors to the fatherland, who deserved a severe punishment for their behavior in this precarious situation. Industrialists in Palestine were soldiers on the furthest front. Their family affairs were thus to be regarded very patriotically.

A photograph kept by Paul shows Aron and Zina, *Nyanya* Sasha, Gita and Monia, who is pushing Victor in a cart with Paul holding on to it. It was taken during the last summer of peace, at the Mont-Dore thermal spa in the Alps of the Department Auvergne-Rhone. Everyone is elegantly dressed, only Sasha and the children are dressed casually. Aron, despite the summer retreat, in a dark suit, with a tie and hat, with dark framed glasses after multiple eye operations looks stiff; Monia, very gentlemanly, is wearing sporty, casual dark pants, a light jacket, white gorget and black and white shoes. Zina and Gita, on the other hand, appear exhilarating in summery dresses, "… as if God had wanted to show the world once again what peace is and what it would lose," as it says in Remarque's novel *The Night in Lisbon*. "The days were filled with the serenity of this summer."

On August 22, 1939, nine days before the outbreak of war, Arusia typed a business letter to Yasha in Tel Aviv, adding in handwriting: "Nomek and Sulamith arrived earlier today, unfortunately at the same time as bad newspapers. Will you still travel to Cyprus under these circumstances?" A week later he wrote to Uncle Aron at the Villa Sanitas in Mont-Dore that the apartment in Vichy was now ready to move in to and that a coupé wardrobe trunk with clothes and linen had been sent there. "Everyone left for Vichy," he wrote. His uncle would also have Rabbi Eisenstadt nearby because he had been transferred to Vichy together with the entire Consistoire, the rabbinic administration. Immediately after France declared war on Germany, the Kahans apparently tried to escape to safety, although they were better off than the migrants with German papers, who, regardless of their attitude to Nazi rule, were considered "enemy aliens" and were interned. They left Paris—perhaps afraid of air raids—and retreated to the province, to the most important spa resort in France, which later, because it had sufficient accommodations with its hotels, was to become the seat of the French puppet government. Aron, Zina, Gita and the children decided to stay in the Auvergne, moving from Mont-Dore to Vichy, about one hundred kilometers away. Their address there was 7 Rue de la Paix. Arusia apparently organized the retreat of the rest of the family in Paris, but was at the same time worried about Edith, who was very pregnant and had gone to her parents in Riga. "There are no more rail or postal connections with Riga," he wrote to Uncle Aron in late August 1939. Only seven years after the second expulsion, the third had begun. The family was disintegrating. Arusia and David also decided to leave France.

On October 18, 1939, Edith, in Riga and far away from Arusia, gave birth to her first son, who was named after his late grandfather Baruch Tanchum.

Meanwhile, war was raging in Europe. The German Wehrmacht had occupied Poland. Nevertheless, in January 1940, Edith and the three-month-old baby set out from Riga on the long, uncertain journey back to Arusia: by rail through the Soviet Union to Romania, from Constanza by ship to Istanbul and from there to Palestine. How many days or weeks might she have been traveling? Another relative, Abram Kagan, fled with his family from Brussels to Toulouse after the occupation of Belgium and Northern France, where he met a friend of his father's and also the Kahans' friend, Rabbi Dr. Moshe Eisenstadt, who had fled from Vichy further south. Through him, Abram found work in the Jewish Refugee Committee, supported by the American relief organization Joint, thus establishing contacts that would save his life.

In Vichy, in February 1940, presumably shortly before Aron and David separated and the family government fell apart, a document was produced in Russian and French, later called in its German translation *The So-Called Constitution*. In his memoirs, Aron claimed authorship, but the Constitution was formulated in the name of the second generation. In it was written what had previously been orally accepted as a consensus: that the history of the family had begun with Chaim and Malka; that the spirit of togetherness was to be upheld; that the "Teutonic barbarism," which was threatening humanity through unprecedented tyranny and the Jewish people with total annihilation, obligated each and every one of them to put the communal interests above their personal ones. The text is a contract and a vow to remain faithful to Jewish tradition as well as to Jewish national interests; to always observe the main rules of the Jewish religion, regardless of individual differences; to be charitable and to provide help to relatives and friends, whereby employees were also to be considered friends. It culminates in complicated mutual moral and material declarations of obligation with the demand to always integrate oneself consciously into the collective, to always care for one another, to fathom and accept the capabilities and limitations of each individual. All members of the family should be able to maintain a similar standard of living, and communications should be maintained beyond the distances between them. The good reputation of the family was an obligation. The constitution was also an appeal to the third generation to uphold the covenant. It invoked the cohesion of the family when it threatened to break apart in the face of extreme threats.

In March 1940, Arusia, who had fled Europe with David via Marseilles a few weeks after Edith's departure from Riga, arrived in Palestine almost simultaneously with his wife and child and was there to welcome them in the port of Haifa. At the same time, Aron, in Vichy, was still trying to settle his finances in view of the danger of the approaching war, which was scattering the family, driving them out of Europe. Arusia was to close all accounts while Rabbi Eisenstadt was to mediate in a renewed dispute over the distribution of wealth. A building in London that brought no revenue was to go into a joint account, but Aron was to receive the proceeds from the execution sale of Mina's tenement building in Berlin-Schöneberg, worth 51,000 Reichsmarks, in stable Western currency—dollars, gold, or pounds sterling according to the exchange rate of 1933—and Monia Ripp was to receive a higher salary than Arusia, since he had to feed a family. Despite the obligation to put the family above the welfare of the individual, Aron apparently did everything possible to assert his own interests at that time of need. Differences that he had long had with his brother David regarding the management of the business deepened in the face of the approaching war, which, as Aron knew, was to put persecuted Jews in mortal danger.

While the family was staying in Mont-Dore and later in Vichy, his father, Monia, regularly went to work in Paris during the week, Victor wrote. Paris was five hundred kilometers away, a few hours by train from Vichy. In the spring of 1940, Monia was to be drafted into the army of the Polish government in exile, which supported the French troops in the fight against the German Wehrmacht, until the capitulation of France. The war was now tearing apart Zina's nuclear family as well. The couples fled the country separately. Lily and Ali with Zina and Aron managed to cross the French-Spanish border into Portugal with Lolia's help before the Battle of France in May 1940. Lolia and Genia, who had already fled from Berlin to Lisbon in the early summer of 1933 but had lived in Tel Aviv in between, had returned to Lisbon in 1939. Victor wrote that Lolia had the necessary contacts in Lisbon so that he could send visas to the family. Ali did well to hurry, because the Armistice Agreement of June 22, 1940 forced the French government to extradite all migrants with German citizenship "on demand." Ali belonged to this group, but, according to his daughters, he also had a Polish passport. Zina and Lily used French alien passports for identification, while everyone else in the family had Polish documents. After the surrender, all Jewish migrants, regardless of their nationality, were directly threatened by the Nazi henchmen, the new masters in occupied France. At first it remained unclear and uncertain how much influence the Nazis would gain in unoccupied France. "In the spring of 1940, we moved to Arcachon, a resort near Bordeaux," wrote Victor Ripp. "We were in Arcachon on May 10, when the Germans invaded France and were still there on June 17 when France surrendered." Monia, Gita and the children were still in Arcachon when the Bordeaux region was taken by the Wehrmacht in early July. "We were lying on the beach and lying next to us were German officers," Gita said in an interview for the Spielberg Foundation. "They were"—she was looking for the right word—"they were correct." When asked, she added "Wehrmacht," by way of explanation.

Gita and her sons recounted that Victor wrote down what numerous other refugees from that time had testified to in their memoirs. It was a hectic time. The situation was confusing, communications were disrupted. The connections were interrupted. People got nervous. An official in Lisbon had accidentally sent the visas for the Ripps to the Portuguese Consulate in Bayonne, not to Bordeaux, the nearest city. "Remember the square in front of the consulate in Bayonne?"—Remarque had his protagonist ask. "Remember the refugees, standing in columns four deep, who then broke away and, in panic, blocked the entrance and desperately groaned and cried fighting for their spot?" Despite numbered tickets, the people would not have been able to be regulated, the door would have been blocked, so that the passports had to be thrown out of the windows. Remarque mentions that the forest of outstretched hands imprinted itself on his character's mind.

But the visas for the Ripps were only valid for a short period of time. Before Victor's parents had even found out that their documents were in Bayonne, they had expired. Thereupon, they tried to get out of the country without visas, trying to obtain an exit permit from the German military administration in Biaritz. When they showed their Polish passports, the official mocked them as dirty Jews, saying that the country no longer existed, and that Poland was a German province. A paradoxical situation arose: France neither accepted the refugees nor let them go. "Looking back at my family's efforts to get out of France, I am struck by how many decisions were involved, how often my parents had to weigh the risks, always with little understanding of the odds," Victor wrote. To get the necessary exit documents, the parents went back to Paris with a confirmation from the Portuguese Consulate of Bayonne that visas were available for them there, even in the lion's den. The commandant's office of the German military administration in France was housed in the Hotel Majestic. The palatial building on Avenue Kléber, today the Peninsula Hotel, is in itself frightening, causing people to feel small. That's where his parents were to present their papers. "The Majestic had a long staircase leading to the administrative offices on the mezzanine floor. It was marble, so each step she [Gita] took resounded like a harbinger of doom. In her mind, Nazis had taken on the form of monsters, unpredictable and dealing in death. But, remarkably, a permit was provided with little trouble. This was October 4. The indicated deadline for leaving France was October 7."

Unlike many other refugees, the Ripps still had time to say their goodbyes to relatives and friends and pack their belongings into containers. After a stop in Bayonne to get their visas, they reached the border town of Hendaye. There the gauge of the railroad tracks changed, and the wagons were shunted. They had to leave the train and walk towards Irun, the town on the Spanish side of the border. Paul remembered that they were crossing a long bridge with their belongings stacked on a cart. It must have appeared endlessly long to them. On the Spanish side, their father was arrested immediately because he had arrived with Polish papers. The Polish government in exile, located in London, was continuing to fight the Nazis, and Monia was, apparently, of conscription age. I could imagine that, after all their efforts to remain in control of the situation and to maintain the upper middle-class lifestyle despite all the adversities and challenges, an abyss was suddenly opening up in front of them. Gita never forgot this moment of fear for the rest of their lives. Victor, two years old, was too young to remember, but maybe when he wrote *Hell's Traces*, something in him remembered. Gita said she felt completely lost. No relief organization was in sight. Her last hope was her brother. He had Portuguese nationality. Paul had had his toy plane taken away at the border, recounted Paul's wife Eleanor, while Victor was allowed to keep his tricycle. Gita spent one night, with the two little boys, full of fear and uncertainty, in a hotel in the Spanish border town. After some hours, Monia was released. As it turned out, a few months earlier, with his fortieth birthday, he had passed the age limit for recruitment into the Polish Armed Forces of the West. The Ripps were allowed to travel on to Lisbon, where their relatives were already waiting for them.

Portugal was a dictatorship, ruled by Prime Minister Salazar. It was anything but safe for the refugees from Nazi Germany, although it was maintaining neutrality for strategic reasons. Some Portuguese consulates, including the one in Bordeaux, still issued visas to persecuted Jews when this already contradicted state policy. "The coast of Portugal had become the last refuge for the refugees, to whom justice, freedom and tolerance meant more than home and existence," wrote Remarque. "Those who could not reach the promised land of America from here were lost. They had to bleed to death in the undergrowth of refused entry and exit visas, unobtainable work and residence permits, internment camps, bureaucracy, loneliness, strangers and the horrible general indifference to the fate of the individual, which is always the result of war, fear and need. Man was nothing at this time; a valid passport was everything." With the occupation of France, a mass exodus had begun into the pro-fascist Portugal, which was maneuvering between the great powers. Salazar probably did not want to jeopardize the centuries-old alliance with Britain. The Portuguese coast also attracted spies and double agents. For Zina and Aron, the port and capital at the mouth of the Tagus in the far southwest of Europe became the fourth exile after the odyssey in revolutionary Russia, then to Berlin and Paris. For little Paul, it was the first. For him it remained linked to the memory of ear infections. Situations of existential insecurity manifest themselves in the weakest parts of the body. He was in constant pain, the family was constantly worried about him, wrote Eleanor. Paul recounted that they had rented a house in Estoril, where they were living with Aron and Zina and Lily and Ali, while trying to get visas for America from there. Estoril is a seaside resort with a pedigree, a refuge for the upper class, about twenty kilometers west of Lisbon. The house they were living in was called Villa Flavia, according to the affidavit for Lily and Ali Feiler.

Even in Lisbon, the family had apparently no financial worries. Apart from the house in Estoril, they rented an apartment in the city at 15 Rua dos Fanqueiros. Immediately after their arrival, Aron, Zina, Lolia and Ali founded a small company, Intercambio Internacional, Limitada, with a share capital of 50,000 escudos, at that time worth less than $2,000, headquartered at 4 Rua Fialho de Almeida. What it wanted to trade with is not stated in the articles of incorporation. Wherever the Kahans went, they rented an apartment, hired a cook and founded a company. This statement, made in Kiev during the First World War by the soldier and later BP manager Hans Ornstein, was even true for the Lisbon escape route. Even in a situation of war and persecution, Aron, now sixty years old and suffering from an eye disease, did not want to give up being a businessman and entrepreneur. "The only business that I know of my parents having in Portugal was a travel agency," wrote Ylana Miller, Lily and Ali's daughter. "I do know that it was an anxious time with concern about getting visas elsewhere."

In Lisbon, Paul was sent to a French lyceum. In France he had grown up with Russian, in Portugal he learned French. It was only in New York that language acquisition and the language of the country coincided, Victor wrote. The family lived in Lisbon for six months. "Twice a week my parents would travel up the coast to Oporto. There was a rumor that the US Consulate there had a more flexible policy regarding passports than the embassy in Lisbon, where the rules were adhered to with maddening precision," Victor described the situation.

For three months, from August to October 1940, until Gita and Monia arrived in Lisbon, Zina's nephew, known as Yasha Rabinovich or Jacob Rabinowitsch, was trying in New York to obtain entry papers for his relatives in Portugal. The lawyer Alexis Goldenweiser, whom the Kahans probably already knew from Kiev or Berlin, supported him. With the help of another lawyer of

Russian origin in Manhattan, a certain Léon Malkiel, Goldenweiser was trying to get Zina and Aron visas for Haiti with transit visas for the USA. However, the immigration laws in Haiti had been changed. That avenue got blocked. Goldenweiser made another attempt, turning to the President's Advisory Committee on Political Refugees for help. Aron himself lobbied the American Consul General in Lisbon for Ali's entry permit. An American businessman, owner of the Atlantic Yeast Corporation, vouched for Aron Kahan. The affidavit with which Lily and Ali Feiler finally succeeded in entering the USA was vouched for by a certain Joachim Ginzberg, who introduced himself as a cousin and partner of M. Golodetz & Co, 91 Wall Street, Manhattan.

The Immigration Act of 1924 limited the number of migrants permitted entry into the USA through a national origins' quota. The quota provided American visas to two percent of the total number of people of each nationality in the United States as of the 1890 census. German, British and Irish citizens, who had no reason to flee at the time, thus had the largest quotas. Victor wrote that, since Poland was occupied and no one could get out of there, his family was lucky that there were hardly any applicants for the Polish quota, although it was small. Nevertheless, it took them five months to get their visas. The American applicant for an affidavit had to vouch for the newcomers and guarantee their livelihood. Therefore Joachim Ginzberg had to disclose his own financial situation. He was the partner of Michael Golodetz. Zina was a born Golodetz and Michael was her relative—an entrepreneur in London and New York who was wealthy and had helped her before, in the early twenties, by providing her with funds for the extension of the attic apartment on Kurfürstendamm. A French translation of a marriage certificate, issued in February 1941 in Marseille by the Office des Réfugiés Russes, identifies Zina as a born Golodetz. She was awaiting her departure in Lisbon at that time. So who could it have been who had vouched for her? If it was Michael Golodetz who had applied for Zina and Aron's American affidavit, she might have needed the marriage certificate to prove her kinship.

Zina and Aron, along with Lily and Ali, left Lisbon first. As Remarque wrote,

> The ship prepared for the journey as if it was an ark at the time of the Flood.
> It was an ark. Every ship that left Europe in those months of 1940 was an
> ark. Mount Ararat was America, and the flood was rising daily. It had long
> since flooded Germany and Austria and was deep in Poland and Prague;

Amsterdam, Brussels, Copenhagen, Oslo and Paris had already sunk into it, the cities of Italy reeked of it, and Spain was no longer safe either.

A ship named after the Portuguese explorer Alexandre Alberto de Serpa Pinto carried Jews and other victims of Nazi persecution overseas under the neutral Portuguese flag from May 1940 until 1942, in return for which Germans, especially those expelled from Brazil, were brought to Europe. At the end of March 1941, Gita, Monia, Paul and Victor received ship tickets for the *Serpa Pinto*.

Uncle Abram Kagan was still in Toulouse at that time. Through Eisenstadt, he had asked his relatives Aron and Zina, who had already been in New York since March 1941, for an American visa, and received a certain amount of money that Eisenstadt handed him before leaving Toulouse for America. Such a short time after their escape, Aron and Zina probably did not have the necessary means or possibilities to obtain the correct papers for their relative. Abram Kagan was arrested, but through the intercession of the bishop of Toulouse, he was released after a short time. With the help of one of his Russian authors, who had been living in the USA for some time, he obtained the desired affidavit. The Kagan family finally reached the USA in early summer 1942 via Casablanca.

CHAPTER 20

Eretz Israel. Tel Aviv

Shortly before his fifth birthday, in April 1933, Eli arrived in Jaffa together with his parents, Nomek and Shula Rosenberg, and brother Michael after a long journey. They had started by train from Berlin to Trieste, and continued from there by ship via Greece and Cyprus. Until today he has not forgotten the landing. The ship was out at sea, far from the port. Arab fishermen came in rowing boats and brought the passengers ashore. The boats rocked on the waves. The sailors took the passengers under their arms and handed them down to the rowers as soon as the waves lifted the boats. Aunt Esther Smoira and Uncle Zalman Rubashov, who had often been a guest of the Kahans in Berlin and called himself Shazar in Eretz Israel, were waiting for them on land. Instead of a belt, Rubashov wore a rope around the waist of his *rubashka*, the Russian peasant shirt. The boy had never seen anything of the sort. In Berlin people were dressed differently. Right after his arrival, Eli was sick for three weeks. During this time, the Rosenbergs were living with Judith and Bendet Kahan in Bezalel Yaffe Street, on the corner of Rothschild Boulevard, in Tel Aviv. The family had a Yemenite cook. The boy didn't know or like what she cooked, especially eggplants, *chatzilim*. Only in kindergarten did he perk up.

The immigration to Eretz Israel is called *aliyah*, the ascent. Although it had been the land of their dreams, it wasn't easy for the Rosenbergs, as for many migrants, because it was an escape, but it was certainly easier for them than for other refugees from Nazi Germany. The Rosenbergs had assets and relatives in the country—like their parents had once in Berlin, like their relatives in Paris and in Lisbon. Consequently, the family was able to prepare for immigration having received entry permits and start-up assistance from various quarters. Esther was married to the president of the Jewish Bar Association under the British mandate, Moses Smoira, and Rubashov was working for the Histadrut, the trade union federation in the *yishuv,* the pre-state Jewish community in Palestine. Rachel Ettinger with her family and Noma Kahan with his wife had already been living there for seven or eight years. Other relatives had arrived shortly before the Rosenbergs: Mina Kahan with her son Joseph; Bendet and Judith with their daughters Lea and Röschen; their eldest, Dora, had arrived ahead of them, rented the apartment in Bezalel Yaffe and welcomed them when they arrived in Jaffa on the *Martha Washington* from Trieste. The five-meter lift with their belongings followed later.

In the late fall of 1933, Rosalia and Baruch Kahan with son Yasha and his family joined them from Paris, and only a year and a half later, in the spring of 1935, Jonas Rosenberg decided to spend the rest of his life not with Anna Kazhdan in Riga, but with his children, Roska and Yasha, in Tel Aviv. At the end of 1935, his nephew Berl Rosenberg, in exile in Belgium, also received permission to enter Palestine. David and Arusia shuttled back and forth between Paris and Tel Aviv until 1940. After fleeing France shortly before its occupation, they too settled in Palestine. As the First World War had already torn the family apart, the Second World War separated Chaim and Malka Kahan's descendants. While the first war had divided them between two hostile European countries, the second one scattered them over two continents, North America and the Middle East, the two new Jewish centers that had formed since the Bolsheviks destroyed the European Diaspora and the Nazis murdered the Jews in Europe. The small group around Aron and Zina fled to New York, the larger one to the *yishuv.* They settled in Tel Aviv and the surrounding area. Aron had been trying to bring David to New York from November 1941. In December, the USA entered the war. Despite the difficult situation, Aron procured an American entry visa for his brother with the help of his lawyer.

The Zionist movement's project, to establish a national home for the Jews in Palestine, had been under British protection since the Balfour Declaration in November 1917, a year before the end of the First World War. The British relied on the support of the Zionists in their fight against the Ottoman Empire. Since the League of Nations' Mandate for Palestine, which entrusted Britain with the administration of the country with due regard for Jewish and Arab interests, the establishment of the Jewish home in Palestine had been internationally accepted. The city of Tel Aviv, no more than twenty-four years old in 1933 and still under construction, formed the heart of the old-new country from which the State of Israel was to emerge.

"Dear Jonas, I never thought I would be writing to you from here. I returned yesterday from a trip to Tiberias with a swollen eye and so I can't get out of the hotel today, am lying on a deck chair, putting on some boracic lotion compresses, dozing off indescribably happy," wrote Chaim Avinoam, just under seventeen years old, to a friend in Tel Aviv. "I am 982 meters above the blue Mediterranean Sea level, and 1200 meters above the surface of Lake Tiberias." In the evening, an icy wind was blowing there, and he hadn't been freezing with such pleasure since leaving Europe. In the late summer of 1937, Chaim Avinoam was travelling around, presumably with his parents Roska and Yasha, to inspect and take possession of his new surroundings, his ancestral and promised land, which had become a refuge. Shortly before the trip, two years after their arrival in Palestine, his parents had officially announced their name change in *The Palestine Gazette*, where there was a special section for this purpose, in order to publicize the new identity, something many new immigrants did in Palestine. They were no longer called Kahan but Haimi-Cohen.

They had been in Acre, and were now staying at the Hotel Canaan in Kiryat Sarah near Safed, intending to go on to Metulla and Mount Carmel. Chaim Avinoam was describing the land to his friend with whom he had once played war games on a map, the battle for the Galilee Mountain Range. He was writing now from the perspective of a ruler who intended to make it bloom. The area was indescribably beautiful. "If anyone comes to me again and tells me that Palestine is a barren land, I'm going to punch him in the face, because that is a lie. He should drive along the Kinereth [Lake Tiberias, or Sea of Galilee] and then tell me that it does not remind him of Lake Geneva. The soil is fertile, reforestation has begun not far from the hotel, and three small woods have already sprung up there, real pine forests." Chaim Avinoam described his contrasting impressions of Safed and Tiberias. He only mentioned the Arab part of the mountain hamlet of Safed, but did not describe it. Perhaps he saw it as a disturbing factor and a dangerous place in the face of the uprisings of the Arabs, who were also organizing themselves nationally against what they saw as the space-consuming Jewish immigrants. The Jewish quarter had made a depressing impression on Chaim Avinoam with its narrow, deserted streets, the old synagogues "where one implores all the blessings of heaven for two piasters," the tiny stores where "Jews of the old type," with side curls, were squatting in caftans and living on charity. On the other hand, he had liked Tiberias, which reminded him of Tel Aviv with its hustle and bustle and its cheerfulness, the palm tree avenues, the hubbub in the streets, stores and cafés.

Haifa on Mount Carmel was the Kahans' first location in Palestine. Rachel and David Ettinger had been living there with their children from 1925 until the sale of the COC subsidiary Chaim Kahan's Successors in 1930, and from 1927

Noma and Rita Kahan were living there, too. As an engineer, Noma had headed a department at Chaim Kahan's Successors before he joined the pioneers and established an orange grove. Waiting for their lifts from Berlin, Mina and Joseph first stayed with Rachel and David, then, for four months, in a guesthouse on the Carmel, before they settled in the immediate vicinity of the Ettingers.

Tel Aviv became the center of the family in the 1930s. Since the spring of 1933, all relatives who sought refuge in Palestine gradually settled there. The Ettingers also moved to Tel Aviv, near the new company, Elite, which had its headquarters in Ramat Gan. As before in Berlin around the Kurfürstendamm, they now lived on Rothschild Boulevard: the Ettingers at number 108, later 114; David Kahan diagonally opposite at number 105; Yasha and Roska with family a few buildings further on at number 85; Baruch and Rosalia in nearby Mazeh. At first also Bendet and Judith, together with the Rosenbergs, stayed in Dora's apartment on the corner of Bezalel Yaffe and Rothschild Boulevard. Later, some moved to the outskirts, others a few streets away. However, the Ettingers—David, Yasha and Roska, Baruch and Rosalia, Dora and Röschen— stayed on Rothschild Boulevard. From Giza I learned that Roska had a trunk under her wardrobe in the hallway, which she had brought from Berlin and in which she kept her personal records, consisting of several thousand letters and documents. A good part of the family history I am writing about is based on them.

Rothschild Boulevard is the oldest, the first major and the most magnificent main street in Tel Aviv. It stretches from Neve Zedek, the first Jewish-Oriental district outside of Old Jaffa, in the south to the cultural center at the Habimah Theater Square in the north. On the boulevard stands the former residence of Mayor Meir Dizengoff, where Ben Gurion proclaimed Israel's independence in May 1948. The Rothschild Boulevard is a reminiscence of Europe and European modernity. It is lined with simple white villas and townhouses, most of which were built in the twenties and the thirties in the style of Bauhaus architecture, to which the center of Tel Aviv owes the nickname White City. Rows of trees separate the two roads from the promenade in the middle. "Tel Aviv: Sea. Light. Azure. Sand, scaffolding, kiosks on the avenues, a Hebrew city, white, linear, growing between orange groves and sand dunes." With these words Amos Oz described the city of the 1940s in *A Tale of Love and Darkness*. At his home—he was living with his parents in Jerusalem at the time—Tel Aviv was spoken about in a mixture of envy and pride, admiration and a hint of secretiveness—as if the city was a secret project of the Jewish people. When the Kahan family settled on Rothschild Boulevard, the trees provided little shade

because they were still small. Today the dense canopy of leaves of the fire aca-
cias protects strollers from the hot Mediterranean sun.

The correspondence between Aron and his lawyer concerning a visa for
David ended in February 1942. Was the visa issued for a visit only or for permanent residence? Did he actually travel to New York in the winter of 1941/1942,
when Palestine was threatened by the advance of German troops and America
was also at war? Or, had there been a dispute between him, Aron and Zina about
the future headquarters of the family business and its management? In any case,
David did not settle in New York, but in Palestine. The times of common, frater-
nally shared patriarchal leadership of the family were over, despite good inten-
tions expressed by both sides and some attempts to continue it across the seas
and countries. The family constitution that Aron and David had formulated in
Vichy in early 1940, shortly before they parted, invoked a cohesion like that of
Berlin, which no longer existed. The flight from the war and the persecution of
the Jews had destroyed it. After the separation from Aron, David led the family
in Tel Aviv, because Baruch had died in 1936, and Bendet, the second oldest
of Chaim's sons, continued to pursue his own interests as before. David's voice
is barely audible in the family archives, his handwriting is known only from a
few documents. But his nephew Arusia spoke for him in his memoirs. Other
descendants supplemented the stories.

Every *rosh chodesh*, the beginning of the month, the family would regularly
get together at David's home, thus continuing the tradition that the Kahans had
cherished in Baku, Kharkov, St. Petersburg, Berlin and Paris. This was also a
large apartment, which did not belong to the family, but to a certain Madame
Ostrowski. David had been living there as a tenant since arriving from Paris;
she also ran the household for him. Eli and Efrat remembered that Madame
Ostrowski always set the table festively. The dominant themes around the table
were probably the war; the disruption to the family; the uncertainty of the fate
of relatives in Poland, Latvia, Lithuania, Belarus and the Ukraine; the destruction of the Jewish townships and *shtetls* in Eastern Europe; the threat to Palestine by the troops of the Axis powers, which had advanced from Tunisia into
Egypt under the leadership of Erwin Rommel and won decisive victories there
in June 1942 against the Allied troops. For Dvora, who considered herself a
born Ettinger and was already a young woman in the 1940s, these meetings of
the Kahans were tiresome obligations. Cousin Yossi, or Joseph, recounted that
he and his mother Mina did not take part in the *rosh chodesh* family meetings.
The trip from Haifa to Tel Aviv was too far for them. When they did join their
relatives on the holidays, they would stay overnight at Bendet's. David, who had

no children himself, had been like a father to him, he added, visibly moved. He had not seen his own father for many years. Aron did not even come to his son's Bar Mitzvah, Eli said.

David, Malka and Chaim's second youngest child and youngest son, remained unmarried. According to Giza, Zina was the love of his life. He was never seen with another woman at his side. In photos he appears as an elegant man. In correspondence with nephews and nieces he comes across as a loving uncle who looked like his mother. He was more interested in literature, culture and the Zionist movement than in the oil business. As a businessman, it was above all he who made sure that the family supported projects that contributed to the formation of a national society and culture and which would stimulate the national economy in Palestine. Such entrepreneurs were in demand in the country. He was thus continuing his father's work.

Immediately before the First World War, Chaim Kahan had generously donated to the Keren Kayemet Le-Israel, the Jewish National Fund, via Mizrachi—for land in Tel Aviv, on which the new Tachkemoni School was built, and in Jerusalem, where a settlement had been established since 1926 and named Mekor Chaim after him, meaning "Chaim's Spring." Mekor Chaim was initially a village with twenty farms along a main road on one hundred and twenty dunams, or twelve hectares, in the southwest of the city, parallel to the railroad. Each property had a house and a garden with plantation, cow sheds and hen houses. In 1931 the settlement had two hundred and two inhabitants in forty-one houses. "Even further south, beyond all these foreign worlds [the realms of Arabic, German and Greek Jerusalem], behind the mountains, at the end of the world, a few isolated Jewish dots were flashing," Amos Oz said in memory of his childhood. One of them was Mekor Chaim. Today it is an urban district of Jerusalem. For the family, Chaim Kahan had purchased a large *pardes*, a citrus plantation in Petah Tikva and other plots of land in Jaffa, Petach Tikva and the Talpiot district of Jerusalem. Immediately after his father's death, David fulfilled his father's wish to donate the tithes of these assets to philanthropic causes. The foundation of the Chaim Publishing House in 1917 in St. Petersburg, where the magazine *Heavar* was published, goes back to David. The Chaim Publishing House reappeared in Palestine after a brief interlude in Weimar Berlin. *Heavar* was also published later in Israel.

Under David's direction, the Kahans had been involved, as early as the 1920s from Berlin, with the Hebrew daily *Haaretz* in Palestine, parallel to their involvement with the publishing houses in Vilna and Berlin. On a trip to Palestine in 1924 David had met up again with Moshe Glücksohn, once a group leader of the Zionist student fraternity in Giessen and now editor-in-chief of the *Haaretz*, whom he adored. He had learned that the newspaper was in financial difficulty and supported it with the consent of his brothers. *Haaretz*, which had evolved from the British military bulletin *The Palestine News*, was initially a weekly newspaper until activists of the Zionist movement from Eastern Europe, supported by the Zionist Organization, financed and directed it. The first one was Isaak Leib Goldberg from Vilna, who grew and distributed citrus fruit in Palestine. From 1919 he published the newspaper in Jerusalem under a new name, *Haaretz*, which now appeared daily. A few years later, in 1922, it was transformed into a cooperative, and the editorial office was handed over to the journalist Moshe Glücksohn, who had gained his doctorate with a thesis on Fichte's theory of the state. Glücksohn was of Lithuanian origin, had studied at the yeshivot in Grodno and Łomża, then at the universities of Marburg and Bern. He had lived and worked in Odessa and Moscow before going to Palestine in 1919. He made it a condition that *Haaretz* be moved to Tel Aviv, because that was where the readership he wanted to address was located. *Haaretz* was and is a non-partisan liberal daily newspaper, one of the largest in Israel today.

At the time, it was David and Baruch who were in correspondence with Glücksohn. In 1925, the Kahans had purchased a plot of land in the center of Tel Aviv, financed the construction of a print shop at 27 Montefiore Street, equipped it with the most modern machines from Germany and leased it to *Haaretz*. From then on, they regularly supported the newspaper with donations, but had also been forced to make savings that were painful for the employees, who protested against them. When further support through donations was no longer possible after the bankruptcy of the COC in the early 1930s, the Kahans had arranged for the cooperative to be converted into a corporation in March 1933, with David taking over the management. "The Liquidation of the *Haaretz* Workers Cooperative Society hereby notify that the winding-up of said Society has been concluded and that its assets now belong to the 'Haim' Publishing Company, Ltd., to which the said assets have been transferred by Mr. DAVID COHEN, the owner of such assets," was the statement of the notaries in *The Palestine Gazette* in early 1934. One of them was Yuda Beham, the confidant from Kharkov, who by now ran a law firm in Tel Aviv and was apparently continuing to advise and represent the Kahans.

When the family lost its domicile in Germany due to the Nazi regime, it increased its investments in Eretz Israel, although its management was still based in Paris. From March 1933, the Kahans were holding a thirty-eight-percent controlling stake in Chaim Publishing House, divided between David Kahan with

22.5 percent and Jonas Rosenberg with 15.5 percent. Other shareholders were the publishing houses Twersky and Eshkol. In addition, the Kahans donated another piece of land and the associated building a few streets away from Montefiore. Two years later, in 1935, under the direction of Chaim Publishing House, *Haaretz* received a new building at 56 Mazeh Street, an unusual modern industrial structure in the white city of Tel Aviv, built by two architects from the Russian Empire. Had David only given the money or had he also influenced the design of the *Haaretz* printing plant? Today the building houses are part of the Hotel Diaghilev. The core section is a monolithic two-story cube, which is loosened up by extensions and insertions. The building is functionally designed in the Bauhaus style. On each floor, four large windows cover the front horizontally. The print shop was located below, the editorial office above. A balcony with rounded corners and see-through tubular steel railings stretches along two windows, elegantly vaulted by a projection of the same shape, which is attached just below the flat roof, barely recognizable as a canopy. Vertically, the building is framed by the glass front of a stairwell, which extends over both floors and the corner of the house, towers far above the cube and perfectly completes the edifice. The Kahans had presented *Haaretz* with an imposing building.

When the newspaper was marking the publication of its five-thousandth issue in December 1935, it was celebrated by political and spiritual leaders of the Zionist movement. Chaim Weizmann, Ben Gurion and Meir Dizengoff wrote greetings, Achad Haam and Chaim N. Bialik were quoted posthumously. *Haaretz* was a serious newspaper committed to Zionist ideals, competing with others, especially the sensationalist *Doar Hayom*, which had been a revisionist-Zionist newspaper from the late 1920s. Moshe Glücksohn headed the editorial office all these years until well into the thirties, when he was already over sixty, maneuvering it through many crises. Twice the Kahan family saved *Haaretz* from insolvency, in the mid-twenties and early thirties, just as they had secured the existence of the publishing houses Romm in Vilna, Petropolis, Obelisk, Shvelen and Stybel in Berlin. In the Kahan era and later, the newspaper attracted ambitious and well-known writers who had arrived from Eastern Europe—the left-liberal native Ukrainian Avraham Shlonsky as well as the conservative Nathan Alterman from Warsaw. Zalman Shazar (Rubashov) also wrote for *Haaretz*. In 1935, the newspaper had seventy employees, including twenty-two journalists, and maintained local editorial offices in Jerusalem and Haifa. It paid good salaries compared to other newspapers in the *yishuv*. Some of the employees, who were active in industry politics, founded and led the Journalists' Association in Palestine.

David was very attached to *Haaretz*. From Paris, he kept in touch with Tel Aviv, ensured the flow of information between the countries and continents and arranged employees from the circle of migrants in Berlin, for example, the journalists Yeshayahu Klinov and Gershon Swet, who was later to honor David's services to the Hebrew press in his obituary. Relatives worked at *Haaretz*. Even David Ettinger, the COC's subsidiary representative in Haifa and Abraham S. Kagan, the publisher in Berlin, had acted as intermediaries between *Haaretz* and the *Berliner Tageblatt* when the newspaper in Tel Aviv needed illustrations and photographs for a weekly supplement. Arusia had been acting as managing director since he had lost his post at Nitag and left Germany. The director of Chaim Publishing House was thus the "financial director" of *Haaretz*, as Giza put it. The special issue of the five-thousandth edition printed photos of David as the founder of Chaim Publishing House and editor of *Haaretz* in recent years and of Arusia as the director of the publishing house. David, still slender and elegant as always, is depicted on the balcony of the new print plant and Arusia, in the office, with a dead-straight parting and a ruler in both hands, at his desk. I later found the photo of Arusia in Efrat's family album. Moshe Ettinger, who changed his name to Moshe Ater in Palestine, began working as a business editor at *Haaretz*.

The family proudly tells of David, who invested not only in *Haaretz*, but also in the *Palestine Post*, since 1950 the *Jerusalem Post*, and in the publishing house Dvir, which was once founded by Chaim N. Bialik in Odessa under the name Moria and migrated to Palestine via Berlin. David was one of those who had attended Bialik's funeral in Tel Aviv in early July 1934, I read in the bulletin of the Jewish Telegraph Agency. Bialik had been the first national poet in Eretz Israel. According to Arusia, David had also worked in the ORT management in Palestine. But six months after *Haaretz* had celebrated its anniversary, the Kahans sold the newspaper to Salman Schocken, a businessman and publisher from Germany. Perhaps the newspaper was too expensive for them in those politically and economically difficult times. Palestine, having survived the Great Depression unscathed and experiencing an upswing in the early 1930s, went through an economic crisis in 1935. Meanwhile, in Paris, Aron Kahan was struggling to keep the family business going in his second exile.

When and where Salman Schocken first met David and Baruch Kahan, whether in Berlin or Marienbad; on the fringes of a Zionist congress in Basel, Zurich, or Karlsbad; or in Palestine, remains uncertain. The Kahans had already had dealings with Schocken in previous years through Chaim Publishing House. The publishing house helped to save Schocken's legendary library from

Nazi Germany and received it in Palestine. Schocken now acted as their key commission agent. The library contained hundreds of valuable manuscripts, a collection of Hebrew incunabula, 60,000 volumes, some first editions, and unique research material. It was shipped to Palestine between January 1934 and December 1935. Rubin Mass, once an employee of Bendet Kahan at Yalkut in Berlin, is said to have supervised the import of the books to Palestine for two years. From an exchange of letters, it appears that the brothers Kahan had offered Chaim Publishing House and *Haaretz* for sale to Schocken at a meeting in Marienbad in the fall of 1935. The negotiations began shortly afterwards at a meeting in Lucerne. In December 1935 they intensified in Tel Aviv. The sale came about in June 1936.

Even under Schocken's leadership, some of Chaim Kahan's descendants continued their work for the *Haaretz*. Moshe Ater remained on the editorial staff until 1950, making a name for himself as a business journalist. Röschen, Bendet's youngest, who had served as an officer in the British Army during the war, was drawing for *Haaretz* maps of Rommel's troop movements, recounted Naomi Loewenthal. After university, Chaim Avinoam was working for *Haaretz* for the rest of his working life as an expert in archaeology and translator of English, French and German articles.

Perhaps the Kahans had relinquished *Haaretz* because they needed capital for their investment in the Elite chocolate factory. Elite was a national project to stand up to Sarotti and Cadbury, according to a study by David DeVries, who conducts research and teaches at Tel Aviv University. David also directed this project. The family's share of the young company's capital was not high, Eli told us; he spoke of twelve and a half percent. The company had been founded in Ramat Gan in October 1933, at a time when the Kahans were reorganizing themselves economically in Paris. A few months later, in January 1934, their brother-in-law David Ettinger had joined the management as the family representative and financial director. One of the eight investors in Elite was Aron Nisse, the Kahans' employee in Riga, with a share of sixty percent, remembered his daughter Judith Shklar. Two former accountants from Nitag were making a new start with Elite. The Kahans' lawyer Yuda Beham became legal advisor to the company. Even though the family did not have a significant financial stake in Elite, they were still present as networkers through their agents. Like a big white ship at anchor, the Elite chocolate factory lay on the meadows of Ramat Gan. Its construction had begun immediately after the company was founded and was completed two years later, in 1935, in the same style and at the same time as the *Haaretz* printing plant and just as aesthetically ambitious. The building, framed by wide streets, surrounded by traffic, with a different company name, is still an eye-catcher and landmark in Ramat Gan today.

Within the family, word is that David Ettinger gave the company Elite its name, which could be understood in Eretz Israel as well as all over the world. According to David DeVries, Chaim N. Bialik was the inventor of the brand. Dvora proudly told us that her father, as a senior manager, had paved the way, opened doors and made it easier for the Latvian confectioners in Palestine to start the company with his knowledge of the country and its languages, and his relations with the mandate administration—as he had previously done for the Kahan family in the oil industry. How did David Ettinger, who had represented the Kahans' oil wholesale in Palestine on his own for years, make out after joining the collective management of a chocolate factory? After the sale of the COC subsidiary in Haifa in April 1930, he had, on his own authority and against the agreements with the buyer Anglo-Persian Oil, attempted to continue the oil business, promising the Soviet Foreign Trade Organization purchases for Palestine. The family was immediately reprimanded by Anglo-Persian Oil for this, and David Ettinger was reigned in and recalled. Her father had been working for Elite for six or seven years, when a quarrel erupted with the chief executive Eliyahu Fromchenko, according to Dvora. In the family it is said that David Ettinger sided with the staff, against the entrepreneurs, and that an inkpot was thrown during the dispute. David Ettinger had temporarily needed a bodyguard to protect himself from Fromchenko. The conflict turned into a family dispute that destroyed the Ettingers' marriage. In the early 1940s David Ettinger withdrew from Elite. David Kahan officially assumed his position on the board of directors. Rachel Ettinger turned against her husband and sided with her brother and her own family.

Had Rachel and David Ettinger's marriage been arranged, or had they found each other by themselves? David came from a Russian acculturated family. His father represented the largest insurance company in the empire, Rossiya, in Uman, Ukraine. The silver elephant, the Viennese centerpiece with the Chinaman, the spice jars on his back, which the family had smuggled out of Soviet Russia and taken with them to Palestine via Berlin, testify to their middle-class origins. In contrast, Rachel came from an upper middle-class family. David had not attended school, as was customary in bourgeois Jewish families at the time, but had received private lessons. Rachel, on the other hand, had gone to a Protestant secondary school for young ladies in Germany after years of home schooling and had lived with her brother David in Marburg for more than a year, away from her parents' home. Did Rachel perhaps resemble the rebellious Russian students that Kurt Blumenfeld described in his memoirs—a modern, educated young woman who spread a spirit of optimism, dreaming of the glorious Russian Revolution? In 1905, Rachel had paid for her participation in the revolution's youth movement in Warsaw with imprisonment. A letter she had written to her oldest brother Baruch in Kharkov shortly after her release from Wiesbaden, where part of the family was taking the waters, speaks of dejection and disorientation. Following her release and the summer retreat in Wiesbaden, the family sent her to her brother Bendet in Antwerp. In 1911 she married David Ettinger, seven years her senior. The wedding took place in Warsaw, in her sister's house, where her mother Malka was also living. Rachel and David Ettinger became hands-on Zionists; it was this and their four children which bound them together. From the time they were together, they planned to emigrate to David's brother in Palestine. But because they were financially dependent on Chaim Kahan, they remained in the Russian Empire. A year and a half after they fled to the West, in the spring of 1925, they were the first of the Kahan family to settle in Palestine. Arusia wrote that Rachel was the most intellectual of Chaim's children, that all her life, up to her old age—she lived to be over eighty—she had studied and taught, had raised four children in Haifa despite her obsession with education and was also involved in social work. One of her projects was the foundation of an organization for the trade in second-hand clothes, Beged Zol.

Chaim Kahan had taken both sons-in-law into the business. Jonas Rosenberg, called by Giza *eidam far yontev* [son-in-law for the holidays], managed to elude him gracefully, but David, a businessman in a dependent position, could hardly please Chaim, let alone his brothers-in-law and their sons. He was considered a stubborn man who obviously needed space. His children recounted a scene from their departure from Soviet Russia: when the train stopped at a small station as it often did en route, their father insisted on going to fetch a pot of water, against their mother's warning. When he got off, he fell, because the train had come to a stop beyond the platform; he got caught between the car and the tracks, and fortunately remained unharmed. While they did not get any water, their father got his way. "Aunt Rochele was a very interesting figure," Giza said. "She was small in stature, with a nice gait, a proud mother, but not a pious woman." Nevertheless, she kept the household kosher. She was bossy and a great critic. Dvora said her parents had been living in the apartment on Rothschild Boulevard side by side for years, without talking to each other. Her voice expressed bitterness, as she took her father's side. The split between the Kahans and the Ettingers continues to have an impact today, said Ayelet Brosh in the Café Lorenz & Mintz in Neve Zedek. She is writing a novel about her great-grandfather.

The *Ha'avara* [Transfer] Agreement of August 1933 between the Jewish Agency, the Zionist Association in Germany and the Reich Department of Commerce made it possible for the Kahans to transfer their assets from Germany to Palestine in an orderly manner. Even though it was controversial in the Jewish world because it recognized the Nazis as a contractual partner and favored Palestine over the rest of the Jewish world, it helped many Jews to secure a livelihood after fleeing to the *yishuv*. The Kahan Vermögensverwaltung in Berlin-Charlottenburg was deleted from the commercial register in 1938. It was then continued under a Hebrew name in Palestine. At the end of January 1941, Agudat Yam Hatikhon Leiskei Mamon, as it was now called, held an extraordinary meeting in Tel Aviv. Bendet, Yasha and Rachel Ettinger were additionally appointed to the management, which until then had consisted of the two managing directors Aron and David, with Arusia and Lolia as board members. Thus, in Palestine, all the children of Chaim and Malka, with the exception of Miriam Rosenberg, were involved in the running of the asset management company. Bendet, Aron, David and Rachel represented their own interests, while Arusia and Lolia were acting for Baruch and Pinchas, their deceased fathers. Yasha, as Roska's husband, might have possibly represented the interests of Miriam, Roska's mother, who had died in Berlin in 1931. Her father Jonas had died in November 1941, nine months after the new composition of the company's management was announced. It is questionable whether Roska and her brother Nomek had agreed with the change in this form—the Rosenbergs being represented by Yasha. Nomek's letter to Aron in 1961 shows his anger at the former family head and economic leader, who had tried to continue to assert his claim to power after the war. Eli recounted that his father had claimed his inheritance through an arbitration court, with Emmanuel Racine acting as arbitrator. The former Paris Racine employee founded the national Israeli oil company Delek in 1951 and headed it until his death in 2020. Eli met him again later at Delek.

In the middle of the war, in 1941, the Kahans' oil business lay idle. Rapide had been sold off, and it remains unclear what happened to the Cie des Carburants du Centre in occupied Paris. In August 1939, Arusia, in Paris, had informed his brother Yasha in Tel Aviv that after the sale of Rapide, the company would continue to operate independently and autonomously, it not yet being certain whether it would be liquidated or sold. Nohaka in Amsterdam was controlled by the German occupying power. After the German Wehrmacht's invasion of the Soviet Union, there was nothing to be learned about the subsidiaries in Memel, Kaunas and Riga.

It is unlikely that the Kahans were involved in Eurotank during the war. The funds of Agudat Yam Hatikhon might not have been great as the family's assets in Palestine were not too flush in 1941. However, it was probably enough to establish small businesses and a relatively carefree life. Even in the bohemian *yishuv*, most of Chaim's descendants continued their bourgeois way of life as far as possible. Immediately after her arrival in 1927, her mother wanted to go to the gym, as in Germany, Efrat said, asking someone on the street for its address; she got asked back, by way of reply, whether she had nothing more important to do in the country. Some of the family installed the heavy Berlin furniture again. An expansive oak buffet filled the Ettingers' dining room, and at the Rosenbergs' the white sanded-lacquer bedroom set from 36 Schlüterstrasse had found a new home. According to Giza, Roska, who like her own mother, Miriam Rosenberg, liked to spend money, ran an elaborate household and was repeatedly admonished by David to be thriftier because here it was no longer like in Berlin. What did become of Roska's childhood dream of becoming a flower arranger in Palestine, when it was not at all customary in Tel Aviv to send flowers on birthdays? "And if so, which flowers?"—Amos Oz asks in his novel *A Tale of Love and Darkness.* "We were allowed to pick as many anemones and cyclamen as we wanted. ... Gladiolas had a fine flair of concerts, of balls, of theater, of ballet, of culture, and of tender, deep feelings." So, at best, one used to give gladiolas as gifts.

Chaim's descendants were easily mistaken in the *yishuv* for Yekkes, but they also adhered to traditions from the Russian Empire. The parents would speak Russian if they wanted to keep something secret from the children. Unlike most Yekkes, they spoke Hebrew, except for the women who had married into the family, came from Königsberg and Memelland and spoke German. Most of them kept a kosher home. At least Roska and her family adhered to the religious customs according to the Orthodox tradition. On festivals, they attended the services of Rabbi Shlomo Ha-Cohen Aronson, whom Chaim Kahan had met at the Mizrachi, who knew Roska and Yasha from Berlin, and who was chief rabbi of Tel Aviv until his death in 1935. Later they used to attend a prayer house that was located nearby.

Bendet and Judith retreated to Petach Tikva, where Chaim Kahans' heirs owned their second center in Palestine, the large citrus orchard. He was living off his inheritance and continued to publish books, traditional writings in Hebrew. Miriam's son Nomek founded a company called Penguin in February

1934, just a few months after his arrival, which produced carbon paper, but business was not good. He loved the theater. Together with his wife Sulamith, who was a trained pianist, he became an impresario for the Cameri, the chamber theater that had opened in Tel Aviv in 1944.

Baruch's sons took different paths. Noma no longer had anything to do with the controversial questions of the distribution of wealth. He had himself paid off, built a house in Herzlia from his inheritance, planted trees and grew citrus fruit. However, their yield was only sufficient to live on because David, the asset manager in Palestine, supported the family of four every now and then. Later Noma became a beekeeper. Not as a farmer, but as a beekeeper he went down in the history of Herzlia. Efrat told later that her mother had had a hard time living on the land. She only found fulfillment in her work helping new immigrants to integrate. On Amos Oz's population scale, which ranged from the pioneers to those afflicted with *zores* (the Yiddish form of the Hebrew word for "misery"), the Kahan family ranked one notch below the pioneers, even though two of them, Noma and Rita, had made the transition to the pioneers. They belonged to the organized *yishuv*, and were on the side not of the workers and union members, but of the entrepreneurs and employers. Yasha, who had once studied philology in Munich and law in Berlin, became a partner of the haberdashery manufacturer Bialer, whom the family knew from Łódź. When they fell out, Yasha founded the company Tamar, which manufactured ribbons of all kinds, in June 1939 in Sarona, now a district of Tel Aviv. His new partner was his brother Arusia, who had undergone many locational and professional changes: in 1933 from Nitag in Cologne to *Haaretz* in Tel Aviv; from there, in 1936, when Schocken took over the newspaper, to the management and handling of the oil business in Paris and then, moving in early 1940, to Tel Aviv. "The ribbons for our wedding from my father-in-law's factory were magnificent," recalled Giza, who had survived the Holocaust in Bucharest under a false identity, had come to Palestine after the war and married Chaim Avinoam in the early 1950s. The two moved in with Grandmother Rosalia.

Of Baruch's sons, only Arusia was a businessman, Dvora claimed. Only he had dared to call on his brothers and cousins in Berlin in the early 1920s to revolt against Aron as the leader of the family and head of the company. Arusia also liked to talk about money, according to Efrat. Even so, he had not become a successful entrepreneur. He later stood his ground against his uncle Aron, merely as the narrator of the family history, putting his own version against his uncle's. In fact, none of Chaim's grandchildren became successful entrepreneurs. Not even Rachel Ettinger's son Moshe Ater, the inventor of the "Nohaks."

He was a leading business editor, first at *Haaretz*, then for fifteen years, from 1960 to 1975, at the *Jerusalem Post*, a critical observer but not a player in the business world. David later appointed his nephew Arusia as heir and, together with Moshe, as administrator of the Kahan assets.

Pinchas's son Lolia was nowhere at home after the Second World War. He told the German restitution authorities that he had fled from Lisbon to England in 1943, served in the British Army and was demobilized in Palestine in 1946. There he worked in a brickworks until he was drafted again when the War of Independence broke out, but only for office work. In 1950 he left Israel, went to the USA and returned to Israel fourteen years later, when he was sixty-two.

The days of Chaim Kahan's heirs as oil entrepreneurs were over. Instead, some of his descendants contributed personally and materially to the Eretz Israel project and to the early idealism of the pioneer immigrants. Two days after the United Nations General Assembly had given its approval in November 1947 for the establishment of a Jewish and an Arab state on the British Mandate territory, war broke out and the fighting for Jerusalem started. Thereupon Nomek's son Eli, who had just begun his studies at the Hebrew University, enlisted in the military together with school friends and joined the Notrim, the kibbutz police in the north of the country. After basic training, he and his friends switched to the Haganah, the Jewish underground army. They belonged to a unit consisting only of students. One day, in January 1948, they were deployed to Gush Etzion, four Jewish settlements in the mountains of Hebron, which were massively attacked by Arabs. In the house of his aunt, Esther Smoira, in the Rechavia District in Jerusalem, he had been waiting all night for transport, fully kitted out and praying together with his aunt. But nobody had come to pick him up. Shortly thereafter, he learned that the entire unit had been wiped out. It was later renamed Lamed He [the Thirty-Five] after the number of soldiers killed. Eli stayed in Jerusalem, defending the last buildings outside the Old City, experienced hunger in the besieged city and was then deployed to Hebron until he injured his arm and became unfit to fight. In an armored vehicle, part of a military convoy, he returned from Jerusalem to his parents in Tel Aviv, an oasis of peace during the War of Independence. Later he fought in the Givati Brigade, laying and defusing mines in the area promised to the Jews by the UN partition plan. But then Ben Gurion, the founder of the state, made sure that the students could return to the universities so that the country's future elite would not risk their lives in the struggle. Eli went to Switzerland to study.

Arusia's son Tanchum Cohen-Mintz, called Tani, over two meters tall, became more popular than any of them as a successful basketball player in the Israeli national team. He got into the sport thanks to his mother Edith Cohen-Mintz, a women's tennis champion in the 1950s. He, too, had started with tennis. He played basketball for Maccabi Tel Aviv. In 1961 he was elected Sportsman of the Year.

Other family members did a great deal for the modernization of the Hebrew language. Efrat recalled that her father, Noma, liked to be distracted from field work by discussions about correct *Ivrit*, the table talk often revolving around the language. After leaving Elite, David Ettinger devoted himself entirely to his linguistic and literary interests, wrote poems, published the first Hebrew pictographic dictionary in 1943, *Sfateinu bemar'ot* [Our Language in Pictures], which was praised by Ben Gurion and continues to provide valuable services to translators today. In addition to and following his work as a business journalist, Moshe, continuing his father's work, founded and directed The Association for Hebrew, the Keren Halashon Ha'ivrit. "The Association was actively involved in various initiatives aimed at strengthening the status and presence of Hebrew within the Israeli society," Moshe's daughter Hagit wrote to me. "For example, it organized conferences, one under the patronage of President Yitzchak Navon, developed a course for teachers in the army, encouraged public broadcasting to raise the level of language skills, donated 400,000 shekels [100,000 euros today] to a foundation for student scholarships and the organization of an annual conference on *Ivrit* at the Hebrew University."

Hagit wrote that her father had also published a book on Hebrew as a modern language and translated books from English and German: Edward Wilson's *To the Finland Station* on the history of revolutionary thought and the emergence of socialism up to the Russian Revolution; Robert Graves's science fiction novel *Seven Days in New Crete*; the major work of the American economist and Nobel laureate Paul Samuelson *Economics: An Introductory Analysis*; poems by Rainer Maria Rilke and Sigmund Freud's *The Man Moses and the Monotheistic Religion*. Apart from Samuelson, whom he probably appreciated as an expert in economics, he probably made books of world literature, which had personally impressed him, accessible to the Hebrew readership. Reading and transcribing Freud's *The Man Moses and the Monotheistic Religion* inspired him in the end to write a monograph in English on Freud and his relationship to religion, thus participating in the debate on the explosive late work of the founder of psychoanalysis. Moshe assumed that the death of Freud's father, which had plunged Freud into a depression and driven him to relentless self-exploration, had initiated psychoanalysis. Moshe's own father had died lonely and impoverished in 1959.

But the family's life in Mandatory Palestine, later Israel, was overshadowed not only by political events in Europe and the rift between David Ettinger and the Kahans. In 1959 Shalom Ettinger's daughter, Shua, was presumably murdered in the Masada region by Arabs from the West Bank, which was part of Jordan at the time. Since then, Chaim Kahan's descendants have been very personally affected by the basic conflict that is still unresolved today—the dispute over the country.

CHAPTER 21

Sanctuaries. The Family Is Alive. New York, Tel Aviv, Ma'agan Michael

A ron wrote from Paris to Alfred Aufhäuser in New York in February 1939,

> I personally am firmly convinced that the idea of creating a service station
> business is perfectly sound from a commercial point of view, notwith-
> standing the fact that service stations in America are an old business, that
> no initiative whatsoever is needed from the outside let alone from afar,
> that it is compatible with the protection of commercial interests and that
> this business should employ exclusively or at least predominantly Jewish
> emigrants who came to America from countries of persecution. I believe
> it can be said, that in a certain respect, the work of these emigrants can be
> of great benefit to the intended business and can contribute a great deal to
> the success of the business. It would therefore be desirable to begin with
> the establishment of this business.

Aron, following Zina, had decided on New York, and had already made preparations for it early in 1939, half a year before the outbreak of the war. But whether
the partnership with Alfred Aufhäuser was ever put into practice remains an
open question. It is possible that Aron was involved in his service stations,
about the existence of which there is no doubt. From the spring of 1941, Aron
and Zina, Gita and Monia, the Russian *Nyanya* Sasha, Lily and Ali lived in
Manhattan on the Upper West Side. To start with, according to Victor Ripp,
Zina's rich relatives, owners of Michael Golodetz & Co, had their office in the

center of the financial world, downtown, at 91 Wall Street. A little later, Aron and Zina moved into an apartment on Sixty-Ninth Street, where, crouched between the high-rise buildings, stand the old brownstone houses, which at that time accommodated immigrants from all over the world; today they are restored and gentrified, expensive city villas. Central Park is in the immediate vicinity. In the fifties, they lived a few streets further away, on Eighty-Forth Street; finally, in the sixties, on West End Avenue, always in apartment buildings with plain brick facades, up to sixteen stories high. Roska's grandson Jonah, who visited the family on Eighty-Forth Street with his parents as a child, remembered a dark apartment in a run-down neighborhood. Paul and Victor might have felt differently about the surroundings. Finally, after the unsettling years of fleeing, their parents had found a place for them to stay. Paul remembered how he started learning English and that Aron often picked him up from school and treated him to a chocolate malt at the drugstore on the corner of Eighty-Sixth Street and Columbus Ave. Victor added that it was "a drink never even imagined anywhere in Europe" and said that Aron showed him how to peel an orange in one piece and advised him to drink hot tea to cool off on hot days.

No sooner had he arrived in New York, than Aron, with the help of his lawyer Alexis Goldenweiser, began to reorganize his assets and business. Goldenweiser, like many other Russian Jewish migrants, had found a new refuge in New York a few years before the Kahans, opening a law firm on the Upper Westside of Manhattan. He apparently represented Aron in various matters. "The Kahans are my good friends," the lawyer wrote to his guarantor in the State Department in Washington, "and I can fully vouch for their excellent character and loyalty." With his help, Aron transferred money from his account at the Central Bank of Portugal in Lisbon to New York and converted it into dollars, which, given the war situation, was only possible with special permission. With Goldenweiser's support, he tried to obtain a license for Paul and Victor's father to produce stencils. With a license, Monia, now called Frank Solomon Ripp, could have built on his former activities in France. Aron himself, with the help of his lawyer, was planning to set up an insurance company that would provide loan securities to owners of apartment buildings against default of payment due to excessive vacancy. In any case, in February 1942, barely a year after his arrival in New York, he already owned a new firm, the Hudson Coast Company, which wanted to export chemicals to South America, despite stricter requirements of the war administration to protect the trade in goods. Aron tried to tie in with tried and tested business structures, even though an existence in the oil trade was out of the question, since the American market was still occupied by the large successor companies after Standard Oil was broken up in 1911. He apparently had made an effort to charter tankers that were transporting oil products from the Gulf of Mexico to the East Coast states, carrying cargo on the return run. Whether he succeeded in this is not clear from Goldenweiser's office documents. In the family archives, Aron and Zina's efforts to gain a foothold in their fourth exile have left no traces. Paul and Victor might have well remembered the Hudson Coast Company, but not what the company was involved with.

Around the same time that Aron was trying to obtain a visa for David, the United States entered the Second World War, while the Nazis began the mass murder of Jews in Eastern Europe. In early 1942, representatives of the National Socialist government and the SS authorities met at the Wannsee Conference in Berlin to organize the barbarity. As long as the war lasted, the family members in Palestine, New York and Eastern Europe were cut off from each other. Only after 1945 did the traffic slowly return to normal. Little by little they learned of the deaths of relatives, friends and former employees in Auschwitz, Grodno, Riga, Treblinka and Łódź. Victor's three-year-old cousin, Alexandre, had been arrested by the French police in July 1942. His father, Aronchik, had been hiding in the Kahans' office in the Rue de la Bienfaisance and escaped. Alexandre's mother and grandmother were also arrested, deported and murdered. Victor later followed the path leading to the death of his cousin and other relatives. He went to Warsaw, Grodno and Paris, visited the memorial at the former Vélodrome d'Hiver, where the Jews had been crammed together before being deported, as well as the camps Beaune-la-Rolande and Drancy. In Riga, Edith's siblings were murdered, and her parents, Arusia's parents-in-law, were deported to Siberia, where Paul Mintz died. In Riga, relatives of Genia, Lolia's wife, were also murdered, like Zina and Mina's relatives in Warsaw. Abram Kagan's partner, the publisher Yakov Bloch, managed to escape to Switzerland. His sister Raissa, however, was arrested while fleeing to her brother, held in the Drancy transit camp and deported from there to the Auschwitz concentration camp where she was murdered. In Treblinka, once the largest Nazi extermination camp in the *Generalgouvernement* [German-occupied Poland] one million people were murdered between July 1924 and August 1943. Speechless, I stood in front of the steles for the Jews from Orla, Grodno, Białystok, Łomża, places where the Baschs, Kamenetskys, Rosenbergs and Kahans—all relatives of the family— had lived. The former employees of the COC in Copenhagen, Abraham Ledermann and Elias Feldmann, had escaped to Sweden, others, employees of Nitag, fled to Palestine, South America, or USA. Emanuel Racine, who had run the Kahans' company in Paris and Orlean, went underground, fought on the side of the Resistance and rescued Jewish children.

The Hanemann brothers in Amsterdam took different paths. Benno Hanemann fled to New York in 1939, Moses Hanemann stayed and continued to run the Nohaka, even under German occupation, until spring 1943, when the company was expropriated and handed over to the Dutch Corporation for the Liquidation of Enterprises and Hanemann was arrested. Their father, a very conscientious man, did not want the employees to leave the company, reported the daughters Ineke in Amsterdam and Dorith in Kiryat Chaim, a suburb of Haifa. Moses Hanemann was deported, together with his wife Gerty, to the Dutch transition camp Westerbork in June 1943 and eight months later, in mid-February 1944, to the Bergen-Belsen concentration camp, north of Hanover. From there, in January 1945, he was sent to the Swabian internment camp Bad Wurzach, where Jewish prisoners were gathered up to be exchanged for imprisoned Germans. In late April 1945, they were liberated by French troops. They had entrusted their one-and-a-half year-old daughter, Bila, to Dutch Christians. They owed their survival to Paraguayan passports, which they had acquired with the help of a business friend, and to the fact that they had relatives in Palestine and consequently a so-called Palestine certificate; they were intended to be exchanged for German civilian prisoners. Bila became Ineke. Her father later described the rescue operation. After the war, in August 1945, she returned to her parents, whom she did not recognize. Her father went back to Nohaka in Amsterdam, after an interlude in Paris, where he recovered and waited months for his recognition as a Dutch citizen. It was thanks to the Dutch coowner Johannes H. Gaukstert that the Nohaka was handed back immediately after the end of the war, the Kahans were recognized as the main shareholders, and Moses Hanemann once again became the company director. Gaukstert had prevented the trustee appointed by the Nazis from plundering Nohaka before leaving his post. The Amsterdam historian Erik Schumacher has recorded the story of Moses and Gerty in a book.

One month after the end of the war, Benno, in New York, had apparently received the first sign of life from his brother. He replied: "I am overwhelmed by joy," described his own situation and listed the names of those mutual friends who had found refuge in New York, naming the Kahans at the top of the list. Aron Nisse was in Canada. He had retired after surviving a heart attack. Benno proudly reported that he had received American citizenship. He had been working with the Kahans for a year and a half. "Our business is a very small one and the main business is the import of diamonds from Palestine; we are acting here as agents for the Palestine factories." Had Aron, in his distress, switched from the wholesale of oil to the import of diamonds? Until the end of 1941, the Eurohandel in Hamburg, led by Carl von Clemm and Hermann Leising, had also imported gemstones from the Netherlands and Belgium into the then still neutral USA via the Pioneer Import Corporation in New York led by Werner von Clemm. Was this coincidence an accident? During World War II, the diamond industry, traditionally considered a Jewish realm and driven out of its European centers, Antwerp and Amsterdam, by the Nazis, had found a new home in Palestine. The British Mandate authorities had actively supported this, similar to the chocolate industry, by facilitating access to African raw material sources, cocoa beans and rough diamonds, through their connections to the colonies of the Empire. Like the chocolate industry in the 1930s, the diamond industry strengthened the booming national Jewish private sector in the 1940s.

"Kahan is, mentally, absolutely unchanged," Benno continued to his brother Moses, "although, unfortunately, he lost his eyesight. He left New York today for a vacation and asked me to give you his and Zlata Kahan's heartiest regards." Aron's American passport, issued in December 1946, also certified his blindness. The man in the passport picture keeps his eyes, especially the right one, half closed and does not look at the photographer. In the following letter Benno Hanemann continued: "Kahan, who, as you know, had all the past years great trouble with his eyes, lost practically his eyesight completely, but he is really admirable, as he tries to ignore that terrible fact, keeping himself and all people around him busy with ideas and plans." The letter to his brother was written on Hudson Coast Company letterhead. Moses Hanemann replied on Nohaka letterhead, telling his brother in New York about his ordeal and Nohaka's fate since the occupation of the Netherlands. From May 1940 to June 1943, he had still managed the company, but under the control of the occupying forces. They had merged seven smaller Dutch petroleum wholesalers into a group called Vereeniging van Importeurs van Petroleum Produkten. This group existed until the postwar period. In August 1945, it was dissolved by a state-controlled sales office, so that the company could once again operate independently.

Shortly after the end of the war, Aron had plans to participate in another national project for Palestine. In late February 1946 he wrote to a certain Lieutenant A. Lachman in Washington: "Dear Mr. Lachman, I refer to the conversation you had with Mr. Goldenweiser regarding the idea of buying American ships from the Surplus for Palestine. ... As you know, a group of Palestinian Jews, including my brother David in Tel Aviv and myself, intends to provide the necessary capital for this purpose." Presumably, he was referring to decommis-sioned warships.

Visas and stamps in Aron's passport bear witness to the first great jour-neys across the Atlantic after the war. Zina and Aron went to places where they had lived and visited their relatives. In 1947 they were for the first time back in France and Switzerland, in 1948, in France, Belgium, England and Israel. In January 1948, Aron tried to reopen the Cie des Carburants du Centre in Paris and offered to do business with the Anglo-Iranian Oil Company. According to his own memoirs, he met up in Paris with Hermann Leising, who had lost his job, home and fortune in the war; in June 1948, immediately after the currency reform, Leising opened a currency exchange in West Berlin, on Budapester Strasse, told his son. In 1949 and 1950 Aron and Zina travelled on the *Queen Mary* and the *Queen Elizabeth*, again to France and Israel. In 1949 they were accompanied by Zina's daughters and their families. They all spent their sum-mer holidays, as had been customary before the war, in a spa, this time in the French town of Vittel en Lorraine. In the years that followed, Zina and Aron continued to be regularly drawn to their relatives in Europe and Israel. Lily's daughters Ylana and Mirriam remembered how the whole family accompanied Aron and Zina each time to the piers of the Cunard Lines on the Hudson. Zina was held in great esteem by her relatives in Israel.

In New York, the Kahans used to attend the nearby small orthodox syn-agogue in one of the brownstone houses, between Broadway and West End Avenue on Ninety-First Street, during the High Holidays. Paul said that a rabbi whom the family knew was leading the services there. It could hardly have been Dr. Moshe Eisenstadt, who, like the Kahans, had fled France to New York, because he had died, aged seventy-four, a few years after his arrival, in December 1943. As before in Berlin and in Paris, and like the family in Tel Aviv, the Kahans in New York used to meet regularly on Shabbat with their relatives and closest friends. Now these gatherings were called Friday night dinner. "Descendants of the Pinchas/Zina branch of the Kahan family would gather together as they always have, for an elaborate, festive dinner," wrote Paul's wife Eleanor. The table was laid with the silver cutlery and the fine Rosenthal porcelain that Miriam Rosenberg had once bought in Weimar Berlin and which was displayed in the exhibition *Berlin Transit* at the Jewish Museum in Berlin in 2012. "When I joined the family in 1962, Zina and Aharon Kahan hosted the dinner. Strict rules of kashrut were kept. Conversa-tion took place in Russian, German, French and a bit of English." There was a seating arrangement, said Ylana and Mirriam, Lily's daughters, with Aron and

Zina at the top of the table and the children at the bottom. Zina and *Nyanya* Sasha shared the housework, baked and cooked elaborately. Victor still keeps Zina's cookbook to this day, which contains two different handwritten recipes for eggs in béchamel sauce, pierogis, chocolate cake, strudel, éclair and filled pastry rolls. Zina had trusted Sasha implicitly. Sasha had remained self-reliant despite her financial dependence. She never sat at the table. The guests were Zina's children—Gita and family, who were living on the same floor as Aron, Zina and Sascha; Lily, Ali and their daughters; from time to time also their brother Lolia with his second wife. He had separated from Genia in Lisbon. Lolia operated a service station in Manhattan in the 1950s. Aron probably got him the job. Zina regularly invited relatives—Cousin Daria Moiseevna Golodetz, her oldest friend in New York, who always used to sit by her side at the top of the table, cousin Yasha Rabinovich with his wife Myrra, who had helped them obtain American visas, and the family doctor, Dr. Dinkin. Invited were also relatives from Aron's side, who lived in Tel Aviv—Eli's older brother Michael, who had first studied in New York and later represented Israel at the United Nations as an economic expert, with his wife. Other guests included Benno Hanemann, Aron's cousin, the publisher Abram Kagan, who, according to Victor, was called "the professor," and a certain Borya, Boris Dembo— Paul remembered a man with a bowler—probably a descendant of Chaim Kahan's first partner in Baku, as well as occasionally Aron's secretary, Genia Wasser. After initial difficulties in New York, Kagan, the Russian-acculturated publisher interested in Christianity, founded another publishing house there. As early as 1917, he had published several books by and about Sigmund Freud in St. Petersburg, and between the wars he had met German and Austrian psychologists in Berlin who were now living in the United States and whom he recruited as authors. Since 1943 he distinguished himself by publishing psychoanalytic and psychological literature in his own publishing house, International Universities Press.

In Victor's memory was etched a picture of Lolia: his uncle was dancing kozachok at his niece's wedding after numerous glasses of vodka; by then he was already over sixty. The immigrants carried their habits with them to foreign countries, exploring and creating islands of familiarity and security for themselves. Like in Berlin and Paris, they ran open houses, founded clubs and associations and relocated organizations that had accompanied them on their escapes to New York. Such was the Association of Russian Jews, which had been founded in Berlin in 1920. In January 1942, the association's president in New York, Julius Brutzkus, announced that Aron was its treasurer.

Lily and Ali lived with their daughters a few streets away from Zina and Aron, on West End Avenue and Eighty-Second Street. After the Shabbat dinner they would stay with their grandmother, Ylana and Mirriam recounted; they would sleep in Zina's room and watch their grandmother comb her long grey hair. She was a fascinating woman, but not a warm-hearted grandmother. They described Aron, however, as a warm-hearted man. They admired how he moved confidently through the rooms as if he could see. Zina had been managing Aron's household, while he provided for her livelihood. The relationship worked, the granddaughters said. On Shabbat mornings they would drink orange juice and watch TV series at the Ripps' next door, things that were not customary in their own home. They described the Ripps as a more Americanized family.

Aleksandra Sokolova, *Nyanya* Sasha, had been living for fifty years, half a century, with the family. First she was Lily's, then Paul's and Victor's and, finally, Ylana's and Mirriam's nanny. In the evenings, she would put cold tea with lots of sugar by their bedside, sing Russian songs to them and, when they were sick, give them *gogel-mogel*, a dessert made from raw eggs, sugar and cocoa, the recipe for which originated in Eastern Europe. Ylana and Mirriam were rejoicing at the sound of the word, laughing loudly, as if they could feel the "homeopathic medicine" melt in their mouths. With the help of *gogel-mogel* she had found her husband, said Mirriam. He had grown up with Polish Yiddish and *gogel-mogel*, and had developed a relationship with the dessert that was as intimate as hers. *Nyanya* Sasha acquired American citizenship and lived in a small apartment of her own in Manhattan in her old age. During her last years, she had moved into a Russian nursing home in New Jersey and was receiving a pension on Lily's initiative.

In the beginning, they had had a very difficult time in New York, Victor said. They had arrived in 1941 completely penniless. In an interview for the Spielberg Foundation, his mother Gita said that in New York she had to earn money for the first time in her life, initially in a chocolate factory. When she would come home from work, the first thing she would do was smell an orange, to get the nauseating smell out of her nose. Later, Gita made costume jewelry. "My mother's costume jewelry business was as a 'contractor,'" Victor said. She made the jewelry that her clients designed, partly with her help, together with six to fifteen employees, depending on the order situation, and sold it to boutiques. She had a talent for it. Her husband Monia took a share in her business, after several unsuccessful attempts to open his own, first together with his brother Aronchik in Paris after the war and then without him in New York, establishing the costume jewelry business together with Gita. He died, prematurely, in

1957, at the age of fifty-seven. Without Aron's support, the new start in New York would probably have been much harder for Gita and Monia.

Her parents, Ylana said, had always tried to remain financially independent of Aron and Zina. In 1949, they went to Tel Aviv with the idea of starting a new life for themselves in the newly founded Israel, where they lived on Rothschild Boulevard in rented accommodation close by their relatives. After a few months, her father decided to return to America. Her mother would have liked to stay; she felt safe and secure in the family circle. Back in New York, Ali became an entrepreneur, like Lily's cousins Nomek, Yasha and Arusia in Israel, but not in the oil industry.

While Cousin Moshe Ater in Tel Aviv was championing a modern Hebrew national culture, Lily was interested in Russian literature. At thirty-four, she resumed her studies, which had been interrupted by war and flight, and took her bachelor's degree, then her master's degree at Columbia University. She worked as a freelancer for radio, the National Broadcasting Company and Radio Free Europe, which was targeting an audience in unfree Eastern Europe, governed by an authoritarian state ideology. After completing her Master's in English studies at the age of fifty at New York University, she became a freelance translator and writer. She translated Soviet Russian avant-garde literature from the revolution period into English—Viktor Shklovsky's Mayakovsky biography, which gained her a nomination for the National Book Award for Translation; in 1995, when she was eighty, she authored a biography of Marina Tsvetaeva subtitled *The Double Beat of Heaven and Hell*. In between, she worked on the translation of Shklovsky's Tolstoy biography, which remained unfinished. I read some of Lily's and Moshe's works. Like Moshe, Lily was apparently fascinated throughout her life by the events that she herself had experienced as a child during the war and revolution, which had upset the Russian society, and in which her relatives had become so entangled that they had had to leave the country. The Russian language and literature remained stronger and longer present with the Kahans in New York than with their relatives in Israel. They continued to live in the diaspora together with *Nyanya* Sasha, who had accompanied them on three escapes through Europe to America. Lily's nephew Victor also shared this passion. He majored in Slavic studies, traveled to the Soviet Union for research and later taught Russian literature. In contrast, Lily's daughter Ylana was drawn to Israel. She chose to focus on Middle East studies, became a Middle East historian and wrote about Palestinian Arabs at the time of the British Mandate.

Let's return to the oil business, which traditionally had formed the family's financial basis. Despite Aron's stubborn attempts to stay in business after the war, its demise could not be stopped. In 1947 the Kahans sold Nohaka in Amsterdam to the Anglo-Iranian Oil Company. For tax reasons, the business was conducted not in the Netherlands, but in Tel Aviv, at 105 Rothschild Boulevard, by the family's asset company, Mediterranean Finance, according to Moses Hanemann. The value of Nohaka was estimated at that time by appraisers commissioned by the prospective buyer, the Anglo-Iranian Oil Company, to be 19,800 pounds sterling.

The following year, in 1948, the British corporation bought another company with which the Kahans had been associated—the Hamburg refinery Eurotank. The owner, William Rhodes Davis, who was suspected of spying for the Nazis, had died in Houston under mysterious circumstances in early August 1941. The Anglo-Iranian Oil Company had acquired Eurotank from the sales assets of the Davis Group. Eurotank was affiliated with the German subsidiary Olex, which had been run since 1950 by Aron and David's old acquaintance Hans Ornstein, who had called himself John Ornstein since his British exile. Anglo-Iranian Oil Company paid $1,800,000 for Eurotank, and Aron received compensation of $45,000, two and a half percent, on the initiative of Davis's former confidant and executor James Lee Kauffman. In a letter of November 1954, Aron reminded John Ornstein of this fact: Eurotank should not have been sold to the Anglo-Iranian Oil Company without his consent. Why had the American management appointed Aron Kahan as sales agent to the British company? A file note of British Petroleum, formerly the Anglo-Iranian Oil Company, from February 1956 states: "Briefly, we first had dealings with Kahan in connection with the purchase of the Eurotank Refinery as he was the founder and, up to Nazi times, owner of the Eurotank Company."

Nowhere in his memoirs did Aron ever mention that he had been the founder and, until the beginning of the Nazi regime, the owner, of Eurotank. This story does not even occur in the family's collective memory, let alone the compensation of 45,000 dollars when the company was sold after the war. At some point I realized what Aron Kahan's share in Eurotank consisted of. After the demise of the COC and in the face of competition from the Benzene Association that had harassed Nitag, he drew up a plan—modelled on the Kahans' companies in the Russian Empire—to set up an integrated oil company with a refinery in Germany. He had probably intended to do this since his arrival in the West, but had not been able to implement it because the acquisition and expansion of the company's premises in Wilhelmshaven was impossible; the tank facilities there stood on unsaleable land leased from the Navy, and the poor transport connections to the hinterland also spoke against the City of Jade as an industrial location. Eurotank was apparently to become the successor to Nitag. After Hitler came to power, Aron had continually tried to exert influence on Eurotank and Nitag, which was not dissolved when the COC went bankrupt; presumably because the majority of shares were held by the bank and no longer by the Kahans. Eurotank had taken over the shares of the German insolvent company and continued the cooperation with its Danish partner. Morten F. Larsen, who is researching the Glad family of entrepreneurs in Copenhagen, assumes that Aron had obtained the preferential treatment for Gica in the exclusive contract with Nitag to compensate Glad for the COC's bankruptcy. It cannot be ruled out that Aron had prepared the sale of Eurotank to Davis, just as sixteen months earlier, in late 1931, Aron had prepared the sale of Nitag to Stanolind in order to salvage capital and connections with which he wanted to continue working in America. It must have been a shame for Aron to see what Davis had made of his project. But if Kauffman used and rewarded him as an agent, Aron is likely to have remained connected to the Davis group of companies through the war years. The compensation was miserable, but it did recognize him as the founder of the company and acknowledged him as a European oil expert, although he was not satisfied with that.

According to the Military Government Act 59, a compensation law had been in effect in the American Occupation Zone since November 1947 and in the British Zone since May 1949. Accordingly, the family had been claiming compensation from the Federal Republic of Germany for personal suffering and loss of property, both individually and as a group, from the early 1950s. Together, Chaim Kahan's descendants demanded compensation for the two buildings at 37 Schlüterstrasse and 32 Wielandstrasse and for the publishing house Romm in Vilna. They received nothing for the buildings in Berlin, based on the argument that the buildings were heavily mortgaged at the time of their expropriation. For the loss of the publishing house in Vilna, they received less than one-tenth of the estimated value of the books looted by the Nazis, 60,000 Deutschmarks. The loss of the publishing houses was not taken into account on the grounds that they had already been expropriated by the Soviet authorities before the Nazi occupation. Together with his brother David, Aron filed an application for compensation of assets with the Lüneburg Regional Court against the Wintershall company in Celle in June 1950. Aron and David Kahan demanded the restitution of Nitag shares valued at three million Deutschmarks, citing Dr. Hermann Leising in Berlin as one person who might have knowledge of the whereabouts of those assets. But only a few months later their lawyer terminated his engagement, and in

May 1951, barely a year after the application was filed, Aron and David withdrew the application.

Years later, Aron claimed that he had been pressured by Hans Ornstein to lodge this compensation claim. He had had no reason to pursue the trial, since he had already sold Nitag in 1932. The application had only served to put Wintershall under pressure. From 1946, the Anglo-Iranian Oil Company had been trying to buy Nitag from Wintershall in order to expand the sales capacity of Olex in Hamburg, which failed in 1949. Had the purchase been successful, the Anglo-Iranian Oil Company would have taken over all the core assets of the former Kahan empire—apart from the COC subsidiary in Haifa in 1930 and Nohaka in 1947; it would have included the entire Nitag, as well as the Eurotank and Wintershall shares, with the exception of the Soviet expropriations in Austria, East Germany and the Baltic Republics. Aron and Leising were involved in the negotiations between the Anglo-Iranian Oil Company and Wintershall in Paris. Three years later, at the end of 1950, during the compensation proceedings between the Kahans and Wintershall, both companies reached an agreement in the dispute over the company colors. Wintershall abandoned the previous Nitag colors green and yellow, so that the Anglo-Iranian Oil Company, later called British Petroleum, could use its green and yellow logo unrivalled around the world. The Anglo-Iranian Oil Company took over the costs of changing all the Nitag emblems to the new company colors of yellow and blue.

Hermann Leising had tried in vain after the war to get his fortune back in the USA, his son recounted. The currency exchange in Budapester Strasse was soon afterwards transformed into the banking business Bankgeschäft Leising & Co. Hermann Leising became a member of the Berlin branch of the Coordination Council for Christian-Jewish Cooperation in 1951. There he stated that he had held neither a leading office nor a leading position in the NSDAP and that he had not been actively involved with National Socialism. He served as treasurer of the Council until 1959.

Sometime in the late 1940s, or early 1950s, Aron fell into one of the basement entrances on the sidewalks of Manhattan, treacherous traps for all pedestrians not at home there. The accident further weakened the blind man.

Aron's letters and schemes from the 1950s are preserved, as are copies of letters in English that had passed through the office of the lawyer Goldenweiser in Manhattan. They had been typed in German and then translated into English by Aron's secretary, Genia Wasser, who had followed him from exile to exile. They all revolve around the Suez crisis after the nationalization of the canal by the Egyptian President Nasser. The heated conflicts between Egypt on the one hand and Great Britain, France and Israel on the other, which began in October 1956, had apparently alarmed Aron, both as an oil expert and as a Jew whose family lived in Israel and whose fortune lay there. His letters are addressed to leading politicians, to the Democrat and ex-president Harry S. Truman in the USA, to the Socialist and Prime Minister Guy Mollet in France, as well as to the top managers of British Petroleum in London and Desmarais Frères in Paris. As he had done before in the People's Republic of Ukraine, in the Weimar Republic and in the interwar Paris, Aron made recommendations as to how the conflicts could be resolved economically and politically. His proposals combined personal and political interests. He criticized the American solo effort, sought possibilities for an alliance of all leading Western powers and considered alliances between Israel and its Arab neighbors. In order to contain the influence of the Soviet Union on the Arab states, he wanted to tie the Iraqi and Saudi Arabian rulers, who had become rich through oil, more closely to their potential customers in the West, and recommended the reopening of the pipeline that had led from Iraq to Haifa and the Mediterranean Sea. This would benefit both Europe and the population of Jordan. He proposed the reorganization and generous financing of refugee aid to Jordan by the United Nations, the United States and Israel, as a political strategy for splitting the Arab camp, and the political reorganization of Jerusalem as Israel's concession to the Arab states and the Christian world. Following the UN partition plan of 1947, the Old City, an area of four to five square kilometers, which at that time was occupied by Jordan, was to become, according to Aron's ideas, an international and interdenominational garden city, administered by the three monotheistic religions under the protection of the United Nations.

Aron fought, increasingly doggedly, for recognition in oil industry circles. For ten years, from the sale of Nohaka in 1948 until 1958, he engaged in heated arguments with leading employees of the Anglo-Iranian Oil Company and later British Petroleum, primarily with his old friend Hans Ornstein in Hamburg and with John Im Thurn at Britannic House in London, the company's headquarters. Aron also knew Im Thurn personally and used to visit him when he was in London, just as he used to meet with Ornstein in Paris and in New York. Aron offered himself as an expert consultant and demanded cooperation or at least adequate compensation for losses suffered during the war and for being treated unfairly by British society. He complained to the managers that, when Eurotank was bought, his compensation had been reduced to half of the originally estimated amount; he was not accepted as a sales agent for Phoenix that same year, whereupon he missed out on a deal. This concerned shares in the

British company Phoenix Oil & Transport Limited, which owned oil fields in Romania. Moreover, they had not acknowledged his help in the dispute with Wintershall over the colors or in the proceedings for reimbursement of concessions expropriated during the war. In August 1953, Aron made Ornstein an offer of collaboration through the Cie des Carburants du Centre in Paris. His company had no debts except those to the French subsidiary of the Anglo-Iranian Oil Company. With this company, the Societé Generale des Huiles de Petrole B. P., he wanted to open gas stations in Paris and asked for a loan. Aron won supporters for the project within the company, including Ornstein, who wrote to Im Thurn: "The poor old man tries by all means to keep himself and his family going, and I admire his courage." But this deal, too, apparently did not materialize.

The more Aron was being fobbed off, the more persistent were his inquiries, his demands becoming seemingly more unrealistic. In the proceedings for Aron's personal compensation, Hans Ornstein had vouched for his former partner, attested to his many years of experience in the petroleum industry and distribution, certifying that he had held a very respected position in the business throughout his entire activity in Germany, and had been the executive director of Nitag, the most important independent distribution organization behind the large international groups and alongside Deutsche Gasolin, which was jointly owned by I. G. Farben, Shell and Esso. He did not mention the gains Aron made for Eurotank with a single word, although Ornstein had led the negotiations when the company was purchased in 1948. In their letters, Ornstein and Im Thurn would reply to Aron politely, but behind his back, in internal correspondence, the top managers agreed, half contemptuously and half compassionately, on the inappropriateness of the demands by the former entrepreneur, the "blind old man."

The Kahans' fortune had grown through the sale of Nohaka, but was now stuck in Israel and no new capital was added. Since then, it has been all about distribution, the legitimacy of claims and quotas. Disputes arose, threatening to tear the family apart. According to statements by the Nazi trustee, which were confirmed after the war by Moses Hanemann from another quarter, Zina and Lolia were the main owners of Nohaka. It was being said within the family in Israel that Nohaka and Elite were connected with each other, and that Nohaka had been bought completely with Elite shares. But Nohaka was older than Elite. From when the two companies were linked and in what form, no one in the family knew, and the Elite archive no longer exists. The export ban on foreign exchange in the newly founded Israel had meant that the Kahans in New York initially received payment for their shares in kind, for example, in Elite chocolate, Victor recalled.

Bendet and Judith died in Petach Tikva at the end of 1952. Rosalia survived Baruch by nineteen years and died in Tel Aviv in 1955. Her son Yasha followed her soon, four years later, in 1959. David Ettinger and David Kahan died during the same year. Rachel Ettinger lived another six years. Aron survived all his siblings. However, he was bitter at the end of his life; Ylana even called his condition paranoid and demented. He often argued with Zina, Victor said. Mirriam remembered that at one of the Friday night dinners, Aron was upset and yelling so much, that Sasha was asked to take him downstairs for a walk to calm him down. Aron even fell out with Lily, his favorite niece. When he promised his last secretary and nurse Maria, a Haitian Catholic, that he would bequeath to her a part of the family fortune, Zina was unable to cope. She separated from him, leaving him in the hands of his son Yossi, who until then had not had much in common with his ever absent father.

Despite his skepticism about the Zionist project, Aron moved to Israel and lived near his relatives, in the Danziger Guesthouse, at 40 Balfour Street, a few steps from Rothschild Boulevard. From August 1967, the mail he was receiving from the Berlin Restitution Office would go to the kibbutz where Yossi lived. The kibbutz Ma'agan Michael, literally translated as "Michael's Anchorage," at the foot of the city of Zichron Ya'akov, thirty kilometers south of Haifa and seventy kilometers north of Tel Aviv, was founded in 1949 by twenty pioneers. Yossi had been one of them. The kibbutz was named after Michael Pollak, the former partner and friend of Aron in Baku, co-owner of the transport company Mazut, which the Pollak family had founded in Nizhny Novgorod, then sold to the Rothschilds, Branobel's competition and later partner. Yossi recounted that once, when he was twelve, his father in Paris had sent him to deliver a letter to Michael Pollak, who was living at the time in a hotel on Mount Carmel in Haifa. The old man had had such an intimidating effect on him that he never forgot the encounter. Pollak was the founder of the largest cement factory in Palestine, later in Israel, Nesher, near Yagur, not far from Haifa.

Pollak had salvaged much of his fortune from the Russian Empire to Palestine, owning Shell shares from the sale of the Mazut company to Shell in 1913, a year before the start of the First World War. With this money he had founded the first cement factory in Palestine in 1923. Dvora, who knew him from her childhood, wrote that he had thus made a decisive contribution to Israel's development. Michael Pollak had made it easier for her father, David Ettinger, to make a new start in Haifa, and the two had had a lot to do with each other. In 1946 Pollak sold Nesher, and since then he has only been a patron of the arts. Among many other things, he financed the start of the kibbutz through the Palestine Immigrant Colonization Association (PICA), for which he had already worked in Paris after fleeing from Russia. Yossi said that Pollak made his donation conditional on the kibbutz being named after him. He met him again in 1950, as a member of a delegation from the kibbutz, this time asking in vain for a donation to a port facility.

The kibbutz, Ma'agan Michael, with 1,500 inhabitants and nearly 800 members, is one of the largest in Israel today. Built on alluvial land, on a small elevation, into an ancient cultural landscape, it is full of bungalows situated idyllically between the sea and the mountains in the midst of well-kept gardens. The majority of the founding generation comes from Germany and Austria. The *kibbutznikim* earn their living with agricultural products from livestock farming—chicken and cows—but above all with fish farming and the manufacture of plastic and fine metal, Plasson and Suron. The production facilities are located between residential areas and the sea, a sober, treeless industrial landscape, unsuitable for walking. The kibbutz is self-governing. It includes an *ulpan* [language school for new immigrants], various social facilities such as a clinic, a kindergarten, a senior citizens' club, a library and primary and secondary technical schools, which prepare for life and work in the kibbutz. Since he was nineteen years old, Yossi has lived as a pioneer on the land. This was an alternative to the military, he said. Since 1949, Ma'agan Michael was his family. In 2010, I met in Ma'agan Michael a tall eighty-eight-year-old man with a broad chest and an open look, who radiated natural authority and warm-heartedness and spoke German to me.

In Ma'agan Michael Yossi raised four children with his wife Lea, née Menuhin. Three of them still live in the kibbutz today. Lea was a socialist, according to Efrat. She once called the Kahans a bourgeois family in decline, and she was probably right.

In his last years, Yossi said, his father was even more obnoxious than before. He often spent Shabbat on the kibbutz and demanded then to have Hermann Struck's painting of his father, Chaim Kahan, in his room. At that time, Aron had been blind for many years, but persistent as always. The oil painting was hanging at Roska's in Tel Aviv. He had agreed with his cousin that the meter-high portrait would be transported every Thursday on a moped—they did not own a car at the time—from Tel Aviv to the kibbutz, seventy kilometers away, and back the same way on Sundays. "We had our peace and quiet, and Hermann Struck saw a part of Israel," Yossi wrote to me.

Since David's death and Aron's decline, there had been quarrelling in the family. Nomek protested against Aron's instruction to reduce the Rosenbergs' inheritance, continuing the dispute of his father Jonas. The fact that David had bequeathed his share to Arusia's nephew, aroused envy in some descendants. Lily and Yossi had to come to an agreement about Aron's heritage. Lily, Aron's foster daughter, represented the interests of her mother Zina, who had cared for Aron for many years. Yossi made claims as his biological son, who had been responsible for his father's upkeep in Israel. Disagreements still came to light at a meeting in Berlin in 2001, when Dvora and her husband, who were national-istically conscious Israelis, met Lily and Ali at an event at Humboldt University in memory of their expelled fellow students from 1933 and, according to Mirriam Rosen, did not exactly welcome their relations from the American Diaspora in a friendly and warm manner.

Aron died in May 1970, a few months before his ninetieth birthday. "The death ... has removed a person both brilliant and tragic, whose long career in a way epitomized the fate of Jewish middle-class abroad," wrote Moshe Ater in the obituary about his uncle in the *Jerusalem Post*, alluding to the price Aron had paid as an entrepreneur in the diaspora under the rule of totalitarian regimes. These had robbed him of his opportunities to act as an entrepreneur in Europe, had deprived him of his existence in Germany from 1933, had restricted his networks, had limited his radius even more tightly with the beginning of the war and had taken away any room for maneuver with the occupation of France. Moshe paid tribute to Aron's life and work. His almost all-consuming passion was the business adventure, not only for the sake of profit; he also wanted to demonstrate courage and dominate people. "His own firms were much too small for his profuse mind and his numerous projects, including world tanker cartels, reform of the oil market, monetary and social matters, Arab refugees, etc."

Aron had provided for his relatives from the time he had been running the family business. He had made the rules, had shown patriarchal family spirit, relying on the authority and legacy of his father, while his brother David had acted as a moderating and corrective influence, working for family cohesion, so that the Kahans were immune to assimilation pressure in the diaspora and could maintain their independence. "What puzzles me is how come that you show such interest in the Kahans," Yossi wrote to me, only to immediately answer the question himself: "they were probably a self-confident and support-ive community that knew how to survive the twentieth century." The family ties had remained intact throughout the Second World War, across the ocean and despite political and cultural differences. David, Aron and Zina used to meet at least once a year in Israel. Zina and Bendet's daughters, Lily and Röschen, and Dora and Gita, remained close friends throughout their lives. Michael Rosenberg and family were absorbed by the Kahans in New York. Lily's daughter Ylana kept closely in touch with the Rosenbergs when she was on research trips to Israel. Uli Cohen-Mintz in Tel Aviv and Paul Ripp in New York and their families still maintain intensive contact to this day. From time to time the descendants organize family reunions in Israel. Shortly after the murder of Shua, before David's death, a group photo with Aron and Zina in the middle, flanked by Rachel and David, in the circle of the descendants was taken at one of these meetings. The photo may have been taken in the orchard or at Ma'agan Michael. Zina is depicted with full, elegantly pinned-up hair, mottled with gray, while Rachel's hair is silky-white. Both women are wearing pearl necklaces and similar blouse dresses. Aron and David are in white shirts, ties closely tied to the neck, while the younger men are wearing open-neck shirts. Aron is keeping his eyes closed, while David is looking seriously into the camera. At that meeting in June 1959, they renewed the Vichy family constitution of 1940, with a request to the following generation "to keep the memory of the deceased alive while at the same time honoring the memory of the noble traditions of our parents in our hearts." Among the signatories, besides the four old people, were Yasha, Roska, Nomek and Arusia. Only the German version of the renewed constitution is preserved among the heirlooms.

In the late 1970s, Arusia and Moshe, as asset managers, sold the plantation and the shares of Chaim Kahan's Successors to Elite. "In the past, we were all employed in the oil industry," Arusia wrote in his memoirs from the 1980s. "Today there are 110 descendants of the family, 13 in New York, 97 in Eretz Israel, and only one is still involved in the oil business: he has a doctorate in geology and works in the oil industry in Eretz Israel." He was referring to Eli Rosenberg, who was involved in the discovery and development of oil wells in Israel. In the nineties he discovered gas fields offshore. He named the first one after his daughter Noa. As we know today, Eli thus initiated a turnaround in Israel's energy industry. He founded his own company, which he named with the Hebrew acronym of his own name, **Eli**jahu **b**en **N**achum **R**osenberg, or Avner for short. Avner works closely with the state-owned oil company Delek. It took years before Eli found recognition and partners willing to start production. On December 25, 2003, the gas from the Noa field (as part of the Tethys field) entered the power supply and has been providing Israel with energy ever since.

Appendix

ABBREVIATIONS

JMB: H-C	Jüdisches Museum Berlin, Archiv Haimi-Cohen
ABRW	Archive Benjamin Ravid, Waltham, Massachusetts
AECJ	Archive Efrat Carmon, Jerusalem
AGRHC	Archive Giza and Raziel Haimi-Cohen, Tel Aviv
AIFA	Archive Ineke Fenger, Amsterdam
ANLR	Archive Naomi Loewenthal, Ramat HaSharon
APRNY	Archive Paul Ripp, New York
ATEJ	Archive Tamar Eshel, Jerusalem
AUCMT	Archive Uli Cohen-Mintz, Tel Aviv
AVRP	Archive Victor Ripp, Princeton, New Jersey
AYMD	Archive Ylana Miller, Durham, North Carolina
AAA	Archiv der Aktiengesellschaft Bad Neuenahr
ACHHR	Amtsgericht Charlottenburg Handelsregister
AGCJZB	Archiv der Gesellschaft für Christlich-Jüdische Zusammenarbeit, Berlin
AJB	Adass Yisroel, Berlin
APW	Archiwum Państwowe, Warsaw
ARDTAM	Azərbaycan Respublikası Dövlət Tarix arxivi Mərkəzi, Baku
ATGK	Archive Thomas Glad, Copenhagen
AWHZ	Archiv der Westsächsischen Hochschule Zwickau
BAB	Bundesarchiv, Berlin-Lichterfelde
BAREEC	Bakhmeteff Archive of Russian & East European Culture, Rare Book & Manuscript Library, Columbia University, New York
BP-AMOCO	British Petroleum Archive, Warwick, England
CDIAK	Tsentralny Derzhavny Istorichny Arkhiv Ukrainy, Kyiv
EAB	Entschädigungsamt Berlin
GAA	Gemeente Achief van Amsterdam
GABO	Gosudarstvenny Arkhiv Brestskoi oblasti, Brest-Litovsk
GARF	Gosudarstvenny Arkhiv Rossiiskoi Federatsii, Moscow
GSPKB	Geheimes Staatsarchiv Preußischer Kulturbesitz, Berlin
HMRA	Henry A. Murray Research Archive, Harvard University, Cambridge, Massachusetts
HWWA	Hamburgisches Welt-Wirtschafts-Archiv

KBK	Det Kongelige Bibliotek København
KS	Københavns Stadsarkiv
LAB	Landesarchiv Berlin
LASA	Landesarchiv Sachsen-Anhalt, Dessau
LBA	Leo Baeck Archives, New York
LVIA	Lietuvos Valstybinis Istorijos Archyvas, Vilnius
NGAB	Natsyyanalny Gistarychny Arkhiv Belarusi, Hrodna
NHAH	Noord-Hollands Archief, Haarlem
NIOD	Archief Instituut voor Oorlogs-, Holocaust- en Genocidestudies, Amsterdam
NLAH	Niedersächsisches Landesarchiv, Hannover
PAAAB	Politisches Archiv des Auswärtigen Amtes, Berlin
RAK	Rigsarkivet, København
RGIA	Rossiisky Gosudarstvenny Istorichesky Arkhiv, St. Petersburg
SAB	Stadtarchiv Bonn
SAH	Stadtarchiv Hannover
SAHH	Staatsarchiv Hansestadt Hamburg
SAK	Stadsarkiv København
SAW	Stadtarchiv Wilhelmshaven
SFA	Stadsarchief Felixarchief Antwerpen
SKB	Staatsarchiv des Kantons Bern
UAJ	Universitätsarchiv Jena

Notes

1. Archives (Haimi-Cohen archives, Jüdisches Museum Berlin, private archives, public archives)
2. Interviews
3. Publications of the Kahan descendants
4. Articles in newspapers, directories and encyclopedias
5. Research literature
6. Memoirs and literature
7. Links

CHAPTER 1
Imprisoned. Jacob Kahan. Berlin

1.

JMB: H-C i: 4: Rosa Langer, Berlin, to Jacob Kahan, München, May/June 1914. H-C i: 18: Rosa Rosenberg, Wiesbaden, to Jacob Kahan, Bad Kissingen, End of July, 1914. i: 42: Aron Kahan, Memoirs, part 1 (Hebrew), 17; part 2 (German), 18. H-C ii: 10: Jacob Kahan, Alexandria, to Baruch and Rosalia Kahan, Jaffa, August 24, 1911. Id., Sofia, to Baruch and Rosalia Kahan, May 7, 1914. H-C 2, folders 13, 19: Collection and album of photographs from the trip to Palestine, April, 1914. H-C 2, folder 17: Hermann Struck, Berlin, to Chaim Kahan, Jaffa, April 2, 1914. H-C 2, folder 18: Letters between Jacob Kahan and the families Kahan and Rosenberg, Berlin, September 19–29, 1914.

AECJ: Hermann Struck, Mizrachi World Organization, Central Bureau, to Baruch Tanchum Kahan, Jerusalem, April 5, 1925.

AAA: Fremdenliste Bad Neuenahr, 1914, no. 11.

CDIAK: Chaim N. Kagan. F. 2034, op. 1, d. 75: Jacob Kahan, Berlin, to Nachum Kahan, Kharkov, October 26, 1913; d. 243–245: Arthur, Amanda and Trude Rosenthal, Berlin, to Jacob Kahan, Kharkov, May 2, 1911; June 22, 1911; December 8, 1911.

LBA: Judith Helfer Collection V. Subseries 1: Arthur and Ludwig Rosenthal, box 2, folder 35, no. 54/1403; folder 37, no. 371/1403; folder 38, nos. 378–380/1403.

2.

Interviews with Dvora Ettinger-Rozenfeld, Ramat Gan, December 8, 2008; November 8, 2010; October 9, 2012. Giza Haimi-Cohen, Tel Aviv, June 24, 2014.

3. ---

4.

"Wiesbaden," *Gemeindeblatt der Israelitischen Gemeinde Frankfurt* 14, no. 9 (1936): 358–359.

"Brückenauer Badebrief," *Frankfurter Israelitisches Familienblatt*, August 14, 1914, 2–3.

"Die Juden im Kriege," *Jüdische Rundschau*, September 4, 1914, 1.

"Zwei Gefangenenlager in Holzminden," *Täglicher Anzeiger Holzminden*, February 28, 2014.

5.

Alfred Marius Duvantier, *L. C. Glad & Co. 1880–1930. December 1930* (Copenhagen, 1930), 174.

Mordekay Eliav et al., *Das Berliner Rabbinerseminar 1873–1938: Seine Gründungsgeschichte— seine Studenten*, trans. Jana Caroline Reimer (Teetz and Berlin: Hentrich & Hentrich, 2008), 199, 225–226.

Ernst Feder, *Politik und Humanität: Paul Nathan, ein Lebensbild* (Berlin: Deutsche Verlagsgesellschaft für Politik und Geschichte, 1929), 110.

Marion A. Kaplan, *The Making of the Jewish Middle Class: Women, Family, and Identity in Imperial Germany* (New York: Oxford University Press, 1991), 122–125.

Hans-Christian Täubrich, *Zu Gast im alten Berlin: Erinnerungen an die Alt-Berliner Gastlichkeit mit Hotelpalästen, Vergnügungslokalen, Ausflugsgaststätten und Destillen* (München: Hugendubel, 1990), 70.

6.

Kurt Blumenfeld, *Gelebte Judenfrage*, ed. Hans Tramer (Stuttgart: Deutsche Verlags-Anstalt, 1962), 105.

Nachum Goldmann, *Mein Leben als deutscher Jude* (Frankfurt/Main et al.: Ullstein, 1983), 98–107.

Sammy Gronemann, *Erinnerungen: Aus dem Nachlass*, ed. Joachim Schlör (Berlin: Philo, 2002), 141.

7. ---

CHAPTER 2
Chaim Kahan. From Orlya to Brest-Litovsk

1.

JMB: H-C i: 3: Eliezer Mosche Basch, Brest-Litovsk, to Miriam Rosenberg, Warsaw, June 24, 1898. H-C i: 26: M. & S. Stok, Warsaw, to Malka Kahan, Warsaw, August–November 1912. H-C i: 43: Rivah Dubinbaum, Brest, to Malka Kahan, Warsaw [191 …]. H-C i: 26: "Z galerji miljonerów. Szkice i sylwetki. Żydowski król naftowy Chaim Kahn," *Nasz przegląd*, April 17, 1929, 5–6. H-C i: 26: Chaim Kahan, Petrograd, to Malka Kahan, Berlin, February 29 / March 13, 1916. Samuel Pomeraniec, Brześć, to Jonas Rosenberg, Berlin, January 21, 1921. H-C i: 15: Obituary for Chaim Kahan, *Haynt* (Warsaw), no. 3, January 3, 1917. H-C ii: 13: Chaim Kahan, Petrograd, to Miriam and Jonas Rosenberg, Berlin,

May 27, 1916. H-C 2, folder 24: Meir Aronsohn, "R. Chaim Kahan, z"l," trans. Raziel Haimi-Cohen, *Heavar* 1 (1918): 34–38.

AECJ: Aaron Cohen-Mintz, *Mishpachat R' Chaim Cohen, z"l ish haneft mi-Brisk de-Lita* (1986, unpublished), 1–40. Id., "Chaim Cohen z"l vebeito im mal'ut 120 shana leholadeto," *Heavar* 18 (1971 / 5731): 1–21 (287–308).

GABO: F. 5, op. 1, d. 5408. l. 10: Zygmuntowska 77 (71) / Jagiellonska 4; op. 3, d. 1050; op. 1, d. 1610, l. 17, 76.

NGAB: F. 492, op. 1, d. 48, l. 14 ob., 19, l. 153/54: Taxes index Brest-Litovsk (1901). Building permits for Chaim N. Kagan. June 1901, 1909/1910. Taxes collection. Kagan's buildings. Ibid., d. 46, l. 60, 60 ob.: Construction plans for Kobrinsky and Volkovyskoye suburbs of Brest (1908). Kagan's ground at Shosseinaya und Medovaya. F. 17, op. 1, d. 344, l. 25 ob.: Index of private buildings and their value for taxes' calculation in the towns of the Grodno Province (1910).

2.

Interviews with Giza Haimi-Cohen, February 14, 2014; Raziel and Giza Haimi-Cohen, June 24, 2014; Jane Rusel, August 14, 2014.

3. ---

4.

"Domovaya kniga. Belostotskaya 66," *Kalendar-spravochnik Brest-Litovsk* (1913).

"Komenda wojewódzka pol. Panstw., Zygmuntowska 71," *Ksiega adresowa Polski* (1928).

"Komenda wojewódzka policji Panstwowej, Zygmuntowska," *Rocznik Miasta Brzesc* (1930).

"Komenda wojewódzka policji Panstwowej, Zygmuntowska," *Brest. Spis abonentów sieci telefonicznych* (1938).

"Orlya," in *Yevreiskaya entsiklopediya*, ed. David Gintsburg, Lev Katsenelson and Avraam Garkavi, 16 vols. (St. Petersburg: Brokgauz-Efron, 1908–1913), vol. 12, 137.

Mark Vishnitser (Wischnitzer), "Brest-Litovsk," in *Yevreiskaya entsiklopediya*, vol. 4, 951–957.

Mordechai Zalkin, "Brest," in *YIVO Encyclopedia*, vol. 1, ed. by Gershon David Hundert (New Haven et al.: Yale University Press, 2008), 236–237.

5.

Meir Bar-Ilan (Berlin), *Fun Volozhin biz Yerushalaim: Epizoden* (New York: Orion Press, 1933), 401.

Verena Dohrn, *Jüdische Eliten im Russischen Reich. Aufklärung und Integration im 19. Jahrhundert* (Cologne et al.: Böhlau, 2008), 196.

Christian Ganzer and Alena Paškovič, "Heldentum, Tragik, Kühnheit. Das Museum der Verteidigung der Brester Festung," *Osteuropa* 58, no. 12 (2010): 81–96.

Das Land Ober Ost. Deutsche Arbeit in den Verwaltungsgebieten Kurland, Litauen und Bialystok-Grodno, ed. on behalf of Oberbefehlshaber Ost, arranged by the press department of Ober Ost (Stuttgart and Berlin: Deutsche Verlags-Anstalt, 1917), 432.

Yohanan Petrovsky-Shtern, *Yevrei v russkoi armii* (Moscow: Novoye literaturnoye obozreniye, 2003), 53–58.

Yevgeny Rozenblat, *Zhizn i sudba brestskoi yevreiskoi obshchiny XIV–XX vv.* (Brest: Belorussky fond kultury, 1993), 11.

Jane Rusel, *H. Struck (1876–1944). Das Leben und das graphische Werk eines jüdischen Künstlers* (Frankfurt/Main et al.: Lang, 1997), 145–198.

Volga Sabaleŭskaya, "Na perakryzhavanni: gabreiskaya supolnasc Berastseishchyny va umovakh madernizatsy (drugaya palova XIX–pachatak XX stst)," *ARCHE* 16, no. 4 (2013): 10–51.

Bea Schröttner, "Hermann Struck im Ersten Weltkrieg," in *Hermann Struck 1876–1944,* ed. Ruthi Ofek and Chana Schütz (Tefen-Berlin: Centrum Judaicum / Open Museum, 2007), 147–195.

Arnold Tänzer, *Die Geschichte der Juden in Brest-Litowsk* (Berlin: Lamm, 1918), 42–53.

John N. Westwood, *A History of Russian Railways* (London: George Allen and Unwin, 1964), 61.

6.

Roman Sliwonik, *Portrety chwil albo uładnianie życia* (Toruń: Adam Marszałek, 2004), 103/104.

Chaim Weizmann, "My Early Days," in *The Golden Tradition. Jewish Life and Thought in Eastern Europe,* ed. Lucy S. Dawidowicz (New York: Holt, Rinehart and Winston, 1967), 375–383.

Pauline Wengeroff, *Memoiren einer Grossmutter. Bilder aus der Kulturgeschichte der Juden Russlands im 19. Jahrhundert,* vol. 1, 2nd ed. (Berlin: Poppelauer, 1913), 2; ibid., vol. 2 (Berlin: Poppelauer, 1910), 16–19.

7.

Michał Mincewicz, "Z historii parafii prawosławnej w Orli," *Nad Buhom i Narvoiu—ukrainsky chasopis Pidlyashshya,* accessed April 30, 2021, http://nadbuhom.pl/art_1928.html.

"Brester Festung," Wikipedia, accessed April 30, 2021, http://de.wikipedia.org/wiki/Brester_Festung.

CHAPTER 3
Life under War Conditions. Berlin

1.

JMB: H-C i: 4: Max Rosenthal to Jacob Kahan. Field postcards 1915–1916. H-C i: 4 and H-C 2, folder 18: Letters from Baruch and Rosalia Kahan, Kharkov, to Jacob Kahan, Berlin, 1915–1918. H-C i: 13: Chaim Kahan, Petersburg, to Miriam Rosenberg, Berlin, June 17, 1914. H-C i: 16: Salo Stock to Herrn Kahan (Rosa Rosenberg), March 22, 1916. H-C i: 13, 24: Correspondence between Jacob Kahan, Berlin, and Rosa Rosenberg, Bad Neuenahr, summer 1916. H-C i: 18, 25: Correspondence between Jacob Kahan, Berlin, and Rosa Rosenberg, Bad Harzburg, August 1915. Jacob Kahan to Rosa Rosenberg [n. p. and n. d.]. H-C i: 42: Aron Kahan, Memoirs, part 1, 5. H-C ii: 22: 100 postcards from Poland, 1915–1918. H-C 2, folder 14: Jonas Rosenberg, merchant's certificate of the Second Guild and certificate about his factories, 1914; folder 15: Dr. Bernhard Kahn, Hilfsverein der Deutschen Juden, to the Königliche Universität Berlin, Berlin, May 4, 1915; folder 16: Identity cards issued by the Berlin police for Jonas and Miriam Rosenberg, Rosa Rosenberg and Jacob Kahan, Berlin; folder 17: Chaim Kahan, Stockholm, to Malka Kahan, Berlin, July 14, 1915; folder 22: Group photograph, Azbil, Berlin, 1922; folder E: Rahel Kahan: Schlüterstraße 36.

AECJ: Cohen-Mintz, *Mishpachat R' Chaim Kahan.*

Archiv eszett GmbH Berlin: Grundbuch Schlüterstraße 36 (32), 10.

ANLR: Dora Kahan, Berlin, to Bendet Kahan, February 26, 1914.

CDIAK: Chaim N. Kagan. F. 2034, op. 1, d. 272: Jacob Kahan, Berlin, to Baruch Kahan, Kharkov, November 27, 1914. Rosalia Kahan, Berlin, to Baruch Kahan, Kharkov, November 30, 1914; d. 246: Jacob Kahan, Berlin, to Baruch and Rosa Kahan, Kharkov, January 21/23, 1916.

EAB: Application for restitution: Reg. no. 68828: Bendet Kahan, Excerpt from the register on marriage (Russian translation).

LAB: Documents on citizenships. Petition for naturalization, Aaron Kahan, A Pr.Br.Rep. 030–06, no. 25576. Bendet Kahan, no. 26195.

LBA: Judith Helfer Collection, V. Subseries 3: Max Rosenthal, Correspondence box 3, folder 8, no. 1117–1180. Subseries 1: Arthur und Ludwig Rosenthal, box 2, folder 39 (Diary/Scrapbook), no. 415–416/1403; no. 478/1403.

PAAAB: R 121090. Press department, Az. P6c: Pressewarte, Lektorate und Pressearchiv, vol. 3, Journalnummer A.N. 15479/1919.

2.

Interview with Dvora Ettinger-Rozenfeld, May 27, 2014; Giza Haimi-Cohen, October 20, 2014; Menachem Perl, Kfar Vradim, February 14, 2014.

3.

Dvora Ettinger-Rozenfeld, *Ha-Ettingerim* (Ramat Gan: self-publication, 2008), 208–209.

4.

"Kahan, Bendet, Kaufm. Schlüterstraße 36," *Berliner Adressbücher* (1915–1917).

"Der Krieg und die deutschen Juden," *Frankfurter Israelitisches Familienblatt*, August 7, 1914, 2.

"Die Juden im Kriege," *Jüdische Rundschau*, September 4, 1914, 1.

"Bücher für jüdische Kriegsgefangene," *Jüdische Rundschau*, July 14, 1916, 231.

"Nachrichten. Berlin. [Lecture of Zalman Rubashov at a meeting of the Cartel of Jewish corporations and of the Herzl Club]," *Jüdische Rundschau*, July 28, 1916, 252.

Dan Miron, "Zalman Shneour," in *YIVO Encyclopedia*, vol. 2, 1714–1716.

Isaak Markon, "Weinberg, Jechiel," in *Jüdisches Lexikon: Ein enzyklopädisches Handbuch des jüdischen Wissens in vier Bänden*, vol. 4, part 2, ed. Georg Herlitz and Bruno Kirschner (Berlin: Jüdischer Verlag, 1927; reprint: Frankfurt/Main: Athenäum, 1987), 1360.

5.

Steven E. Aschheim, *Brothers and Strangers: The East European Jews in Germany and German Jewish Consciousness, 1800–1923* (Madison et al.: University of Wisconsin Press, 1982), 157–168.

Feder, *Paul Nathan*, 110–111.

Christoph Kreutzmüller and Björn Weigel, *Nissim Zacouto: Jüdischer Wunderknabe und türkischer Teppichgroßhändler* (Berlin: Hentrich & Hentrich, 2010), 12.

Karl-Heinz Metzger, "Juden in Charlottenburg," in *Juden in Charlottenburg: Ein Gedenkbuch*, ed. Verein zur Förderung des Gedenkbuches für die Charlottenburger Juden (Berlin: Textpunkt-Verlag, 2009), 12–28.

Tamara Or, *Heimat im Exil: Eine hebräische Diasporakultur in Berlin 1897–1933* (Göttingen: Wallstein, 2020), 115.

Moritz Pineas (Pinkus), "Zum Tode von Rabbiner Dr. Weinberg," in *Adass Jisroel. Entstehung, Entfaltung, Entwurzelung, 1869–1939*, ed. Max M. Sinasohn (Jerusalem: Sinasohn, 1966), 175–177.

Marc B. Shapiro, *Between the Yeshiva World and Modern Orthodoxy: The Life and Works of Rabbi Jehiel Jacob Weinberg 1884–1966* (London and Portland: The Littman Library of Jewish Civilization, 1999), 51–56.

Max M. Sinasohn, *Die Berliner Privatsynagogen und ihre Rabbiner, 1671–1971* (Jerusalem: Sinasohn, 1971), 74.

Richard B. Speed, *Prisoners, Diplomats, and the Great War* (New York: Greenwood Press, 1990), 68–79.

Egmont Zechlin and Hans Joachim Bieber, *Die deutsche Politik und die Juden im Ersten Weltkrieg* (Göttingen: Vandenhoeck & Ruprecht, 1969), 126–138.

6.

Goldmann, *Mein Leben*, 103–109.

Gershom Scholem, *Von Berlin nach Jerusalem: Jugenderinnerungen*, trans. Michael Brocke and Andrea Schatz (Frankfurt/Main: Jüdischer Verlag, 1994), 93–94.

7.

"Wohnhaus Schlüterstraße 32. Charlottenburg," *Berliner Architekturwelt* 11, no. 7 (1909): 258, accessed April 30, 2021, http://opus.kobv.de/zlb/volltexte/2006/598/pdf/BAW_1909_07.pdf.

"Gefechtskalender Erster Weltkrieg," Wikipedia, accessed April 30, 2021, http://de.wikipedia.org/wiki/6._Division_%28Deutsches_Kaiserreich%29#Gefechtskalender.

Gedenkbuch des Reichsbund jüdischer Frontsoldaten, ed. Reichsbund jüdischer Frontsoldaten (n. p., 1932), accessed April 30, 2021, http://www.denkmalprojekt.org/Verlustlisten/rjf_wk1.htm.

CHAPTER 4
On the Move. Vilna, Warsaw, Kharkov, Saratov

1.

JMB: H-C: i: 6, 20, 26; ii: 13, 17: Chaim Kahan, Russian Empire (Petrograd, Kharkov, Baku, Saratov, Kislovodsk), to the families Kahan and Rosenberg, Berlin (via Stockholm and Copenhagen), 1915–1916. H-C i: 20: Postcards addressed to Mr. Stigell, Helsingfors, 1882; Steinicke to company Hugo Däubler, Toruń, 1877. i: 21, H-C ii: 1: Envelopes addressed to Fedor Fedorovich Danilovich, Kharkov. H-C i: 26: Żydowski król naftowy Chaim Kahn. H-C i: 42: Aron Kahan, Memoirs, part 1, 5. H-C 2, folder 10: Photographs of the refinery in Knyazevka near Saratov; folder C: Chaim Kahan, merchant's certificate of the First Guild (copy), Petersburg, 1917.

AECJ: Cohen-Mintz, "Chaim Cohen z"l vebeito," 1.

ANLR: Invitations to the wedding of Bendet Kahan and Judith Bramson, Poreche, February 23, 1904.

ARDTAM: Kaspiiskoye chernomorskoye neftepromyshlennoye i torgovoye obshchestvo: F. 587, op. 1, d. 25.

CDIAK: Chaim N. Kagan. F. 2034, op. 1, d. 39, 42, 47, 48, 49, 52, 200.

RGIA: Binagadinskoye neftepromyshlennyoe i torgovoye o-vo akts. 1915–1917: F. 23, op. 14, d. 296. Kavkazsko-Volzhskoye torgovo-promyshlennoye o-vo akts.: F. 23, op. 28, d. 867. Petrogradsky chastny kommerchesky bank: F. 597, op. 2, d. 225.

2.

Interview with Raziel and Giza Haimi-Cohen, June 24, 2014.

3. ---

4.

"Kharkov," in *Kratkaya yevreiskaya entsiklopediya*, vol. 9, ed. Itschak Oren, Michael Zand, Naphtali Prat and Ari Avner, 10 vols. (Jerusalem: Keter, 1976–2001), 647–655.

"Die kaukasische Petroleumausbeute im Jahre 1882," *Export. Organ des Centralvereins für Handelsgeographie* 5, no. 36 (1883): 621.

"Handelsnachrichten," *Chemiker-Zeitung. Fachzeitschrift u. Handelsblatt für Chemiker, Ingenieure* … 10, no. 1 (1886): 29, ibid., 11, no. 1 (1887): 2.

"Kagan Kogan Chaim," *Spravochnaya kniga o litsakh petrogradskogo kupechestva* (1911): 264, ibid. (1916): 114.

Otchet Saratovskogo birzhevogo komiteta za 1885 god (Saratov, 1886), 15.

Plan goroda Baku, ed. A. N. Suvorov (Baku, 1892), 12.

"Russian Petroleum. The Trade Depression Considered in Convention at Baku," *Bradstreet's: A Journal of Trade, Finance, and Public Economy*, May 1, 1886, 275–276.

"Kuptsy-yevrei," 1. Polnoe sobranie zakonov, vol. 28, no. 21.547, § 28.

"Kuptsy-yevrei," 2. Polnoe sobranie zakonov, vol. 10, no. 8.054, §§ 48–64, ibid., §§ 51–53, vol. 23, no. 22.057, vol. 34, no. 34.248.

Grigory Voltke, "Kuptsy-yevrei po russkomu zakonodatelstvu," in *Yevreiskaya entsiklopediya*, vol. 9, 916–922.

5.

Vagit Alekperov, *Oil of Russia: Past, Present, and Future*, trans. Paul B. Gallagher and Thomas D. Hedden (Minneapolis, MN: East View Press, 2011), 49–54.

Boris V. Ananich, *Bankirskie doma v Rossii 1860–1914 gg.* (Leningrad: Nauka, 1991), 60–62.

Verena Dohrn, "Akkulturation und Patriotismus. Die ersten modernen Juden im Russischen Reich Leben in zwei Kulturen," in *Akkulturation und Selbstbehauptung von Nichtrussen im Zarenreich*, ed. Trude Maurer and Eva-Maria Auch (Wiesbaden: Harrassowitz, 2000), 61–81.

Aleksandr A. Fursenko, *The Battle for Oil. The Economics and Politics of International Corporate Conflict over Petroleum, 1860–1930* (Greenwich et al.: Jai Press, 1990), 47–51.

Lutz Häfner, *Gesellschaft als lokale Veranstaltung. Die Wolgastädte Kazan und Saratov (1870–1914)* (Cologne et al.: Böhlau, 2004), 10–13, 85–95, 100.

Yevgeny Kotlyar, *Yevreisky Kharkov. Putevoditel* (Kharkov: Tsentr vostokovedeniya, Kharkovskaya gosudarstvennaya akademiya dizaina i iskusstv, 2011), 8–17.

H. Landoy, "Yidn in ruslender naft-industrie un naft-handl," *Yivo-bleter* 14, nos. 3–4 (1939): 269–284.

Arthur von Mayer, *Geschichte und Geographie der deutschen Eisenbahnen 1835–1890*, (Berlin: Baensch, 1891), vol. 4, 1223.

Andrij Portnov and Tetjana Portnova, "Die 'jüdische Hauptstadt der Ukraine'. Erinnerung und Gegenwart in Dnipropetrovsk," trans. Christiane Körner, *Osteuropa* 62, no. 10 (2012): 25–40.

Alfred Rieber, *Merchants and Entrepreneurs in Imperial Russia* (Chapel Hill and New York: University of North Carolina Press, 1991), 220–221.

Frithjof Benjamin Schenk, *Russlands Fahrt in die Moderne. Mobilität und sozialer Raum im Eisenbahnzeitalter* (Stuttgart: Steiner, 2014), 232–238, 248–257.

Viktor. N. Semenov and Nikolai N. Semenov, *Saratov kupechesky* (Saratov: Izd-vo zhurnala "Volga," 1995), 13–144, 66–92.

Walter Sperling, *Der Aufbruch der Provinz. Die Eisenbahn und die Neuordnung der Räume im Zarenreich* (Frankfurt/Main: Camous-Verlag, 2011), 129–145.

Westwood, *Russian Railways*, 150–152.

6.

Meir Bar Ilan, *Fun Volozhin biz Yerushalaim*, 400–401.

Ilya Golts, *Po dorogam i ukhabam zhizni (Posledny menshevik)* (Jerusalem: Lira, 2003), 34–36.

Aron Klein, ed., *Mi-Baku le-Eretz Israel. Sipura shel mishpachat Itskovich* (Tel Aviv: self-publication, 1998), 28.

Martin D. Kushner, *From Russia to America: A Modern Odyssey* (Philadelphia: Dorrance, 1969), 79–85.

Yakov L. Teitel, *Iz moei zhizni. Za sorok let* (Paris: Ya. Povolotsky i Ko, 1925), 170–176.

7.

Olga V. Frolova, "Iz istorii mestnoi telefonnoi svyazi v Rossii: Zemskiye telefonnyye seti," *Elektrosvyaz: istoriya i sovremennost* 3, no. 1 (2007): 7–11, accessed April 30, 2021, http://www.computer-museum.ru/connect/zemsk.htm.

CHAPTER 5
Citizenships and the World of Education—Berlin, Bonn, Frankfurt, Marburg, Antwerp

1.

JMB: H-C: i: 20: Postcard from an unknown, Rue Jacobs, Antwerp, to Chaim Kahan and Jonas Rosenberg, Warsaw, November 12, 1905. H-C 2, folder H: Dora Löwenthal, comment regarding the school Philanthropin in Frankfurt/Main.

AECJ: Cohen-Mintz: "Chaim Cohen z"l vebeito," 1–3, 6, 9, 14–15.

ANLR: Judith Kahan, Circular letter to the parentship, Antwerp [n. d.].

AUCMT: Baruch Kahan's certificate of Wöhlerschule, Frankfurt/Main, 1927; Arusia Kahan, Notebooks, Jaffa, 1914.

AVRP: Gita Ripp, [reminiscences], Family Reunion, January 4, 1997, 2–3.

AESM: Rachel Kahan, enrollment form, roll of the Jewish pupils, no. 77.

BAB: Documents of the Allgemeine Deutsche Schule Antwerpen. Report about the sixty-seventh school year (1906/1907): R 901 no. 38699 (December 1907–July 1908).

CDIAK: Chaim Kagan. F. 2034, op. 1, d. 247: B. Kahan, list of losses, Antwerp, 1907; d. 649: Photograph of Baruch Kahan, Frankfurt/Main [n. d.].

LAB: Aaron (Arusia) Kahan, Jacob Kahan, Bendet Kahan, documents on citizenships. Petitions for naturalization in Germany: A Pr. Rep. 030–06 nos. 16105, 25576, 26195.

SFA: Foreigner files 481, no. 121.716, no. 116.746, no. 121.389.

SKB: Mosche Glücksohn, documents for doctorate, CV: BB IIIb 1297, vol. 23 (1907).

2.

Interviews with Dvora Ettinger-Rozenfeld; Josef (Yossi) Cohen, Ma'agan Michael, March 15–17, 2011; Menachem Perl, February 14, 2014.

3.

Ettinger-Rozenfeld, Ha-Ettingerim, 50, 206.

4.

Marcus Cohn, "Misrachi," in Jüdisches Lexikon, vol. 4, part 1, 231–235.

Nathan Michael Gelber, "Chibat Zion," in Jüdisches Lexikon, vol. 4, part 2, 1585.

Georg Herlitz, "Isaak Rülf," in Jüdisches Lexikon, vol. 4, part 1, 1527–1528.

Jakov Shabad, "Brest-Litovsk," in Yevreiskaya entsiklopediya, vol. 4, 951–960.

Hugo Hillel Schachtel, "Kattowitzer Konferenz," in Jüdisches Lexikon, vol. 3, 626–627.

"Zeitungsnachrichten und Correspondenzen. Marburg. Israelitisches Schülerheim," Der Israelit 42, no. 35 (1901): 797; ibid., nos. 40–41 (1901): 924; 44, no. 39 (1903): 875.

5.

Allgemeine Deutsche Schule zu Antwerpen: 12 Photographische Ansichten, ed. Allgemeine Deutsche Schule zu Antwerpen (Brüssel: Nels, 1914).

Brita Åsbrink, Imperiya Nobelei, trans. Tatyana Dobronitskaya (Moscow: Tekst, 2003), 181–189, 247–256.

Mordechai Breuer, Jüdische Orthodoxie im Deutschen Reich, 1871–1918: Sozialgeschichte einer religiösen Minderheit (Frankfurt/Main: Jüdischer Verlag bei Athenäum, 1986), 18–23, 58–59, 73, 352.

Rosine De Dijn, Antwerpen, Mechelen und Lier die Schönen von Brabant (Bergisch Gladbach: Lübbe, 1992), 85.

Greta Devos and Hilde Greefs, "The German Presence in Antwerp in the Nineteenth Century," IMIS-Beiträge 14 (2000), 105–128.

Jakob Engel, Die hebräische Mittelschule Tachkemoni in Jaffa (Hamburg: Ackermann & Wulff, 1918).

Axel Erdmann, *Die Marburger Juden: Ihre Geschichte von den Anfängen bis zur Gegenwart* (PhD diss., Philipps University, Marburg, 1987), 143–152, 167–173.

Jack Fellman, *The Revival of a Classical Tongue: Eliezer Ben Yehuda and the Modern Hebrew Language* (The Hague et al.: Mouton, 1973), 103.

Judah L. Fishman (Maimon), *The History of the Mizrachi Movement* (New York: The Mizrachi Hatzair of America, 1928).

Gertrud Heinemeyer, "Die Elisabethschule im Kaiserreich 1878/9–1918," in *Reform und Tradition: Die Elisabethschule Marburg 1879'2004, Festschrift zum 125-jährigen Jubiläum*, ed. Elisabethschule (Marburg: self-publication, 2004), 11–28.

Andrea Hopp, *Jüdisches Bürgertum in Frankfurt am Main im 19. Jahrhundert* (Stuttgart: Steiner, 1997), 20–34, 66–67, 121–122, 239.

Esther Huhn, *Die allgemeine deutsche Schule. Beiträge zur Geschichte der Auslandsdeutschen in Antwerpen* (PhD diss., Rijksuniversitair Centrum, Antwerpen, 1973), 3–27, 79–81, 132–137.

Thomas Jürgens, *Diplomatischer Schutz und Staatenlose* (Berlin: Duncker & Humblot, 1987), 83–101.

Steven M. Lowenstein, "Das religiöse Leben," in *Deutsch-jüdische Geschichte in der Neuzeit*, ed. Michael A. Meyer and Michael Brenner, vol. 3: *Umstrittene Integration: 1871–1918*, ed. Steven M. Lovenstein et al. (München: C.H. Beck, 1997), 114.

Samuel Rosenblatt, *The History of the Mizrachi Movement* (New York: Mizrachi Organization of America, 1952).

Michael R. Marrus, *The Unwanted: European Refugees in the Twentieth Century* (New York et. al.: Oxford University Press, 1985), 51–121.

Jochen Oltmer, *Migration und Politik in der Weimarer Republik* (Göttingen: Vandenhoeck & Ruprecht, 2005), 238–269.

Miriam Rürup, *Ehrensache: Jüdischen Studentenverbindungen an deutschen Universitäten 1886–1937* (Göttingen: Wallstein, 2008), 112.

Anne-Christin Saß, *Berliner Luftmenschen: Osteuropäisch-jüdische Migranten in der Weimarer Republik* (Göttingen: Wallstein, 2012), 88–101.

Inge Schlotzhauer, *Das Philanthropin 1804–1942: Die Schule der Israelitischen Gemeinde in Frankfurt am Main* (Frankfurt/Main: Kramer, 1990), 5–10, 47–68, 89.

Dov Schwartz, *Religious-Zionism: History and Ideology*, trans. Batya Stein (Boston: Academic Studies Press, 2009), 1–33.

Robert W. Tolf, *The Russian Rockefellers: The Saga of the Nobel Family and the Russian Oil Industry* (Stanford, CA: Hoover Institution Press, 1976), 133–135.

Oliver Trevisiol, *Die Einbürgerungspraxis im Deutschen Reich 1871–1945* (PhD diss., University of Konstanz, Konstanz, 2004), 155–156, 162–163, 189–190.

Gudrun Westphal, "Die jüdischen Schülerinnen der ehemaligen Höheren Töchterschule, heute Elisabethschule (1878 bis 1938)," *Experiment*, special issue: *Die jüdischen Schülerinnen der Elisabethschule, 1878 bis 1938. Zeitung der Elisabethschule* (November 1992): 4–23.

Idem, "Verzeichnis der jüdischen Schülerinnen der ehemaligen Höheren Töchterschule, heute Elisabethschule, 1878 bis 1938," ibid., 24–48.

6.

Boris Pasternak, *Sommer 1912: Briefe aus Marburg*, trans. Sergej Dorzweiler (Marburg: Blaue-Hörner-Verlag, 1990), 29–30, 40.

7.

Dinur (Dinaburg), "Benzion Jawitz, Ze'ev," Jewish Virtual Library, accessed April 30, 2021, https://www.jewishvirtuallibrary.org/jawitz-ze-x0027-ev.

"Invitations and Annual Reports" of the Realschule der Israelitischen Religions-Gesellschaft Frankfurt on Main, 1884–1904, Compact Memory, accessed April 30, 2021, www.compact-memory.de.

"Philanthropin," Wikipedia, accessed April 30, 2021, http://de.wikipedia.org/wiki/Philanthropin_%28Frankfurt_am_Main%29.

"Wöhlerschule," Wikipedia, accessed April 30, 2021, http://de.wikipedia.org/wiki/W%C3%B6hlerschule.

"Chaim Kagan and Malka in Antwerp," Family Search, 481 # 116746, accessed April 30, 2021, https://familysearch.org/pal:/MM9.3.1/TH-1971-28172-26995-17?cc=2023926&wc=MMPF-2G9:713352896.

"Bendet Kahan and Judith in Antwerp," Family Search, 481 # 121716, accessed April 30, 2021, https://familysearch.org/pal:/MM9.3.1/TH-1961-28150-56423-81?cc=2023926&wc=MMPF-2P7:n1959937090.

"Baruch Kagan and Rosalia in Antwerp," Family Search, 481 # 121389, accessed April 30, 2021, https://familysearch.org/pal:/MM9.3.1/TH-1942-28150-32011-60?cc=2023926&wc=MMPF-2P3:n492122453.

CHAPTER 6
To Baku

1.

JMB: H-C: i: 3: Oil company of the brothers Nobel, board of directors (M. Shteyn), trade department in Russia N4, to Mr. Ch. N. Kagan, Warsaw, June 17, 1906. H-C i: 28: Aaron Kahan, *Die Reorganisation des deutschen Petroleumhandels nach dem Kriege* (unpublished). H-C i: 42: Aron Kahan, Memoirs, part 1, 2–20.

ARDTAM: F. 46, op. 4, d. 306, l. 215–222. Kaspiiskoye chernomorskoye neftepromyshlennoye i torgovoye obshchestvo F. 587, op. 1, d. 223 (telegramms).

CDIAK: Chaim N. Kagan. F. 2034, op. 1, d. 21; d. 22; d. 37; d. 218–236.

RGIA: F. 23, op. 14, d. 296: Kavkazsko-volzhskoye torgovo-promyshlennoe aktsionernoye obshchestvo, 1913–1917.

2.

Interviews with Raziel and Giza Haimi-Cohen, June 24, 2014; July 2, 2014.

3. ---

4.

"Promysl," in *Yevreiskaya entsiklopediya*, vol. 13, 5.

"Rossiya," ibid., vol. 13, 659–660.

"Baku," in *Kratkaya yevreiskaya entsiklopediya*, vol. 1, 282–283. "Baku," in *Yevreiskaya entsiklopediya*, vol. 4, 119–120. "Baku," in *Meyers Lexikon*, vol. 2 (Berlin: Bibliographisches Institut, 1905), 291.

"Beilin, Arkadii," in *Kratkaya yevreiskaya entsiklopediya*, vol. 1, 283. See also ibid., vol. 10, 937.
Plan goroda Baku i yego raionov (Tiflis, 1913).
"Petrol," *Spravochny yezhegodnik Baku i yego raionov* (1910): 145–146. See also ibid. (1913): 183, 185, 307–309.
"Petrol," "Itskovich i Petrol," *Spravochny yezhegodnik Baku i yego raionov* (1914): 302, 342. Ibid., supplement, 103.
"Leopold Feygl," in *Kratkaya yevreiskaya entsiklopediya*, vol. 1, 282; ibid., vol. 10, 548.
"Goldlust & Feigl, Batum. Agentur der Kaiserlich-königlichen landesbefugten Lampen-Fabrik von R. Ditman in Wien," *Oestreichische Monatsschrift für den Orient* 13, no. 1, supplement (1887): II.

5.

Bakhman Yu. Akhundov [Bəhman Yusif oğlu Axundov], *Monopolistichesky kapital v dorevolyutsionnoi bakinskoi neftyanoi promyshlennosti* (Moscow and Leningrad: Izdatelstvo sotsialno-ekonomicheskoi literatury, 1959), 7–111.
Alekperov, *Oil of Russia*, 74–97.
Åsbrink, *Imperiya Nobelei*, 113, 137.
Eva Maria Auch, *Öl und Wein am Kaukasus: Deutsche Forschungsreisende, Kolonisten und Unternehmer im vorrevolutionären Aserbaidschan* (Wiesbaden: Reichert, 2001), 42–47, 53–66, 102–119.
Salo W. Baron, Arcadius Kahan, et al. *Economic History of the Jews* (Jerusalem: Keter, 1975), 179–181.
Moisei Bekker, "Istoriya formirovaniya yevreyskoi etnicheskoi gruppy na territorii Azerbaidzhana," in *Özümüzü və dünyani dərkenmə yolunda* (Baku: n. p., 2012), 16–43.
Aleksandr N. Bochanov, *Delovaya elita Rossii 1914g.* (Moscow: Rossiiskaya akademiya nauk, 1994), 203, 239–240.
Bertram Brökelmann, *Die Spur des Öls: Sein Aufstieg zur Weltmacht* (Berlin: Osburg, 2010), 69–98.
Khachatur Dadayan [Xachatur Dadayan], *Armyane i Baku (1850–1920)* (Yerevan: Nof Noravank, 2007), 5–41, 58–67.
Shamil S. Fatullayev [Şamil S. Fatullayev], *Gradostroitelstvo i arkhitektura Azerbaidzhana XIX–nachala XX veka* (Leningrad: Stroiizdat, Leningradskoe otdeleniye, 1986), 424.
Fursenko, *Battle of Oil*, 9–13, 26/7, 44–51, 68–73, 159.
Aliovsad N. Guliyev [Aliovsad N. Quliyev], ed., *Monopolistichesky kapital v neftyanoi promyshlennosti Rossii 1914–1917: Dokumenty i materialy* (Leningrad: Izdatelstvo Akademii nauk SSSR, 1973), 542, 544.
Leo Gurwitsch, *Wissenschaftliche Grundlagen der Erdölbearbeitung* (Berlin: Springer, 1913), 102–107.
Marat Dzhafar Ibragimov [Marat Cəfər İbrahimov], *Neftyanaya promyshlennost Azerbaydzhana v period imperializma* (Baku: Elm, 1984).
David Itskhak, *Istoriya yevreev na Kavkaze*, vol. 1 (Tel Aviv: Kavkasioni, 1989), 478–481.
Aidin M. Kadyrli [Aydin M. Qadirli], *Iz istorii razvitiya dorevolyutsionnoi bakinskoi neftepererabatyvayushchei promyshlennosti* (Baku: Elm, 1970), 38–73.

Arcadius Kahan, "Notes on Jewish Entrepreneurship in Tsarist Russia," in *Entrepreneurship in Imperial Russia and the Soviet Union*, ed. Gregory Guroff and Fred V. Carstensen (Princeton: Princeton University Press, 1983), 104–124.

Andreas Kappeler, *Russland als Vielvölkerreich: Entstehung, Geschichte, Zerfall* (Frankfurt/Main and Vienna: Büchergilde Gutenberg, 1993), 145–149.

Landoy, "Yidn in ruslender naft-industrie," 269, 273–276, 281.

Joseph A. Martellaro, "The Acquisition and Leasing of the Baku Oilfields by the Russian Crown," *Middle Eastern Studies* 21, no. 1 (1985): 80–88.

Joseph Mendel, *Die Entwicklung der internationalen Erdölwirtschaft in den letzten Jahren* (Leipzig: K. F. Koehler, 1922), 12–13, 49–58.

Mir-Yusif Mir-Babayev, *Kratkaya khronologiya istorii Azerbaidzhanskogo neftyanogo dela* (Baku: Sabah, 2004), 3–73.

Idem, *Concise History of the Azerbaijani Oil*, 3rd ed. (Baku: self-publication, 2010), 21–49, 57–71, 108–120.

Lev Polonsky, *Bankirsky dom br. Rotshild v Baku* (Baku: self-publication, 1998), 3–70.

Georg Spies, *Erinnerungen eines Ausland-Deutschen*, ed. Wolfgang Sartor (Sankt Petersburg: Olearius, 2002), 251–252, 261–262.

Georg Spies, *Zwei Denkschriften zum Petroleummonopol* (Berlin: Puttkammer & Mühlbrecht, 1913), 2.

Ronald G. Suny, "Eastern Armenians under Tsarist Rule," in *The Armenian People from Ancient to Modern Times*, ed. Richard G. Hovannisian, vol. 2 (Basingstoke et al.: Macmillan, 1997), 109–137.

Tolf, *The Russian Rockefellers*, 129.

Westwood, *Russian Railways*, 302.

Daniel Yergin, *The Prize: The Epic Quest for Oil, Money, and Power* (New York et al.: Simon & Schuster, 1991), 129–133.

6.

Essad Bey [Lev Nussimbaum], *Kaukasus: Seine Berge, Völker und Geschichte*, 2nd ed. (Berlin: Deutsche Buchgemeinschaft, 1931), 76.

Mi-Baku le-Eretz Israel, 13, 30.

Kurban Said [Lev Nussimbaum], *Ali und Nino* (Vienna et al., 1937, reprint: Hamburg: Gruner and Jahr, 2010), 21–22.

7. ---

CHAPTER 7
Zina and the Oilfields. Baku

1.

JMB: H-C: i: 42: Aron Kahan, Memoirs, part 1, 5–7; part 2, 20, 32–34. H-C 2, folder 5: Zina Kahan, photo, Baku [n. d.].

AVRP: Paul Ripp, Victor Ripp, interview with Zina Kahan (1881–1976), New York, March 23, 1974. Ripp Family Reunion: Conversation in Israel in about 1970 with Zina Kahan, Dora

Rosenfeld, Arusia Cohen-Mintz, Chaim Avinoam Haimi-Cohen, Giza Haimi-Cohen, Lolia Kahan, Shulamit Rosenberg, Tani Cohen-Mintz, trans. Gita Ripp, New York, November 8, 1992.

ARDTAM: L. E. Itskovich & Petrol: F. 755, op. 1, d. 2, d. 3. Petrol: F. 768, op. 1, d. 4.

RGIA: Binagadinskoe: F. 23, op. 14, d. 296.

2.

Interview with Gita Kahan-Ripp for the Spielberg Foundation, conducted by Naomi Rappaport, New York, January 30, 1997.

3.

Victor Ripp, "My Fabulous Baku Fortune," *The Antioch Review 60, no. 2 (2002): 312–330*.

Idem, "Baku," *The Ontario Review. North American Journal of Arts* 59 (2003–2004): 95–111.

4.

"Shchedrin," in *Yevreiskaya entsiklopediya*, vol. 16, 141.

Plan goroda Baku, 1913.

Bakinsky sputnik (1913): 494–495.

"Petrol," "Petrol i Itskovich," *Spravochny yezhegodnik Baku i yego raionov* (1914): 302, 342.

5.

Parvin Ahanchi [Pərvin Ahənçi], *Neftepromyshlennye rabochie Baku (konets XIX–nachalo XX vekov)* (Tambov et al.: Mezhdunarodny informatsionny nobelevsky tsentr, 2013).

Dadayan, *Armyane*, 42–57, 71–148.

Dohrn, *Jüdische Eliten im Russischen Reich*, 66.

Glenn Dynner, *Men of Silk: The Hasidic Conquest of Polish Jewish Society* (Oxford et al: Oxford University Press, 2010), 5–17.

Lazar Golodetz, *History of the Family Golodetz*, trans. Shlomo Noble (New York: n. p., 1954).

Hassan Hakimian, "Labor and Migration: Persian Workers in Southern Russia 1880–1914," *International Journal of Middle East Studies* 17, no. 4 (1985): 443–462.

James D. Henry, *Baku: An Eventful History* (London: A. Constable & Co., 1905).

Kappeler, *Russland*, 145–149.

Nikolai E. Makarenko, *Lyalichi: Starye gody* (n. p., 1910).

Hans-Heinrich Nolte, *Religiöse Toleranz in Rußland 1600–1725* (Göttingen et al.: Musterschmidt, 1969), 90–91.

Suny, "Eastern Armenians," 109–137.

6.

Eva Broido, *Wetterleuchten der Revolution* (Berlin: Der Bücherkreis, 1929, reprint: Berlin: Guhl, 1977), 120–125.

Essad-Bey, *Öl und Blut im Orient: Meine Kindheit in Baku und meine haarsträubende Flucht durch den Kaukasus* (Stuttgart et al., 1929, reprint: Freiburg/Breisgau: Maurer, 2008), 21–22.

Maxim Gorki, *Durch die Union der Sowjets. Tagebuchnotizen und Skizzen*, trans. Irene Wiedemann and Charlotte Kossuth, vol. 15 of his *Gesammelte Werke in Einzelbänden*, ed. Eva Kosing and Edel Mirowa-Florin (Berlin and Weimar: Aufbau Verlag, 1970), 301–304.

Mi-Baku le-Eretz Israel, 28.

Solmaz Rustamova-Togidi [Solmaz Rüstəmova-Tohidi], *Mart 1918. Baku. Azerbaidzhanskie pogromy v dokumentakh* (Baku: n. p., 2009).

Kurban Said, *Ali und Nino*, 10, 21–22, 33, 37, 45, 60, 62, 74, 92, 105, 117, 126, 153, 222, 235–236, 315.

7.

Parvin Ahanchi [Pərvin Ahənçi], "Ethnic Relations in Baku during the First Oil Boom," *Biweekly Azerbaijan Diplomatic Academy* 4, no. 4 (2011), accessed April 30, 2021, http://biweekly.ada.edu.az/vol_4_no_4/Ethnic_relations_in_Baku_during_the_first_oil_boom.htm.

"Lyalichi," Gosudarstvenny arkhiv Bryanskoi oblasti, accessed April 30, 2021, http://www.archive-bryansk.ru/lyalichy.

CHAPTER 8
Aron and the Black Gold. Baku

1.

JMB: H-C: i: 18: Rosalia Kahan, [Petrograd], to family Kahan-Rosenberg, Berlin, April 22, 1917. H-C i: 26: Ilya I. Pines, Moscow, to Jonas Rosenberg, Warsaw, February 20, 1912. i:42: Aron Kahan, Memoirs, part 1, 9–16. H-C 2, folder 23: Chaim N. Kahan, Wilna, to Malka Kahan, Warsaw, March 22, 1911; Chaim N. Kahan, Petersburg, to Malka Kahan, Warsaw, December 25, 1911; Chaim N. Kahan, Petersburg, to Malka Kahan, Warsaw, May 21, [1912]; Chaim N. Kahan, Petersburg, to Malka Kahan, Warsaw, October 12, 1912; Meir Yakovlevich Aronson, Kharkov, to Chaim N. Kahan, February 27, 1913; Chaim Kahan, [Bad Neuenahr], to his sons, June 2, [1914]; B. Kahan, Charlottenburg, draft of a telegram to Petersburg, May 17, 1914.

AVRP: Ripp Family Reunion; Moshe Ater, "In Memoriam Aharon Kahan, Oil Pioneer," *Jerusalem Post*, May 14, 1970, 5.

ARDTAM: Petrol, F. 768, op. 1, d. 3; Branobel: Production and Trade Of Sulfuric Acid, F. 798, op. 1, d. 267, d. 600; op. 2, d. 3640, d. 3641, d. 2224.

BAREEC: Abram S. Kagan papers 1902–1952, no. BA#136, box 7: Interview conducted by Marc Raeff ([beginning of the 1980s,] microfilmed 1998), 55.

CDIAK: Chaim N. Kagan. F. 2034, op. 1, d. 60: Aron Kahan, Baku, to Baruch Kahan, [Petrograd or Kharkov], October 1, 1917; d. 173: Aron Kahan, Baku, to David Kahan, [Petrograd or Kharkov], June 27, 1916.

RGIA: Petrol: F. 23, op. 28, d. 1631–1632; op. 14, d. 222. Azovsko-Donskoi kommerchesky bank: F. 616, op. 1, d. 615. Petrogradsky chastny kommerchesky bank: F. 597, op. 2, d. 225. Sibirsky torgovy bank: F. 638 op. 1, d. 638. Kavkazsko-Volzhskoye torgovo-promyshlennoye o-vo akts.: F. 23, op. 14, d. 296; op. 28, d. 867.

2. and 3. ---

4.

"Dembo, Iosel Abramovich," *Spravochnaya kniga o litsakh petrogradskogo kupechestva* (1916): 74.

"Petrol," and "Itskovich i Kagan," *Spravochny yezhegodnik Baku i yego raionov* (1914): supplement, 155–201.
"Petrol," *Spravochnaya kniga o litsakh petrogradskogo kupechestva* (1916): 188.
Plan goroda Baku, 1913.

5.
Akhundov, *Monopolistichesky kapital*, 88–97.
Ilkham Aliyev [Ilham Aliyev] and Akif Muradverdiyev, *Azerbaidzhanskaya neft v politike mira*, vol. 2 (Baku: Azerbaidzhan, 1997), 55.
Åsbrink, *Imperiya Nobelei*, 181, 184, 189, 247, 256.
Bochanov, *Delovaya elita*, 157.
Duvantier, *L. C. Glad & Co.*, 157–163.
Fursenko, *Battle for Oil*, 73, 107–125.
Yury P. Golitsyn, *Deutsche Bank: 125 let v Rossii* (Moscow: Alpina Business Books, 2008), 76–91.
Michail Ya. Gefter, ed., *Monopolistichesky kapital v neftyanoi promyshlennosti Rossii 1883–1914: Dokumenty i materialy* (Moscow and Leningrad: Izdatelstvo Akademii nauk SSSR, 1961), 444–446, 718, 738–739.
Guliyev, *Monopolistichesky kapital*, 330, 502, 540.
Klaus Heller, "Typen und Rechtsformen großgewerblicher Unternehmen in Rußland im 18. und in der ersten Hälfte des 19. Jahrhunderts," in *Unternehmertum in Rußland*, ed. Klaus Heller (Berlin: Akademie-Verlag, 1998), 19–20.
Joseph Mendel, *Die Entwicklung der internationalen Erdölwirtschaft in den letzten Jahren* (Leipzig: Koehler, 1922), 149–150.
Polonsky, *Bankirsky dom*, 30.
Wolfgang Sartor, "Die Europäische Petroleum-Union G.m.b.H 1906–1914," in *Unternehmertum in Rußland*, ed. Klaus Heller (Berlin: Akademie-Verlag, 1998), 147–173.
Fritz Seidenzahl, *100 Jahre Deutsche Bank 1870–1970* (Frankfurt/Main: Deutsche Bank, 1970), 205–227.
Tolf, *The Russian Rockefellers*, 133–135, 184–187, 190–193.

6.
Schalom Asch, *Die Sintflut*, trans. Siegfried Schmitz (Berlin, Wien and Leipzig: Zsolnay, 1930), 40–57, 983–985, 1259–1273.

7. ---

CHAPTER 9
Summer Resorts during the War. Bad Harzburg, Bad Neuenahr, Bad Polzin

1.
JMB: H-C i:4: Receipt of luggage and check-in, address: Kahan, Bad Neuenahr, Vienna, September 1, 1913. H-C i: 16: M. Zettel, Zurich, to Chaim N. Kahan, Bad Neuenahr, June 16,

1914. H-C 2, folder 23: Chaim N. Kahan, Bad Neuenahr, to Miriam und Jonas Rosenberg, St. Moritz, August 6, 1912; Chaim N. Kahan, Baden-Baden, to Miriam and Jonas Rosenberg, Bad Kissingen, August 9, 1912. Correspondence summer 1915: Rosa Rosenberg, Harzburg, to Jacob Kahan, Berlin: H-C i: 14: August 18, 1915; H-C i: 18: August 29; September 1, 1915. Correspondence summer 1916: Rosa Rosenberg, Bad Neuenahr, to Jacob Kahan, Berlin: H-C i: 10: July 20 (via Trude Rosenthal); July 21 (ditto); July 24 (ditto); July 26 (ditto); July 28; August 9; August 18, 1916; H-C i: 13: July 17 (ditto); July 25; August 6, 1916; H-C i: 18: July 20 (ditto); July 26; August 10; August 15; August 23, 1916; H-C i: 24: July 28; August 4; [August 7]; and August 9, 1916; H-C ii: 9: July 31, 1916. Correspondence summer 1917: Rosa Rosenberg, Bad Polzin, to Jacob Kahan, Bad Harzburg: H-C i: 10: August 20; August 27, 1917; H-C i: 13: August 17; September 2, 1917; H-C i: 18: July 26; August 29, 1917; H-C i: 24: August 21, September 6, 1917; H-C i: 25: September 7, 1917; H-C i: 30: August 15, 1917; H-C ii: 9: August 22, 1917. Rosa and Miriam Rosenberg, Polzin, to Jonas Rosenberg, Berlin: H-C i: 30: August 18; August 19; August 22; August 24; August 30; August 31; September 2, 1917. Jacob Kahan, Bad Harzburg, to Rosa Rosenberg, Polzin: H-C i: 39: August 14; August 16; August 17; August 18; August 23; August 27; August 31; September 2; September 4; September 6, 1917. H-C i: 14: Jacob Kahan, Bad Harzburg, to Regina Petruschka, Leipzig, August 22, 1917; Jacob Kahan, Bad Harzburg, draft of a letter [no address, n. d.]. H-C 2, folder E: leaflet of the Hotel Parkhaus Bad Harzburg, 1917; picture postcards 1915: Rosa Rosenberg, Bad Harzburg, to Jacob Kahan, Berlin, August 17; August 20; August 24; August 26, 1915; picture postcards 1917: Jacob Kahan, Bad Harzburg, to Rosa Rosenberg, Polzin, August 19; August 22; August 26; September 3; September 5; September 9; September 10; September 11, 1917; Rosa Rosenberg, Polzin, to Jacob Kahan, Bad Harzburg, September 4, 1917. H-C i: 14: Dr. I. Beham to J. Kahan and N. Rosenberg, Bad Harzburg, Hotel Parkhaus, August 24, 1917. H-C i: 16: Salo Stock to Mr. Kahan (Rosa Rosenberg), March 22, 1916. H-C i: 18: Feldhilfsarzt Aron, Münster, at present Charlottenburg, to Jacob Kahan, Bad Harzburg, September 7, 1917; Pinchas Kahan to the family in Berlin, August 01/14, 1917; Rosalia Kahan, Petrograd, to Jacob Kahan, Bad Harzburg, July 17/30, 1917; Trude Rosenthal, Berlin, to Jacob Kahan, Bad Harzburg, [August 8]; September 10, 1917. H-C ii: 9: Max Lew, Berlin, to Jacob Kahan, Bad Harzburg, August 27, 1917. H-C ii: 13: Jacob Kahan, [Bad Harzburg], to Rosalia Kahan, [Petrograd], September 8, 1917. H-C 2, folder 16: Miriam Rosenberg, Russian passport. Correspondence summer 1918: Rosa Rosenberg, Polzin, to Jacob Kahan, Bad Salzbrunn: H-C i: 7: July 29, 1918; H-C i: 10: August 13, 1918; H-C i: 25: August 5; August 8; August 10, 1918. H-C i: 18: Lewstein, Altheide, to Jacob Kahan, Bad Salzbrunn, August 11, 1918; H-C i: 24: August 18, 1918.

2. ---

3.
Jacob Kahan, "Die nationalen Forderungen des jüdischen Volkes in Rußland und seine politischen Parteien," *Yeshurun* 4, nos. 7–8 (1917): 353–375; nos. 9–10 (1917): 483–509.

4.
"Notstandsaktion für Palästina, Gerhard Scholem z. Zt. Berlin," *Jüdische Rundschau*, August 31, 1917, 293.

"Herzlwald, Jacob Kahan dankt S. L. Fuchs f. d. wiedergef. Kneifer," *Jüdische Rundschau,*
September 21, 1917, 319.

"Rede des Reichskanzler Georg Michaelis über Friedenskundgebung des Papstes im Hauptausschuss des Reichstages," *Berliner Tageblatt,* August 22, 1917, 4.

"Staatssekretär Richard von Kühlmann über die auswärtige Politik. Rede im Hauptausschuss zur
Amtseinführung," *Berliner Tageblatt,* August 23, 1917, 3–4.

AG Bad Neuenahr, Kur- und Fremdenlisten, nos. 19, 31, July/August 1907; nos. 20, 26, July/
August 1911; nos. 18, 20, June 1912; no. 34, August 1913; no. 11, June 1914.

Meyers Reisebücher: Der Harz (Leipzig and Wien: Bibliographisches Institut, 1907), 119–120.

L. Perlmutter, "Neuenahrer Badebrief," *Die neue jüdische Presse Frankfurter Israelitisches Familienblatt,* September 5, 1913, 10.

Verzeichnis von Hotels, Sommerwohnungen and Geschäften in Bad Harzburg, ed. Herzogliches
Badekommissariat (Bad Harzburg: Bad Harzburg Rosdorff, 1915).

5.

Bad Polziner Schulfreunde: Gedenkschrift Bad Polzin. 650 Jahre Stadt, 300 Jahre Bad ([Osnabrück]:
self-publication, 1988), 10, 36, 68–69.

Bad Polziner Schulfreunde: Geschichtliches über Bad Polzin (n. p., 1982), 9.

Frank Bajohr, *"Unser Hotel ist judenfrei": Bäder-Antisemitismus im 19. und 20. Jahrhundert*
(Frankfurt/Main: Fischer-Taschenbuch-Verlag, 2003), 180–182.

Gronemann, *Erinnerungen,* 215–216.

Uwe Hager, "Bad Harzburg," in *Historisches Handbuch der jüdischen Gemeinden in Niedersachsen
und Bremen,* ed. Herbert Obenaus et. al., vol. 1 (Göttingen: Wallstein, 2005), 807–812.

Kaplan, *The Making of the Jewish Middle Class,* 122–125.

Rürup, *Ehrensache,* 83–84.

Gerhard Salinger, "Jüdische Gemeinden in Hinterpommern," in *"Halte fern dem Lande jedes Ver-
derben …," Geschichte und Kultur der Juden in Pommern,* ed. Margret Heitmann and Julius
Schoeps (Hildesheim et al.: Georg Olms, 1995), 59–60.

Heinz Schönewald, *Bad Neuenahr: Weltbad der Kaiserzeit* (Erfurt: Sutton, 2009), 2, 105.

Thea Sternheim, *Tagebücher,* ed. Thomas Ehrsam and Regula Wyss (Göttingen: Wallstein, 2011),
vol. 1, 223.

Mirjam Triendl-Zadoff, *Nächstes Jahr in Marienbad: Gegenwelten jüdischer Kulturen der Moderne*
(Göttingen: Vandenhoeck & Ruprecht, 2007), 49–56.

Markus Weber, *"Das ist Deutschland … und es gehört uns allen." Juden zwischen Akzeptanz und
Verfolgung im Kurort Bad Harzburg* (Braunschweig: Appelhans, 2016), 38–41, 76–78.

Wolfgang Wilhelmus, *Geschichte der Juden in Pommern* (Rostock: Koch, 2004), 252.

6.

Gaito Gasdanow [Gaito Gazdanov], *Ein Abend bei Claire,* trans. Rosemarie Tietze (München:
Hanser, 2014), 68–70.

Scholem, *Von Berlin nach Jerusalem,* 102, 108.

7.

150 Jahre Festschrift der Aktiengesellschaft Bad Neuenahr, 38–39, accessed April 30, 2021, https://
issuu.com/bad-neuenahr/docs/festschrift.pdf.

"Kultussteuer-Umlagerolle der Synagogengemeinde Bad Neuenahr von 1909," Alemannia Judaica, accessed April 30, 2021, http://www.alemannia-judaica.de/bad_neuenahr_synagoge.htm.

Jochen Tarrach, "Erster Weltkrieg. Aus feudalen Hotels wurden Lazarette," *Rhein Zeitung online*, accessed April 30, 2021, http://www.rhein-zeitung.de/region/der-erste-weltkrieg_artikel,-Erster-Weltkrieg-Aus-feudalen-Hotels-wurden-Lazarette-_arid,1123273.html.

CHAPTER 10
Economic Management in Times of War and Revolution. Petrograd

1.

JMB: H-C i: 6: Chaim Kahan, Petrograd, to Kahan-Rosenberg, Berlin, December 23, 1915; Chaim Kahan, Petrograd, to Kahan-Rosenberg, Berlin, via L. C. Glad & Co., Copenhagen [March 17, 1916]. H-C i: 18: Baruch Kahan, [Petrograd], to Kahan-Rosenberg, Berlin, October 21, 1916; Rosalia Kahan, [Petrograd], to Kahan-Rosenberg, Berlin, February 17, 1917; Baruch Kahan, Tsarskoe Selo/Petrograd, to Kahan-Rosenberg, Berlin, May 24, 1917; June 24, 1917; October 17, 1917; Baruch Kahan, [Tsarskoe Selo], to W. Finkelstein, Stockholm, June 5, 1917; Baruch Kahan, Petrol Moscow, to Kahan-Rosenberg, Berlin, July 8, 1918. H-C i: 26: Chaim Kahan, Moscow, to Kahan-Rosenberg, Berlin, via L. C. Glad & Co., Copenhagen, September 25, 1915. H-C i: 42: Aron Kahan, Memoirs, part 1, 16, part 2, 18/9.

RGIA: Binagadinskoe: F. 23, op. 28, d. 245-246. Petrol: F. 23, op. 14, d. 222. Russisch-Baltische Mineralölwerke, Riga: F. 23, op. 12, d. 2038. Petrol: F. 23, op. 28, d. 1631-1632. Azovsko-Donskoi kommerchesky bank: F. 616, op. 1, d. 615. Petrogradsky kommerchesky bank: F. 597, op. 2, d. 225.

CDIAK: Chaim N. Kagan. F. 2034, op. 1, d. 42: Contracts with the Russisch-Baltische Waggonfabrik AG, Riga, 1893–1897; d. 237–241: Trade relations with Goldlust, 1896; d. 250: Jacob Kahan, Berlin, to Baruch and Rosalia Kahan, [Petrograd], October 12, 1917; d. 248: [Jonas Rosenberg, Berlin,] to Baruch Kahan, Kharkov, October 21, 1917.

ARDTAM: Branobel: F. 798, op. 1, d. 600; d. 2224; op. 2, d. 3640, d. 4575: Trade relations with Shifrin and Goldlust. Kaspiiskoye chernomorskoye nefteproryshlennoye i torgovoye obshchestvo: F. 587, op. 1, d. 151: Trade relations with Shifrin and Goldlust.

2. and 3. ---

4.

"Kagan, Aron Chaim., Troitskaya 23, direktor prav. Aktsionernogo obshchestva Petrol," *Ves Peterburg* (1914).

"Kagan, Chaim Nachum., Stremyannaya 6, preds. prav. Obshchestva Petrol," *Ves Peterburg* (1914).

"Liquidation russischer Unternehmungen," *Handels-Zeitung des Berliner Tageblatts*, October 4, 1917, 4.

Obzor bakinskoi neftyanoi promyshlennosti za 1915 (Baku, 1916), vol. 1, 173–186.

"Russko-Baltiiskikh neftepromyshlennykh zavodov akts. o-va," *Spravochnaya kniga o litsakh petrogradskogo kupechestva* (1916): 193.

5.

Rudolf Agstner, "Österreich im Kaukasus 1849–1918," in *Occasional Papers,* ed. Diplomatische Akademie Wien (Wien: Diplomatische Akademie Wien, 1999), 52–58.

Bochanov, *Delovaya elita,* 120, 127, 144, 166, 228–229, 233.

Dadayan, *Armyane,* 34.

"Inneres Wirtschaftsleben," *Der Deutsch-Russische Wirtschaftskrieg* 20 (1917): 4.

Gefter, *Monopolistichesky kapital* (1961), 738/9.

Iosif F. Gindin, *Russkiye kommercheskiye banki: Iz istorii finansovogo kapitala Rossii* (Moscow: Gosfinizdat, 1948), 220–222.

Guliyev, *Monopolistichesky kapital* (1973), 330, 502, 510, 547/8.

Marat Dzhafar Ibragimov [Marat Cəfər İbrahimov], *Bakinskaya neftyanaya promyshlennost v gody pervoi mirovoyi voyny (1914–Fev. 1917)* (PhD diss., Baku, 1972), 21, 34–37.

Jury N. Netesin, "Evakuatsiya promyshlennosti Latvii v pervuyu mirovuyu voinu (1915–1917 gg.)," *Problemy istorii* 1, no. 6 (1962): 27–75.

Polonsky, *Bankirsky dom,* 30–31.

Kornely F. Shatsillo, *Russky imperializm i razvitiye flota: Nakanune pervoi mirovoi voiny (1906–1914 gg.)* (Moscow: Nauka, 1968), 215–216.

Lewis H. Siegelbaum, *The Politics of Industrial Mobilization in Russia: A study of the War-Industries Committees* (London: Palgrave Macmillan, 1983), 121–158.

Tolf Russian, *Rockefellers,* 194.

6.

Asch, *Die Sintflut,* 45, 56–60, 982–985.

Sholem Asch, *Briv,* ed. Mordekhay Tzanin (Bat Yam: Bet Shalom Ash, 1980), 67–73.

7.

"Sankt Petersburg Stremyannaya No. 6," Save-SPb, accessed April 30, 2021, https://www.save-spb.ru/page/houses/houses/stremyannaya_6.html.

"Ukazatel deystvuyushchikh v Imperii aktsionernykh predpriyatii, Sankt Peterburg 1903," Our Baku, accessed April 30, 2021, https://www.ourbaku.com/index.php/%D0%97%D0%B0%D0%B3%D0%BB%D0%B0%D0%B2%D0%BD%D0%B0%D1%8F_%D1%81%D1%82%D1%80%D0%B0%D0%BD%D0%B8%D1%86%D0%B0.

CHAPTER 11
Across the Front Line. Berlin, Warsaw, Baku, Moscow, Vilna, Kharkov, Kiev

1.

JMB: H-C i: 14: Baruch Kahan, Moscow, to Jonas Rosenberg and Bendet Kahan, Berlin, June 11/24, 1918. H-C i: 15: Chaim N. Kahan, obituaries. H-C i: 16 & 17, H-C i: 20 & 26: Chaim

N. Kahan and Jonas and Miriam Rosenberg, addresses in Warsaw, November, 1904-1914. H-C i: 18: Baruch Kahan, [Kharkov], to family Rosenberg, Berlin, October 21/November 3, 1916; November 5, 1918; Rosalia Kahan to Jacob Kahan, Berlin, Moscow, July 8, 1918; Kharkov, December 17, 1918. H-C i: 21: Joseph Schreiber, Yekaterinoslav, to Boris E. Kagan [Baruch Kahan], Kharkov, September 4, 1918. H-C i: 25: Rosa Rosenberg, Bad Polzin, to Jacob Kahan, Bad Salzbrunn, August 8, 1918. H-C i: 26: David Kahan, Kiev, to the families Kahan and Rosenberg, Berlin, December 26, 1918. H-C i: 42: Aron Kahan, Memoirs, part 2, 19, 21, 26. H-C ii: 13: Rosalia Kahan, Kharkov, to Jacob Kahan, Berlin, January 18, 1919. H-C ii: 17: Baruch Kahan, Kharkov, to family Rosenberg, Berlin, January 8, 1919. H-C ii: 22: Postcards from Poland 1916–1918, among others: S. Ebin, Warsaw, to Jonas Rosenberg, Berlin, May 1, 1916; Mosche Pisarewitz, Warsaw, to Jonas Rosenberg, August 12, 1918. H-C 2, folder 4: Photographs of family Rosenberg, Warsaw, 1894–1912; folder 14: Merchant Jonas Rosenberg, certificates of guild membership, Warsaw, 1914; G[erson]. Oppenheim (company L. C. Glad & Co), Copenhagen, to Bendet Kahan, Berlin, November 23, 1916; October 19, 1917; folder 16: Jonas Rosenberg, Russian passport, 1914; folder 23: Fragment of a letter [Chaim Kahan to Jonas Rosenberg, fall 1913]; Chaim Kahan, Berlin, to Malka Kahan and his sons, [Warsaw], December 1, 1913; Chaim Kahan, Berlin, to Malka Kahan, Miriam and Jonas Rosenberg, [Warsaw], December 14, 1913.

AECJ: Cohen-Mintz, "Chaim Cohen z"l vebeito," 3.

AVRP: Paul Ripp and Victor Ripp, interview with Zina Kahan.

APW: No. 72/1136, d. 86, 85: Warszawski gubernalny urząd do spraw podatku przemysłowskogo 1908–1912 (commercial tax). No. 72/1151, d. 1425: Starszy Inspektor fabrychnych Guberni Warszawskiej w Warszawie.

CDIAK: Chaim N. Kagan. F. 2034, op. 1, d. 246, d. 250, d. 251, d. 263: Jacob Kahan, Berlin, to Baruch and Rosa Kahan, [Petrograd], January 21–23, 1916; [Kharkov], October 12, 1917; December 14, 1917; September 5, 1918; d. 248, 257: [Jonas Rosenberg, Berlin] to Baruch and Rosalia Kahan, [Kharkov], October 21, 1917; May 29, 1918; d. 176: Aron Kahan, Baku, to David Kahan, [Moscow], April 16, 1918; d. 258: Jacob Kahan, Berlin, to David Kahan, [Kharkov or Kiev], June 26, 1918; d. 259, d. 260, d. 266, d. 264: Jacob Kahan, Berlin, to Baruch and Rosalia Kahan, to brother Arusia, to David and Aron Kahan, [Kharkov], July 1, 1918; July 12, 1918; September 27, 1918; d. 262: Bendet Kahan, Berlin, to Baruch Kahan, [Moscow or Kharkov], July 5, 1918; d. 261: Jacob Kahan, Berlin, to Baruch Kahan, [Kharkov], July 22, 1918; d. 279–294.

EAB: Application for restitution: Reg. no. 68875: Leonid Kahan (Kagan).

LAB: Restitution offices of Berlin, restitution affair: B Rep. 025–01, no. 11/13 WGA 13660/59: Jacob Haimi-Cohen and others (publisher Rom) versus Deutsches Reich, 1961.

LVIA: F. 517, op. 1, d. 964: Podatnye prisutstviya Vilenskoi Gubernii. Spiski vladeltsev torgovykh i promyshlennykh predpriyatii, Vilna, 1894 (taxpayers in the Vilna province, roll of trademen 1894).

2. and 3. ---

4.

"Kahan, Boruch, Nowolipki 19, Dom handlowy," *Księga adresowa Miasta Warszawy* (1896).

"Rosenberg, E., Franciszkanska 30, Przedsiebiorca Nafta," *Księga adresowa Miasta Warszawy* (1896).

"Kaspiisko-Chernomorskoye neftopromyshlennoye torgovoye o-vo, Senatorska 10," *Księga adresowa Miasta Warszawy* (1896).

"Kahan Ch. (wl. Rozenberg, Jonas) (hurt.), Ogrodowa 3," *Adresy Warszawy* (1909, 1910).

"Rosenberg, J., Skórzana ul. 4," *Adresy Warszawy* (1909, 1910).

"Nasledniki Zhuka, D., Zavalnaya 43," *Vsya Vilna* (1896, 1909).

"Bentsel, Chaim. Kagan, Kavkazskaya 10," *Vsya Vilna* (1914).

"Kagan, Ch. N., Kavkazsko-Volzhskoye torgovo-promyshlennoye aktsion. o-vo, Zhandarmsky pereulok 10," *Vsya Vilna* (1914, 1915).

5.

Genrikh Agranovsky, *Oni zdes zhili … Zametki o yevreiskom nasledii Vilnyusa* (Vilnius: Versus Aureus, 2014), 23–24.

Stephen D. Corrsin, *Warsaw before the First World War: Poles and Jews in the Third City of the Russian Empire 1880–1914* (New York: Columbia University Press, 1989), 1–6, 13–14, 31–38, 45–46, 89–106.

Vladas Drėma, *Lost Vilnius* (Vilnius: Versus Aureus, 1991).

Ewa Małkowska-Bieniek, *Warszawa—Warsze: Jewish Warsaw, Warsaw's Jews*, exhibition at the Museum of the History of Polish Jews, March 27–June 6, 2014.

"Tätigkeitsbericht unseres Vertrauensmanns Robert Skutezk, Warschau," *Polen-Russland* 1 (1916): 19.

Jarosław Zieliński, ed., *Prewar Jewish Warsaw in Historic Photographs* (Warsaw: Wydawnictwo RM, 2012).

Jarosław Zieliński, *Atlas dawnej architektury ulic i placów Warszawy* (Warsaw: Towarzystwo Opieki nad Zabytkami, 1996–2011), vol. 4 (Graniczna), vol. 5 (Karmelicka), vol. 8 (Królewska), vol. 15 (Ogrodowa).

"Zweiter Halbjahrsbericht unseres Vertrauensmanns Robert Skutezky, Warschau," *Königreich Polen* 2 (1916–1917): 15–26.

6.

Asch, *Die Sintflut*, 1259–1273.

Alexander A. Carlebach, "German Rabbi goes East," *Leo Baeck Yearbook* 6 (1961): 60–121.

Alfons Paquet, *Im kommunistischen Rußland. Briefe aus Moskau* (Jena: Diederichs, 1919), 19, 62.

Isaac Bashevis Singer, *A Day of Pleasure: Stories of a Boy Growing up in Warsaw* (New York: Farrar, Straus and Giroux, 1969).

7. ---

CHAPTER 12
Expulsion from Russia. Baku, Kharkov, Yekaterinoslav, Moscow

1.

JMB: H-C i: 13: Rosalia Kahan, Baku, to Jacob and Rosa Kahan, Berlin [n. d.]; David Kahan, Baku, to the families Rosenberg and Kahan, Berlin, June 11, 1919; Baruch Kahan, Yekaterinodar,

to the families Rosenberg and Kahan, Berlin, July 16, 1919; Rahel Ettinger, [Kharkov], to Zina Kahan, Baku, July 28, [1919]; [early in August 1919]; David Ettinger, Kharkov, to David Kahan, Baku, August 1, 1919; Arusia Kahan, Kharkov, to Baruch Kahan, [n. p.], August 8, 1919; David Kahan, Baku, to the families Rosenberg and Kahan, Berlin, [summer 1919]; David Kahan, Baku, to the families Rosenberg and Kahan, Berlin, September 17, 1919. H-C i: 14: Rosalia Kahan, Baku, to Jacob and Rosa Kahan, Berlin, [n. d.]; Baruch Kahan, Baku, to the families Rosenberg and Kahan, Berlin, August 8; September 2; September 4; September 8, 1919; David Kahan, Baku, to Rosa and Jacob Kahan, Berlin, September 15, 1919; Abram (Abraham) Ledermann, Copenhagen, to Rosa Kahan, Berlin, September 30, 1919. H-C i: 17: Baruch Kahan, Kharkov, to family Rosenberg, Berlin, January 8, 1919. H-C i: 42 Aron Kahan, Memoirs, part 2, 24–27, 30–32, 40–41. H-C i: 43: Baruch Kahan, Kharkov, to the families Rosenberg and Kahan, Berlin, October 8, 1918. H-C ii: 13: Rosalia Kahan, Kharkov, to Jacob Kahan, Berlin, January 18, 1919. H-C 2, folder 16: Marriage certificate of Jacob and Rosa Kahan; folder E: Arusia Kahan, Kovno, to Aron Kahan, [Berlin], July 20, 1921.
ATGK: Letter of thanks by Russian refugees to Carl Frederik Glad, 1916.
AVRP: Paul Ripp and Victor Ripp, interview with Zina Kahan.
AUCMT: Aaron Kagan (Arusia Kahan), certificate of exemption from conscription, Kharkov, May 6, 1919.
CDIAK: Chaim N. Kagan. F. 2034, op. 1, d. 63: Rosalia Kahan, Petrovsk, to Boris (Baruch) Kahan, November 11, 1919; d. 67: Rosalia Kahan, Petrovsk, to Boris (Baruch) Kahan, November 15, 1919. d. 178–179: Bendet Kahan, Charlottenburg, to David Kahan, [Moscow], May 28, 1918; d. 253: Jacob Kahan, Berlin, to David Kahan, [Moscow], May 13, 1918; d. 254: Jacob Kahan, Berlin, to Baruch and Rosalia Kahan, [Moscow], May 27, 1918; d. 257: Jonas Rosenberg, Berlin, to family Kahan, [Moscow], May 29, 1918; d. 260: Jacob Kahan and Rosa Rosenberg, Berlin, to family Kahan, [Moscow], July 12, 1918.
KBK: Judaica-Collection: Aron Kahan to L. C. Glad & Co, Copenhagen, May 16, 1919.
LAB: Documents on citizenships: Petition for naturalization, Aaron (Arusia) Kahan.
SAK: The Caucasian Oil Company, Batumi, Mai–August, 1920, F. 17 N 198. Batum, konsulær repræsentation 1902–1922: Vizeconsul Heinrich Warnecke F. 2–0679.

2.
Interview with Dvora Ettinger-Rozenfeld; interview with Gita Kahan-Ripp for the Spielberg Foundation.

3.
Ettinger-Rozenfeld, *Ha-Ettingerim*, 195–205.

4. ---

5.
Esther Aksel-Hansen, *Breve fra Petrograd, 1917–1918*, ed. Bernadette Preben-Hansen, (Copenhagen: Det Kongelige Bibliotek, 2007), 189, 212–213, 216–217.
Oleg V. Budnitsky and Aleksandra Polyan, *Russko-yevreisky Berlin 1920–1924* (Moscow: Novoye literaturnoye obozreniye, 2013), 343.

Oleg V. Budnitsky, *Rossiiskiye yevrei mezhdu krasnymi i belymi (1917–1920)* (Moscow: Rosspen, 2006), 175–279.

Duvantier, *L. C. Glad & Co.*, 162–176.

Nikolaus Katzer, *Die weiße Bewegung in Russland: Herrschaftsbildung, praktische Politik und politische Programmatik im Bürgerkrieg* (Cologne et al.: Böhlau, 1999), 123–138.

Joachim Tauber and Ralph Tuchtenhagen, *Vilnius: Kleine Geschichte der Stadt* (Cologne et al.: Böhlau, 2008), 178–179.

"Winter, David Alexander, Dr. (1878–1953)," in *Biographisches Handbuch*, vol. 2: *Die Rabbiner im Deutschen Reich 1871–1945*, ed. Michael Brocke, Julius Carlebach, et al. (Berlin: Saur, 2009), 659.

6.

Asch, *Die Sintflut*, 1260–1261.

Simon Dubnow, *Buch des Lebens: Erinnerungen und Gedanken. Materialien zur Geschichte meiner Zeit*, ed. Verena Dohrn, on behalf of the Simon-Dubnow-Institut, vol. 2, trans. Barbara Conrad (Göttingen: Vandenhoeck & Ruprecht, 2005), 345–362.

Paquet, *Im kommunistischen Rußland*, 3–5.

7.

"Soobshchenie svidetelnitsy P. O. Taslitskoy predstavitelyu Yeobshchestkoma o pogrome otryadom generala Shkuro v g. Yekaterinoslav v nachale iyulya 1919 g.," Scepsis Library (copy of a document in GARF: F. R-1339, op. 1, d. 419), accessed April 30, 2021, http://scepsis.net/library/id_1870.html.

Aleksandr Bystryakov, "Chronika zhizni yevreev Yekaterinoslava–Dnepropetrovska," *Yevreiskaya starina* 2 (2015), accessed April 30, 2021, http://berkovich-zametki.com/2015/Starina/Nomer2/Bystrjakov1.php#1.3._1906-1919_gody.

"Moskva," Rossiiskaya yevreiskaya entsiklopediya, accessed April 30, 2021, https://www.rujen.ru/index.php/Москва.

"H. F. Ulrichsen," in *Dansk Biografisk Leksikon*, 2nd ed., (København: Schultz, 1933–1944), accessed April 30, 2021, http://denstoredanske.dk/Dansk_Biografisk_Leksikon/Samfund,_jura_og_politik/Myndigheder_og_politisk_styre/Politiker/H.F._Ulrichsen.

CHAPTER 13
Fresh Start in the West. *Caucasian Oil Company*. Copenhagen, Berlin, London, Hamburg, Wilhelmshaven

1.

JMB: H-C: i: 13 David Kahan, Baku, to the Rosenberg family, Berlin, September 17, 1919; [fall 1919–spring 1920]; Baruch Kahan, Baku, to the Rosenberg family, Berlin, July 16, 1919. H-C i: 14: Baruch Kahan, Baku, to the Rosenberg family, Berlin, August 8; September 2; September 4; September 8, 1919. H-C i: 26: David Kahan, Kiev, to the Rosenberg family, Berlin, December 26, 1918. H-C i: 42: Aron Kahan, Memoirs, part 2, 27–32, 34–35.

LAB: Commercial Register files, A Rep. 342-02 no. 62699: Caucasian Trade Company.

BAB: Reich's Ministry of Finance: Property Sande near Wilhelmshaven. Caucasian Trade Company: R2, no. 8815, vol. 2, 1921–1924.

RGIA: Purchase contract, Russian-Baltic oil producing companies, Riga: F. 23, op. 12, d. 2038.

RAK: Udenrigsminiseriet: Caucasian Oil Company, Batumi 1920: F. 17 nos. 189–207.

SAK: Politiets Registerblade: Station 7 (Østerbro), Filmrulle 0024. Registerblad 21 (unikt id: 2238106): Abraham Ledermann.

SAW: File 3620: note of emergency currency of the Jade Cities Wilhelmshaven-Rüstringen. October 1922.

2. Interview with Thomas Glad and Morten F. Larsen, Copenhagen, May 10, 2016.

3. ---

4.

"Lehner, Dr. Ernst, Direktor, Lietzenburger Str. 27," *Berliner Adressbücher* (1922); "Ornstein, Hans, Kaufmann, Wilmersdorf, Berliner Str. 4," ibid.

"Caucasian Oil Company," in *Registreringstidende for Aktieselskaber*, ed. Handelsministeriet (Copenhagen, 1919), no. 6, 307–308, reg. no. 1856, no. 9, 529–530, reg. no. 1920, no. 8, 464.

"Caucasian Oil Company," *Sø-og Handelsrets-Tidende*, new series 14, no. 20 (August 1923): 210.

"Caucasian Oil Company," *Oil Paint and Drug Reporter* 99, no. 7 (1921): 14.

"Caucasian Oil Company," *National Petroleum News* 14 (October–December 1922): 104.

"Caucasian Oil Company," in *Erstes Revaler Handels-Adressbuch* (Tallinn, 1921), 99, 123, 125.

"Itskovich i Kagan," *Spravochny yezhegodnik Baku i yego raionov* (1914): supplement, 183–186.

"Jensen & Glad, København," in *Kraks Vejviser* (Copenhagen, 1906), 736.

"A/G Russisch Baltische Mineralölwerke Riga," *Berlingske Tidende*, October 8 and 21, 1920.

"Russisch-Baltische Mineralöle Rektifikations Akz. Ges.," in *Lettlands Adressbuch für Handel, Industrie u. Gewerbe* (Riga, 1922–1923), 231.

"Jacob Eskjeld Salomon," in *Candidati og Examinati Juris 1736–1936, Candidati politices 1852–1936, Candidati Actuarii, 1922–1936*, ed. A. Falk-Jensen and H. Hjorth-Nielsen, vol. 4 (Copenhagen, 1958), 8.

George Wenzel, "Max Lew," in *Deutscher Wirtschaftsführer: Lebensgänge deutscher Wirtschaftspersönlichkeiten* (Hamburg et al.: Hanseatische Verlagsanstalt, 1929), 342.

"Mittelamerika–Wilhelmshaven. Die Ankunft des Tankdampfers *Lucellum*," *Wilhelmshavener Zeitung*, April 29, 1922, 2.

"Estlands Ind- og Udførsel. 1. Juli–31. December 1920," *Udenrigsministeriets Tidsskrift*, February 15, 1921, 66.

"Caucasian Oil Company," *Commerce Reports* 3, nos. 27–39 (July–December 1922), 402.

"Caucasian Oil Company," *The Petroleum Times*, January 22, 1927, 143.

"Nitag," *Adressbücher Wilhelmshaven* (1922, 1926–1927, 1928–1929, 1931–1932).

"Paul Niehuß," *Wilhelmshavener Zeitung*, January 18, 1955, 3.

5.

Duvantier, *L.C. Glad & Co.*, 158, 262–265.

Jens Graul, *Die Stadt auf Befehl: Strukturwandel und Konversion in Wilhelmshaven* (PhD diss., University of Oldenburg, Wilhelmshaven, 1996), 61–84.

Rainer Karlsch and Raymond G. Stokes, *Faktor Öl: Die Mineralölwirtschaft in Deutschland 1859–1974* (München: Beck, 2003), 112–120, 162.

Die Oelbehälteranlagen in Rüstringen-Wilhelmshaven, vol. 2, ed. Städtisches Industrieamt Rüstringen (Rüstringen: Paul Hug & Co., 1921).

Walter Suhren, *Die wirtschaftliche und soziale Entwicklung Rüstringens* (Rostock: Oldenburg, 1926), 904–905.

Tolf, *The Russian Rockefellers*, 213–217.

6.

Essad Bey, *Das Weiße Russland: Menschen ohne Heimat* (Leipzig and Weimar: Kiepenheuer, 1991), 71–75.

7.

"Novemberrevolution. Wilhelmshaven und Rüstringen machten 1918 Geschichte," *Gegenwind. Zeitung für Arbeit*Frieden*Umweltschutz*, December 6, 2000, 1, accessed April 30, 2021, http://www.gegenwind-whv.de/novemberrevolution-2/.

"Klasson R. E. nashel sposob delat benzin i masla iz torfa," Semeinyye istorii, accessed April 30, 2021, http://www.famhist.ru/famhist/klasson/0022482a.htm.

"History 1910s," Sinclair Oil & Refining Corporation, accessed April 30, 2021, https://www.sinclairoil.com/history/1910.html.

CHAPTER 14
Family in Exile. Berlin

1.

JMB: H-C i: 4 Rosa Kahan, Berlin, to Jacob Kahan, Hamburg, October 9, 1921; Arusia Kahan, Wiesbaden, to Rosa Kahan, Berlin, November 25, 1921; Rosa Kahan, the steamboat "Cranz" on its way to Schwarzort, to Jacob Kahan, Hamburg, June 29; Schwarzort, June 30; July 3; July 7; July 18; July 26; Memel, July 28, 1922. H-C i: 8: Interim agreement of Nitag, June 1923. H-C i: 12 Rosa Kahan, Bad Harzburg, to Jacob Kahan, Hamburg, July 22; August 1, 1921; Berlin, August 14, 1921; Babelsberg, September 7; September 9; September 14 (together with Arusia Kahan); September 17; September 23; Berlin, October 2; October 7; October 9; [October 11]; [October 13]; October 30; October 31; November 4; November 6; November 8; November 18; [November 20]; November 22; November 24; [November 25]; November 27; November 28; December 1; December 4; [December 5]; December 6; December 9, 1921. January 6; February 1; February 3; February 10; February 24; February 27; March 1; March 2; March 3; March 7; March 10; March 19; March 21 & 22; March 24; March 27; March 28; March 30; April 3; April 29; May 2; May 5; May 8; [May 14]; May 15; May 19; May 23; May 26, 1922; Arusia Kahan, Berlin, to Rosa and Jacob Kahan, Hamburg, November 14, 1921; Arusia Kahan, Wiesbaden, to Jacob Kahan, Hamburg, November 26, 1921; Arusia Kahan, Berlin, to Rosa Kahan, Hamburg, December 15, 1921; Dora Kahan,

Berlin, to Rosa Kahan, Hamburg, December 18, 1921; Nachum Kahan, Zwickau, to Jacob Kahan, Hamburg, April 26, 1922; Arusia Kahan, Berlin, to Rosa Kahan, Hamburg, December 16, 1922. H-C i: 42: Aron Kahan, Memoirs, part 2, 41. H-C 2, folder 3: Photograph of Nachum Kahan, Zwickau, 1922; Honeymoon of Rosa and Jacob Kahan, Memel, June, 1919; folder 5: Photograph of Rosa Kahan with the family of Zina Kahan, Bad Harzburg, summer 1921; folder 7: Photographs of Mina Levstein, Berlin, 1919, and of Aron Kahan [n. d.]; folder 16: Jacob Kahan and Rosa Rosenberg, marriage certificate; folder A: Jacob Kahan, certificate of enrollment at Friedrich-Wilhelms University Berlin, spring semester 1919; folder B: Photographs of Chanukah in Logenhaus, Berlin, December 1922; picture postcard on occasion of Aron Kahan's and Mina Levstein's engagement, New Year's Eve, 1920.

AECJ: Cohen-Mintz, "Chaim Cohen z"l vebeito," 7.

ATEJ: Invitation to the wedding party of Rosa Rosenberg and Jacob Kahan, March 20, 1919; Kahan and Rosenberg families, Berlin, telegram to Salzmann, Copenhagen, for Zilla Feinberg [n. d.].

AWHZ: Ingenieurschule Zwickau, matriculation register 1921–1923, records of Leon Kahan, no. 3155, and Nahum Kahan, no. 3164.

EAB: Application for restitution: Reg. no. 68.830: Jakob Kahan.

GABO: Aron and Mina Kahan, marriage certificate, Berlin-Wilmersdorf, March 9, 1921; David Kahan, petition for naturalization in Poland, September 1925: F. 2, op. 1, d. 1021.

LAB: Restitution offices of Berlin, restitution affairs B Rep. 025–04 no. 1941 and no. 1942/50.

WGA: Tenement Wielandstraße 32, Berlin-Charlottenburg: Documents of citizenships: A Pr. Br. Rep. 030–06 no. 14185: Zlata (Zina) Kahan.

2. ---

3.
Ettinger-Rozenfeld, Ha-Ettingerim, 199, 205.

4.
"Cassierer, Alfred, Dr. Rechtsanwalt, Kurfürstendamm 225," Berliner Adressbücher (1921); "Goldberg, Salomon, Prof. Dr. jur. Syndikus, Wilmersdorf, Kurfürstendamm 150," ibid.

"Funcke, Eugen, Landmesser, Vermess. Büro, Grundst. U. Hypothek. Makler, Steinmetzstr. 57," Berliner Adressbücher (1922); "Uhl, Bruno, Dipl.-Ing., Charlottenburg, Leibnizstr. 221," "Holz, Ignatz, Just. Rat, Fasanenstr. 28," ibid.

"Chaim Avinoam Kahan," announcement of birth, Jüdische Rundschau, September 20, 1920, 509.

"Rachel [Rosa] and Jacob Kahan," announcement of marriage, Jüdische Rundschau, March 21, 1919, 162.

Carl von Ossietzky, "Komödienhaus 'Karussell,'" Berliner Volks-Zeitung, January 5, 1922.

Peter Panter (Kurt Tucholsky), "Massary and Roberts," Die Weltbühne, September 29, 1921, 330.

Jörg Plath, "Das KaDeWe lag mal in Petersburg," Taz. Berlin lokal, March 18, 1995, 35.

"21. 11. 1921. Abend des 'Obshchestvo russkikh yevreev' im Marmorsaal," in Chronik russischen Lebens in Deutschland 1918–1941, ed. Karl Schlögel et al. (Berlin: Akademie- Verlag, 1999), 1061.

"29. 11. 1921. Guest Performance by the Moscow Art Theater on Königgrätzer Straße, Berlin. Anton Tschechow 'Three Sisters,'" in *Chronik russischen Lebens*, 1087.

5.

Verena Dohrn and Anne-Christin Saß, "Einführung," in *Transit und Transformation: Osteuropäisch-jüdische Migranten in Berlin 1918–1939*, ed. Verena Dohrn and Gertrud Pickhan (Göttingen: Wallstein, 2010), 9–11.

François Guesnet, "Russian-Jewish Cultural Retention in Early Twentieth-Century Western Europe Contexts and Theoretical Implications," in *The Russian Jewish Diaspora and European Culture, 1917–1937*, ed. Jörg Schulte, Olga Tabachnikova and Peter Wagstaff (Leiden et al.: Brill, 2012), 2.

Fred Oberhauser and Nicole Henneberg, *Literarischer Führer Berlin* (Frankfurt/Main and Leipzig: Insel-Verlag, 1998), 414–415.

Saß, *Berliner Luftmenschen*, 88–89.

Hans Dieter Schreeb and Detlef Schaller, *Kaiserzeit—Wiesbaden und seine Hotels in der Belle Epoque* (Wiesbaden: Verlag Horst Axmann, 2006), 221, 228.

6.

Andrej Bely, "Wie schön es in Berlin ist," in *Russen in Berlin: Literatur, Malerei, Theater, Film 1918–1933*, ed. Fritz Mierau (Leipzig: Reclam, 1987), 56–58.

Moische Kulbak, "Ein Ball …," in *Unter Emigranten. Jiddische Dichtung und Prosa aus Berlin*, ed. Andrej Jendrusch (Berlin: Edition Dodo, 2003), 103.

Viktor Šklovskij, *Zoo oder Briefe nicht über die Liebe*, trans. Alexander Kaempfe (Frankfurt/Main: Suhrkamp, 1980), 75–76.

7.

Minutes of the Reichstag debates on housing shortage, 1919–1923, sessions 99, 169, 306, accessed April 30, 2021, http://www.reichstagsprotokolle.de/.

"*Prinzessin Olala*," announcement, *Berliner Tageblatt*, December 4, 1921, 23, accessed April 30, 2021, http://zefys.staatsbibliothek-berlin.de/kalender/auswahl/date/1921-12-04/27646518/.

"Isa Kremer," announcement, *Berliner Tageblatt*, April 30, [1922], 21, accessed April 30, 2021, http://zefys.staatsbibliothek-berlin.de/kalender/auswahl/date/1922-04-30/27646518/.

I. V. Zenkevich, "A. K. Kulidzh—popularizator rusistiki v SShA," *Iazyk i tekst* 3, no. 3 (2016): 78–85, accessed April 30, 2021, http://psyjournals.ru/langpsy/2016/n3/Zenkevich_full.shtml.

CHAPTER 15
Nitag. Berlin

1.

JMB H-C i: 3: United Caucasian Oil Company London, to Jonas Rosenberg, Merano, October 29; November 8, 1924. H-C i: 8: Interim Nitag agreement, Berlin Charlottenburg, June 11, 1923. H-C i: 26: Dr. Jakob Rabinowitsch, business card. H-C i: 27: Rheinische Nitag, company reports 1926–1931. H-C i: 28: Aaron Kahan, *Die Reorganisation des deutschen Petroleumhandels nach dem Kriege* [Berlin, 1924]; [Aron Kahan], *"Friedenspreis". Wie kann Friede und Gedeihen für Deutschland und Europa durch internationale Zusammenarbeit gesichert werden?* [Berlin, 1924]. H-C i: 33: Nachum (Nomek) Rosenberg to Aron Kahan, Tel Aviv, March 7, 1961. H-C i: 42: Aron Kahan, Memoirs, part 2, 29, 36–37, 39, 41. H-C 2, folder 10: Photograph of the Nitag staff in celebration of the inauguration of the new office accommodation, Keithstraße 11, Berlin-Schöneberg, September 13, 1927; folder 14: Nitag, June, 1923.

AECJ: Cohen-Mintz, "Chaim Cohen z''l vebeito," 11. Id., *Mishpachat R' Chaim Cohen*, 10.

LAB: Documents on citizenships, A Pr. Br. Rep. 030–06 no. 25576: Aaron Kahan. Commercial Register files, Nitag. A Rep. 342–02 no. 60671. Caucasische Handelsgesellschaft m.b.H.: A Rep. 342–02 no. 62699: Vollbrot: A Rep. 342–02 no. 59659. Debag: A Rep. 342–02, no. 59214.

EAB: Applications for restitution: Bendet Kahan. Leonid Kahan. Jakob Kahan. Reg. no. 68.871: Aharon Cohen-Mintz. Reg. no. 68.832: Aron Kahan. Reg. no. 68.831: David Kahan. Reg. no. 402.511: Deborah Loewenthal, nee Kahan. Reg. no. 78.565: Nachum Rosenberg. Reg. no. 345.016: Dr. Boris Schirmann [Schirman]. Reg. no. 78.515: Gita Rosenzweig. Reg. no. 57.331: Israel Estrin. Reg. no. 162.628: René Henri Lew. Reg. no. 273.735: Sara Weissberg, nee Rubinow. Reg. no. 257.403: Vera Alexander, nee Murawtchik.

BP-AMOCO: Quotas in the German motor fuel convention from August 27, 1932, no. 68318.

BAB: Rheinische Naphta-Industrie-AG: R 8127 no. 1691.

HWWA: Pressemappe 20. Jahrhundert. Company Archive: Naphta-Industrie und Tankanlagen AG (Nitag), company reports 1923–1937, newspaper articles 1926–1932.

SAB: Commercial Register, no. 1984/59: Rheinische Naphta-Industrie-AG.

SAH: Niedersächsische Betriebsstoff-Gesellschaft: HR 7/ no. 1676.

SAHH: Nitag, Hamburg branch: Commercial Register, department B, no. 1837. Restitution office, no. 351–11_47105: Dr. Berl Rosenberg. Ocean Vessel Register. Motortankschiff *Malkah*, no. 231–4_69, vol. 66, 6856.

LASA: Mitteldeutsche Kraftstoff: C 110 Halle, no. 1352. Commercial Register, department B, no. 1018.

2. ---

3.

Aron Kahan, *Erläuterungen zu der vorgeschlagenen Reform des Geldverkehrs in Deutschland* (Berlin: self-publication, 1923).
Idem, *New Scheme for Settlement of Reparations Problem* (London: self-publication, 1923).

4.

"Caucasische Handelsges. m. b. H., Schlüterstr. 36," *Berliner Adressbücher* (1921–1922).
"Naphta Industrie- und Tankanlagen Aktien-Gesellschaft (Nitag), Kleiststr. 31," *Berliner Adressbücher* (1923–1927).
"Naphta Industrie- und Tankanlagen A.-G. (Nitag), Keithstr. 11," *Berliner Adressbücher* (1928–1931).
"Naphta Industrie- und Tankanlagen A.-G. (Nitag) Filiale Hamburg, Speersort 8/10. Postadresse: Mönckebergstr. 19/21," *Hamburger Adressbücher* (1926–1928).

"Rosenberg, B. [Berl], Dr. Geschäftsführer, Brahmsallee 14," *Hamburger Adressbücher* (1926–1927).

"Dembo, Wulf, Direktor, Xantener Str. 4," *Berliner Adressbücher* (1925, 1930).

"Dembo, Wulf, Kaufmann, Duisburgerstr. 3," *Berliner Adressbücher* (1933).

"Estrin, Israel, Prokurist, Steglitz, Holsteinische Str. 9," *Berliner Adressbücher* (1930, 1933).

"Estrin, Israel, Prokurist, Wilmersdorf, Laubacherstr. 43," *Berliner Adressbücher* (1934).

"Die neuen Konzentrationen in der deutschen Erdölindustrie," *Petroleum* 19, no. 20 (1923): 687–699.

"Naphta-Industrie und Tankanlagen A.-G., Nitag, Berlin," *Petroleum* 20, no. 29 (1924): 1526. "Finanzielle Chronik. Naphta-Industrie und Tankanlagen A.-G., Nitag, Berlin," *Petroleum* 22, no. 24 (1926): 9; ibid. 23, no. 4 (1927): 131; no. 15 (1927): 625; ibid. 24, no. 23 (1928): 1025.

"Firmennachrichten," *Oel und Kohle* 11, no. 28 (1935): 497.

"Limicana," *Berliner Börsenzeitung*, August 29 (1927), 10.

"Limicana," *Hamburgischer Correspondent und Neue Hamburgische Börsenhalle*, October 18, 1923, 24; October 24, 1923, 21; June 10, 1925, 23; September 15, 1926, 16.

"Limicana," *Hamburger Nachrichten*, September 17, 1926, 8.

"Nitag," *Berliner Handels-Register. Verzeichnis der in den Amtsgerichtsbezirken Berlin-Mitte, Charlottenburg … wohnenden eingetragenen Einzelfirmen, Gesellschaften und Genossenschaften* 67 (1931), 899.

"Nitag," in *Wilhelmshavener Heimatlexikon*, ed. Werner Brune, Heike Coldewey et al. (Wilhelmshaven: Brune, 1986–1987), vol. 2, 354.

"Schiffsverkäufe," *Hansa. Deutsche Nautische Zeitschrift* 64, no. 3 (1927): 417.

"Orient Mineralölwerke," *Berliner Börsenzeitung*, June 2, 1928, 10.

"United Oil Importers, Ltd.," *The Petroleum Times*, January 22, 1927, 143.

"Wirtschaftsberichte. Erdölwirtschaft," *Technik und Wirtschaft. Zeitschrift für Wirtschaftskultur* 26 (1933): 20–23.

5.

Erich Achterberg, *Berliner Banken im Wandel der Zeit: Eine Schrift zum 75jährigen Bestehen des Bankhauses Hardy & Co. GmbH Frankfurt-Berlin* (Darmstadt: Hoppenstedt, 1956), 62–63, 82–84.

Patrick Bormann, Judith Michel and Joachim Scholtyseck, "Einleitung," in *Unternehmer in der Weimarer Republik*, ed. Patrick Bormann, Judith Michel and Joachim Scholtyseck (Stuttgart: Franz Steiner Verlag, 2016), 7–14.

Karlsch and Stokes, *Faktor Öl*, 112–154.

Titus Kockel, *Deutsche Ölpolitik 1928–1938* (Berlin: Akademie-Verlag, 2005), 29–30.

Ingo Köhler, *Die 'Arisierung' der Privatbanken im Dritten Reich: Verdrängung, Ausschaltung und die Frage der Wiedergutmachung* (München: Beck, 2005), 11–17.

Annette Schlapkohl and Theo Müller, *100 Jahre Schindler: Chronik einer Hamburger Firma* (Hamburg: Husum Verlag, 2008), 9–28.

Suhren, *Die wirtschaftliche und soziale Entwicklung*, 904–905.

6. ---

7.

"*Grete Glad*," Project "Transportschiffe bei Operation Weserübung," Historisches Marinearchiv, accessed April 30, 2021, https://www.historisches-marinearchiv.de/projekte/weseruebung/ausgabe.php?where_value=74.

"O.V. Ch. N. KAHAN," Richardson, Duck & Company, Thornaby, accessed April 30, 2021, http://www.teesbuiltships.co.uk/view.php?official_number=&imo=&builder=5025&builder_eng=&year_built=1917&launch_after=&launch_before=&role=&type_ref1=&propulsion=&owner=&port=&flag=&disposal=&lost=&ref=167393&vessel=BEECHLEAF.

CHAPTER 16
Devotion to Books. Petrograd, Vilna, Berlin

1.

JMB H-C i: 12: Rosa Kahan, Berlin, to Jacob Kahan, Hamburg, May 15, 1922. H-C ii: 12: Dr. Ing. Gustav Birstein [Gustaw Birsztein], Warsaw, to Jonas Rosenberg, July 9, 1923.

AECJ: Cohen-Mintz, "Chaim Cohen z"l vebeito," 9.

ANLR: Bendet Kahan, Karlsbad, to Dora Kahan, Berlin, August 28, 1925.

ABRW: Simon Rawidowicz, Tel Aviv, to Esther Klee, Berlin, February 25; March 12; July 29, 1925; Rabbiner Professor David Simonsen, Copenhagen, to Simon Rawidowicz, Berlin, September 11, 1925.

BAREEC: Abram Kagan papers, interview conducted by Marc Raeff, 5, 54–56.

LAB: Restitution offices of Berlin. Restitution affair Jacob Haimi-Cohen et al. versus Deutsches Reich, 1961: B Rep. 025–01, no. 11/13 WGA 13660/59.

2. ---

3.

Ettinger-Rozenfeld, *Ha-Ettingerim*, 206.

Verzeichnis für den jüdischen Buchhandel, ed. Bendet Kahan (Berlin: Jalkut, 1927).

4.

"A. J. Stybel Verlag," *Berliner Börsenzeitung*, September 10, 1927, 4; November 3, 1927, 4; November 18, 1927, 4; April 7, 1930, 8.

"Abraham Josef Stybel Verlag," *Jüdische Rundschau*, August 9, 1927, 453; November 8, 1927, 633.

"Damenkomitee des 'Bet am ivri,'" *Jüdische Rundschau*, November 6, 1931, 514.

Miron, "Zalman Shneour."

"Statut Spółki Akcyjnej pod firmą 'Spółka Akcyjna Wydawniczo-Drukarska Rom,'" *Monitor polski*, January 8, 1924, 3–6.

"Hotzaot Sefarim Me'uchadot," *Official Gazette of the Government of Palestine*, September 16, 1925, 479–480.

"Kagan, Bentsel Chaim," *Vsya Vilna. Adresnaya i spravochnaya kniga g. Vilny* (1914): section 7: inhabitants, 125–126.

5.

Mikhail Beizer, *Yevrei v Peterburge* (Jerusalem: Biblioteka Aliya, 1990), 301.

Olga Demidova, "'Chochu byt iskrennim': Zhizn i vospominaniya Abrama Kagana," in Abram Kagan, *Vospominaniya*, ed. Olga Demidova (St. Peterburg: Petropolis, 2016), 3–29.

Gottfried Kratz, "Der Berliner russische Verlag Slovo (1920–1935)," in *Archiv für Geschichte des Buchwesens*, ed. Monika Estermann and Ursula Rautenberg on behalf of Historische Kommission des Börsenvereins des Deutschen Buchhandels e. V., vol. 64 (Berlin and New York: De Gruyter, 2009), 193, 202.

Idem, "Russische Verlage und Druckereien in Berlin 1918–1941," in *Chronik russischen Lebens*, 522, 538, 542–544, 549–550, 553–554, 569.

Maria Kühn-Ludewig, *Jiddische Bücher aus Berlin (1918–1936)* (Nümbrecht Bruch: Kirsch, 2006), 173–174, 198–201.

Idem, *Johannes Pohl (1904–1960): Judaist und Bibliothekar im Dienste Rosenbergs. Eine biographische Dokumentation* (Hannover: Laurentius, 2000), 160–161.

Jürgen Plähn, "Signets russischer Verlage in Berlin," in *Russische Autoren und Verlage in Berlin nach dem Ersten Weltkrieg*, ed. Thomas R. Beyer, Gottfried Kratz and Xenia Werner (Berlin: Spitz, 1987), 151–186.

Leon Shapiro, *The History of ORT* (New York: Schocken, 1980), 94, 148.

6.

Abram Kagan, *Vospominaniya*, ed. Olga Demidova (St. Peterburg: Petropolis, 2016), 69–96.

Rubin Mass, "Perakim michayai," in *Ve'im bigvurot Fourscore Years. A Tribute to Rubin and Hannah Mass on Their Eightieth Birthdays*, ed. Abraham Eben Shushan et al. (Jerusalem: Yedidim, 1974), 351–353.

7.

Agnes Grasffa, "Raisa Bloch-Gorlina (1898–1943). Put istorika-mediyevista v chernye dni yevropeiskoi istorii," Rusofil. Russkaya istoriya, filosofiya i kultura, accessed April 30, 2021, http://russophile.ru/2016/07/21/.

Abraham Z. Idelsohn, "My Life," *Jewish Music Journal* 2, no. 2 (1935): 8–11, accessed April 30, 2021, http://www.jewish-music.huji.ac.il/content/abraham-zvi-idelsohn.

A. Kentler, "Po serdtsu idet parokhod," part 1, e3e5. Shakhmaty v Peterburge, accessed April 30, 2021, http://www.e3e5.com/article.php?id=1720.

"Romm Publishing House," Wikipedia, accessed April 30, 2021, https://en.wikipedia.org/wiki/Romm_publishing_house.

CHAPTER 17
36 Schlüterstrasse, Expulsion from Paradise. Berlin

1.

JMB: H-C i: 11: Family letter, Swinemünde, n. d. [August 1923]. H-C i: 19, H-C i: 38: Summer resorts and trips 1924–1935. H-C ii:18: Kahan Vermögensverwaltung 1927. H-C ii: 19: Rosa Kahan, Berlin, to Jonas Rosenberg [Riga], June 11, 1933. H-C 2, folder 03: Photograph of Baruch Kahan's family, Schlüterstrasse 37, January 30, 1927; photograph of Noma and Lolia

Kahan with fiancés. Alkazar, Hamburg, Reeperbahn, October 31, 1927; folder 4: Photograph of statuettes of Miriam and Jonas Rosenberg; folder 8: Photograph of Chaim Avinoam Kahan, KaDeWe Berlin [n. d.]; folder 12: Photograph of Jacob's and Roska's apartment, Wielandstrasse 32, around 1931; folder 18: Pusztinsky family, greeting card; folder 20: Malka's funny sayings, 1928–1929, documented by Rosa Kahan; folder A: Rosa Kahan, Leporello with Chaim Avinoam's witticisms, 1925; folder B: Photograph of Lily and Chaim Avinoam Kahan, Berlin, summer 1925; folder E: Rachel Kahan: Schlüterstrasse 36; folder F: Bluma Altbaum, greeting card for the Kahans and the Rosenbergs.

AECJ: Family photo album.

AGRHC: Chaim Avinoam Kahan to Rosalia and Baruch Kahan, Passover, [n. d.]; Chaim Avinoam Kahan, Wiesbaden, to Jacob Kahan, Berlin, March 4, 1932; Chaim Avinoam Kahan, drafts for the Bar Mitzvah celebration, September 1933.

ANLR: Wedding newspaper for Gita and Salomon Ripp, Berlin, October 1932.

AJB: Card file of the Adass Yisroel cemetery: Malka Kahan / Malka bat Eliezer Moshe, deceased January 15, 1922; Miriam (Mirla) Rosenberg / Miriam bat Moreinu Ha-Rav Chaim Ha-Cohen, deceased August 23, 1931.

EAB: Applications for compensation: Aharon Cohen Mintz, Aron Kahan, Bendet Kahan, David Kahan, Deborah Loewenthal, Jacob Kahan, Leonid Kahan, Nachum Rosenberg. Reg. no. 257.299: Shalom Ettinger. Reg. no. 344.103: Sulamith Rosenberg. Reg. no. 354.345: Zlata Zina Kahan.

GABO: Aron Kahan, David Kahan, Zina, Gita and Lily Kahan, petitions for naturalization in Poland 1924–1925: F. 2, op. 1, d. 1021, l. 371–435.

LAB: B Rep. 025–03 Restitution offices of Berlin no. 2829 (1950): Lawsuit of Mina Kahan, represented by Jewish Restitution Successor Organization Inc., versus Walter Weymann. Charge: Forced sale of ground and tenement Gutzkowstrasse. 2. Documents on citizenships: Aaron Kahan, Bendet Kahan, Jacob Kahan. Ebd. A Pr.Br.Rep. 030–06 no. 14185: Zlata Zina Kahan.

2.

Interviews with Dvora Ettinger-Rozenfeld; Gita Kahan-Ripp for the Spielberg Foundation; Efrat Carmon, Jerusalem, December 4, 2008; November 14, 2010; Eli Rosenberg, Berlin, March 14, 2010; Tel Aviv, December 2, 2009; October 9, 2012; Giza Haimi-Cohen, December 8, 2008; November 8, 2010; March 18, 2011; Naomi Loewenthal, Ramat Aviv, December 9, 2008; Yossi Cohen, December 5, 2009; November 11, 2010; Raziel Haimi-Cohen, New Jersey, June 24, 2014; Michal Froom, Ma'agan Michael, September 21, 2016; Tamar Eshel, Jerusalem, January 1, 2017.

Video films: Howard Rosen, *Gabe's Interview*, Madison, WI, 1997; Amos Cohen, *Josef Cohen Speaks of His Family* [Hebrew], Tel Aviv, April 2012.

3.

Victor Ripp, *Hell's Traces: One Murder. Two Families. Thirty-Five Holocaust Memorials* (New York: Farrar, Straus and Giroux, 2017), 34, 171.

4.

"Rosenberg, Jonas, Kaufm., Charlottenburg, Schlüterstr. 36" *Berliner Adressbücher* (1918–1930).
"Kahan, Bendet, Kaufm., Charlottenburg, Niebuhrstr. 67," *Berliner Adressbücher* (1918).

"Kahan, Bendet, Kaufm., Charlottenburg, Niebuhrstr. 10," *Berliner Adressbücher* (1921–1927).

"Kahan, Bendet, Kaufm., Charlottenburg, Dahlmannstr. 5," *Berliner Adressbücher* (1928–1933).

"Kahan, Baruch, Kaufm., Charlottenburg, Schlüterstr. 37," *Berliner Adressbücher* (1925–1933).

"Kahan, Aron, Direktor, Charlottenburg, Wielandstr. 32," *Berliner Adressbücher* (1923–1926).

"Kahan, David, Direktor, Charlottenburg, Schlüterstr. 43," *Berliner Adressbücher* (1924).

"Kahan, Jakob, Kaufm., Charlottenburg, Schlüterstr. 36," *Berliner Adressbücher* (1924).

"Kahan, Jacob, Prokurist, Charlottenburg, Wielandstr. 32," *Berliner Adressbücher* (1931–1934).

"Kahan, Sina, Kaufmswtw., Kurfürstendamm 47," *Berliner Adressbücher* (1924–1931).

"Kahan, Sina, Wtw., Bleibtreustr. 32," *Berliner Adressbücher* (1932–1933).

"Kahan, M., Frau, Charlottenburg, Wielandstr. 32," *Berliner Adressbücher* (1928–1933).

"Ettinger, David, Charlottenburg, Schlüterstr. 37," *Berliner Adressbücher* (1925).

"Rosenberg, Nachum, Charlottenburg, Wielandstr. 32," *Berliner Adressbücher* (1927–1933).

"Grundstücksgesellsch. G.m.b.H. (Schlüterstr. 37), Wielandstr. 32," *Berliner Adressbücher* (1925–1927).

"Kahan, Vermögensverwalt. G.m.b.H., Wielandstr. 32," *Berliner Adressbücher* (1928–1933).

"Kahan, Vermögensverwalt. G.m.b.H., Keithstr. 11," *Berliner Adressbücher* (1929–1933).

"Kahan, Vermögensverwalt. G.m.b.H., Charlb., Schlüterstr. 37," *Berliner Adressbücher* (1934–1935).

"Michael Rosenberg," announcement of birth, *Jüdische Rundschau*, April 9, 1926, 203.

"Malkah Kahan," announcement of birth, *Jüdische Rundschau*, December 3, 1926, 693.

"Elijahu Rosenberg," announcement of birth, *Jüdische Rundschau*, May 11, 1928, 271.

"Nachum Kahan and Rita Kahn," announcement of marriage, *Jüdische Rundschau*, December 2, 1927, 685.

"Kahan Vermögensverwaltung GmbH," *Berliner Börsenzeitung*, July 13, 1927, 10.

"Nachum Rosenberg and Sulamith Hurwitz," announcement of engagement, *Jüdische Rundschau*, October 17, 1924, 507.

5.

Verena Dohrn and Anke Hilbrenner, introduction to *Buch des Lebens* by Simon Dubnow, vol. 3, 40–42.

Verena Dohrn, "'Wir Europäer schlechthin': Die Familie Koigen im russisch-jüdischen Berlin," *Osteuropa: Impulse für Europa. Tradition und Moderne der Juden Osteuropas* 58, nos. 8–10 (2008): 229–30.

Idem, "Die Familie Chaim Kahan und ihre Unternehmen im Weimarer Berlin," in *Berlin Transit. Jüdische Migranten aus Osteuropa in den 1920er Jahren,* ed. Jüdisches Museum Berlin (Göttingen: Wallstein, 2012), 100–105.

Edward K. Kaplan and Samuel H. Dresner, *Abraham Joshua Heschel: Prophetic Witness* (New Haven: Yale University Press, 1998), 129–137.

Dieter Schwab, "Gleichberechtigung und Familienrecht im 20. Jahrhundert," in *Frauen in der Geschichte des Rechts: Von der Frühen Neuzeit bis zur Gegenwart,* ed. Ute Gerhard (München: Beck, 1997), 792.

6.

Vera Broido, *Tochter der Revolution: Erinnerungen,* trans. Jürgen Schneider (Hamburg: Ed. Nautilus, 2004), 136–137.

Eleonore Hertzberger, *Durch die Maschen des Netzes: Ein jüdisches Ehepaar im Widerstand gegen die Nazis* (München: Heyne, 1996), 12.

Mary-Kay Wilmers, *The Eitingons: A Twentieth-Century Story* (London: Faber and Faber 2009), 186–187.

7. ---

CHAPTER 18
The Mavericks between the Wars—European Corporate Networks: Berlin, Hamburg, Copenhagen, London, Riga, Paris, Amsterdam

1.

JMB: H-C i: 3: United Caucasian Oil Company, London, to Jonas Rosenberg, Meran, October 29, 1924. H-C i: 27: David Kahan, Paris, to Moritz Hanemann, Amsterdam, March 10 and 13, 1939; August 23, 1939; to Ch. Karl Kondor, Anvers, March 13, 1939; to Helge Lühr, Malmö, March 13, 1939; to A. Milman, Bucharest, March 13, 1939; to M[ordechai]. Rosenberg, Anvers, August 29, 1939. Aron Kahan, Paris, to A[lfred] Aufhäuser, New York, February 10, 1939; to J[akob] A. Rabinovich [Rabinowitsch], London, March 11, 1939. H-C i: 42: Aron Kahan, Memoirs, part 2, 36–39.

AECJ: Cohen-Mintz, "Chaim Cohen z"l vebeito," 13.

AIFA: Moses Hanemann, Amsterdam, to Lothar Nachman, New York, September 29, 1964.

AUCMT: Picture story "Ahron Rolle," Cologne, 1928.

AYMD: Aron Kahan, "Did I Accomplish Anything in My Lifetime and If So—What Exactly?," 16–17.

BAB: Reich's ministry of finance 8V8—Mineral oil tax, equalization tax. Suggestions for composition and modification of the mineral oil tax et al. Formation of a fuel monopol, R2/10629, vol. 3: 1930–1932. Deutsche Revisions- u. Treuhand AG, Berlin, report on Eurotank AG 1931–1935; Report on Eurotank AG, 1931–1941: R/8135/, sig. 4114.

BP-AMOCO: Quotas, 1932; Agreement between the Caucasian Oil Company (Copenhagen) and Anglo–Persian Oil Company (Egypt), March 28, 1930, no. 111922; Algemeen Noord-Hollandsch Handelskantoor (NOHAKA), Amsterdam: Balance Sheet, August 5, 1947, no. 95869; C.N.V. Algemeen Noord-Hollandsch Handelskantoor (NOHAKA), Amsterdam: Report on Investigation together with Balance Sheet, November 30, 1946, no. 95802.

EAB: Applications for restitution: Reg. no. 261.105: Moses (Moritz) Hanemann, David Kahan, Aron Kahan.

GAA: Persoonskaarten: Gaukstert Johannes Hendricus.

GSPKB: Application of Bankhaus Hardy & Co. for Nitag to Reich's ministry of finance: Deduction of Gesellschaftssteuer, Berlin, December 9, 1931. Reich's minister of finance to the Prussian minister of trade and industry, Berlin, December 18, 1931: I. HA Rep. 120 Prussian ministry of trade and industry: C VIII 1 no. 66 vol. 18; C V Nr. 100A vol. 7.

HMRA: Judith B. Walzer, interview conducted by Judith Shklar, July 16, 1981, 2 parts. Walzer, Judith B., 1975–01–01, "Oral History of the Tenured Women in the Faculty of Arts and Sciences at Harvard University, 1981 (Log# 00709)," hdl:1902.1/00709," part 1, 4–13, 17–18.

HWWA: "Presseberichte Nitag," *Frankfurter Zeitung*, December 25 and 29, 1931, Sign. N 96. "Naphta Industrie und Tankanlagen AG (Nitag)," *Frankfurter Zeitung*, October 15 and November 1, 1932, Sign. N 96.

LAB: Eurotank, company reports 1932–1937: A Rep. 342–02 no. 60841. Restitution offices of Berlin. Restitution affair Kahan Vermögensverwaltung versus Deutsche Nitag: B Rep. 025–04 no. 1938 + 1939/50.

NHAH: Commercial register van de Kamer van Koophandel en Fabrieken, toegang 448, Amsterdam 1958, Algemeen Noord-Hollandsch Handelskontoor (Nohaka) N. V, no. 38492.

NIOD: Omnia Treuhandgesellschaft m.b.H. Nohaka, F. 94, no. 4372. Archief Moses Hanemann: Box 142.

SAB: Trade card file: Trade card of Rheinische Naphta-Industrie AG: no. 1984/59.

RAK: Udenrigsminiseriet: *The Caucasian Oil Company. Engelske Myndigheders Beslaglæggelse af Olie i Batoumi, 1920*. Gruppeordnede sager 17–78 (1909–1945): 17, nos. 189–207, 198.

Erhvervsarkivet, Vyborg: Det Danske Petroleums Aktieselskab, Direktør Chr. Holm (1902–1938): Correspondence (official), 1902–1938: Ole Simonsen, Copenhagen, to consul general Christian Holm, Vedbæk, July 23, 1932, no. 22; business correspondence (official) m 1914–1936: Director Christian Holm, Copenhagen, to Director V. O. Helander, Helsingfors, April 18, 1934, no. 57; Christian Holm, [Copenhagen], to F. Klasen, Hamburg, October 18, 1935; Christian Holm, [Copenhagen], to J. A. Mowinckel, Paris, October 18, 1935, no. 60. Statoil A/S (1932–1939), Memoranda vedr. "Outsiderne" (1932–1939). Ole Simonsen, Intern report, October 25, 1935, no. 229.

SAK: Politiets Registerblade: Station 6 (*Nørrebro*), Filmrulle 0007, Registerblad 3258 (unikt id 1641280): Elias Feldmann.

2.

Interviews with Thomas Glad and Morten F. Larsen, May 10, 2016; Daniella Wexler, née Racine, Jerusalem, May 28, 30; June 1, 2016; November 10, 2017.

3. ---

4.

"Litpetrol, A.-G. Marktstr. 20," *Adressbuch für die See- und Handelsstadt Memel* (1929).

"Barrow's Oil Industry. Hope of Development," *The Petroleum Times*, July 25, 1925, 153.

"Caucasion Oil Co., Ltd., Establishes Oil Pipe-Line in Haifa Harbor," *Jewish Telegraph Agency*, February 4, 1927, 4.

"Benzinen kan sælges billigere," *Politiken*, August 8, 1928, 2.

"Benzin-Krig," *Jydsk Motor. Officielt organ for Jydsk Motor Union*, November 16, 1928, 6.

"Elias Feldmann mod C. F. Glad," *Sø- og Handelsrets-Tidende*, October 1, 1942, 251–260.

"Elite, Chocolate and Sweets Company Ltd.," *The Palestine Gazette*, February 8, 1934, 118.

"Elite," *The Palestine Gazette*, September 26, 1934, 862.

"Gica," *Registreringstidende for Aktieselskaber* 12 (1930): 384.

"Mere billig Benzin," *Motor. Medlemsblad for Forenede Danske Motorejere*, November 10, 1928.

"Nitag," *Zentralhandelsregisterbeilagen zum Reichsanzeiger*, November 29, 1937, 1.

Dr. Th., "Der Erdölmarkt Lettlands," *Der Ost-Europa-Markt. Organ des Wirtschaftsinstituts für Russland und die Oststaaten* 17 (1937): 286.

"Ny billig Benzin-Tank," *Social-Demokraten*, April 10, 1929.

"Priman," *The Palestine Gazette*, January 9, 1941, 30.

"Tankstellenverzeichnis," in *Deutschland: das Land der schönen Autostraßen*, ed. NITAG, Deutsche Treibstoffe Aktiengesellschaft (Dresden: Dr. Güntzsche Stiftung, [1938]).

"The United Caucasian Oil Co., Ltd.," *Banque Ottomane, Circulaire Mensuelle* (March 1927): 121.

David Filitz and Armenak Bahaturianz, "Notice," *The London Gazette*, October 20, 1931, 6730.

"United Oil Importers, Ltd.," *The Petroleum Times*, January 22, 1927, 143.

"Union General des Naphtes," *The Petroleum Times*, August 24, 1929, 363.

"United Caucasian Oil Company Ltd., Haifa," *Official Gazette of the Government of Palestine*, September 16, 1925, 480.

"Various Matters," *The Petroleum Times*, April 2, 1927, 626; ibid., October 8, 1927, 684.

"Wintershall übernimmt Tankstellennetz der Nitag," *Öl und Kohle* 11, no. 28 (1935): 497.

5.

Hannes Bajohr, "Judith N. Shklar (1928–1992): Eine Werkbiographie," in Judith Shklar, *Ganz normale Laster*, trans. Hannes Bajohr (Berlin: Matthes & Seitz Berlin, 2014), 277–319.

Avraham Barkai, *Vom Boykott zur 'Entjudung': Der wirtschaftliche Existenzkampf der Juden im Dritten Reich 1933–1943* (Frankfurt/Main: Fischer-Taschenbuch, 1987), 18–21.

Duvantier, *L.C. Glad & Co.*, 262–265.

Dale Herrington, *Mystery Man: William Rhodes Davis: American Nazi Agent of Influence.* (Dulles, VI: Brassey's, 1999), 11–37, 73, 187–211.

Karlsch and Stokes, *Faktor Öl*, 155, 168/9.

Titus Kockel, *Geologie und deutsche Ölpolitik, 1928 bis 1938: Die frühe Karriere des Erdölgeologen Alfred Theodor Bentz* (PhD diss., Technical University, Berlin, 2003), 236–254.

Kockel, *Deutsche Ölpolitik*, 61–67.

Morten F. Larsen, *The History of the Entrepreneurial Family L. C. Glad* (Copenhagen, project in progress).

Gerald D. Nash, *United States Oil Policy 1890–1964: Business and Government in Twentieth Century America* (Pittsburgh: University of Pittsburgh Press, 1968), 112–127.

Gregory P. Nowell, *Mercantile States and the World Oil Cartel 1900–1939* (Ithaca et al.: Cornell University Press, 1994), 260.

Benjamin Siew, *Lettlands Volks- und Staatswirtschaft* (Riga: Müllersche Buchdruckerei, 1925), 145.

Steven C. Topik and Allen Wells, "Warenketten in einer globalen Wirtschaft," in *Geschichte der Welt: 1870–1945. Weltmärkte und Weltkriege*, ed. Akira Iriye and Jürgen Osterhammel, (München: C. H. Beck, 2012), 613.

Klaus Volland, *Das Dritte Reich und Mexiko: Studien zur Entwicklung des deutsch-mexikanischen Verhältnisses 1933–1942 unter besonderer Berücksichtigung der Ölpolitik* (PhD diss., University of Hamburg, Hamburg, 1976), 83–164.

Yergin, *The Prize*, 267.

6. ---

7.

"Compagnie Industrielle Maritime Stockage et Services Pétroliers," CIM-CCMP, accessed April 30, 2021, http://www.cim-ccmp.com/fr/le-groupe-cim-ccmp.php#histoire.

"Mum and me. Mum's Family-History," Marion Kane [website], accessed April 30, 2021, https://www.marionkane.com/mum-and-me/.

"Von Clemm v. Smith. United States District Court S. D. New York, 23. November 1965," *Court Listener*, accessed April 30, 2021, https://www.courtlistener.com/opinion/1818210/von-clemm-v-smith/.

"Pommereul, Marguerite, mar. Rouvier," *Instrumentalistinnen-Lexikon*, accessed April 30, 2021, http://www.sophie-drinker-institut.de/cms/index.php/pommereul-marguerite.

CHAPTER 19
The Third Expulsion. Paris, Lisbon

1.

JMB: H-C i: 27: David Kahan, Paris, to Jacob Chaimi-Cohen, Tel Aviv, April 19; April 29; May 10; May 11; June 5; June 27; June 28; August 16; August 18; August 19; August 22; August 23; August 25, 1939; to Rosa Haimi-Cohen, Tel Aviv, May 4; June 6; June 23, 1939; to Jacob and Rosa Haimi-Cohen, Tel Aviv, June 23; June 6, 1939; to Fr. Graupe, Amsterdam, April 19, 1939; to Theresa Sacharyewna-Levitt, Brüssel, April 19; May 3; June 6, 1939; to Moritz Hanemann, Amsterdam, March 10; March 13; August 23, 1939; Arusia Kahan, Paris, to Aron Kahan, Mont-Dore, August 29, 1939; René Lew, Antwerp, to Arusia Kahan, Paris, May 1, 1939; Theresa Sacharjewna-Levitt, Brüssel, to David Kahan, Paris, May 2; June 4; June 17, 1939; Benno Hanemann, Amsterdam, to Jacob Haimi-Cohen, Tel Aviv, March 20, 1939. H-C i: 28: The "Family Constitution," Vichy, February 1940; Tel Aviv, June 1959; Chaim [?], Paris, March 18, 1940, to David [Kahan]. H-C i: 32 Correspondence between Jonas Rosenberg, Berlin, and Anna Kazhdan, Riga [et al.], the 1920s. H-C i: 35: Arusia Kahan, Riga, to Jacob and Rosa Haimi-Cohen, Noma and Rita Cohen, Tel Aviv, November 8; November 12; November 29; December 16, 1937. H-C i. 42: Aron Kahan, Memoirs, part 2, 20, 38. H-C ii: 6 Rabbinical court proceedings, Paris, 1934–1935. H-C ii: 18, 19, 20: Correspondence between Jonas Rosenberg, Berlin, and Anna Kazhdan, Riga, 1932–1933. H-C 2, folder A: Gitti Hamburger, Riga, April 3, 1940, to Edith and Arusia Kahan, Tel Aviv; folder 12: Photograph of Anna Kazhdan, Jonas Rosenberg and Simon and Ida Dubnow, Berlin [before 1933].

AGRHC: Chaim-Avinoam Kahan, "Abteilung Briefe," Paris, September 18, 1934; to Rosalia and Baruch Kahan, Tel Aviv, September 23, 1934.

APRNY: Family photograph of Aron and Zina Kahan, Gita and Salomon Ripp with their children Paul and Victor and Sasha Sokolov, Mont-Dore, summer 1940.

AYMD: French version of the "Family Constitution," February 1940. Affidavit for Lia (Lily) and Alfred Feiler, New York, November 26, 1940. Aron Kahan, Lisbon, to the consul general of the USA, Lisbon, [n. d.]. The Atlantic Yeast Corporation, Brooklyn/New York, to the consul general of the USA, Lisbon, December 5, 1940. Charter of the Intercambio Internacional, Limitada. O Jornal do Comércio e das Colónias, May 8, 1940, 2.

BAREEC: Alexis Goldenweiser papers no. BA#136, box 57: Aron and David Kahan, 2 folders: folder 1: Addressees: Aron Kahan, Rua Dos Fanqueiros 15, 5, Lisbon; Jacob and Myrra Rabinowitch c/o M. Golodetz & Co, 91 Wall St., New York; Alexis Goldenweiser, New York, to Dr. E. v. Hofmannsthal, Buenos Aires, August 9, 1940; Dr. E. v. Hofmannsthal, Buenos Aires, to Alexis Goldenweiser, New York, August 15, 1940; Léon Malkiel, New York, draft of a letter to Goldenweiser, New York, August 15, 1940; Léon Malkiel, New York, to Frederic Roland, Port-au-Prince, August 29, 1940; to Maitre E. Bouland, Port-au-Prince, September 13, 1940; [Alexis Goldenweiser], draft of a letter to President's Advisory Committee on Political Refugees, New York [n. d.]; Frederic Roland, Port-au-Prince, to Léon Malkiel, New York, October 9, 1940; Max Immanuel, New York, to Alexis Goldenweiser, New York, June 15, 1941; Jacob Rabinowitch, New York, to Alexis Goldenweiser, New York, September 11, 1940; Zlata Kahan, Treasury Department, Application for a license to engage in a foreign exchange transaction, April 15, 1943, no. NY 531859.

EAB: Applications for restitution: Zina Kahan, Aron Kahan, Jakob Kahan, Gita und Frank-Salomon Ripp, Lia (Lily) Feiler, Leonid Kahan.

GABO: House and ground in Brest-Litovsk, Zygmuntowska/Jagiellonska 1937'1939: F. 5, op. 1, d. 3330, l. 1–4.

LAB: Restitution offices of Berlin. Restitution affairs. JRSO for Mina Kahan (Gutzkowstraße 2) versus Walter Weymann, Berlin-Charlottenburg, 1950: B Rep. 025–03 WGA no. 2829 (1950). Jacob Haimi-Cohen et al. (publishing house Rom) versus Deutsches Reich, 1961. Pinchas Kahan and Zina Kahan, née Golodetz, marriage certificate (copy of the French translation), Marseille, February 7, 1941: B Rep. 025–01 no. 11/13 WGA 13660/59.

2.

Interviews with Gita Kahan-Ripp for the Spielberg Foundation; Giza Haimi-Cohen, December 8, 2008; Paul and Eleanor Ripp, Victor Ripp, New York, May 3, 2015; Mirriam Rosen and Ylana Miller, New York, May 8, 2015; Mirriam Rosen, Madison, WI, August 5, 15; Ylana Miller, Durham, NC, July 13, 16, 2017; Yossi Cohen, December 16, 2010; January 26, 2011. Video films: Mirriam and Howard Rosen, *Gita's Album*, Madison, WI, 1997.

3.

Ripp, *Hell's Traces*, 3–5, 51, 60–61, 165, 175–187.

4.

"Kahan (Jacob). Villa George-Sand, 1," *Annuaire téléphonique à Paris* (1935); "Kahan (Lina), r. Jean-Carriès, 6," ibid.; "Carbur. du Centre (Cie des), r. Bienfaisance, 17", ibid.
"Kahan (Mme Sina), 3, r. Marbeau," *Annuaire téléphonique à Paris* (1938).
"Kahan Vermögensverwaltung," *Zentralhandelsregisterbeilagen zum Reichsanzeiger*, no. 2, January 3, 1936, 1; no. 47, February 25, 1936, 1; "Jalkut," ibid.

5.

Hannah Arendt, *Elemente und Ursprünge totaler Herrschaft* (Frankfurt/Main: Europäische Verlagsanstalt, 1958), vol. 1: *Antisemitismus*, 130.
Richard D. Breitman and Alan M. Kraut, *American Refugee Policy and European Jewry, 1933–1945* (Bloomington et al.: Indiana University Press, 1987), 236–249.

Thomas Stephan, "Exil oder Heimat? Palästina im Spiegel der Berichterstattung," in *Rechts und links der Seine: Pariser Tageblatt und Pariser Tageszeitung 1933–1940*, ed. Hélène Roussel and Lutz Winckler (Tübingen: Niemeyer, 2002), 339.

6.

Lion Feuchtwanger, *Exil* (Berlin and Weimar: Aufbau-Verlag, 1994), 278.

Hanni Mittelmann, *Sammy Gronemann: Ein Leben im Dienste des Zionismus* (Berlin: Hentrich & Hentrich, 2012), 41.

Erich Maria Remarque, *Die Nacht von Lissabon* (Berlin and Weimar: Aufbau-Verlag, 1986), 5–6, 30, 110, 196.

Gershon Swet, "Tsiunim. David Kahan z'l. Ehad milamed vav," *Hado'ar* 39, no. 7 (5720/1959): 107.

7.

"*Serpa Pinto*," Wikipedia, accessed April 30, 2021, https://de.wikipedia.org/wiki/Serpa_Pinto_ (Schiff).

CHAPTER 20
Eretz Israel. Tel Aviv

1.

JMB: H-C 2, folder 14: List of the former collaborators of the Nitag in Berlin, later living in Tel Aviv; folder E: Arusia Kahan, Paris, to Jacob Haimi-Cohen, Tel Aviv, August 5, 1939.

AECJ: Cohen-Mintz, "Chaim Cohen z"l vebeito," 10, 15, 16. University of Tel Aviv, 1968: Announcement for a grant on behalf of David Ben Chaim Cohen, z"l, promoted by his nephew Ahron Cohen-Mintz. List of the family Kahan's donations, of which the main initiator was David Kahan. Jubilee edition of *Haaretz*, December 27, 1935.

AGRHC: Chaim-Avinoam Haimi-Cohen, Hotel Kanaan, Kiriath Sarah, Safed, to Jonas Bing, Tel Aviv, August 2, 1937.

ACHHR: Kahan Vermögen GmbH: Commercial Register, department B, no. 21593.

BAREEC: Abram S. Kagan papers: Interview conducted by Marc Raeff, 56. Alexis Goldenweiser papers: Aron and David Kahan, box 1: Visa for David Kahan, November 1941–February 1942.

BP-AMOCO: Agreement, 1930.

CDIAK: Chaim N. Kagan. F. 2034, op. 1, d. 56: Rahel Kahan, Wiesbaden, to Baruch Kahan, [Kharkov], October 30, 1906.

EAB: Application for restitution: Leonid Kahan.

HMRA: Judith B. Walzer, Interview conducted by Judith Shklar, 19.

2.

Interviews with Dvora Ettinger-Rozenfeld; Giza Haimi-Cohen, December 8, 2008; November 8, 2010; November 29, 2015; October 26, 2017; Joseph (Yossi) Cohen, November 11; December 16, 2010; Naomi Loewenthal, December 1, 2015; Efrat Carmon, December 4,

2008; November 14, 2010; December 2, 2015; October 20, 2017; Eli Rosenberg, Tel Aviv, October 9, 2012; November 30, 2016; October 26, 2017; Berlin, February 14, 2018; Uli Cohen-Mintz, Tel Aviv, December 1, 2015; July 20, 2016; Hagit Benziman, Jerusalem, December 20; December 24; December 31, 2017; January 4; January 9, 2018; Danielle Wexler, Jerusalem, May 28; May 29; May 30; June 1, 2016.

3.
Efrat Carmon, "Misadut haneft leshchunot Mekor Chaim: Chaim Kahan, po'elo vemishmachto," *Mekor Chaim. Sipura shel shchuna bedroma shel Yerushalaim*, ed. Yossi Spanier, Eyal Meiron and Reuven Gafni (Jerusalem: Keren Kayemet Le-Israel, 2015), 105–116.
Moshe Ettinger, *The Man Freud and Monotheism* (Jerusalem: Magnes Press, 1992).
Ettinger-Rozenfeld, *Ha-Ettingerim*, 104–107, 170, 214–219.

4.
"Agudat Yam Hatikhon Leiskei Mamon Beeravon Mugbal," *The Palestine Gazette*, May 22, 1941, 493.
"Elite," *The Palestine Gazette*, September 25, 1941, 965; August 27, 1942, 980; August 5, 1943, 678; January 17, 1946, 72.
"Haaretz, Haim Publishing Company, Ltd.," *The Palestine Gazette*, January 18, 1934, 45.
"Haaretz," *The Palestine Gazette*, June 28, 1934, supplement no. 2, 536.
"Public Notice. Persons Changing Their Names," *The Palestine Gazette*, June 17, 1937, 594.
"Penguin Company Ltd.," *The Palestine Gazette*, March 15, 1934, 219.
Oren Soffer, "Haaretz," in *Enzyklopädie jüdischer Geschichte und Kultur* (Stuttgart and Weimar: Verlag J.B Metzler, 2002–2017), vol. 2, 488–490.
"Tamar Elastic Bands Factory Ltd.," *The Palestine Gazette*, June 22, 1939, 638.
"Trieste-Lloyd Liner to Carry Body to Holy Land," *Jewish Daily Bulletin* (New York), July 8, 1934, 1, 11.
Yfaat Weiss, "Ha'avara-Abkommen," in *Enzyklopädie jüdischer Geschichte und Kultur*, vol. 2, 490–494.

5.
Yehoshua Ben Arie, "Mekor Chaim: Korotia, betia, vetoshavia," in *Mekor Chaim*, 15–33.
Volker Dahm, *Das jüdische Buch im Dritten Reich*, rev. ed. (Frankfurt/Main: Buchhändler-Vereinigung, 1982), vol. 2, 727.
Anthony David, *The Patron: A Life of Salman Schocken, 1877–1959* (New York: Metropolitan Books, 2003), 237–241, 253–257.
David De Vries, "Capitalist Nationalism and Zionist State-Building, 1920s–1950s: Chocolate and Diamonds in Mandate Palestine and Israel," *Journal of Modern European History* 18, no. 1 (2020): 48–54.
Idem, *Society and Economy in State Building. The Social History of Chocolate in Palestine and Israel* (Tel Aviv, project in progress).
Ouzi Elyada, "Miiton mimsadi leiton mischari: 'Haaretz', 1918–1937," *Kesher* 12, no. 29 (2001): 59–68.

Hagit Lavsky, *The Creation of the German-Jewish Diaspora: Interwar German-Jewish Immigration to Palestine, the USA and England* (Berlin: De Gruyter, and Jerusalem: Magnes Press, 2017), 19–24.

Stefanie Mahrer, "'Much More Than Just Another Private Collection': The Schocken Library and its Rescue from Nazi Germany in 1935," *Naharaim* 9, nos. 1–2 (2015): 5, 9–16.

6.

Kurt Blumenfeld, *Erlebte Judenfrage: Ein Vierteljahrhundert deutscher Zionismus* (Stuttgart: Deutsche-Verlags-Anstalt, 1962), 47.

Amos Oz, *Eine Geschichte von Liebe und Finsternis*, trans. Ruth Achlama (Frankfurt/Main: Suhrkamp, 2008), 16, 24–25, 33, 72.

7.

"Oral History Interview with Emmanuel Racine," United States Holocaust Memorial Museum's Collections, accessed April 30, 2021, https://collections.ushmm.org/search/catalog/irn49598.

"Givati Brigade," Wikipedia, accessed April 30, 2021, https://en.wikipedia.org/wiki/Givati_Brigade

"Gusch Etzion," Wikipedia, accessed April 30, 2021, https://de.wikipedia.org/wiki/Gusch_Etzion

"Mekor Chaim," Wikipedia, accessed April 30, 2021, https://en.wikipedia.org/wiki/Mekor_Chaim.

"Tanhum Cohen-Mintz," Wikipedia, accessed April 30, 2021, https://en.wikipedia.org/wiki/Tanhum_Cohen-Mintz

CHAPTER 21
Sanctuaries. The Family Is Alive. New York, Tel Aviv, Ma'agan Michael

1.

JMB: H-C i: 27: Aron Kahan, Paris, to Alfred Aufhäuser, New York, February 10, 1939.

AECJ: Ahron Cohen-Mintz, List of the family donations.

AIFA: Moritz Hanemann, Amsterdam, to Lothar Nachman, New York, September 29, 1964.

AVRP: Ater, Aharon Kahan, oil pioneer.

AGCJZB: Enrollment declaration of Hermann Leising, June 14, 1951.

BAB: Reich's ministry of finance. Sande/Wilhelmshaven: R2, Nr. 8815, Bd. 2, 1921–1924.

BAREEC: Goldenweiser papers: Aron and David Kahan, box 2: Aron Kahan, New York, Projects: Addressees: Hon. Harry S. Truman, Independence, MO, November 1956; Mr. Robert Cayrel, c/o Desmarais Frères, Paris, December 1956; Abba Khan, Ambassador of Israel, New York, [n. d.]; Board of management of the British Petroleum, London, December 1956; Presidium of the British Petroleum, London, February 1957; A. N. Spaniel, New York, March 1957; Guy Mollet, Paris, April 1957. "A Plan for the Liberation of Europe from the Middle East Blackmail," February 1957.

BP-AMOCO: Mr. Aron Kahan, correspondence 1948–1958, no. 45255. Aron Kahan, Compagnie des Carburants du Centre, Paris, to John Im Thurn, Anglo-Iranian Oil, London, January 29, May 21, 1948; Aron Kahan, Hudson Coast Company, New York, to John Im Thurn, Anglo-Iranian Oil / British Petroleum, London, November 6, 1951; April 2; December 16, 1953; July 12, 1955; May 7; May 9, 1956; Aron Kahan, Hudson Bay Company New York, to John (Hans) Ornstein, Olex, Hamburg, June 18; November 12, 1952; August 20, 1953; November 5; November 19; November 27, 1954; John (Hans) Ornstein, Olex, Hamburg, to John Im Thurn, Anglo-Iranian Oil, London, August 24, 1953; R. Norman Tottenham-Smith, Societe Generale des Huiles de Petrole B. P., S. A., Paris, to Hector Watts, Anglo-Iranian Oil, London, August 25, 1953; Aron Kahan, Hudson Coast Company, New York, to John E. M. Davies, Societe Generale des Huiles de Petrole B. P., S. A., Paris, February 2; March 10, 1954. Dossier "Mr. Aron Kahan," February 13, 1956. Nohaka Report, 1946.

EAB: Applications for restitution: Aron Kahan. Moses (Moritz) Hanemann.

LAB: Restitution offices of Berlin. Restitution Affairs: B Rep. 025–04 no. 4 WGA 1938 + 1939/50: Bendet, Aron, David Kahan, Jonas Rosenberg, Tel Aviv (tenements Schlüterstrasse 37, Wielandstrasse 32, Berlin-Charlottenburg) versus Deutsche Nitag, Berlin, 1950. B Rep. 025–04 no. 1941 + 1942/50 WGA: (tenements Wielandstrasse 32, Berlin-Charlottenburg) Aron Kahan, Tel Aviv, versus Paul Riedel, Berlin, 1950. B Rep. 025–05 no. 51 WGA IRSO/902: Jakob Kahan, Berlin (Portfolio at Hardy &Co GmbH, Frankfurt/Main) versus Deutsches Reich, 1951. B Rep. 025–01 no. 11/13 WGA 13660/59: Jacob Haimi-Cohen a.o. (publishing house Rom) versus Deutsches Reich, 1961.

NHAH: Commercial Register files, Nohaka.

NIOD: Archief Hanemann, Nohaka, Amsterdam, to Moses (Moritz) Hanemann, [Paris], June 7, 1945; Johannes H. Gaukstert, Amsterdam, to Moses (Moritz) Hanemann, Paris, July 10, 1945; Benno Hanemann, New York, to Moses (Moritz) Hanemann, [Paris], June 20; 28, 1945; Moses (Moritz) Hanemann, [Paris], to Benno Hanemann, New York, [June 11, 1945].

NLAH: Restitution affairs. Application for restitution: Aron and David Kahan, Tel Aviv, versus Wintershall, Celle, 1950/51: Nds. 720 Lüneburg Acc. 2009/128 no. 318.

2.

Interviews with Victor Ripp, Hannover, August 18; August 19, 2014; Ylana Miller, January 9, 2014; Paul and Eleanor Ripp, Victor Ripp, May 3, 2015; Mirriam Rosen and Ylana Miller, May 8, 2015; Diana Franzusoff-Peterson, Merion, PA, June 1, 2015; September 26, 2017; Morten F. Larsen, July 11, 2017.

Video films: Mirriam and Howard Rosen, *Gita's Album*, Madison, WI, 1997.

3.

Ettinger-Rozenfeld, *Ha-Ettingerim*, 80, 81.

Lily Feiler, *Marina Tsvetaeva: The Double Beat of Heaven and Hell* (Durham, NC: Duke University Press, 1994).

Ylana Miller, *Government and Society in Rural Palestine, 1920–1948* (Austin, TX: University of Texas Press, 1985).

Ripp, *Hell's Traces*, 165–166, 186–187.

4.

"Leising, Hermann Dr. jur. et rer. pol., Kaufmann, Charlottenburg, Sophienstr. 30," *Berliner Adressbücher* (1943).

"Leising & Co., Bankgesch., Budapester Str. 42," *Amtliches Fernsprechbuch für Berlin* (1950, 1954).

"Abraham Ledermann," obituary, *Holstebro Dagblad*, June 9, 1947 (information: Morten F. Larsen).

5.

De Vries, *Society and Economy in State Building*.

Idem, "Capitalist Nationalism and Zionist State-Building," 55–58.

Graul, *Die Stadt auf Befehl*, 70–71.

Harrington, *Mystery Man: William Rhodes Davis*, 199–211.

Joachim Joesten, *Öl regiert die Welt: Geschäft und Politik* (Düsseldorf: Rauch, 1958), 128.

Karlsch and Stokes, *Faktor Öl*, 264–265.

Lucien Lazare, *Rescue as Resistance: How Jewish Organizations Fought the Holocaust in France*, trans. Jeffrey M. Green (New York: Columbia University Press, 1996), 201.

Bo Lidegaard, *Die Ausnahme, Oktober 1943: Wie die dänischen Juden mithilfe ihrer Mitbürger der Vernichtung entkamen*, trans. Yvonne Badal (München: Blessing, 2013), 265.

Peter Nolte, *Spurensuche: Kommilitonen von 1933* (Berlin: Humboldt-Universität, 2001), 25, 50–51.

Peter Salwen, *Upper West Side Story: A History and Guide* (New York: Abbeville Press, 1989), 67, 126, 231.

Erik Schumacher, *Mau en Gerty: Een Joodse liefdesgeschiedenis tussen volksverhuizingen en wereldoorlogen* (Amsterdam and Antwerpen: Em. Querido's Uitgeverij, 2016), 174–177.

6.

Moses (Moritz) Hanemann, "Ein Kind wird gerettet," in *Die unbesungenen Helden: Menschen in Deutschlands dunklen Tagen*, ed. Kurt R. Grossmann (Berlin: Arani-Verlag, 1957), 194–198.

7.

"Ma'agan Michael," Wikipedia, accessed April 30, 2021, https://en.wikipedia.org/wiki/Ma%27agan_Michael.

"The Nesher Haifa Plant," Nesher, accessed April 30, 2021, https://www.nesher.co.il/en/factories/.

"NITAG," Wikipedia, accessed April 30, 2021, https://de.wikipedia.org/wiki/NITAG

"Wurzacher Schloss, Bad Wurzach," NS Dokumentation Oberschwaben: Erinnerungswege, accessed April 30, 2021, http://www.dsk-nsdoku-oberschwaben.de/de/erinnerungswege/ergaenzungsheft/bad-wurzach-wurzacher-schloss.html

"Von Clemm v. Smith. United States District Court S. D. New York, 23. November 1965," *Court Listener*, accessed April 30, 2021, https://www.courtlistener.com/opinion/1818210/von-clemm-v-smith/.

THE FAMILY TREE

Chaim Kahan Orlya 1850 – St. Petersburg 1916
∞ **Malka Basch** Brest-Litovsk 1847 – Berlin 1922

Baruch-Tanchum Brest-Litovsk 1866 – Tel Aviv 1936
∞ Rosalia Berlin, Vilna 1873 – Tel Aviv 1955

- **Jacob (Yasha)** Warsaw 1895 – Tel Aviv 1959
  ∞ Rachel (Rosa) Rosenberg, Warsaw 1898 – Tel Aviv 1981
- **Nachum (Noma)** Vilna 1897 – Jerusalem 1985
  ∞ Rita Kahn, Memel 1905 – Jerusalem 1985
- **Aron (Arusia) Cohen-Mintz** Vilna 1899 – Tel Aviv 1987
  ∞ Edith Mintz, Riga 1913 – Tel Aviv 2003

Miriam Brest-Litovsk 1869 – Berlin 1931
∞ Jonas Rosenberg, Łomża 1869 – Tel Aviv 1941

- **Rachel** Warsaw 1898 – Tel Aviv 1981
  ∞ Jacob Haimi-Cohen, Warsaw 1895 – Tel Aviv 1959
- **Nachum (Nomek)** Warsaw 1899 –Zurich 1963
  ∞ Sulamit Hurwitz, Minsk 1904 – Tel Aviv 1985

Pinchas Brest-Litovsk 1870 – Baku 1917
∞ Zina Golodetz, Shchedrin, Belarus 1881 – New York 1977

- **Leonid** Shchedrin 1902 – Tel Aviv 1969
  ∞ Eugenia Pines, Riga
- **Gita** Baku 1909 – New York 1998
  ∞ Solomon Ripp, Grodno 1900–New York 1957
- **Lily** Kislovodsk 1915 – Durham, NC 2004
  ∞ Alfred Feiler, Berlin 1912–Durham, NC 2003

Bendet Brest-Litovsk 1877 – Petah Tikva 1952
∞ Judith Bramson Weissee (Suwałki) – Petah Tikva 1877

- **Dora** Kursk 1905–Ramat Gan 2001
  ∞ Walter Loewenthal, Hamburg 1900– Ramat Gan 1975
- **Lea** Antwerp 1907– Magdiel 1989
  ∞ Chaim David Perl, Luhansk–Israel 1980
- **Shoshana (Röschen)** Berlin 1914–Tel Aviv 1994
  ∞ Itzchak Pinchas gest. in Tel Aviv

Aron Brest-Litovsk 1880 – Tel Aviv 1970
∞ Mina Levstein, Łódź 1892–Tel Aviv 1948

- **Yossi (Joseph) Cohen** Berlin 1922–Ma'agan Michael 2013
  ∞ Lea Menuhin Petaluma, CA 1923– Ma'agan Michael 1987

David Brest-Litovsk 1882– Tel Aviv 1959

Rachel Brest-Litovsk 1885 – Ramat Gan 1965
∞ David Ettinger, Uman, Ukraine 1878 – Ramat Gan 1959

- **Moshe Ater** Warsaw 1911–Jerusalem 1990
  ∞ Chava Buchsbaum Nowy Sącz 1913–Jerusalem 1990
- **Shalom** Yekaterinoslav 1912–Israel 2003
  ∞ Rivka
- **Dvora** Yekaterinoslav 1914–Ramat Gan 2016
  ∞ Paul Rozenfeld, Berlin 1912–Ramat Gan 2009
- **Chaim Ater** Yekaterinoslav 1917–Ramat Gan 1965
  ∞ Miriam, Berlin 1921–Israel 1993

Index

CPSIA information can be obtained
at www.ICGtesting.com
Printed in the USA
JSHW030606260422
25280JS00004B/6

9 781644 697559